Palgrave Studies in the History of Finance

The study of the history of financial institutions, markets, instruments and concepts is vital if we are to understand the role played by finance today. At the same time, the methodologies developed by finance academics can provide a new perspective for historical studies. Palgrave Studies in the History of Finance is a multi-disciplinary effort to emphasise the role played by finance in the past, and what lessons historical experiences have for us. It presents original research, in both authored monographs and edited collections, from historians, finance academics and economists, as well as financial practitioners.

More information about this series at
http://www.palgrave.com/gp/series/14583

Stephen Pierpoint

The Success of English Land Tax Administration 1643–1733

palgrave
macmillan

Stephen Pierpoint
Bartlett School
University College London
London, UK

Palgrave Studies in the History of Finance
ISBN 978-3-030-07977-2 ISBN 978-3-319-90260-9 (eBook)
https://doi.org/10.1007/978-3-319-90260-9

Cover credit: Courtesy of Kent History and Library Centre, Maidstone
Cover design by Laura de Grasse

Printed on acid-free paper

This Palgrave Macmillan imprint is published by the registered company Springer International Publishing AG part of Springer Nature
The registered company address is: Gewerbestrasse 11, 6330 Cham, Switzerland

Preface

This book attempts a reassessment of the underappreciated and misunderstood land tax. Whether I am being entirely fair in my judgement of the historiography will be for the reader to decide, but I believe there are a number of explanations for this state of affairs. One of the problems is that the last major reassessment of the land tax was in the year of the current writer's birth and that was a very long time ago indeed. I am referring to William Ward's 'The English Land Tax in the Eighteenth-Century' of 1953. Another difficulty is the very nature of the historical evidence itself, but the main problem concerns the overpowering nature of some major historical narratives and the particular form of English state they contemplate.

The title of this book may cause some surprise for two reasons. I use the word 'success' to describe land tax administration, and my time frame starts earlier than most would have it. There are many historical texts but surprisingly few describe English land tax as successful—certainly without considerable equivocation. And yet successful it was because it could raise greater sums than other contemporary levies and far more than previous direct taxes. Land tax as such is not normally considered to have been levied before the Glorious Revolution of 1688. However, if historians are reluctant to use the term 'land tax' prior to this, contemporary writers during the Restoration and Interregnum were quite content to do so. It was used by them to describe highly productive direct taxes sometimes otherwise called 'assessments' or 'aids', mainly levied on real estate and virtually identical to post-revolutionary land tax. I stand by those writers and believe their views were sound based on the detailed arguments I provide below. The objective of this book then is to show how, when and why land taxes were so successful between their 1643 introduction and their temporary threatened demise at the time of the excise crisis of 1733. Although this period was a time of tension, with an English population divided by political and religious affiliations, unprecedented amounts of tax were still collected. I will try and explain how this was possible.

Despite the lack of a recent detailed review, land tax and other fiscal records continue to be objects of fascination for historians. A state's tax records often survive in some form. Surely those documents must tell us something about contemporary politics, the economy, the state and the people. Certainly, England's tax records have been drawn upon by historians of every stripe to discuss all these matters. After all, the period under review here is usually seen as one featuring important changes and historians have been keen to explore the tax evidence. The economy was developing relatively quickly or perhaps rather more slowly depending on your taste. Society was changing and becoming more commercial and urbanised. The Civil War was waged or rather the Wars of the Three Kingdoms. The monarch had to concede considerable authority to Parliament, some during the Restoration, and more after the Revolution. The English state was developing and flexing its muscles in foreign lands and on distant oceans. The English and British nations were being forged. In discussing these topics, historians have tapped into the state's tax records to make their case. Indeed, some very powerful historical narratives are in play and must be engaged with or should I say crossed swords with in this book.

The fiscal role of the English economy is another significant theme of this book. Sometimes a taxation system lags behind economic development and growing sectors of an economy might largely escape the net of tax legislators. Indeed, this might be an additional incentive for their development. Today's chancellor might therefore worry about the taxation of tech businesses, personal service companies, big brand coffee shops, and indeed the service sector in general. At least he should. The seventeenth-century English economy was expanding, but there had been growth in sectors which were little troubled by the traditional archaic tax system. There had been significant increases in the production of consumer goods, and greater wealth was being extracted from agricultural and urban real estate. There were fiscal opportunities here, and legislators in the United Provinces had already exploited the similarly expanding Dutch economy via land taxes and excise. How would the seventeenth-century English Parliament respond to growing militarisation and increasing financial needs?

Land tax is difficult because of the nature of the historical records and their survival. These taxes have left scanty remains in central document repositories because they were administered locally in cities, towns, hundreds, wapentakes and parishes. In the period considered here, there was no strong requirement or need to retain local land tax records, certainly in the long term, and great quantities of documents were simply discarded. Survival is extremely patchy and fortuitous, but much better in some places than others. This book largely relies on three of those better places, backed up by data from elsewhere when available. The early modern English state, like many others, kept some detailed records of its central administration and was a reasonable custodian in its archives of such material. Such document retention includes taxes where significant government control was exercised as was the case with the excise. However, it is surely a mistake, and one perhaps made too often, to believe that the scarcity of central archival records is a testament to a failing tax. And it would likewise be a mistake to view a tax as successful simply because it leaves much documentation behind. I believe that such a focus on central bureaucratic records would perhaps create the misapprehension that those central state officials were more effective or more important than they actually were. Then, perhaps that was precisely the intention of those early modern administrators.

I have tried to be as analytical and dispassionate as possible, but like the vast majority of the thousands of tax officials in this period, I am a middling-sort white English male. Tax administration in seventeenth- and eighteenth-century England was a patriarchal male affair, and some of the characters involved can be glimpsed in the index and the following pages of this book. There was much diligence, but this book is not looking for heroes. A national tax that relied on individual excellence would surely fail, when tens of thousands of land tax officials were involved each and every year. No this had to be a tax that could be operated by the average middling-sort of seventeenth-century man given the right tools and incentives. I am also interested in the resulting human interactions and alongside graphs, tables and statistics I discuss how individuals worked and strived.

I myself have spent decades in tax management and educational governance, and there is a strong emphasis in this book on process improvements and administration. It is what I know best. Fortunately, as the acknowledgements relate, I have had much help and support along the way, which I hope has avoided the focus of this work becoming too narrow.

London, UK Stephen Pierpoint

Acknowledgements

This work is based on a PhD thesis at the University of Cambridge. I would like to express my particular thanks to my two supervisors who were of immense help, showed great patience, and who have given tremendous encouragement during the completion of this project. Professor Craig Muldrew has helped me turn broad thoughts and ideas into a workable thesis. His promptings and cajoling, I greatly value. I have of course been inspired by his work on debt and cashflow. I am deeply obligated. Professor D'Maris Coffman has been immensely patient and good-humoured as I grappled with the detailed issues around land tax administration, and especially in finding my third case study, which for so long seemed impossible. Her detailed knowledge has been inspirational. My special thanks to Anne Davison whose PhD thesis at Canterbury Christ Church University has been of immense help to me, and she has also provided me with additional material, thoughts and ideas. The assistance of staff at the Kent History and Library Centre I immensely value. I would like to thank staff at the National Archives, the London and Metropolitan Archives and the Bristol Record Office. Some of the material studied here is fragile and I am very grateful that I have been allowed to see and handle so much original documentation. I would like to thank: Dr. David Harris Sacks, Dr. Stephen Hipkin, Dr. John Broad, Dr. Craig Spence, and Imogen Wedd for information and helpful suggestions.

On a more personal level, the completion of this work owes much to the support of my family and particularly my wife Louise Murray who has shown great fortitude, as at times research became all-consuming. Finally, the responsibility for any errors and shortcomings, of which I am sure there are many, are entirely my own.

Contents

Epigram

'As to the manner, Sir, of raising taxes upon the people, it is a certain maxim, that that tax, which is most equal and the most general, is the most just, and least burdensome; where every man contributes a small share, a great sum may be raised for public service, ... Upon the other hand, there is no tax that ever was laid upon the people of this nation, that is more unjust and unequal than the land-tax. The land-holders bear but a small proportion to the people of this nation, or of any nation; yet no man contributes any the least share to this tax, but he that is possessed of a land-estate; and yet this tax has been continued without intermission, for above these 40 years. It has continued so long, and has lain so heavy, that I may venture to say, many a landed gentleman in this kingdom has thereby been utterly ruined and undone.' [Robert Walpole 1732][1]

[1]William Cobbett, *Cobbett's Parliamentary History of England: From the Norman Conquest, in 1066 to the Year 1803*, vol. 8 (London: T.C. Hansard, 1806–1820), p. 944.

Abbreviations

A&O	Acts and Ordinances of the Interregnum
BRO	Bristol Record Office
CAMPOP	The Cambridge Group for the History of Population and Social Structure
CTB	Calendar of Treasury Books
ECCO	Eighteenth Century Collections Online
EEBO	Early English Books Online
ESFD	The European State Finance Database
GDHC	Grey's Debates of the House of Commons
HOCJ	Journal of the House of Commons
HOLJ	Journal of the House of Lords
HoP	History of Parliament
HPHC	The History and Proceedings of the House of Commons
JP	Justice of the Peace
KASMI	Kent Archaeological Society Memorial Inscriptions
KHLC	Kent History and Library Centre
LMA	London Metropolitan Archives
Mayor	The Lord Mayor in the City of London, but the term 'Mayor' is normally used
MP	Member of Parliament
Oxford DNB	Oxford Dictionary of National Biography
SMV	The Society of Merchant Venturers
SoR	Statutes of the Realm
TNA	The National Archives
VCH	Victoria County History

Other Abbreviations

£ s d, Pounds, shillings and pence, when referring to contemporary sources is written as £x-xs-xd or alternatively in analysis as £xx.xx. Thus, £14-10s-6d becomes £14.53 in analysis.

List of Figures

List of Tables

CHAPTER 1

Introduction

1.1 Preamble

The aims of this book are to attempt the rehabilitation of English land taxes and explain the chronology of their success. Colin Brooks attempted something similar in 1974, despite his own modesty, against a tide of land tax denigration from Ward and others.[1] Ward's flawed, but well-established 1953 analysis has been widely accepted, and Brooks largely ignored, by historical narratives focusing on state institutions, bureaucracy and the excise tax with its paid officials. This has led to a misunderstanding of the origins, chronology and reasons for the success of English land taxes. Indeed, reading some texts it is difficult to understand how land taxes raised such remarkably large amounts of money for English state coffers. Part of the challenge is to look in the right place and at the right time. Central state records are sparse because land taxes were administered locally in cities, towns, hundreds and parishes. Local tax record survival is generally poor because there were few legal requirements to protect them. Survival is patchy at best. Three case studies are the main, but not sole focus here because of their better document quality and heavy tax burdens: the county of Kent and the cities of London and Bristol. The weight of tax is important. Land taxes were paid against an amount or quota set by parliament, and some parts of the country for historical reasons escaped lightly. Perhaps too much land tax research has targeted such lightly taxed areas where old methods

S. Pierpoint, *The Success of English Land Tax Administration 1643–1733*, Palgrave Studies in the History of Finance,
https://doi.org/10.1007/978-3-319-90260-9_1

of tax-gathering persisted. The three case study areas were all heavily taxed, and their combined contribution represented over ten per cent of national direct taxation throughout this period. It is only by studying such areas where significant tax sums were levied and raised that it is possible to comprehend the scale of fiscal challenges and measure success. It is also important to consider the right period. Many historians rightly point out the debt owed by post-revolutionary levies formally termed 'Land Tax' in contemporary statutes to the earlier 'assessments' and 'aids' going back to the 1640s. This book goes slightly further and argues that all the main features of the later 'Land Tax' were created during the Civil War and Interregnum and the term 'land tax' was in common usage. It is therefore right to use the term 'land tax' from 1643 to describe all these taxes.

England's avoidance of significant military engagement for decades prior to the Civil War meant the state was sparsely funded by outdated and declining traditional taxes despite the country's increasing wealth. A series of seventeenth-century military engagements required new sources of funding, and fresh levies were designed to meet this demand. Land taxes, excise and reformed customs were deployed which could tap into the wealth of the developing English economy and successfully fund civil wars, trade wars and continental conflicts over the next 70 years. The assessment or land tax emerged in the 1640s and was arguably the most successful seventeenth-century levy as the primary supply for three Anglo-Dutch wars, the Nine Years' War and the War of the Spanish Succession. These new land taxes were successful because in many parts of the country they were, contrary to some accounts, a 'radical departure'[2] in direct tax form, mechanics and process from what had preceded them and were capable of tapping growing cashflows from commerce and rent for the services of the state. Many of those who had benefitted most from England's economic growth now filled traditional local authority roles as justices of the peace, aldermen, mayors, sheriffs and common councilmen and could be pressed into tax administrative service for the state. Administration was patriarchal and if often diligent in land tax-gathering, a few officials evaded or avoided other forms of taxation. But these same men also championed the reform of poor relief, the repair of highways, street lighting, the administration of justice and the development of their local economies.

This book was partly inspired by the diligent Interregnum efforts of Joshua Pix, Anthony Webb and Thomas Catlett, high-collectors in the sub-lathe of Upper Scray in Kent, who promptly collected far greater amounts of direct taxation from far more people than any of their predecessors.[3] How did they achieve this? Fortunately, they created excellent and still extant documentary records which can be interrogated. There appeared to be something markedly different about this new tax, and it was described in different terms by contemporaries as a rent-tax and soon after as a land tax. These Kentish individuals and dozens like them across the county and thousands countrywide were a fundamental part of successful tax-gathering. This book was also inspired by the author's professional career first as a tax inspector witnessing appeal cases to the local General Commissioners[4]—those extraordinary unpaid volunteers so unfairly derided in direct tax historiography—and later as a tax manager in industry.

The argument expounded here is that the widely recognised mid-seventeenth century and later English fiscal success (Fig. 1.3) was founded on the growth of an 'Atlantic economy' with London and Amsterdam at its heart, featuring: urban expansion, higher wages, greater liquidity, more commercialised land markets and the purchase of consumer goods particularly alcohol and tobacco, generating significant flows of value which could be exploited by the fiscal state.[5] Civil War supply needs provided the trigger for the state to tap these cashflows and generate tax growth in England, and similarly the Dutch Revolt in the Netherlands. This laid new foundations for the creation of sustainable, well-targeted and broadly based taxation which was hard to avoid, paid by both those who 'willingly contributed' as well as those who did not.[6] This new land tax took the point of taxation much closer to monetary flows and commercial cycles in the developing English economy when cash was scarce. Economic development was a necessary condition for fiscal growth, but it required extensive innovation and re-engineering of tax form and process to find a successful solution. Fundamental changes in tax form were forged by innovative legislation at the centre and met by creative tailored responses in many localities, but particularly in the South and East where burdens were heaviest. If they were sometimes self-interested, the unremunerated local governors in charge were often experienced and capable. They were assisted by others within the local community both paid and unpaid, thus land taxes were remarkably cheap to collect because the state could exploit these considerable human resources at minimum cost.[7] The resulting bargain between state and locale was that as long as a fixed tax amount or*quota* was met, local governors could allocate it as they saw fit. Tax officials as well as taxpayers therefore had some process ownership.

Civil War militarisation required regular and substantial revenues and fiscal experimentation quickly focussed on tapping accessible cashflows, rent in the case of the land tax[8] and product supply chains for the excise, at a time when physical cash was significantly constrained after a period of high inflation.[9] If the immediate target of the new direct tax legislation was the rent paid by occupiers of real property,[10] its broader aim was on cashflows and what the land could produce, the shops could sell, the workshops manufacture, the warehouses store or the occupiers could earn. This revolutionary cashflow exploitation strategy had remarkable longevity and established more regular supply than had seemed possible before and foreshadows modern tax-gathering.[11] These two powerful new levies, land taxes and excise, became indispensable weapons of the fiscal state, despite regular outbreaks of political anguish at their sheer power, accompanied by rhetorical flourishes from landowners, country MPs and sceptical politicians. Such rhetoric was endlessly recycled particularly during the excise crisis of 1733. As fiscal burdens increased, land taxes underpinned: the post-1688 Financial Revolution, military success and the growth of parliamentary authority. Some authors mistakenly view land taxes as little different from previous direct levies[12] and therefore coercive central authority,[13] rising consent,[14] a process of negotiation or some combination,[15] must explain the creation of the highly taxed English state.[16] What is contended here is that English state authority relied upon and was strengthened by reliable revenue flows from effective tax mechanisms and related government debt.[17] This was boosted by a Civil War and Interregnum fiscal transformation[18] which created effective tax structures administered through local institutional and non-institutional governance,[19] which was probably generally honest and lacking in corruption.[20] In this changing world, continued fiscal success and even heavier tax burdens required fresh waves of innovation, adaption and commitment both centrally and locally. Over time innovation included the better use of human resources, delegation, empowerment and process simplification. At the heart of the arguments advanced here are the effectiveness and adaptability of local administration in responding to innovative land tax legislation against a background of economic change. Tax form and process, the role of local administration and the importance of the economy and cashflow have been significantly underestimated in historiographical explanations of fiscal growth.

In February 1732, Walpole argued, in supporting a reduction of the land tax to a historically low rate of one shilling in the pound that the levy unjustly targeted a small proportion of the landed classes and most people escaped any payment at all (see the Epigram).[21] Walpole was considerably overstating his case as he knew full well, but he understood that whereas excise was paid by few merchants, manufacturers and importers who could spread their tax burden through a markup on price to many, land taxes worked in reverse. Many paid, and could be forced to pay, but the burden could be shared with far fewer landlords, although the precise tax incidence is far less clear than Walpole's rhetoric allows. The following February Walpole complained of the personal attacks that 'all the Means human Industry was capable of, have been employed to raise the Clamours against me in all parts of the Kingdom'. If he still put this down to 'artful Falsehoods, Misrepresentations and Insinuations',[22] he may have been reminded of Sir Robert Carr's 1670 urging that unfair as land taxes were 'not [to] take a worse way'.[23] Land tax was raised to two shillings in 1734 and four in 1740 on Walpole's watch and at war with Spain. Three national taxes: excise, customs and land taxes were dominant in our period and despite reservations and tainting with adverse political rhetoric, all were essential in maintaining state supply. None could seriously be dispensed with.

1.2 Historiography

Historians of state formation have often relied heavily on taxation studies to support competing models. Because such fiscal enquiries were substantially founded on the post First World War works of Joseph Schumpeter,[24] who believed the state was primarily created by financial need, tax and state narratives are deeply entwined in early modern historical debate. If Charles Tilly's phrase the 'War made the state and the state made war'[25] is rather narrow, then the notion that modern states achieved a 'monopoly of violence, a bureaucratic administration [and] … a more rational fiscal system'[26] is widespread in the literature. The 'New Fiscal History' with its global reach also owes much to Schumpeter but has moved beyond 'foregrounding the modern state as the thing ultimately to be explained.'[27] As an important counterpoint, other writers including Hindle suggest people, community, networks and governance have been overlooked in the state formation historiography because of an overemphasis on taxation and finance.[28]

Because of the profound impact of post-Schumpeterian writing on taxation historiography, it is important to consider the subject in some detail here, because such narratives have created distinct views of land taxes. Much early modern European research has focussed on how tax and debt resourced states emerged when modestly taxed medieval kingdoms were substantially funded by income from the monarch's own capital assets and rights—their *domains* or *demesnes*. There is at least some consensus that the change from *domain state* to *fiscal state* was rooted in the financial crisis resulting from growing expenses of early modern warfare. More contested is the extent to which such a transition would necessarily require some ceding of authority from monarch to representative bodies to support and authorise higher tax burdens. In England, this is often portrayed in terms of a seventeenth-century monarchical crisis with some resolution after 1688. These discussions were taken forward in John Brewer's seminal 1989 work, *The Sinews of Power*, where he developed the powerful notion of a post-1688 British *fiscal-military state*, which was an institutional and central bureaucratic state capable of raising and deploying enormous resources for war through debt and taxes, but where 'bookkeeping not battles' was to the fore and the establishment of administrative routine more significant than the clash of weapons.[29] *The Sinews of Power* has been hugely and widely influential,[30] but it was not written in isolation[31] as Brewer himself acknowledges, and contemporary work included O'Brien's important and independent contribution.[32] Brewer's work ultimately owes something to Max Weber, who viewed the state's bureaucratic coordination as the distinctive mark of the modern era.[33] The extent to which taxation or debt was the more important financial support for the state has been long debated, but Brewer believed Dickson, in another classic work,[34] 'underestimates the importance of taxes to the so-called financial revolution', whilst at the same time supplementing much of the latter's work.[35] Such a post-revolutionary institutionalised state coincidentally[36] underpins North and Weingast's powerful post-revolutionary model of 'credible commitment' to 'secure property rights, protection of their wealth, and the elimination of confiscatory government', which facilitated economic growth and the development of markets. 'Credible commitment' has been another long-enduring and influential if not uncontested discourse, sometimes referred to as the *new institutional economics*.[37]

These very powerful historiographies, which are both institutional and post-revolutionary, create difficulties for understanding land tax development which, as will be argued here, substantially began in the 1640s and relied on delegated local authority. Much late twentieth-century fiscal historiography emphasised the post-revolutionary excise, whereas the land tax, with its largely local administration, appears incongruous in the rise of a centralised institutional and bureaucratic state. Customs administration, seen as bedevilled by prevailing corruptions, was also devalued in this narrative, and contrary views of the land tax such as those of Brooks were largely ignored.[38] Brewer downplays direct taxes, because he firmly believed the advancement of tax collection over the course of the long eighteenth century came from a move 'from a fiscal system marked by heterogeneity and amateurism to a tax system characterised by the orderly collection of public moneys by a predominantly professional body of state officials'.[39] Thus, the orderly world of the excise replaced the disorderly one of land taxes. Brewer devotes few pages, and no figures or tables to direct taxes, and he believes they 'scarcely had an administration at all', and were run by a 'hodge-podge of amateur and local officials',[40] even though for long periods they fiscally outperformed 'professional' bureaucrats, and land taxes were the primary supply for the Nine Years' War and the War of the Spanish Succession, as has long been recognised.[41]

This negative narrative of land tax administration is compounded by a major secondary source, Ward's *The English Land Tax in the Eighteenth Century*.[42] Although rather dated, it remains a significant influence on the historiography of land taxes despite long-standing criticism by Brooks.[43] It is deeply flawed. Ward's use of data is sometimes defective (as discussed below), evidence is frequently anecdotal in style, and he can be self-contradictory, and much evidence presented seems better interpreted in an entirely contrary way. Ward is his own best critic when admitting, regarding the 1690s, that 'although in administrative study breakdown and conflict inevitably loom large, and the abnormal receives fuller attention than the normal, the achievements of the land-tax administration in these years must not be forgotten'.[44] In any case, land tax achievements are very much relegated to the background. Instead, Ward's work is littered with cases of failed receivers, dishonest collectors and tales of incompetence, but he is nowhere able to show this was typical of land tax administration in general, and not the inevitable consequence of a vast administration which suffered periodic local failure. Indeed, the fact that such incidents were being recorded suggests they were also being dealt with. This was not lost on

Brooks who recognised the 'misleading impression of perpetual strife'.[45] As regards contrary explanations of Ward's evidence, a few important examples must suffice here, although there is more detailed criticism to follow particularly in Chapter 5. Ward complains that 'the decay of the local administration was very great'[46] after 1715 and cites as examples the declining numbers of tax commissioners' meetings. He highlights mid-eighteenth century Wingham in Kent[47] and criticises Bristol's commissioners for being 'loath to appear for land-tax business',[48] probably because there were far fewer minuted meetings after the 1690s. Even without the detailed reconsideration of this material below, it is difficult to support Ward's belief that a greater number of meetings at such a senior level must demonstrate a more effective tax process. Indeed, prima facie this evidence might be more readily explained as an excellent example of what might be termed 'working smarter not harder' in modern business parlance, because in this case the paid clerks did more of the work, leaving commissioners only to make essential decisions. His further criticism of Kent's rigid commissioners' agendas[49] is probably better seen as evidence of the good administrative practice of standard agendas making sure that business was done.[50] Ward's noting of contemporary complaints about the fairness of tax quotas are surely better seen as local participation and ownership, particularly when those complaints often resulted in change as shown here. When Ward presents evidence of a system in chaos because of Treasury interventions, Commons' request for reports, or even the removal of receivers, he is at his weakest. Much of this evidence is better understood as appropriate stakeholder action, involvement and intervention. Make no mistake, Ward is right that, despite his poor use of data, the tax remittances from receivers were slower, often much slower, in the second half of the eighteenth century than the first,[51] but it is impossible from Ward's account to understand why. Crucially, it is also impossible to understand how the eighteenth-century land tax brought in so much of the state's supply year after year. Ward cites as an example of failure the fact that between 1715 and 1770, £82,500 was lost because of failing receivers. This writer believes that a loss of $<0.1\%$ of gross taxes over this long period is a startling testament to success. Because receivers required others to provide surety in case of failure or corruption Treasury could and did protect itself as shown by examples here. Ward's model of a land tax administration in chaos has significantly coloured later historiography.

Brewer's broader institutional paradigm has survived remarkably well, if not unchallenged,[52] but more recent studies have tended to push back the English fiscal-military state's life at least to the Restoration,[53] focussed on expenditure as well as income, upgraded the contribution of the customs[54] and developed a multi-state perspective within the British Isles. This important latter point will not be a focus of this analysis because of the chosen case studies. More fundamentally, the bureaucratic and institutionalised core of Brewer's model has been challenged by several writers including Graham, who argues it was not war but 'society made the state'[55] and accuses bureaucratic narratives of 'purging private interests from official structures'. In Graham's view, bureaucratisation was 'the outcome rather than the cause' of state formation and was often highly inefficient.[56] Hoppit criticises the new institutional economics model for 'exaggerating the modernity of Britain's "state" structures and its capacity to devise and implement economic policy'. He points out the state's heavy reliance on not always cooperative 'revenue offices, local government and the courts to implement its measures'.[57] Brewer, whilst proclaiming the success of the bureaucratic excise, recognised that substantially increased tax extraction began in mid-seventeenth century England (Fig. 1.3), a period when the two main taxes were not the excise, but land taxes and the sometimes-farmed customs. Using Beckett's data, in the period 1671–1688, customs contributed more than any other tax and land taxes most in the periods between 1643–1670 and 1689–1714.[58] Land taxes were close to meeting their considerable tax targets throughout the Restoration.[59] If the origins of fiscal expansion, and the origins of the fiscal-military state itself, cannot be explained by post-revolutionary state bureaucratisation how can they be explained? And does this imply a different kind of English state?

In considering early fiscal success, Braddick sensed a rising 'level of consent beyond acquiescence',[60] and many stress greater willingness (see footnote 14) as a part of the answer, brokered during the Restoration by local middlemen in the shires seeking 'to secure status through government service'.[61] O'Brien with a more top-down perspective believed it was the rise of 'sovereign authority with sufficient political coercive and administrative capacities' that was the key.[62] Acemoglu has somewhat squared this consent/coercion circle by arguing that states that are 'politically weak', such as that of Restoration England, can impose higher tax burdens if there is 'consensually strong state equilibrium', suggesting a balance between coercion and 'participation' might be important.[63]

Unfortunately for such narratives, the notion that coercion or cooperation might be newly developed enabling factors behind increased tax extraction has proved difficult to demonstrate in practice, despite something of an historiographical industry focussed on the overcoming of seventeenth-century popular 'tax resistance' which permeates voluminous late twentieth-century writing chronicling every minor 'tax riot', abused tax-gatherer, and anti-taxation pamphlet. Coffman has done much to show how such contemporary anti-taxation discourses were usually linked to special-interest groups or the political activities of royalists rather than any serious general unrest.[64] The profound difficulty for such 'tax resistance' narratives is the very early success of both excise and land tax during the Interregnum, a period which Coffman believes is under-researched.[65] Indeed, Braddick broadly[66] rejects the simplistic 'tax resistance' model and instead cites the 'remarkable lack of evidence of direct opposition to central government'[67] which in turn echoes Brewer's view of the 'extraordinary lack of resistance in the nation as a whole to such a high level of fiscal imposition'.[68] Coffman[69] goes further and points to the marked success of the Commonwealth excise, but this was completely eclipsed by that of the contemporary land tax or assessment.[70] At best, the coercion or cooperation explanations of early fiscal growth appear unproven. Conrad Russell made this very point in a review of Braddick's *Parliamentary Taxation*, where he felt the author's work 'gives very little indication of why or how it was possible to raise such immense sums with so little disturbance. There is still a question to be answered here'.[71]

Part of the answer to Russell's conundrum probably lies in English local governance often unfairly maligned in institutional narratives. Brewer's characterisation of local administration as a 'hodge-podge of amateur and local officials',[72] or Ward's as 'haphazard',[73] Braddick's 'underdeveloped bureaucracy'[74] or traditional views of localism[75] are challenged by other studies.[76] The disparaging term 'amateur' is so widely used in the historiography of land taxes that it is important to challenge its excessive and inappropriate use head-on now.[77] There are three main reasons why it should be used sparingly. Firstly, there is no apparent contemporary usage.[78] Secondly, it masks the important role of paid staff who did much of the day-to-day work, namely the collectors, clerks and receivers. Finally, the term is regularly used in a deliberately disparaging way particularly to make adverse comparison with the bureaucratic excise, which in contrast is treated kindly in the historiography, as an early modern tax with an increasingly professional bureaucracy required for forging and forming the English state. Importantly, Brooks, often overlooked in bureaucratic narratives, swims against this tide by recognising the 'professional' responsibility of land tax officials.[79]

As Daunton has pointed out, it was precisely such non-institutionalised governance structures which facilitated the success of the early income tax and remained part of the tax system until recently.[80] Non-institutionalised governance structures were valued throughout the early modern period and beyond because of their local voice and independence. Seventeenth-century local administration is well understood through a series of important works, and its effectiveness during the seventeenth century has long been recognised in some historical narratives. Joan Kent amongst others has shown the contemporary importance and efficiency of many areas of local and parish administration and she notes that by around 1700 'reforms not only had been implemented, but had taken root; and many aspects of local administration seem to have settled into established patterns, to have become more uniform, almost routine' and cites the role of magistrates in improving and tightening the chain of command.[81] Hoppit's local Restoration administrators 'could find ways to maintain the highways, repair bridges, and care for the poor'.[82] Innes, for the eighteenth century, notes that local administrators 'had much experience behind them and a well-developed and increasingly ambitious and reflective culture of public service'.[83] Local administration has been shown to be effective earlier still in implementing central policy, in areas of legal matters and poor law administration. In broader studies, Sng has pointed to the effectiveness of, for example, 'the decentralized fiscal structure of Austria [which] contributed to the stability of the multi-ethnic empire and did not hamper its long-term economic development'.[84] Central control was not required to ensure effective processes were in place.

There are significant and well-established narratives that point to a more complex English state rooted in its people and communities rather than in its bureaucrats. These narratives are being revisited in more recent historiography of the fiscal-military state.[85] As long ago as 1982, Wrightson maintained that in the late sixteenth and seventeenth centuries, 'local communities were penetrated more deeply than had been the case previously by forces of economic, administrative and cultural integration which bound them into a national society and economy'.[86]

Braddick in his later work stresses the importance of 'a network of offices exercising political power coordinated under the Tudor and Stuart crown'[87] and stresses the role of local officeholders in any 'understanding of the early modern English state'.[88] Hindle also looked to the period before 1640. He criticised the overemphasis on taxation in state formation and rejected the notion that the state was simply created by financial needs, and instead sees a 'growth of governance' impetus, which was 'less a matter of institutional innovation at the centre than of social and cultural development in the localities'.[89] For Hindle, 'the state was a reservoir of authority on which the populace might draw, a series of institutions in which they could participate, in pursuit of their own interests'.[90] The degree to which individuals were self-serving or acting out of duty to their fellows might be debated, but the operation of Hindle's state required the 'active participation of thousands of private individuals who assumed public responsibility'.[91] Direct taxes relied on such delegation of authority to local officials with an occasional audit or prompting letter from the Exchequer or Board of Taxes by way of central control. Therefore, Hindle's notions of a state employing 'the delegation of central authority to men of quite humble status across thousands of parishes'[92] has significant resonance when considering land taxes. This chimes with Goldie's unacknowledged republic of 'officeholding', where one-twentieth of all adult males at around 1700 were involved in governance in any one year.[93] However, if the development of pre-1640s local governance capability was important this could not have been the only critical success factor. If capable local administration was well established then why were pre-1640s national taxes unsuccessful and declining? Why did traditional forms like the *subsidy* and *fifteenth and tenth*[94] fail in the seventeenth century? Braddick highlights this conundrum when he points to the 'failure of the [pre-1640] state in some functions and its success in others'.[95] Perhaps the simple answer is that the economy had moved on, but forms of taxation had not.

What then of economic factors behind tax growth? Contemporaries recognised seventeenth-century economic development, including Gregory King who proclaimed, 'England did mightily advance between the years 1600 and 1688'.[96] There are very broadly two current views of the British economy in the historiography of the late medieval and early modern period. One sees the period as one of general stagnation, albeit with some fluctuations following Phelps Brown and Hopkins[97] and Clark,[98] based substantially on real wages. The other, favoured by de Vries and others,[99] considers broader measures of wealth to suggest modest but sustained growth, again with considerable fluctuations. The literature here is enormous and revolves around whether there was a pre-1800 'Little Divergence' prior to the 'Great Divergence' of the nineteenth century, and its form and impact, and whether there was an 'Industrious Revolution'.[100] Were such changes supply-side driven or consumer led? Broadberry et al. report English per capita real GDP growth of 0.18% p.a. for the period between 1270 and 1700, 0.48% for the period 1700 and 1870, but stronger growth for the period 1650–1700 of 0.82%.[101] Following this modest growth narrative, as this work does, the early modern period was already characterised by a 'respectable lifestyle'.[102] There are numerous supporting indicators of changing living standards including a growing diversity of diets including meat, beer and imported sugar; the broader availability of new and cheap consumer goods including tobacco and soap; imported luxuries including silks[103]; the growing wealth of testators[104]; the virtual elimination of dearth; the growth of publicly funded welfare provision; increasing literacy; higher wages[105]; the growing diversity of occupations; urbanisation with far less people involved in agriculture[106]; the 'Great Rebuilding'[107]; more commercialised land markets,[108] particularly in the South-East; expanding grain exports; a booming re-export market[109]; rapidly growing labour productivity[110]; and a growth in the services and industrial sectors at the expense of agriculture. The early growth of the secondary sector (manufacturing and construction) is increasingly clear thanks to the pioneering work of the CAMPOP group.[111]

Later seventeenth-century, real GDP growth is estimated by Broadberry et al.,[112] at 0.78% p.a., but this is eclipsed by estimates of fiscal growth and as O'Brien points out, 'the fact that Britain's national product and urbanization rate probably rose by ratios of around three between the Glorious Revolution and the [1815] Treaty of Vienna, while tax receipts at the Exchequer multiplied some 15 times in real terms, degrades any suggestion that purports to explain Britain's fiscal success as a product of economic growth'.[113] Should economic developmental explanations of fiscal growth be dismissed? O'Brien himself does not go so far, only ruling them out as 'major forces behind the marked upswing in revenues'.[114] Sng summarises a broad consensus that 'Empirically, it has been observed that modern economic growth was associated with the rise of the fiscal state and the presence of strong central governments in Western Europe'.[115] What is contested is the nature of that relationship. Did the rise of a strong fiscal state foster economic growth or did growth provide the engine for tax expansion, alternatively was the relationship symbiotic? From different perspectives, both Acemoglu and O'Brien see economic growth as enabled by 'participation' or 'coercion'.[116] Although O'Brien recognises the importance of 'the gains from overseas trade',[117] specialisation[118] and markets,[119] he ultimately explains increased taxation in terms of coercive powerful elites.[120] He downplays economic changes and believes they are not 'major forces behind the marked upswing in revenues from taxes and loans'.[121] His primary evidence and one implied in much historiography of this period is that because tax growth is very much larger than any of the accepted measures of economic growth, it cannot be a major explanatory factor.[122] On the other hand, Fine argued that the development of the excise evolved closely in line with society and economy.[123] Brewer also takes a rather more positive stance believing that the ease with which post-revolutionary England raised supply was for three reasons: a powerful representative body, fiscal expertise and 'a commercialised economy whose structure made it comparatively simple to tax'.[124] This last seems important. After all, prima facie, the three most successful levies of the seventeenth century were those most closely related to contemporary cashflows from product supply chains and the tenanting of land in this growing 'commercialised economy'. There was also some fiscal learning from the pioneering Dutch as t' Hart[125] proposes, and both land taxes and excises were established earlier in the United Provinces where fiscal growth began over 50 years earlier.[126] Exploiting cashflows effectively reduced the optionality risk of traditional tax-gathering where local administrators acted as 'good neighbours rather than as effective representatives of the national government's interests'.[127] As economic development is likely to be a necessary condition for fiscal growth, then it is important to investigate those parts of the country which bore a significant weight of tax and are most likely to have been forced to adopt new taxation methods (Table 1.1). Many local land tax studies in the past have focussed on parts of the country where traditional tax-raising methods could continue because direct tax burdens remained low because they were set low land tax quotas. The important and neglected question is how did highly taxed regions respond to those heavier burdens? The heavily taxed county of Kent and cities of London and Bristol make up the three chosen case studies (and see Sect. 2.4 below).[128]

It is argued here that new forms of taxation were required to exploit England's developing economy and fund increasing seventeenth-century militarisation. There are alternative views. Thus, as far as Braddick was concerned, it was rather a matter of 'harnessing the existing structures and applying more effective pressure'.[129] Perhaps this was coupled with 'the respectable paternity of the [land] tax'.[130] For Braddick, and O'Brien and Hunt, seventeenth-century legislative forms were nothing new, although they have a slightly more positive view of excise.[131] Land taxes were 'traditional forms' whose quota system was 'hardly changed since the middle ages'. Besides, for some, land taxes were also wholly inconsistent in application.[132] Perhaps it is unsurprising and inevitable that these and similar models which seek explanations of fiscal growth in terms of coercion or consent downplay the importance of the mechanics and processes of taxation.[133] However, these latter questions are given greater scope in the broader fiscal literature. Excises were widely and successfully levied in early modern Europe and are enormously widespread across modern developing nations as discussed by Cnossen, precisely because they are almost universally easy to deploy where there is material product supply.[134] Excises were certainly raised at far higher rates by the Dutch than the English.[135] Thus, how far can the excise's success in England be explained by bureaucratisation, consent or coercion and how much simply by fiscal opportunism and increased consumption of alcohol and tobacco?[136] In the context of 'stable state formation', direct taxes, such as the land taxes (or 'internal' revenues), are potentially far more interesting than indirect levies, according to Blanton and Fargher, because they often appear to require some delegation of authority and collective action to achieve success.[137] This is a very general point, but provides one of the reasons for the detailed focus on legislation, governance, tax form and mechanics in this book.

Land tax records have also been much studied by agricultural and social historians, particularly for the late eighteenth and early nineteenth centuries when there is significant survival of parish assessments. This material is plundered here, including debates about the strength and consistency of correlations between land tax and acreage.[138] Extensive use has been made of some of Spence's work and the associated database for London.[139] However, discussion of these issues is included in the general text and not here in the historiography.

In conclusion, the historiography of land taxes and their administration has been significantly coloured by powerful narratives which focus on the post-revolutionary development of England's institutions and bureaucracy. The understanding of land taxes has also been hampered by the lack of a detailed review since Ward's work of 1953. These are taxes looking for a narrative. Land taxes were not bureaucratic, they were not institutionalised, and they had little by way of a professional administration.[140] Further, some historical narratives argue that they were nothing new, they were not modern,[141] they were not equitable,[142] and yet they were hugely successful at delivering cash to the Exchequer. The objective of this current work is to explain that success. Furthermore, because direct levies relied heavily on local administration, they have escaped the attention of many fiscal scholars busy with central records in recovering evidence of the machinery of state formation left by state bureaucrats. Land taxes have thus been both seriously overlooked and misjudged, because central records contain relatively little information. This book will focus substantially on local administrative records to consider how changing tax form, capable governors and improving fiscal processes contributed to the success of the land tax in a developing economy.

1.3 Methodology, Research Aims and Sources

1.3.1 Methodology

Approaches to early land taxes usually focus either on the study of central records such as Chandaman's[143] or of individual local administration such as Beckett's.[144] Ward attempted to cover both, but largely skimmed the surface of local administration.[145] Because administration was overwhelmingly local, central record studies often overlook local process developments and refinement and where they seek depth become anecdotal, whilst individual local studies have the difficulty of arriving at broad conclusions. Survival of local land tax documentation before the late eighteenth century is very poor. Even in areas where survival is relatively good, as in the chosen case study areas, there are difficult challenges because of significant archival gaps. Any analysis must recognise the shortcomings of such data, but be innovative in the use of surviving material.

The method adopted here is to critically consider in great detail the surviving administration records produced in three selected cases study areas and by comparison between them and other published material, draw broader conclusions. The first objective is to understand local administrative responses to legislative change. In particular, is there evidence that the new 1640s legislation prompted the creation of new tax mechanisms and processes on the ground? Were changes linked to economic and political developments? How did administrators deploy human resources to gather these successful and long-lived direct taxes and what adjustments, if any, needed to be made over time as burdens grew and populations changed? What were the backgrounds, capabilities, roles and responsibilities of the administrators themselves? What can the flows of funds from taxpayer via tax-gathering officialdom to the Exchequer divulge about the nature and efficiency of tax-gathering? The questions asked of the primary sources used in this study are who did what and when and how effective were such efforts? The overriding objective is to understand to what extent these local efforts contributed to the success of land taxes. Both rural and urban case studies were chosen to permit comparison. Good surviving records from the City of London, the much smaller City of Bristol, and the tiny 'town and port'[146] of New Romney provide urban comparatives.[147]

The land tax process required the production of prolific amounts of documentation across the nation. Over the period considered, there were between 60 and 130 separate statutory tax quotas set by parliamentary legislation across England and Wales, to be paid by counties, boroughs and other local administrations, and each of these required one or more tax summaries or ***duplicates*** to be despatched to the Exchequer.[148] Clerks and receivers-general would also require copies. Each duplicate suggests several printed copies of the statute would have been distributed by the Exchequer to the responsible local commissioners to be read at inaugural meetings, together with other pre-printed material including warrants and receipts. Each commissioner group employed a clerk who probably took meeting minutes. London and Bristol had only one statutory quota, but Kent had eleven in 1673[149] and an increasingly subdivided 28 by the early eighteenth century.[150] Each tax duplicate showed the individual totals from all parishes, boroughs, tax precincts or other subdivision which added up to one local statutory quota. Thus, Kent's 11–28 statutory quotas, and some quotas had multiple duplicates, were subdivided further on the face of these documents into parishes, precincts and boroughs. Each of these lesser subdivisions would have employed assessors who would already have drawn up a separate tax assessment with the names of numerous individual taxpayers and their dues. There were 18 such parish tax assessments in Bristol, up to 56 in the single lathe of Wingham in Kent and somewhere between 77 and 146 in the City of London. The fact that there are over ten thousand parishes in England alone gives some indication of the number of tax assessments produced nationwide on a quarterly or annual basis.[151] Each tax assessment implies at least one authorising assessor's warrant and one or more collectors' warrants. The county receivers-general needed to be appointed and warranted to gather the resulting cash. Receivers would give collectors cash receipts over the year and a further commissioners' receipt at process end. Receivers in turn expected Commissioners' or Exchequer receipts. Various officials kept accounts. This is to say nothing of the correspondence between receiver and clerk, clerk and collector, clerk and commissioners, receiver and Exchequer, clerk and assessor, and the clerk and Exchequer. For the period 1643–1733, hardly any of this material remains, but a critical mass of documents survives in the three case study areas.[152] Survival is limited and partial. It is the duplicate*s* that comprise a key element of surviving records from the period, being retained as part of central records from counties across the land.[153] There is surprisingly good if fragmentary survival of a variety of early local tax documentation amongst the Commonwealth Exchequer Papers.[154] In local archives in Kent, London and Bristol, there are a varied and extensive range of documents used by local administrators including commissioners' minutes, accounts, officials' warrants, tax assessments, receipts and correspondence. Through diligent conservation efforts, much material is in good or very good condition. Wherever possible this study has utilised original documents[155] rather than microfiche or third-party photographic reproductions. The major exception to this is the use of the Ancestry.co.uk website, which has excellent reproductions of City of London tax assessments after 1692 if somewhat confusingly catalogued.[156] Other photographic reproductions have proved problematic because signatures are often difficult to read or may be lost if written on the reverse. This is a study of these locally produced documents and is dependent on their chance retention and survival in the hands of local officials and on archival preservation.[157] Different documentary material ranges survive in each study area, gaps are numerous, and comparison is never straightforward. Civil War and Interregnum documents from locations beyond the three case study areas have been utilised to add to a limited evidence base.[158] A major secondary database has been extensively utilised in this study for the London 1693–1694

Four Shilling Aid,[159] but no new databases were created for evidence presented here. Data were processed using Microsoft® Excel, and all graphical images are in that form.

1.3.2 *Identifying the Tax Officials*

Tax commissioners were named in readily accessible legislative statutes and ordinances.[160] Because these were usually prominent men involved in local or national politics the vast majority can be readily identified as MPs named in the History of Parliament (HoP),[161] civic officials known from local accounts such as Beaven in Bristol[162] or Woodhead in London,[163] supplemented by the Oxford Dictionary of National Bibliography (Oxford DNB) and other local and online sources.[164] Individuals active in the process can be identified through their signatures on duplicate*s*, warrants, assessments and other documents as well as by their minuted attendance at commissioners' meetings. The vast majority of signatures are legible and are readily identified with names in the sources described. Commissioners' minutes survive well in Bristol and St. Augustine Lathe, East (better known as Wingham, Fig. 3.1)[165] in Kent and very occasionally in the City of London. Throughout, there are familiar difficulties of common names and those of fathers and sons, but at the commissioner level these difficulties can usually be readily overcome.[166]

Tax-collectors were usually named in the land tax duplicate*s* retained at The National Archives (TNA).[167] During the early eighteenth century, duplicate*s* were often written on high-quality parchment, so almost all names are legible. Collectors may also be named in commissioners' minutes, on warrants, assessments and other documents. Therefore, it is often possible to trace the continuity of collectors and assessors from one year to the next. The names of assessors appear on many of these sources, but not the duplicate*s*. On occasion, the occupations of individual assessors and collectors were given in the assessments themselves or on contemporary polls or marriage duty assessments. From other contemporary documents, it has sometimes been possible to track other responsibilities that these individuals had, for example in the case of Bassishaw in London, where local ward documents survive.[168] Some individual tax officials are better documented where they went on to take broader civic or national roles.

1.3.3 *Tax Accounts*

Several local financial accounts are used in this study. Chandaman questions the reliability of any Restoration accounts not destined for Exchequer scrutiny, claiming the 'majority are of doubtful provenance'.[169] Whilst accepting that caution is required, because City of London accounts were closely scrutinised themselves, they may be considered relatively reliable. In Kent, the keen Interregnum oversight of Receiver-General Charles Bowles created consistency and conformity in the production of Interregnum accounts from various lathes which encourages some confidence. Receivers and their deputies and head/high-collectors often kept accounts, but few survive. London has the most complete records because the City Chamberlain was usually the receiver[170] and for most years from the Restoration onwards there are accounts showing payments to the receiver from collectors and from the receiver to the Exchequer.[171] These provide the dates of payments and the amounts remitted and were recorded by city ward and precinct. Numerous high-collectors' accounts survive from Interregnum Kent and indeed from several other south-eastern counties in the Commonwealth Exchequer Papers.[172] There are no surviving accounts for Kent after 1660, and no tax accounts were traced for Bristol, largely because receivers were rarely resident there. Here, tax efficiency can be mapped through receipts sent to commissioners by receivers at annual process close and through correspondence between receivers and clerks.

1.3.4 *Taxpayers and Tax Assessments*

In 1700, there were about 23,000 land taxpayers in the City of London, more than 3,800 in the City of Bristol, and approximately 27,500 in Kent.[173] Numbers increased somewhat over time. Some paid in respect of their offices or personal estates, but most paid as occupiers of land whether held for domestic, commercial or agricultural purposes. Most taxpayers are named on assessments for land taxes, polls, other taxes and in returns or *estreats*[174] and some as appellants against their tax charges.[175] There are well-known and serious difficulties with land tax assessments, noting in particular Mingay's concerns over the 'grave limitations'[176] of this source, and particularly Ginter's strictures on 'these nasty little documents, which at the outset seemed so simple, proved treacherous'.[177] In 17 pages, he sets out the 'minor problems', and then, in a further 22 sets out the 'major problems'[178] which he deemed 'for the most part unresolvable'. Because Ginter has chosen the relatively lightly taxed county of Yorkshire (near the bottom of Table 1.1), his conclusions are not entirely representative of England as a whole. Nevertheless many points are well made. Thus, individual tax charges often reflected more than a single property (up to 80 in Bristol, see below), sometimes the landlord pays directly, many properties were untaxed and individuals listed as occupier may be nothing of the sort.[179] One taxpayer may appear many times, and those who paid the tax may not suffer it because they were often able to deduct from their rent. Tax incidence is far from clear, as William Petty speculated.[180] Taxed 'rent' does not necessarily represent the rent paid or the annual value of land, but evidence presented below suggests in many areas a discounted approximation was normal and that land values were used flexibly to meet quotas.[181] The questions in this work are not about land ownership or social structure, but about who paid tax to the collector, and also who did not. It seems probable that in the great majority of cases, the individual named against a tax charge would be expected to pay. In London and Bristol, landlords sometimes paid on behalf of tenants and in Kent landlords and tenants were usually both named, with a clear implication that the tenant would pay initially. No doubt, some collectors and perhaps other officials dipped into their own pockets to complete their tax round by making short-term loans or gifts to the hard-up as Brooks recognised.[182]

Broad estimations of taxpayers and non-payers are made here by comparing the mid-1690s marriage duty lists, which may provide a more comprehensive list of resident individuals, with contemporary land tax assessments as discussed below.[183] There is also assistance from contemporary polls and in the case of London, alternative methods of population calculation from secondary sources using the *Bills of Mortality* and birth records.

1.4 The Role of Women in the Tax Process

It is well established that by the seventeenth-century English women were able to become scholars, philosophers or writers, they ran businesses, prosecuted cases in the courts, lent money and enjoyed wealthy lifestyles without the necessary accompaniment of men. Unmarried women and widows could own property, buy financial assets, sue and be sued.[184] In contemporary London, almost all wives, according to court records, were gainfully employed even if often female businesses were run under the name of their husband.[185] However, in a deeply patriarchal society it remained exceptionally difficult to take on any overtly political or administrative role whether nationally or locally. The control of money matters was also very largely a male preserve. English tax-gathering was both financial and political, and it is perhaps unsurprising that women appear to have been almost entirely excluded from land tax administration. However, some 10–15% of land taxes were paid by women usually as occupiers of urban or rural land.

Considering the tens of thousands of tax officials named in contemporary documents from three case study areas, it is noteworthy that virtually all named individuals were men. The official documents almost always give the forename and surnames of individuals, and occasionally, a title so the identification of male and female officials is usually straightforward. Of course, not all names are fully decipherable on contemporary documents and in a few cases only a surname can be made out. It is worth noting that the legislation itself appeared not to discriminate overtly as to the choice of male or female officials. Statutes normally referred to the appointment simply of persons as tax officials, but according to common law under the rules of 'coverture'[186] women's separate legal existence was restricted and 'a wife could not technically enter into economic contracts in her own right and in order to make basic purchases on credit had to do so in her husband's name'.[187] There were many ways to work around this restriction, but as the main powers of discipline and control over all tax officials were in levying penalties and seizing assets, the naming of married women as tax officials would carry with it some difficulty and financial risk. It was certainly avoided in the cases and documents studied here. Women are never named as tax commissioners in the land tax statutes, hardly ever as collectors in tax duplicates, or on tax warrants. Could it be that some married women worked as lead players or assistants under the name of a husband or relative without being named as such? Naming a married female tax official's husband in tax documents would be a practical solution to the issue of discipline and control. It is certainly likely that some married women remain hidden in this way, but the sources considered here are largely silent on the matter and there has been no attempt here to look at broader material, but this finding appears to mirror the experience of others.[188] There was no similar common law restriction for spinsters or widows, and the three cases of women identified and named in tax documents below were all widows. Nevertheless, the number of identified individuals is tiny and it seems clear that tax administration was overwhelmingly a male preserve. Only three women emerge from the documents studied as acting in any official capacity. An Henman, widow, was a joint tax-collector with John Younge in the parish of Murston in Upper Scray in 1671 according to the tax duplicate.[189] Widowed and remarried Mary Echlin was involved in sorting out the tax accounts of her deceased receiver-general husband for the year 1711.[190] Widowed Elizabeth Ashurst signed the receipts for poundage due to the commissioners' clerk for her deceased husband Henry who had also been Town Clerk.[191] There is no evidence that either of these latter two were involved in detailed administration, other than resolving issues from their late husbands' estates. These three women appear an exception to the rule because land tax administration was overwhelmingly a male bastion.

1.5 Historical Context

The chosen period is from the 1643 introduction of the innovative Weekly Assessment, triggered by Civil War, to the excise crisis of 1733 when the very existence of land taxes seemed under threat. The innovative 1643 legislation was followed by numerous further assessments which were soon called land taxes in common parlance and in Parliament itself. This long perspective has been selected to consider the particular challenges that local land tax administrators faced, and the resulting many and varied adaptations made in three comparative study areas. In particular, considering such a long period allows consideration of improvements in the tax process including, simplification, delegation and the increasing experience of personnel. In the later eighteenth century, land tax contribution to supply declined and the value of real estate for tax purpose was not re-rated as land values soared. Consideration of these later periods would be for another work.

Parliament was invariably involved in authorising all land taxes on an annual or more frequent basis. The text of most of these parliamentary ordinances and statutes are well preserved. The terms 'land tax', 'assessment', 'rent-tax' or 'aid' are used in this study and by contemporaries, but the terms are virtually synonymous, as is often recognised in the historiography, including both Turner and Beckett.[192] The current study favours the term land tax, and this would have been a term widely understood in the Interregnum (and see below), because they all contained similar and distinctive legislative features set out in detail below (Table 2.1). This continuity of pre- and post-revolutionary land tax is generally well understood in the literature. The 24 February 1643 First Weekly Assessment was itself the product of fiscal experimentation over the previous year, but significant legislative adaption continued for another decade. Key legislative features remained part of administration hereafter, including the broad basis of taxation focussed primarily on occupiers of land; the potential deduction of tax suffered by tenants from their landlords' rent; the broad shape of fixed amounts due to be paid by counties and cities—or quotas (Fig. 1.2)[193]; the mechanism for reassessment; the deadline-driven process; and the name 'land tax'. Land taxes were easily the most burdensome tax of the period from 1643 to1659 levied every year and raising perhaps £12.2m in total compared with £5m for the excise and £1.8m for sequestrations.[194] At the Restoration, both the assessment and the excise were tarnished by association with the Commonwealth, even though royalists had dabbled with both, and dramatic royalist rhetoric such as this from the future Charles II in 1659 seemed to herald abolition: '… our long enslaved subjects, under the Egyptian bondage of Taxes, Excise, unusual Customs, Assessements, and Free-quartering'.[195]

Royal promises of Restoration abolition of both the assessment and the excise were never delivered, nor likely to be. Political anguish expressed in Parliament in the 1660s, 1670s, 1690s and the 1730s over these two powerful[196] and uncompromising levies, which might create an overly powerful military-backed monarchy, was easily quelled by their sheer effectiveness. Whereas the excise became part of ordinary revenue, so the king could in theory 'live of his own',[197] land taxes were still raised only as extraordinary supply and required ongoing parliamentary approval in years of mobilisation. In fact, land taxes were levied in most years until the Exclusion Crisis, and the distinction between ordinary and extraordinary revenues became increasingly blurred, as is widely recognised.[198] Post-Interregnum demobilisation and later mobilisations had to be funded, and parliament accepted that only land taxes, however tarnished, could reliably generate sufficient sums, sometimes alongside a poll.[199] Chandaman believes 96% of expected Restoration assessment yields were delivered, a far higher proportion than any other direct levy, and this represented 86.5% of all contemporary direct taxes (Fig. 1.1).[200]

Sir Robert Carr MP, a tax commissioner himself, expressed the dilemma created by this tarnished but powerful tax in the House of Commons in November 1670: 'Hears great objections against a Land-Tax, but would not take a worse way. Would have it debated whether a Land-Tax be not a way much more certain and less burthensome'.[201]

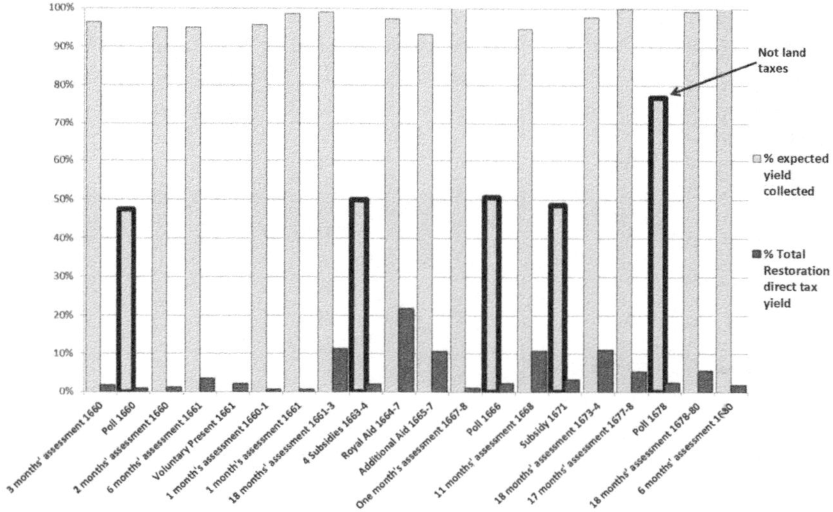

Fig. 1.1 Restoration direct tax yields after Chandaman[202] *Note* The graph shows both the proportion of expected yield gathered for each tax and the proportional contribution to the £11.4m direct taxes collected in the period. Land taxes outperformed all others on both measures

Land tax effectiveness was put significantly to the test during the Second Anglo-Dutch War requiring significant sums to be levied in four related legislative statutes with a maximum annual charge of over £1,450,000 across England and Wales.[203] These taxes were virtually identical in form to the Interregnum assessment, with some additional burden on the taxation of offices and some modest adjustments of earlier quotas (see Fig. 1.2).[204] Such adjustment created some fierce debate, but rather modest movement.[205] Land taxes levied in the four years from December 1664 comprised the largest amount of direct tax ever levied in the country and would not be surpassed until after the

Glorious Revolution, making up over 44% of all Restoration direct levies (Fig. 1.1). More short-lived heavy burdens had been raised in the early 1650s as Civil War ended, and there was engagement in the First Anglo-Dutch War.[206]

Restoration land taxes were so successful at cash generation that an Exchange Office was created in 1667 to provide limited supervision, manage payments and cash delivery to London, and facilitate increased paper transfers of funds.[207] In the interim, supply experiments included a not so 'free and voluntary present',[208] and a final hugely unsuccessful attempt to replace the land tax with an old-fashioned quadruple subsidy in 1663–1664.[209]

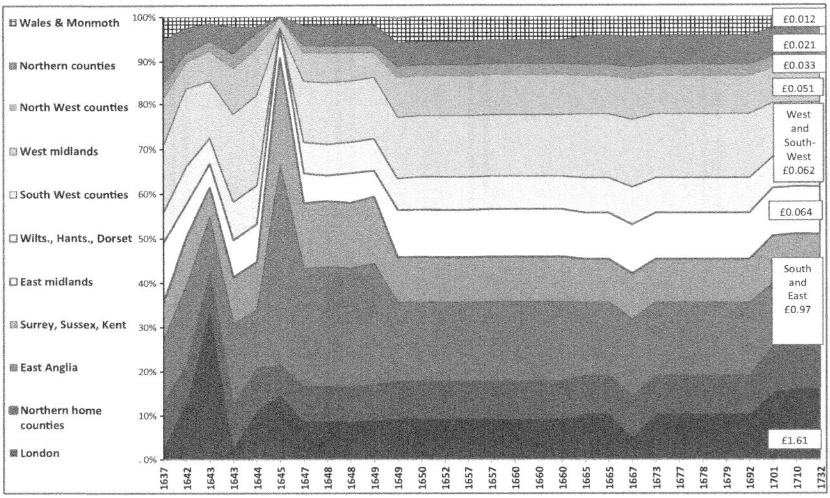

Fig. 1.2 The regional basis of county tax quotas 1637–1732 for ship money, subsidies, assessments and land taxes[210] *Note* Tax weight per acre order. Far right, £1.61 = tax per acre at four-shilling/£ rate based on contemporary sources[211]

In 1671, there was a further piece of innovative legislative experimentation with a new form of subsidy[212] which actually bore many features of the assessment, including the focus on occupiers and rent. However, there was an attempt to broaden the personal estate element of the tax including a tax on bankers and interest. The dominant real estate part of this novel tax was raised at 12d/£ so there were no fixed quotas or amounts to be raised in each county and town unlike the land taxes. This meant that for the first time, in many parts of the country, there would have been a new valuation of real estate. This was then estimated at between £9 and £18 million annual value in England and Wales which at one shilling/pound should have raised £450,000–£900,000 plus further amounts from stock, money and offices, making up contemporary yield estimates of £569,620–£1,139,241 in all.[213] In fact, it raised only £365,000, which even allowing for perceived declining land values, was wholly unsatisfactory. This failure was perhaps because, as Chandaman believed, 'in practice it never related to the real value of property',[214] it allowed the deductions of expenses to alleviate tax burdens, and amounts were effectively self-assessed (Fig. 1.1).[215] More important however was the lack of statutory quotas. Several areas failed to revalue, but legislators had provided for this by the long-established exemption that allowed the 'usual' methods to prevent 'Obstructtions and Delayes in assessing and collectting'. This largely unsuccessful fiscal experiment yielded less than half the ambitious anticipated yield.[216] It was not repeated, in what became more perilous times for state finance following the Stop of the Exchequer—the repudiation of state debt in 1672.

After this subsidy failure, Parliament resorted to the tried and trusted conventional land tax assessments which were levied again on four further occasions during the 1670s, particularly to fund the Third Anglo-Dutch War. Where 1671 real estate valuations had taken place, these could be utilised as the basis for the later assessments with quotas in 1673–1674 (*18-months' assessment*),[217] 1677–1678 (*17-months' assessment*),[218] 1678–1679 (*18-months' assessment*)[219] and 1680 (*6-months' assessment*).[220] Legislators for these late Restoration levies innovatively increased the pay of officials and empowered collectors by delayering administration with the abolition of the high-collector role which sat between receiver and sub-collector. The 1680 assessment provided a final payment of tax on 24 August 1680—the last of the Restoration, as the Exclusion Crisis prevented further levies as parliament was not successfully reconvened. Fortunately for the monarchy, trade and commerce prospered in the succeeding period and indirect tax receipts were buoyant which together with asset sales substantially made up any shortfall from direct taxes.[221]

Land taxes or aids were quickly reintroduced after 1688 against multiple military threats, including the 'Defence of Your [majesty's] Realmes for the Reduceing of Ireland and for the Vigorous Prosecution of the Warr against France both by Sea and Land'.[222] The legislation was virtually identical to what had gone before, including the precise shape of quotas (Fig. 1.2),[223] with some new provisions for the taxation of shareholding, that is corporate taxes. On the other hand, the unsuccessful *hearth tax* was quickly abolished. This provided a useful opportunity for overblown political rhetoric to explain the reasons for abolition in terms of the generosity of the new monarch. Hearth tax was: 'not onely a great Oppression to the Poorer sort but a Badge of Slavery upon the whole People'.[224] In fact, hearth tax produced modest returns which were more trouble than they were worth.

With regular parliaments, land tax funding became the major supply for the Nine Years' War and thereafter effectively a permanent levy. The higher levels of remuneration for tax officials were continued from the Restoration and increasingly experienced paid receivers, collectors and clerks took most of the administrative burden. Land tax's Restoration record tax burdens were quickly broken as they reached annual rates of £1,651,702-18s-0d in 1692.[225] However, this was levied against a background of economic tightening in time of war. The pressure of a huge war effort led to significant fiscal experimentation with both indirect and direct levies as tax burdens doubled, and there was a renewed currency crisis. Food prices escalated, and the price of wheat tripled in the decade after 1688.[226] Post-revolutionary land taxes, like many of their Restoration and Interregnum predecessors, were collateralised by state borrowing against future receipts with interest rates of 6–7%. Supply was still difficult and national quotas were dispensed with for the 1693–1694 Four Shilling Aid, as they had been in 1671. This act instead, applied a pound rate of 4s/£ on land and offices in an attempt to bring in about two million pounds in a single year.[227] This new act also launched a nationwide revaluation of real estate purportedly to reduce perceived unfairness, although it contained the usual exemption override to allow traditional taxation methods thus 'avoideing all Obstruc[i]ons and Delayes'. Achievements as regards reducing perceived unfairness were limited as tax became even more heavily skewed towards the South-East of the country and particularly urban areas (Fig. 1.2).[228] As well as being skewed by the historic 'Commonwealth' shape of quotas as Davenant claimed,[229] there was probably some significant basis in the underlying economy because the South-East land markets were more commercialised than those elsewhere and producing cashflows which could be exploited by the state. The shape of land tax quotas bears clear resemblance to the geography of agrarian capitalism mapped and described by Shaw-Taylor.[230] Spence's Londoners, Davison's and Grover's Kentish farmers, and Habakkuk's Northamptonshire and Bedfordshire landowners all seem to be paying tax either at a rate close to the statute on their rents or at least slightly discounted.[231] Further north and west taxpayers paid less, often very much less, but there was little consistency and traditional tax methods persisted there.[232] Important at this time too was the role of statisticians like Gregory King who could make better estimates of the tax capacity of the country than ever before.

The last years of the Nine Years' War coincided with what has been termed the *Financial Revolution*. These years saw the formation of the Bank of England, the issuance of government bonds, the widespread use of paper bills, the Civil List, a currency crisis and the Great Recoinage, but also widespread public fiscal conversation and debate.[233] With even higher demands for supply and falling land tax receipts, probably because of the lack of fixed quotas, there was further fiscal experimentation including a broadly based tax on marriages, births and burials (1695),[234] and a duty on houses or *window tax* (1696).[235] Unfortunately, none of these levies could remotely match the effectiveness of the traditional land taxes at raising state supply and a land tax with quotas was raised again from 1698.[236] Quotas were now based on the 1693–1694 Four Shilling Aid. Land taxes continued to be deployed throughout the period considered here, varying from nominally 4s/£ on land briefly down to one shilling in 1732 and 1733.[237] The plethora of direct levies created a mid-1690s challenge for the local governors who were already charged with the administration of land taxes. There was also the matter of political opposition to high taxation, against a background of economic difficulties, in a brief period of peace between the Nine Years' War and the War of the Spanish Succession, which saw the Standing Army Controversy and troop levels sharply reduced.

During the War of the Spanish Succession, land tax was the major supply, but was permanently overtaken by the excise as a revenue source

Table 1.1 Percentages of National land tax quotas by county 1643–1710[238]

Order by tax per square mile in 1702 as estimated by 1745 sources

	1643 (%)	Nov 1650 (%)	1657 (%)	Royal Aid (%)	1673–1674 (%)	1679 (%)	1692 (%)	1701 (%)	1710 (%)	1650-Royal Aid % Quota movement (%)	Royal Aid to 1692 movement (%)	Royal Aid-1710% movement (%)	Tax per square mile 1702 sources (£)	MPs 1702	1702 land tax per MP (£)
Metropolitan London	**35.9**	**9.5**	**9.5**	**10.7**	**10.7**	**10.7**	**10.7**	**15.5**	**16.4**	**12.4**	**0.00**	**53.8**	**27,422.18**	**8**	**38469.25**
Bristol	**0.2**	**0.2**	**0.2**	**0.3**	**0.3**	**0.3**	**0.3**	**0.4**	**0.4**	**18.6**	**0.00**	**27.8**	**6412.61**	**2**	**3695.77**
Surrey	1.2	2.2	2.2	2.3	2.3	2.3	2.3	3.4	3.3	3.9	0.00	44.0	91.18	14	4786.71
Bedfordshire	0.7	1.3	1.3	1.3	1.3	1.3	1.3	1.4	1.4	−2.2	0.00	9.8	88.40	4	7138.50
Buckinghamshire	1.2	1.9	1.8	1.9	1.9	1.9	1.9	2.4	2.4	−0.2	0.00	24.3	86.97	14	3404.29
Hertford	1.3	2.0	2.0	2.0	2.0	2.0	2.0	2.2	2.1	−2.1	0.00	9.1	76.74	6	7162.17
Northants	1.2	2.0	2.0	2.1	2.1	2.1	2.1	2.4	2.4	2.8	0.00	17.1	70.43	9	5345.22
Berkshire	1.6	1.6	1.6	1.6	1.6	1.6	1.6	2.1	2.1	5.9	0.00	25.0	62.77	9	4561.56
Suffolk	3.7	5.2	5.2	4.8	4.8	4.8	4.8	3.7	3.7	−8.2	0.00	−23.0	59.72	16	4613.69
Norfolk	3.7	5.4	5.4	5.2	5.2	5.2	5.2	4.3	4.2	−5.2	0.00	−17.8	59.37	12	7055.00
Oxford	1.9	1.6	1.6	1.6	1.6	1.6	1.6	2.0	2.0	2.5	0.00	18.9	59.10	9	4353.67
Essex	3.3	5.0	5.0	4.5	4.5	4.5	4.5	4.6	4.5	−9.9	0.00	−0.3	59.10	8	11,375.88
Kent	**3.7**	**5.2**	**5.2**	**4.8**	**4.8**	**4.8**	**4.8**	**4.2**	**4.2**	**−7.4**	**0.00**	**−13.6**	**53.83**	**18**	**4635.72**
Huntingdon	0.6	0.9	0.9	0.9	0.9	0.9	0.9	0.8	0.8	3.7	0.00	−15.7	50.64	4	3874.25
Worcester	1.7	1.8	1.8	1.6	1.6	1.6	1.6	1.7	1.7	−9.3	0.00	4.6	50.22	9	3744.00
Leicester	0.5	1.6	1.6	1.6	1.6	1.6	1.6	1.8	1.7	1.4	0.00	10.5	50.17	4	8717.75
Somerset	3.1	3.9	3.9	4.0	4.0	4.0	4.0	3.3	3.3	3.6	0.00	−19.0	48.79	16	4067.59
Warwickshire	1.8	1.8	1.8	1.7	1.7	1.7	1.7	2.0	2.0	−2.5	0.00	15.3	47.91	6	6644.00
Gloucester	2.4	2.6	2.6	2.7	2.7	2.7	2.7	2.4	2.4	5.1	0.00	−11.3	47.81	8	5940.25
Wiltshire	2.1	2.8	2.8	2.9	2.9	2.9	2.9	2.6	2.6	3.0	0.00	−9.4	47.49	34	1519.76
Cambridgeshire & Ely	1.5	2.1	2.1	2.0	2.0	2.0	2.0	1.7	1.6	−5.1	0.00	−17.4	46.36	6	5471.00
Sussex	1.8	2.7	2.7	2.6	2.6	2.6	2.6	3.1	3.0	−2.7	0.00	14.7	42.95	28	2172.14
Rutland	0.2	0.4	0.4	0.3	0.3	0.3	0.3	0.3	0.3	−10.1	0.00	−20.8	40.63	2	2762.50

(continued)

Table 1.1 (continued)

Order by tax per square mile in 1702 as estimated by 1745 sources

	1643 (%)	*Nov 1650 (%)*	*1657 (%)*	*Royal Aid (%)*	*1673–1674 (%)*	*1679 (%)*	*1692 (%)*	*1701 (%)*	*1710 (%)*	*1650-Royal Aid % Quota movement (%)*	*Royal Aid to 1692 movement (%)*	*Royal Aid-1710% movement (%)*	*Tax per square mile 1702 sources (£)*	*MPs 1702*	*1702 land tax per MP (£)*
Nottinghamshire	0.5	1.3	1.3	1.3	1.3	1.3	1.3	1.4	1.4	−4.3	0.00	7.7	39.30	8	3409.50
Hampshire, Southampton, Isle of White	2.2	2.9	2.9	3.2	3.2	3.2	3.2	2.8	2.8	10.2	0.00	−13.1	37.26	26	2122.62
Devon	5.4	4.4	4.4	4.9	4.9	4.9	4.9	4.2	4.1	9.5	0.00	−14.9	34.63	26	3176.27
Dorset	1.3	1.9	1.9	2.0	2.0	2.0	2.0	1.7	1.7	4.4	0.00	−15.8	34.53	20	1655.80
Lincoln	2.4	3.9	3.9	3.7	3.7	3.7	3.7	3.6	3.6	−3.7	0.00	−3.4	33.41	12	6018.83
Cheshire	0.7	1.2	1.2	1.2	1.2	1.2	1.2	1.4	1.4	−4.7	0.00	23.1	31.99	4	7149.75
Derbyshire	0.5	1.3	1.3	1.3	1.3	1.3	1.3	1.2	1.2	−5.9	0.00	−3.7	28.51	4	6023.25
Staffordshire	0.6	1.3	1.3	1.3	1.3	1.3	1.3	1.4	1.4	−5.6	0.00	8.0	26.96	10	2712.10
Cornwall	1.8	2.3	2.3	2.2	2.2	2.2	2.2	1.6	1.6	−4.0	0.00	−28.4	26.82	44	726.70
Shropshire	1.1	1.9	1.9	1.7	1.7	1.7	1.7	1.5	1.5	−7.3	0.00	−16.8	26.27	12	2421.67
Hereford	1.3	1.7	1.7	1.6	1.6	1.6	1.6	1.0	1.0	−1.3	0.00	−37.8	24.89	8	2551.13
Monmouth	0.2	0.7	0.7	0.6	0.6	0.6	0.6	0.5	0.5	−14.9	0.00	−13.2	23.25	3	3270.67
Yorkshire	3.4	4.4	4.4	5.0	5.0	5.0	5.0	4.6	4.6	13.5	0.00	−9.0	19.56	30	3054.40
Lancaster	1.5	1.3	1.3	1.5	1.5	1.5	1.5	1.1	1.1	9.8	0.00	−28.1	14.69	14	1499.21
Durham	0.2	0.2	0.2	0.5	0.5	0.5	0.5	0.5	0.5	128.9	0.00	12.8	13.98	4	2649.25
Northumberland	0.2	0.3	0.3	0.5	0.5	0.5	0.5	0.7	0.7	78.4	0.00	34.6	8.55	8	1818.50
Wales	1.3	4.9	4.9	3.7	3.7	3.7	3.7	2.2	2.2	−25.1	0.00	−40.5	6.67	24	1830.46
Westmorland	0.1	0.1	0.1	0.2	0.2	0.2	0.2	0.2	0.2	63.9	0.00	−9.5	4.81	4	761.25
Cumberland	0.1	0.2	0.2	0.2	0.2	0.2	0.2	0.2	0.2	58.6	0.00	−23.9	2.87	6	618.83

in 1714.[239] This return of England to the European theatre of war saw land taxes at 4s/£ until 1713 when the Tory administration halved the rate for three years. The end of war, fluctuations in the political fortunes of Whigs and Tories, and the 1715 Rising all created challenges for local direct tax administrations. The bursting of the South Sea Bubble ruined many, and ended political careers, but created opportunities for others. Walpole's handling of the post-Bubble aftermath assisted his rise, and if land taxes were generally lower under his leadership, it was partly because of his policy of detachment from foreign battlefields. Key aspects of the 1733 legislative form were little changed from 90 years earlier (Table 2.1). Even Walpole ultimately found it impossible to dispense with the land tax as the 'sturdy beggars'[240] and satirists enjoyed their 1733 revenge.[241] Whatever the political rhetoric, the fiscal truth was that, only excise, land tax and customs were capable of raising the millions of pounds required to meet the state's need for supply. This was as true in 1733 as in 1660, 1672, 1688, 1701, 1715 or 1643.

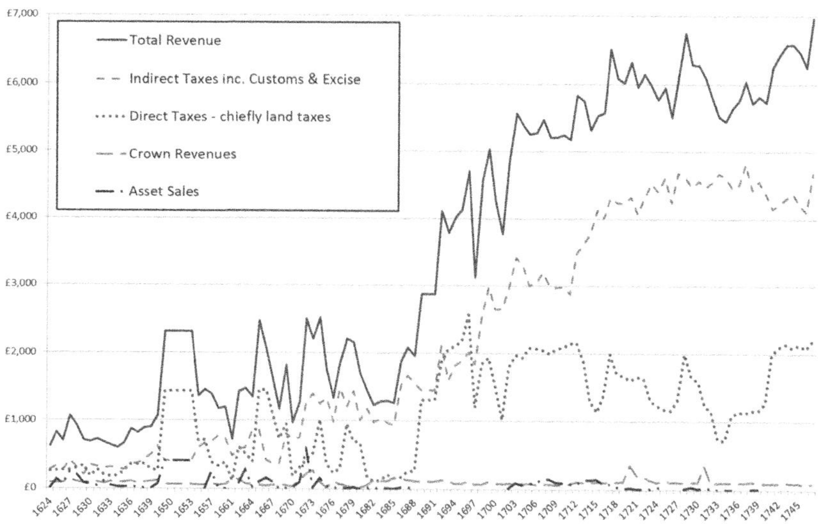

Fig. 1.3 English state taxes and other revenues after O'Brien and Hunt. Gross revenue (thousands) 1624–1745[242]

Notes

1. Colin Brooks, 'Public Finance and Political Stability: The Administration of the Land Tax, 1688–1720,' *Historical Journal*, vol. 17, 1974, pp. 281–300. Brooks on page 281 said 'I do not intend to attempt a rehabilitation of the Land Tax as a "fiscal weapon"', but his work does much to do so as a critique of William R. Ward, *The English Land Tax in the Eighteenth Century* (London: Oxford University Press, 1953).
2. To contradict Michael J. Braddick, *Parliamentary Taxation, Local Administration and Response*, The Royal Historical Society Studies in History (Woodbridge: Boydell Press, 1994), p. 150.
3. Upper Scray was sometimes called 'Milton and Tenham hundred'.
4. Department for Constitutional Affairs, *Tax Appeals: A Guide to Appealing Against Decisions of the Inland Revenue on tax and Other Matters*, http://webarchive.nationalarchives.gov.uk/20060820083451/hmrc.gov.uk/leaflets/tax-appeals.pdf. In fact, the General Commissioners have now been subsumed into HM Courts & Tribunals Service, but some local independence is still maintained.
5. For example, Patrick K. O'Brien and Philip A. Hunt, 'The rise of a fiscal state in England, 1485–1815', *Historical Research*, vol. 66, 1993, pp. 129–176.
6. Recognised in contemporary legislation which noted much tax was 'yet unpaid … to the great discouragement of those who have willingly contributed'. Ordinance: 'June 1645: An Ordinance for the more speedy getting in of the Moneys in Arrear', A&O, pp. 697–700.
7. The low cost was widely recognised by contemporaries.
8. See below, the term 'land tax' was in use at least by the 1650s.
9. Following Craig Muldrew, 'Wages and the Problem of Monetary Scarcity in Early Modern England', in Jan Lucassen (ed.), *Wages and Currency: Global Comparisons from Antiquity to the Twentieth Century* (Bern: Peter Lang, 2007), pp. 391–410; Craig Muldrew, *The Economy of Obligation: The Culture of Credit and Social Relations in Early Modern England* (Basingstoke: Palgrave, 1998), pp. 98–103.
10. Rack-rent is usually taken to mean full annual value.
11. The term 'revolutionary' is used in relation to the excise by D'Maris Coffman, *Excise Taxation and the Origins of Public Debt*. Palgrave Studies in the History of Finance (Basingstoke: Palgrave Macmillan, 2013).
12. Braddick, *Parliamentary Taxation*, p. 150 sees land taxes as 'far from a radical departure' from the past.
13. Coercive authority, e.g., according to Patrick K. O'Brien 'The nature and historical evolution of an exceptional fiscal state and its possible

significance for the precocious commercialization and industrialization of the British economy from Cromwell to Nelson', *The Economic History Review*, vol. 64, 2011, pp. 408–446, 439.

14. The terms 'consent', 'willingness' and 'tax morale' are all widely used by various authors. Michael J. Braddick, *The Nerves of the State: Taxation and the Financing of the English State 1558–1714* (Manchester: Manchester University Press, 1996), p. 185, uses the term 'consent'; Brooks, 'Public Finance and Political Stability', p. 282 has 'The levying of the Land Tax depended not upon force, but upon consent', p. 282. Henry Roseveare, *The Financial Revolution, 1660–1760* (London: Longman, 1991), p. 2, describes the transformation of the 'willingness, rather than the ability, of the English people to pay high taxes, lend large sums of money and above all repose trust in the financial institutions of their parliamentary government'; Ward, The English Land Tax, p. 4 has 'consent' of the 'propertied classes to fairly regular taxation upon incomes and trained to work the local tax machinery'; Prak and van Zanden propose the concept of 'tax morale' in contemporary Holland. Maarten Prak and Jan Luiten van Zanden, 'Tax Morale and Citizenship in the Dutch Republic', in Oscar Gelderblom (ed.) *The Political Economy of the Dutch Republic* (Farnham: Ashgate, 2009), pp. 143–166. Beyond this taxpayer consent is central to the 'New Fiscal Sociology'. It is suggested 'that taxpayer consent is best explained not as coercion, predation, or illusion, but as a collective bargain in which taxpayers give up resources in exchange for collective goods', Isaac W. Martin, Ajay K. Mehrotra, and Monica Prasad, 'The Thunder of History: The Origins and Development of the New Fiscal Sociology', in Martin, Mehrotra and Prasad (eds.), *The New Fiscal Sociology: Taxation in Comparative and Historical Perspective* (Cambridge: Cambridge University Press, 2009), pp. 1–27, 14.
15. Daron Acemoglu, 'Politics and Economics in Weak and Strong States', *Journal of Monetary Economics*, vol. 52, 2005, pp. 1199–1226.
16. Others believe that the role of highly taxed states in economic development has been hugely overstated, e.g. Gregory Clark review: 'Money, banks, government bonds, taxes, naval organization—did any of these make the British Industrial Revolution? To a sceptic it all seems on a par with those fervent believers who see Weeping Madonnas in tree stumps. But with belief every institution becomes wondrous'. Review of Leandro Prados de la Escosura (ed.). *Exceptionalism and Industrialization: Britain and its European Rivals, 1688–1815* (Cambridge: Cambridge University Press, 2004), *The Journal of Economic History*, vol. 66, 2006, pp. 833–834.

17. Peter G. M. Dickson, *The Financial Revolution in England. A Study in the Development of Public Credit 1688–1756* (London: Macmillan, 1967).
18. Transformation or 'fiscal revolution' according to D'Maris Coffman, 'The Fiscal Revolution of the Interregnum: Excise Taxation in the British Isles, 1643–1663' (PhD thesis, University of Pennsylvania, 2008). Alternatively, this was simply the 'groundwork' for the post-revolutionary Financial Revolution following Cecil D. Chandaman, *The English Public Revenue 1660–1688* (Oxford: Clarendon Press 1975), p. 1.
19. Following, e.g. Stephen Hindle, *The State and Social Change in Early Modern England c.1550–1640* (Basingstoke: Palgrave, 2000).
20. As argued by several authors. During the Interregnum 'when it came to handling public revenue, the "honest-radicals" were indeed scrupulously honest' according to Stephen K. Roberts, 'State and Society in the English Revolution', in Michael J. Braddick (ed.), *The Oxford Handbook of the English Revolution* (Oxford: Oxford University Press, 2015), pp. 294–311, 301. See also Alan Everitt, *The Community of Kent and the Great Rebellion 1640–1660* (Leicester: Leicester University Press, 1966), p. 181, who describes the Committeemen as probably 'relatively honest stewards'. This general honesty of land tax administration may have been long-lasting, e.g. Donald E. Ginter, *A Measure of Wealth, The English Land Tax in Historical Analysis* (London: Hambledon Press, 1992), pp. 143–148 recognises little evidence of favouritism or manipulation in the nineteenth century.
21. William Cobbett, *Cobbett's Parliamentary History of England: From the Norman Conquest, in 1066 to the Year 1803*, vol. 8 (London: T. C. Hansard, 1806–1820), p. 944.
22. William Coxe, *Memoirs of the Life and Administration of Sir Robert Walpole, Earl of Orford*, vol. 2 (London, 1800), p. 248.
23. Debates in 1670: November (1st–15th), GDHC, vol. 1 (1769), pp. 272–289.
24. Joseph A. Schumpeter, *The Crisis of the Tax State* (International Economic Papers IV, 1954), pp. 5–38, http://www.scribd.com/doc/36871535/Schumpeter-The-Crisis-of-the-Tax-State. See also the narrative in E. Ladewig Petersen, 'From Domain state to Tax state, synthesis and interpretation', *Scandinavian Economic History Review*, vol. 23, 1975, pp. 115–148.
25. Charles Tilly, 'Reflections on the History of European State Making', in Charles Tilly (ed.), *The Formation of National States in Western Europe* (Princeton, 1975), p. 42.

26. In their critique of this narrow position, Stephen Pincus and James A. Robinson, 'Challenging the Fiscal-Military Hegemony: The British Case', in Aaron Graham and Patrick Walsh, *The British Fiscal-Military States, 1660–c.1783* (Abingdon: Routledge, 2016), pp. 229–261. The authors in fact take the view that 'Politics not war made the British state'.
27. For example, Andrew Monson and Walter Scheidel, *Fiscal Regimes and the Political Economy of Early States* (An International Conference Sponsored by the Department of Classics, Stanford University, and the Alexander Hamilton Center, New York University, 2010); Andrew Monson and Walter Scheidel (eds.), *Fiscal Regimes and the Political Economy of Premodern States* (Cambridge: Cambridge University Press, 2015); Richard Bonney (ed.), *Economic Systems and State Finance* (Oxford: Oxford University Press, 1995); Richard Bonney (ed.), *The Rise of the Fiscal State in Europe: c.1200–1815* (Oxford: Oxford University Press, 1999); and Philip T. Hoffman and Kathryn Norberg (eds.), *Fiscal Crises, Liberty, and Representative Government 1450–1789* (Stanford: Stanford University Press, 1994).
28. Hindle, *The State and Social Change*.
29. John Brewer, *The Sinews of Power: War, Money and the English State* (London: Unwin Hayman, 1989). Quotations: p. xvi.
30. It has led to searches for fiscal-military states across Europe *Inter alia*: Christopher Storrs (ed.), *The Fiscal-Military State in Eighteenth-Century Europe, Essays in honour of P.G.M. Dickson* (Farnham: Ashgate, 2009); Christopher Storrs, *War, Diplomacy and the Rise of Savoy, 1690–1720* (Cambridge: Cambridge University Press, 2000); Bonney, *The Rise of the Fiscal State in Europe*; Mark Ormrod, Margaret Bonney, and Richard Bonney (eds.), *Crises, Revolutions and Self-sustained Growth in European Fiscal history, 1130–1830* (Stamford: Paul Watkins Publishing, 1999); John Brewer and Eckhart Hellmuth (eds.), *Rethinking Leviathan: the Eighteenth-Century State in Britain and Germany* (Oxford: Oxford University Press, 1999); and Stephen Conway and Rafael Torres Sanchez (eds.), *The Spending of States; Military Expenditure During the Long Eighteenth Century: Patterns, Organisations and Consequences, 1650–1815* (Saarbrucken: LIT Verlag, 2011).
31. John Brewer, 'Revisiting "The Sinews of Power"', in Aaron Graham and Patrick Walsh (eds.), *The British Fiscal-Military States, 1660–c.1783* (Abingdon: Routledge, 2016), pp. 27–34; also Aaron Graham and Patrick Walsh 'Introduction', in the same work.
32. Patrick K. O'Brien, 'The Political Economy of British Taxation, 1660–1815', *The Economic History Review*, vol. 41, 1988, pp. 1–32.

33. Brewer himself cites Michael Mann as a main influence in his introduction to 'The Sinews of Power' and in 'Revisiting', p. 28. Michael Mann, *The Sources of Social Power*, 1, *of A History of Power from the Beginning to AD 1760* (Cambridge: Cambridge University Press, 1986).
34. Dickson, *The Financial Revolution in England*.
35. Brewer, *The Sinews of Power*, p. 88.
36. Brewer, 'Revisiting' denies any direct influence from Douglass North and Barry Weingast, 'Constitutions and Commitment: The Evolution of Institutions Governing Public Choice in Seventeenth Century England', *The Journal of Economic History*, vol. 43, 1989, pp. 803–832.
37. North and Weingast's 'credible commitment' paradigm has faced criticism because key aspects of their 'England in 1688 model' were not unique: property rights were already substantially protected before 1688, institutional reforms were not quickly reflected in the markets, and many less-institutionalised European states could borrow at similar interest rates. See Julian Hoppit, 'Compulsion, Compensation and Property Rights in Britain, 1688–1833', *Past & Present*, vol. 210, 2011, pp. 93–128; D'Maris Coffman, Adrian Leonard, and Larry Neal (eds.), *Questioning credible commitment: perspectives on the rise of financial capitalism* (Cambridge: Cambridge University Press, 2013); Nathan Sussman and Yishay Yafeh, 'Institutional Reforms, Financial Development and Sovereign Debt: Britain 1690–1790', *The Journal of Economic History*, vol. 66, 2006, pp. 906–935; Robert C. Allen, 'Progress and Poverty in Early Modern Europe', *The Economic History Review*, vol. 56, 2003, pp. 403–443, 403–406, provides a useful summary of the criticism. For more supportive texts, see Stephen Pincus and James A. Robinson, *What Really Happened During the Glorious Revolution?*, in Sebastian Galiani and Itai Sened (eds.), *Institutions, Property Rights and Economic Growth: The Legacy of Douglass North* (Cambridge: Cambridge University Press).
38. Noting Brewer's response in 'Revisiting', p. 31. Brooks, 'Public Finance and Political Stability'.
39. Brewer, *The Sinews of Power*, p. 91.
40. Brewer, *The Sinews of Power*, pp. 100–101, although he also calls them 'gifted amateurs…with a strong sense of public duty', p. 250. Brewer in 'Revisiting', p. 33, notes the 'local and social origins of political power, and the primacy of issues of public order and regulation as spurs to governance' based on Michael J. Braddick, 'The Early Modern English State and the Question of Differentiation from 1550 to 1700', *Comparative Studies in Society and History*, vol. 38, 1996, pp. 92–111, 94.

41. The strong performance of land tax has long been recognised, e.g. Maurice Ashley, *Financial and Commercial Policy Under the Cromwellian Protectorate* (Oxford: Oxford University Press, 1934), p. 80.
42. Ward, *The English Land Tax.*
43. Brooks, 'Public Finance and Political Stability'. Brook's approach is gentle criticism of Ward, but his overall analysis is largely damning. He claims on pp. 281–282, 'I do not intend to attempt a rehabilitation of the Land Tax as a "fiscal weapon"'; nor to deny either its unequal incidence or its frequently wayward supervision'. He nevertheless makes a significant effort in rehabilitation.
44. Ward, *The English Land Tax*, p. 56.
45. Brooks, 'Public Finance and Political Stability', p. 282. This comment referred not only to Ward, but also to some of his sources.
46. Ward, *The English Land Tax*, p. 90.
47. (1) Wingham or St. Augustine Lathe, East and see below. (2) His analysis is based on the excellent survival of commissioners' minutes KHLC: Sa/ZO3. These are discussed further below.
48. Ward, *The English Land Tax*, p. 90.
49. Ward, *The English Land Tax*, p. 88.
50. These commissioners' 'resolves' are KHLC: Q/C/Tc2.
51. Ward, *The English Land Tax*, p. 101, Diagram I.
52. For example, Hoppit questions the efficiency of the fiscal-military state in: Julian Hoppit, 'Review of the Sinews of power: war money and the English state by John Brewer and War and the economy in the age of William III and Marlborough by D. W. Jones', *Historical Journal*, vol. 33, 1990, pp. 248–250.
53. Graham and Walsh (eds.), *The British Fiscal-Military States*, take the fiscal-military state back to 1660, but [p. 7] also point to 'a wider pattern of fiscal innovation stretching back to the 1640s at least'. See also Coffman, 'The fiscal revolution of the interregnum'.
54. Hoppit relying on Beckett's data believes that the significance of the customs, with its 'traditional corruption' narratives, has been significantly underestimated. Julian Hoppit. Unpublished paper given at the British Fiscal States conference, Oxford, 2013 cited in Graham and Walsh, 'Introduction', p. 9; John V. Beckett, 'Land Tax or Excise: The Levying of Taxation in Seventeenth-and Eighteenth-Century England', *The English Historical Review*, vol. 100, 1985, pp. 285–308, Table 2. See Brewer, 'Revisiting', p. 31, who notes this criticism by arguing that the proposition that 'a politically biased or unfair system must necessarily be inefficient was not true'.

55. Aaron Graham, *Corruption, Party, and Government in Britain, 1702–1713* (Oxford: Oxford University Press, 2015), Chapter 1. Quote (1) p. 229; Quote (2) p. 3.
56. Ibid., p. 245.
57. Julian Hoppit, 'Political Power and British Economic Life, 1650–1870', in Roderick Floud, Jane Humphries, and Paul Johnson (eds.), *The Cambridge Economic History of Modern Britain, Volume 1, 1700–1870* (Cambridge: Cambridge University Press, 2014), pp. 344–367; especially pp. 348–350, 'Rethinking the state'.
58. Beckett, 'Land Tax or Excise', Table 2, and over the period 1643–1733 customs revenues contributed only 3% less than direct taxes which themselves were a similar percentage behind excises.
59. Chandaman, *The English Public Revenue*, Appendix 2.
60. Braddick, *The Nerves of the State*, p. 185, although in more recent work Braddick prefers the term 'legitimation' and even recognises 'the unreasonable acquiescence and compliance of the English taxpayer' in Michael J. Braddick 'Fiscal transformation and political compliance: England, 1550–1700', *Illes I Imperis*, vol. 13, 2010, pp. 21–37.
61. Braddick, *Parliamentary Taxation*, p. 126.
62. O'Brien, 'The Nature and Historical Evolution', p. 439.
63. Acemoglu, 'Politics and economics in weak and strong states'. This article in itself is part of a decades old debate around 'strong' and 'weak' states.
64. For example, Coffman, *Excise Taxation*.
65. A point stressed by Coffman, *Excise Taxation*, e.g., p. 9, because 'much less attention has been paid to the mid-century experience'.
66. Braddick, *Parliamentary Taxation*, but especially in Chapter 4 he still provides numerous examples of the very tax resistance he elsewhere rejects as to material significance.
67. Braddick, *Parliamentary Taxation*, p. 17*ff.*
68. Brewer, *The Sinews of Power*, p. 22.
69. Coffman, *Excise Taxation*, p. 79*ff.*
70. Based on data from Patrick K. O'Brien and Mr Philip A. Hunt. 'Data prepared on English revenues, 1485–1815', European State Finance Database, http://www.esfdb.org/.
71. Conrad Russell, review of Michael J. Braddick, *Parliamentary Taxation in 17th-Century England. Local Administration and Response* (Woodbridge: Boydell Press, 1994), *The English Historical Review*, vol. 110, 1995, pp. 1215–1216.
72. Brewer, *The Sinews of Power*, pp. 100–101.

73. Ward, *The English Land Tax*, pp. 58 and 175; John V. Beckett, *Local Taxation National Legislation and the Problems of Enforcement* (Dorchester: Bedford Square Press, 1980), p. 1.
74. Braddick, *Parliamentary Taxation*, p. 150.
75. After Everitt, *The Community of Kent*, but the historiography is immense.
76. Discussed in Jacqueline Eales and Andrew Hopper (eds.), *The County Community in Seventeenth-Century England and Wales* (Hatfield: University of Hertfordshire Press, 2012) and Clive Holmes, review of Anthony Fletcher, *A County Community in Peace and War: Sussex 1600–1660* (London and New York: Longman), in *The American Historical Review*, vol. 82, 1977, pp. 632–633.
77. Ward, *The English Land Tax*, pp. 41 and 58; Beckett, *Local Taxation National Legislation*, p. 1; Michael Turner, John V. Beckett, and Bethanie Afton, *Agricultural Rent in England, 1690–1914* (Cambridge: Cambridge University Press, 1997), p. 61; Michael Turner and Dennis Mills (eds.), *Land and Property: The English Land Tax 1692–1832* (Gloucester: Alan Sutton, 1986), p. 176, 'At the heart of the problem was the amateur administration'; John V. Beckett, 'Land Tax Administration at the Local Level 1693–1798', in Michael Turner and Dennis Mills (eds.), *Land and Property: The English Land Tax 1692–1832* (Gloucester: Alan Sutton, 1986), pp. 161–179, see p. 176; Robert W. Unwin, *Search Guide to the English Land Tax* (Wakefield: West Yorkshire County Records Office, 1982), p. 3, 'cumbersome and far from efficient at a time when it was becoming apparent that the successful administration of the State demanded regular sources of revenue'…'it was characterised by amateurism'; Brewer, *The Sinews of Power*, p. 100; Andrew M. Coleby, *Central Government and the Localities: Hampshire 1649–1689* (Cambridge: Cambridge University Press, 1987), pp. 43–44; and Chandaman, *The English Public Revenue*, p. 174.
78. EEBO searches.
79. Brooks, 'Public Finance and Political Stability', p. 288.
80. As has been pointed out by Martin Daunton, *State and Market in Victorian Britain: War, Welfare and Capitalism* (Woodbridge: Boydell Press, 2008), p. 83.
81. Joan Kent, 'The Centre and the Localities: State Formation and Parish Government in England, c. 1640–1740', *Historical Journal*, vol. 38, 1995, pp. 363–404, 390. Kent also cites increased use of printed forms and the circulation of legislative texts, ibid., p. 394.
82. Julian Hoppit, 'Patterns of Parliamentary Legislation, 1660–1800', *Historical Journal*, vol. 39, 1996, p. 129. See also Anthony Fletcher, *Reform in the Provinces: The Government of Stuart England* (London:

Yale University Press, 1986) who states that local administration was 'untidy and often inconsistent, but ultimately coherent'.

83. Joanna Innes, 'The Domestic Face of the Military-Fiscal State: State and Society in Eighteenth-Century Britain', in Lawrence Stone, *An Imperial State at War: Britain 1688–1815* (Abingdon: Routledge, 1994), p. 102.
84. Tuan-Hwee Sng, review of Bartolomé Yun-Casalilla and Patrick K. O'Brien, with Francisco Comín Comín (eds.), *The Rise of Fiscal States: A Global History, 1500–1914* (Cambridge: Cambridge University Press, 2012), *The Economic History Review*, vol. 67, no. 1, February 2014, pp. 310–311. He is referring to Renate Pieper and Chapter 7 in this volume 'Financing an Empire: the Austrian composite monarchy, 1650–1848', pp. 164–191.
85. For example, Graham and Walsh, 'Introduction'; Brewer, 'Revisiting'; Graham, *Corruption, Party, and Government*.
86. Keith Wrightson, *English Society 1580–1680* (London: Hutchinson, 1982), p. 21.
87. Michael J. Braddick, *State Formation and Social Change in Early Modern England, c.1550–1700* (Cambridge: Cambridge University Press, 2000), p. 427.
88. Braddick, 'The Early Modern English State'. Graham also looks to networks and sees state formation deriving from 'political consolidation and interest aggregation'. Graham, *Corruption Party and Government*, p. 31.
89. Hindle, *The State and Social Change*, p. 36.
90. Ibid., p. 16.
91. Ibid., p. 24.
92. Ibid., p. 29.
93. Mark Goldie, 'The unacknowledged republic: officeholding in early modern England', in Tim Harris (ed.), *The Politics of the Excluded, c.1500–1850* (Basingstoke: Palgrave, 2007), p. 161. He calculates around half of all adult males so involved in any one decade around 1700.
94. Sometimes called just the fifteenth by contemporaries and here.
95. Braddick, 'The Early Modern English State', p. 97.
96. Quoted in Paul Slack, 'Government and information in seventeenth-century England', *Past and Present*, vol. 184, 2004, pp. 33–68, 67. Colley makes a similar point that 'commerce, especially foreign commerce, was the engine that drove a state's power' Linda Colley, *Britons: Forging the Nation 1707–1837* (New Haven: Yale University Press, 1992), p. 62.
97. Henry Phelps Brown and Sheila V. Hopkins, *A Perspective of Wages and Prices* (London: Methuen, 1981).

98. For example, Gregory Clark, *A Farewell to Alms: A Brief Economic History of the World* (Princeton: Princeton University Press, 2007).
99. Jan de Vries, *The Industrious Revolution: Consumer Behavior and the Household Economy, 1650 to the Present* (New York: Cambridge University Press, 2008); Mark Overton, Jane Whittle, Darron Dean, and Andrew Hann, *Production and Consumption in English Households, 1600–1750* (London: Routledge, 2004).
100. De Vries, *The Industrious Revolution*; Robert C. Allen and Jacob Weisdorf, 'Was There an 'Industrious Revolution' Before the Industrial Revolution? An Empirical Exercise for England, c. 1300–1800', *The Economic History Review*, vol. 64, 2011, pp. 715–729.
101. Stephen Broadberry, Bruce M. S. Campbell, Alexander Klein, Mark Overton, and Bas van Leeuwen, *British Economic Growth, 1270–1870* (Cambridge: Cambridge University Press, 2015), Table 5. See also Robert C. Allen, *The British Industrial Revolution in Global Perspective*, New Approaches to Economic and Social History (Cambridge: Cambridge University Press, 2009).
102. Stephen Broadberry, Bruce M. S. Campbell, Alexander Klein, Mark Overton, and Bas van Leeuwen, *Rethinking England's Economic Past*, https://www2.warwick.ac.uk/fac/soc/economics/research/centres/eri/bulletin/2010-11-1/broadberry/, Warwick University, 15 November 2010 (accessed 12 January 2017).
103. Barry Supple, *Commercial Crisis and Change in England, 1600–1642: A Study in the Instability of a Mercantile Economy* (Cambridge: Cambridge University Press, 1959).
104. For example, Overton et al., *Production and Consumption in English Households 1600–1750*, pp. 7–8, refer to 'significant changes in domestic comfort, changes in diet with the widespread adoption of imported goods such as sugar and tea, and changes in cooking and eating behaviour'.
105. The contrary views on this of: (1) Broadberry et al., *British Economic Growth 1270–1870*. (2) Allen, *The British Industrial Revolution in Global Perspective*; and the importance of the country's 'unique structure of wages and prices', p. 2. (3) Judy Z. Stephenson, 'Real' Wages? Contractors, Workers and Pay in London Building Trades, 1650–1800', *The Economic History Review*, 2017, http://dx.doi.org/10.1111/ehr.12491; https://doi.org/10.1111/ehr.12491.
106. Leigh Shaw-Taylor and E. Anthony Wrigley, 'Occupational Structure and Population Change', in Roderick Floud, Jane Humphries, and Paul Johnson (eds.), *The Cambridge Economic History of Modern Britain, Volume I, 1700–1870* (Cambridge: Cambridge University Press, 2014), pp. 53–88.

107. William G. Hoskins, 'The Rebuilding of Rural England, 1570–1640', *Past and Present*, vol. 4, 1953, pp. 44–59. The precise dating is contested by others.
108. This was a long-term process occurring right across Northwestern Europe according to Bas J. P. van Bavel, 'The Organization and Rise of Land and Lease Markets in NorthWestern Europe and Italy, c. 1000–1800', *Continuity and Change*, vol. 23.1, 2008, pp. 13–53; Jane Whittle, 'Conclusion', pp. 216–221, in Jane Whittle (ed.), *Landlords and Tenants in Britain, 1440–1660, Tawney's Agrarian Revolution Revisited* (Woodbridge: Boydell Press, 2013).
109. Supple, *Commercial Crisis and Change*, pp. 90–93.
110. Robert C. Allen, 'Economic Structure and Agricultural Productivity in England', *European Review of Economic History*, vol. 3, 2000, pp. 1–25.
111. The Cambridge Group for the History of Population and Social Structure, http://www.campop.geog.cam.ac.uk/.
112. Broadberry et al., *British Economic Growth 1270–1870*, Table 5.07.
113. O'Brien, 'The Nature and Historical Evolution', p. 420. The period discussed is 1688–1864.
114. Ibid.
115. Sng, review of 'The rise of fiscal states a Global History'. See also Allen, 'Progress and Poverty in Early Modern Europe', p. 429, 'representative government did not accelerate growth'. See also Robert C. Allen, 'Why the Industrial Revolution was British: Commerce, Induced Invention, and the Scientific Revolution', *The Economic History Review*, vol. 74, pp. 357–384.
116. The main exposition of this view is perhaps in Daron Acemoglu and James A. Robinson, *Why Nations Fail: The Origins of Power, Prosperity and Poverty* (London: Profile Books, 2012); O'Brien, 'The Nature and Historical Evolution', p. 420, notes 'that the dramatic rise of a strong fiscal state was significant for the growth of the domestic economy'.
117. O'Brien, 'The Nature and Historical Evolution', p. 438.
118. Ibid., p. 420: 'Furthermore, the concentration of households and producers in towns and regions of specialization not only increased taxable outputs flowing through organized markets, but also rendered the imposition and collection of such taxes easier to administer. Larger and denser zones of production, together with established and regular circuits for distribution and exchange (which accompanied the growth of industrial market economies), are prerequisites for the collection of more revenue in the form of indirect taxes'.
119. Ibid., p. 423.
120. Ibid., p. 420, 'Rising agricultural productivity, industrialization, and the relocation and reorganization of production must be regarded as

contributory and not as major forces behind the marked upswing in revenues from taxes and loans'.

121. Ibid., p. 420. Although O'Brien, recognises that 'development came on stream in large part as the outcome of civil war and an interregnum of fiscal state formation in 1642–1688'.
122. O'Brien, 'The Nature and Historical Evolution', p. 420.
123. Selma Evelyn Fine, 'Production and Excise in England, 1643–1825' (PhD thesis, Radcliffe College, 1937).
124. Brewer, *The Sinews of Power*, p. 42.
125. Marjolein 't Hart, 'The Devil or the Dutch? Holland's impact on the Financial Revolution in England, 1643–1694', *Parliaments, Estates and Representation*, vol. 11, 1991, pp. 39–52. Although 't Hart sees it more as a model than a direct copy.
126. Ibid., p. 46. This seems to have been a direct landlord tax with rates fixed at 20% of rural land rents and 8.5% of house rents. See also (1) de Vries et al., The First Modern Economy, p. 106*ff.* (2) Wantje Fritschy, *Public Finance of the Dutch Republic in Comparative Perspective. The Viability of an Early Modern Federal State (1570–1795s)* (Leiden: Koninklijke Brill, 2017), especially Figs. 3.7C and 3.8A.
127. Braddick, 'The Early Modern English State', p. 93. Although Braddick ultimately sees this as resolved because 'Internal resistance to tax raising had been reduced, at least partly due to a greater differentiation of magisterial roles, a recognition of the autonomous needs of the state, and a greater sense of responsibility', p. 102.
128. Both Norfolk and Southampton were also considered, but ruled out on quality of data grounds.
129. Braddick, *Parliamentary Taxation*, p. 126.
130. Braddick, *Parliamentary Taxation*, p. 158. The 'respectable paternity' notion is echoed in O'Brien's argument, 'The Nature and Historical Evolution', p. 428.
131. Braddick, *Parliamentary Taxation*, p. 150, as discussed sees no 'radical departure'—although he recognises some innovation, but on p. 126 he described the excise as 'a radical departure in theory and practice'. On the other hand, Patrick K. O'Brien and Philip A. Hunt, 'The emergence and consolidation of excises in the English fiscal system before the Glorious Revolution', *British Tax Review*, vol. 1, 1997, pp. 35–58, argue that excises '... hardly introduced anything innovatory into the English fiscal system'.
132. Ginter, *A Measure of Wealth*, p. 114, 'There seems to have been no general pattern whatever in the ways the mechanisms for assessment were employed—not within any county, not within any region, not even among the townships of any parish'. Although, it should be noted,

Ginter chose for his study a lower tax county which widely used traditional or 'usual' methods. See Table 1.1 of this book.

133. O'Brien, 'The Nature and Historical Evolution', p. 426, 'a political consensus among England's wealthy elites for an altogether stronger and more centralized state'. Braddick, 'The Early Modern English State'.
134. 94% of countries today have excises representing 25% of global tax-take, levied in various political contexts including dictatorships and democracies and are especially successful in developing countries with moderate or high levels of illiteracy and poverty. After Sijbren Cnossen, *Excise Systems: A Global Study of the Selective Taxation of Goods and Services* (Baltimore: John Hopkins University Press, 1977), p. 23. Of countries surveyed, India had the highest proportion of such taxes at 50% in 1977; Cedric Sandford, *Why Tax Systems Differ; A Comparative Study of the Political Economy of Taxation* (Bath: Fiscal Publications, 2000).
135. Jan de Vries and Ad van der Woude, *The First Modern Economy. Success, Failure, and Perseverance of the Dutch Economy, 1500–1815* (Cambridge: Cambridge University Press, 1997), especially pp. 102–105 and Table 4.6.
136. Allen, *The British Industrial Revolution in Global Perspective*, p. 128. Allen has attributed England's growing power to an 'intercontinental trade boom' beginning in the sixteenth century.
137. Richard Blanton and Lane Fargher, *Collective Action in the Formation of Pre-Modern States* (New York, Springer, 2008). In their analysis of pre-modern states, they distinguish between 'external' and 'internal' revenues, the former derived from a small base or few collection points (such as trade taxes on foreign imports/exports) and the latter from a broad base (such as farmers).
138. Gordon E. Mingay, 'The Land Tax Assessments and the Small Landowner', *The Economic History Review*, vol. 17, 1964, pp. 381–388; J. M. Martin, 'Landownership and the Land Tax Returns', *The Agricultural History Review*, vol. 14, 1966, pp. 96–103; David B. Grigg, 'The Land Tax Returns', *The Agricultural History Review*, vol. 11, 1963, pp. 82–94; Ginter, *A Measure of Wealth*.
139. Spence, *London in the 1690s*. And the related database: Derek Keene, *Metropolitan London in the 1690s: Four Shillings in the Pound Aid, 1693–1694; For the City of London, the City of Westminster, and Metropolitan Middlesex. 1966* (Database). The UK Data Service. Persistent identifier: https://doi.org/10.5255/ukda-sn-3497-1, https://discover.ukdataservice.ac.uk.
140. But see Sect. 1.2 regarding the use of the terms 'amateur' and 'professional' in this period.

141. O'Brien, 'The Nature and Historical Evolution', p. 428, 'traditional forms'; Ginter, *A Measure of Wealth*, p. 151, has them 'deeply embedded in the most ancient governmental traditions of the local community …'.
142. For example, William Kennedy, *English Taxation 1640–1799* (London: G. Bell & Sons Ltd, 1913; Elibron Classics edition 2007), various, but p. 64*ff* quoting Petty and Locke.
143. For example, Chandaman, *English Public Revenue*.
144. For example, John V. Beckett, 'Local Custom and the "New Taxation" in the Seventeenth and Eighteenth Centuries: The Example of Cumberland', *Northern History*, vol. 12, 1976, pp. 105–126.
145. Ward, *The English Land Tax*. Brooks, 'Public Finance and Political Stability', has done the same but with greater finesse.
146. As local administrators described it.
147. Nearby Lydd also has good records, but it has been utilised far less in this study because of the fragile nature of these documents. See Felix Hull, *Guide to the Kent County Archive Office* (Maidstone: Kent County Council, 1958).
148. Contemporaries used the term 'duplicate' to describe other copies including the parish assessments themselves, and the term 'duplicate' is variously used in the secondary literature. TNA usually refer to them as communal assessments. Tax assessments and summary duplicates were both termed 'duplicate' in ordinances and statutes at various times, and this confusion has passed into modern usage. Common contemporary usage in Kent is applied here that 'duplicates' represent the summary duplicate only.
149. TNA: E179/129/745.
150. As additional boroughs or small towns were given their own separate quota.
151. Sometimes biannual or other irregular patterns.
152. Some lists are available. Particularly useful are Jeremy Gibson, *The Hearth Tax and Other Later Stuart Tax Lists and the Associated Oath Rolls* (Birmingham: Federation of Family History Societies, 1985) and Jeremy Gibson, Mervyn Medlycott, and Dennis Mills, *Land and Window Tax Assessments*, Second Edition (Birmingham: Federation of Family History Societies, 1998). See also Dennis Mills, 'Appendix. Survival of Early Land Tax Assessments', in Turner and Mills, *Land and Property*, pp. 219–234.
153. Kent: TNA: E182/430 (1694–1697)—E182/436 (1731–1733); London & Middlesex: TNA: E182/594 (1689)—E182/604 (1733–1737); Bristol TNA: E182/837 (1689–1692)—E182/842 (1730–1734).

154. TNA: SP/28 various.
155. And working largely from this author's own photographic record.
156. However, the website requires organisational attention, particularly because assessments are not always filed under the correct City wards.
157. Archives used: Kent History and Library Centre (KHLC), London Metropolitan Archives (LMA), Bristol Record Office (BRO), The National Archives (TNA).
158. For the City of London, various metropolitan documents have been considered. For Kent, comparative material from: Hertfordshire: TNA: SP 28/156; Sussex: TNA: SP 28/181; and Buckinghamshire: SP 28/148–149.
159. Keene, *Metropolitan London in the 1690s* (Database).
160. Chiefly from Statutes of the Realm (SoR) and Acts and Ordinances of the Interregnum (A&O), but some from Early English Books Online (EEBO).
161. History of Parliament (HoP)—British Political, Social & Local History, http://www.historyofparliamentonline.org/.
162. Alfred B. Beaven, *Bristol Lists. Municipal and Miscellaneous. Compiled by the Rev. A. B. Beaven* (British Library, Historical print Edition, 1899).
163. J. R. Woodhead, *The Rulers of London 1660–1689 A Biographical Record of the Aldermen and Common Councilmen of the City of London* (London, 1966), British History Online, http://www.british-history.ac.uk/no-series/london-rulers/1660-89. Supplementary material from Oxford DNB.
164. For example, Kent Archaeological Society database of individuals, http://www.kentarchaeology.org.uk/Research/research.htm.
165. The contemporary and familiar name from the historiography named after the place where commissioners met.
166. For example, there were three active Bristol commissioners named John Knight with some overlapping periods of office. Identification is almost always possible though year or title.
167. City of London: TNA: E182/594 (1689)—E182/604 (1733—1737); Kent: TNA: E182/430 (1694–1697)—E182/436 (1731–1733); Bristol: TNA: E182/837 (1689–1692)—E182/842 (1730–1734). A few local copies also survive by way of comparison. There are some exceptions, e.g., in Bristol where the commissioners' minutes will allow lists to be completed.
168. Sources: *The Bassishaw Record and Assessment Book*—LMA: P69/MIC1/B/006/MS03505. See also Christine M. Fox, *A History of Bassishaw Ward: c. 1200–c. 1600* (London: eBook Partnerrship.com, 2014).
169. Chandaman, *The English Public Revenue*, Appendix I, p. 281.

170. At least until 1733 or 1734.
171. Chamberlains' audit papers LMA: COL/CHD/LA/02/various.
172. TNA: SP 28, various. There are some accompanying receipts.
173. Based on the mid-point between the 1705 counts from St. Augustine Lathe, East (2461 taxpayers = 10.7% of Kent quota grossed up = 23,041) and St. Augustine Lathe, West (c. 1667 taxpayers = 5.5% of Kent quota grossed up = 32,221).
174. Returns of non-payment, which may or may not imply enforcement action is required.
175. Some were tax officials themselves.
176. Mingay, 'The land tax assessments and the small landowner'.
177. Ginter, *A Measure of Wealth*, p. xxv and Chapters 2 and 3.
178. Ibid., Chapter 3. These included: the unit of analysis, properties missing, tenurial status, residence, who paid the tax, occupancy and so on.
179. Ibid., pp. 46–47 has relevant discussion.
180. William Petty, *A Treatise of Taxes & Contributions, shewing the Nature and Measures of Crown Lands, Assessments, Customs, Poll-Money, Lotteries, Benevolence, Penalties, Monopolies, Offices, Tythes, Raising of Coins, Harth-Money, Excize*, etc.... (Printed for N. Brooke, at the Angel in Cornhill, 1662). His broad conclusion was rather that the incidence was with the consumer of the produce of the land.
181. Kent: From Anne Davison, 'The Agrarian Economy of Romney Marsh and its Hinterland, with special reference to the Knatchbull Estate, c.1730–1790' (PhD thesis, Canterbury Christchurch University, 2011), p. 58 and personal communication; Bristol: Sample property records mainly in Temple parish see below and personal communication David Sacks; London: Craig Spence, *London in the 1690s: A Social Atlas* (London: Centre for Metropolitan History, 2000), and personal communication.
182. Brooks, 'Public Finance and Political Stability', p. 289.
183. Alternatives would be polls and the Restoration hearth tax, but these have not been extensively used here.
184. After Ann M. Carlos and Larry Neal, 'Women in the City: London 1720–1725', 200 XIV International Economic History Congress, 21 to 25, August 2006, Helsinki, Finland, http://www.helsinki.fi/iehc2006/papers3/Carlos.pdf (accessed 24 April 2017).
185. Amy Louise Erickson, 'Married Women's Occupations in Eighteenth-century London', *Continuity and Change*, vol. 23, no. 2, 2008, pp. 267–307.
186. Under the laws of coverture, a husband and wife were one person under the name of the husband.

187. Joanne Bailey, 'Favoured or Oppressed? Married Women, Property and 'Coverture' in England, 1660–1800', *Continuity and Change*, vol. 17, no. 3, 2002, pp. 351–372, 352.
188. Women were invisible, but may have played a larger role than is evident from official documents. (1) Personal email communication Jonah Miller, Project: The Male State: Officeholding and Gender in England, 1660–1750, Kings College London (7 February 2018); 'The problem of invisible women sounds very similar to what I have found with other kinds of officeholding … [but] various members of male officers' households (including but not only their wives) were actively involved in carrying out official duties'. (2) Personal email communication Alice Blackwood, Research Topic: "Lytul Maidens", Householding and Wardenship: Changing Perceptions of Female Leadership in English Parishes, 1540–1650 who believe 'there is just very little evidence to be found of female involvement in these administrative positions at all in the early modern period'. (8 February 2018). (3) Dr. John Broad of the CAMPOP group confirms by email a similar picture; 'I haven't found women acting as Land Tax collectors' (14 February 2018).
189. TNA: E179/301/5.
190. TNA: E182/432. She signed a technical document, a certificate of arrears for the year 1711 sent to the Exchequer on 18 February 1714. It suggests an understanding of accounts, and it is signed under her hand and seal. Her husband was the Kent receiver William Fausett who died in 1711, and she had by this latter date married Lieutenant-General Robert Echlin according to a note on her oil painting by Thomas Sadler referred to at the 27 November 2014 Chorley's auction. http://www.ukauctioneers.com/auction_catalogue.cfm. Walker Weldon and Edward Bathurst had split Kent into two parts as they took over from Faussett according to CTB, vol. 25, 29 November 1711, p. 568, but were apparently only handling accounts from 1712.
191. LMA: COL/CHD/LA/03/080/007 & 008 and LMA:COL/CHD/LA/03/111/06. 4 warrants for payment to the town clerk for poundage acknowledged as received for the years 1702–1705.
192. Beckett, 'Land Tax or Excise' describes the land tax as really 'an extension of earlier levies' and Turner's view that it was 'indistinguishable in some ways from earlier taxation'—Michael Turner, 'The Land Tax, Land and Property: Old Debates and New Horizons', in Turner and Mills, *Land and Property*, p. 1; Ward, *The English Land Tax*, p. 3.
193. Each county, borough or city named in the statute would pay a fixed sum, but with no national tax rate.
194. Ian Gentles, *The English Revolution and the Wars in the Three Kingdoms, 1638–1652* (Harlow: Pearson Longman, 2007), p. 108.

195. November 1659 'gracious message to General Monck' from Charles II. Thomason/669.f.22[22], EEBO. Such rhetoric was far from unique and Secretary Bennet wrote in 1664 claiming that the Assessment '*had been renounced*' since the Restoration. Chandaman, *English Public Revenue*, p. 145, quoting from Cobbett's *Parliamentary History of England.*
196. Chandaman, *The English Public Revenue*, p. 141 calls the assessment 'strong'.
197. For example, Ibid., p. 2.
198. For example, Ward, *The English Land Tax*, pp. 1 and 16.
199. Chandaman, *The English Public Revenue*, p. 162*ff.* Chandaman believes that polls were sometimes levied during the Restoration to charge incomes not touched by land taxes.
200. Chandaman, *The English Public Revenue*, p. 189 and Appendix 2. At over £10m for the period 1660–1680 land taxes, even though collected only for some years, compare well with the total for all ordinary revenue both permanent and temporary (but excluding extraordinary direct taxes) at £24.5m.
201. Debates in 1670: November (1st–15th), GDHC, vol. 1 (1769), pp. 272–289. Thomas Culpeper the younger in his new 1668 preface to his father's 1621 '*Tract on Usury*' uses similar language: 'Even by a Land Taxe (if better expedients be not offered)', EEBO, Wing (2nd ed., 1994)/C7555.
203. The main levies being the Royal Aid which ran for three years and the Additional Aid overlapped for the last two years, but both were somewhat reduced by the Great Fire.
204. The quotas had south-eastern bias mirroring earlier areas of parliamentary support. The shape of quotas bears a strong resemblance to the distribution of parliament supporting MPs in the Long Parliament; Douglas Brunton and Donald H. Pennington, *Members of the Long Parliament* (London: Allen & Unwin, 1954), p. 187.
205. The first of which was termed the 'Royal Aid'. Chandaman, *English Public Revenue*, pp. 161–162 provides the background.
206. A series of ordinances raised £120,000 per month or £1,440,000 annually and had briefly been almost as heavy as the Royal Aid.
207. William R. Ward, 'The Office of Taxes 1665–1798', *Bulletin of the Institute of Historical Research*, vol. 25, 1952, pp. 204–205; Chandaman, *The English Public Revenue*, pp. 186–187.
208. 13 Car. II, St. 1, c. 4, voluntary present, 1661, SoR, vol. 5, p. 307. This 'present' was not so voluntary because there are accounts of London arrears e.g. TNA: E179/252/18.
209. 15 Car. II, c. 9, 4 subsidies, 1663–1664, SoR, vol. 5, pp. 453–481.

210. Ship money 1636—1637, TNA: SP16/376, No. 104; SoR, various; A&O, various; 5 Geo. II, c. 5, Land Tax for 1732. Note the general stability, after 1649—1650, other than for a special reduction for London's Great Fire and increased taxes on urban populations especially London and Middlesex from the 1690s
211. Anon., *Land Tax at 4s in the Pound Paid by England & Wales in 1702, & 1744, Proportion'd and Compar'd by 513 Parts, According to ye no. of members of Parliament, and ye Square Miles in Each County: Also ye Members Sent, & Land Tax Paid by Scotland* (London, 1745). Eighteenth Century Collections Online. Gale. Cambridge University Library. BL. Harleian 4226 ff. 15–16. It is quoted in Turner and Mills, *Land and Property*, p. 169. It declared 'when it is at four shillings, a man perhaps in Kent or Essex shall pay the full, or sometimes more; in Norfolk or Lincolnshire he shall pay three shillings; in Staffordshire and Shropshire two; in Devonshire and Yorkshire fifteen pence; in Cornwall and Wales nine pence'.
212. 22 & 23 Car. II, c. 3, subsidy, 1671. SoR, vol. 5, pp. 693–703.
213. Based on Chandaman, *The English Public Revenue*, pp. 167 and 193.
214. Chandaman, *The English Public Revenue*, p.159, believed most of the subsidy burden fell on land.
215. See Chandaman, *The English Public Revenue*, p. 167.
216. Chandaman, *The English Public Revenue*, p. 151 and Appendix 2 suggests just under half of the anticipated yield was realised. A major problem was the low real estate rate of 1s/£.
217. 25 Car. II, c. 1, 18-months' assessment, 1673–1674, SoR, vol. 5, pp. 752–782. Chandaman, *The English Public Revenue*, terminology applied for Restoration taxes.
218. 29 Car. II, c. 1, 17-months' assessment, 1677–1678, SoR, vol. 5, pp. 802–836.
219. 30 Car. II, c. 1, 18-months' assessment, 1678–1680, SoR, vol. 5, pp. 867–883.
220. 31 Car. II, c. 1, 6-months' assessment, 1680, SoR, vol. 5, pp. 897–934.
221. E.g. O'Brien and Hunt, 'Data prepared on English revenues, 1485–1815'.
222. 1 Wm. & Mar., Sess. 2, c. 1, Two Shilling Aid, 1690, SoR, vol. 6, pp. 104–142.
223. In fact very similar to the 1650s.
224. It went on to say '… Wee Your Majestyes most Dutifull and Loyall Subjects the Commons being filled with a most Humble and Gratefull sence of Your Majestyes unparallell'd Grace and Favour to Your People not onely by Restoreing their Rights and Liberties which have beene Invaded contrary to Law but in desireing to make them Happy and at

Ease by takeing away such Burthens as by Law were fixed upon them by which Your Majestie will Erect a lasting Monument of Your Goodnesse in every House in the Kingdome'. 'William & Mary 1688: An Act for the Takeing Away the Revenue ariseing by Hearth-Money', SoR, vol. 6, pp. 61–62.

225. O'Brien and Hunt, 'Data prepared on English revenues, 1485–1815'. 2 Wm. & Mar., Sess. 2, c. 1, £1,651,702 Aid, 1690–1691, SoR, vol. 6, pp. 180–218; and 3 Wm. & Mar., c. 5, £1,651,702 Aid, 1691–1692, SoR, vol. 6, pp. 259–301.
226. Brodie Waddell, 'The Politics of Economic Distress in the Aftermath of the Glorious Revolution, 1689–1702', *The English Historical Review*, vol. 130, 2015, pp. 318–351, 324.
227. Four shillings to the pound according to 4 Wm. & Mar., c. 1, Four Shilling Aid, 1692–1693, SoR, vol. 6, pp. 323–372. The inaugural meeting was 15 February 1693 and payments were due to the Exchequer by 25 March 1693, the last by 25 December 1693.
228. This was recognised by Ward, *The English Land Tax*, Table I.
229. Writing in 1695 according to Ward, *The English Land Tax*, pp. 8–9.
230. Leigh Shaw-Taylor, 'The Rise of Agrarian Capitalism and the Decline of Family Farming in England', *The Economic History Review*, vol. 65, 2012, pp. 26–60. His rather later maps of the decline of family farming show a marked similarity to land tax quotas in terms of farm sizes and the number or presence of workers employed. He is also very clear that critical developments came later in the North of England than in the South and East.
231. Spence, *London in the 1690s*; Davison, *The Agrarian Economy of Romney Marsh* and personal communication; Richard Grover, 'Early Land Tax Assessments Explored (2) Kent and Sussex', in Michael Turner and Dennis Mills (eds.), *Land and Property: The English Land Tax 1692–1832* (Gloucester: Alan Sutton, 1986), pp. 204–218; and H. John Habakkuk, 'English Landownership, 1680–1740', *The Economic History Review*, vol. 10, 1940, pp. 2–17.
232. Mingay, 'The Land Tax Assessments and the Small Landowner'; Davison, *The Agrarian Economy of Romney Marsh*, p. 130; Ginter, *A Measure of Wealth*, p. 113 notes in his Yorkshire case study, 'It is simply not true that in general landlords paid the land tax …' Ginter, *A Measure of Wealth*, p. 114, says 'There seems to have been no general inclination to assess on full valuations … no general pattern whatever'.
233. Waddell 'The Politics of Economic Distress', pp. 318–351.
234. 6 & 7 Wm. III, c. 6, Marriage Duty Act, 1695, SoR, vol. 6, pp. 568–583. It ultimately applied from 1695–1706 and was also 'upon Batchelors and Widowers'.

235. 7 & 8 Wm. III, c. 18, Duties upon Houses, 1696, SoR, vol. 7, pp. 86–94.
236. After long debates, see Philip Loft, 'Political Arithmetic and the English Land Tax in Reign of William III', *Historical Journal*, vol. 56, 2013, pp. 321–343.
237. This is better understood as a quota equivalent to the four-shilling rate of 1693–1694, three-quarters of that (=three shillings), half (=two-shillings), and a quarter (=one shilling).
238. Note some counties had quotas for boroughs, towns, and cities which have been amalgamated with county totals here. Sources: SoR various, A&O various. Anon., *Land tax at 4s in ye pound paid by England & Wales in 1702, & 1744*, Bristol = 737.7 acres/640 = 1.15 square miles (after Ralph and Williams, *The Inhabitants of Bristol in 1696*, p. xxii). This includes some areas not built up. Metropolitan London = 7182.6 acres = 11.22 square miles (After Spence, *London in the 1690s*, Appendix III, pp. 176–177).
239. After Beckett, 'Land Tax or Excise', Table 2.
240. The London Merchants, those 'sturdy beggars … engaged in fraud … supported by another [more dangerous] set … fond of improving every Opportunity … for stirring up the People of Great Britain to Mutiny and Sedition'. Walpole 14 March 1733 First Parliament of George II: Sixth session (part 3 of 5, from 27 February 1733), HPHC, vol. 7: 1727–1733 (1742), pp. 304–353.
241. Paul Langford, *The Excise Crisis, Society and Politics in the Age of Walpole* (Oxford: Clarendon Press, 1975); Paul Langford, *Walpole and the Robinocracy* (Cambridge: Chadwyck-Healey, 1986).
242. O'Brien and Hunt, 'Data prepared on English Revenues, 1689–1727.'

CHAPTER 2

Legislation for a New Tax on Land

2.1 Preamble

Two important aspects of land tax historiography and chronology will be discussed in this chapter. First, traditional tax narratives of the English state have focussed on post-revolutionary developments to align with the Financial Revolution and the formation of a fiscal-military state. The terminology of land taxes also reflects this with a post-revolutionary 'Land Tax' and earlier related 'assessments' and 'aids'. Second, commentators on the earlier pre-Revolutionary land tax forms, the aids and assessments, have argued that there was nothing new about these taxes and that they were little different from the ancient subsidies and other direct levies which preceded them. It will be argued here that neither of these approaches has significant merit. It will be shown here that the main innovative features of land taxes were created by 1640s legislators aided by feedback loops from administrators in the English regions. Crucial legislative features, discussed in detail here, were created, or at least uniquely assembled, in the decade after 1642–1643, and remained a fundamental part of legislation thereafter (Sects. 2.2–2.3 below). These features characterise what contemporaries, such as William Petty[1] and others called the 'land-tax'.[2] It will be further argued, on the basis of case study evidence (Sect. 2.4), that these innovative legislative features were understood and followed to a substantial extent in many localities and adapted on the ground, to ensure tax effectiveness. The result was

S. Pierpoint, *The Success of English Land Tax Administration 1643–1733*, Palgrave Studies in the History of Finance,
https://doi.org/10.1007/978-3-319-90260-9_2

productive taxation that could efficiently target income principally from land and included innovations around: clear deadlines, enforcement, logistics and process. These taxes were markedly different from what had gone before.[3] The importance of the exploitation of cashflows from production and around financial cycles was vital to the success of the early land taxes when physical cash was scarce (see Sect. 2.5). There is evidence from the case studies and beyond that land taxes were a highly effective tax form which could deliver large sums to the Exchequer long before the Restoration.

Civil War created an urgent need for supply and saw parliamentary ordinances for two taxes new to England's fiscal landscape in 1643, the excise and the assessment or land tax. The excise had been deployed in the Netherlands for over a hundred years,[4] and widely in Europe and even in England, there had been consideration of the taxation of inland product supply.[5] The Dutch also levied heavy land taxes from the 1570s on landlords and tenants.[6] Land acreage had long been usefully employed in England in calculating local rates by the taxation of occupiers, and this method had a long history in Kent and elsewhere, including the 'marsh tax system'.[7] Occupier rates were fundamental to the poor law by levies on 'every inhabitant, parson, vicar, or other, and of every occupier of lands, houses, tithes impropriate, propriations of tithes, coalmines of saleable underwoods',[8] and Cannan believed that by the beginning of the seventeenth century local taxes and rates were often levied according to '(1) the incomes of landlords identical with the rents; and (2) the incomes of the tenants, not identical with, but merely assumed to be equal in proportion to the rents'.[9]

2.2 Legislative Features of Land Taxes

There were many familiar aspects to the new 1643 First Weekly Assessment, including the appointment of local commissioners, assessors, collectors and receivers. The setting of tax quotas, disciplinary procedures, and the distraint of non-payers were ancient. However, older direct taxes had failed to raise expected yields because they sought to raise supply by one of two distinct and rather ineffective methods. First, they targeted small numbers of the more visible wealthy and usually less mobile inhabitants with a theoretically heavy subsidy. The ancient English subsidy supposedly taxed land values but legislation allowed taxpayers to pay on the greater of either land or goods, not both, and taxpayers could effectively choose and self-assess with costs deductible. Very many taxpayers especially in towns paid tax on their goods only, and land was in practice lightly taxed. Payers may even have gained some prestige for such generosity.[10] Second, they employed a very low level but broader taxation, the fifteenth and tenth, which many taxpayers could pay, and it was less likely to be avoided or evaded. It had a quota, but it was very low at just £600 for the whole City of London, for example.[11] Polls were similarly a broadly based levy but at a low rate. Neither strategy was appropriate when a heavy burden of taxation was necessary.

Braddick and Chandaman[12] rightly point to the decreased effectiveness of the subsidy and the need for multiple levies to raise meaningful amounts as in the case of the five subsidies of 1627.[13] Extra-parliamentary ship money was deployed nationwide, and in times of peace in the 1630s. It may have 'reached far deeper down into local society', as Sharpe claims, but met with mixed success and modest national amounts were levied, compared with what was to come.[14] Although more than £200,000 was raised annually in the early years, returns declined thereafter.[15] As the Wars of the Three Kingdoms began, it is not surprising that the first parliamentary supply statutes were in the form of six traditional subsidies in 1640[16] and a poll tax.[17] As relations between monarch and parliament broke down, parliament set about a period of fiscal experimentation with ordinances that of course no longer required the authority of the king.

The Weekly Assessment was introduced in an ordinance of 24 February 1643 for the 'maintenance of the army'.[18] This introduction was no doubt the work of John Pym and his allies as they built up military supply capacity. It followed fiscal experimentation in the build-up to war including a voluntary request for at least theoretically repayable monies,[19] sometimes called 'the propositions' in June 1642.[20] Many donated,[21] but by November, it was perhaps only a modest exaggeration to claim that Parliament's army was 'for the most part maintained by the voluntary contributions of divers well-affected persons, who have freely contributed according to their abilities'. However, 'considering there are divers others within the Cities of London, and Westminster, and the suburbs of the same and also within the Borough of Southwark, that have not contributed at all', fresh measures were needed. Therefore, 'the propositions' was made a compulsory levy, sometimes called the 'fifth and twentieth part'[22] with a metropolitan London focus.[23] The rules for collection were sparse.[24] The First Weekly Assessment ordinance followed but was compulsory, comprehensive, and nationwide, or at least reaching those areas under parliamentary control. Fine-tuning was quickly required,[25] and more modest levies were soon added nationally, for example regarding maimed soldiers[26] and in London, to 'stop and fortify all highways leading to the City'.[27]

The 24 February 1643 ordinance for the First Weekly Assessment was highly detailed and broadly based in terms of the taxable individuals specified, because both persons and corporates were potentially liable on all forms of real and personal property.[28] This in itself was not greatly different from the traditional subsidy[29] and included 'Fee-simple, Fee-tail, for term of life, term of years, by Execution, Wardship, or by copy of Court-Roll, of and in any Honors, Castles, Mannors, Lands, Tenements, Rents, Services, Tithes, Oblations, Obventions, Annuities, Offices of Profit, Fees, Corrodies, or other yearly Profits or Hereditaments'. However, unlike the subsidies, there was neither provision for deductible expenses, nor for optionality. Taxpayers would pay on both their land and personal estates. Early flows of funds may have been slow judging from the fact that in May, parliament issued a further ordinance[30] to appoint two individuals per county to ensure 'such expedition as the emergent and present necessities doe require'. The county committees[31] targeted those 'that have not Contributed or Lent at all towards the maintenance of the said Army'.[32]

2.2.1 National Quotas, Local Quotas, and the Inaugural Meeting of Commissioners

What immediately distinguished the 1643 First Weekly Assessment was both the presence and the weight of national quotas seeking £410,000 in just three months.[33] Ship money and even the fifteenth and tenth had had quotas, but these new assessment taxes were even heavier than the '£400,000 Levy' of March 1642[34] intended to be for a full 12 months.[35] The order of taxable locations in the Weekly Assessment is pertinent. First cited was the City of London which was to pay £10,000 weekly (or £120,000 over three months), then Westminster £1,250, Middlesex £750, Kent £1,250, Essex £1,125, Surrey £400, Southwark and adjoining £300,[36] Sussex £625, Hertfordshire £450, Cambridgeshire £375, the Isle of Ely £147.50, Suffolk £1,250, Norfolk £1,250, Huntington £220, Buckinghamshire £420, and Bedfordshire £250. These made up almost 60% of the total. It is perhaps unsurprising that metropolitan

London headed the ordinance followed by Kent and other south-eastern counties, given political realities, although 'high rates on London and Westminster [were] not to be a precedent'. The fact that these areas and counties remained the major contributors to land taxes thereafter is perhaps more remarkable (see Fig. 1.2).

The ordinance also includes another long-enduring feature, the setting of an inaugural meeting of commissioners appointed by Parliament at the start of the tax process by county, city or borough. Commissioners were to meet and then 'sever and divide themselves' into smaller groups 'for the execution of the said Service'.[37] By February 1645, this inaugural meeting had been given a deadline so that 'Committees hereby appointed … shall within eight dayes next ensuing the publication hereof, meet together at some convenient place in every of the said Cities, Counties and places respectively' specified.[38] This was soon permanently replaced by a stated date: 'That the several and respective Commissioners hereby appointed … shall meet together at the most common and usual place of meeting in each of the said Counties, Cities and Towns respectively, on or before the Tenth day of December, One thousand six hundred and fifty'.[39] Such inaugural meetings quickly became an opportunity to divide national quotas to create local ones as commissioners apportioned their county, borough or city quota to parishes, lathes, hundreds, wards and other subdivisions. This was despite the fact that contemporary legislators also sought a county-wide tax rate; 'Commissioners or the major part of them then present, shall upon view and perusal of the said several Surveys, cast up the true Revenue and yearly Profits of the whole county or city, to the end that an equal pound rate may be apportioned'.[40] In terms of fairness across a county, this seems reasonable, but reconciling a local quota with a county-wide pound rate was difficult. In fact, Kent continued to attempt to do so throughout the Interregnum and the Restoration as shown on the faces of successive and relatively continuous runs of tax assessments from the county.[41] Such apportionment was doubtless the product of serious negotiation between residents in their respective locales. In the City of London, a local ward quota system was certainly in place from at least 1644,[42] although apportionment remained in a state of flux until the early 1700s (see Fig. 5.9). Because City of London authorities had long subdivided national quotas on a ward basis,[43] it is likely that local assessment quotas applied from 1643[44] and this was probably true of many parts of the country.[45]

2.2.2 *Land Taxes on Tenants and Landlords*

Although all forms of property were to be taxed, there were innovative plans for real estate contained in both the '£400,000 Levy' of 1642[46] and the 1643 First Weekly Assessment legislation. If the land was let at or near 'yearly value thereof'[47] then the 'person or persons to whom the rent thereof belongeth, [was or were] to be solely chargeable therewith'. On the other hand, if the land was 'let at any easie or small rent or under-value, then the sum taxed to be apportioned betweene the party or parties' as agreed. This wording clearly acknowledges and attempts to tax income from real estate against a background of highly varied contemporary land tenures and payment arrangements nationwide, including, quit, peppercorn and rack-rents according to Turner et al.[48] This contrasts with the subsidy which focussed rather vaguely on the 'yearly profits of the yearly value' of land possibly implying a direct tax on owners. The new wording was still a challenge for assessors who might have had to reasonably apportion tax for each property, and discover and assess distant landlords. One solution in Kent and Surrey was to apply a standard formula to apportion taxation between landlord and tenant. Legislators understood these problems and knew that local assessors would often by default assess the occupier for the full amount of the tax whether they were owner or not. Thus, legislation provided that where such tenant was charged:

> with any summe of money contrary to the true intent and meaning of this Ordinance, That it shall and may be lawfull to and for such Tenant or occupier to stop and detaine the same, from and out of his rent due for the same Land, or to take his Lawfull remedy.[49]

This deduction for the tenant was confusing and unwieldy and left the tenant with the possibility of having to go to law. The wording was quickly amended in the London ordinance of 7 March 1643[50] to make occupiers the taxable party and give tenants automatic deduction rights. It states that houses were to be valued and '... The said money [is] to be paid by the said Tenant or Inhabitant where houses are inhabited, who is to deduct the same out of his next Rent payable to the Landlords, if it be a rack-Rent, and by the Landlords where houses shall stand empty'.[51] Of course, this appears to omit anybody paying any other sort of rent that was not a rack-rent. The standard long-term legislative form appeared two years later in February 1645[52] whereby the tax became effectively an occupiers' levy, thus:

> … the Tenants of all Houses and Lands, which shall be rated by vertue of this Ordinance, are hereby required and authorized, to pay such summes of Money, as shall be Rated upon such House and Lands, and to deduct out of their Rents, so much of the said Rates, as in respect of the Rents of every such House and Lands the Landlords should or ought to pay and beare; and the Landlords both mediate, and immediate, according to their respective interest, are hereby required to allow such deductions and payments, upon the receipt of the residue of their Rents. And be it provided, That every Tenant paying the said Assessement, shall be acquitted and discharged for so much Money as the said assessment shall amount unto, as if the same had been actually paid unto such person or persons, unto whom his Rents should have been due and payable.

It was for the commissioners to resolve 'any difference [that] shall arise between Land-lord and Tenant' as a result of this.[53] There was of course one entirely current, practical and mundane rationale behind this, and it was expressed in the *House of Lords Journal* (HOLJ) for 24 August 1643 which complained 'there is no Provision made that the Tenants shall pay the several Sums of Money that shall be assessed upon the Landlords … [and] that many of the said Landlords are gone out of the Country, and many others of them have not sufficient Goods to be found'.[54] Tenants and other occupiers were easier to locate and tax and they would have the ability to deduct tax paid from their rent—with a statutory special brief to commissioners to resolve any disputes arising.[55] Braddick reports that 329 such disputes went on to be heard by the Indemnity Committee.[56] Of course, the assessment also taxed personal estates,[57] but partly by design and partly fortuitously, legislators and administrators had discovered a practical real estate tax that was to have a very long life.

2.2.3 Usual and Equal Method

The taxation of rents methodology did not work everywhere, but this was no matter as long as quotas were met. Legislators therefore allowed local officials to use traditional means thus: 'for the removal of all Obstructions, and the more speedy and effectual Execution of this Act, to proceed according to the most just and equal way' in such cases. Such wording appears in the 1649 legislation,[58] but it seems that local practices applied in many places particularly where the burdens were light (see Table 1.1; and Fig. 1.2) and this may be particularly the case in Cumberland.[59] In such cases, this merely codified existing practice. This 'usual and equal' method wording or something like it remained a permanent feature of land tax legislation thereafter.[60]

2.2.4 Reassessments and Appeals

The subsidy had long allowed taxpayers to complain where they were overassessed, and the 1643 First Weekly Assessment followed suit permitting 'Persons over-rated to be relieved on complaint to Committee' of commissioners.[61] However, a successful and material appeal could mean that the local quota would not be met. There was also the considerable matter of those assessed who had died, left the district or were simply unable or unwilling to pay. Such difficult challenges were recognised by administrators across the London metropolis in the early 1640s.[62] Collectors were given a formidable armoury of tools[63] to deal with defaulters including an authority to enter premises and 'break open any House, Chest, Trunck, Box, or other thing wherein any such Goods are'[64] to distrain and sell such personal property so that tax would be paid. Nevertheless, it would have quickly become clear that not all amounts in the assessment could be collected, but as fixed quotas had to be met, there could be a shortfall. Was it simply a matter of where there were successful appeals of being able 'to charge the same upon such other person or persons as they [the commissioners] shall see cause'?[65] In other words, tax someone—anyone else. This would not be straightforward if the initial assessment had been proportionate. Although this latter wording was common in late 1640s legislation, and continued throughout the 1650s and 1660s, it appears unspecific and potentially unjust. The considered 1652 legislative response was to statutorily allow a full reassessment of the parish or wapentake, or other subdivision for amounts to make up the quota, and this became the standard form thereafter, so that 'the several and respective Commissioners, Assessors and Collectors aforesaid ... are hereby Authorized and required to assess the full quota, but where the same shall be unassessed, not collected, levied or not paid, the said new Assessment to be made, collected, levied and paid in such manner and by such means as in this Act for the assessment is declared'.[66] All taxpayers would thus pay a little more. Reassessment was certainly used by local administrators long before this 1652 legislation, but was a key part of the land tax process thereafter recognised in all case studies and places beyond. The earliest identified reassessment in this study is dated 9 May 1644 from Paddington in Middlesex.[67]

2.2.5 Payment Deadlines and the Importance of Summary Duplicates

Early ordinances delegated tax-gathering authority to local commissioners who were to meet regularly 'once in every week at the least'[68] and were expected to manage the process locally with few set deadlines around collection, although there were some around making assessments.[69] They were nevertheless expected to 'Monethly or oftner, as there shall be occasion, are to give an accompt of their proceedings and actions to the Parliament or Councel of State'.[70] Such loose control might be appropriate where significant tax funds were spent locally, to fund garrisons say, rather than being returned to the centre, but as the Civil War ended this was less useful particularly after the Battle of Worcester on 3 September 1651. Already on 16 April 1651, Parliament had asked 'That Mr. Speaker do write the like Letters to the Commissioners in the several Counties as formerly, to quicken the Collection of the Assessment'.[71] Whether this intervention was decisive is unclear, but subsequent ordinances, including that agreed on 2 September 1651[72] normally contain clear payment deadlines and in Kent, these deadlines are stated on the few surviving collectors' warrants[73] at least from Anthony Webb's of March 1654.[74] These national deadlines appeared on warrants across the country thereafter, although local deadlines had been set from the 1640s (Table 2.1).[75]

One important symbolic and practical change concerns the breadth of the tax base and reporting to the Exchequer. For centuries, for taxes like the subsidy, the complete tax roll could normally be returned to the Exchequer containing the full list of all individual taxpayers and their tax

Table 2.1 Land tax legislative initiatives 1643–1652 still current in 1733[76]

Initiatives	*First Ordinance*	*Acts and Ordinances or Statutes of the Realm*	*Text of Statute of Ordinance*
National quota	1642: £400,000 levy & February 1643: First Weekly Assessment ordinance	SoR, vol. 5, pp.145–167, A&O, pp.85–100	
Weight of tax	1642: £400,000 levy & February 1643: First Weekly Assessment ordinance	SoR, vol. 5, pp.145–167, A&O, pp.85–100	
Division of tax between landlord and tenant	1642: £400,000 levy & February 1643: First Weekly Assessment ordinance	SoR, vol. 5, pp.145–167, A&O, pp.85–100	'...if the Land be set or let to or neere the yearly value thereof, in the possession of any Tenant, for life, lives, or years, or at will, such person or persons to whom the rent thereof belongeth, to be solely chargeable therewith; But if the same be let at any easie or small rent or under-value, then the sum taxed to be apportioned betweene the party or parties to whom the rent belongeth; And the Tenant or occupier of the Lands, Tenements, or Hereditaments, as the Taxers shall thinke meet. And if they or any of them shall doe any injury, the same to be rectified by the said Committees, or any two of them within their severall limits or divisions, according to their discretion: And if any such Tenant or occupier of Lands, Tenements, or Hereditaments, shall or may be charged with any summe of money contrary to the true intent and meaning of this Ordinance, That it shall and may be lawfull to and for such Tenant or occupier to stop and detaine the same, from and out of his rent due for the same Land, or to take his Lawfull remedy against such person or persons to whom the said rent is or shall be due or belonging...'
Dated inaugural meeting of commissioners	February 1645: Fairfax Army	A&O, pp. 614–626	'...shall within eight dayes next ensuing the publication hereof, meet together at some convenient place in every of the said Cities, Counties and places respectively...'

(continued)

Table 2.1 (continued)

Initiatives	*First Ordinance*	*Acts and Ordinances or Statutes of the Realm*	*Text of Statute of Ordinance*
Automatic tenant deduction of tax from landlord's rent. Commissioners to resolve disputes	February 1645: Fairfax Army	A&O, pp. 614–626	'... the Tenants of all Houses and Lands,..., are hereby required and authorized, to pay such summes of Money, as shall be Rated upon such House and Lands, and to deduct out of their Rents, so much of the said Rates, as in respect of the Rents of every such House and Lands the Landlords should or ought to pay and beare; and the Landlords both mediate, and immediate, according to their respective interest, are hereby required to allow such deductions and payments ...'
Local tax quotas	April 1649: An Act For Raising Ninety thousand pounds per Month, but implied in earlier ordinances	A&O, pp. 24–57	'The said Commissioners or the major part of them then present, shall upon view and perusal of the said several Surveys, cast up the true Revenue and yearly Profits of the whole county or city, to the end that an equal pound rate may be apportioned.'
Usual' or traditional assessment approved where 'obstructions or delays' may happen	April 1649: An Act For Raising Ninety thousand pounds per month, but implied in earlier ordinances	A&O, pp. 285–319	'... Commissioners...where such Obstructions shall be or happen, shall appoint a general meeting together, and the major part of them then meeting, may, and are hereby authorized (for the removal of such obstructions, and the more speedy and effectual execution of this Act) to proceed according to the most just and equal of Rates held in such places.'
Clear deadlines for collectors' payments	September 1651: An Act For Raising one hundred and twenty thousand pounds per Month. But implied in earlier ordinances	HOCJ, vol. 7, 2 September 1651, p. 10	'The Parliament have, by their Act, herewith sent you, continued the Assessments of 120,000£. a Month, for Three Months, from the Nine-and-twentieth of September next; and ordered, That the same be at once assessed, and the Collection thereof so disposed, and effectually prosecuted, that one Moiety, at the least, may be paid in to the Treasury on or before the Twentieth of October next; and the other Moiety, on or before the First of December next.'
Reassessment where quota not met	December 1652: An Act For Raising one hundred and twenty thousand pounds per Month. But implied in earlier ordinances	A&O, pp. 653–688	'... where the same shall be unassessed, not collected, levied or not paid, the said new Assessment to be made, collected, levied and paid in such manner and by such means as in this Act for the Assessment is declared...'

dues.[77] The assessment taxed far more people and sending copies of such voluminous documentation was impractical, unnecessary and time-consuming. By the mid-1640s in Kent[78] and many other counties,[79] it was common practice to send just a summary duplicate for each sub-lathe to the Exchequer, including only the parish (or other division), the names of collectors and amounts of tax due—but not a long list of taxpayers' names.[80] This summary became codified into legislation in the 1660s and was described in the *Royal Aid* statute of 1664[81] which stated that this 'Duplicate soe to be returned into the King's Remembrancer's Office in the Exchequer is intended to containe noe more then the summes in grosse to be collected by each Sub Collector and the severall Names of the said Sub Collectors'.[82] The development of the duplicate is one clear example of local administration developing tax solutions which were later codified into legislation. Reassessment would be another, but much of the evolving detailed structure described above, probably developed in this way.

2.3 The Tax Process

A very broad outline of the resulting tax process described in the legislation discussed and intended for national application follows. The process was built on more ancient statutes, but was also highly innovative as is identifiable in all three case study areas throughout much of the study period.

Parliament appointed unpaid bodies of commissioners on a county by county or city by city basis,[83] who were largely responsible for administration. After the inaugural meeting at a 'usual place', the commissioners divided themselves into smaller groups to administer manageable areas: hundreds or wapentakes, for example, and in the case of Kent, lathes, sub-lathes and boroughs. In many towns and cities, there was no need for subdivision, but both London and Bristol saw some delegation to wards and parishes. The local commissioners appointed and paid a clerk to handle correspondence, copy and produce documents and organise meetings. Paid officials received 'poundage', a small proportion of the monies they paid up. Commissioners selected and warranted unremunerated parish assessors to compile the names of those assessed and their tax dues in a formal written assessment. Then, paid collectors or sub-collectors were chosen, although the two roles of assessor and collector were sometimes combined. Until the 1670s,[84] high- or head-collectors were appointed to gather monies from local sub-collectors. There would also be a paid treasurer or receiver-general variously appointed, chiefly responsible for gathering county money from officials down the tax-gathering chain and passing it to central authorities.

Once assessors had compiled their assessment, with its list of individual names and tax amounts, it was passed to the clerk for copying. One copy, once 'seen and allowed' by commissioners was for the collector, and given to them along with their empowering warrant.[85] By the mid-1640s as discussed, summaries or duplicates[86] were produced for the Exchequer containing only the names of parishes, collectors and tax dues. Collectors had the task of garnering monies from taxpayers, but would resort to distraint if necessary. Once gathered, monies were passed up the tax-gathering chain and receipts or 'acquittances' down. These latter documents were invaluable in protecting collectors from further liability or disciplinary action. Land taxes evolved from weekly assessments to monthly quarterly and annual levies by statute and local practice, but it is unclear how often collectors went on their rounds. Throughout the Restoration and beyond, delivery to the receiver was generally on a quarterly basis.[87]

State authority implicitly and explicitly permeated tax legislation as it cascaded down from parliament to tax-gathering officialdom—'the allocation of responsibility from the top to the bottom'.[88] Such legal authority was undoubtedly a fundamental part of financial controls and also gave investors the confidence to lend to the state on the strength of ordinances which had been collateralised since the 1640s, as Coffman also observes for the excise.[89] Commissioners appointed by king or parliament in statute or ordinance signed and sealed warrants empowering collectors and assessors to act and telling them what to do and when. They then approved, signed and sealed assessments and duplicates as part of process monitoring. Assessments, warrants and duplicates regularly cited the legislation authorising the tax-gathering or the commissioners' powers.[90] Auditors were periodically involved in the checking process and outcomes. Abatements of tax, certified by commissioners' warrants, were possible, and in Upper Scray and elsewhere in Kent, involved a mixture of genuine mitigation of overassessment and uncollectable amounts.[91] From the 1670s onwards, on receipt of all tax monies due, the receiver would send a final commissioners' receipt to indicate collection was complete.[92]

2.4 Background to the Case Studies

2.4.1 *The City of London*

Mid-seventeenth-century English population had peaked at over five million, but urban populations continued to grow in England as a whole and particularly in London. In City wards, the population had doubled in a century (Fig. 2.1).[93] The importance of urban London in changing Britain's society and economy, particularly from the mid-seventeenth century, has long been discussed by Wrigley and others.[94] It contributed a significant proportion of ordinary state revenue.[95] Metropolitan London at the end of the seventeenth century comprised an urban population of well over half a million souls.[96] It was the largest city in Western Europe and probably contained more people than all the other urban areas of England combined.[97] It is estimated that by the end of the seventeenth century, perhaps one-sixth of English people had resided in London at some time in their lives.[98]

Contemporaries typically viewed the whole conurbation including the City, Westminster, parts of Middlesex and Southwark, as London.[99] Royal London, political London and the commercial City were bound together in networks of streets, personal relationships, trade and exchange. This was the political, royal, financial, banking, legal, commercial, professional, communications, shipping, import, export, and re-export, industrial, manufacturing, artistic, theatrical and shopping capital of the country.[100]

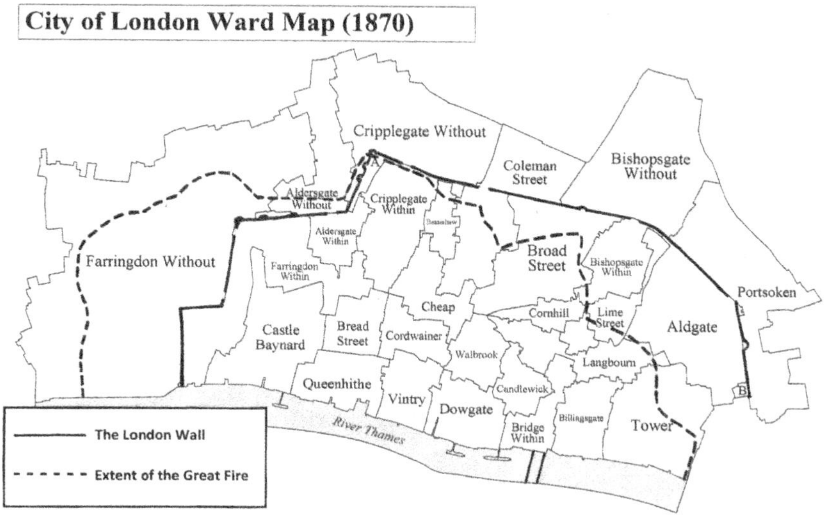

Fig. 2.1 The wards of the City of London and extent of the Great Fire[101]

In many of these areas, London was utterly dominant in the nation by the end of the seventeenth century with perhaps 80% of imports and 85% of re-exports.

Contemporary John Graunt[102] famously described it as 'perhaps a head too big for the body'—a capital too big for the country. People, goods, water supply, power, transport and road links were drawn into this metropolitan City and it in turn emitted waste, pollution and mortal remains. London would often be under a blanket of 'great stinking fogs' caused significantly by emissions from the burning of wood and Newcastle coal for domestic and commercial purposes.[103] The tax case study chosen is the City itself with its 25 wards within and without the ancient city walls.[104] Some comparison is made throughout with data from the broader metropolis.

2.4.2 *The County of Kent*

Kent was also seen as wealthy by contemporaries:

> A Knight of Wales, a Gentleman of Cales [or Calais], a Laird of the North Country: a Yeoman of Kent, with his yearly rent, will put them out all three.[105]

Kent's traditional gavelkind land tenure was unusual. It was essentially a system of partible inheritance which militated against the formation of large estates. According to Hipkin,[106] here was a relatively fluid and commercialised land market where tenants could build viable farms through 'market-sensitive leasehold deals' in a county dominated by the mid-seventeenth century by such farms, many of which supplied London's growing demands[107] and were already recognised for their distinctive produce. For example, Teynham in Upper Scray in Kent was noted for its fruit-growing by the early seventeenth century as in Michael Drayton's Poly-Olbion[108]:

> Rich Tenham undertakes thy Closets to suffize,
> With Cherries, which wee say, the Sommer in doth bring,
> ...
> Whose golden Gardens seeme th'Hesperides to mock:
> Nor there the Damzon wants, nor daintie A[p]ricock,

> Nor Pippin, which we hold of kernell-fruits the king,
> The Apple-Orendge; then the sauory Russetting:
> The Peare-maine, which to France long ere to vs was knowne.[109]

Substantial parts of seventeenth-century Kent were tenanted, and income from rent could 'underwrite credit', finance the expansion of businesses and meet tax bills.[110] The county also benefitted significantly from state investment in the naval dockyards on the Medway.

London's seventeenth-century growth far exceeded any other, but towns and urban living had grown substantially in England by 1700 and about 25 larger towns had between 5,000 and 20,000 inhabitants. There were numerous smaller towns in Kent which had separate commissioner groups named in statutes by the 1670s, including Canterbury, Dover, Folkestone, Fordwich, Faversham, Tenterden, Sandwich, New Romney, Lydd and Hythe.[111] Several of these had less than a thousand inhabitants including the small town and port of New Romney in Kent which along with Lydd kept and retained excellent tax records. There are various estimates of the urban population of England and Wales by 1700; some have it as over a third, but this might be too high, following Shaw-Taylor and Wrigley.[112] The Land Tax Act for 1710 gave separate tax quotas to 63 cities, towns and boroughs,[113] making up 21% of the tax assessment—over 16% in the metropolis of London alone. Of these, only London and Norwich (0.43%) then had a national land tax quota share greater than Bristol's (0.37%). New Romney's share was a mere 0.013%. In Kent, Dover had the largest quota at 0.097% closely followed by Canterbury's 0.089%.[114]

2.4.3 *The City of Bristol*

The City and County of Bristol, 'metropolis of the West',[115] the country's second port, a great regional trading centre,[116] faced many of the land tax-gathering challenges of the City of London itself, albeit on a smaller scale, chiefly how to levy a broadly based tax on a large and mobile population in an expanding and developing urban environment. By 1700, the City's population had passed 20,000,[117] and may have reached 50,000 by 1750.[118] Its population was continuing to be swelled by immigration from the countryside, Ireland and smaller towns as the City's importance as a regional centre and international port grew. Bristol profitably imported *inter alia*: fish, timber and furs from North America; sugar, cotton and ginger from Barbados, Antigua and Jamaica; and wine and oil from Spain and Portugal. It manufactured soap, brewed beer and produced sugar and tobacco. As Sacks and others have shown, Tudor and Stuart Bristol was both an outward-reaching but sometimes inward-looking City, as it responded to developments in England and across the post-medieval world to play an important role in the Atlantic economy.[119] Bristol was profoundly impacted by the discovery of the New World, overseas empire building, the Reformation and Civil War. Bristol was also affected by the rapid growth of London and economic and political developments there. By 1700, a change in economic focus towards the Atlantic had brought riches and employment to the City. Bristol's governors, influenced by dissenting opinions, had pioneered educational provisions for the young, and had established the most advanced system of poor relief in the country. The City was said by contemporaries to be the best port after London even if some of its citizens were already profiting from the notorious triangular trade[120] and the trade in indentured servants.[121]

Bristol's civic administrative structure was rather like London's with its mayor, sheriffs, aldermen and common councilmen also forming the core of tax commissioners throughout the period from the 1640s and into the eighteenth century.[122] Late seventeenth-century administration was dominated by the merchant classes supported by wealthier grocers, drapers, mercers and the like. To label many of them with a single epithet probably does scant justice to their diverse commercial activities. Most were significant taxpayers themselves, but many could deduct tax from their landlords' rent. Few, even of these wealthy merchants, artisans and shopkeepers, owned freehold property rights on their urban dwellings, shops or storehouses. What freehold there was, in the confines of the City, came into private hands from dissolved ecclesiastic holdings, most of which were owned by absentee gentry and institutions.[123] Bristol's civic officials and its burgesses probably comprised the majority, but by no means all of the City taxpayers across 18 parishes (Fig. 2.2).[124]

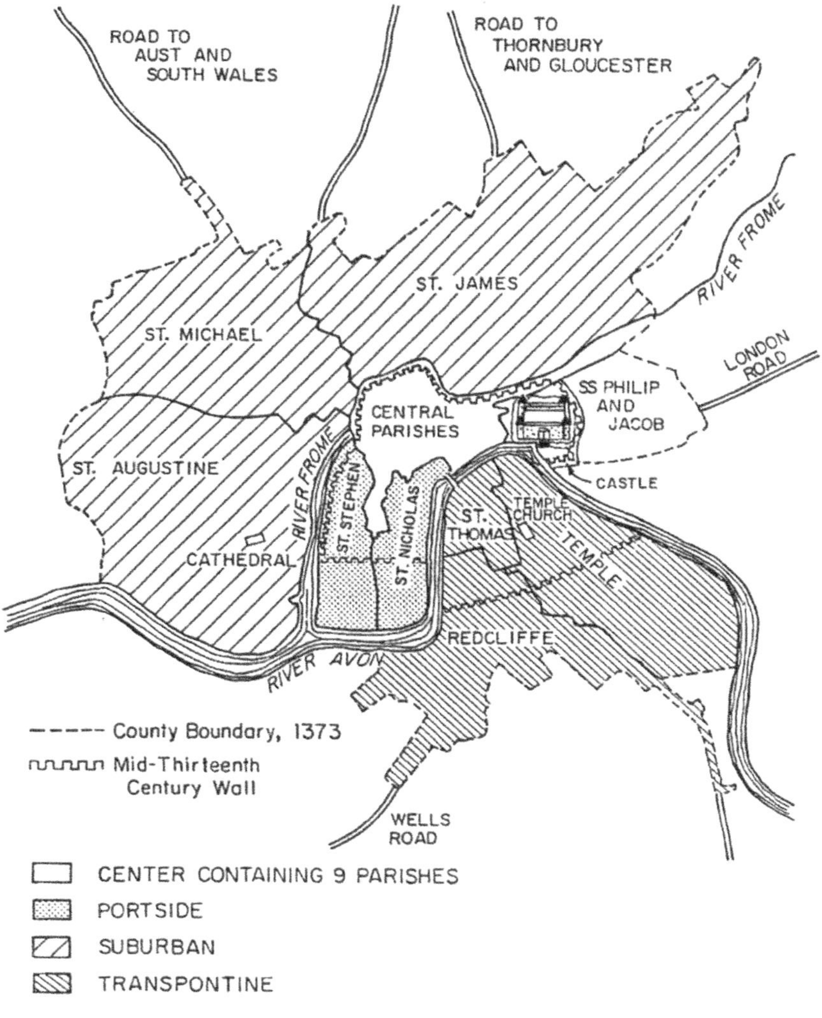

Fig. 2.2 Bristol's Ecclesiastical Geography after Sacks, *The Widening Gate*, Fig. 1.3[125] (With copyright permission from Sacks 1991)

2.5 The Importance of Cashflow Exploitation

> The want of Money, which like an Epidemicall disease, hath over-run the whole land.[126]

It is argued here that because seventeenth-century cash was so scarce, when legislators created two new taxes in 1643, the assessment and the excise, they designed them to be well placed to exploit two contemporary cashflows of growing importance: rent and product supply chains. The argument is mainly based on implication from the legislative texts and the tax outcomes in the case study areas. For land taxes, this intent is clear from the intricate focus on tax deduction in parliament's legislative ordinances. Both new taxes charged individuals who were likely to generate cash, including farmers, shopkeepers, producers and merchants, but allowed them some means to shift the immediate tax burden elsewhere—on to consumers or landlords. In both cases, it took some amount of legislative tinkering to make the taxes effective. The resulting large volumes of tax monies created remittance challenges which helped foster the development of paper bill transactions and London and regional banking facilities.

The broadly based land taxes depended largely on physical cash payments by hundreds of thousands of taxpayers to local collectors up and down the land. Some did not or could not pay, some fled to avoid payment, and others no doubt borrowed to pay as the quotas had to be met. To make matters worse, physical cash, in the form of gold and silver coin, was tightly constrained in a growing English economy, and paper bill alternatives were only available to a small minority. Over the century and more, prior to the Civil War, the physical money supply situation had been exacerbated by high inflation and low coinage growth. This further drove the creation of an economy, described by Muldrew,[127] as substantially based on credit, with cash largely reserved for certain limited activities, including the payment of rents, tithes and taxes as well as remittances by merchants as recognised by Coates in Civil War London.[128] As far as taxes were concerned, 'because of the small scale of each payment, and the fact that the collection was centralised … credit or payment in kind, was made virtually impossible'.[129] The greater commercialisation of land by the mid-seventeenth century and growing consumer demand for alcohol, tobacco and other merchandise created more accessible rent-flows and product supply chains that the fiscal state could exploit by innovative taxation. Complaints that high taxation was stripping coin from a county or City during the seventeenth century carried more than a grain of truth as tax receipts were often physically transferred in wagons under armed guard to London. The success of the assessment meant that enormous sums moved this way and there were failed pleas that taxes could be paid in commodities instead of cash.[130] When during the mid-1660s, land taxes annually raised over £1.4 million overwhelmingly in coin, it should be remembered that Samuel Pepys estimated that there was only seven million pounds of coinage in circulation.[131] Indirect levies may have taken the tax total to £3.6 million.[132] This provided a significant seventeenth-century and later fiscal challenge.

Long-established business networks and forms of credit allowed limited tax monies to be transmitted from the provinces to the Exchequer in paper bill form at least since the 1590s.[133] Such facilities were boosted by the establishment of an Exchange Office in 1667 to handle record amounts of tax receipts.[134] This was indeed the genesis of the later Tax Office, allowing transfers to London, by the use of bills of exchange, 'to lessen the charge and clamour of the waggons'.[135] The Treasury view a year later in August 1668 praised 'the good success of the Office of Exchanges having already very much lessened the number of waggons and for the few remaining waggons horses can be more cheaply hired'.[136] Nevertheless, physical transfers of cash to London continued from many counties long after the Revolution.[137] The Treasury specifically requested payment in specie during the Bubble Crisis.[138] Bristol's taxes were still transferred to London in coin in the 1670s[139] as were Kent's, according to Sir Edward Dering MP who had been a local tax commissioner there since 1660.[140] Nevertheless, there is some suggestion from the fact that so many payments by Kentish high-collectors in the 1640s and 1650s were in the form of round sum amounts (Fig. 3.10) that some transfers were already in paper bill form. It is hard to be sure, but various forms of paper transactions were possible by mid-century of more or less formality, assignability and legal enforceability. Kerridge suggests London goldsmith-bankers' notes[141] were issued as early as 1650[142] and bills of exchange and other hybrid forms of paper long before that.[143] Bankers like Edward Backwell were hugely involved as fiscal agents, farming customs and excise and even acting as tax commissioners.[144] Nevertheless, the vast majority of taxpayers still paid in coin and complaints of a shortage of coin lasted long into the eighteenth century.[145]

Receivers-general stood as intermediaries between tax-collectors and the Exchequer and could profit from that position. They gained considerable credit in the money market and probably promoted the circulation of paper bills according to Roseveare,[146] but they might have been tempted to hold on to cash longer than was necessary and deploy it for their own purposes as MPs and Westminster officials long suspected. Doubtless, one reason that customs, excise and hearth tax were brought under direct Treasury control during the Restoration was to end such exploitation. Treasury could mitigate delays in tax payments by collateralising expected fiscal cashflows and borrowing against them in the money markets, thus partly shifting the liquidity risk to investors, as it had indeed long done so. The price of shifting this risk as well as any non-payment risk was in the 6% or higher interest rates paid on such instruments during the Restoration.[147] Numbered Treasury Orders, often with the more ancient nomenclature of 'tallies'[148] were secured on tax-flows from the *Additional Aid* of the 1660s at 6%,[149] and such Orders were for the first time assignable and tradeable, making them attractive then to 900 subscribers. They were also issued to government officials as security for their own short-term borrowing as in the case of Samuel Pepys as Treasurer of the Tangier garrison.[150]

Physical cash constraints remained throughout the century and illegal forgery and coin clipping reduced the quality of coin in circulation leading to the Great Recoinage with important legislation in 1696[151] and 1697,[152] to encourage the redemption of old hammered silver at face or fixed value as tax payments amidst threats to reject such coin as legal tender. Receiver-generals were pressed into service to accept clipped coin as long as they were paid to the Exchequer by 4 May 1696 and in the second act by 1 June 1697 to qualify.[153] The intention was to encourage taxpayers to pay early, and this was certainly achieved as was the broader objective of bringing in large amounts of clipped coinage.

Did the legislation also encourage dishonesty by collectors or receivers? Ward certainly believed so and claims there was one prosecution and at least eleven other receivers were suspected, but apparently no further action was taken.[154] The current author is more sceptical on this point.[155] It is certainly true that coins that were devalued in normal circulation might be redeemed at full or fixed value, but Treasury knew this when the legislation was enacted. Even so the Treasury Lords wrote to the 'Commissioners of every county that my Lords have great reason to suspect that more clipt money has been paid by the collectors of the 4 shilling Aid to the Receiver General [of each respective County] than they, the said collectors, actually received from the King's subjects'.[156] Receivers usually had financial networks and anyone in a county, city or town would have been able to make use of this opportunity to cash in their clipped coinage with the receiver whether they were a taxpayer or not. The receiver would simply be acting like a bank or intermediary between the taxpayer and those with cash by taking deposits from those with clipped coin. Such cash along with any actual tax receipts would be paid up by the deadline and collectors would then collect the remaining taxes to balance the receiver's account and he could then settle his depositors' accounts. Did this amount to dishonesty? The receivers would presumably have argued not and the fact, if Ward is right, that there was only a single prosecution suggests that this was not seen as a serious misdemeanour. Treasury had money early and clipped money was removed from circulation.

The incentives for early payment of clipped silver achieved success in Bristol, and in London, significant amounts of hammered silver were quickly remitted to receivers particularly from commercial wards (Fig. 5.4). How much of this was tax money and how much was from deposits, to be recouped from later tax receipts, is impossible to establish. In any case, threats of non-redemption contained in the legislation may have rung somewhat hollow to those who could exploit the value of silver on the continental markets. Neither act was entirely successful in dealing with the fundamental difficulties of reconciling the value of coinage in everyday circulation with the volatilities of commodity markets.

Strikingly, throughout our period, tax-flows in metropolitan London, which made up one-sixth of the post-revolutionary national tax total, were intimately linked to and tightly constrained by the annual financial cycle and the settlement dates of Lady Day and Michaelmas when bills were paid, debts settled and cash in coin freed up (Fig. 5.4). The establishment of the Bank of England and the increasing use of inland bills of exchange, after legislative changes at the turn of the century, provided significant alleviation of the difficulty of transferring tax balances, as did the creation of local banking facilities suggested by Pressnell,[157] particularly in the mid-to-late eighteenth century, sometimes with receivers-general behind them.[158] Even post-revolutionary tax-collectors were soon paying receivers using bills of exchange as they were legally allowed to do, and two deputy-receivers were prosecuted in 1697 for refusing to accept them.[159] Others were warned 'to observe the law in taking such bills'.[160] Collectors would know that Exchequer bills might be purchased at a discount, but were accepted at face value if used for the payment of taxes which provided further opportunity for profit.[161] If receivers had the advantage of being able to delay cash remittances and deploy funds for their own purposes, they also had considerable expense in remittance and in administration including the payment of deputies.[162] Some went under, as Ward reports, but he significantly underestimates the success of the policy of calling in their sureties when this occurred.[163]

Perhaps Pressnell has a point when he argues that 'a considerable volume of public money swelled the funds of private bankers, and in this indirect fashion helped to fructify private enterprise',[164] as receivers profited. However, this might also explain the slower flows of revenues to the Exchequer as the eighteenth century progressed. The Baker family, residing at Hawkhurst Lodge, included two eighteenth-century receivers-general for Kent. In 1790, John Baker, with others, founded the Union Bank, but this family had been local financiers long before that.[165] Eighteenth-century liquidity was aided by an inflow of foreign coin, particularly Portuguese, which was widely accepted and in circulation.[166] Taxpayers and collectors sometimes attempted to pay their tax dues by foreign currency or invalid Commonwealth coin and Boxer reports that the Cornwall receiver was accepting Portuguese coin in 1737.[167] However, Kent's Receiver-General George Baker repeatedly reminded Kentish collectors that 'No broad gold[168] or [Portuguese] Moidores[169] can be taken' in respect of tax receipts.[170]

The early modern success of customs, excises and land taxes owes much to their fiscal positioning close to cashflows, particularly physical payments in coin, cash-generating activities and economic flows of value. All three levies involved some element of deduction of tax from a revenue stream whether rent or product supply chains and are part of often deployed and highly successful fiscal strategies including value-added taxes, withholding taxes on dividends, deduction of tax at source on interest and employers' deduction of tax from emoluments. Such strategies have a number of advantages, not least because they potentially somewhat separate the incidence and payment of tax. It is more palatable for someone to pay if they do not feel they are suffering the fiscal burden themselves, and it is more difficult to avoid tax if someone else has already paid it on your behalf as seventeenth-century tenants did for their landlords or brewers for their customers. This makes such taxes more efficient and cheaper to collect. This tax deductions strategy was widely and demonstrably understood in the early 1640s by tax officials in several counties. After all it would be spelt out to them in printed legislation distributed countrywide. One very early tax warrant from Newnham in Kent dated 11 October 1644 is typical and states that 'the tenants & occupiers of lands are hereby required to pay the rent tax & deduct the same out of their landlords' rent'.[171] Kent was not alone in understanding the significance of deduction in the new tax rules as the following order from Surrey shows even earlier, on 6 January 1644:

> Order to the High constables of the hundred of Elmbridge … to send your warrant to the petty constables of the severall places and parishes within the hundred to collect money for horses and soldiers specified in the ordinances … And this tax so assessed to be paid by the severall tenants of any landlords, the Tenants abating two [parts] of three as to be divided to his landlord out of his saide rent … Non payers who 'refuse to pay' to be 'distrayned the goods of the said [person] so refusing and to sell the same …[172]

This example brings out the importance of local knowledge and negotiation. There are similar references from Kingston in Surrey and elsewhere in the same county.[173] In Buckinghamshire at the county committee sitting at Aylesbury on 23 February 1649, it was 'ordered that the severall tennants to Sir John Pakington's lands in Elsborough[174] doe pay the arrears charged upon these lands to this garrison which shall be defalked [deducted] out of their rents …'.[175] This presumably refers to Sir John Pakington, 2nd Baronet (1621–1680) who was a staunch royalist during the Civil War.[176] He would have been extremely reluctant to pay any parliamentary taxes himself even if he could be found. However, if his tenants paid up, they could deduct from his rent and he would be indirectly taxed anyway, which was the purpose of the commissioners' action and indeed the purpose of the legislation.

Did land tax legislation and administration ensure the tax burden was always passed to the landlord? Of course, they did not. Nevertheless, the principle was well established in the South-East by the 1640s. Statute always allowed the use of traditional methods and expediency where 'Obstructions shall be or happen'[177] as long as quotas were met. Legislation from the Restoration onwards formally allowed landlord and tenant to agree different terms regarding where the tax burden lay, if they saw fit,[178] and the landlord might deploy the simple expedient of raising the rent to push the burden back on to the tenant.[179] In any case, the tax incidence is unclear, because the market impact of the tax is uncertain. In a land of quit rents, customary tenures as well as rack-rents deduction of tax was not always physically possible. If some, for political reasons, were sure that fiscal incidence was with the owner or freeholder '... that the Land should pay a most grievous unequal tax',[180] the reality was much more complex. The power of excise and land taxes inevitably made them 'potential weapons in the hands of any politician'[181] throughout this period. Nevertheless, the land tax relied on the productive utilisation of urban and rural real estate and the precise tax incidence was far less important to administrators. It also required local knowledge on the part of assessors to estimate the value of land and buildings and the revenue they or their occupants produced as well as the rent paid. Crucially, they might also know how much people could actually afford to pay—a wonderful advantage to this tax, significantly overlooked in the historiography. Ultimately, enforcement action might be required, and there is plenty of evidence up and down the land that these powers were used. There was nothing new in the 1640s assessment legislation and its power to distrain goods against unpaid taxes. However, broader numbers of people had distrainable goods as the century advanced, whether stock and crop in the field, shop wares, goods in the warehouse or simply household goods. These were all items that could be sold to meet a tax bill. More people than ever before had something to lose and could be targeted by broadly based taxation.

It has been argued here that land taxes were created by early 1640s legislators as a new and innovative tax better engineered to exploit England's wealth and increasing cashflows from agricultural production, business, trade and commerce. The nature and timing of those cashflows had a significant impact on the effectiveness of the new land taxes. Despite negative historiography, highly effective new taxes were delivering significant sums in the case study areas and in many parts of the country before the Restoration. They remained highly effective throughout the period discussed here as they delivered the vast bulk of their required Restoration statutory quotas.

Notes

1. He referred to 'Assessement, or Land-taxe', working very much in tandem with an excise. William Petty, *A Treatise of Taxes & Contributions.*
2. There is no evidence that the term was materially used before 1643, but it was relatively common by the early Restoration. Source: EEBO searches on 'land-tax' and 'land tax'.
3. The process substantially invented in the seventeenth century seem little changed to those employed in 1821 and described to the Parliamentary Select Committee of 1821, Session 23 January to 11 July 1821, vol. viii, pp. 5–169, *Reports from Committees (5). Militias; Receivers General; Malt; Royal Burghs; Ireland*, etc. 'Report from the Select Committee of the Duties of the Receivers General of Land and Assessed taxes'.
4. The 1583 *gemene middelen* taxed a largely familiar range of commodities, particularly: wine, beer, meat, peat, salt, soap, grain, woollen cloth and spirits. It was also adopted in German states, Denmark, some Italian city-states and tried in Scotland in the 1590s.
5. O'Brien and Hunt 'The emergence and consolidation of excises'. Land taxes had also been long used in the Netherlands, but excise was a far more important levy there. James D. Tracy, *The Founding of the Dutch Republic. War, Finance, and Politics in Holland 1572–1588* (Oxford: Oxford University Press, 2008).
6. Fritschy, *Public Finance of the Dutch Republic*, Part 1, 2.2 and personal email communication 27 February 2018. Land taxes were levied so that '2/3 of the amount had to be paid by the owner, 1/3 by the tenant'. Fritschy is uncertain about the method of levying these early taxes, but the current author would speculate that the occupier deduction of tax from rent is a possibility.
7. Rather 'the Laws and Customs of Romney Marsh'. The use of acreage as an equitable means of assessing local poor rates or sewer levies is discussed in Davison, *The Agrarian Economy of Romney Marsh.* It was ancient in Romney Marsh and beyond. Davison believes the system was used in many other parts of England for drainage or sea defence rates, pp. 5–6, and originates in the thirteenth century. Land values had long figured in statutes as recognised by Edwin Cannan, *The History of Local Rates in England* (London: Longmans, Green, 1896) p. 114ff, and yearly land values in statutes from the fifteenth century, Peter Harris, *Income Tax in Common Law Jurisdictions: Vol. 1, From the Origins to 1820* (Cambridge: Cambridge University Press, 2006), p. 99.
8. 40 Eliz. I, c. 2 after Cannan, *The History of Local Rates*, p. 3.
9. Cannan, *The History of Local Rates*, p. 85; Spence, *London in the 1690s*, pp. 6–7 suggests there was a long-standing tradition in London of tax

on inhabitants by the 'rental value of their properties, [which] extended back at least 600 years' before 1693.

10. After, Chandaman, *The English Public Revenue*, Chapter 5. The prestige element is discussed in Jeremy Boulton, *Neighbourhood and Society: A London Suburb in the Seventeenth Century*. Cambridge Studies in Population, Economy and Society in Past Time (Cambridge: Cambridge University Press, 1987), p. 107. Boulton maintains that contribution to the subsidy 'itself qualified the person assessed to a particular social and economic standing which was recognised in the parish'.
11. In urban areas, there had long been additional material civic levies. Archer points to civic, military levies and tithes in London. Ian W. Archer, 'The Burden of Taxation on Sixteenth-Century London', *Historical Journal*, vol. 44, 2001, pp. 599–627.
12. Braddick, *Parliamentary Taxation*; Chandaman, *The English Public Revenue*, Chapter 5.
13. 3 Car. I, c. 8, 5 subsidies, 1627 SoR, vol. 5, pp. 39–53.
14. Kevin Sharpe, *The Personal Rule of Charles I* (London: Yale University Press, 1992), p. 570.
15. Henrik Langelüddecke, '"I finde all men & my officers all soe unwilling": The Collection of Ship Money, 1635–1640', *Journal of British Studies*, vol. 46, 2007, pp. 509–542.
16. (1) 16 Car. I, c. 2, 4 subsidies, 1640. SoR, vol. 5, pp. 58–78. (2) 16 Car. I, c. 4, 2 further subsidies, 1641. SoR, vol. 5, pp. 79–101. (3) See also 'February 1643: Order for assessing divers Persons in London, according to the Ordinance of 29 November', A&O, pp. 77–79.
17. 16 Car. I, c. 9, poll, 1641, SoR, vol. 5, pp. 105–110.
18. 'February 1643: An Ordinance for the speedy raising and levying of Money for the maintenance of the Army Raised by the Parliament, And other great Affaires of the Commonwealth, by a Weekly Assessement upon the Cities of London and Westminster, and every County and City of the Kingdome of England, and Dominion of Wales', A&O, pp. 85–100.
19. At least in theory at 8% interest, but in practice little or nothing.
20. The stated purpose was to 'excite all well-affected Persons to contribute' plate, money and horses to Parliament's cause according to 'June 1642: Ordinance of both Houses, for bringing in Plate, Money, and Horses', A&O, pp. 6–9.
21. TNA: SP 28/158 Commonwealth Exchequer Papers e.g. has an account for Ashford Town in Kent showing who had given and in what form. Mrs Knight, a widow, for example, had given £1-10s-0d in plate and ten shillings in money.
22. Not more than a twentieth part of 'estates'.

23. It was intended to have national impact see Braddick, *Parliamentary Taxation*, pp. 131–132.
24. 'November 1642: An Ordinance for the assessing of all such as have not contributed upon the Propositions of both Houses of Parliament, for the raising of Money, Plate, Horse, Horsemen, and Armes, for defence of the King, Kingdom and Parliament, or have not contributed proportionably to their Estates', A&O, pp. 38–40. The name 'fifth and twentieth part' comes from the fact that sums were not to 'exceed … the twentieth part of their estates' presumably against a normal four shilling in the pound rate.
25. 4 March 1643 ('March 1643: Ordinance to explain some Things in the One for the Weekly Assessment', A&O, p. 100); 11 April 1643 ('April 1643: An Ordinance for the Explanation of the Weekely Assessement in London. And that the City of London shall have the publike Faith of the Kingdom, for the repayment of 24000li. for every 40000li. that shall be monethly collected, and paid in by the said City, upon the said Ordinance', A&O, pp. 128–129).
26. 6 March 1643 ('March 1643: An Ordinance for an Assessment to be made in the several Parishes of England, for the relief of maimed Soldiers Widows, and fatherless Children', A&O, pp. 102–103).
27. 7 March 1643 ('March 1643: An Ordinance and Declaration that the Lord Major and Citizens of the City of London, for the better securing and safety thereof, shall have full power and authority according to their discretion, to trench, stop, and fortifie all high-waies leading into the said City, as well within the Liberties as without, as they shall see cause, And for the better effecting thereof, shall impose upon all the Inhabitants within the same, upon every house worth 5l. a yeare, sixpence, and every house of greater rent after the rate of two pence in the pound', A&O, pp. 103–104).
28. 'every other person and persons borne within this Realme of England, Wales, or other the Kings Dominions, as well Ecclesiasticall as Temporall, and every Fraternity, Guild, Corporation, Mystery, Brotherhood, and Cominalty Corporate, or not Corporate'.
29. And the listed taxable property was comparable to the subsidies of, for example, 1625, 1627, and 1641 which typically included every 'Fraternity, Guild, Corporation, Mystery, Brotherhood, and Cominalty Corporate, or not Corporate'.
30. 'May 1643: An Ordinance with the Names of the Knights and Gentlemen entrusted in every County to bring up a speedy Account of the Weekly Assessement, and to return the names of all such Persons as refuse to pay', A&O, pp. 139–141.

31. 'May 1643: An Ordinance for the speedy raising and levying of money thorowout the whole Kingdome of England, and dominion of Wales for the relief of the Common-wealth, by taxing such as have not at all contributed or lent, or not according to their Estates and Abilities', A&O, pp. 145–155.
32. Parliament had made a compulsory levy on Westminster and the City but was already experiencing difficulties in collections because collectors were engaged in other 'Public Affairs of the State' and some 'well-affected Persons are still occasionally pressed to further Contributions, whilst those that have not contributed, or not in Proportion to their Estates, do not make a proportionable Supply' according to 'February 1643: Order for assessing divers Persons in London, according to the Ordinance of 29 November', A&O, pp. 77–79.
33. Actually 12 weeks.
34. 16 Car. I, c. 32, £400,000 levy, 1642, SoR, vol. 5, pp. 145–167.
35. Payable in May and November.
36. As well as the parishes of '*Redderith, Newington-Butts, and Lambeth*'.
37. This is also implied in the '£400,000 Levy' [16 Car. I, c. 32, £400,000 levy, 1642, SoR, vol. 5, pp. 145–167]—'and that afterwards they may by theire assents and agreements sever themselves for the execution', but the application is less clear.
38. 'February 1645: An Ordinance for Raising and maintaining of Forces for the defence of the Kingdome, under the Command of Sir Thomas Fairfax, Knight', A&O, pp. 614–626.
39. 'November 1650: An Act for raising of One hundred and twenty thousand pounds per Mensem for Four Moneths, To commence the Five and twentieth of December 1650. for Maintenance of the Forces in England, Ireland and Scotland, Raised by Authority of Parliament for the Service of this Commonwealth', A&O, pp. 456–490.
40. 'April 1649: An Act For Raising Ninety thousand pounds per Mensem, For the Maintenance of the Forces raised by Authority of Parliament, for the Service of England and Ireland, For Six Moneths, from the 25th of March 1649 to the 29th of September, 1649', A&O, pp. 24–57.
41. Especially, New Romney and Lydd: KHLC: NR/RTa9 New Romney assessment for the Royal Aid compares the tax assessed with the town and port's proportion, Lydd (1663–1680), KHLC: Ly/9/3-15& KHLC:NR/ZLy1.
42. According to the Bassishaw Record and Assessment Book. LMA: P69/MIC1/B/006/MS03505.
43. Notably for the fifteenth and tenth.
44. See John Stow, *A Survey of London. Reprinted From the Text of 1603.* Edited by C. L. Kingsford. John Stow's survey, reprinted from the 1603

edition. British History Online, http://www.british-history.ac.uk/no-series/survey-of-london-stow/1603. The fifteenth was raised both as a national tax and a local City of London rate. The quotas varied slightly according to Stow.

45. For example, A letter from the tax commissioners to the high-constables of the hundred of Kingston, Surrey dated 16 July 1644 asks them to 'apporcon the fifteene pounds upon the several parishes' (TNA: SP 28/244/pt.2).
46. 16 Car. I, c. 32, £400,000 levy, 1642, SoR, vol. 5, pp. 145–167.
47. February 1643, First Weekly Assessment. A&0, pp. 85–100.
48. Turner et al., *Agricultural Rent*, Chapter 1.
49. February 1643, First Weekly Assessment, A&0, pp. 85–100.
50. 'March 1643: An Ordinance and Declaration that the Lord Major and Citizens of the City of London, for the better securing and safety thereof, shall have full power and authority according to their discretion, to trench, stop, and fortifie all high-waies leading into the said City, as well within the Liberties as without, as they shall see cause, And for the better effecting thereof, shall impose upon all the Inhabitants within the same, upon every house worth 5l. a yeare, sixpence, and every house of greater rent after the rate of two pence in the pound', A&O, pp. 103–104.
51. The wording is complex and starts 'Upon every house that shall be let for, or may be valued worth five pound per yeare, sixpence: and for every house of greater rent after the proportion of two pence in the pound that the tenant of the said house, paieth …'. Unfortunately no tax assessment survives for this levy.
52. February 1645: Fairfax Army, A&O, pp. 614–626.
53. Restoration legislation allowed landlords and tenants to negotiate alternative divisions of the tax.
54. HOLJ, vol. 6, 24 August 1643, p. 195.
55. And the rules were extended to fee-farm rents or other rents due to his Majesty.
56. Braddick, *Parliamentary Taxation*, p. 128. The Indemnity Committee 1647–1656, was intended to provide indemnity for acts committed in the name of Parliament including tax collection. Braddick does not acknowledge that this large number of cases suggests a material change in tax form as proposed here.
57. 'Coine, in Plate, stocke of Merchandize, any manner of Corne and Graine, Householdstuffe, & of all other goods, movables' according to the February 1643, First Weekly Assessment, A&O, pp. 85–100.
58. 'December 1649: An Act for an Assessment for six Moneths, from the Five and twentieth of December, 1649, for maintenance of the Forces

raised by Authority of Parliament for the Service of England and Ireland, at the rate of Ninety thousand pounds per mensem for the first three Moneths, and at the rate of Three score thousand pounds for the last three Moneths', A&O, pp. 285–319.

59. For example, Beckett, 'Local Custom and the "New Taxation"'. The current author's initial analysis of documents from Lancashire seems to show a traditional roll-out of ancient quotas, similar to Cumberland, for assessments throughout the interregnum: TNA/E179 various.
60. Ward, *The English Land Tax*, p. 3, is wrong to suggest this form only emerged in 1677.
61. February 1643, First Weekly Assessment wording, A&0, pp. 85–100.
62. As early as 1 July 1643 in St. James Clerkenwell (TNA: SP 28/169/pt.1).
63. The relevant section in the statute for the '£400,000 Levy' was 2,300 words long.
64. February 1643, First Weekly Assessment wording, A&0, pp. 85–100.
65. The wording appears in several statutes before 1652. For example, April 1649: An Act For Raising Ninety thousand pounds per Mensem, A&O, pp. 24–57.
66. 'December 1652: An Act for an Assessment at the Rate of One hundred and twenty thousand Pounds by the Moneth for Six Moneths, from the Five and twentieth day of December, One thousand six hundred fifty two; to the Four and twentieth day of June next ensuing, towards the Maintenance of the Armies in England, Ireland and Scotland; as also for the Navy', A&O, pp. 653–688.
67. TNA: SP 28/167/pt.2.
68. April 1649: An Act for Raising Ninety thousand pounds per Month, A&O, pp. 24–57.
69. Some subsidies, because they were isolated events, also had deadlines for the delivery of monies.
70. For example, 'July 1650: An Act for Setling of the Militia of the Commonwealth of England', A&O, pp. 397–402.
71. HOCJ, vol. 6, 16 April 1651, p. 561.
72. HOCJ, vol. 7, 2 September 1651, p. 10. Two payments with deadlines were specified, 20 October and 1 December 1651.
73. Upper Scray: Anthony Webb, TNA: E179/128/678; Joshua Pix, TNA: E179/128/679; William Catlett, TNA: E179/128/685.
74. The latest 1651 warrant dated December contained no deadline. There are no surviving Upper Scray warrants between this date and May 1654, so it is unclear if the new format appeared earlier.
75. For example, the warrant from Newnham (TNA: SP/28/158, part 3) and dated 11 October 1644 has a deadline of 5 November.

76. Sources: A&O, SoR, Chandaman, *English Public Revenue*.
77. There are numerous subsidy rolls showing such, e.g. Kent, TNA: E179/128/609. Roll dated 22 August 1628 for the first two subsidies of the five granted in 1628 for Upper Scray, Kent.
78. For example, from the 1640s: TNA: E179/128/65, 29 April 1643, for February 1642 '£400,000 Levy', St. Augustine Lathe; TNA: E179/128/664, 20 June 1643, for the 24 February 1643 weekly assessment, Canterbury; TNA: E179/128/665, 30 April 1643, for the 1642 February grant of '£400,000 Levy', St. Augustine Dover; E179/128/666 [dated July 1645 or later], February 1645, Fairfax army, Canterbury; TNA: E179/128/669 [dated February 1645 or later], February 1645, monthly assessment for the Scottish army, Canterbury; TNA: E179/128/671 [?13 August 1645 or later], 18 October 1644, weekly assessment for relief of the British Army in Ireland, Canterbury.
79. TNA: SP 28 contains local tax assessments from many counties, but few after the 1640s.
80. Tax assessments and summary duplicates were both termed 'duplicate' in ordinances and statutes at various times. Common contemporary usage in Kent is applied here. The term 'duplicate' is reserved for the summary duplicates only, unless clearly specified.
81. Chandaman, *The English Public Revenue*, p. 185 wrongly attributes this change to the 18-months' assessment of 1673–1674.
82. 16 & 17 Car. II, c. 1, Royal Aid, 1664–1667, SoR, vol. 5, pp. 525–552.
83. Their names were contained in successive statutes, which were often printed and distributed.
84. They were briefly resurrected in the 1690s.
85. The warrant and assessment might be combined in a single document.
86. For example, the commissioners' minute book KHLC: Sa/ZO3 used the term 'duplicate' for this summary only.
87. It is the clerk's copies of tax assessments that most commonly survive, but a few collectors' copies remain and these were sometimes marked with monthly ticks suggesting monies gathered.
88. Harris, *Income Tax in Common Law Jurisdictions*, p. 99.
89. D'Maris Coffman, 'Towards a New Jerusalem: The Committee for Regulating the Excise, 1649–1653', *The English Historical Review*, vol. 128, 2013, pp. 1418–1450. The assessments were collateralised e.g. 'February 1648: An Ordinance For raising of Twenty thousand pounds a Moneth for the Relief of Ireland', A&O, pp. 1072–1105. This ordinance provided that 'Persons that lending on this Ord. to be repaid at 8% interest; Committee for Irish Affairs may borrow on security of this Ord. up to £30,000'.

90. With the familiar phrase 'By virtue of an ordinance [or act] of Parliament…'.
91. 'Overassessed', 'land drowned' or 'houses empty' may be genuine adjustments, but, 'not to be had' is surely a write-off of an unrecoverable sum. TNA: E179/128/685, William Catlett's account of 25 December 1656 from Upper Scray.
92. 'That every Receiver Generall from time to time within the space of one Moneth next after he shall have received the full summe that shall be charged upon any Hundred or Division for each particular payment that is to be made to such Receiver Generall by vertue of this Act shall give to the Commissioners that shall act in such Hundred or Division a Receipt under his hand and seale acknowledgeing his Receipt of the full summe charged upon such Hundred or Division'. 30 Car. II, c. 1, 18-months' assessment, 1678–1680, SoR, vol. 5, pp. 867–883.
93. Vanessa Harding, 'City, capital, and metropolis: the changing shape of seventeenth-century London', in Julia F. Merritt (ed.), *Imagining Early Modern London: Perceptions and Portrayals of the City from Stow to Strype, 1598–1720* (Cambridge: Cambridge University Press, 2001), pp. 117–143, p. 124.
94. Recognised by many including E. Anthony Wrigley, 'A Simple Model of London's Importance in Changing English Society and Economy, 1650–1750', *Past & Present*, vol. 37, 1967, pp. 44–70, and his model of a rapidly developing metropolitan society driving social and economic change on a national scale is widely followed.
95. Chandaman, *English Public Revenue*, p. 89, believed it may have been as much as 40%; Joan Thirsk and John P. Cooper (eds.), *Seventeenth-Century Economic Documents* (Oxford: Clarendon Press, 1972), Chapter 8, pp. 751–815; O'Brien, 'The Political Economy of British Taxation', pp. 8–10 believe as much as 47% in the 1690s, up from 9% in 1685.
96. For example, Vanessa Harding, 'The Population of London, 1550–1700: A Review of the Published Evidence', *London Journal*, vol. 15, 1990, pp. 111–128. Although any measure is an estimate and requires judgement as to where the boundary of London as opposed to the City of London lies. Gregory King in 1695 has an estimate of 527,560 which would be mid-range with Harding's own rough figures for 1700 based on the Bills of Mortality at 556,000–641,000. Wrigley has 575,000 in Wrigley, 'A simple model of London's importance'; Finlay and Shearer have 490,000 in Roger Finlay and Beatrice R. Shearer, 'Population Growth and Suburban Expansion', in A. L. Beier and Roger Finlay (eds.), *London 1500–1700: The Making of the Metropolis* (London: Longman, 1986), pp. 37–59.

97. Probably around 60% of England's total, according to: Spence, *London in the 1690s*, p. 1.
98. For example, Wrigley, 'A Simple Model of London's Importance', p. 49.
99. Spence, *London in the 1690s*, p. 41 estimates that c. 180 of 940 hectares of the 1690s metropolitan City was not built-up, including tenter grounds, burial grounds, squares, markets and rope walks.
100. And see, e.g., Perry Gauci, *Emporium of the World: The Merchants of London 1660–1800* (London: Hambledon Continuum, 2007).
101. The 1870 ward map is little changed from two hundred years earlier. Based on the Ordnance Survey Town Plan of London (1871–1876) at 1:1056 scale. Accessed at https://creativecommons.org/licenses/by-sa/4.0/. This work is licensed under the Creative Commons Attribution-ShareAlike 4.0 International License. To view a copy of this license, visit http://creativecommons.org/licenses/by-sa/4.0/ or send a letter to Creative Commons, PO Box 1866, Mountain View, CA 94042, USA.
102. John Graunt, Natural and Political Observations mentioned in a following index, and made upon the Bills of Mortality (Printed by Tho: Roycroft, for John Martin, James Allestry, and Tho: Dicas, at the Sign of the Bell in St. Paul's Church-yard, 1662). Similar phrases were used even earlier by others including Captain John Gaunt in 1603 according to Robert Owen and Robert Dale Owen, *Letterpress the Crisis; or, the Change from Error and Misery to Truth and Happiness* (London, J. Eamonson, Gray's Inn Road, 1833).
103. As described by John Gadbury a late seventeenth century astronomer quoted in Spence, *London in the 1690s*, p. 29.
104. As defined in Harding, 'The population of London, 1550–1700' and excluding Bridge Without in Southwark. The City had its own land tax quota as did Middlesex, Westminster and Southwark, as sometime did Sergeant's Inn, Chancery, Inner Temple, Inns of Chancery, Middle Temple, Lincoln's Inn, Gray's Inn and together Whitehall, Saint James and Somerset House.
105. This is widely quoted in Kent's historical writing *inter alia*, Jacqueline Bower, 'The Kent Yeoman in the Seventeenth Century', *Archaeologia Cantiana*, vol. 14, 1994, p. 156. It is found in primary sources at least as early as the early seventeenth century; EEBO: 'Anglorum speculum or The worthies of England'. Author: G. S. probably George Sandys (1578–1644). Republished 1684; Bibliographic name/number: Wing (2nd ed.)/S22B; Copy from: Harvard University Library. Reel position: Wing/2002:01.
106. See, e.g., Stephen Hipkin, 'Tenant Farming and Short-Term Leasing on Romney Marsh, 1587–1705', *The Economic History Review*, New

Series, liii (2000), pp. 646–676; Stephen Hipkin, 'The Structure of Landownership and Land Occupation in the Romney Marsh Region, 1646–1834', *Agricultural History Review*, vol. 51, 2003, pp. 69–94; Davison, *The Agrarian Economy of Romney Marsh*; Hipkin, *'The Structure of Landownership'*, Believes the buying and selling of property in Kent was commonplace at least a hundred years earlier accelerated by the availability of ex-monastic lands and encouraged by an unusual form of gavelkind.

107. Ormrod, David; Gibson, James M.; and Lyne, Owen, City and Countryside Revisited. *Comparative Rent Movements in London and the South-East, 1580–1914*. Studies in Economics 1117, Working paper. Department of Economics, University of Kent, 2011.
108. Everitt, *The Community of Kent*, p. 25 quoting Michael Drayton's, *Poly-Olbion*, published in 1612.
109. Michael Drayton, *Poly-Olbion*, EEBO, STC (2nd ed.) / 7226. This was a topographical poem covering England and Wales.
110. Jane Andrewes, 'Industries in Kent', in Michael Zell (ed.), *Early Modern Kent 1540–1640*. Kent County Council (Woodbridge: Boydell Press, 2000), pp. 105–140.
111. First in 29 Car. II, c. 1, 17-months' assessment, 1677–1678, SoR, vol. 5, pp. 802–836.
112. Shaw-Taylor and Wrigley, 'Occupational Structure and Population Change', pp. 53–88. They have 16.3% in towns over 5000 in 1700, Table 2.10.
113. 8 Anne, c. 1, Land Tax for 1710. The Act provides far from a complete list of all urban centres, many of which were simply undifferentiated in county totals, but some 'urban' taxation would have fallen on cultivated land, as on a small scale in Bristol's case.
114. 12 & 13 Wm. III, c. 10, Land Tax for 1701, SoR, vol. 7, pp. 648–716.
115. Walter E. Minchinton, 'Bristol: Metropolis of the West in the Eighteenth Century: The Alexander Prize Essay', *Transactions of the Royal Society*, vol. 4, 1954, pp. 69–89.
116. William B. Stephens, *The Seventeenth-Century Customs Surveyed. William Culliford's Investigation of the Western Ports 1682–1684* (Farnham: Ashgate, 2012), pp. 36–38.
117. Based on Elizabeth Ralph and Mary E. Williams, *The Inhabitants of Bristol in 1696* (Bristol: Bristol Record Society Publications XXV, 1968), but see arguments below for a higher figure.
118. E. Anthony Wrigley, 'Urban Growth and Agricultural Change: England and the Continent in the Early Modern Period', in Wrigley, *People, Cities and Wealth* (Oxford: Blackwell, 1987), pp. 157–193, p. 160.
119. David H. Sacks, *The Widening Gate: Bristol and the Atlantic Economy, 1450–1700* (Berkeley: University of California Press, 1991).

120. It particularly did so after 1698 when the Royal African Company's monopoly over the slave trade ended.
121. For example, Patrick McGrath, *Merchants and Merchandise in Seventeenth-Century Bristol* (Bristol: Bristol Record Society Publications XIX, 1955), pp. 237–238.
122. Especially Beaven, *Bristol Lists*.
123. Sacks, e-mail communication.
124. Taxpayer numbers and freemen numbers are similar: Restoration (c. 2,900), 1690s–1700s (c. 3,500), and mid-century (c. 4,500) according to HoP.
125. Sacks, *The Widening Gate*. Sts. Philip and Jacob is regarded as Suburban by Sacks and here. Central parishes were: All Saints, Castle Precinct, Christchurch, St. Ewen, St. John, St. Leonard, St. Mary-le-Port, St. Peter, and St. Werburgh.
126. Henry Peacham, 'The Worth of a Penny: Or, A Caution to Keep Money. With the causes of the scarcity and misery of the want hereof in these hard and mercilesse Times: As also how to save it in our Diet, Apparell, Recreations, &c. And also what honest Courses men in want may take to live'. London, printed by R. Hearne, 1641. Quoted in Carl Wennerlind, *Casualties of Credit: The English Financial Revolution, 1620–1720* (Cambridge, MA: Harvard University Press, 2011).
127. Muldrew, *The Economy of Obligation*, pp. 98–103.
128. 'Cash flow was very important in the early modern economy and every merchant's nightmare was a wave of bankruptcies, one triggering another', p. 21; Ben Coates, 'The Impact of the English Civil War on the Economy of London, 1642–1650' (PhD thesis, University of Leicester, 1997).
129. Muldrew, *The Economy of Obligation*, p. 91.
130. Chandaman, *The English Public Revenue*, pp. 181–182, fn5 based on CTB, vol. 1, 27 December 1665, pp. 700–701.
131. Quoted in Muldrew, *The Economy of Obligation*, p. 102, this was partly because of hoarding. This was despite a re-coinage of republican silver in 1662. Chandaman, *The English Public Revenue*, p. 206.
132. Muldrew, *The Economy of Obligation*, p. 90.
133. Eric Kerridge, *Trade and Banking in Early Modern England* (Manchester: Manchester University Press, 1988), p. 55, citing John V. Beckett, *Coal and Tobacco: The Lowthers and the Economic Development of West Cumberland, 1660–1760* (Cambridge: Cambridge University Press, 1981), pp. 115–117.
134. It was closed in 1670, but a similar office was operational three years later. See also Ward, *The English Land Tax*, pp. 14–15.
135. CTB, vol. 2, 5 June 1667, p. 8.

136. CTB, vol. 2, 26 August 1668, p. 611.
137. Chandaman, *The English Public Revenue*, p. 182, fn2; CTB, vol. 2, April–August 1668, pp. 307, 330, 421, 612. Chandaman believes the office was discontinued in 1670.
138. Ward, *The English Land Tax*, p. 107.
139. It is difficult to be sure why this method was chosen when the Bristol Corporation (Kerridge, *Trade and Banking*, p. 64) and local merchants were already using bills of exchange quite widely.
140. Quoted in Kerridge, *Trade and Banking*, p. 57, citing Bodleian Library, MS Top. Kent a.1 fo.26v; Dering, Sir Edward, 2nd Bt. (1625–1684), of Surrenden Dering, Kent and Bloomsbury, Mdx. Source: HoP (accessed 3 May 2017).
141. They were '... the first bankers in the West to loan the funds deposited with them in the form of transferable paper money' according to Jongchul Kim, 'How modern banking originated: The London goldsmith-bankers' institutionalisation of trust', *Business history*, vol. 53, 2011, pp. 939–959; J. Keith Horsefield, 'The Beginnings of Paper Money in England', *The Journal of European Economic History*, vol. 6, 1977, pp. 117–133.
142. Kerridge, *Trade and Banking*, Chapter 5.
143. Ibid., Chapter 4.
144. Edward Backwell, 12 Car. II, c. 9, Poll, 1660, SoR, vol. 5, pp. 207–225.
145. The Restoration also saw other markets in paper instruments including mortgages and annuities but few of these would have been used in the payment of taxes, see Roseveare, *The Financial Revolution*, p. 22.
146. Roseveare, *The Financial Revolution*, pp. 24–25.
147. Reducing to 3% by the 1720s.
148. See Chandaman, *The English Public Revenue*, Appendix I, for an account of how these worked during the Restoration.
149. Roseveare, *The Financial Revolution*, pp. 14–21.
150. Ibid., Document 4, p. 80.
151. 7 & 8, Wm. III, c. 1, Recoinage, 1695–1696, SoR, vol. 7, pp. 1–4.
152. 8 & 9 Wm. III, c. 6, Land Tax & subsidies, 1696–1697, SoR, vol. 7, pp. 166–189, s. LXXXII stated that 'Rates may be paid before 1st June 1697 in hammered Silver Monies. 'And whereas several Persons who shall be assessed by this Act for or in respect of their Manors Lands Tenements Rents Offices Persons Stocks Debts or other Matters or Things hereby intended to be charged may be willing and desirous to pay or satisfie att once in ha[m]mered Silver Moneys att the Rate of Five Shillings and Eight Pence an Ounce all or several of the Monthly Payments by this Act intended to be satisfied by them Be it further enacted by the Authority aforesaid That it shall & may be lawfull to and

for any p[er]son or Persons att any time before the First Day of June One thousand six hundred ninety and seven to satisfie and pay to the respective Collector or Collectors in such ha[m]mered Silver Moneys att such Rate as aforesaid all or any of the said Monthly Payments'. The 1696 Act had a similar proviso but this time with 'Proviso for Payment of Assessments in Clipt Silver before 4th May 1696'.

153. TNA: E182/596 has a pre-printed receipt dated 3 July 1697 for £2,964-6s-1d from Thomas Cuddon Receiver-General of Middlesex (and London) for 10,462 ounces and 5 pennyweights of 'hammered silver' which at 5s-8d per ounce gives this amount. Presumably this was received before the 1 June and it appears to have been issued only after weighing by Thomas Neale Esquire Master and Worker of his Majesty's Mints.
154. Ward, *The English Land Tax*, pp. 44–45.
155. Although a slightly different view is expressed in Pierpoint, 'The Administration of the Land Tax', pp. 72–73.
156. CTB, vol. 11, 12 August 1696, p. 46.
157. Leslie S. Pressnell, 'Public Monies and the Development of English Banking', *The Economic History Review*, vol. 5, 1953, pp. 378–397.
158. See Parliamentary Select Committee of 1821, Session 23 January to 11 July 1821, vol. viii, pp. 5–169, *Reports from Committees (5). Militias; Receivers General; Malt; Royal Burghs; Ireland:* etc. 'Report from the Committee of the Duties of the Receivers General of Land and Assessed taxes'.
159. See Ward, *The English Land Tax*, p. 45 and CTB, vol. 12, 10 September 1697, p. 313. Richard Cobb and William Oades of the County of Southampton were the parties and had presumably refused because of the extra value of clipped silver at this time. The county was warned about 'further abuse of this kind'.
160. CTB, vol. 13, 1 November 1697, p. 22.
161. There are relevant notes in the biography of John Knight I MP (c.1656–1708), of Beaufort Buildings, Strand, and Somerset House, London. Source: HoP (accessed 4 May 2017).
162. Throughout the Restoration and beyond they claimed expenses.
163. Ward, *The English Land Tax*, pp. 49–50. Sureties were effectively third-party receiver guarantees.
164. Pressnell, 'Public Monies', p. 378.
165. Obituary in *The Gentleman's Magazine*: 1831, vol. 101, Part 1, p. 176. The bank was originally known as Baker, Denne, Kingsford, Wigzell & Kingsford and was founded by John Baker, John Denne, Sampson Kingsford, (forename unknown) Wigzell and William Kingsford, http://heritagearchives.rbs.com/companies/list/halford-baldock-and-co.html#jq35K56qbrSY2TFl.99.

166. Nuno Palma, *Anglo-Portuguese Trade and Monetary Transmission During the Eighteenth Century*, Nova School of Business and Economics. Current draft (incomplete, not for circulation): October 21, 2012; Charles Ralph Boxer, 'Brazilian Gold and British Traders in the First Half of the Eighteenth Century', *Hispanic American Historical Review*, vol. 49, 1969, pp. 454–472; Ward, *The English Land Tax*, pp. 108–109.
167. Ibid.
168. Commonwealth gold.
169. A Portuguese gold coin current in England in the early eighteenth century.
170. KHLC: NR/RTL2 various 1726–1731.
171. TNA: SP 28/158, part 3. Commonwealth Exchequer Papers, Kent.
172. TNA: SP 28/149, part 4. Commonwealth Exchequer Papers, Surrey.
173. TNA: SP 28/152, Part 1. Commonwealth Exchequer Papers, Surrey.
174. See TNA: 705:349/12946/502712. Lease for eighty years from Sir John Pakington of Hampton Lovett, co. Worc., knt. This document of 1607 refers to Ellesborowe or as it is now known Ellesborough. This is presumably Sir John Pakington (1549–1625).
175. TNA: SP 28/220 Buckinhgamshire, volume 1: Correspondence from committee regarding accounts.
176. Sir John, 2nd Bt. (1621–1680), of Westwood Park, Worcs. Source: HoP (accessed 9 February 2018).
177. 'December 1649: An Act for an Assessment for six Moneths, from the Five and twentieth of December, 1649, for maintenance of the Forces raised by Authority of Parliament for the Service of England and Ireland, at the rate of Ninety thousand pounds per mensem for the first three Moneths, and at the rate of Three score thousand pounds for the last three Moneths', A&O, pp. 285–319.
178. For example, 16 & 17 Car. II, c. 1, Royal Aid, 1664–1667, SoR, vol. 5, pp. 525–552, s. XXVI 'Provided alwayes That noe thing in this Act contained shall be construed to alter change determine or make void any Contracts Covenants or Agreements whatsoever betweene the Landlord and Tennant touching the payment of Taxes or Assesments Any thing herein before mentioned to the contrary notwithstanding'.
179. Evidence from Kent and Surrey shows Interregnum and Restoration tenants often retained some modest proportion of the charge on 'stock-in-crop', or stock-in-trade, e.g. in New Romney KHLC: NR/RTa1-27.
180. Anon, *A Letter to a Freeholder on the Late Reduction of the Land Tax to One Shilling in the Pound, by a Member of the House of Commons* (London: Printed for J. Peele, 1732).
181. Ward, *The English Land Tax*, p. 1.

CHAPTER 3

Fiscal Innovation and Local Response 1643–1680

The distinctive innovatory responses to parliamentary legislation in the three case study areas is described in this chapter as local administrators created solutions primarily to tax land that would work in each area. There are common features including delegation to local sub-teams administrative delayering the deployment and empowerment of officials with greater experience and the greater use of the transfer of monies in paper form rather than coin. Traditional administrative roles including mayors sheriffs aldermen and justices of the peace were now populated by those doing well from a growing English economy. These men were appointed as the chief administrators of the new levies and if they had to pay more tax they would at least have a degree of process ownership and control. Such important and extensive changes imply similar innovations in many parts of the country and quash any notion that the pre-Revolutionary period was characterised by fiscal administrative inertia.

3.1 Land Tax 1643–1660

Contrary to some authors, this period saw marked successful fiscal experimentation, particularly in the South and East, as local officials, grappling with the new real estate tax legislation described above, focussed on the economic flows of value around the occupiers of land. Both Kent (Fig. 3.1) and the City of London witnessed considerable tax innovation in this period as described below, but they were not unique. Bristol

S. Pierpoint, *The Success of English Land Tax Administration 1643–1733*, Palgrave Studies in the History of Finance,
https://doi.org/10.1007/978-3-319-90260-9_3

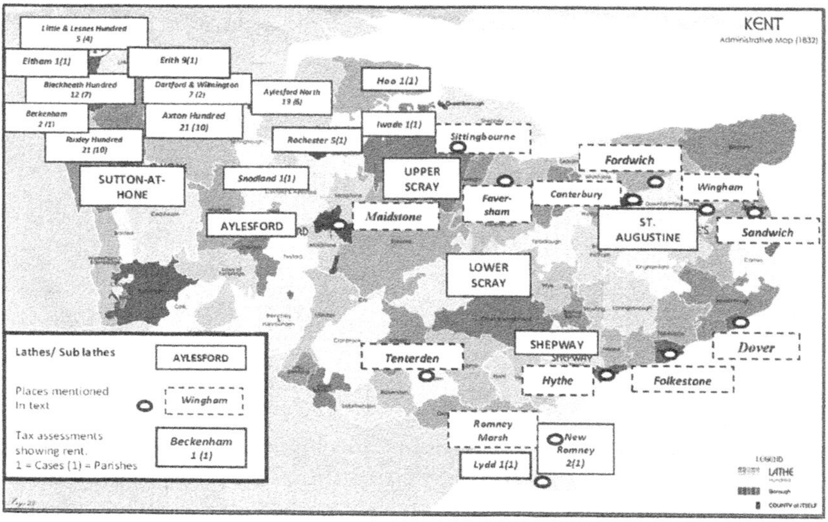

Fig. 3.1 Kent and its lathes showing places with surviving tax assessments prior to 1650 indicating taxed rent[1]

administrators were probably also creative judging by its well-organised processes in existence in the 1660s, but evidence is too slight to make any detailed judgement.

The Commonwealth Exchequer Papers for south-eastern counties have numerous references to new forms of taxation, tenants' ability to deduct tax from their landlords' rent and high-collectors' accounts suggesting a broad understanding of the new legislation across many parts of the country as well as high levels of tax collection success.[2] The new legislation targeted immovable property and its occupiers in respect of real estate value as well as their personal wealth, but over time, the fiscal importance of the first grew as the latter declined. The increasingly commercialised urban and rural land markets of South-East England bore much of the national tax burden (Fig. 1.2). London administrators instigated regular process maintenance and upgrading to maintain tax effectiveness and meet the challenges of this demanding urban environment with its seemingly vast numbers of taxpayers, highly mobile and diverse populations and catastrophic events including fire and plague. Kent's large tax burdens meant that it also witnessed significant innovation and developed a tax process robust enough to overcome the most difficult of times, including a 1648 royalist 'rebellion'.

Targeting immoveable property was not fiscally novel, but as these case studies show, it was the systematic and diligent administrative effort expended, the weight of charge and the breadth of tax that provided a decisive break from the past. Both London[3] and Bristol[4] saw upward pressure on land values responding to the demand for accommodation from mushrooming populations clamouring for a share in these cities' international and domestic commercial success.[5] City population growth was built on immigration because in City of London parishes, deaths often exceeded births.[6] Kent and the other south-eastern counties in London's hinterland benefitted significantly from the capital's growth and were intimately linked economically with it spurring increasing real estate values, according to Ormrod et al.[7]

Seventeenth-century and earlier developments in the legal and commercial enjoyment of land allowed future Chancellor Heneage Finch to say in 1671 that, 'every house, and nearly every farm, in England had at least two titles (and often many more), the present tenant's and the landlord's, which might itself be a tenancy, or subtenancy, freighted with encumbrances'.[8] Such increasingly commercialised relationships created cashflows which the fiscal state might exploit. Finch, as an early supporter of Restoration land taxes, a Kentish tax commissioner and justice of the peace himself, would have understood all of this very well. This chimes with Hoyle's[9] 'fluidity and rising volume of the land market in the sixteenth and early seventeenth centuries' and Shaw-Taylor's observation that the 'the dominance of family farming had been broken long before the beginning of the seventeenth century' and 'agrarian capitalism was dominant in southern and eastern England by 1700'.[10] Land tax records of the 1780s, when extensive records at last survive, show over 80% of land tenanted, and Shaw-Taylor asks how much earlier did such patterns emerge.[11] In a marked departure from the old subsidy and other tax rolls, the 1640s tax assessments from metropolitan London, Kent, Surrey,[12] and other counties proclaim this very complexity and how it could be taxed. Kent's assessments now usually show the names of both landlords and tenants, together with their tax and annual rent for the first time (Table 3.1), and in metropolitan London, tax amounts in respect of 'occupiers' or 'tenants' and anonymous '*out-landlords*'. Similar new methods were almost certainly widespread given the many references in the Commonwealth Exchequer Papers from many counties and the numerous landlord and tenant disputes centring on taxation before the contemporary Indemnity Committee.[13] In London too, a new approach is visible in both the City and the broader metropolis.[14] There may even be a clear reason for the City of London/Kent divergence. Kent and other southern counties, including Surrey, developed their new tax processes early, on the basis of the 1643 legislation which proposed that the tax for landlord and tenant should be 'apportioned betweene the party or parties … as the Taxers shall thinke meet'.[15] Such apportionment continued throughout the Restoration.[16] This may explain why both landlords' and tenants' names appear almost universally on Kentish assessments hereafter. They would share the tax cost. The City probably based its developed process after a 1646 City revaluation of property, and so used the later post-1645 legislation which only required information regarding 'the Tenants of all Houses and Lands, which shall be rated'. Landlords were only taxed via a deduction 'out of their Rents'.[17] The names of landlords were not required and so they appear as anonymous out-landlords on City assessments. Hipkin's 'successful tenant farmers' in Kent's Romney Marsh had built portfolios of land for commercial farming and grazing.[18] The establishment of such commercial agricultural value flows and supporting industrial and service sectors were obvious fiscal targets for the innovative legislators of 1640s Parliament. So successful was the outcome that the land taxes, as they quickly became known, became an indispensable mainstay of state finance.[19]

Contrary to some authors who see no 'radical departure'[20] from earlier levies, or that 'there is little reason to believe the process of valuation was any more realistic or effective in the assessment than in the subsidy',[21] it is argued that the evidence presented here demonstrates that there was indeed a fresh and structured approach in many areas. The broad tax base enshrined in the assessment legislation and enacted in all three case study areas provided the new tax with an appropriate link, with means to pay and cashflow. This tax was also hard to avoid. Property was immoveable, fairly stable in value, and could readily be appraised and approximated by knowledgeable local assessors, creating some perception of fairness. After all, tax assessments were often public documents perhaps pinned to the church door.[22] Inhabitants were chargeable and any crops or stock in the fields, timber in the wood or goods in the house, shop or warehouse could be and were seized and sold if payment was not forthcoming. Real estate's relative stability and visibility contrasted with the volatility of personal wealth. The inevitable outcome was that there were constant

Table 3.1 Implementation of the 'rent-tax' in Kent as shown by tax assessments indicating: landlord, tenant, rent and tax due, 1642–1650[23]

The tax assessment shows (bold if rent is shown)	*1642*	*1643*	*1644*	*1645*	*1646*	*1647*	*1648*	*1649*	*1650*	*Total*
Taxpayer and tax only	12	24	4	0	2	0	0	0	0	42
Landlord, tenant, and tax but not rent	1	4	2	0	0	0	0	0	0	7
Taxpayer, rent, and tax	**1**	**12**	**8**	**4**	**3**	**0**	**0**	**0**	**0**	**28**
Showing landlord, tenant, rent, and tax	**3**	7	**17**	**22**	**22**	0	**2**	0	**2**	**75**
Total	17	47	31	26	27	0	2	0	2	152

appeals regarding the latter, so visible in Bristol, which ensured that the rent element of the assessment became progressively greater over time, particularly as fixed quotas had to be met nationally and locally.

3.1.1 *The Rent Tax in 1640s Kent*

The early 1640s Parliament, desperate for supply, saw London and the south-eastern counties in its control as being at the heart of its plans for fiscal success and experimentation. They are named first in early legislation (Sect. 2.2.1). By contrast, Bristol quickly fell into the hands of Royalists until September 1645. Kentish officialdom responded quickly and adroitly to the new taxation and by the mid-1640s had developed a broadly based real estate levy predominantly focussed on tenants, landlords and their rent (Table 3.1). The fact that there is so much Kentish material amongst Exchequer papers may even suggest that the county's methods were known and perhaps even seen as a model.[24] That some reasonable estimation of land values was now taking place is supported by the good correlation between the amount of tax assessed in the parishes and acreage, which contrasts with the traditional subsidy even if there is still variation between parishes.[25] The calculation of the correlation coefficients between the land tax rent and *Victoria County History* (VCH) acreage in Upper Scray 1627–1730 shows a significant relationship (Fig. 3.2) as do similar calculations for St. Augustine Lathe, West (24 parishes), and St. Augustine Lathe, East (54 parishes), in 1673.[26] The VCH figures are imprecise, and the relationship between land acreage and tax has been intensively debated in eighteenth-century agricultural history by Martin, Mingay, Grigg, Ginter and others.[27] Ginter's demonstration of widespread inconsistency in Yorkshire contrasts with Martin's description of a close relationship between acreage and tax in Warwickshire. It seems likely that in areas which were lightly taxed such as Ginter's Yorkshire and Beckett's[28] Cumberland, traditional[29] methods of assessment could still be employed in the 1640s and such lightness of tax continued in the quotas ever after. It is argued here that in areas like Kent and Warwickshire, which were heavily taxed, new methods had to be developed (Table 1.1). More importantly, the argument here is not for a precise correlation, but a reasonably good apportionment of a heavy burden that would be acceptable locally to better exploit rent flow and the produce of the land.

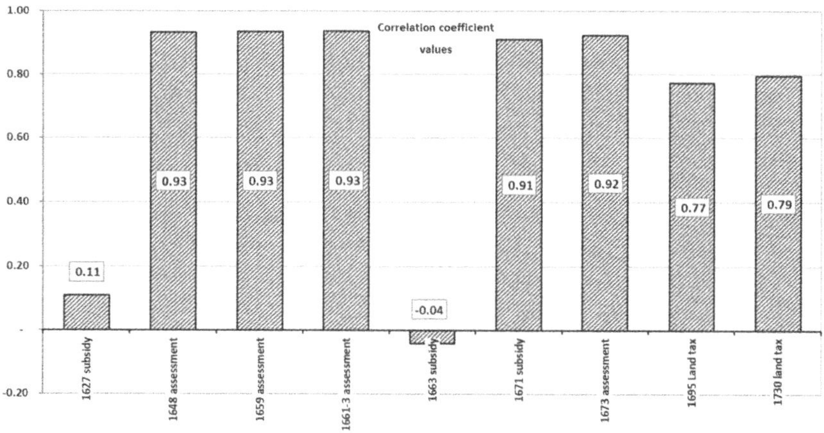

Fig. 3.2 Upper Scray, Kent. Regression analysis of the relationship between VCH parish acreage in 27 parishes and the amounts of tax paid 1627–1730. Land tax and subsidies compared.[30] *Note* The tax on rent for the land taxes and assessments correlates well with acreage. The subsidies do not apart from that of 1671 which employs land tax valuation methods

Of course, acreage is not the same as rent, and taxable rent may not be the same as the physical rent paid. Turner et al. demonstrate that in the seventeenth century, alongside rack-rents,[31] there were numerous forms of 'rent', including copyhold, customaryhold and life leasehold.[32] Although such forms were common in the North and West, they were found nationwide. Neither is rent synonymous with income from land, it is more the landlord's share. Turner et al. quote one nineteenth-century Yorkshire source: 'It has long been a prevailing opinion that the produce of a farm should be equal to three rents; one for the landlord, one for the expenses of cultivation and another for the farmer'. Contemporaries in Kent had varying and inconsistent views about how much of their income went on taxation.[33] Nevertheless, it was the intention of 1640s legislators to tax deemed or actual rack-rents and there are strong indications from the evidence presented here that officials in Kent and elsewhere made significant efforts to oblige them.

Tax officials understood what was required by the new legislation, because as they implemented this novel 'rent-tax', as they termed it, they created new tax processes. Prior to 1642, Kentish tax assessments, as was the case countrywide, were little more than lists of individuals and their tax liability in just two columns, frequently with little guidance as to how tax had been calculated. This changed rapidly in Kent with the legislative focus on rent from 1642 to 1643, and the principle of tenants' tax deduction from rack-rent was firmly established by 1644–1645.[34] The names of landlords, tenants, tax and most importantly their annual rent quickly appeared on tax assessments across the county by the mid-1640s (Table 3.1). This was so widespread that it was clearly the implementation of policy directives from senior Kentish commissioners.[35] This form remained the Kentish standard[36] thereafter and is visible in neighbouring Sussex, according to Grover, long before it became normal nationally in the 1780s and beyond.[37] Kentish documents repeatedly refer to tax on landlord and tenant, and this is true of several other south-eastern counties including Surrey and Buckinghamshire.[38] The amount of taxed 'rent' is stated on over one hundred Kentish tax assessments from this period (Table 3.1). Across the county during the 1640s and 1650s, rates of pence/pound tax on rent were frequently stated and appear preprinted on the receiver-general's receipts and accounts. This suggests a Kent-wide tax rate was being attempted.[39] Kent had used similar local rating methods for centuries, but not for national taxation.[40] In Kent, the use of land acreage as an equitable means of assessing poor rates or sewer levies had ancient ancestry in Romney Marsh.[41] Davison notes the 'marsh taxation system' and methods were also used in many other parts of the country for local drainage or sea defence rate assessments. This is supported by Cannan (see above Sect. 2.1).[42] A big part of the success of the early land tax therefore appears to have been an adaption of the methods used to divide a local rate burden across the community for national taxation.

Available evidence from over one hundred surviving pre-Restoration Kentish tax assessments shows that the great majority of tax, c.78%,[43] probably fell on tenanted land. Much of the rest may have fallen on owner-occupiers because no separate landlord was shown, but following Ginter care is required in making such an assumption.[44] Only very modest amounts were levied on personal estates. The original February 1643 legislation, described above, had tried to apportion the charge between landlord and tenant depending on the type of ownership and rent (see Sect. 2.2.2). As discussed, this was far too complex to implement and was abandoned by 1645 legislators for the simpler remedy of taxing the occupiers and allowing them to deduct tax from rent.[45] In fact, it was common in Kent and Surrey to tax the occupier and allow most tax to be deducted, but leave a small charge for the occupier for 'stock' or the tenants' share. In Surrey, this was as high as a third[46] but less in Kent.[47] The commissioners in Kent and probably in Surrey too regularly set both a county-wide policy of such apportionment and a guide tax rate, as is clear from the high-collectors' accounts and other documents.[48] The 28 December 1650 tax assessment for Iwade parish in Upper Scray in Kent, for example, shows 12d/£ for the landlord and 3d/£ for the tenant for 'stock on the land'.[49] This Kentish policy demonstrably applied county-wide in rural parishes and small towns such as New Romney.

Legislative adherence and coordination were enabled by the country-wide distribution of printed copies of legislative ordinances, pre-printed pro forma warrants (surviving from as early as 1645),[50] receipts and the like, which as described, contained detailed instructions.[51] The strong national presence of MPs amongst commissioners in Kent and elsewhere could ensure Parliament's wishes were fulfilled.[52] The other major visible change was the vast increase in taxpayer numbers compared with the traditional subsidy, as was the case in London and Bristol discussed below. Iwade parish in Upper Scray in Kent had just 39 different taxpayers in 1650 paying 4.7% of the sub-lathe's tax. This suggests very approximately 830 taxpayers in all for the sub-lathe compared with around 200 for the subsidy in 1628 and 1640.[53] In comparison, Kent had been a relatively dutiful payer of the relatively modest demands for 1630s ship money according to Langelüddecke, typically paying up more than the national average proportion of its allocated quota, 77% of the 1635 charge and perhaps as much as 97% in 1636.[54] It paid 89% of the 1637 quota, if somewhat slowly by April 1639, and a similar proportion of the 1638 charge by May 1640, but like most counties its contribution for the 1639 levy collapsed and it probably never paid more than a third.[55] Kent's ship money levies of £8,000 per year were meagre indeed compared with the £70,000 levied by the assessment in 1645, and it took a year or 18 months to bring in substantial amounts of ship money.[56]

3.1.2 *Bristol's Subsidy and 'Town Dues'*

Bristol has little comparable documentation, but its 1663–1664 subsidy,[57] which probably mirrors earlier levies, shows only around 500 taxpayers, compared with over two thousand for the Royal Aid one year later.[58] Most of those subsidy payers were charged the very minimum taxable amount above the exemption threshold of £3 and almost all the rest paid at just £4. Virtually, all tax paid was in respect of goods not land.[59] This goods figure was then used for the slightly later Royal Aid assessment, but a much larger real estate element was then added. As in Kent, local rates in Bristol were more broadly based and had attempted to tax real estate. Bristol has ancient records of 'town dues' which include local taxes on the rent of 180 tenements, gardens, burial grounds dating back to the fifteenth century, but the weight of tax is very modest in scale.[60]

3.1.3 *Out-Landlords in 1640s London*

The City of London took slightly longer than Kent to develop a real estate-based tax strategy even though metropolitan taxation was a major priority for parliament. Parliament produced numerous contemporary ordinances either for London alone or with the City as primary target.[61] Initially, City administrators in the 1640s focussed mainly on the taxation of personal estates and stock as they always had for the subsidy, and there was only modestly increased taxation of real estate. However, in adjacent metropolitan Westminster and Middlesex, where perhaps there was less opportunity to tax commercial businesses and stock, the new legislation, as in Kent, initiated an early and substantial tax focus on land and rent.[62] There are detailed parish accounts surviving for the First Weekly Assessment and other later 1643 assessments[63] for the Westminster parishes of St. Clement Danes, St. Giles in the Fields Holborn, Westminster St. Margaret and the Middlesex parishes of St. Andrew Holborn[64] and St. Sepulchre.[65] These show taxation on tenants for their landlords, 'Tenants rated according to their rents and for their goods', or 'Rents and Estates'.[66] A single assessment from Chelsea, Middlesex, indicates that similar real estate and personal estate assessments were deployed for the earlier 1642 '£400,000 Levy' with its assessment-like features (Sect. 2.2.1).[67] These documents imply the taxation of occupiers who can deduct the tax paid from rent as per statute or sometimes the direct taxation of landlords. Similar practices can be identified within two years in several other parishes in the greater metropolis.[68] The transformation of metropolitan London's tax assessments in the period 1642–1645 into new forms required by statute is similar in many ways to practices in Kent, except here, the names of landlords are rarely shown. A few parishes initially retained traditional forms of tax assessment[69] but most of these show that a separate calculation had been made on both land and personal estates.[70] Unfortunately, few metropolitan assessments or accounts survive after 1646 until the Restoration.[71]

These early metropolitan assessments reveal familiar features from later land taxes. It is not clear if such methods were used for earlier local rating across the greater metropolis, but in the City ward of Bassishaw where good evidence survives, and as is further discussed below, the methods appear to be entirely new.

The 1643 City of London had in living memory witnessed several forms of local and national taxation levied on people living in its 25 wards, the main administrative divisions shown in Fig. 2.1 The small Bassishaw Ward, with its excellent tax records, is exemplar here in revealing evidence of all of them, although there is supporting evidence from elsewhere. The subsidy had been theoretically heavy, but because only the wealthy few were taxed perhaps only 5–10% of the population were troubled by it. Only between 36 and 57 households ever paid anything in Bassishaw or about a quarter of all householders in Fig. 3.3.[72] Taxpayers were also effectively self-assessed and therefore subsidies raised modest amounts, a maximum of £250 annually in Bassishaw.[73] Taxing only the wealthy few is well known in other contemporary cities including Evans' Norwich.[74] The ancient fifteenth and tenth were far broader and variously reached 95–111 Bassishaw taxpayers, but the burden at c. £600 for the whole City and just £7 for this ward was exceptionally light (Fig. 3.4). This lightness could be mitigated by levying multiple fifteenths together, as many as six together in 1608–1609, but the burden was still very modest. The 1630s ship money was as broadly based as the fifteenth and in one instance heavier at £335 than any subsidy (Fig. 3.4).[75]

There is a valuable and almost contemporary comparative source, the well-known 1638 settlement of tithes list, which lists inhabitants and their 'moderated rents' from most parishes within the City.[76] Its intent was to improve the collection of tithes and the exercise focussed on household rental value. Judging from the jagged profile shown in Fig. 3.5, it is likely to be something of a broad estimation. Nevertheless, it is clearly a substantial effort to value city property and one that can be used as a benchmark for how land was valued for the later land tax assessments. Bassishaw's 1636 ship money assessment[77] survives in its entirety and names individual taxpayers many of whom are familiar from the 1638 tithes list. None of those shown as being below £4 rent in this latter list (53 of these or over one quarter) and a few of those between £4 and £5—appear on the ship money roll, suggesting a link to rental values and exemption for the poorest.[78] In fact, virtually all tax appears to have been levied on the top 50% of households in terms of their rental amounts (Fig. 3.3). Although there is little indication on the face of the assessment itself of what was being taxed by the 1636 ship money, there is a generally good level of correlation between the amount of 'moderated rent' in 1638 and the amount of ship money levied (correlation coefficient = 0.77)[79] suggesting that some form of real estate valuation indeed played a significant part.[80] The ship money assessments from Bassishaw share another element familiar from the post-1643 assessments, the taxation of landlords in respect of their tenants. Two significant landlords were named and taxed for ship money: George Cornish was taxed £1 for eight tenements in Crowne Alley and Martyn Pinder £1 for nine in Bell Alley. However, it should be noted that the amount of 1636 ship money levied was less than half of the lightest of the later assessments (Fig. 3.4).

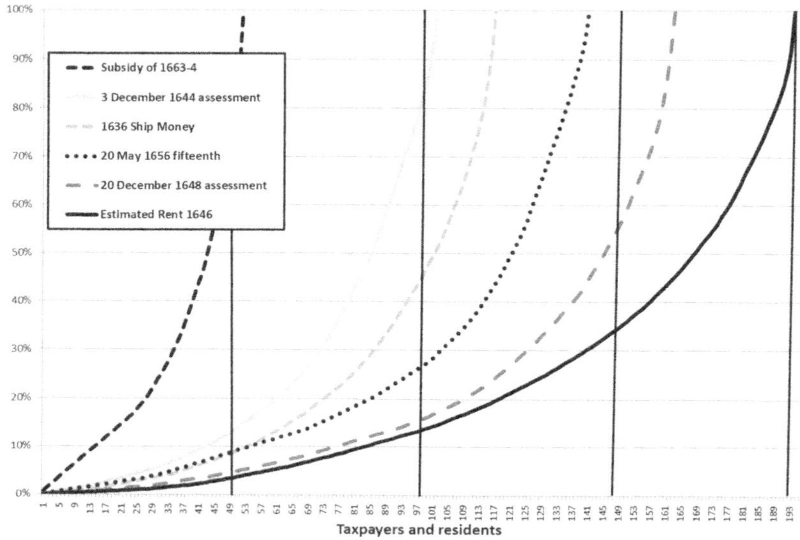

Fig. 3.3 City of London, Bassishaw Ward, tax quartiles for the 1636 ship money, the assessments of 1644 and 1648, the 1656 fifteenth and tenth, and the 1663–1664 subsidy compared with a contemporary 'estimate' of annual rental values 1646.[81] *Note* Tax quartiles shown by vertical lines. Cumulative proportions of taxation (vertical scale). Households to the right of the relevant curved line were not taxed. The 1663–1664 subsidy taxed least households and the 1648 assessment the most. Assumption: The estimated rent for 1646 is probably a list of all households

Collectors in St. Margaret's Westminster recognised in an account dated 31 July 1645 one typical and long-lived urban challenge when they produced a list of amounts unpaid, because of 'those that are gonne, that are poore, that are dead and those that are in arrears'.[82] The great majority were gone or poor. Officials in St. James Clerkenwell recognised the same in June 1646[83] and the church wardens had earlier on 1 July 1643 compiled a list of those 'poore hereunder named [who do not] paye any tax nor duty to church or poore neither have they any lands or tenements to the value of twenty shillings nor any goods or chattels to the value of twenty pounds'.[84] This list of people would presumably be land tax exempt. St. James Clerkenwell also shows another recurrent extra-statutory feature, the taxation of landlords for their tenants. If the legislation was aimed at occupiers, there was little point in trying to gather taxes and rates from poor tenement dwellers who had been growing in number as larger houses were divided. It was much better and much more practical to tax their landlords directly. For the ordinance for the present relief of the British Army in Ireland which was levied from 1 September 1644, 'John Walker [was taxed presumably as his agent] for his landlord Mr Price for these 21 ten[a]nts' at the rate of 3 shillings per week.[85]

The very earliest weekly assessments reached a similar number of Bassishaw taxpayers, at 92–129, as the traditional fifteenth and tenth.

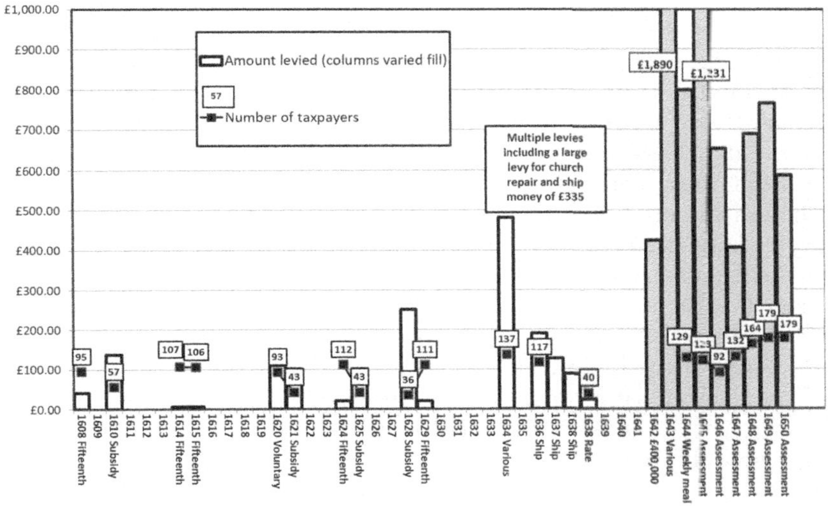

Fig. 3.4 City of London, Bassishaw Ward 1608–1650. Comparison of the amount of tax assessed and the number of taxpayers for various seventeenth-century taxes[86]

However, the City tax weight over the three months of the First Weekly Assessment of February 1643 was far greater at £120,000[87] and £1,200 for Bassishaw than any previous levy. In fact, only £114,246.06 of the City's large quota was ever assessed,[88] but because of the great weight of tax, City inhabitants were excused some later levies because 'of the great proportion laid upon them by the late Weekly Assessment for three moneths'.[89] The City's national quota share was quickly reduced thereafter. This First Weekly Assessment had some success, although collection appears slow because it took from February to July for about half of the City monies to be paid up. This was probably assisted by the coincidence of the timing of this levy with the City's annual financial cycle of Lady Day settlement discussed in Chapter 5 (Sect. 5.1 and Fig. 5.2).[90] This was one of the main times of the year when debts were settled in the City and monies freed up.

The earliest detailed surviving Bassishaw assessment is from March 1644 for the Earl of Essex's army.[91] It shows that a local quota had been allocated to the ward of £66 per month, although the sum actually assessed was slightly less at £64.33.[92] This demonstrates that a city-wide local quota system was already operational (see Sect. 2.2.1) and continued thereafter. This, like other surviving early City assessments, retained the traditional focus on the personal assets of the wealthy, but there was a modest new charge on 'inhabitants' and their 'out-landlords' reflecting the new legislation's intent and implying that tenants could deduct tax from their landlord's rent.[93] Legislation rarely specified tax rates, although the ordinance of 7 May 1643 provides 'so as for their Lands they bee not rated above the fift part of their yeerly Revenue [4s/£], and for their goods and chattels, and personall estate, not above the twentieth part of the value of them [1s/£]'.[94] The tax rate on personal wealth is difficult to judge from the evidence considered here. If real property values were being taxed consistently, it should be possible to identify this by comparison with contemporary property valuations. However, the tax in respect of out-landlords that represents rent for the 1644 Earl of Essex levy shows only a modest correlation with the 1638 tithes list.[95] This suggests that these early assessments were not applied at consistent rates and were not closely related to real estate. Compared with the 1638 tithes list, the individual taxpayers' assessed amounts vary widely suggesting anything from a 4% to a 51% real estate tax rate. Indeed, the correlation with rent is much less clear than for the 1636 ship money, even though taxpayer numbers were similar.

In 1644, the out-landlord's share, or real estate part, was a very modest 14% in Bassishaw[96] and the mean of 20 surviving mid-1640s assessments in other City wards was only slightly higher at 19%.[97] This contrasts with much higher real estate proportions in the contemporary broader metropolis beyond the City at 60–70% estimated from the accounts discussed (Sect. 3.1.3).[98] These latter figures are largely based on accounts for those paying money for the Scotch Army in 1645.[99]

City taxpayers were relatively few in number at this time, according to surviving documents, comprising only between a quarter and a half of the numbers assessed in the 1660s in the wards of Aldgate, Portsoken, Dowgate, Tower, Walbrook, Coleman Street, Vintry, Cornhill, Langbourn and Cripplegate Without, and the precincts of St. Martin Ludgate, St. Andrew Holborn, Whitefriars and Smithfield in Farringdon Without Ward.[100] Portsoken Ward is usually viewed as one of the poorest City wards and its Restoration and later tax assessments were dominated by rent taxation.[101] However in this early period, for the two ward precincts where documents survive in Houndsditch and Covent Garden, only 16 and 19% of the tax were in respect of real estate. The main charge was on personal estates. Indeed, in Houndsditch, although the 1638 inhabitants' list contained some 278 householders, the 1645 tax roll had just 80 taxpayers. This suggests that most householders, most real estate and most income remained untaxed. In the seven years between 1638 and 1645, there would have been much movement of population, but it seems likely that those not being taxed in Portsoken Ward included landlords listed in 1638 as owning considerable numbers of properties including John Claybrooke's tenements (£16 rent), Mr. Green's 16 tenements (£20 rent) and even Mr. Webster's house and rents consisting of 45 tenements (£123 rent). Of the taxpayers that can be identified in 1638 and 1645, many appear to be local tradesmen because they include one each of the following: grocer, goldsmith, distiller, ironmonger, bricklayer, founder, courier, needle-maker, brasier, shopkeeper and broker, two tailors and smiths, and three upholsterers and chandlers. Thus, the taxpayer base was small because it was largely confined to tradesmen and their goods mirroring the subsidy form of taxation.

According to contemporary texts, it was Parliament's supporters who contributed most to this and other levies, loans and requests for contributions, as similarly recognised in contemporary Norwich.[102] It is suggested by the evidence presented here that the collection problem was not just a matter of unwillingness to pay as some contemporaries imagined, but the application of traditional subsidy-like methods that had long been ineffective in the City and were simply outdated compared with what was happening elsewhere in the broader metropolis. Assessment of goods often required elements of self-assessment and of goodwill, and taxes that relied on such were unlikely to maintain historically high tax burdens in the long term. Between December 1644 and

July 1645, a further three parliamentary ordinances were passed to chase any arrears that arose.[103] A June ordinance allocated the blame to officials. It asserted that problems arose:

> chiefly through the default of the several Collectors, Sub-Collectors and other Officers appointed for those services, to the great discouragement of those who have willingly contributed and paid their several Rates and Assessments imposed upon them, to the great disservice of the Commonwealth.[104]

Although the initial assessments were 'weekly', by March 1644 in Bassishaw and in legislative ordinance by December, amounts were accounted for on a monthly basis.[105] This does not mean that tax-gatherers actually collected on this basis, but there are suggestions that collectors did collect smaller amounts from taxpayers more often in the 1640s than in later years. There are indications from the 1645 Treasurers at War accounts[106] that collectors were making payments to receivers far more frequently than their Restoration counterparts, at least monthly or more often.[107] On average the 72 tax precincts listed in these accounts each made between three and six payments to the Treasurers in just three months, between June and August 1645, with an average of four but there was no consistent pattern.[108] If such frequent collection was indeed taking place, it would perhaps have encouraged assessors and collectors to focus on the easier targets of traders and the traditionally wealthy. A broader levy with more and poorer doors to knock on would only have become feasible with less frequent collections but longer collection rounds.[109] Whatever the case, in 1645, Parliament remained dissatisfied with performance:

> And forasmuch as the Lord Mayor, Aldermen and Commons of the City of London, in Common-Councel Assembled, out of their care to advance the publique service, have by several Acts and Orders of the said Common-Councel, nominated and appointed several persons, Members of the said Common-Councel, to be a Committee for the gathering in of Arrears, which said Committee for want of a sufficient power, as well to compel Collectors and Officers heretofore appointed for the service aforesaid, to bring in to them their Accompts and Moneys received, as also the persons Rated and Taxed to pay the said several sums in Arrear, could not perform such service as otherwise they might have done ...[110]

This was despite the fact that the Committee for the Advance of Money for the Service of the Parliament, had according to Coates, appointed 'special distraining collectors from different wards to collect arrears. Additionally, Parliament ordered regular soldiers to help the collectors'.[111] No doubt it was a challenging process to apportion tax burdens and gather arrears across the City. A 1645 petition to the Common Council stated: 'Assessments Are made very unequal, whereby the Taxes laid upon the City, are made burthensome, and paid with much repining'.[112] There was nothing new about such complaining of inequity, although Parliament's eventual May 1648 response was blunt and unequivocal in proposing further empowerment of civic authority to clear the arrears as the Second Civil War began: 'Whereas severall summs assessed within the City and Liberties thereof are yet in Arrear, and unpaid, by reason of disaffection to the Parliament, and some other Obstructions, viz: Upon pretence of being unequally rated'.[113]

Responses to the mid-1640s arrears problems were both local and parliamentary. As discussed, the early assessments had been narrowly based and substantially taxed personal estates (Figs. 3.3 and 3.4).[114] Could the City develop more broadly based levies like those already operating in Middlesex and Westminster? There may have been some attempt in 1646. An apparently City-wide mayoral precept of 3 October 1646[115] required the ward deputies and common councilmen to estimate the 'true yearly value' or 'estimate and cess' of property values.[116] Only in Bassishaw Ward is there evidence that it was carried out, but there is no reason to suppose it did not take place in other wards. After all as discussed, City parishes had successfully undertaken a similar exercise in 1638 in compiling an inhabitants' list for tithes.[117] This 1646 'estimate' records 195 Bassishaw households and halls compared with the similar figure of 197 in 1638 and a total 1646 'rent' value of £2,462.00 compared with £2,350.83. There is a close relationship between the two (correlation coefficient = 0.85).[118] Use of this valuation was not immediate, probably because parliamentary pressure had been reduced as the First Civil War ended. Indeed, there were no further parliamentary ordinances complaining of London arrears until 1648. The next assessment in the Bassishaw assessment book was dated 7 September 1647. It did not apply the new 'estimate' in any discernible way, indeed it appears similar to that of March 1644 described above with a focus on personal estates.[119] With Civil War recommencing,

Parliament made various efforts to reform officialdom. Only a dozen tax commissioners had been appointed in February 1645[120] but this was increased to 29 in June 1647 at a time of relative peace.[121] With peace threatened, there was a further and more urgent attempt by Parliament in April and May 1648 to empower local ward officials, this time by making them fully fledged tax commissioners.[122] This gave them much more authority to hire and fire officials and approve documents. This created a two-tier commissioner structure in the City with the appointment of local officials in the wards and a higher tier of aldermen above them, thus empowering the traditional local governance arrangements. The ordinance gave authority to a lower tier of the 'Deputy [Aldermen] and Common Councilmen in wards of London' to operationally intervene with collectors, 'and take notice who have paid, and who not, and the reasons given by them that have not paid' and if that was unsuccessful, it further authorised the higher tier of the Lord Mayor and aldermen 'to remove such obstructions as they shall be informed, are not remedied by the said' lower-tier Committee. This latter group were to recognise 'any persons obstinately refusing the payment of their Assessments, according to the limitations aforesaid, and by their evill examples become an incouragement unto others to do the like', and were to refer them to the Committee for Sequestrations.

This two-tier structure was not novel, but it went well beyond the ward official empowerment of 1645 and for the earlier subsidies. The new rules gave commissioner status to common councilmen and provided them with extensive and clear responsibilities and authority.[123] Although common councilmen and deputies in later ordinances lost their full commissioner powers, their vital ward administrative role congruent with local government in the capital had been fully recognised by Parliament and they remained a powerful City land tax force thereafter.[124] A two-tier structure became the norm throughout the Restoration and beyond, with the deputy and common councilmen acting as local officialdom but with ultimate authority in the offices of mayor and aldermen.[125] Such recognition led to the need for further control and thus the December 1648 ordinance 'for the chusing of Common Councilmen And other Officers' to disqualify anyone suspected of Royalist sympathies or who would simply not toe the line.[126]

Freshly empowered administrators in Bassishaw had more power, but they could also do things in a different way, and with limited evidence, the same thing was happening in other wards. In particular, Bassishaw officials significantly broadened the tax base for their December 1648 assessment which finally employed the 1646 'estimate' for rents.[127] It is unclear if post-1648 assessments were more successful, but there were no further parliamentary ordinances chasing London arrears.[128] The out-landlords' or rent share of tax in the City rose sharply from below 20% to over 45%, based on only a few legible assessments including those from Bassishaw (six assessments, 45–51%)[129] and Coleman Street (three assessments, 42–48%).[130] The 164–179 Bassishaw households subject to tax charges in 1648 and 1649 meant that most were now assessed, and this was approximately a 50% increase on earlier assessments (Fig. 3.4). There were numerous references now to lodgers and tenements and one to a warehouse in the 1648 Bassishaw assessments. In seven cases, landlords were taxed on their tenements. All landlords had at least two tenements, one had three, and three had 'several'. In fact, in two of these latter cases, it is possible to estimate tenement numbers from the ship money lists. Here, George Cornish had eight tenements and Martyn Pinder nine there. Both men were omitted from the 1647 Assessment, but not in December 1648 when at least 26 tenements were being taxed on their landlords in the ward. By comparison with the 1646 'estimate', an annualised two-shilling rate appears to be commonly charged on rent in this latter assessment, but some pay less whilst several pay more, some considerably more, suggesting there was some partial re-rating. Landlords of tenements were a major target.[131] Of the five individuals apparently paying more than a five-shilling rate compared with the 1646 'estimate', three were landlords with multiple tenements: Robert Bethell (two tenements), John Whitehead (three) and Barnard Clapshaw (several). Unfortunately, the 1646 'estimate', if it was ever completed, has not survived elsewhere in the City. There are strong indications from Coleman Street Ward that by 1648 there was also a much more determined effort to tax out-landlords' rents and tenements than before to make up the local quota.[132] In Bassishaw, the new broadly based assessment form characterises all the later assessments in the period up to 25 March 1650, after which there are no surviving assessments until the Restoration. There is one further important difference in the December 1648 Bassishaw assessment compared with any previously. The Company Halls of the Girdlers, Coopers, Weavers and Masons were no longer assessed in the inhabitants' column on their wealth but in the out-landlords' column on their rental value.

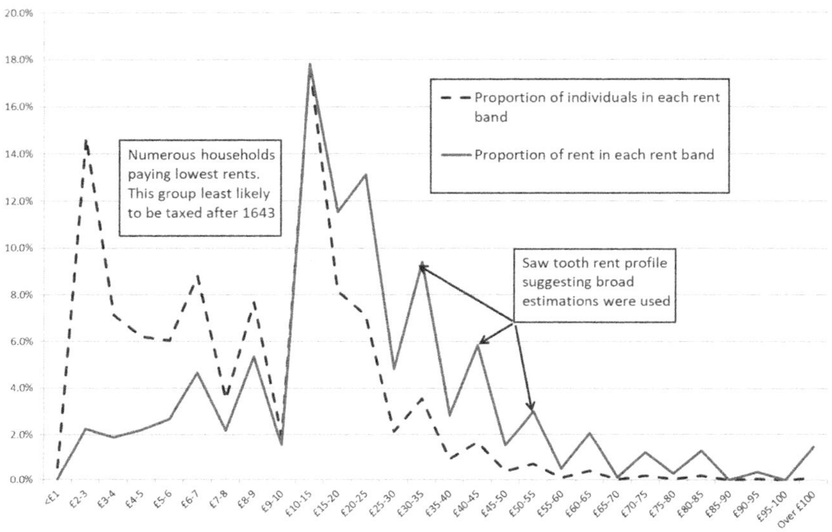

Fig. 3.5 The inhabitants of London in 1638. Distribution of rents and individuals compared[133]

By 1648, Bassishaw suffered heavier taxation than it had ever done before (Fig. 3.4). Neither this nor other direct taxes attempted to tax all Bassishaw homes directly and it is clear by comparison with the 1646 'estimate' and the 1638 tithes list, that properties omitted were the poorest or had the lowest values.[134] At least 26 of these were tenements but a further 41 inhabitants were omitted in December 1648. Most were probably too poor to pay or were taxed on landlords not identified as such. It seems unlikely that they were simply omitted in error.[135] Such patterns of landlord taxation and the omission from charge of poor households are familiar from the more detailed records of post-revolutionary London and Bristol described below. To consider the distribution of taxpayers amongst general householders, it is worth looking at who paid and who did not. Taxpayers can be allocated to rent quartiles and compared with the 1646 'estimate' as in Fig. 3.3. If the rent quartiles are assumed to correspond to wealth, and recognising Alexander's important caveats on this point, then the top 10% paid most tax to their collectors.[136] In the figure, only the December 1648 assessment troubled the lowest quartile of households.[137] The 1663–1664 subsidy, like others in the Bassishaw assessment book, troubled only the wealthiest households but employing customary amounts with no serious attempt to tax actual income or value.[138]

The City alone raised at least £513,867 in direct taxation in the 1640s according to Coates, and the metropolis in excess of £100,000 p.a.[139] This compares with total metropolitan values of £1,323,158 and £1,525,010 for excise and customs, respectively. London was therefore something of a cash cow for parliamentary taxation, but it also housed the greatest numbers of bankers, merchants and wealthy individuals prepared to lend money to Parliament against expected tax receipts. A number of ordinances show this practice was well-established.

The tax-collectors themselves are less well known than the more senior officials, but in Bassishaw during the 1640s, they lived in properties of middle, but not the very highest taxed rental value (Fig. 3.6). The individuals living in properties with the highest rent were aldermen, deputies and other men apparently much too wealthy for menial tax-collecting. None of the 20 collectors identified lived in a property valued at less than £6, based on the 1646 valuation, with a maximum of £26. The collectors' mean rent at £13.75 was modestly more than the inhabitants'

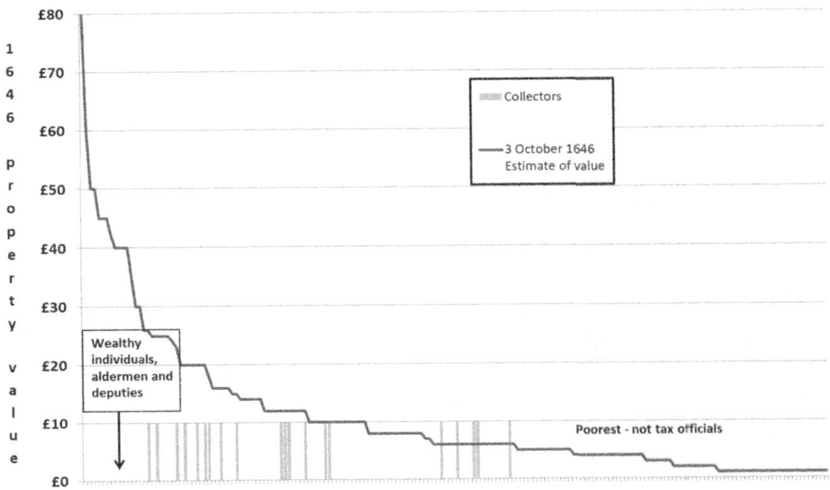

Fig. 3.6 City of London, Bassishaw Ward. The 1640s tax-collectors and annual value of properties from the 1646 'estimate'[140]

mean of £10.35. Collectors, as during the Restoration, were rotated for each new assessment so men of even middling means took their turn.

In summary, based on the evidence available, the City took about five years to develop a real estate-based assessment tax, probably after initially relying on a relatively narrowly based subsidy-style tax on goods and personal estates. The results of these early methods were unsatisfactory for Parliament. Parliament tried to blame unwilling taxpayers or reluctant officials, but this was probably not the main problem. The real difficulty was that traditional forms of tax-gathering aimed at small numbers of visibly wealthy individuals and their goods would never be able to deliver the large amounts of taxation Parliament expected from the City. The supply demands of the Second Civil War appear to have generated new impetus and a fresh approach and new empowerment of local ward officials who could do things in a different way. Through numerous cajoling and empowering parliamentary ordinances and a mayoral precept seeking land valuations, officials in the City developed forms of assessment taxation more focussed on real estate, which were much more broadly based, and similar to the tax forms already established in the broader London metropolis and across the adjacent counties including Surrey and Kent. Tax would now normally be paid by most occupiers, with some ability to deduct from landlords' rent. The poor would be exempted, or their landlords' taxed directly. This City tax form developed in the 1640s was very similar to that deployed during the Restoration and post-revolutionary periods. These early City officials had created a workable urban land tax.

3.1.4 County Coordination in 1650s Kent

The evidence presented so far suggests that in metropolitan London, the City of London and the county of Kent, slightly different routes were taken, but each area produced workable real estate taxes. But what can be learned of broader tax organisation and what of the Interregnum? Only Kent provides extensive evidence. However, this evidence shows that tax-gathering could be closely coordinated across broader areas to minimise tax collection times. This hints that similar efforts were likely across England, particularly the South-East, resulting in the high efficacy of Restoration land taxes discussed by Chandaman and shown in Fig. 1.1.[141]

Everitt recognised there was something different about the new assessment in Kent and proclaimed 'the efficiency of the tax was remarkable', and as discussed below this seems to be an accurate reflection on the work of seventeenth-century officials in all parts of the county.[142] Analysis of evidence comprising the high-collectors' dated receipts and the accounts of Joshua Pix, Thomas Catlett and Anthony Webb, all of Upper Scray, William Polehill of Aylesford South and others in Kentish lathes show that very high tax-gathering rates, close to 100%, were regularly achieved right across the county throughout the Interregnum. In 20 Upper Scray (Fig. 3.1) tax collections over the period 1648–1660 in 29 parishes, each with many individual collectors and assessors, an overall collection rate of 99.6% was achieved, from *c.* 830 taxpayers.[143] William Polehill's 22 slightly larger Aylesford South collections were almost equally effective at 99.5%.[144] Robert Joseph, John Rabson, Edward Whitton and Thomas Rooke in Sutton-at-Hone, Lower Scray, Aylesford North and Shepway, respectively, appear to have fared little worse even if data are more limited. Everitt believed similar feats were achieved in the period 1643–1648. This earlier material is more fragmentary and recorded in a rather less consistent manner, and collection success was probably *c.* 2–5% lower in the mid-1640s than in later periods. There are suggestions from other authors that similar standards were eventually achieved across South-East England during the 1650s, for example, in Hampshire and Norfolk.[145] High-collector Anthony Webb's 1648 efforts in Upper Scray should not be passed over lightly. In fact, this was a remarkable success story in itself.[146] This was the year of royalist-backed disturbances, sometimes termed the 'Kentish Rebellion', culminating in the Battle of Maidstone on 1 June 1648, where Fairfax's Parliamentary forces triumphed. The battle and other activity took place nearby. Sittingbourne on Webb's collection round was seized by royalists on 21 May. The 18 May 'Petition of the County of Kent' called king and Parliament to negotiate and declared 'That according to the Petition of Right, our property may not be invaded by any Taxes or Impositions whatsoever'.[147] Even staunch Parliamentarian, Sir Anthony Weldon complained in July 1648 that the 'Kentish rebellion' could be partly blamed on the 'extraordinary and unpropotionable [tax] burthen … upon this county, made use of by malignants to exasperate the people against parliament'.[148] Despite such doubts, there was but a short gap in the flow of Upper Scray's tax receipts, between 18 April and 3 July and an estimated loss of just £66 in uncollected taxes. Robert Joseph and Thomas Rooke,

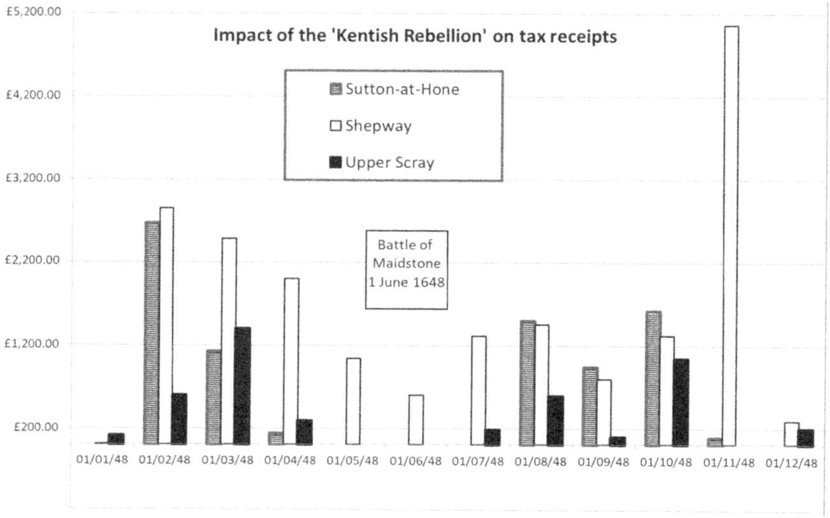

Fig. 3.7 Receipts (dates and amounts) given to high-collector Anthony Webb in Upper Scray in 1648, showing only a short gap in collection around the time of the Battle of Maidstone. *Note* Collection in Sutton-at-Hone and Shepway shown as a comparative. For sources, see Endnote 172

in possibly less troubled Sutton-at-Hone and Shepway, respectively, may have faced fewer difficulties, but enjoyed minimal reductions in receipts (Fig. 3.7).[149]

Was this collection success simply achieved by force or 'at the point of a sword'?[150] It seems unlikely given that tax commissioners and military commanders Michael Livesey, Colonel William Kenrick and Lieutenant-Colonel John Bix sent concerned letters to high-collector Webb in 1648 urging him to bring in cash 'sometime tomorrow or the next day', but offering no military support.[151] Of course, there was some implied military threat for non-payers, but Webb's achievements were still remarkable. To reinforce this picture of administrative efficacy, just twelve years later in 1660, diligent Upper Scray high-collector Joshua Pix, armed with his 27 February warrant and supported by his team of sub-collectors, gathered 100% of the last Protectorate assessment with remarkable efficiency and in short order between March and July 1660.[152] This was achieved despite royalist anti-assessment proclamations and sentiment, the rump parliament's dissolution of 16 March, the Convention Parliament's 25 April first meeting, the 4 April declaration of Breda, the proclamation of the king at Canterbury on 11 May and his landing at Dover on 25 May.[153] There is no evidence here of any pre-Restoration 'tax strike' to bring down the government once promoted by Hill and others,[154] but long discounted by Hutton.[155]

Further important changes took place during the early-1650s as the Civil War ended, trade wars resurfaced, and new peaks of national taxation were reached, but unfortunately only Kent of the case studies provides detailed evidence. The ending of domestic hostilities meant national tax quotas could become settled (Fig. 1.2). Further, Parliament was becoming increasingly restive over the delivery of tax to the Exchequer. As mentioned above (Sect. 2.2.5), from September 1651, after the Battle of Worcester, legislative ordinances contained regular deadlines for the delivery of tax monies and these deadlines were soon spelt out on Kentish high-collectors' warrants.[156] Indeed, warrants become increasingly involved, specifying the detailed requirements of the legislation. It was at about this time, or somewhat before (see Fig. 3.8), that the flows of cash in Kent take on a remarkable regularity of pattern suggesting well-coordinated county-wide efforts to meet deadlines and to deliver timely money to the receiver-general. From at least 1650, not only were tax monies promptly collected with stated tax rates identical across the county, but the process commenced at similar dates and remittances appear to be coordinated across the whole county. After 1650, coordination across the county is marked (see Fig. 3.8). Tax collection times were falling across Kent, from around 30 weeks from the start of the collection period to bring in 90% of assessed amounts in the mid-1640s, to around twelve weeks by the early-1650s. Although much money was still late, this was not really the fault of collectors or commissioners, but rather one of Parliament's overambition. It took Kent's Interregnum commissioners and assessors about a month from the date of the parliamentary ordinance to produce verified assessments and place warrants and assessments in the hands of the high-collector. Collectors generally garnered most monies within a further two months. The setting of clear deadlines also coincided with a legislative move towards more regular quarterly assessments.

The demands of this process should not be underestimated. Soon after each successive ordinance was passed, Kent commissioners met by the stipulated legislative date to agree general county policy at their inaugural meeting. They then split up into their lathes and sub-lathes (the traditional administrative districts) and these subgroups met again in their localities and summoned and then warranted their high-collectors. So, for example, the 'Act for continuing the monthly assessment of £120,000'[157] was approved by Parliament on 15 April 1651 and ordered to be 'forthwith printed and published' to be placed in the hands of local officials.[158] Such printed texts would no doubt take days to reach all corners of the land. Yet county commissioners were to meet within a few days that is 'on or before' 30 April, and then divide into their local administrative areas.[159] At their undocumented[160] Kent-wide inaugural meeting, commissioners agreed a 19d/£ tax in Kent,[161] and the local quotas for each lathe and sub-lathe, and then subdivided for local implementation.[162] Given what was to follow, this first meeting probably took place around the statutory date of 30 April. There would then have been further commissioners' meetings in the lathes, amongst other things, to summon the assessors and high-collectors to be warranted. And yet on 12 May, the high-collectors already had their warrants in both Upper Scray[163] and Lower Scray[164] and on 19 May in the sub-lathe of Aylesford South[165] as well. There is no dated warrant for Shepway Lathe, but Thomas Rooke[166] was the first of these four high-collectors to make payment of gathered taxes to receiver-general Charles Bowles of £1,000 on 11 June. This was exactly eight weeks from the ordinance publication, but the other three high-collectors all made payments by the end of that month. The fact that payments were made means that local parish assessments had meanwhile been carried out and approved, parish sub-collectors had been appointed and probably warranted, and had collected monies against those assessments to pay to the high-collector. It is this coordinated efficiency of process that is reflected in Fig. 3.8. Within the space of less than a decade, Kent administrators had thus established a remarkably effective tax process which continued throughout the Interregnum and for years after. If deadlines were not always met, very high collection rates and regular flows of revenue for the Exchequer were possible.[167] Other counties may have achieved success for similar reasons, given the clear focus on rent in many counties in the Commonwealth Exchequer Papers.[168] Braddick's Norfolk figures are slightly poorer than Kent's collection rates, but by the late Protectorate the county's flows were also on a par with Kent.[169] In Hampshire, by 1656 'the assessment was apparently being paid in its entirety'.[170] Hertfordshire, Buckinghamshire and Sussex also all show high levels of collection success during the Interregnum.[171] The Interregnum English state appears to have created a national tax which, though operated locally, could substantially deliver legislated tax quotas to a parliamentary timetable.

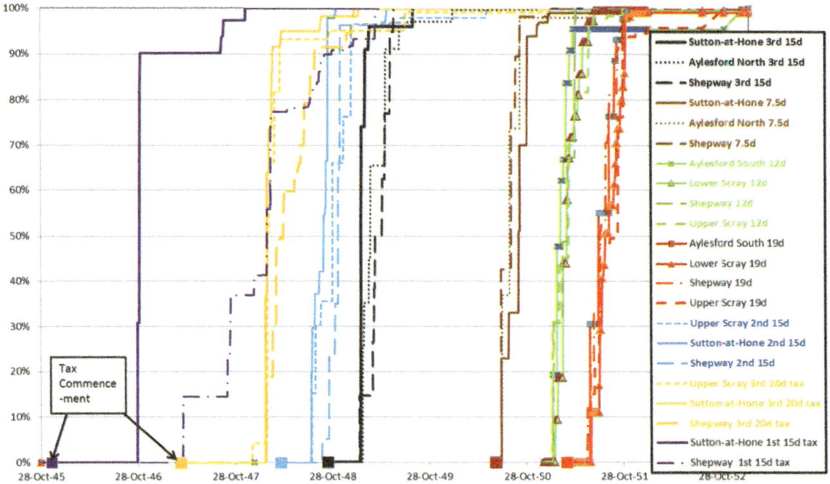

Fig. 3.8 Kent's coordinated tax collection patterns 1645–1652 showing seven levies and flows of tax monies (cumulative percentage tax) paid by multiple sub-lathe high-collectors to the receiver.[172] *.Note* 'Tax commencement' shown in the figure is the statutory date for the first commissioners' meetings

In rural counties, cash to pay tax bills was most available when agricultural produce was sold or rent paid, but it is hard to be precise. Nevertheless, flows of Interregnum cash paid to receivers in Kent and other south-eastern counties show marked seasonal patterns where high-collectors' accounts survive (Fig. 3.9). Although these are somewhat varied between Kentish lathes and other counties, there are some common themes with payment peaks in February and autumn but a trough in March/April. Because this correlates poorly well with the collection deadlines set out in 1650s legislation, there must be another explanation.[173] It is suggested here that the autumnal peak may be linked to the normal Michaelmas (29 September) rent and payment settlement date (compare London Fig. 5.2), when cash was freed up, but there was no similar peak after Lady Day (25 March) the other main settlement

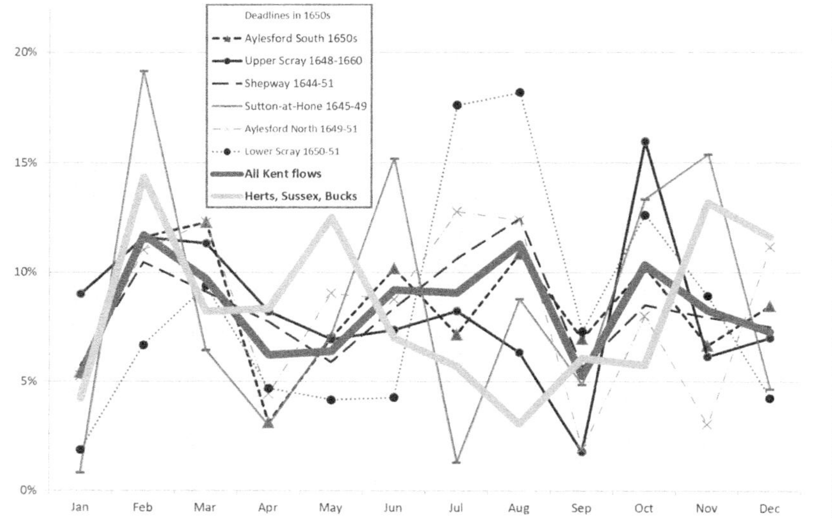

Fig. 3.9 Kent in the 1650s. Seasonality of Interregnum flows of tax monies to the receiver-general in Kentish lathes and three other south-eastern counties compared with 1650s payment deadlines[174]

day. The most likely explanation might be that tax monies were made available from the proceeds of sales of commercial agricultural production allowing taxes and other debts to be settled. The heavy fiscal burdens at the time of the First Anglo-Dutch War probably drove the national real estate-based portion of land taxes higher still compared with tax on personal estates. This was not a legislative change, but the inevitable outcome of making the delivery of local quotas more reliable. Personal estates were too volatile and prone to evasion to provide a reliable base of taxation. By Restoration, tax on the real estate portion of land tax constituted c.60% in the City of London, over 70% in Bristol and higher still in Kent.

3.1.5 *Round Sum Tax Payments as Evidence for Paper-Based Transactions*

Were other factors at work to improve tax efficiency? One issue will be considered briefly here, the question of money transfer from taxpayer to the Exchequer. Kentish high-collectors each gathered tax from dozens of parish sub-collectors who in turn collected small sums from hundreds of local taxpayers. High-collectors themselves often had a more general treasurer role within the county committees. Thomas Rooke in Shepway, for example, had further responsibility for sequestrations and local defence spending. Tens of thousands of pounds were received and paid on by such men who had significant local standing, broad networks and substantial financial capabilities. In what form were these financial transfers? Commissioner Sir Edward Dering MP claimed Restoration Kent monies were paid in cash.[175] However, it is likely that some payments from high-collectors to receivers were in some sort of paper form as early as the 1640s.

This is very tentative and based on the fact that the recorded payments in the accounts and receipts were often in the form of a round sum. Information is sketchy at best, but most of the Kentish Interregnum payments were in round sum form (Fig. 3.10), particularly from the late 1640s.[176] Of course, paper bills were not always in

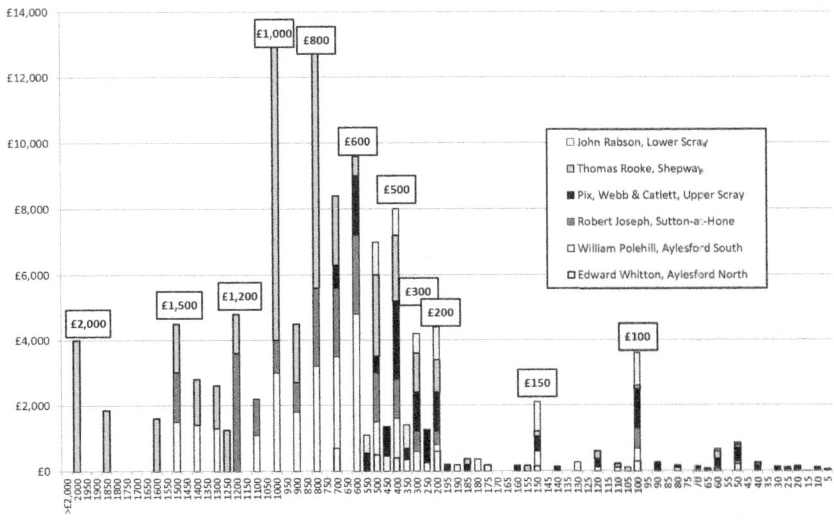

Fig. 3.10 Kent 1644–1660. Payment of round sum amounts from high-collectors to the receiver-general. Horizontal scale the round sums considered, vertical scale, the total money paid in those amounts. For sources, see Endnote 176

round sums, although following Kerridge they often were, and it is clear that physical cash could sometimes constitute a round sum payment.[177] Nevertheless, a very few acquittances/receipts appear to be for multiple amounts and these indicate some payments in paper as well as cash.[178] Such round sum payments are not only visible in 1640s Kent, but also London, Sussex (74% rounds sums average payment £1,133.37)[179] and Hertfordshire (49% rounds sums average payment £691.19).[180] Further research is clearly required in this area, but it seems likely that officials in Kent and other southern counties were making significant use of paper transfers to circumvent physical cash shortages. Because these early land taxes were so much heavier than their direct tax predecessors, this would have been a very important development.

3.2 Empowerment, Administration and Real Estate Taxation 1643–1688

3.2.1 1643–1660

> Anyone reading the legislation could be forgiven for thinking that here was a smooth, well-oiled machine for efficient annual assessment and collection, but it was quite one thing for central government to lay down the rules and regulations, and quite another for it to enforce them.[181]

Because much local land tax research has been in areas where tax quotas were low, process efficiency in highly taxed areas in the South and East has been somewhat overlooked. In Bristol and the City of London, the traditional civic authorities, long employed in implementing national and local initiatives, formed the assessment administration. Thus, mayors, sheriffs, aldermen and common councilmen were empowered or sometimes removed to meet the needs of the time and political compromise was required from individuals. In Kent, parliament's newly established county committee, justices and local MPs were at the heart of tax administration.[182] In all three case study areas, it is argued there is good evidence of adherence to parliament's instructions with modification to meet local needs.

Legislative adherence and coordination were facilitated by the countrywide distribution of numerous printed statute copies, which were to be read to officials and excerpts made available to taxpayers, containing detailed instructions about the tax process. Many examples of such documents have been identified in Bristol, London and Kent and can doubtless be discovered in archives across the country. In all three case study areas, there is evidence of both innovation and adherence to Parliament's instructions. The long and highly detailed assessment legislation set out the significant sums demanded from each county, city and borough by tax quota and soon specified clear targets and dated deadlines.[183] With 'to-do' lists, named parties and deadlines, the legislation of the seventeenth and eighteenth century reads almost like a piece of modern process-engineering designed to improve business efficiency by creating an easy to follow step-by-step process.[184] Was this legislation adhered to or was this a case of barking unheeded orders from the bridge of state as Beckett implies above? Legislation would have been ineffective without appropriate response and capable implementation by the traditional, but according to Hindle and others, increasingly effective local governors—the local, better and middling male sort, who already *inter alia* dispensed justice, administered the poor law and raised local taxation.[185] To what extent would these individuals, with their traditional roles, help or hinder implementation, particularly as they and their networks would be some of those most heavily taxed? For example, London's government at the time was variously viewed as hidebound and fractured[186] or alternatively stable.[187] The evidence presented here and in succeeding sections is that in the case study areas there were determined efforts to follow the legislation, to meet on a timely basis, discipline officials and implement parliament's legislation. After all, some of these individuals had been involved in administering national legislative innovation including the poor law for decades and as justices in many cases they carried significant local authority. Many also benefitted from the developing state and the growing English economy.

3.2.2 Kent

In rural Kent, local tax administration was often in the hands of MPs and JPs who traditionally acted as governors to administer justice, licensing and the poor law. Some of the smaller boroughs like New Romney were much smaller corporations but with civic officials acting in a way not unlike London or Bristol. New Romney even returned two MPs.[188] Kent's rural real estate ownership was never dominated by very large landowners; although there were numerous medium-sized ones, as well as substantial tenants, some of whom had leased large portfolios of land themselves.[189] Such men became MPs and justices and comprised the great majority of tax commissioners. Kentish MPs were clearly expected to be or become tax commissioners. Of over two hundred MPs identified in the period 1643–1733, at least 95% did so.[190] Very many of these were not just listed in the legislation, but like: Michael Livesey and William Kenrick[191] in Upper Scray; Augustine Skinner and William James[192] in Aylesford South; and Sir Thomas Walsingham and Augustine Skinner in Sutton-at-Hone; were active tax commissioners attending meetings and signing numerous documents to make sure parliamentary legislation was implemented. Sir Michael Livesey, the well-known regicide, and elected MP for Queenborough in Upper Scray, though a prominent military commander,[193] still made time for tax committees and paperwork between 1644 and 1660. He was disparaged for his pains as 'Collonel, Sequestrator, and Plunder-Master General of Kent'.[194] In fact, over half of Kent's 18 commissioners listed in the February 1643 statute[195] were MPs and whilst commissioner numbers increased to over four hundred by the 1700s, MPs remained prominently active throughout.

Many of these men were involved in the tax process as taxpayers as well as administrators and knew the tax process intimately as the following small example illustrates. As discussed, legislation permitted the 'Tenant or Occupier to stop and detain' tax paid out of the rent especially and specifically according to a 1648 ordinance 'on fee-farm and other rents due to king'.[196] Further: 'Landlords, both mediate and immediate, according to their respective interest are hereby required to allow such deductions and paiments'[197] from rents received. Sir Edward Hales of Tunstall, commissioner for the first assessment in 1643 and MP for Queenborough in Upper Scray for many years until April 1648, wrote, or probably his clerk, a highly detailed and pertinent acknowledgement of his fiscal responsibility as landlord and tenant of the king in respect of a long list of successive assessed taxes on 18 November 1648 concluding: 'And [lastly] the other tax of six pence in the pound whereby the landlord beareth five pence and the tenant one penny. And the said Sir Edward Hales have paid and allowed the said taxes accordingly to his tenants that have paid him their Rents due at our Lady Day and Michae[lmas] last, and especially for Neates farme att Mynster within the Isle of Sheppey in the said county, which he holdeth by lease from his Maj[es]^{tie} by yearly rent of seventy pounds one penny halfe penny ….'[198] In other words, as statute demanded, he acknowledged and permitted tax deduction by his tenants from their rent due to him and paid tax himself as tenant of the king.

Across Kent and across the country, many had gained administrative experience through local, and parish work as well as state endeavours, and according to Hindle, there were, 'thousands of private individuals who assumed public responsibility'.[199] Many individuals became involved with county committees set up by Parliament in 1642 for local administration at time of civil war but which according to Everitt had much earlier parentage in Kent and elsewhere to coordinate justice and probably raise ship money.[200] The Kent County Committee had sub-committees in the five county lathes,[201] and these would have provided the immediate subdivisions for tax collection and vital experience for those involved in fiscal administration.[202] Thus in Shepway, Thomas Rooke became sub-committee Treasurer and, as mentioned, high-collector of the assessment from 1644–1651.[203] It was probably the Kent County Committee itself that drove the creation of the new form of assessments in response to legislation. Charles Bowles was the likely key figure in this development of tax process from the mid-1640s to the late 1650s holding multiple county roles.[204] He was not unique in the country, but busier than most. He was receiver-general for Kent and treasurer and commissary for the Kent County Committee. His signature is on thousands of surviving documents. Everitt believes he did much to standardise the high-collectors' accounts and very much besides.[205] He had been a member of the Committee for Sequestrations, a Commissioner for 'ejecting Scandalous, Ignorant and insufficient Ministers and Schoolmasters',[206] a bridge warden, a militia commissioner in 1651, an assessment commissioner,[207] a governor of the Sir John Hawkins Knight Hospital in the 1650s and High-Sheriff of Kent in 1658, and had risen from being 'minor gentry' and keeper of naval stores in Chatham[208] to 'a man of great estate got in these times'.[209] David Polehill became Kent's new receiver-general in 1659 after Bowles' death.[210] If few Kentish tax commissioners survived the Restoration, more sub-collectors did so ensuring continuity of process and suggesting the skill and ability to operate tax processes were more important than politics at this level. Of 116 Upper Scray sub-collectors for the 18-months' assessment of 1661–1663, 28 or 24% appear to be familiar names—a turnover broadly similar to the Interregnum.[211]

The steady flow of duplicates to the Exchequer, surviving from sub-lathes across Kent, testifies to the Restoration continuance of tax process including remarkably, an almost complete book of Kent duplicates from all parts of the county for the six quarterly assessments of 1673–1674, which again shows a strong presence of commissioner MPs as signatories.[212] In New Romney[213] and Lydd,[214] a continuing tax-gathering process can be discerned between the 1640s and the eighteenth century, thanks to the excellent survival of assessments, warrants and other documents.

3.2.3 Bristol

Bristol's Corporation had the official and ancient title of 'The Lord Mayor, Aldermen and Burgesses of Bristol'. As in many towns and cities, Bristol's seventeenth-century civic authorities were oligarchic and self-nominating, with occasional bouts of parliamentary or monarchical interference.[215] The structure is well known and described by others.[216] At the heart of Bristol's early modern civic administration were its dozen aldermen,[217] who normally served for life and the annually selected mayor[218] and two sheriffs. Its chief executive officers were the chamberlain, whose significant financial role was based on the City of London's counterpart,[219] and the town clerk who was also the City's legal adviser and clerk of the peace.[220] Beyond this were a broader group of 30 common councilmen, a body established in 1373 to help the mayor and sheriffs 'ordain and establish reasonable remedies against any deficiencies or defects and levy taxes on rents and merchandise to be expended for the common good'.[221] In other words, they had significant authority in gathering taxes and as long recognised the main sources of those revenues would be from trading and real estate. This normally made 43 officials in all with a fiscal purpose exercised in the subsidies, land taxes and poor rates thereafter. Beyond them were the burgesses of very ancient standing who usually had the privilege of electing the City's two Members of Parliament sometimes along with the freeholders.[222] Although the number of Restoration tax commissioners expanded from about a dozen to 32 by 1679, they were still almost exclusively drawn from this narrow group of civic officials.

The aldermen also served as the local board of justices of the peace, a body which nationally had important tax functions. Many individuals had a variety of roles advancing from burgess to common councilman, alderman, sheriff and mayor. As Sacks has pointed out, the major merchant-retailers or 'mere' merchants had a prominent place in civic administration as well as the commercial life of the City. Brooks has identified similar participation in other English towns.[223] Over a third of all Bristol's post-revolutionary tax commissioners were members of the Society of Merchant Venturers and many served as master, warden and/or treasurer.[224] Some of these merchants were the most active tax commissioners according to incomplete minuted meeting attendance records.[225] Commissioners were also prominent in others areas, including the Bristol Corporation of the Poor, the Admiralty Court, in the Court of Orphans, the Trained Bands and the Bristol Volunteers.[226] The City was wealthy, 'amongst the richest Corporations of the land',[227] and had purchased monastic and other estates in the sixteenth century and continued to acquire land and wealth.[228]

Once Bristol was recaptured by parliament on 11 September 1645 what was to be done with those civic officials who had been too close to the royalist commanders? It was realised by parliament that there were many in civic authority, 'so as their Continuance in the Magistracy, Government, and Common Council of the City (of so great Concernment to the whole Kingdom) will be altogether inconsistent with the Safety and Welfare thereof in these Times of War and Danger' and must be 'suspended from their respective Places and effectively replaced by the Committees of Parliament in the said City, who have hereby as full Power and Authority, together with them to all Intents and Purposes'.[229] This was partially amended in November with the re-instatement of three men: Alderman Richard Aldworth, Common Councilmen Richard Vickris and Luke Hodges.[230] By December, the City had been placed under martial law under Major-General Philip Skippon as Governor of Bristol with a Bristol Garrison funded by a local assessment of £3,000 per month on the City and neighbouring counties of which Bristol was to pay just £200.[231] Little evidence of these early levies survives, but this brief history provides some indication of the challenges faced by Bristol's middling and sometimes better male sort who were responsible for local government and tax collection. Could they retain their positions in times of changing political allegiances? Well-to-do tax commissioners across the nation had strong incentives to make the land taxes a success for their own safety and prestige and to secure advantages for their local communities in Parliament and no doubt also for themselves. Aldworth, Vickris and Hodges, all aldermen by 1645[232] had proved their 'Fidelity to the Parliament … having received full and ample Testimony of the[ir] Integrity and Ability'.[233] All were already or were to become tax commissioners.[234] These three Bristolians were not unique in the City in their ability to adapt. Merchant Venturer and MP, Sir Robert Cann was an Interregnum common councilman and sheriff, but one amongst many 'ready to express his loyalty and good affection'[235] to his majesty at the Restoration even though his father had proclaimed the Commonwealth as mayor in 1649.[236] He continued to be an active Restoration tax commissioner, alderman, mayor and sheriff and in 1678 MP. Cann's political balancing act was not repeated by all Bristolians. By orders of 19 June 1660 and 4 October 1661, four aldermen and some common councilmen displaced in the 1640s were restored and a similar number of others 'unduly brought in' during the Commonwealth were removed including Richard Vickris himself, although many others were retained.[237] As far as tax commissioners were concerned, the cull of the potentially disloyal was more brutal.[238] In very early Restoration statutes, only a handful of commissioners known to be loyal to the King were named.[239] The 18-months' assessment of 1661–1663 is the first to herald a change, and only 5 of the 28 listed commissioners had acted during the Interregnum.[240] By comparison, hardly any survived in Kent after 1660.[241]

Throughout the seventeenth century and beyond, Bristol's mayor, its sheriffs and aldermen were usually the first appointments listed in the tax statutes as commissioners. The common councilmen were the other major group given their tradition taxation role mentioned above. During the Restoration, the number of commissioners listed in statutes was small.[242] The statute for the Royal Aid (1664–1667) lists only 15 names in Bristol: the mayor, nine of the aldermen and five common councilmen; 13 of these were recoded as attending one or more minuted meetings.[243] Commissioner numbers increased thereafter. For the 1679 Aid, there were 32, including all 12 aldermen, one of whom was also mayor, two sheriffs and 17 members of the Common Council and one other.[244] The result of all this was that during the Restoration direct taxation was almost entirely administered at commissioner level by the aldermen, sheriffs and mayors with a few common councilmen and this is confirmed by the commissioners' meeting attendance figures for the period.[245] The duplicates and assessments were usually signed by between three and six of this group including the mayor and two or more aldermen.[246] This action would no doubt have taken place in the council house at the Tolzey.

3.2.4 London

London civic structure is also well known.[247] As discussed, City of London officials were empowered and controlled by London-specific late 1640s legislation, which, after much tinkering, re-enforced and modified a two-tier structure of tax bureaucracy (see page 75).[248] Local common councilmen and deputies would be responsible for assessment and administration in the 25 local wards, and aldermen and other tax commissioners had City-wide oversight and responsibility.[249] This administrative structure remained in place throughout the Restoration and beyond, but it was not static as will be later outlined. The City's Interregnum commissioners survived into the Restoration at slightly better rates than in Bristol or Kent, based on the 1661–1663 18-months' assessment, where around 18 out of 63 commissioners also served during the Interregnum.[250] The relatively good survival of land tax officials in London can be compared with the similar evidence, described by Coffman, where a number of London-based customs and excise officials continued in post no doubt due to their capability and experience.[251]

3.3 The Restoration

3.3.1 Restoration Administration

Despite a loss of experienced officials in Royalist culls, tax administration in London, Bristol and Kent provided a settled Restoration process routine with the support of survivors, civic authorities, justices, clerks, MPs, receivers and increasing numbers of commissioners.

London had the significant advantage of the administrative, legal and financial experience and expertise contained in the offices of Town Clerk and Chamberlain and their staff. The City Chamberlain had for centuries performed an accounting and treasury function, and it is not surprising that this office now often provided such a function for the assessment right across the metropolitan area and beyond. Sir Thomas Player senior was receiver-general for the Royal Aid across metropolitan London as well as official collector of the hearth tax and had been City Chamberlain since 1651—a remarkable political survival no doubt aided by his ability to fund the government via civic loans and by his skills as a financier and banker.[252] In the early 1660s, national Restoration receipts were to be paid to the Chamber of London and not the Exchequer, partly, no doubt, in recognition of Player's formidable abilities.[253] His payments to the Exchequer against tallies were recorded.[254] By 1660, City tax accounts were organised into a regular day book, where receipts were recorded in sequence by date, but recording the collector and the City ward or precinct.[255] These amounts were then transferred into a ward book showing how much each tax precinct had paid and how much was left owing against the quota to be chased up.[256] There was also a further account of the payments made to the Exchequer.[257] Restoration collectors were obliged to make returns of any uncollectable amounts to the ward officials (not the commissioners themselves) for immediate approval, and these would be submitted to the chamberlain to add to his ledgers as amounts he could not expect to receive.[258]

Throughout the Restoration, the City of London's Lord Mayor and aldermen were appointed as commissioners in successive ordinances, but the commissioners' list began to broaden to include others. Professional men, including lawyers, begin to appear and other relevantly experienced individuals who were not otherwise civic officials.[259] In 1664 for the Royal Aid,[260] there were only 37 named commissioners, but there were 93 for the last Restoration assessment in 1680.[261] There are a few noteworthy aspects to this evolving composition of commissioners.[262] The Lord Mayor and aldermen remain prominent throughout. In 1664, seven commissioners had been Lord Mayor before and nine would become so in future. The current Mayor Sir John Lawrence, 25 other aldermen and five former aldermen make up the bulk of commissioners (84%). In 1680 although there were more aldermen and former aldermen (47), they make up much less of the total (51%). Many individuals were current or former sheriffs. In 1664, there were 23 (62%) and in 1680, 32 (34%). It is these most senior civic officials who were the main signatories of assessments; warrants for collectors, clerks and assessors; and duplicates which guaranteed the authority of the City.[263] The fact that town clerks were also commissioners' clerks was a considerable advantage when there were numerous documents to be signed throughout the year by civic officials doubling as commissioners.

Only two of four London MPs were listed in the 1664 statute (and seven former MPs), but all were listed in 1680 legislation (and six former MPs). MPs representing other parts of the country (both current and former) with homes in London often became City commissioners. The 1664 statute had at least ten current and two former non-City MPs (32%), compared with 23 and 6, respectively, in 1679 (31%).

There was a continuation of the 1640s two-tier structure. The local common councilmen performed the lower-tier assessor role in each ward, and the aldermen/commissioners the higher tier city-wide oversight role. This was a useful separation of powers, but, as local officials were rarely commissioners themselves, actions, for example, the warranting of collectors and approval of assessments, had to be constantly referred to the higher tier for agreement and signature.[264] If few deputies and common councilmen became Restoration commissioners themselves, there were some exceptions. For example, in the 1657 ordinances, Sir Christopher Pack of Bassishaw was a tax commissioner as alderman, but Common Councilman Abraham Church, for the same ward, was also named.[265] There was no significant group of common councilmen or deputies acting as commissioners in 1664, but in 1680, 14 common councilmen and three deputies were named.[266] This may have given more independence to some wards, but there is no evidence of any reduction in the need to refer to the higher tier for document approval.[267] In 1664, of the remaining non-aldermanic group one was the City Recorder Sir William Wilde and two cannot be identified significantly further. By 1680, far more individuals were becoming commissioners beyond the normal civic officials and MPs. At least seven were senior lawyers or judges, and many others were wealthy merchants, both groups common into the eighteenth century. However, it is not clear from surviving documents that these individuals had a significant role in the tax process, but they may have added greater weight, breadth of knowledge and skill sets to the City commissioner body.

There was significant continuity. Aldermen, once appointed, usually kept the role for life. Sometimes, they worked their way up through the meanest ward roles to become senior civic dignitaries and lived and worked for many years in the City. The aldermen, common councilmen and deputies would all be freemen of the City, and by the time the assessment was introduced only freemen[268] were allowed to vote in the elections for common councilmen and aldermen. Common councilmen in Bassishaw ward were elected by annual meetings of the wardmote, where the freemen gathered.[269] One main function of such meetings was to select local officials for the coming year, including the wardmote jury, as well as constables, beadles, scavengers, secretaries, clerks and other local roles, and to nominate an alderman if there was a vacancy. Wardmotes had local legislative power and assumed tax-raising authority, according to Pearl, almost as a bulwark against the aldermen.[270] There were 237 City common councilmen in 1646, a role which no doubt provided a source of personal power and authority for such individuals, who often tended to be the wealthiest in the ward.[271] Unlike the aldermen, common councilmen were selected annually, but individuals were often reselected for years, which was no doubt an advantage to tax process continuity. Aldermen were the wealthiest individuals with a property qualification of £10,000[272] by the mid-seventeenth century, and as Pearl maintains, the Court of Aldermen was 'oligarchic and almost self-perpetuating', with powerful legal and administrative authority.[273] Local government of each ward was carried out by these officials but in practice there was much day-to-day delegation by the alderman to their deputies in each ward including taxation. Although some individuals moved from ward to ward, civic officials of all types comprised some of the least mobile individuals, which helped them retain local power, influence and personal networks.[274]

Usually, the deputy alderman and common councilmen were in charge of the ward process including assessing their fellow citizens to taxation, the approval of returns or *estreats* of uncollected amounts and no doubt chivvying the collectors.[275] They would sign the completed assessments for final checking by the town clerk's office at Guildhall. However, at least one copy of the tax assessments was always signed off by higher-tier commissioners before the collectors could act according to surviving documents—the appropriate statutory procedure.[276] There were three copies of each assessment, one each for the clerk, the collector and the receiver. Most surviving documents appear to be the clerk's paper copies but with a few collectors' copies readily identifiable because they were usually on more durable parchment. The other important difference is in signing. Whereas the clerk's copies were signed only by ward officials, the collectors' copies also include an attached warrant and were signed by higher-tier tax commissioners, usually the mayor and aldermen.[277] This was of course because only commissioners could appoint and warrant collectors under the act. For example, the collector's warrant for the first quarter of the 18-months' assessment of 1673–1674 for Portsoken Ward nominated Robert Moore and Robert Wright to:

> collect and gather with all possible speed according to the monthly tax or sums of money before [assessed?] and from time to time after receipt thereof pay the same unto Richard Reeves Esquire Receiver general of s[ai]

> d quarterly paym[en]t at the house of John Linsey Esq In Lombard Street so that the same quarterly payment may be paid in by the time limited & appointed by the s[ai]d Act of Parliament. And if any those p[er]son shall refuse neglect or delay to pay the money wherat he or she is assessed then this s[ai]d Collector and forthwith to levy the same by distress & sale of the goods of the p[er]son for refusing neglecting or delaying to pay as by the s[ai]d Act is prescribed & directed. In Witness whereof we have hereon to set our hands & seals the xxiii day of May 1673.[278]

64% of surviving Restoration assessments, which may not be entirely representative, were signed by a serving deputy and 89% by at least one common councilman as assessors. For historical reasons, the typical City ward structure did not quite apply in all parts. As the City had expanded, particularly in parts of Farringdon Without[279] and St. Martin's Le Grand,[280] assessment responsibilities lay with headboroughs (1% of all assessment signing officials), jurors (3%), constables (1%) and church wardens (1%).[281] All these officials had to be appointed and warranted by commissioners named in legislation even if, as on the August 1673 assessment for Broad Street Ward, local officials ambitiously claimed to be 'sub-commissioners'. They were nothing of the kind as no such role existed.[282]

Bristol's civic leaders were often keen to promote the City's trading interest and even remunerated its MPs[283] and other civic officials.[284] Sir Richard Crump received '£17-13s-4d in parliamentary wages' from the corporation, making clear to him that they expected a 'sedulous care in their concerns'.[285] Kent's Restoration MPs were active land tax commissioners themselves. Indeed, across the nation, such landowners, businessmen and professionals, who attempted to influence events at Westminster, to promote their communities, and no doubt to benefit themselves and their fellows, were often directly responsible for collecting national taxation and were substantial taxpayers themselves.[286] At the same time, such commitment would not always trump self-interest. The visible 'pretence of his service'[287] for the monarch's land taxes might mask substantial and less-visible customs evasion as was the case in Bristol.[288] William Culliford's 1682–1684 investigation of the customs in the western ports including Bristol exposed substantial fraud and incompetence including the collusion of merchants with customs officials.[289] These merchants appear to have included Aldermen Sir Richard

Crump, Sir John Knight and William Crabb, all three of whom went on to distinguished civic careers achieving the offices of mayor and sheriff and Crumpe was elected MP. All were land tax commissioners, but none were charged or punished. Many other tax officials were probably involved and such frauds continued despite occasional whistleblowing. Sacks believes it was 'just par for the course in the conduct of business' and Stephens recognises 'a long tradition of illicit trading and of customs … fraud'.[290] McGrath was in no doubt that 'a considerable amount of [tax] fraud went on in seventeenth-century Bristol' particularly involving tobacco. Nor should it be imagined that tax commissioners were always without rancour.[291] In Bristol, bitter enmities ebbed and flowed between Whig and Tory, high churchman and dissenter, but at least all could agree the land tax quota must be met.

By the 1660s, a routine of commissioners' meetings had been established in Bristol: to carry out tax business, approve parish quotas, appoint and warrant assessors and collectors, and agree and sign parish assessments. This is clear from the incomplete minute book and assessments.[292] All 37 surviving Restoration parish assessments were signed by groups of senior commissioners including the mayor.[293] This document survival is modest, and these assessments contain the names of assessors on only 19 occasions and mentioned collectors five times.[294] However, there are better data from the commissioners' minute book where the assessors and collectors were almost always named.[295] Unfortunately, even here less than half of the expected records of quarterly appointments survive. These incomplete records make clear that, unlike London's, Bristol's assessors and collectors were not otherwise civic officials themselves, even if all were burgesses, but were nominated by the parishes and comprised wealthier local men with businesses, trades and professions.[296] In parts of the country where there were no such civic authorities, MPs, ex-MPs and the local boards of local justices could fill the gap by becoming tax commissioners as in Kent.[297] Other variant local governance arrangements were in place up and down the land.

Receivers-general were responsible for transmitting county or City tax receipts to the Exchequer and were generally appointed by Treasury. They were rewarded by poundage on sums remitted. The City of London Chamberlain's office provided the natural and usual choice as receiver-general for the direct taxes of the whole metropolis—not just the City.[298] They were invariably men of means who individually, or through their networks, could provide adequate sureties to the Exchequer,[299] which would be checked before they could take office.[300] Such sureties were seized if receivers defaulted (see Sect. 5.2). There was even a limited audit function performed by the Auditors of Land Revenue.[301] Many such were also receivers for other taxes including window taxes and even for customs and excise.

Bristol was too small to have its own receiver and shared one with Somerset. Kent had its own, serving all the lathes and boroughs. Receivers often lived a considerable distance from tax-collectors and commissioners' clerks and from London. Remitting Restoration tax revenue to London from places such as Bristol often meant the physical transfer of cash under guard. Bristol and Somerset Receiver-General John Tooker was recognised as having 'diligently and faithfully executed his said office' in conveying monies to the Exchequer and paid expenses.[302] Tooker's money was conveyed 80 miles over land to Exeter via Tiverton and then 350 miles by sea, which was probably safer and faster than by land.[303]

The City of London Town Clerk's office, with its ancient recording obligations, assumed the role of tax commissioners' clerk and accounting back office thus together with the receiver/chamberlain (in most years) centralised the City's administrative and accounting effort at the Guildhall. Bristol employed a series of lawyers until 1701 after which it also permanently employed its own town clerks in the role. Lawyers often played this role in Kent and across the nation.

3.3.2 *Restoration Process Innovation and Resilience*

The Restoration is sometimes mistakenly seen as a relatively static period of land tax development, a period of 'inertia' as Braddick calls it. There were in fact important changes centrally and locally as record annual amounts of tax were collected, the speed of collection improved, tax on rent became more important than ever, the role and stature of collectors developed, the Treasury was given fresh authority and responsibility for supervision, London's administration was resilient despite plague and fire, and paper transfers of tax monies developed apace. This section will consider the detailed impacts in the case study areas.

London

Restoration land taxes were quickly successful, even if they were tainted by their Commonwealth roots. They were certainly preferred after the disappointing returns of an old-fashioned subsidy levied in 1663–1664 (see Fig. 1.1). This subsidy proved to be a City, and according to Chandaman[304] national failure, because as argued here, it was a tax form past its time.[305] The subsidy rate was the usual 4s/£ on the value of land over 20s value per year or 2s-8d/£ on goods, but double for aliens and Popish Recusants. According to the 1638 inhabitants' lists, and the 1646 'estimate', there were approaching 200 'housekeepers' or households in Bassishaw, but a meagre 12 were assessed for land by this subsidy.[306] Perhaps this was simply because very few inhabitants owned their own homes and landlords were institutions or absentees. For subsidies, individuals were taxed on the higher of land or goods, not both, and if it is assumed that all those taxed on goods would have been assessed on lands if the goods figure had not been higher, then the total is still just a paltry 51. This suggests massive under-assessment was taking place as in every previous seventeenth-century subsidy.[307] Two pairs of subsidies were to be raised. The Act stipulated that the two subsidies were to be paid into the 'Exchequer in one entire Sum' on 1 May 1663 with a further payment of the other pair on 1 May 1664. Nevertheless, Bassishaw raised a meagre £226.67 in four subsidies which was far less than that for the single assessment of 20 December 1648 at £484.

After this failed subsidy, London's Restoration land tax assessment processes were quickly re-established taking the City's full statutory quota and dividing it 'according to such rates, rules and proportions' as determined by the commissioners following Interregnum practice.[308] Local ward quotas were applied, but pound rates were nevertheless set out as a guide for assessors. A rate of 2d/£ per month or 2s/£ per year appears to have been the Restoration standard during a period when the City's national quota was static.[309] The evidence is as follows:

1. The 1664 Tower Ward assessment of two months states that 'The rate for Landlords not exceeding 2d per month per pound' or 2s/£ annually. The authority for this rate came from 'his Majesty's lieutenants dated February 1664' and therefore this would have been City-wide.[310]
2. The May 1666 assessment for Bridge Ward's two contemporary taxes the Royal and Additional Aid unusually includes a separate

column showing the rent for each taxpayer in Kentish style and a calculation at 2d per month for the former tax and 1 1/2d for the latter or 2s and an additional 1s-6d annually—3s-6d in all.[311]

3. The Militia Money assessment for 1663–1664 for Vintry Ward has a 2d per month rate equivalent to a 2s/£ rate.[312]
4. The £70,000 tax per month of 1663 also refers to a monthly rate 'not above 2d p[er] £' in Billingsgate.[313]
5. The preamble text for the 18-months' assessment of 1673—1674 from Aldersgate Without[314] states that the monthly quota for the City according to legislation was £5,091-11s-4d 'of which £130 p[er] month is by the Commissioners in the said Act of Parliament named apportioned on the ward of Aldersgate Without' and 'Att the rate of 2d p[er] pound upon the rents of houses to the yearly value' or 2s/£.[315]
6. Although the 18-months' assessment of 1673–1674 was quota driven, and no documents show a separate figure for rent, it nevertheless appears to be based substantially on the 1671 subsidy which had a 1s/£ rate. From a study of sample assessments, it is clear that the 18-months' assessment was levied generally applying twice that rate or 2d/month or 2s annual rate. Indeed, this 2s/£ rate is stated on the face of the assessment for Aldersgate Without above.[316]

The City's Restoration assessments were in the format established in the 1640s with the inhabitants or occupiers taxed on their own personal estates, and in respect of the land value which could be deducted from rent paid to landlords, if terms permitted.[317] The precise terminology varies, but the result is the same, a tax on both personal and real estate. Whereas pre-Restoration assessments often refer to occupier and out-landlord, they now variously refer to: real and personal estates, landlord and stock, landlord and tenant, landlord and personal estates, and landlord and inhabitant, although the last two were most popular.[318] As in the 1640s, landlords were taxed directly for some tenements, but because the assessments are incomplete and sometimes in poor condition, it is difficult to estimate accurate numbers.[319] Normal powers of distraint applied, but the mobility and poverty of population—the poor, dead and gone—remained a challenge as they had since 1643.[320] The overassessment solution to this problem (discussed in detail in Sect. 4.2 (b)) was in use, where local officials assessed more than the set quota to prevent shortfalls, but this was cautiously applied as it was non-statutory.[321] The average tax quota overassessment for the 1664–1667 Royal Aid at 0.7% compares with 0.6% in 1703 but 6.2% in 1733 and 0.3% in Restoration Bristol.[322]

The common councilmen and deputy were responsible for approving the returns releasing collectors from future liability where money could not be collected.[323] It could also mean collectors would get paid their poundage. Sometimes, a single local common councilman took on this task. In Farringdon Within, for example, in respect of the 18-months' assessment of 1673–1674, Thomas Adams approved the uncollectability of seven shillings and six pence in St. Michael-le-Quern precinct where he lived[324]; similarly, John Brand in Sadlers Hall; William Hall, the current deputy for Goldsmith Row precinct; Edward Clarke in St. Peter precinct; Humphrey Curtis in Monkwell Street precinct; and Robert Gilbert in St. Augustine precinct. There are numerous similar examples.[325] Officials would also identify errors. In St Sepulchre, Farringdon Without, for the 11-months' tax in 1668, Deputy Thomas Tunman said: 'I have examined this role and find that in the Dolphin yard ... you have put down 2s-4d and it should be £2-4s-0d'. There were further errors on the assessors' part and Tunman required 'I pray you to amend the roll and [put] it back to the Beadle'.[326]

It was not inevitable that the common councilmen would agree such returns even in wards like Cripplegate Without where the poor, dead and gone loomed large. Significant sums could sometimes not be collected there 'by reason of the poverty of some and the absence of others being gone out of the ward or dead & cannot be collected'. Common councilmen were not fools and could do their maths. They knew from the collectors' accounts how much has been collected and how much was still to pay. On 26 November 1679, four Cripplegate Without officials, including the deputy Augustus Newbold and three common councilmen, accepted some amounts were uncollectable but refused to approve the collectors' returns of uncollectable amounts for John Graytricks and Samuell Smith of Red Cross and White Cross precinct and of John Bennett and Francis Parret for Fore Street and Grub Street precinct at least until they paid the remaining balances of £57-14-6d and £21-18-8½d, respectively, 'being still in their hands they remaine charged for the same until they make payment thereof Accordingly'.[327]

The Second Anglo-Dutch War forced tax rates higher than ever. London's highest Restoration rates on annual land values reached a guide level of 3s-6d/£ (estimated at example 2 above) although quickly disrupted by the Great Plague and the Great Fire. This significant levy was decades before the 4s/£ land taxes of the 1690s. The distribution of the City's statutory tax quota remained flexible between wards, but had to be met in full (Fig. 5.9). Flexibility usually resulted from a process of negotiation, but was ultimately decided by senior commissioners, for example, in 1661 matters were 'referred to the Alder[men] of the several wards together with several com[ission]ers hereafter named, or any 7 to apportion the several Quotas upon the several wards and take an estimate of the real and personal estates & other interests chargeable … having regard to the pensions in Langbourn[e] and all other wards that have public offices exercised in them …' [328] When this was done, the mayor, on behalf of the commissioners, would issue a precept to the ward officials to start their assessment work. Although less than 20% of surviving Restoration ward assessments were dated at completion, it is possible to estimate from this group that the assessment process took about six weeks to complete, with little recognisable difference caused by the time of year the process began.[329] These dated assessments show that local ward assessors delivered assessments rather more quickly from precept date over time and there was some quickening of the reaction of commissioners to legislation, but there was no uniform pattern across the City, and the mid/late 1660s was much impacted by plague and fire.[330] Predictably, the poorer extra-mural and riverside wards with their generally more numerous and mobile taxpayer populations took somewhat longer to assess at seven to eight weeks than the central wards which generally took three to four.[331] This variation cannot be entirely explained by taxpayer numbers because some wards had increased human resourcing to compensate. Some wards had two teams of assessors (Aldersgate Within[332] and Aldgate[333]) but Farringdon Without had up to eight.[334] There were also more assessors at work in some wards than others. The data are however insufficient to decipher deeper granularity.

Direct tax collection in the City was effective and resilient despite drastic interruption by plague and fire as evidenced by accounting data for the three-year Royal Aid (Fig. 3.11).[335] Restoration collection started effectively enough as Sir Thomas Player's accounts for four earlier levies in 1660 and 1661 show. The arrears are at only 1% of £60,666.67 charged, although the speed of collection was variable.[336] This is slightly better than Chandaman national averages, but not wholly exceptional.

For the plague and fire interrupted Royal Aid of 1664–1667,[337] London was charged £5,091-11s-4d per month. The accounts for the first quarter are incomplete, which may be linked to the Great Plague and after the fifth quarter there was considerable disruption from the Great Fire of 2–5 September 1666.[338] For the intermediate three quarters, there are good data, and monies were due to the Exchequer for these, respectively, on 1 August and 1 November 1665 and 1 February 1666 (Fig. 3.11).[339]

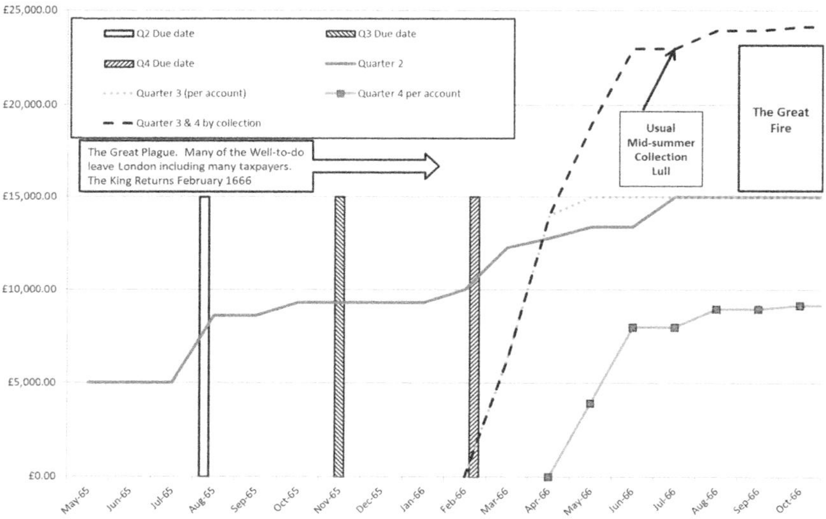

Fig. 3.11 City of London 1665–1666. Cumulative Royal Aid payments for quarters 2–4 made by the receiver-general to the Exchequer compared with statutory due dates[340]

Second quarter collection was well under way, with over half the money collected by the statutory payment deadline of 1 August 1665, despite the fact that plague was well-established that summer with thousands dying every week across the metropolis. Initially, the plague's impact was largely beyond the City, but matters were worsening into the early autumn. Many of the well-to-do, including some substantial taxpayers, left the City. Tax collection stalled. The king did not return to

London until February 1666 coinciding with the resumption of City collection for that second quarter and the next two.[341] Understandably, second quarter collection had been exceptionally slow, taking well over a year to complete, yet 94% of the full amount had been gathered by the eve of the Great Fire (Fig. 3.11).[342] It was the collection speed in the third and fourth quarters that gives us a glimpse of the efficiency and rapid recovery of the City's tax-gathering machinery in the most difficult of times. According to his own records, the receiver-general paid up the entire third-quarter quota in short order between 13 March 1666 and 5 May 1666, although speed varied between wards (Fig. 3.12a) and the poorer riverside wards struggled most and richer central wards did best. Third-quarter results are somewhat misleading, however, because third- and fourth-quarter amounts were collected together, and he allocated all the initial receipts to the third quarter until that quota total (£15,000) had been made up and any subsequent payments to the fourth quarter. On the eve of the Great Fire, a substantial £23,950 (of the £30,000 two quarters total) had been collected.[343] This analysis shows rapid collection until the end of May, slightly reduced pace in June and then a slow pace of collection in July and August marking the normal slack period in the City's seasonal financial cycle (see Fig. 5.2) before an almost dead stop with the Great Fire in September. Because of the Fire, it was decided by Parliament that:

> All the sum & sums of money which were charged or allotted upon the several Wards & places of the said City burnt down in the late dismal fire for their portion [quota] of the said Royal Aid and Additional Supply shall be permitted & forever pardoned and discharged.[344]

The decision may have followed this unsigned and undated petition, which also summarises the remarkable efforts made by the City:

> For as much as by reason of visitation of the plague in the Cittie of London & Liberties therof and the … removal of the Citizens & inhabitants there upon into the country severall quarterly payments of the Royall Aid and Additionall Supply granted to his Majesty by the Parliament in the 16th 17th & 18th yeares of his Majesty's happy raign could not be timely rated or assessed as in and by the said severall Acts of Parliament were appointed & directed. And after that the same were rated & assessed a great part thereof could not by reason of the dismall fire ensuring

> thereupon bee levyed & paid nor can now be Levyed & paid unless it should be raised upon the inhabitants of the standing parts of the Citty who have already paid their part & portion ... and ask for pardon and discharge.[345]

The speed of rebuilding and recovery was remarkable. Assuming a 2s/£ rate (see page 98 above), the taxed annual value of City real estate fell from c. £372,051 in the pre-Fire 1660s (Table 3.2)[346] to about £324,967 for the post-Fire 1671 subsidy[347] before rising again to £424,999 in 1673–1674 and £452,794 in 1693–1694.[348] With statutory exemptions, estimations and accidental omissions, none of these figures are likely to represent a complete or accurate picture, but broad patterns are clear. As long recognised, land values in central wards are highest and lowest in extra-mural and riverside areas.[349]

The 14 wards less damaged by fire (Fig. 2.1) were still required to gather land taxes and pay up as a post-Fire 1672 precept makes clear, but there was much disruption to contend with.[350] A copy of a letter to the deputy and common councilmen of Bishopsgate in the less damaged north and east of the City (Fig. 2.1) acknowledges that many wards could not pay for obvious reasons, but stated that 'several parts of this city which were not burnt down or demolished in the late dismal fire' should pay the four principal and partly overlapping levies 1664–1668: the Royal Aid, the Additional Supply, the one-month's assessment and the 11-months' assessment.[351] It points out that 'a very great sum of money whereof £450-19s-1d is in arrears upon the ward of Bishopsgate' and insisted that 'you deliver unto us on or before the eighth day of July next ensuring one copy of your said assessment under your hands fairly written in a book with the names of able and fit persons to be collectors and their exact sums of their collection set down ...', and urges the same not to 'fail as you will avoid the penalty [to] be incurred for refusal or neglect thereof'. There were to be no excuses despite the difficult times. In Langbourn, tax assessments could only be on 'that part of the ward

Fig. 3.12 **a** City of London 1665–1666, cumulative percentage tax collection for the third and fourth quarters of the Royal Aid by ward showing coordinated collection across the City despite plague and fire. **b** Comparison of payments received and paid by the receiver showing money was quickly paid on to the Exchequer[352] ▶

(a)

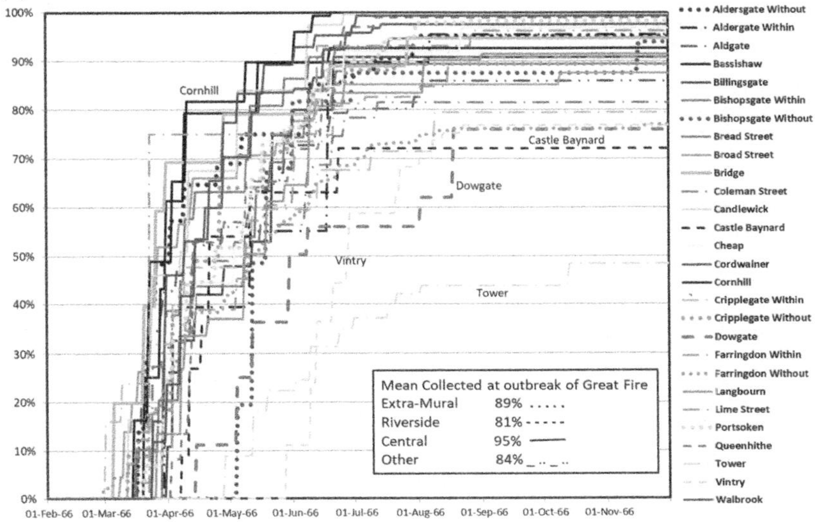
100%
90%
80%
70%
60%
50%
40%
30%
20%
10%
0%
01-Feb-66
01-Mar-66
01-Apr-66
01-May-66
01-Jun-66
01-Jul-66
01-Aug-66
01-Sep-66
01-Oct-66
01-Nov-66
Cornhill
Castle Baynard
Dowgate
Vintry
Tower
Mean Collected at outbreak of Great Fire
Extra-Mural 89%
Riverside 81%
Central 95%
Other 84%
Aldersgate Without
Aldergate Within
Aldgate
Bassishaw
Billingsgate
Bishopsgate Within
Bishopsgate Without
Bread Street
Broad Street
Bridge
Coleman Street
Candlewick
Castle Baynard
Cheap
Cordwainer
Cornhill
Cripplegate Within
Cripplegate Without
Dowgate
Farringdon Within
Farringdon Without
Langbourn
Lime Street
Portsoken
Queenhithe
Tower
Vintry
Walbrook

(b)

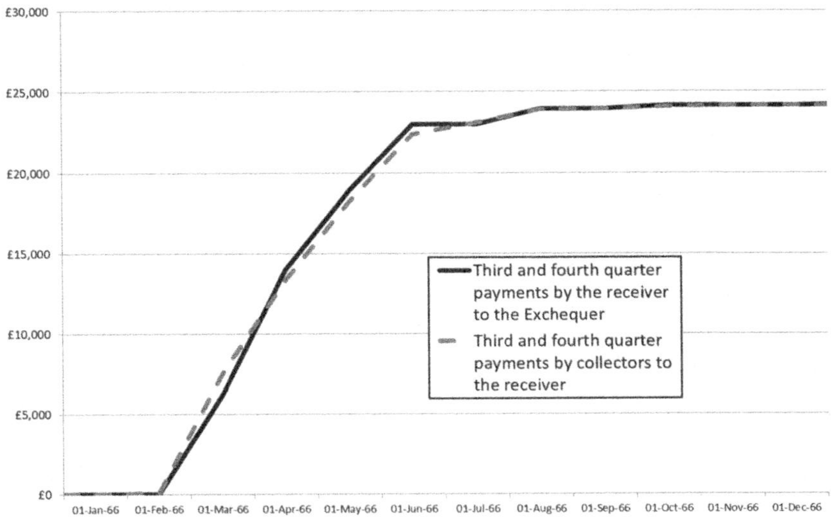
£30,000
£25,000
£20,000
£15,000
£10,000
£5,000
£0
01-Jan-66
01-Feb-66
01-Mar-66
01-Apr-66
01-May-66
01-Jun-66
01-Jul-66
01-Aug-66
01-Sep-66
01-Oct-66
01-Nov-66
01-Dec-66
Third and fourth quarter payments by the receiver to the Exchequer
Third and fourth quarter payments by collectors to the receiver

Table 3.2 City of London wards. Estimated annual rent per ward 1665–1701 and rent per hectare[353]

City Ward	*1665 Estimated rent assuming 2s/£ tax rate (rent share = 60% of quota where no surviving assessment)*	*Rent tax charge 1671 [from 1671 Duplicate] 1s/£ rate*	*Percentage empty houses and tofts 1673–1674 (%)*	*1673–1674 Taxed rent assuming 2s/£ rate*	*1693–1694 Taxed rent [after Spence, App.III, p. 176]*	*1701 Land Tax from Duplicate at 3s/£ rate*	*Rent per hectare 1673–1674*	*Rent per hectare rank 1673–1674*	*Rent per hectare rank 1693–1694*	*Rent per hectare 1693–1694 (After Spence App III)*
Aldersgate Within	£7,013	£3,848.00	36%	£8,742	£6,928	£6,797	£2,362.71	7	16	£1,872.43
Aldersgate Without	£7,916	£8,992.50	7%	£9,867	£7,485	£7,527	£1,265.02	24	24	£959.62
Aldgate	*£16,282*	£19,364.50	1%	£19,249	£18,893	£19,350	£1,436.52	23	23	£1,409.93
Bassishaw	£3,080	£2,381.00	1%	£3,572	£4,188	£4,172	£1,488.33	21	17	£1,745.00
Billingsgate	£11,172	£10,069.00	13%	£12,720	£14,800	£15,192	£2,399.95	6	5	£2,792.45
Bishopsgate Within	£8,449	£9,339.00	5%	£11,699	£13,302	£13,045	£1,746.11	16	15	£1,985.37
Bishopsgate Without	£7,148	£13,244.00	10%	£12,626	£15,545	£15,689	£701.43	28	27	£863.61
Walbrook	£10,771	£8,564.00	28%	£12,035	£9,975	£10,326	£3,085.90	2	8	£2,557.69
Broad Street	£25,784	£18,249.00	14%	£22,792	£25,545	£23,666	£1,981.90	13	10	£2,221.30
Bridge	£10,125	£8,325.00	22%	£11,329	£13,733	£13,823	£2,221.37	9	6	£2,692.75
Coleman Street	*£9,596*	£8,541.50	13%	£11,013	£11,425	£11,955	£888.14	26	26	£921.37
Candlewick Street	*£7,288*	£4,781.00	10%	£6,954	£8,148	£8,151	£2,781.59	4	3	£3,259.20
Castle Baynard	£11,891	£6,777.00	39%	£18,736	£17,083	£16,751	£1,718.89	17	19	£1,567.25
Cheap	*£16,433*	£10,064.00	22%	£12,361	£16,693	£16,851	£2,332.26	8	4	£3,149.62
Cordwainer Street	£8,617	£4,104.00	29%	£9,215	£8,738	£8,948	£2,142.92	10	14	£2,032.09
Cornhill	£8,693	£9,144.00	0%	£10,637	£13,266	£13,416	£4,431.98	1	1	£5,527.50
Cripplegate Within	£13,271	£11,034.00	5%	£11,947	£16,722	£16,427	£1,551.60	19	12	£2,171.69
Cripplegate Without	£9,985	£16,653.50	7%	£17,311	£13,752	£13,689	£967.09	25	28	£768.27
Dowgate	£9,819	£4,271.00	48%	£9,756	£8,503	£8,739	£1,625.95	18	22	£1,417.17
Farringdon Within	*£27,778*	£19,883.75	31%	£29,904	£32,049	£32,500	£2,062.36	11	11	£2,210.28
Farringdon Without	£60,928	£62,441.67	5%	£73,039	£77,983	£73,210	£1,457.87	22	20	£1,556.55
Langbourn	£14,714	£12,870.00	11%	£19,401	£23,202	£22,326	£3,031.37	3	2	£3,625.31

(continued)

Table 3.2 (continued)

City Ward	*1665 Estimated rent assuming 2s/£ tax rate (rent share = 60% of quota where no surviving assessment)*	*Rent tax charge 1671 [from 1671 Duplicate] 1s/£ rate*	*Percentage empty houses and tofts 1673–1674 (%)*	*1673–1674 Taxed rent assuming 2s/£ rate*	*1693–1694 Taxed rent [after Spence, App.III, p. 176]*	*1701 Land Tax from Duplicate at 3s/£ rate*	*Rent per hectare 1673–1674*	*Rent per hectare rank 1673–1674*	*Rent per hectare rank 1693–1694*	*Rent per hectare 1693–1694 (After Spence App III)*
Lime Street	£5,436	£5,374.00	0%	£5,942	£6,603	£7,586	£1,916.71	15	13	£2,130.00
Portsoken	£8,985	£13,722.00	1%	£14,042	£15,300	£15,387	£872.20	27	25	£950.31
Queenhithe	£7,005	£6,424.67	33%	£8,544	£8,087	£8,079	£1,499.03	20	21	£1,418.77
Tower	£24,593	£18,353.00	20%	£23,518	£26,853	£31,583	£2,027.45	12	9	£2,314.91
Vintry	£7,015	£3,031.00	51%	£8,636	£7,653	£7,716	£1,919.18	14	18	£1,700.67
Walbrook	£12,265	£5,121.00	16%	£9,411	£10,340	£10,366	£2,413.18	5	7	£2,651.28
	£3,72,051	£3,24,967	14%	£4,24,999	£4,52,794	£4,53,266	£,1615.35			£1,721.00

of Langbourn standing' according to officials in 1669.[354] Elsewhere, collectors were partly discharged from payment, as in the case of Roger Stackhouse, a London Merchant appointed for the fourth Precinct of Coleman Street Ward in the north of the City for the fifth and sixth quarterly payments of the Royal Aid and the contemporary first and second quarters of the Additional Aid. He had applied his 'utmost endeavours' to collect 'the money upon his Roll' and paid £130. Coleman Street was only partly destroyed by fire, so his discharge was only £5-5s-5d, partly for reason of the 'poor dead & gone' but 'especially by reason of the fire'. Tax collections continued but on a slightly less coordinated basis than before, judging by payments from the wards.[355]

If the Great Plague brought delay and the Great Fire disruption and a cut in the City's statutory quota, normal service was quickly resumed in the early 1670s. The 1671 post-Great Fire subsidy was to be levied at 1s/£ on land and thus provided an opportunity for a revaluation of City property following rebuilding, even though there remained numerous building sites or plots of ground ('tofts' in contemporary documents) and yet to be occupied 'empty' houses. The 1671 assessment from Broad Street calls it a: 'Valuation and assessment of and upon the Lands, offices and stock of the inhabitants'.[356] Less than half of these 1671 City of London ward tax assessments survive, but those that do, all provide a separate calculation of rent showing that there was probably a consistent post-Great Fire revaluation.[357] The City duplicate, signed on 12 September 1671, provides summary totals for all wards and their precincts for both taxed 'Stocke' and 'Rents', in two separate columns, again suggesting a universal re-rating; 78% of the tax was levied on rents and the rest on personal estates.[358] The duplicate's tax on rent figure was £16,248 which, at a 1s/£ rate, was equivalent to a City annual land value of £324,967 (Table 3.2). As the 1671 subsidy was levied on vacant plots, building sites and empty properties, it can be surmised that it encouraged redevelopment. This revaluation was used as the basis for the 18-months' assessment (with quota) of 1673–1674. In a sample, 47% of cases, exactly the same rent figure was used in 1671 and 1673–1674 and a further 25% were within 20%.[359] Assessments were covered with crossings-out almost invariably increasing the tax assessed. Taxpayers would have to pay a little more tax to make up the new ward quotas no doubt because rebuilding was not yet complete. Queenhithe Ward's administrators, which had much the highest proportion of empty houses and tofts in the sample, did not use the 1671 figures at all but reassessed for the later levy. By the late 1670s, the City's share of tax based on real estate rent compared with personal estates exceeded 70%[360] as its commissioners and common councilmen mobilised 200 tax-collectors to gather sums large and small from 20,000 doors.[361]

Given that wards were allocated varying quotas throughout the post-Fire Restoration, officials might have to plead for an adjustment when their local quota seemed too high. The inhabitants of St. Giles, Cripplegate Without, petitioned the Lord Mayor and City of London commissioners regarding the 18-months' assessment of 1673–1674, claiming that a quota at £200 overrated them 'being almost double the rate usually allotted upon that ward … the former dividend never exceeded one hundred pounds p[er] month or thereabouts … the said ward at present in it above two hundred empty houses and those inhabitants who do therein reside, are most of them handicrafts trades; and of meane degree not able to beare the burden of so great tax; the most able inhabitants having left the said ward …' and further, Cripplegate Without 'is a great measure poorer than it was before the late dreadful fire …'[362] Table 3.2 suggests that such petitioning later minimised the quota in this ward. Given the above caveats, it nevertheless appears to have been in the central wards of the City and the commercial thoroughfares described by Alexander[363] where rents appear to have risen most rapidly during the late seventeenth century as is suggested in Table 3.2.[364]

The receivers quickly paid on monies received to the Exchequer according to Fig. 3.12b much as they did after the Revolution.[365] There was to be no holding on to cash. The City receivers' accounts show evidence of seasonal financial tax-flows in spring and autumn, though much disturbed by fire, which have much in common with those after the Glorious Revolution. Monies were most often paid up after Lady Day (25 March) or Michaelmas (29 September) which seem to be linked with City seasonal financial cycles (see Sect. 5.1 below), that is the commencement of the legal/financial year starting on 25 March when legal obligations and rent payments often fell due.[366] Lady Day and Michaelmas were also the normal days for the collection of the hearth tax so any 'double-hatting' collectors could collect two taxes at once. These tax collection flows suggest that any instructions that amounts were 'to be collected in every month monthly' were largely ignored.[367] Ward suggests that two collection cycles rather than the four specified by statute were an important sign of the 'decay' of land tax administration in the mid-eighteenth century, but in the City this was simply normal practice a century earlier.[368] It was normal across the whole of metropolitan London by the 1690s and probably much earlier judging by the accounts. Such patterns probably pertained across many areas of England because of the importance of Lady Day and Michaelmas in the settling of debts and the payment of rents.

Bristol

Restoration commissioners soon re-established their tax processes even if most of the faces at commissioners' meetings had changed. Bristol's Restoration land tax commissioners' minutes survive commencing 8 March 1665. Of the seven Restoration inaugural commissioners' meetings for new taxes, where records are extant, six were by the statutory deadline, and one was three days late, but probably with good reason.[369] The first recorded meeting was by Parliament's statutory deadline of 10 March 1665, but already this has the feel of a well-established routine.[370] There was also a generally close following of legislation via the printed statute which was read out at that first meeting. In 1665, monthly parish quotas for the next quarter were agreed at the first meeting and assessors appointed the following day and their warrants issued. The form of assessors' warrants was set out in the minutes and included a tight 21 March deadline for delivery of the completed assessments. The assessments must have been returned on time because on 22 March, commissioners met again to appoint and name parish collectors, sign their warrants and issue them with copies of completed parish assessments as the act required. Thus, 'a Copy of Assessment subscribed by them [assessors] to Commissioners, who are to sign and seal Two Duplicates thereof, and deliver one to [the] Sub-collector'. Collectors' warrants were also detailed, telling collectors what to do and what powers they had, including those of distraint. They were not to fail under a £20 penalty 'to doe and performe according as by the said Act'[371]; 12 of the 18 parishes have at least one surviving assessment from the Royal Aid and many have several (see Table 3.3).[372] They all appear to be clerk's copies (rather than collector's copies) and almost all were signed by several commissioners.[373] There is also extensive parish quota data from the commissioners' minute book.[374]

Even with a local as well as a national quota in place, pound rates could sometimes be employed across county or city as discussed for Interregnum and Restoration Kent (Fig. 3.8).[375] The practice of showing the taxed annual rent on the face of Kentish assessments continued during the Restoration[376] was occasional in London, but was totally absent in Bristol until the 1690s.[377] Local quotas might suggest that

Table 3.3 City of Bristol. Tax and taxpayer growth 1660s–1693[378]

Parishes	*Location (see Fig. 2.2)*	*Real estate taxpayer growth 1660s–1693*	*Taxed rent per acre in 1693–1694 assessment*	*Taxed Rent per acre in the 1660s [estimated]*	*Rent per acre rank 1693–1694*	*Rent per acre rank 1660s*	*Taxed rent per acre growth 1660s to 1693–1694 [est.] (%)*	*Number of tax charges % growth 1660–1693–1694*	*Average tax charge on rent movement 1660s to 1693–1694*	*Increase in parish share 1660s–1693 rank*
All Saints	Central	Missing	£714.08	*£573.85*	1	1	*24*	Missing	Missing	16
Castle Precinct	Central	117	£131.87	£68.61	10	12	92	107%	−£1.00	2
Christchurch	Central	Missing	£530.00	*£295.13*	2	5	*80*			13
St. Ewen	Central	9	£512.86	£561.00	3	2	−9	50%	−£7.00	10
St. John	Central	22	£129.37	£139.83	11	9	−7	16%	−£1.24	17
St. Leonard	Central	Missing	£123.33	*£139.25*	12	10	*−11*	Missing	Missing	12
St. Mary-le-Port	Central	Missing	£374.40	*£327.51*	4	4	*14*	Missing	Missing	11
St. Peter	Central	Missing	£152.12	*£140.78*	9	8	*8*	Missing	Missing	14
St. Werburgh	Central	10	£215.07	£184.24	6	7	17	22%	£1.35	15
St. Nicholas	Portside	61	£260.80	£345.92	5	3	−25	22%	−£3.72	8
St. Stephen	Portside	46	£180.14	£92.20	8	11	95	14%	£3.61	1
Sts. Phillip & Jacob	Suburban	120	£47.12	£16.66	17	18	183	138%	£0.69	3
St. Augustine	Suburban	Missing	£37.30	*£26.30*	18	17	*42*	Missing	Missing	4
St. James	Suburban	463	£63.10	£39.25	14	14	61	259%	−£5.40	5
St. Michael	Suburban	24	£47.64	£38.42	16	15	24	14%	£0.52	9
St. Mary Redcliff	Transpontine	11	£54.29	£31.40	15	16	73	5%	£2.50	7
St. Thomas	Transpontine	100	£182.91	£190.79	7	6	−4	52%	−£4.81	18
Temple	Transpontine	89	£83.30	£48.51	13	13	72	57%	£0.63	6
All			£106.09	£81.92			30			

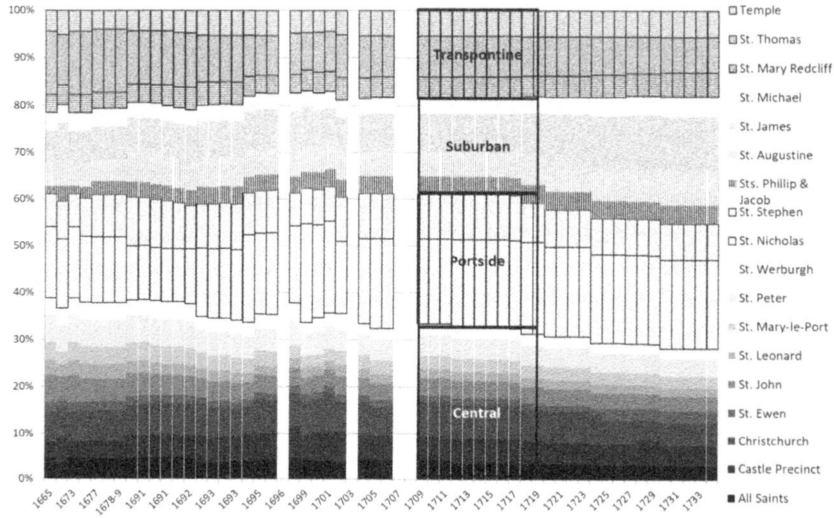

Fig. 3.13 City of Bristol. The changing shape of land tax parish quotas 1665–1734. Central, suburban, transpontine and portside divisions after Sacks (see Fig. 2.2)[379]

reasonable apportionment had taken place so that different areas would not be taxed significantly more heavily than others. Whether or not such apportionment was actually reasonable was a constant source of national complaint and debate. But such complaint allowed some degree of local process ownership and adjustment. There were also problems of arrears and non-payment. With the process of reassessment well-established, the legislation required others to make up the quota for those who did not or could not pay and this might vary from year to year depending on the success of particular businesses and trades or the general economic climate.[380]

In Bristol (Fig. 3.13), the City of London (Fig. 5.9) and Upper Scray in Kent, there was constant tinkering with local quotas during the Restoration, often on a quarterly basis. However, even in the City of London, some central wards suggest declining population into the eighteenth century and extra-mural wards some population increases.[381] Expansion in Westminster caused taxed parishes to petition Parliament about new and untaxed developments.[382] Bristol was fortunate because it could apportion its statutory quota across all City parishes and as the suburban City grew there was less of a burden on central parishes but more elsewhere (Fig. 3.13). Nevertheless, Bristol's Restoration proportion of tax raised on land increased from 70 to 80% by 1680.[383]

Kent

Tax burdens were probably heavier in Kent than London or Bristol judging from its county-wide rate of 3s-10d/£ at their 1666–1667 peak, according to assessments from New Romney and Lydd, which probably explains why the county enjoyed a quota reduction in the 1700s (Table 1.1).[384] Thomas Player's accounts for the 18-months' assessment of 1661–1663 show that the county had, despite this heavy burden, paid up its tax dues ahead of London, Berkshire, Devon, Middlesex, Southampton, Surrey, Southwark, Essex and Exeter.[385] Perhaps this was because Kent continued its effective Interregnum tax processes after the Restoration. Its tax assessments continued to show the names of landlord and tenant and the amount of rent as discussed elsewhere by this author.[386]

3.3.3 Restoration Administrative Delayering

After the 2 January 1672 Stop of the Exchequer and the unsuccessful 1671 subsidy, land taxes were redeployed, but there were significant changes. The legislation delayered tax administration by stripping out the head-collector role. This provided additional responsibilities and rewards for collectors, clerks and receivers across the nation, but impacted the case study areas in different ways. This and additional central oversight led to the reduction in the rotation of collectors and the deployment of more experienced individuals which appears to have improved amounts collected and reduced tax process times.

The Restoration saw administrative change at local and central levels. In 1667, a London Exchange Office was created,[387] later replaced by the similar Treasury's 'Agents for Taxes', with its own commissioners and solicitors.[388] These central offices had roles for chasing arrears, for exchange and for arranging transfers of physical cash to London. Chandaman believes that this had the effect of speeding delivery of cash to the Exchequer as Coleby also recognises in Hampshire in the 1670s.[389] There were also legislative changes. Restoration legislation placed much more onus on local collectors and the receiver, but also the clerk. Prior to the Restoration, high-collectors had full responsibility to extract local tax revenues from numerous parish sub-collectors to pay on to the receiver as Joshua Pix and his colleagues had done in Kent in the 1640s and 1650s. From 1661, both local collectors and their head-collectors[390] were statutorily obliged to pay money to the receiver even if the head-collectors continued as go-betweens.[391] The 1672 legislation for the 18-months' assessment of 1673–1674, after the Stop of the Exchequer, removed the head/high-collector role entirely but specified that no local collector would have to travel more than ten miles to deliver monies to the receiver. This meant the onus was now on the receiver to visit each locale which was a significant additional burden.[392] This administrative delayering created responsibilities for receiver and collector which were rewarded by increased remuneration or poundage: 1d/£ collected raised to a normal 3d/£ for collectors, and 1d raised to 2d for receivers. Nevertheless, clerks still received 1d/£. The extra resources for the receivers meant that they could deploy deputies to collect money in local boroughs and parishes whilst the receivers themselves visited London to arrange transfers of monies in specie or paper form. Could it be argued that the delayering was less significant because the head-collector's job was replaced by a deputy-receiver? This is really not the case. Responsibility for cash transfer from locale to Exchequer was now firmly with the receivers and they could organise that as they saw fit. Collectors were now directly accountable to the tax commissioners themselves not via an intermediary, and this was the crucial aspect of this delayering.

The changes may have improved process efficiency. Overall national collection rates, according to Chandaman, speeded up and increased from c.96 to c.99% (and see Fig. 1.1). This legislation remained the norm hereafter, although briefly a head-collector role was reintroduced in the period 1688–1696 but this was soon permanently abandoned in 1698.[393] The 1672 statute typically meant that the receiver or deputy would announce his attendance at a particular place, at a specified date and time on a quarterly basis, often at an inn, in Bristol or Kent, for example, and the collector was obliged to deliver *all* collected tax monies to him as thus appointed. In practice, the receiver would tell the clerk, who would be obliged to inform all the local collectors probably usually in writing of the place, date and time, for example, in the 18 Bristol parishes,[394] the 29 in Upper Scray or the 56 parishes in Wingham in Kent, and similarly for 10,000 parishes nationally.

These legislative changes also had other impacts on the ground. The tradition that men of all but the poorest means had a duty of service to the locale and the nation, witnessed in many parts of the country, meant that the roles of collector and assessor, together with the non-tax roles of constable, scavenger, secretary and the like, were often endlessly rotated.[395] Thus, collectors were often inexperienced. During the Restoration, tax was still usually assessed quarterly and collectors authorised or warranted to act only for this short period and were then replaced by others.[396] There was some exception to this in London, as quarters began to be combined around seasonal financial cycles (see Table 3.4), but normally Restoration collectors in Bristol and Kent were rotated quarterly. This was also something Braddick noted in late sixteenth- and early seventeenth-century Norfolk and Cheshire.[397] If this rotation helped men feel they had fulfilled their duty of obligation to the country, it can hardly have helped the efficiency or continuity of the tax process. It is true that rotation may have had a slight advantage in precisely identifying which payment was for which quarter, and this was a matter of importance for the Treasury and the receiver in matching payments and the debt they had secured on them. This was referred to on 5 April 1673 by Lord High Treasurer Thomas Clifford when he asked each receiver of the 18-months' assessment to make sure he was 'taking care to pay his receipts into the Exchequer by or before the days appointed by the Act, taking care that the payments on each of the six quarters be kept distinct and the tallies struck accordingly'.[398] A greater concern was the speed of collection itself, and the administrative delayering inspired different developments in Bristol and Kent on one hand and in London on the other.

In Bristol, there was a sharp lessening of the quarterly rotation of petty officials, and this was not only true of the paid collectors, but particularly of unpaid assessors (Table 3.5). There is some indication that this meant that the assessor and collector roles became increasingly confined to the better-off taxpayers, or at least those who lived more commonly in accommodation with higher annual taxed rent. In newly developed Castle Precinct, the officials' monthly tax mean in the 1660s was £0.188[399] which was only slightly more than the all taxpayer mean of £0.155 compared with the 1690s figures of £0.94 and £0.50, respectively.[400] In St. James parish, the 1660s[401] differences were greater at £0.182 and £0.078, and this was only slightly less than that

Table 3.4 City of London, showing cases where the normal quarterly basis of assessment did not apply. Two or more quarters might be amalgamated and one set of named collectors was responsible for the whole period. The table shows only the major statutes[402]

Legislation		*12 Car. II, c. 27, 6 months' Assessment, 1661. SoR, vol. 5, pp. 269–277*	*13 Car. II, St. 2, c. 3, 18 months' Assessment, 1661–1663. SoR, vol. 5, pp. 325–348*	*Royal Aid 1664–1667 [16 & 17 Car. II, c. 1] and Additional Aid [17 Car. II, c. 1]*	*18 & 19 Car. II, c. 13, 11 months' Assessment, 1668. SoR, vol. 5, pp. 616–623s*	*18 & 19 Car. II, c. 13, 11 months' Assessment, 1668. SoR, vol. 5, pp. 616–623*	*29 Car. II, c. 1, 17 months' Assessment, 1677–1678. SoR, vol. 5, pp. 802–836*	*30 Car. II, c. 1, 18 months' Assessment, 1678–1680. SoR, vol. 5, pp. 867–883*	*31 Car. II, c. 1, 6 months' Assessment, 1680. SoR, vol. 5, pp. 897–934*
Assessments under the Act	1	Q1 & 2	Q1	Q1 & 2	1st 5 months	Q1	Q1	Q1 & 2	Q1
	2		Q2	Q3 & 4	Last 6 months	Q2 & 3	Q2	Q3 & 4	Q2
	3		Q3 & Q4	Q5 & 6		Q4	Q3	Q5 & 6	
	4		Q5 & 6	Q 7, 8 & 9		Q5	Q4		
	5			Q10 & 11		Q6	Last 5 months		
	6			Q12 & arrears					

for the 1690s at £0.61 and £0.25, respectively. Brooks recognised similar reduced rotation of officials after 1674 in Southampton.[403]

Less-marked reduction in the rotational of officials is visible in Kent, and there is no evidence in the City of London during the Restoration.[404] In London, it was the assessors, who frequently remained in post for numerous quarters and for various taxes, and provided a backbone of experience for the tax process. But this stability predated the Restoration.

Table 3.5 City of Bristol. Restoration continuity of collectors and assessors where individuals named were the same as the previous quarter[405]

City districts	*Mean collector continuity pre 1671 (%)*	*Mean collector continuity post 1671 (%)*	*Mean assessor continuity pre 1671 (%)*	*Mean assessor continuity post 1671 (%)*
Centre	5	28	6	73
Portside	9	13	0	65
Suburban	6	6	7	72
Transpontine	22	30	4	72
Total	**16**	**21**	**5**	**72**

London was different from both Kent and Bristol, and indeed most of the rest of the country, because payments could be made at any time to the chamberlain's office at the City Guildhall, not only at an appointed time when the receiver was in town. Thus, Archibald Townson and John Sands, collectors for both the fifth and sixth quarters of the Royal Aid and Additional Aid in Vintry Ward, according to their warrant dated 26 July 1666, had to 'collect and gather according to the monthly tax on sumes of money before expenses from tyme to tyme after receipt thereof & to pay the same severally to Mr William Avery [Head Collector] att the office of Sir Thomas Player kn[igh]t, Chamberlaine of the Citty'.[406] Thus, there was no specific payment date other than the statutory deadline. Except for that collectors could pay from time to time as they saw fit. The pre-1672 head-collectors had no specific role in the City. Whereas they probably still had to travel from parish to parish in Kent to gather local tax monies, in London William Avery worked in the same place as the receiver. Kent collectors were paid 1d/£ poundage, but presumably so was Avery. It may have been good grounding, however, because he went on to become Town Clerk in November that same year and tax commissioners' clerk.

In London, the 1670s legislation changes described had minimal impact on the tax process itself. There was almost identical language on the City warrant for Robert More and Robert Wright in Barrs precinct in Portsoken Ward, dated 23 May 1673 for the first quarter of the 18-months' assessment of 1673–1674.[407] They would pay from 'time to time' in accordance only with 'the tyme lymited by the s[ai]d Act', or by 3 June in this case and they were thus encouraged to act 'with all possible speed'.[408] Therefore, whereas in most parts of the country, collectors received increased poundage for the additional responsibility of directly delivering gathered taxes to the receiver on a fixed date and at a fixed place, there was no material extra responsibility in London. Here, the pattern of collector rotation continued as it always had done, probably since the inception of land taxes. Based on 329 City assessments bearing collectors' names, there were 865 Restoration collectors, but only 20 appear more than once.[409] These exceptions almost entirely occur in two wards where there were government offices and where state employees were taxed and perhaps more specialist knowledge or greater consistency was required. Thus, in the St. Dunstan-in-the-West precinct of Farringdon Without Ward, Danyell Langley and Robert Olarentia were repeat 1660s collectors for government offices in The Strand.

Nevertheless, there was change in London too. Some process simplification had already taken place in 1660s London as multiple quarters often appeared on these assessments with one team of collectors. This seems to be connected to the twice yearly financial cycles around Lady Day and Michaelmas discussed in Sect. 5.1. For example, for the 36 months of the Royal Aid of the 1660s, there were only six assessments and not the normal twelve (Table 3.4) and therefore only six teams of collectors.[410] St. Dunstan-in-the-West, Farringdon Without, with a continuous run of tax assessments naming collectors between 1658 and 1671, provides a useful example for further analysis.[411] St. Dunstan-in-the-West had three sub-precincts and sometimes an extra team of collectors solely handling the government offices in The Strand mentioned above. Collection was almost always by a pair of collectors in each precinct. Here, there are 141 named individuals: 114 individuals collected only once; 23 performed twice, mostly back-to-back where the City had amalgamated quarters (Table 3.4); three appear thrice; and one, four times.[412] This high rotation of local administrative burdens is familiar

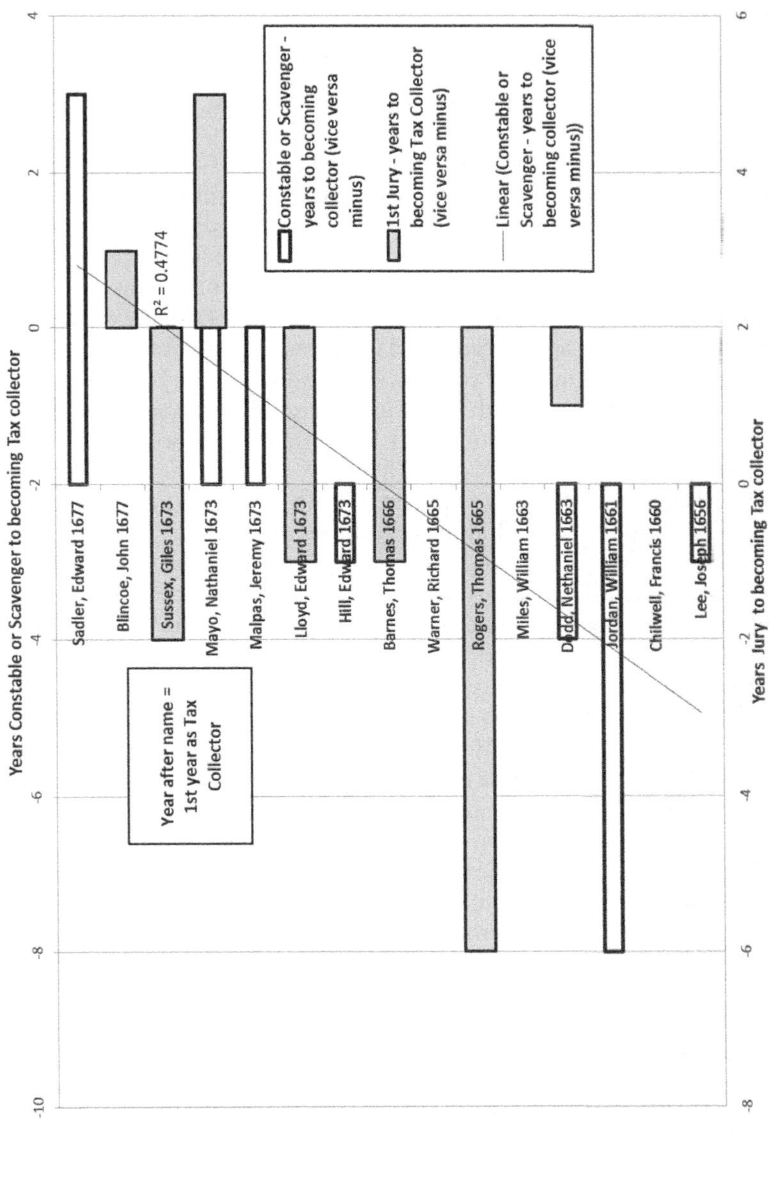

Fig. 3.14 Restoration tax-collectors in Bassishaw Ward showing that over time more experienced individuals from the wardmote became tax-collectors[413]

from Boulton's description of members of the seventeenth-century Southwark community who willingly participated in local government by taking on a variety of parish and ward roles, both unpaid and paid.[414]

Wards and precincts usually nominated one or two Restoration collectors per round, occasionally more. Sometimes, it is clear that one collector was senior to the other. For example, the Cordwainer Ward assessment for the first and second quarters of the 1678–1679, 18-months' assessment, nominates Anthony Greene and Owen Crafts as collectors,[415] but assessors were asked to 'hand the Roll to Crafts' who was presumably senior and responsible for keeping accurate records.[416] Of the 865 named collectors, at least 146 were identified as to their business including nine victuallers, eight drapers, seven cheesemongers, six merchants and five apothecaries. Many seem to have been involved in food, brewing, clothing and small-scale manufacturing, but the range was wide. Such individuals with commercial experience may have been ideally placed as collectors, because they knew their neighbours and were used to handling cash.[417]

City of London collection was not static as Bassishaw evidence demonstrates. Bassishaw's middling-sort of men had served in local government on the Wardmote Inquest long before mid-seventeenth-century records begin and throughout the eighteenth century.[418] Wardmote juries were at the core of governance by hearing and resolving local issues. Individuals often served for decades, normally on a three-year rolling basis (one year on followed by two years off).[419] Most male heads of household were expected to and were willing to perform additional ward duties such as constable and moved from such junior roles to more senior ones. The very wealthiest men were often exempted, as they functioned at a higher level within and beyond the City, as were all women (even though they made up around 15% of household heads), and the poorest, many of whom did not pay tax anyway.[420] Unlike most ward roles, tax-collectors were chosen by common councilmen directly and not at the wardmote.[421] Nevertheless, it is valuable to compare the collector role with roles chosen there. In Bassishaw, tax collection in the 1660s was a junior role where little prior ward experience was evident or required. It was one of the earliest civic duties individuals could perform, on average, slightly earlier than those other junior roles chosen by the wardmote, constable and scavenger.[422] Like these latter roles, individuals often became tax-collectors before they ever served on the wardmote jury or just after their first appearance. Two of Bassishaw's earliest

Restoration tax-collectors, Francis Chilwell and William Miles, had little prior experience and had never served on the jury. Things were changing. Before the 1672 Act, collectors normally had little or no prior wardmote experience, afterwards most were seasoned individuals (Fig. 3.14). The role of collector had thus changed from being one of the most junior to being one of the most senior ward posts in the space of just a few years. Increased experience continued to be important after the Glorious Revolution and the rotation of collectors sharply decreased as the job became not an obligation for one or two collections rounds, but a calling for years and decades as the City developed a highly experienced cadre of these and other officials.

If the frequent rotation of Restoration collectors persisted in London, longer than Bristol or Kent, they were clearly more experienced men. The development of bodies of officials at all levels in the tax process, with years and even decades of experience, was a strong feature in all three case study locations suggesting real commitment to delivering the state's supply. In London, the more senior roles of common councilman, deputy and alderman and of course tax commissioner were usually only accessible to those who had served on the wardmote for years. On average, Bassishaw individuals became tax assessors (ten individuals) six years after their first wardmote, and for commissioners it was sixteen years (three individuals).[423]

The City of London Chamberlain's office at Guildhall, usually the receiver's office as well, developed standard forms of tax accounting under the mid-century reigns of the Sir Thomas Players, father and son. At ward level, there were modest improved turnaround times during the Restoration for assessment completion reducing from a mean 51 days to 38 days.[424] If officials in the prosperous central wards were rather prompter than those in poorer extra-mural or riverside wards, it may have had more to do with the size, mobility and mortality of the taxpayer population than assessor efficiency. The chamberlain's front office accounting function was supported by the town clerk's back office activities, and town clerks always acted as commissioners' clerks, including Sir John Weld (1660–1666), William Avery (1666–1672) and William Wagstaffe (9 February 1672–1690) . There is evidence of Wagstaffe's effective involvement in the tax process in checking assessments. For example, he found several mistakes 'in casting up the Booke' in the 18-months' assessments for 1673–1674, but these were often of a relatively minor nature suggesting keen scrutiny.[425] He asked the commissioners to 'rectify the Duplicate accordingly'. In his letter to the ward commissioners dated 15 September 1674 regarding the sixth quarterly assessment, he complained of overrating in Cheap Ward for Honey Lane Market as being 'too high & unreasonable and raised tene shillings p[er] month above their proportion'.[426] The letter went on to demand the sum 'bee reduced & abated … unlesse the said assessors shall show good cause to the contrary on Thursday next'.[427] Less is known of accounting in Bristol and Kent, but the documents suggest well-organised administration and regular processes.

The interregnum and Civil War period witnessed new land tax processes developed in many parts of the country including the three case studies with a focus on taxing land and rent with sums to be gathered from a broad base of occupiers. Local governors were freshly empowered or dismissed if their loyalty was in question. Activities and actions could be coordinated across counties and indeed across the country as commissioners sought to commence by the inaugural date set by Parliament. The Restoration saw further important developments in London, Bristol, Kent and across the nation. London's tax administration proved most resilient despite fire and plague. Record amounts of direct taxation were reliably delivered to the Exchequer from across the nation through processes of improved oversight, enhanced financial transfer facilities including paper transactions, and better rewarded and more experienced officials. If local responses varied somewhat, then the result was the same, nearly all the tax demanded was paid up to the centre. These remarkable results contrasted with the ancient taxes such as the subsidy which continued to fail and newer levies such as the hearth tax which could never produce more than a modest supply.

Notes

1. Sources: KHLC: NR/RTi1, New Romney; KHLC: Ly/9/2/1-2, Lydd; TNA: SP/28/157-160, Commonwealth Exchequer Papers—numerous assessments; TNA: E179/128/685, Iwade. Base map: English: Administrative map of the ancient county of Kent in 1832. Showing Lathes, Hundreds, Boroughs and the County of Itself of Canterbury. Source data on parish boundaries—Kain, R.J.P. and Oliver, R.R. (2001), 'Historic Parishes of England and Wales: Electronic Map—Gazetteer—Metadata', Colchester: History Data Service. ISBN 0 9540032 0 9. Source data for Boroughs: H.M.S.O. Boundary Commission Report

1832 (courtesy of www.visionofbritain.org). Date: 9 March 2013, 12:21:46; Source: Own work, Author, XrysD. This file is licensed under the Creative Commons Attribution-Share Alike 3.0 Unported license.

2. TNA: SP 28 Commonwealth Exchequer Papers Various.
3. Ormrod et al., 'City and Countryside Revisited'.
4. D.M. Livock (ed.), *City Chamberlain's Accounts in the Sixteenth and Seventeenth Centuries* (Bristol: Bristol Record Society Publications XXIV, 1966), pp. xv–xvi, shows a 39% increase in income from the City's own lands between 1556/1557 and 1627/1628. The further increase to 1693 BRO: F/AU/1/62 is a much more modest 14% if the new developments in the marsh and Castle Precinct are removed.
5. References in, e.g. Ormrod et al., '*City and Countryside Revisited*'; Derek Keene, 'A New Study of London Before the Great Fire', *Urban History Yearbook* (1984), pp. 15–16.
6. But see Neil Cummins, Morgan Kelly, and Cormac Ó Gráda, 'Living Standards and Plague in London, 1560–1665', *Economic History Review*, vol. 69, 2016, pp. 3–34. The authors show that this was very variable and in richer central areas this reversed in non-plague years.
7. Derek Keene, 'Changes in London's Economic Hinterland as Indicated by Debt Cases in the Court of Common Pleas', in James A. Galloway, *Trade, Urban Hinterlands and Market Integration c. 1300–1600* (London: Centre for Metropolitan History Working Papers Series No. 3, 2000), pp. 59–81; Ormrod et al., 'City and Countryside Revisited', Tables 2 and 3.
8. Quoted in Christopher Brooks, 'The Agrarian Problem in Revolutionary England', p. 185; Whittle, *Landlords and Tenants in Britain, 1440–1660*, pp. 183–199; HEHL Hastings Manuscripts Box 26/19. See also HoP.
9. Richard Hoyle, 'Tenure and the Land Market in Early Modern England: Or a Late Contribution to the Brenner Debate', *Economic History Review*, vol. 43, 1990, pp. 1–20, 14.
10. Shaw-Taylor, 'The Rise of Agrarian Capitalism', p. 32 and abstract, summarises the debate. He points to a number of studies which found high tenancy rates before 1700 particularly in the South and East which 'suggest the dominance of agrarian capitalism at the end of the seventeenth and the opening of the eighteenth century' based on the ratio of farmers to farm workers from sources, 1697–1720 (p. 52). See also Robert C. Allen, *Enclosure and the Yeoman* (Oxford: Clarendon Press, 1992), p. 21 who sees a slightly different pattern of change to large farms and has a different view as to what constitutes a large farm.
11. Shaw-Taylor, 'The Rise of Agrarian Capitalism', p. 45.

12. No exhaustive search of the Commonwealth Exchequer Papers has been carried out, but there are also two assessments from Surrey of this form in TNA: SP 28/200 f60.
13. Sources: TNA: SP 24 Committee and Commissioners for Indemnity: Books and Papers 1647–1656. See also Braddick, *Parliamentary Taxation*, pp. 151–158. He cites 329 disputes between landlord and tenant over tax liability, but only a few of these can be identified as to location.
14. For example, TNA: SP 28/163 pt.11 has an account or outturn statement from St. Giles in the Fields, Holborn dated 18 September 1645 showing 'landlords' and 'goods' in respect of a September 1643 ordinance and another for the First Weekly Assessment from St. Clement Danes showing 'Tennants rated according to their rent' and 'for their goods'.
15. February 1643: First Weekly Assessment, A&O, pp. 85–100.
16. Evidence from New Romney assessments, KHLC: NR/RTa27 6 April 1980. The landlord/tenant ratio was 5:1.
17. 'February 1645: An Ordinance of the Lords and Commons assembled in Parliament, for the raising and levying of the Monthly Sum of One and Twenty Thousand Pounds, towards the Maintenance of the Scotish Army under the Command of the Ear[l] of Leven, by a Monthly Assessment upon the severa[l] Counties, Cities, and Towns, of the Kingdom of England therein mentioned', A&O, pp. 630–646.
18. Ormrod et al., 'City and Countryside Revisited'.
19. The term 'rent-tax' was current in Kent by the mid-1640s and 'land-tax' appeared in legislation in the 1650s and was used by Petty in the 1660s (William Petty, *A Treatise of Taxes & Contributions*). TNA: SP 28/158, part 3, Newnham warrant previously discussed.
20. Braddick, Parliamentary Taxation, p. 150, 'far from a radical departure' from earlier levies and was bedevilled by post-Restoration 'inertia' although he recognises some innovation.
21. Chandaman, *The English Public Revenue*, p. 141 and the assessment's success was more due to fixed quotas and protracted periods of application.
22. As suggested by Davison, *The Agrarian Economy of Romney Marsh*, based on contemporary observations in 1734; also Ginter, *A Measure of Wealth*, p. 17; the ordinance for a 6-months' assessment from 25 December 1653, EEBO, Thomason.158: E.1062[28] states that commissioners must give 'publique notice… to the Inhabitants of such parish or place, to the end that the people concerned therein may be acquainted therewith …' [Printed in 1653].
23. Sources: TNA: SP 28/157-160 & 234.
24. If so, the model was never rolled out nationally.

25. As is well established from, e.g. Grover, 'Early Land Tax Assessments Explored', p. 213ff and more widely; Mingay, 'The Land Tax Assessments and the Small Landowner'; Ginter, *A Measure of Wealth*.
26. The correlation coefficient of two arrays of numbers was calculated using the CORREL function of Microsoft Excel for St. Augustine Lathe, West (24 parishes), and St. Augustine Lathe, East (54 parishes), sub-lathes to two decimal places for 1673 of 0.86 and 0.89, respectively. Good correlations can be seen elsewhere. The figure for Rutland in 1712 by similar calculation is 0.64 with 56 entities (parishes and villages) based on Table 6 in T.H. McK Clough (ed.), *The 1712 Land Tax Assessments and the 1710 Poll Book for Rutland* (Rutland: RLHRS Occasional Publication No. 7, 2005). In one parish, Brooke, ibid., p. 22, acreage was used as a Land Tax measure.
27. Mingay, 'The Land Tax Assessments and the Small Landowner'; Martin, 'Landownership and the Land Tax Returns'; Grigg, 'The Land Tax Returns'; and Ginter, *A Measure of Wealth*, p. 270ff, Chapter 6 and p. 114. Martin saw a close correlation between land tax and acreage in late eighteenth-century Warwickshire. Mingay saw no such correlation in Nottinghamshire for a similar period.
28. Beckett, 'Local Custom and the "New Taxation"'.
29. 'Usual' in the legislation.
30. Note the 1671 subsidy employed assessment methodology. The correlation coefficient of the two arrays of numbers was calculated using the CORREL function of Microsoft Excel for 27 Upper Scray parishes rounded to two decimal places. Kent Archaeological Society database of individuals, http://www.kentarchaeology.org.uk. Two parishes listed in assessments, but not wholly within Upper Scray, Headcorn and Stockbury, have been excluded from calculations because acreage figures are not available. There are concerns about the detailed accuracy of VCH figures, therefore, this analysis should be considered as indicative only, e.g. Ginter, *A Measure of Wealth*, p. 270*ff.*
31. Following Ormrod et al., *City and Countryside Revisited*, p. 10, rack-rents did not necessarily reflect productivity.
32. *Agricultural Rent*, pp. 19–26.
33. See, e.g. Everitt, *The Community of Kent*, p. 160.
34. For example, February 1645: Fairfax Army, A&O, pp. 614–626.
35. It remained so hereafter, e.g. (1) Iwade. TNA: E179/128/685; (2) St. Mary Cray. TNA: E179/249/18; (3) Snodland. TNA: E179/128/682; (4) New Romney. KHLC: NR/RTi1 12 July 1648 and run of assessments after 1662 KHLC: NR/RTa9-28; (5) Lydd. KHLC: Ly/9/3/3-15 and KHLC: NR/ZLy1; (6) Various TNA: SP 28/157-60.

36. The only significant exceptions are small parishes. See Grover, 'Early Land Tax assessments Explored', Table 2, p. 206, which has figures from St. Augustine Lathe, East.
37. Separate landlord and tenant columns were also present in neighbouring Sussex (Grover, 'Early Land Tax Assessments Explored', Table 2, p. 206) but see Ginter, *A Measure of Wealth*, p. 135 states that 'in most wapentakes of Yorkshire, and probably in most counties of England, rents were not commonly reported on the land tax duplicates until the later 1820s'.
38. For example, Surrey: several references in TNA: SP 28/152 & 245; Buckinghamshire: TNA: SP 28/220.
39. For example, the 6-months' assessment from 25 December 1654 was the '10d tax', TNA: E179/128/678.
40. Several subsidy rolls can be perused at TNA, but none contain any evidence of use of such forms, e.g. TNA: E179/128/609, August 1628; TNA: E179/128/618, April 1629; TNA: E179/127/547, ? February 1610.
41. Davison, *The Agrarian Economy of Romney Marsh*, e.g. for 'scots' pp. 5–6. She states the method was established at least by the thirteenth century and was known as 'the Laws and Customs of Romney Marsh'. Acreage did not only apply to scots, but was, for example, used as a means of assessing for the cost of the Cinque Port Charter in 1634, KHLC: Sa/RTz4.
42. Cannan, *The History of Local Rates*, p. 85.
43. This is assumed to be those assessments where the names of landlord and tenant are different. Commonwealth Exchequer Papers, TNA: SP 28/157–160.
44. Ginter, *A Measure of Wealth*. Because of the complexity of land ownership which might, for example, include sub-tenancies, tenants and ultimate owners, the 'landlord' on the face of the assessments could be the owner or tenant.
45. 'February 1645: An Ordinance of the Lords and Commons assembled in Parliament, for the raising and levying of the Monthly Sum of One and Twenty Thousand Pounds, towards the Maintenance of the Scotish Army under the Command of the Ear[l] of Leven, by a Monthly Assessment upon the severa[l] Counties, Cities, and Towns, of the Kingdom of England therein mentioned', A&O, pp. 630–646.
46. This is the same proportion as levied for Dutch land taxes. Fritschy, personal email communication 27 February 2018.
47. Evidence from Kent and Surrey shows Interregnum and Restoration tenants often retained some modest proportion of the charge on 'stock-in-crop', or stock-in-trade, e.g. in New Romney KHLC: NR/RTa1-27.
48. The precise apportionment varied slightly over time. Rates were set, for example: the 20d tax, 12d tax, 15d tax and so on.

49. TNA: E179/128/685, f7.
50. The earliest pre-printed London warrants are dated July 1645. This includes one from Islington and two from Middlesex dated 10 July 1645 (TNA: SP 28/169/pt.2 and pt.3) and LMA: COL/CHD/LA/O3/017/008 [Land Tax and Subsidies (8 Wm III c.6) Commissioners' certificates of payment by individuals of the amount assessed on them, 1697] has several for 1690s London.
51. Very many receipts survive as early as the 1640s in Kent. Thomas Catlett's receipt of 1 April 1656 was a typical example, TNA: E179/128/685/f92. Taxpayer receipts only occasionally survive. One from the Duchy of Lancaster in Middlesex was signed by Sir Edward Barkham and Sir William Roberts on 25 July 1645. TNA: SP 28/170. By comparison, there is one from Cambridgeshire dated 16 October 1644 (TNA: SP 28/152).
52. Commissioners named in ordinances in A&O have been compared with HoP, Brunton and Pennington, *Members of the Long Parliament*, and other sources.
53. The assessment has 46 taxed amounts and 26 different Landlords. Subsidy estimates from TNA: E179/128/609 Subsidy 22 August 1628 and TNA: E179/128/648 December 1640.
54. Thirsk and Cooper, *Seventeenth-Century Economic Documents*, p. 618, based on TNA: SP16/376, no. 104, 'Totals for the Counties 1636/7'. The figure here was an annual charge of £8,000.
55. Langelüddecke, '"*I finde all Men*"', Tables A6, p. 542. The respective national figures for comparison are 87% (1637), 80% (1638), and 21% (1639).
56. Sums levied were smaller in some years, for example, only £2,750 for 1638.
57. BRO: F/Tax/M1 & 2, 'The Subsidy Booke for Bristol' 1663.
58. BRO: F/Tax/2. Various parishes with estimates for missing parishes.
59. BRO: F/Tax/M/1. The goods figure in the 1663–1664 subsidy assessment appears to be used for the Royal Aid. Thus Robert Clifford (St. Ewen) was charged 16s-8d on Goods for two subsidies and 1s-4d per month in the Royal Aid or 1s-4d × 12 = 16s. The total subsidy value taxed was £526.13 on a property value of £1,999.50. This was for two subsidies at a rate of 2s-8d × 2. This compares with the £1,348.63 for the non-traditional subsidy of 1671, the annual charge for the Royal Aid and Additional Aid of £4,203.91 and £7,391.53 for the 1704 land tax at a 4s rate. There is a stark change from the subsidy of 1663–1664 where most of the 500 individuals paid a few shillings each to 1704 where over 3,500 taxpayers paid c. £2 each.

60. Henry Bush, *Bristol Town Duties: A Collection of Original and Interesting Documents* (Bristol, 1828), British History Online, http://www.british-history.ac.uk/no-series/bristol-duties.
61. Archer, 'The Burden of Taxation on Sixteenth-Century London'.
62. 'The City of Westminster with the liberties thereof, and all the parishes and houses which are now within the weekly Bill of Mortality, within the County of Middlesex' according to the February 1643, First Weekly Assessment, A&O, pp. 85–100.
63. Most of the material for this period was from accounts produced after the assessment was made, rather than the assessments themselves, but almost all those cited here were set out like an assessment. Some contain separate lists of non-payers and the reasons for non-payment. The surviving assessments from this early period, where they do exist, are often in poor condition and difficult to decipher.
64. A divided parish part within and without the City.
65. A divided parish part within and without the City.
66. Various accounts: TNA: SP 28/162–170. London, Middlesex, and metropolitan London: St. Clement Danes (TNA: 28/163—two accounts including one for the First Weekly Assessment); St. Giles in the Fields, Holborn (TNA: 28/163; three accounts); St. Margaret's Westminster (TNA: SP 28/162 and 165; two accounts); St. Martin-in-the-Fields (TNA: SP 28/164 and 165; eight accounts); St. Andrew Parish, High Holborn (TNA: SP 28/167—five accounts including the First Weekly Assessment); and St. Sepulchre, Middlesex (TNA: SP 28/163).
67. Chelsea, Middlesex (TNA: SP 28/163).
68. St. James Clerkenwell (TNA: SP 28/167; four assessments); Duchy of Lancaster, The Strand, Middle and Savoy wards (TNA: SP 28/165; two accounts); Hampstead, Middlesex (TNA: SP 28/165; 2 accounts); Islington, Middlesex (TNA: SP 28/167 & 169, two accounts); High Holborn (TNA: SP 28/170); Hendon, Middlesex (TNA: 28/162, 1 assessment).
69. They have two columns, one for the taxpayer and the other for the tax amount.
70. Willesden, Middlesex (TNA: 28/169, one assessment 1644); St. Pancras, Middlesex (TNA: 28/167, one assessment 1643); St. Giles without Cripplegate (TNA: 28/170, one assessment); Islington, Middlesex (TNA: 28/165-169); Lordship of Finsbury (TNA: SP 28/170). Those that did not: St. Giles without Cripplegate (TNA: 28/162, five assessments); Paddington, Middlesex (TNA: 28/167, four assessments); 'Old Brentford' (TNA: 28/162, one assessment); and Hornsey, Middlesex (TNA: 28/165).
71. Sources checked: TNA: SP 28/162-170, London, Middlesex and metropolitan London; E179 database; LMA: searches.

72. An approximation from the London subsidy rolls, two documents give the names of 3,433 residents of London valued and assessed for the subsidy in 1541 and 5,900 in 1582 listed by ward and parish and supported by Bassishaw evidence. 'Introduction', in R.G. Lang (ed.), *Two Tudor Subsidy Rolls for the City of London, 1541 and 1582* (London, 1993), pp. xv–lxxvii. British History Online, http://www.british-history.ac.uk/london-record-soc/vol29/xv-lxxvii.
73. Sources: The Bassishaw Record and Assessment Book. LMA: P69/MIC1/B/006/MS03505.
74. John T. Evans, *Seventeenth-Century Norwich: Politics, Religion and Government, 1620–1690* (Oxford: Clarendon Press, 1979), who also notes that 'Only a minority of the inhabitants were obligated to contribute even to the most minor taxes, such as the poor rate and the collection for the river and streets' pp. 14–15.
75. It is worth noting that ward inhabitants in assessing ship money pledged loyalty to the king in their assessment book by noting the legality of the legislation LMA: P69/MIC1/B/006/MS03505, 'May it please your most excellent Majesty' and signed by 12 prominent citizens. The 1638 Inhabitants list is very similar in terms of names and order (although the order was reversed) to the Bassishaw assessments for ship money. Unfortunately, the 1638 ship money list is damaged, but that for 1636 is clear and complete.
76. Thomas Cyril Dale, *The Inhabitants of London in 1638* (London: Centre for Metropolitan History, 1931). British History Online, http://www.british-history.ac.uk/no-series/london-inhabitants/1638/.
77. The contemporary 1638 Bassishaw ship money roll appears incomplete and has not been used here.
78. 79 out of the 117 ship money names can be matched with a high degree of confidence with the 1638 tithes list. Deviant spellings have been accepted. Most of the remaining variation and omissions can probably be explained by inhabitants moving away or by death. The latter may explain why there is a John Dunn on the tithes list, but George Dunn appears on the ship money roll, Thomas Harrison appears on the 1638 tithes, but John Harrison on the ship money roll.
79. The correlation coefficient of two arrays of numbers was calculated using the CORREL function of Microsoft Excel with 117 cases rounded to two decimal places. The same calculation for the 1638 (possibly incomplete ship money assessment) correlates with the 1638 tithes less well and is based on only 57 cases. The correlation coefficient=0.61 rounded to two decimal places.
80. If so, a two-shilling/pound rate on rent is the best fit with the 1638 rents, but a three-shilling rate is possible. The ship money distribution may suggest a three-shilling rate because two-thirds of the numbers

are at three-shilling intervals. The resulting volatility and uneven distribution suggest both broad estimation at work and other measures of wealth in play.

81. Sources: The Bassishaw Record and Assessment Book. LMA: P69/MIC1/B/006/MS0350 and TNA: E179/314/27—summary City of London account.
82. TNA: SP 28/162/pt.1.
83. TNA: SP 28/169/pt.2.
84. These were traditional exemptions from the subsidy, but not the early assessments.
85. It appears to be tenants rather than tenements.
86. Sources: The Bassishaw Record and Assessment Book, LMA: P69/MIC1/B/006/MS03505. Data include estimates where sources are incomplete. Note the hugely increased 1640s burden created by the assessment.
87. At £10,000 per week for 12 weeks according to the February 1643, First Weekly Assessment, A&O, pp. 85–100.
88. TNA: 28/170, Mr Collins' book 'Collectors of the Weekly Assessment', has £114,576-2-10d as the total, but there are some arithmetical errors here. The figure quoted above is the totals from each ward as given in this book.
89. 'August 1643: An Ordinance for the speedy Raising and Levying of Money, for the Maintenance of the Army raised by the Parliament, and other great Affairs of the Commonwealth', A&O, pp. 223–241.
90. According to TNA: 28/170, Mr Collins' book. Ben Coates, *The Impact of the English Civil War on the Economy of London, 1642–50* (Farnham, Surrey: Ashgate, 2004), Table 2.1, p. 51, has possibly £157,997 raised in the City in c. 1643–1644 from the Twentieth part and the First Weekly Assessment, and £513,867 in total up to December 1650 or c. £64,000 per year in direct taxes.
91. The Bassishaw Record and Assessment Book, LMA: P69/MIC1/B/006/MS03505. The first surviving post-1643 assessment in the Bassishaw tax book dates from March 1644, but this was an unusual levy for a 'weekly meal', but the first major assessment followed soon afterwards also in 'March 1644: An Ordinance for the speedy compleating and maintaining of the Army under the immediate Command of Robert Earle of Essex, Lord Generall of the Forces raised by the Parliament', A&O, pp. 398–405.
92. The legislative City quota was £5,485.74 and Bassishaw was allocated 1.2% of this.
93. 'Tenants to pay rates and deduct Landlord's share from rent' according to March 1644: Earl of Essex Army, pp. 398–405.

94. 'May 1643: An Ordinance for the speedy raising and levying of money thorowout the whole Kingdome of England, and dominion of Wales for the relief of the Common-wealth, by taxing such as have not at all contributed or lent, or not according to their Estates and Abilities', A&O, pp. 145–155.
95. The correlation coefficient of two arrays of numbers was calculated using the CORREL function of Microsoft Excel = 0.37 rounded to 2 decimal places for 31 cases.
96. The Bassishaw Record and Assessment Book, LMA: P69/MIC1/B/006/MS03505.
97. Sources: TNA: SP 28/162-170 and TNA/E179/147/607; TNA/E179/147/602; TNA: E179/147/601; there are 20 examples from the following Wards: Dowgate, Tower, Coleman Street, Farringdon Without (Smithfield, St. Martin Ludgate, Whitefriars, St. Andrew Holborn), Vintry, Cheap (St. Mary-le-Bow), Portsoken (Houndsditch[2]), Walbrook, Aldgate (2), Cornhill (4), Langbourn and Cripplegate Without. There are additional assessments which are not sufficiently legible to make any calculations.
98. They average from 60 accounts examined for Westminster and Middlesex is c. 68%, but as these are accounts rather than assessments, this figure should be treated with caution. A 1643 account book for the 5 September 1643 assessment for arms in Westminster and Middlesex (TNA: E179/253/12) for similar parishes gives a figure of 63%.
99. TNA: SP 28/162-170; February 1645: Scottish Army, A&O, pp. 630–646. There are some surviving assessments for this period, but their condition is poor and they are difficult to decipher in the TNA: E179 series comprising many cases for the February 1645, 21 monthly assessment for the Scottish army. E179/147/576, 579-616; E179/252/16-17.
100. Counts based on: Restoration, LMA: COL/CHD/LA/03/various; 1640s, TNA: SP 28/162–170.
101. It is situated outside the City walls to the East.
102. Evans, *Seventeenth-Century Norwich*, especially Table 21 and 22 on pp. 147–148.
103. (1) 'December 1644: An Ordinance for bringing in the Areares of the Monethly Assessment, formerly charged upon the Cities of London and Westminster, and all other Parishes and places within the Lines of Communication and County of Middlesex', A&O, pp. 580–582; (2) 'June 1645: An Ordinance for the more speedy getting in of the Moneys in Arrear, formerly Imposed upon the Bill of Four hundred thousand pounds; the Ordinances for the Fifty Subsidies, Weekly Assessment, and weekly Meal, within the City of London and

Liberties thereof', A&O, pp. 697–700; (3) 'July 1645: An Ordinance for the Leavying and Collecting of Money in Arrear in the County of Middlesex, and Cities of London and Westminster, Borough of Southwark and places adjacent', A&O, pp. 736–738.

104. HOLJ, vol. 7, 12 June 1645, p. 427.
105. Ward quotas were already calculated on a monthly not weekly basis by December 1644. 'December 1644: An Ordinance for the Raising of Money to pay the Charge of the Fortifications and Guards, and for other necessary uses', A&O, pp. 574–578.
106. TNA: E101/67/11A.
107. Friday and Saturday were favoured payment dates. On average, precincts made payments once per quarter for the Restoration Royal Aid.
108. The 1645 payments for the fifth, sixth and seventh months [June–August] of the earlier ordinance were to be paid directly by collectors to these Treasurers and if that was not enough then moneys from the eighth, ninth and tenth months [September-November] and if necessary for further months beyond that. See February 1645, Fairfax Army, A&O, pp. 614–626. Even if November was the last month in the original ordinance, there was a further extension for six months and the Treasurers continued to receive amounts of arrears up until 1652.
109. In terms of collection, the poorest performing were the extra-mural and riverside wards with lower average rents.
110. 'June 1645: An Ordinance for the more speedy getting in of the Moneys in Arrear, formerly Imposed upon the Bill of Four hundred thousand pounds; the Ordinances for the Fifty Subsidies, weekly Assessment, and weekly Meal, within the City of London and Liberties thereof', A&O, pp. 697–700.
111. Coates, *The Impact of the English Civil War*, p. 27. 'July 1645: An Ordinance for the Leavying and Collecting of Money in Arrear in the County of Middlesex, and Cities of London and Westminster, Borough of Southwark and places adjacent', A&O, pp. 736–738.
112. John Lilburne, *England's Birth-Right Justified*, in Coates, *The Impact of the English Civil War* (2004), p. 28.
113. (1) 'April 1648: An Ordinance for the speedy bringing in the Arreares of the Assessements in the City of London and Liberties thereof', A&O, pp. 1128–1131; (2) 'May 1648: An Ordinance for the speedy getting in the Arreares of such Money as is Assessed on the Citie of London and Liberties thereof, for the maintaining of the Forces raised by Authority of Parliament', A&O, pp. 1145–1147.
114. The Bassishaw Record and Assessment Book, LMA: P69/MIC1/B/006/MS03505.
115. The only evidence is from Bassishaw. Ibid.

116. LMA: CLC/W/GA 1608–1907.
117. Dale, *The Inhabitants of London in 1638*.
118. The correlation coefficient of two arrays of numbers was calculated using the CORREL function of Microsoft Excel for 77 matched cases. Of these 18 (23%) have precisely the same rent figure and 49 (63%) are within £1.
119. LMA: P69/MIC1/B/006/MS03505.
120. February 1645: Scottish Army, A&O, pp. 630–646.
121. 'June 1647: An Ordinance for the raising of Moneyes to be imployed towards the maintenance of Forces within this Kingdome, under the Command of Sir Thomas Fairfax Knight. And for the speedy transporting of, and paying the Forces for the carrying on the Warre of Ireland', A&O, pp. 958–984.
122. 'May 1648: An Ordinance for the speedy getting in the Arreares of such Money as is Assessed on the Citie of London and Liberties thereof, for the maintaining of the Forces raised by Authority of Parliament', A&O, pp. 1145–1147.
123. From the mid-sixteenth-century, London's subsidy commissioners had appointed two layers of assessors. The 'high book' was compiled for the entire City by six aldermen and six commoners and recorded the City's most prominent and wealthy citizens by ward, and the 'low book' by local ward assessors including the 'second rank' of such citizens. For example, the 1572 high assessors' book, LMA: CLC/281/MS02942 1572. The whole of the City of London assessed over a mere 48 pages of taxpayer lists. And see Valerie Pearl, *London and the Outbreak of the Puritan Revolution. City Government and National Politics 1625–1643* (Oxford: Oxford University Press, 1964), who explains in detail how the City administration was structured and how it evolved structurally and politically.
124. That is not to say these officials were not active earlier, because from the archival material earlier assessments were signed by ward officials and were referred to in the accounts of Mr Collins of the Weekly Assessment in 1643, TNA: SP 28/170.
125. For the Interregnum beyond c. 1650, the picture is far less clear given the lack of documentation, but the continuance of this two-tier structure seems likely, given that it is readily apparent by 1659–1660. It is important to note that throughout, none of the commissioner group or assessor group was ever paid, but collectors (usually 1d/£), high-collectors (usually the same), clerks (1/2–1d/£) and receivers (usually 1d/£) were all rewarded proportionately to amounts remitted.
126. 'December 1648: An Ordinance for the chusing of Common Councilmen, And other Officers within the City of London, and Liberties

thereof for the yeare ensuing', A&O, pp. 1252–1253. It was broad and applied to the 'Lord Major, Alderman. Alderman's Deputy, Common Councell-man, or into any Office, or other place of trust'.

127. LMA: P69/MIC1/B/006/MS03505. This was for 12 months from 25 March 1648 @ £40-8s-4d, although the barely legible quota should apparently have been £40-11s-0d.
128. Based on searches of A&O, which is not necessarily a complete record.
129. Sources: The Bassishaw Record and Assessment Book, LMA: P69/MIC1/B/006/MS03505.
130. TNA: E179/269/37 Part 1–2; TNA: E179/252/17, April 1649: An Act For Raising Ninety thousand pounds per Mensem, A&O, pp. 24–57.
131. Of course 'popish recusants' always paid double tax, but this probably does not explain the patterns here.
132. Evident in Bassishaw and the taxing of probable tenements in Chimney Alley in Coleman Street Ward. See TNA: E179/252/17 [1649 assessment].
133. Dale, *The Inhabitants of London in 1638.*
134. Most are £5 and under, but because of population movement it is difficult to be precise.
135. There are 195 tax charges in the 'estimate' + 1 reference to 2 houses less 6 non domestic = 190. December 1648 assessment = 163 less 16 lodgers + 19 tenements (26 tenements—7 tax charges)—5 non domestic = 123. Therefore, there were 67 inhabitants apparently untaxed.
136. James M.B. Alexander, 'The Economic and Social Structure of the City of London, c. 1700' (PhD thesis, London School of Economics, 1989). Alexander argued that the richest did not always live in the most valuable properties.
137. There are two later assessments in the book one undated (162 taxpayers) and one of 1649–1650 (179 taxpayers).
138. This is based on only five cases where the subsidy has taxed lands, and the 1646 estimate has identical names. The mean value of these five for the subsidy list is £14.20, much lower than the £33.40 in the 1646 estimate.
139. Coates, *The Impact of the English Civil War*, p. 23.
140. Valuation of the livery halls and Guildhall were excluded.
141. Chandaman, *English Public Revenue*, Chapter V and p. 330
142. *The Community of Kent*, p. 159.
143. (1) Iwade had 39 different taxpayers in its 1650 assessment paying 4.7% of Upper Scray's tax which grosses-up to 830 Upper Scray taxpayers. This is a broad extrapolation from a small amount of data. If the numbers were similar to the 1664 hearth tax, this might be a higher figure of over 1,200 taxpayers according to: Hearth Tax Online. Centre for Hearth Tax Research. University of Roehampton, London, http://www.hearthtax.org.uk/communities/kent/; (2) The figure is 99.5%

if minor uncleared account balances are treated as arrears and for Aylesford South 98.9%.

144. Upper Scray: c. 6.5–7%, Aylesford South: c. 8.5–9% of Kent's tax.
145. *The Community of Kent*, p. 158. These other counties were not researched in detail, but see TNA: SP 28/various. Braddick's Norfolk figures (*Parliamentary Taxation*, pp. 137–140) are slightly lower, but by the late Protectorate, the county was on a par with Kent. Coleby, *Central Government and the Localities*, Chapter 2. He claims earlier returns were disappointing, but improved sharply thereafter.
146. TNA: E179/128/678/f3 (duplicate). It may even be a case of lost receipts, but this seems unlikely.
147. EEBO, Thomason/69:E.441[25]. There were similar contemporary petitions from elsewhere.
148. From Everitt, *The Community of Kent*, p. 140.
149. Collection success was at 97% in Shepway and 100% in Sutton-at-Hone.
150. Stephen Dowell's phrase actually in relation to the excise in, *A History of Taxation and Taxes in England* (London: Longmans, Green & Co., 1884), II, p. 11.
151. TNA: E179/128/678, 8 March 1648.
152. 'January, 1659/60: An Act for an Assessment of One hundred Thousand Pounds by the Moneth, upon England, Scotland, and Ireland, for Six Moneths', A&O, pp. 1355–1403.
153. Albeit Parliament passed an effectively continuing ordinance on 29 May: 12 Car. II, c. 2, 3-months' assessment, 1660, SoR, vol. 5, pp. 179.
154. Christopher Hill, *Some Intellectual Consequences of the English Revolution* (London: Weidenfeld and Nicolson, 1980), p. 17; Austin Woolrych, 'Historical Introduction', in Don M. Wolfe (ed.), *Complete Prose Works of John Milton*, 8 vols. (New Haven CT: Yale University Press, 1953–1982), vii, p. 144.
155. Ronald Hutton, *The Restoration: A Political and Religious History of England and Wales 1658–1667* (Oxford: Clarendon Press, 1985), p. 92.
156. From at least as early as Anthony Webb's of March 1654, TNA: E179/128/678. The last December 1651 warrant contained no deadline. There are no surviving Kentish warrants between this and March 1654, so it is unclear if the new format appeared earlier.
157. 'Act for continuing the monthly assessment of £120,000 (levied by the Act of 29 November, 1650) for six months from the 25th March, 1651, for maintenance of the Armies in England, Scotland and Ireland'; HOCJ, vol. 6, 15 April 1651, p. 561.
158. EEBO; Thomason / E. 1061[47].
159. Ibid.
160. No minutes survive.

161. Confusingly, it was either a 19d or 23d tax suggesting different rates were approved or perhaps a range.
162. Bowles Accounts TNA: SP 28/130. Proportions varied. Kent commissioners subdivided its quota of £6,266.67 between the lathes so a county-wide pound rate would have been impossible.
163. TNA: E179/128/685 f138. There was probably a single body of commissioners for both sub-lathes.
164. Lower Scray: John Rabson, TNA: 179/128/680.
165. Aylesford South: William Polehill, TNA: E179/128/681-2 and E179/249/20.
166. Shepway: Thomas Rooke, TNA: E179/249/16 and SP 28/158-60.
167. See, e.g. Everitt, *The Community of Kent*, Table V.
168. TNA: SP/28.
169. Braddick, *Parliamentary Taxation*, pp. 137–140.
170. TNA: SP 28/154. Thomas Gallet's account in Coleby, *Central Government and the Localities*, p. 46.
171. Hertfordshire: TNA: SP 28/156; Sussex: TNA: SP 28/181; Buckinghamshire: SP 28/148-49.
172. Sources: (1) Upper Scray: Anthony Webb, TNA: E179/128/678; Joshua Pix, TNA: E179/128/679; William Catlett, TNA: E179/128/685; (2) Aylesford South: William Polehill, TNA: E179/128/681-2 and E179/249/20; (3) Aylesford North: Edward Whitton, TNA: E179/128/672; (4) Lower Scray: John Rabson, TNA: 179/128/680; (5) Shepway: Thomas Rooke, TNA: E179/249/16 and SP 28/158-60; (6) Sutton-at-Hone: Robert Joseph, TNA: SP 28/159 & 259.
173. Deadlines vary, but the end of the months of January, April, July and October was most common.
174. TNA: SP 28/130, Charles Bowles's receiver-general account book; Hertfordshire: TNA: SP 28/156; Sussex: TNA: SP 28/181; Buckinghamshire: SP 28/148-49.
175. Quoted in Kerridge, *Trade and Banking*, p. 57 citing Bodleian Library, MS Top. Kent a.1 fo.26v. Dering, Sir Edward, 2nd Bt. (1625–1684), of Surrenden Dering, Kent and Bloomsbury, Mdx. Source: HoP (accessed 3 May 2017).
176. Charles Bowles' account books TNA: SP 28/130 shows few round sums received, but these increased from c. 1647–1648. Some of the receipts themselves represent multiple payments, e.g. Catlett's 1 April 1656 for £515 from Charles Bowles [TNA: E179/128/685] has a calculation showing this was three separate payments (1) £265 'cash this day', (2) £50 'Treasurers at War' and (3) £200 illegible. Both (2) and (3) may involve paper transactions.

177. Kerridge, *Trade and Banking*, pp. 53–54. Kerridge quotes William Cavendish making a specie payment of £13,500 from Derbyshire to London because it was too large for a single credit transaction, Kerridge, *Trade and Banking*, p. 50.
178. For example, in Upper Scray Joshua Pix's receipt of 3 September 1650 for £119 actually represents payment of £50 and £69 with a total shown on the receipt TNA: E179/128/679 f6.
179. Sussex: TNA: SP 28/181.
180. Hertfordshire: TNA: SP 28/156.
181. Beckett, 'Land Tax Administration at the Local Level', p. 163 and Beckett, *Local Taxation: National Legislation.*
182. The importance of justices nationally is recognised widely including Ward, *The English Land Tax*, p. 4 and Ginter, *A Measure of Wealth*, p. 139, 'land tax was administered by the local resident magistracy and their peers'.
183. And from at least 1644 was governed by internal City ward quotas—The Bassishaw Record and Assessment Book, LMA: P69/MIC1/B/006/MS03505. Local quotas were prescribed in the earliest legislation which should be 'according to the usuall proportions and divisions of Rates in the said places'. March 1644: Earl of Essex Army: A&O, pp. 398–405. Significantly these ward quotas for the assessment were quite unlike that of that other quota tax the fifteenth and tenth.
184. After Michael Hammer and James Champy, *Reengineering the Corporation: A Manifesto for Business Revolution* (London: Nicholas Brealey Publishing, 1993).
185. Hindle, *The State and Social Change*, p. 36.
186. For example, Gary S. De Krey, *A Fractured Society, The Politics of London in the First Age of Party, 1688–1715* (Oxford: Clarendon Press, 1985); Valerie Pearl, 'Change and Stability in Seventeenth-Century London', *London Journal*, vol. 5, 1979, pp. 3–34.
187. For example, Steve Rappaport, *Worlds Within Worlds: Structures of Life in Sixteenth-Century London* (Cambridge: Cambridge University Press, 1989).
188. Edward Hasted, 'The Town and Port of New Romney', in Edward Hasted, *The History and Topographical Survey of the County of Kent.* Volume 8 (Canterbury, 1799), pp. 446–464. British History Online, http://www.british-history.ac.uk/survey-kent/vol8/pp446-464.
189. For example, Stephen Hipkin, 'Property, Economic Interest and the Configuration of Rural Conflict in Sixteenth and Seventeenth-Century England', *Socialist History*, vol. 23, 2003, pp. 67–88; Hipkin 'The Structure of Landownership'.
190. Sources: HoP; Brunton and Pennington, *Members of the Long Parliament.* This includes special cases where MPs died soon after

taking political office such as Mildmay Fane in 1715 who never became a commissioner. Some may have been commissioners in other counties and no analysis has been undertaken for such cases.

191. MP for Hythe in the third Protectorate parliament, sources above.
192. TNA: E179/249/20, approving accounts. Both were Protectorate MPs in Kent.
193. Jason T. Peacey, 'Livesay, Sir Michael, First Baronet (1614–1665?)'. *Oxford Dictionary of National Biography*, Oxford University Press, 2004, http://www.oxforddnb.com/view/article/16797, accessed 25 April 2017.
194. 'A More exact and necessary catalogu[e] of pensioners in the Long Parliament', EEBO, Wing (2nd ed.) / M2697A.
195. Including those designated commissioners for either Canterbury or Rochester.
196. February 1648: Relief of Ireland, A&O, pp. 1072–1105.
197. June 1647: Maintenance of Fairfax's Forces, A&O, pp. 958–984.
198. Source: TNA: SP 28/234.
199. Hindle, *The State and Social Change*, p. 24.
200. Everitt, *The Community of Kent*, p. 129.
201. The lathes: Shepway, St. Augustine, Scray (Upper and Lower), Aylesford (North, South and East), Sutton-at-Hone (Upper and Nether) and later Thanet and Canterbury. There was a separate Sequestration Committee and an Accounts Committee. Everitt, *The Community of Kent*.
202. As discussed, where tax commissioners divided themselves up to administer smaller regions.
203. TNA: SP 28/159-60 Account Books.
204. Roberts, 'State and Society', p. 298 states 'Furthermore, it is amply clear from a mass of surviving narratives of those called to account at the court of Exchequer after 1660 for their handling of wartime revenues that the same individuals held multiple and often diverse offices'.
205. Everitt, *The Community of Kent*, p. 158.
206. 'August 1654: An Ordinance for Ejecting Scandalous, Ignorant and Insufficient Ministers and Schoolmasters', A&O, pp. 968–990.
207. He was named in: 'November 1650: An Act for Raising of One Hundred and Twenty Thousand pounds per Mensem for Four Moneths, To Commence the Five and Twentieth of December 1650. For Maintenance of the Forces in England, Ireland and Scotland, Raised by Authority of Parliament for the Service of This Commonwealth', A&O, pp. 456–490.
208. Catharina Clement, 'Political and Religious Reactions in the Medway Towns of Rochester and Chatham During the English Revolution, 1640–1660 (PhD thesis, Canterbury Christchurch University, 2013)'.

209. According to High Justice, BM, Add. MS 5494, quoted in Everitt, *The Community of Kent*, p. 179.
210. TNA: E179/129/706 and TNA: E179/313/7. TNA: E179/128/679 was signed by Polehill on 26 July 1659. Coffman, *The Fiscal Revolution of the Interregnum*, observes similar survivals amongst lower ranks within the excise, but also sees much greater survival amongst senior ranks.
211. 13 Car. II, St.2, c. 3, 18-months' assessment, 1661–1663, SoR, vol. 5, pp. 325–348; TNA: E179/129/699-700 duplicates. A continuity long recognised, e.g. Dowell, *History of Taxation*, II, p. 46.
212. TNA: E179/129/745; 25 Car. II, c. 1, 18-months' assessment, 1673–1674. 52% of the sub-lathe duplicates were signed by current/former MPs.
213. New Romney KHLC: NR/RTi1 12 July 1648 and run of assessments after 1662 KHLC: NR/RTa9-28.
214. Lydd: KHLC: CP/Z3/18, 1677, Lydd assessment for tax for raising: £584,978-2s-2½d for building 30 ships of war; KHLC: Ly/9/3-15 and KHLC: NR/ZLy1, Lydd (1663–1680); KHLC: NR/RTa28, Lydd 1680; KHLC: NR/ZLy1/5, Memoranda of meetings of commissioners of taxes at Lydd, 1715–1718.
215. For example, Evans, *Seventeenth Century Norwich*, p. 30; 'Political oligarchy was pervasive in the towns of Tudor and Stuart England'.
216. Especially Beaven, *Bristol Lists.*
217. Established at 12 in 1581, Elizabeth Ralph, *Guide to the Bristol Archives Office* (Bristol: Bristol Corporation, 1971), p. 5. This number included the recorder.
218. First recorded in about 1216.
219. Established in 1499 according to Livock, *City Chamberlain's Accounts*, p. xii.
220. Livock, *City Chamberlain's Accounts*, p. xii.
221. Quoted in Ralph, *Guide to the Bristol Archives Office*, p. 5.
222. Historically, the right of election was exercised by the members of the City Corporation, on the grounds that the Corporation itself owned the freehold of the City, although there were objections to such a claim. So Bristol oscillated between being a Corporation borough and a Freemen borough. See Bristol and Avon Family History Society. *Index to the Bristol Burgess Book Volumes 1 to 21 1557–1995.* www.bafhs.org.uk.
223. Brooks, 'Public Finance and Political Stability', p. 291, specifically Southampton, Ludlow, and Richmond.
224. Calculations made using Beaven, *Bristol Lists.*
225. Comparing Beaven, *Bristol Lists* with tax commissioners' minutes 1689–1748, BRO: 04798, BRO: 09374, and BRO: F/Tax/M/3. There is further discussion below concerning gaps in the minute books.

226. Beaven, *Bristol Lists.*
227. Livock, *City Chamberlain's Accounts*, p. xiii.
228. BRO: F/AU Audit papers.
229. 'October 1645: An Ordinance of the Lords and Commons for the better Securing and Government of the City of Bristoll', A&O, pp. 797–798.
230. 'November 1645: Ordinance to settle the Magistracy of the City of Bristol', A&O, pp. 801–802.
231. 'December 1645: An Ordinance for the Constituting and Appointing of Sergeant-Major-General Philip Skippon, to be Governor of the City and Garrison of Bristol', A&O, pp. 811–812.
232. Aldworth reconfirmed by the December ordinance and Vickris and Hodges elected that year.
233. December 1645: Appointing Sergeant-Major-General Philip Skippon, A&O, pp. 811–812.
234. Richard Vickris only in 1652, Luke Hodges and Richard Aldworth continuously from 1643–1652. Both the latter became MPs for Bristol and militia commissioners according to Beaven, *Bristol Lists.*
235. Source: HoP.
236. 'An Act declaring England to be a Commonwealth', 19 May 1649.
237. Beaven, *Bristol Lists.*
238. A&O, SoR, various.
239. There were only seven in 12 Car. II, c. 27, 6-months' assessment, 1661, SoR, vol. 5, pp. 269–277.
240. 13 Car. II, St.2, c. 3, 18-months' assessment, 1661–1663, SoR, vol. 5, pp. 325–348.
241. Exceptions were Sir Robert Hales, 1st Bart., Sir Robert Honeywood and Sir Thomas Stiles who had very long careers as commissioners. Sources: SoR.
242. Sources: A&O, SoR, various.
243. BRO: F/Tax/M2 Restoration commissioners' minute book.
244. 31 Car. II, c. 1, 6-months' assessment, 1680, SoR, vol. 5, pp. 897–934. All calculations based on Beaven, *Bristol Lists.*
245. BRO: F/Tax/M2 minute book.
246. BRO: F/Tax/2.
247. For example, Ian W. Archer, 'The Government of London, 1500–1650', *London Journal*, vol. 26, 2001, pp. 19–28.
248. For example, potential Royalist sympathisers were excluded.
249. After the early experiment with ward officials as commissioners in 1648 as discussed—which prefigures these post-revolutionary developments.
250. 13 Car. II, St.2, c. 3, 18-months' assessment, 1661–1663, SoR, vol. 5, pp. 325–348.
251. Coffman, 'Towards a New Jerusalem', p. 1435.

252. Gary S. De Krey, 'Player, Sir Thomas (d. 1672)', *Oxford Dictionary of National Biography*, Oxford University Press, 2004; online edition, Jan. 2008, http://www.oxforddnb.com/view/article/22363 (accessed 25 April 2017).
253. Chandaman, *The English Public Revenue*, p. 174.
254. LMA: COL/CHD/LA/02/028, Royal Aid accounts City receipts book—3. See Chandaman, *The English Public Revenue*, Appendix I, pp. 286*ff.*
255. LMA: COL/CHD/LA/02.
256. Cash books survive from the 1640s and accountants have allocated sums by ward, but no separate ward books survive, e.g. TNA: 28/162 Part 1, 'London Receiver's Book' for light horse 1645, and TNA: 28/162 Part 2, 'Alex Jones book for the Relief of Taunton'.
257. Debt was secured on many of the taxes and the receiver at this time had the role of matching tallies and payments made. Whereas the receiver-general's receipts for the Royal Aid might constitute 3–400 payments from collections, payments to the Exchequer would be far less frequent comprising perhaps 12–20 payments.
258. For example, LMA: COL/CHD/LA/03/16/03 [Royal and Additional Aids. Returns of collectors as to deficiencies. Copy order regarding quarterly payments unpaid in the City of London owing to the Plague and Fire] has returns and related documents for the Royal Aid. All the returns of uncollectable amounts of the 'poor, dead, and gone' were signed by common councilmen and addressed to William Avery the head-collector at his house in Gresham College.
259. Sources throughout this section: (1) Biographical detail from Woodhead, *The Rulers of London*; (2) Supplementary material from Oxford DNB; (3) Named commissioners from SoR.
260. Commencing for the period from December 1664.
261. 31 Car. II, c. 1, 6-months' assessment, 1680, SoR, vol. 5, pp. 897–934.
262. Identification of individuals from the statute is not always straightforward given the presence of some common names and issues with several members of the same family, although most ward officials are readily identifiable.
263. (1) Assessment sources: LMA: COL/CHD/LA/03/various. Legible signatures compared with secondary sources including Woodhead, *The Rulers of London*; (2) The collectors' assessments usually doubled as warrants as, for example, that from Portsoken Ward dated 23 May 1673, LMA: COL/CHD/LA/03/014/011 [25 Car. II, c. 1, 18-months' assessment, 1673–1674. Assessments: for the first quarter Portsoken Ward]. This states: 'The commissioners authorise and appoint…' and containing the usual warnings that any taxpayers 'shall

refuse, neglect or delay to pay the said money… then the said collectors are to forthwith to levy the same by distress @ sale of the goods of the person or persons …'; (3) the 1645 duplicate (TNA: E179/147/600) was signed by the Mayor Thomas Atkins and Aldermen John Wollaston and Thomas Adams. That of 30 September 1660 for the one-month's assessment (TNA: E179/147/607) was signed by the newly appointed Mayor Sir John Frederick and Aldermen Anthony Bateman and Thomas Alleyn.

264. As evidenced by numerous surviving documents in LMA: COL/CHD/LA/03/various. Signatures have been checked for all surviving documents in this series.
265. This ordinance of 9 June, 1657 ('June 1657: An Act for an Assessment upon England at the Rate of Sixty thousand Pounds by the Moneth, for three Moneths', A&O, pp. 1058–1097.) names 'all the Aldermen for the time being'. He was not separately named in the ordinance. Church was named in the ordinance.
266. LMA: COL/CHD/LA/03/various signatures identified from Woodhead, *The Rulers of London.*
267. Ibid.
268. In theory, such householders paid at least £10 a year in rent and 30 shillings a year in taxes.
269. Minutes survive from various wards at different times, e.g. that from Bassishaw 1655–1752, LMA: CLC/W/GA/002, Bassishaw Wardmote Inquest minutes. Because many wards had become very large, there were further ancient subdivisions into precincts which claimed many of the functions of the full Wardmote. It was a peculiarity that often there was a poor match between parishes and sub-precincts. See Pearl, *London and the Outbreak*, p. 53*ff.*
270. According to Pearl, *London and the Outbreak*, p. 56.
271. Ibid.
272. £15,000 by 1710.
273. Pearl, *London and the Outbreak*, p. 60.
274. Based on the assessments LMA: COL/CHD/LA/03/various.
275. Sources: signed assessments and other documents largely from: LMA: COL/CHD/LA/03/various, compared with Woodhead, *The Rulers of London.* Individuals recognised—593; signatures identified—1,436; assessments and other documents considered—357; assessments without signatures—25; and mean signatures per assessment—4.39.
276. Based on the assessments LMA: COL/CHD/LA/03/various.
277. The Royal Aid assessment for the fifth and sixth quarters for Vintry Ward (LMA: COL/CHD/LA/03/066/025, Royal and Additional Aids, fifth and sixth quarters. Assessments for the first and second quarters Vintry) includes both the local assessors' paper copy of the assessment signed

off only by local ward officials (Deputy Philip Dakins and Common Councilmen: William Fellowes, Arthur Bray, Richard Batson, William Powney, Walter Sykes, Thomas Dorebar, John Hobby(?) and Richard Greene [the latter two may be from other wards]) and the collector's copy in more durable parchment which, because it empowered the collector, had to be signed off by commissioners named in the statute: Sir Thomas Bludworth, by then Lord Mayor, and Aldermen Sir Thomas Adams and Sir William Hooker. There are also collectors' copies for the same quarters for: (1) Bread Street Ward (LMA: COL/CHD/LA/03/066/006, Royal and Additional Aids, fifth and sixth quarters. Royal Aid; first and second quarters Additional Aid. Bread Street, signed by the Mayor Sir Thomas Bludworth and Aldermen Sir Richard Ford and Sir Robert Hanson); (2) Langbourn Ward (LMA: COL/CHD/LA/03/066/020, Royal and Additional Aids, fifth and sixth quarters. 1 and 2 quarters Langbourn, signed by Mayor Sir Thomas Bludworth, and Aldermen Sir Thomas Adams and Sir John Frederick). The earlier Quarters 1–2 Royal Aid collector's copies from; (3) St. Dunstan-in-the-West, Farringdon Without (signed by the Major Sir John Lawrence and Aldermen Sir Thomas Adams and Sir Richard Brown); (4) the Portsoken Ward assessment for Q1 of the 18-months' assessment of 1673–1674 was also a collectors' copy signed by Mayor Sir Robert Hanson, and Aldermen Sir John Frederick and Sir William Peake (LMA: COL/CHD/LA/03/014/011, 25 Car. II, c. 1, 18-months' assessment, 1673–1674).

278. LMA: COL/CHD/LA/03/014/011 [25 Car. II, c. 1, 18-months' assessment, 1673–1674, SoR, vol. 5, pp. 752–782. Assessments: for the first quarter Portsoken Ward]. This was signed by Mayor Robert Hanson and Aldermen Sir John Frederick and Sir William Peake. A further signature is illegible.
279. St. Bartholomew-the-Great and St. Bartholomew-the-Less had parish officials in charge and the assessment for Whitefriars states 'Wee the Constables and other the inhabitants … chosen for this Assessment' [LMA: COL/CHD/LA/03/015/001].
280. Here, headboroughs and chief constables were the relevant officials.
281. As they were each named on the face of the assessments.
282. LMA: COL/CHD/LA/03/022/018 [25 Car. II, c. 1, 18-months' assessment, 1673–1674, assessments: for the second and third quarters Broad Street].
283. According to Livock, *City Chamberlain's Accounts*, p. xxiv.
284. BRO: F/AU/1/36, 1666, chamberlains' audit, has, for example: £52 for the Mayor, £20 for the Recorder, £15 for the Town Clerk, and £12.50 for the Chamberlain.

285. Crumpe, Sir Richard (c. 1628–1700), of Ballan Street, Bristol. Source: HoP (accessed 4 May 2017).
286. Of course, they may have been able to deduct tax from their own rent.
287. TNA: Treasury Papers, T/27/7. pp. 262, 263 quoted in McGrath, *Merchants and Merchandise*, p. 222.
288. David Sacks personal communication, E-mail discussion.
289. Stephens, *The Seventeenth-Century Customs Surveyed*, especially pp. 35–54.
290. Sacks personal communication and Stephens, *The Seventeenth-Century Customs Surveyed*, p. 38.
291. McGrath, *Merchants and Merchandise*, p. 216.
292. BRO: F/Tax/M/2, commissioners' minutes 1665–1680.
293. Sources: (1) BRO: F/Tax/A/1 [15 Car. II, c. 9, 4 subsidies, 1663–1664, SoR, vol. 5, pp. 453–481]; (2) BRO: F/Tax/A/2, Royal Aid [16 & 17 Car. II, c. 1, Royal Aid, 1664–1667, SoR, vol. 5, pp. 525–552] and the Additional Aid [17 Car. II, c. 1, Additional Aid, 1665–1667, SoR, vol. 5, pp. 570–574]; (3) BRO: F/Tax/A/3, Poll [18 & 19 Car. II, c. 1, Poll, 1666, SoR, vol. 5, pp. 584–597]; (4) BRO: F/Tax/A/4, Assessment [30 Car. II, c. 1, 18-months' assessment, 1678–1680, SoR, vol. 5, pp. 867–883].
294. They were rarely named as assessors as such, but this seems the likely conclusion given that they were putting their signatures at the end of the parish assessments.
295. BRO: F/Tax/M/2.
296. On the basis of land taxes paid. Further detail on this is provided below.
297. Beckett, 'Local Custom and the "New Taxation"'. Also Ward's Buckinghamshire commissioners, *The English Land Tax*, p. 4.
298. London receivers, usually the chamberlain, were typically named on City duplicates and often their deputies.
299. See Ward, *The English Land Tax*, pp. 10–14, provides examples.
300. For example, LMA: COL/CHD/LA/03/003/013. This is a letter from Peter Rich to Town Clerk William Wagstaffe dated 21 April 1689, stating that he and associates will 'give Bond' to the City Receiver General for the '3 M^{o}[nth] tax' in the City as 'good security'. There are numerous references in CTB.
301. Ward, *The English Land Tax*, p. 13.
302. TNA: E179/172/436. This includes a warrant dated 5 May 1675 for payment issued by the Exchequer. It allowed John Tocker an additional £60 towards his expenses incurred in delivering the monies raised in this grant to Exeter and Tiverton in order that they could be conveyed more speedily to London'.
303. For example, Muldrew, 'Wages and the Problem of Monetary Scarcity', p. 399.

304. Chandaman, *The English Public Revenue*.
305. (1) 15 Car. II, c. 9, 4 subsidies, 1663–1664, SoR, vol. 5, pp. 453–481; (2) In Bassishaw, there appears to be a draft and a final version. The total for land is £160 and for goods £182. The tax calculation for land and goods is as set out in the statute for 2 subsidies; (3) its predecessors were no better. The 1663–1664 subsidy (51 taxpayers) has been selected here, but there are similar results for 1541 (48), 1582 (69), 1610 (57), 1621 (60), 1622 (60), 1625 (43) and 1628 (36). A 'brief account' [TNA: E179/314/27] of the first two 1663–1664 subsidies for the City indicates only £7,567-9s-3d paid into the Exchequer.
306. This was a 'moderated rent' and therefore presumably discounted.
307. The same appears true in St. Dunstan-in-the West (Farringdon Without) where 66% of taxpayers paid a flat rate of 16s and another 15% or £1-1s-4d, LMA: P69/DUN2/C/002/MS02969/002.
308. LMA: COL/CHD/LA/03/111/012 [Assessments: 12 Car. II, c. 29, one-month's assessment, 1661, SoR, vol. 5, pp. 282–287]. Cripplegate Without: Fore Street & Grub Street Precincts.
309. This usual rate was increased by c. 75% during the Second Anglo-Dutch War to 3s-6d/£.
310. LMA: COL/CHD/LA/03/088/006 [Tower ward assessment: 14 Car. II, c. 3, Militias 1662, SoR, vol. 5, pp. 358–364. This London Militia tax was raised in conjunction with land taxes and the assessments were made for both contemporaneously. The Militia tax was under a precept from the Lieutenancy].
311. LMA: COL/CHD/LA/03/066/007 [Bridge assessment: 14 Car. II, c. 3, Militias 1662, SoR, vol. 5, pp. 358–364].
312. LMA: COL/CHD/LA/03/018/007 [above].
313. LMA: COL/CHD/LA/03/088/002 [Billingsgate assessments: 14 Car. II, c. 3, Militias 1662, SoR, vol. 5, pp. 358–364].
314. LMA: COL/CHD/LA/03/024/001 [25 Car. II, c. 1, 18-months' assessment, 1673–1674. Assessments: for the second and third quarters Aldersgate Without]. In fact, the assessors repeat this text for this ward in other quarters, e.g. in the fourth quarter according to LMA: COL/CHD/LA/03/036/013 [25 Car. II, c. 1, 18-months' assessment, 1673–1674. Assessments: for the fourth-quarter Aldersgate].
315. The £5,091-11s-4d figure for the City was common for many assessments and is equal to the amount apportioned to the City under the Royal Aid per month see, e.g. COL/CHD/LA/03/066/008 [Royal and Additional Aids, fifth and sixth quarters, Castle Baynard].
316. LMA: COL/CHD/LA/03/024/001 [above] and LMA: COL/CHD/LA/03/036/013 [above].

317. As discussed above, the Restoration saw the introduction of a clause allowing landlord and tenant to agree different terms to that in the act. 13 Car. II, St.2, c. 3, 18-months' assessment, 1661–1663, SoR, vol. 5, pp. 325–348, s. XXIX. 'Proviso for Agreements as to Taxes between Landlord and Tenant'.
318. LMA: COL/CHD/LA/03/various Restoration assessments; Ancestry.co.uk, post-revolutionary assessments.
319. LMA: COL/CHD/LA/03/various. Mention of tax charges on: alleys, courts and houses in the assessments may also suggest landlords and multiple tenants.
320. TNA: E179/252/22 shows the 1650 assessment for Coleman Street Ward signed off by commissioners giving powers of distraint 'And if any the said persons shall [refuse] or neglect to pay the money [that] is so assessed then the said collectors [according] to the Act [?] to levy the same by distress & sale of the Goods of such persons so refusing or neglecting to pay'.
321. Overassessment is where the tax assessed is greater than the quota, so successful appeals and non-payments do not result in an underpayment and the need for a reassessment. Estimates of overassessment are based on the assessment with the most complete records for the period, the 18-months' assessment of 1673–1674 where complete assessments are available from 22 of 28 wards and sub-wards. The mean overassessment rate is 0.7%, but riverside Vintry Ward was overassessed by 5.1% and extra-mural Portsoken by 3.3%. Sources: LMA: COL/CHD/LA/03/various.
322. Based on the Royal Aid and the 12 of 18 parishes with a complete decipherable assessment. Source: BRO: F/Tax/2 various assessments. These have been compared with quotas from the Restoration commissioners' minute book BRO: F/Tax/M/2.
323. There were some exceptions particularly in the smaller precincts where constables, church wardens and other officials might sign off. In Whitefriars for the third and fourth quarters of the 18-months' assessment of 1679–1680, the constables Robert Gosling and Robert Britton, amongst others, approved the returns. In St. Anne Blackfriars, Farringdon Within for the same quarters, George Woulfe and Peter Williamson signed off as Church Wardens; LMA: COL/CHD/LA/03/125/002 [18 months' deficiencies and other papers] and LMA: COL/CHD/LA/03/056/010 [Royal and Additional Aids St. Bartholomew- the-Less].
324. Woodhead, *The Rulers of London*.
325. Including John Pope resident in St. Michael Wood Street precinct signing off Cripplegate Within return for this precinct on 27 November 1679.

326. LMA: COL/CHD/LA/03/113/005 [18 & 19 Car. II, c. 13, 11-months' assessment, 1668, SoR, vol. 5, pp. 616–623. Assessments: for the first quarter or first 5 months. Farringdon Without precincts: Smithfield, Holborn Cross and Church Precincts of St. Sepulchre].
327. LMA: COL/CHD/LA/03/125/002 [above]. It was signed by Augustus Newbold the Deputy for Cripplegate Without, as well as common councilmen Richard Knight, Edward Winston and Edward Dermer.
328. LMA: COL/CHD/LA/03/111/012 20 June 1661 assessment for Bread Street the one-month's assessment.
329. Sources: LMA: COL/CHD/LA/03/various.
330. This trend does not seem to be connected with other factors such as when the precept was issued.
331. Based on 1673 data, the extra-mural parishes averaged over c. 1,500 taxpayers, the central wards c. 400–450 and riverside c. 550–600. The surviving assessments suggest similar numbers in the 1660s. Without wards: Aldersgate Without, Bishopsgate Without, Cripplegate Without, Farringdon Without and Portsoken. Riverside: for example, Castle Baynard, Queenhithe and Vintry. Central: Billingsgate, Bread Street, Broad Street, Bridge, Candlewick, Cheap, Cordwainer, Cornhill, Langbourn and Walbrook.
332. Including St. Martin's Le Grand.
333. Including Duke's Place.
334. St. Andrew Holborn, St. Bartholomew-the-Great and the Less, St. Sepulchre, St. Brides Fleet Street, Holborn Cross, Whitefriars and St. Martin Ludgate.
335. There is some limited earlier material showing payments into the Exchequer in the early 1660s particularly TNA: E179/323/23. The first of these is dated to 1660–1661 (12 Car. II, c. 21, one-month's assessment, 1660–1661, SoR, vol. 5, pp. 252–253.) was only three quarters collected four years later. The next two levies (12 Car. II, c. 27, 6-months' assessment, 1661, SoR, vol. 5, pp. 269–277; and 12 Car. II, c. 29, one-month's assessment, 1661, SoR, vol. 5, pp. 282–287) show 97–98% collection rates but amounts trickling in over a period.
336. Source: LMA: COL/CHD/LA/02/029. Based on: (1) 12 Car. II, c. 2, 3-months' assessment, 1660, SoR, vol. 5, pp. 179; (2) 12 Car. II, c. 21, one-month's assessment, 1660–1661, SoR, vol. 5, pp. 252–253; (3) 12 Car. II, c. 20, two-months' assessment, 1660, SoR, vol. 5, pp. 250–251; (4) 12 Car. II, c. 27, 6-months' assessment, 1661, SoR, vol. 5, pp. 269–277; (5) 12 Car. II, c. 29, one-month's assessment, 1661, SoR, vol. 5, pp. 282–287. Received £59,075.20 against quotas

of £60,666.67=£1,591.47 less allowances £1,001.27=arrears of £590.20.

337. And see Justin A. Champion, *London's Dreaded Visitation: The Social Geography of the Great Plague in 1665* (London: Historical Geography Research Monograph No. 31, 1995).
338. There are later summary accounts for first quarter of Jeremy Snow who was metropolitan London's receiver-general in the late 1660s (TNA: E179/314/32). These suggest that payments were delayed and disrupted by the plague and there were some arrears as late as 1668.
339. 16 & 17 Car. II, c. 1, Royal Aid, 1664–1667, SoR, vol. 5, pp. 525–552.
340. LMA: COL\CHD\LA\02\026 Royal Aid City Receipts book.
341. Ward tax collection was largely suspended until February, although money continued to trickle in from some wards and less impacted parts especially Bridge (October), Farringdon Without (several small payments in December), Coleman Street (late August) and Castle Baynard (September).
342. Both poor performing Vintry and Tower were worse hit by the plague than central wards, but not as badly as most extra-mural areas which seemed unaffected. Sources including ward quotas: Head-collector William Avery (and Town Clerk) accounts: LMA: COL/CHD/LA/O3/044/001 [Royal and Additional Aids. Head-collectors' accounts of receipts from the ward collectors showing quarterly arrears etc.]. Postings per LMA: COL/CHD/LA/02/026, a book of the Royal Aid accounts for London, http://alchemipedia.blogspot.co.uk/2009/09/great-plague-london-1665-geographical.html.
343. £15,000 for the third quarter and £8,950 for the fourth.
344. LMA: COL/CHD/LA/03/16/003 [Royal and Additional Aids. Returns of collectors as to deficiencies. Copy order re quarterly payments unpaid in the City of London owing to the Plague and Fire]—unsigned document amongst the Head-collector's/Receiver-General's papers.
345. LMA: COL/CHD/LA/03/016/03 [above].
346. Estimated from surviving assessments assuming a 2s/£ rate and broader estimates where no assessments survive but ward quotas are available (estimated as [land + personal estates] * 60%).
347. TNA: E179/252/22, City duplicate. There is at least one abatement, LMA: COL/CHD/LA/03/057/004 for Cornhill, and it is not clear if this is before or after the duplicate. The duplicate itself is generally of good quality, but a small number of figures are difficult to decipher.
348. Thomas Fiddian Reddaway, *The Rebuilding of London After the Great Fire* (London: Jonathan Cape, 1940).

349. David V. Glass, 'Introduction', *London Inhabitants Within the Walls 1695* (London Records Society, 1966). British History Online, http://www.british-history.ac.uk. Alexander, 'The Economic and Social Structure of the City of London'. Extra-mural = Portsoken, Farringdon Without, Cripplegate Without, Aldersgate Without, and Bishopsgate Without; Riverside = Castle Baynard, Dowgate, Queenhithe, and Vintry; Central = Bassishaw, Billinsgate, Bishopsgate Within, Bread Street, Broad Street, Bridge, Candlewick, Cheap, Cordwainer, Cornhill, Langbourn and Walbrook.
350. (1) Less damaged wards were: Aldersgate Without, Aldgate, Bishopsgate Within, and Without, Bread Street, Broad Street, Coleman Street, Farringdon Without, Langbourn, Lime Street, Portsoken, Queenhithe and Tower. They all continued to pay something. LMA: COL/CHD/LA/03/078/011 [Arrears Draft precept for assessment to be made on the Ward of Bishopsgate for the arrears of the Royal and Additional Aids. The 1-month's Tax for the Duke of York, and the 11-months' assessment]. It is undated, but was probably compiled in 1672.
351. The Royal Aid [16 & 17 Car. II, c. 1, Royal Aid, 1664–1667, SoR, vol. 5, pp. 525–552]; the Additional Aid [17 Car. II, c. 1, Additional Aid, 1665–1667, SoR, Vol. 5, pp. 570–574]; the one-month's assessment [17 Car. II, c. 9, one-month's assessment, 1667–1668, SoR, vol. 5, pp.580–583]; and the 11-months' assessment [18 & 19 Car. II, c. 13, 11-months' assessment, 1668, SoR, vol. 5, pp. 616–623] were a group of related taxes making a period of four years continuous assessment from 1665 to 1668.
352. Percentages are of sums collected not the entire quota. a) Sources: Head-collector William Avery (and Town Clerk) accounts, LMA: COL/CHD/LA/O3/044/001 [above]. Ward Quotas; b) Postings per LMA: COL/CHD/LA/02/026, chamberlain's accounts 1665–1672. A book of the Royal Aid accounts.
353. Sources: Roger Finlay, *Population and Metropolis: The Demography of London 1580–1650, Cambridge Geographical Studies* (Cambridge: Cambridge University Press, 2009); LMA: COL/CHD/LA/O3/044/001 [above], Head-collector's list of quotas for quarters 1–2 of the Royal Aid; TNA: E179/252/22, 1671 duplicate showing real and personal estates; Keene, *Metropolitan London in the 1690s* (Database); 1701: LMA: COL/CHD/LA/03/108/007 [Assessments: 12 & 13 Wm. III, c. 10, Land Tax for 1701, SoR, vol. 7, pp. 648–716; duplicate assessments of parishes in the City of London, Middlesex and Westminster under Act of Parliament]. Copy duplicate showing real and personal estates.

354. LMA: COL/CHD/LA/03/065/020 [11-months' assessment returns and certificates of collectors as to deficiencies c. 1688].
355. As, for example, with the accounts for quarters 10–11 of the Royal and Additional Aid in mid-1667, LMA: COL/CHD/LA/02/026, p. 40*ff*, Royal Aid accounts City Receipts book.
356. LMA: COL/CHD/LA/03/057/007 [22 & 23 Car. II, c. 3, subsidy, 1671, SoR, vol. 5, pp. 693–703].
357. Surviving sources: Billingsgate, Bishopsgate Without, Bridge, Broad Street, Candlewick, Cripplegate Within and Cripplegate Without, Farringdon Without (St. Bartholomew-the-Great, St. Bartholomew-the-Less, St. Andrew, Holborn, Holborn Cross, and St. Dunstan-in-the-West), Langbourn, Portsoken, Queenhithe and Tower. Sources: LMA: /COL/CHD/LA/03/various.
358. TNA: E179/252/22. There is also a list of abatements on appeal (LMA: COL/CHD/LA/03/125/008 [Subsidy on land offices and stocks. 22&23 Car. II c. 3 Abatement of assessments on appeals]), which should be reflected in the duplicate, but as the latter is undated it is not completely clear. The rate was 1s/£1 on land and 15s/£100 on personal estates.
359. This is based on a small unscientific sample of 50 cases from each ward.
360. Various assessments: LMA: COL/CHD/LA/03/062/028 [29 Car. II, c. 1, 17-months' assessment, 1677–1678. Ward returns of deficiencies first and second quarters].
361. Tax-collector numbers varied between 150 and 200 according to duplicates. The number of doors estimated from surviving various assessments LMA: COL/CHD/LA/03/various.
362. LMA: COL/CHD/LA/03/078/010 [25 Car. II, c. 1, 18-months' assessment, 1673–1674. Petition of the Ward of Cripplegate Without against the allotment of £200 per month assessed in the ward. The former dividend never exceeding £100 per month approx]. Undated but c. 1674.
363. Alexander, 'The Economic and Social structure of the City of London', produced similar results with his work based on tax precincts. His Map 3.02 based on the 1693 data shows that the highest rental areas were even more strongly clustered along the two or three main streets of the City. These consisted of the streets at both ends of Cheapside, Gracechurch Street and the overlapping block surrounded by Threadneedle Street, Gracechurch Street and Lombard Street. Alexander went on to plot the personal estate or stock tax wealth from the same dataset and found pockets of wealth more heavily concentrated: 'Those districts immediately adjacent to the two main arterial routes through the City, the Cheapside and Cornhill east-west axis, and

the route up from London Bridge northwards along Gracechurch Street and Bishopsgate, can now be seen to be somewhat secondary in terms of taxpaying wealth to the areas set back from the main thoroughfares'.

364. Glass used the £20 figure as a measure of wealth in his classic analysis and this has been roughly compared with the 1638 tithes list, the Royal Aid, the 1671 subsidy, the 1673–1674 assessment and the 1593–1694 4s Aid in this text. Glass, *London Inhabitants Within the Walls 1695*. The main thoroughfares were along Cheapside (Cheap and Bassishaw Wards) and between Bishopsgate and the river (Bishopsgate Within, Cornhill, Langbourn, Candlewick, Lime Street, Billingsgate and Bridge Wards) showed the greatest increases.
365. Indeed, payments were slightly anticipated.
366. The tax year began on 6 April in England under the Gregorian calendar from 1752.
367. LMA: COL/CHD/LA/03/007/014 [25 Car. II, c. 1, 18-months' assessment, 1673–1674. Assessments: for the first quarter Aldersgate Within Ward] c. May 1673.
368. Ward, *The English Land Tax*, p. 90.
369. The first meeting of the tax cycle, BRO: F/Tax/M1 and M2, Restoration commissioners' minutes 1663–1664 and 1665–1680. The one late meeting should have taken place on 4 September, but actually took place on the seventh, and there may have been a last minute delay given preparatory documents was dated 4 September.
370. 16 & 17 Car. II, c. 1, Royal Aid, 1664–1667, SoR, vol. 5, pp. 525–552, s. III.
371. Ibid., s. VII.
372. BRO: F/Tax/2, tax assessments. Strictly there were 17 parishes and one precinct—Castle Precinct, but 18 parishes are often referred to in the secondary literature and here.
373. There are also some surviving for the one-month's assessment and the 11-months' assessment which immediately followed the Royal Aid and Additional Aid with virtually identical parish quotas.
374. BRO: F/Tax/M/2, Restoration commissioners' minutes.
375. Chandaman, *The English Public Revenue*, p. 160, argues that both pound rates and local quotas were intended by the legislation during the Interregnum, but the pound rate was generally abolished in land tax legislation after 1657 until the Revolution.
376. Sources: chiefly from New Romney: KHLC: NR/RTa1-27; and Lydd, KHLC: ZLY/1-2 & NR/RTa28.
377. Although, as the 1671 subsidy required a pound rate, it may have done so at this point, but unfortunately no parish assessments survive. Otherwise, unlike Kent or London, although the Bristol authorities set

parish quotas, they never proposed a Restoration pound rate of any kind according to surviving commissioners' minute books and tax assessments. Sources: BRO: F/Tax/M/2, Restoration commissioners' minutes; BRO: F/Tax/A/1-4, Restoration assessments.

378. 1660s: BRO: F/Tax/A/2; 1693–1694: BRO: F/Tax/A/14. 1660s real estate is based on parish tax quotas from the Restoration commissioners' minute book, BRO: F/Tax/M/2 * 71.23% = average proportion of real estate as opposed to personal estates in parishes for which assessments survive; 1693–1694 real estate figures are based on the surviving assessments from 1693 or 1694 if unavailable. Occupied acreage after Ralph and Williams, *The Inhabitants of Bristol in 1696*, p. xxii.

379. Sacks, *The Widening Gate*: Fig. 3 for City divisions. Sources: Bristol duplicates, TNA: E182/837 (1689–1692)–E182/842 (1730–1734). For earlier periods; BRO: F/Tax/M/2 Restoration commissioners' minutes.

380. Non-payers were not just the familiar widows and aged poor. On the face of the 1677 assessment in Castle Baynard Ward, someone, probably a collector, had written in the margin those that were poor and probable non-payers. In this case, it included Giles Munkton, a poor cloth-drawer; Richard Foote, a tailor; James Salter, another cloth-drawer; William Lane, a plasterer; Edward Morris, a victualler; Thomas Claridge, a labourer; Richard Bishop, a journeyman carpenter; and John Wilmott a bookbinder. Source: LMA: COL/CHD/LA/03/061/022 [29 Car. II, c. 1, 17-months' assessment, 1677–1678. Assessment for first quarter Cripplegate Without, Red Cross Street, White Cross Street Precincts].

381. Sources: John Smart of Guildhall, *A Short Account of the Several Wards, Precincts, Parishes, &c in London* (London, 1742), Eighteenth Century Collections Online. Gale. Cambridge University Library; Finlay and Shearer 'Population Growth and Suburban Expansion', pp. 37–59, https://www.locatinglondon.org/static/Project.html.

382. HOCJ, vol. 21, 4 March 1728, p.71, where the vicar, churchwardens, vestry, and other inhabitants and landholders of the parish of St. Martin-in-the-Fields petitioned parliament that the newly carved out parish of St. George, Hanover Square was untaxed.

383. BRO: F/Tax/A/4, assessment for 30 Car. II, c. 1, 18-months' assessment, 1678–1680, SoR, vol. 5, pp. 867–883.

384. KHLC: NR/RTa9, New Romney assessment has the Kent-wide rates per quarter: The Royal Aid rate was: 5½d/£ Landlord and 1d/£ stock and crop on tenants; Additional Aid rate: 4d/£ Landlord and 1d/£ stock on crop for the tenants = 3s-10d/£ in all. There are identical figures for Lydd, KHLC: Ly/9/2/4-8, assessments for the Royal Aid.

385. LMA: COL/CHD/LA/02/028, 'The Accompt of Thomas Player' for 13 Car. II, St.2, c. 3, 18-months' assessment, 1661–1663, SoR, vol. 5, pp. 325–348.
386. As in the book of duplicates for all six quarters of the 18-months' assessment of 1673–1674, TNA: E179/129/745. See also Stephen J. Pierpoint, 'The importance of direct taxation to the Fiscal-military state in Early Modern Britain', *Structural Change and Economic Dynamics*, vol. 40, 2017, pp. 13–28.
387. The Exchange Office was sometimes known as the Tax Office, CTB, vol. 3, 27 July 1669, p. 120. It was at Great St. Helens.
388. Ward, 'The Office of Taxes', pp. 204–205. It ceased to function in 1670, but it was effectively replaced by the similar Treasury's 'Agents for Taxes' with its own Exchange Office and by 1673 this office had supervisory control over hearth money and direct taxes.
389. Chandaman, *The English Public Revenue*, p. 182; Coleby, *Central Government and the Localities*, Chapter 2.
390. 'Head-collector' was the normal term used during the Restoration and 'high-collector' during the Interregnum and earlier. Sometimes reference is simply to 'collector' and 'sub-collector'.
391. According to: 13 Car. II, St.2, c. 3, 18-months' assessment, 1661–1663, SoR, vol. 5, pp. 325–348. '[Head]-Collectors and sub collectors are hereby required to pay in all and every the su[m]ms so received by them to the said Receivers-Gen[er]all'.
392. The 18-months' assessment [25 Car. II, c. 1, 18-months' assessment, 1673–1674, SoR, vol. 5, pp. 752–782], copied the 1671 subsidy [22 & 23 Car. II, c. 3, subsidy, 1671, SoR, vol. 5, pp. 693–703], in this regard.
393. The first of the new land taxes with a quota, 9 Wm. III, c. 10, £1,484,015 Land Tax, 1698, SoR, vol. 7, pp. 307–364.
394. There are examples of such correspondence in Bristol.
395. Some roles appear more permanent, e.g. that of beadle.
396. The assessment might cover one quarter, but following the 1640s tradition of monthly assessments the amounts were usually stated as a monthly amount.
397. Braddick, *Parliamentary Taxation*, p. 66*ff*.
398. CTB, vol. 4, 14 April 1673, pp. 110.
399. BRO: F/Tax/A/2/CP a-b assessments.
400. BRO: F/Tax/A/14/CP and 18/CP assessments.
401. BRO: F/Tax/A/2/StJ and BRO: F/Tax/A/14/StJ assessments.
402. There are a very small number of exceptions to this pattern. Source: LMA: COL/CHD/LA/03/various. Statute names after Chandaman, *The English Public Revenue*, Chapter V, pp. 138–195.
403. Brooks, 'Public Finance and Political Stability', p. 289.

404. Restoration: based on 357 assessments in LMA: COL/CHD/LA/03/various. Earlier: Pre-Restoration continuities and discontinuities are hard to establish given scant survival of evidence other than for Bassishaw Ward with a continuous run of assessments and named officials. In the period 1643–1650, twenty collectors can be matched with names on the 3 October 1646 'estimate'. Here, tax collection rotated between the middle to upper ranks (in rent terms) of male householders, but not the top rank. Only two names appear more than once and that for the two assessments in 1644, probably collected at the same time.
405. BRO: F/Tax/A/2 Restoration assessments various from surviving quarters. BRO: F/Tax/M2 Restoration commissioners' minute book
406. LMA: COL/CHD/LA/03/066/025[above] Warrant attached to the collectors' copy of the assessment signed by Sir Thomas Bludworth by then the Lord Mayor and Aldermen Sir Thomas Adams and Sir William Hooker. There are also surviving collectors' copy assessments and warrants for the same quarters for Bread Street Ward (LMA: COL/CHD/LA/03/066/006[above]) and Langbourn Ward (LMA: COL/CHD/LA/03/066/020[above) with identical language.
407. The Portsoken Ward assessment for the first quarter of the 18-months' assessment of 1673–1674 is a collectors' copy signed by the Mayor Sir Robert Hanson and Aldermen Sir John Frederick and Sir William Peake (LMA: COL/CHD/LA/03/014/011[above]), 25 Car. II, c. 1, 18-months' assessment, 1673–1674, SoR, vol. 5, pp. 752–782.
408. In this case to pay Richard Reeves Esquire the receiver-general for this 18-months' assessment, 1673–1674, in Lombard Street.
409. LMA: COL/CHD/LA/03/various.
410. LMA: COL/CHD/LA/03/various wards, quarters 1–2, 3–4, 5–6, 7–9, 10–11, and 12.
411. LMA: P69/DUN2/C/002/MS02969004/002, *local assessment book*. In a very few cases, names are missing or illegible. This contains 24 varied assessments from 29 November 1660–1671 including the subsidy, an assessment (militia tax), and an assessment for pavements. It also lists and gives a summary of a further 13 earlier assessments for the period from 25 December 1657.
412. This last was Robert Olarentia for The Strand offices already mentioned.
413. LMA: COL/CHD/LA/03/various. R^2 linear regression calculation of displayed data from Microsoft Excel.
414. Boulton, *Neighbourhood and Society*.
415. Located in Watling Street[?] and near St. Mary-le-Bow churchyard respectively.

416. LMA: COL/CHD/LA/03/059/002 [30 Car. II, c. 1, 18-months' assessment, 1678–1680. First and second quarters Cordwainer].
417. LMA: COL/CHD/LA/03/various.
418. LMA: CLC/W/GA/002, Bassishaw Wardmote Inquest minutes commencing in 1655.
419. Based on the author's detailed analysis of Bassishaw's detailed Wardmote account LMA: CLC/W/GA/002.
420. After Carlos and Neal, 'Women in the City'.
421. Evidence: the nomination of collectors by common councilmen/assessors is visible on the face of numerous assessments, LMA: COL/CHD/LA/03/various. It should be noted also that many collectors acted at ward precinct level and not across the ward.
422. Both chosen by the Wardmote. Examples here from Bassishaw Wardmote Inquest minutes 1655–1752 LMA: CLC/W/GA/002 1655–1688.
423. There are certainly exceptions for wealthy incomers, for example.
424. Sources: LMA: COL/CHD/LA/03/various. This figure is from the date of the precept starting the tax process to the assessment completion date.
425. COL/CHD/LA/03/014/004 [25 Car. II, c. 1, 18-months' assessment, 1673–1674, SoR, vol. 5, pp. 752–782; Ward returns of deficiencies, first—sixth quarters].
426. LMA: COL/CHD/LA/03/014/004 [above].
427. Other examples include (1) Cripplegate Without £2-9s-6d per quarter (first quarter 27 December 1673); (2) Broad Street £4-17s-0d (sixth quarter); (3) Aldgate fifth precinct, 5s-6d per month [sixth quarter 15 December 1674]; (4) St. Mildred Bread Street, £1-10s-0d per quarter (sixth quarter); (5) Fore Street & Grub Street precinct of Cripplegate Without, 2s-4d per month (sixth quarter); and (6) Broad Street lower, unstated error but countersigned by Broad Street commissioner, William Savage.

CHAPTER 4

After the Glorious Revolution

Heavier and more permanent post-revolutionary tax burdens created fresh challenges for officials in south-eastern counties and urban areas which bore much of the fiscal weight (Fig. 1.2). Parliament and Treasury, anxious for success, improved their oversight and assurance processes. Administrators in urban settings, particularly in poorer parishes, witnessed taxpayer populations more mobile, mortal and impoverished than elsewhere which perhaps made it more difficult to bring tax monies in, particularly as money also had to be found for substantial local rates. By the early 1700s, officials in London, Bristol and Kent, had developed bespoke solutions to these challenges which relied *inter alia* on increased human resources, more experienced officials, a practical choice of taxpayer, process flexibility and simplification, and increased delegation and empowerment. Process improvement did not cease in 1700; it must be stressed. More of the administrative work was now delegated to long-serving paid officials who had appropriate skills and capabilities. Clerks became a key resource and were given additional rewards. Paid clerks and collectors were overseen by an increasingly experienced body of senior officials.

The post-revolutionary land tax was very substantially levied on real estate, with lighter burdens on personal property. Government salaries became a particular target not only in urban locations like London and Bristol, but also in Kent where perhaps two-thirds of all England's riding officers for the customs were stationed including men at New Romney

S. Pierpoint, *The Success of English Land Tax Administration 1643–1733*, Palgrave Studies in the History of Finance,
https://doi.org/10.1007/978-3-319-90260-9_4

and Winchelsea.[1] A proportion of such tax costs were transferred back to the government.[2] Interest rates on state debt secured on land taxes fell from 7 to 8% in the 1690s to 3% by 1723—of course interest rates also declined on other forms of state debt.[3] Central coordination and scrutiny was available from the Board of Taxes established in 1688 with its experienced officials.[4] The House of Commons regularly asked for details of arrears of taxes,[5] set up committees to investigate shortfalls[6] and exposed corruption as in the case of Morgan Whitley, receiver for North Wales and Cheshire.[7] Such Treasury and Commons scrutiny of arrears, cited as evidence of decline by Ward, on the contrary suggest improved assurance processes at work across a vast enterprise.[8] In some years, full accounts of payments or arrears were presented to the Commons from all county receivers,[9] and regular general summaries were made available.[10] The Tax Agents also frequently reported to Treasury about the performance of receivers in robust terms. The minutes from 1 July 1701 state:

> The Agents for Taxes are called in. They think the Cobs will run further in debt if they be kept in [as Receivers][11]: and say that Mason [Receiver] of Oxfordshire has been slow in his payments. Mr. Austen is to be [put in as Receiver] in the place of Cob.
>
> They say Kent is a good Receiver [for Lincolnshire] and therefore my Lords will continue him.
>
> Tho. Lloyd is to be Receiver of Cheshire and North Wales.
>
> They say that Mr. St. Johns is not fit to be entrusted as a Receiver.[12]

Restoration land taxes were occasionally substantial, but levied only in years of mobilisation and demobilisation and when Parliament would grant them. After the Glorious Revolution, the tax became effectively permanent and often at a four-shilling rate which was heavier than ever before. These post-revolutionary levies were the major supply for the Nine Years' War and the War of the Spanish Succession, and metropolitan London's[13] specified contribution rose to almost one-sixth of the nation's total by 1698.[14] London's share of national population had grown to exceed one-tenth, but only a quarter of them now lived in the 25 City wards as the metropolis expanded.[15] The detailed shape of Restoration regional land tax quotas survived until 1692 (Fig. 1.2). There then followed four years of experimentation without a quota at a fixed tax rate in the pound as already attempted in 1671. As then, this pound rate method was unsuccessful and income declined from

c. £1.92 m in 1693 to £1.66 m in 1697.[16] Nevertheless, the detailed assessment for the Four Shilling Aid of 1693–1694 formed the basis for the re-imposed, but modified 1698 national quotas which remained substantially fixed thereafter.[17] The City fathers in London extended this quota 'fixing' to apply to their local ward quotas as well (see Fig. 5.9).[18] The new fixed national quotas did not resolve perceived and real injustices that the South and East were more heavily taxed than the North and West; in fact, it made matters worse. The former would pay two shillings tax per acre, according to near contemporary sources, compared with a few pence in the latter (Fig. 1.2).[19] The new quotas were also much greater than the historic ones for the growing urban centres including metropolitan London (50% increase), Bristol (28%), Norwich (60%), Exeter (40%) and dozens more towns and boroughs nationally.[20] Even the little Kentish town and port of New Romney saw its quota increased by 20%.[21] The county of Kent, which had been historically very heavily taxed as discussed above, actually saw its quota share modestly declined by 13%, but it still paid 4.2% of national taxation. Most other southern counties saw heavier quotas (Table 1.1).[22] Population was probably static or declining in some central City of London wards,[23] although in extra-mural wards and the wider metropolis it continued to expand. The 25 City ward's 23,000 taxpayers[24] paid 6.2% of national land taxation,[25] an annual average at a four-shilling rate of £5.30 each.[26] In comparison, Bristol could spread its 0.37% share of national quota more thinly across newly developed suburban greenfield and central brownfield sites with their expanding populations. Here, taxpayers grew in number from 3,800 in 1693 to 4,600 by 1733 (Fig. 4.3; Table 4.1).[27] In 1693, they would at 4s/£ pay an average of £1.95 each[28] falling to £1.60 by mid-century. The figure in New Romney[29] was similar at about £2.00, but this was less than Wingham in Kent at £3.09.[30] A four-shilling national tax charge produced about two million pounds.[31] Broadly, if as in the case studies, about one-sixth or one-seventh of English inhabitants paid tax, and assuming a population of England and Wales of 5.2 million, then there were about 740,000–860,000 land taxpayers paying £2.30–£2.70 annually on average.[32] Those actually suffering the tax burden, because of occupiers' deduction of tax from rent, and the impact of the tax on land markets, are much more difficult to quantify. However, Walpole (see epigram) was certainly incorrect, as he would have been well aware, when he maintained that the land tax fell on only 1% of the population which would imply about £38 tax annually at a four-shilling rate.[33] Archibald Campbell, the first Earl of Ilay was scarcely less extreme in 1732[34]:

> We all know what a small proportion the landed gentlemen of this nation bear to the rest of the people; we all know what a number of rich merchants, tradesmen, stock-holders, money-lenders, and other sorts of people there are in this nation, who have no landed estate, or but a very small land estate, in proportion to their other estates. None of these pay a farthing, or but a mere trifle towards the land tax … for the landed interest … taken together … do not make above a hundredth part of the people of this nation … [but pay] one third part of the whole money that has been raised for the public use.

The real estate element of land tax certainly became dominant nationwide. Land was importantly stable for a quota system and, if somewhat under-assessed, could minimise the likelihood of taxpayer appeal. Davison's Kentish analysis from the Furnesse estate in 1710 demonstrates this underassessment at work. Her data 'show a close relationship between the rent paid and "taxable rent" … [but at] … around 71.5% of their market rents'.[35] The real estate portion of land taxes reached 80% in the City of London and slightly more in Bristol.[36] In rural Kent, it was over 95%, as it had long been, with small amounts of tax on government salaries and stock.[37] As government officials proliferated, there was a greater proportion of tax raised from their salaries in urban locations as evident in Bristol (8–9% of all land tax),[38] the City of London[39] and New Romney (3–5%).[40] In 1701, Bristol commissioners had to adjust their quotas to accommodate them. 'This apportionment was afterwards altered because there was noe consideration of the Customs in the parish of St. Nicholas nor of the offices of the excise'.[41] London taxed incomes outside its ward structures including corporate profits, post office and excise office salaries and pensions in a separate category, often termed rather vaguely, 'Waters, etc.'[42] There was also tax on staff salaries at the Custom House and the Navy Office in Tower Ward. Tax on such incomes varied considerably from year to year but usually comprised over 10% of City land tax throughout the eighteenth century.[43] This sector even had its own specialist collection team, and one of their warrants survives dated 5 June 1700.[44] Those specialists included the City's chief accountant John Smart (1702–1737?), Daniel Mann (1689–1706), John Hutton (1696–1711) and Robert Walker (1696–1716). After 1716, John Smart was the sole collector (and see Sect. 4.5.3).

Local Urban Rates Employing National Land Tax Methodology

Land tax methods were so successful and seen to be so by contemporaries that they were used for local rates replacing customary methods. This was particularly true in urban areas.

Urban taxpayers had additional burdens with the poor to support, streets to clean, highways to repair and lamps to light. If these levies were lighter than land taxes, they could be considerable. The innovatory Bristol Poor Act of 1696, the first of its kind nationally, established a new body, the Corporation of the Poor, and transferred responsibility for poor relief to City authorities from parishes. Bristol merchant, financial author and sometime tax commissioner himself, John Cary was the main instigator of this measure for the better maintenance and employment of the poor.[45] He was strongly supported by Bristol's MPs, Sir Thomas Day and Robert Yate. The new Corporation's governors and deputy governors, like the aldermen and tax commissioners, were substantially drawn from the wealthy merchant classes.[46] The new rating method applied across the city and owed much to land taxes, and this may even have been promulgated by Cary himself. The old parish poor rate appears to have been a rather formulaic personal estate tax. In the parish of St. John in 1672 for instance, each ratepayer would suffer a specific rate, in this case 1s 1d, multiplied by an unspecified personal wealth measure, probably often stock in trade.[47] John Bradway paid the lowest amount that year, 2s-2d (2 × rate), and Edward Hearne and Mr James Cade the highest at £1-1s-8d (20 × rate). Far fewer people, apparently the wealthiest, paid this traditional rate in the parish in 1672 than contemporary land taxes. One hundred and fifty paid land tax, but only half that number paid the poor rate. Following the 1696 Act, Bristol's poor rate base was broadened and a real estate element, virtually identical to the land tax, was levied on occupiers. It is unclear, but there may have been a broader national transformation in local rates along these lines because Humphrey Prideaux, the Dean of Norwich, said in 1713 that 'the general usage now is to make a rate … on persons in respect of the lands … for this reason the farmer or occupier, not the landlord, is to pay the same'.[48] The 1698 poor rate for the parish of St. John included the old formulaic measure, but with a much larger charge on real estates at 9d/£ per half year. The real estate values were taken and strongly correlate with contemporary land taxes.[49] The other poor rate development was that the numbers assessed increased in the parish to about 150, the same as for the land tax. This initial city-wide poor rate was substantial and amounted to about a third of the land tax at £2,316, but this gap narrowed, until after 1767 the poor rate was always greater than a four-shilling land tax.[50] Bristolians paid annual local rates of various kinds amounting to more than £1,000 for much of the seventeenth century.[51] In 1705, lamp and scavenger rates amounted to approximately one quarter of the four-shilling land tax in Castle Precinct. Unlike the poor rate, these taxes did not apply land tax methodology.[52] If required, a highway rate might be levied as in St. Mary Redcliffe for 'Repairing the Highwayes in the said Parish beginning att the foot of Red Cliffe hill'. This costs £24, but the rate was not to 'exceed the sume of a 3d in the pound of the yearly value of the lands and tenements'.[53] In other words, land tax methods were in use here too.

The heavy post-restoration tax burdens in the City of London raised concerns about maintaining them in the face of falling rents and loss of trade when a new Thames bridge was proposed at Westminster which might divert commercial traffic away from the City itself. A note was drafted in January 1722 in the town clerk's office.[54] It correctly proclaimed that the City alone 'pays near a sixteenth part of the land tax charged on the whole Kingdom of Great Britain' and questioned 'how shall the Tax be paid if the rents be lessened & the citizens impoverished by the Bill'. On top of this, the City institutions including the Livery Companies contributed significantly to charity 'to educate the youth, maintain schools & hospitals, to pay stipends to ministers & to support the aged and impotent; most of their rents [income] consist in houses in London, which if this bill do pass will not be sufficient to do so many charitable acts'.

4.1 An Urban Challenge

Post-revolutionary urban land tax administrators in London and Bristol rose to the challenge of heavier burdens, frozen quotas, and growing and diverse populations. Processes were simplified, skilled clerks and experienced collectors employed, and taxpayers chosen and assessed with care and sensitivity.

Bristolians were concerned about sharp rises in new tax quotas after 1700. Robert Yate wrote to fellow Bristol MP Sir William Daines on 14 February 1702 bemoaning the new quota of £7,391-10s-8d caused by a rise from three to four shilling in the pound for 1702.[55] 'If wee doe not get an abatement for the personal estates and the offices, Sallaries and perquisites of the Customs and Excise', the City would be forced to levy a five-shilling tax on land to meet the quota. He urged the town clerk to assist using the historic 'Duplicates remaining in the Counsell house' to make appropriate calculations. This work was done, but the quota remained unchanged. As the 1702 quotas employed the 1693–1694 four-shilling assessment, it appears that Yates' worst fears were ill-founded. A contemporary and similar exercise took place in the City of London.[56] Non-payers, through death, poverty and removal, remained a long-term collection problem. The first remedy was to use the powers of distraint contained in the Act. Collectors enforced payment through the seizure and selling of goods. Indeed, these draconian powers, if slightly toned down, remain part of modern UK taxing powers. A note in the Bristol commissioners' minute book of c. 20 April 1717 indicated that a warrant was issued to seize goods 'a bagg of hopps and one cask of powdered sugar' of Joseph Waters and was sold to the Innholder at the appraised value of £10-11s-6d.[57]

The early 1700s saw the freezing of land tax quotas in the City of London, whilst underlying incomes and rents varied, for example, where there had been improvement or structures 'rebuilt [and] very much advanced'.[58] It was fortunate then that in the first decades of the new land tax the City saw only modest rental movement.[59] As rent levels rose rapidly later in the century, tax long ceased to reflect property value. The growth of metropolitan London's population beyond the City, coupled with modest population falls in some City wards, created the problem that, with a fixed quota, City dwellers were over-taxed compared with their near metropolitan neighbours. As London further expanded, there were questions as to how to tax new building developments when quotas were fixed. This pattern contrasts with the continuing flexibility of Bristol's parish quotas across the whole city (Fig. 3.13).

In Bristol, real property was principally domestic dwellings, but also included multiple forms of land-use according to the land tax assessments themselves.[60] It included: workshops, meeting houses, warehouses, soap houses, glass houses, timber yards, brew houses, offices, dock facilities,[61] shops, cellars, lofts, yards, stables, gardens, paddocks, orchards and animal pens, comprising at least 7% of the 1693–1694 real estate charge.[62] Some parish assessors probably did not trouble to distinguish non-domestic real estate, so this figure probably underestimates the full extent. In the transpontine parish of Temple, there is unusually detailed assessment information showing non-domestic property comprising 15% of real estate by annual value including land and gardens (5%), warehouses, soap houses and sugar houses (4%). Some real estate property had dual uses as dwellings and commercial premises by way of lofts, cellars, gardens and the ubiquitous 'house and shop'. If the very many individuals listed as having trades and occupations in the 1694–1695 poll and 1693–1694 assessment partly used domestic space for business use, then in St. Mary-le-Port parish this dual usage could have amounted to as much as 60% of the value of real estate and in St. Ewen, 55%.[63] Of course, these were central City parishes where retail and business premises proliferated, and any individuals no doubt paid tax from such commercial income. Elsewhere in suburban or transpontine parishes, such commercial usage was probably very much less.

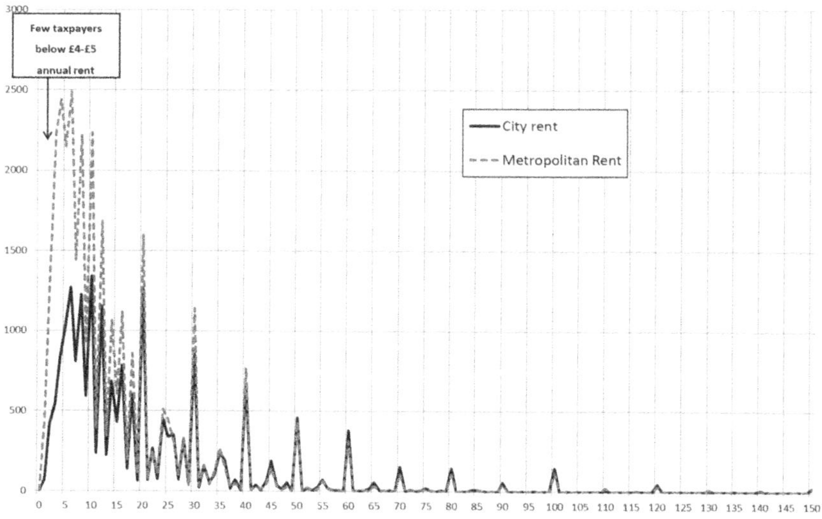

Fig. 4.1 The 1693–1694 distribution of city and metropolitan London rents £0–150 from land tax assessments showing both the uneven and likely rounded estimated rental values in both areas and the rapid decline below c. £4–5. Number of real estate taxpayers—vertical axis, rent in pounds—horizontal scale[64]

There were many valid reasons advanced for non-payment of taxes. People had moved or died, but often people could simply not afford to pay. Why assess poor people if getting money from them would be troublesome? The tremendous advantage of local assessment was that it could be sensitive to individual difficulties as shown in all three case study areas. In general, poorer people living in property just above the minimum statutory 20 shillings annual rent could be exempted. In the City, few were taxed below a rent of £4–5 in the 1690s (Fig. 4.1), and this was probably true even earlier. It was probably true in Bristol considering the taxed rent profiles (Fig. 4.2). Adjustments were often required. In London's St. Bartholomew-the-Great precinct, Farringdon Without Ward, for the first quarter of the 17-month assessment of 1677, William Barret and Widow Lammas were excused 2s 2d tax because: 'Both their houses fell down (being rotten) … & some people killed therein'. On the same return, dated 22 August, William Ford had been charged 'by mistake' because his house belonged to a neighbouring parish.[65] In 1717 Bristol, 'The Commissioners in consideration of the late fire in the parish of Christ Church have thought fit for this yeare to ease the same the summe of £15 with intent that th[e] houses of Mathew Bown and John White should be eased and that the houses and stock of Mr Anthony Plomer, the widow Baker and Mr William Salmon lately burnt down be not charged'.[66]

4.1.1 *Identifying Taxpayers and Inhabitants*

Post-revolutionary legislation still broadly taxed all 'Mannors, Messuages, Lands, Tenements, [and] Hereditaments or other the Premisses',[67] with annual rents of 20 shillings and above, and 'required'[68] occupiers to pay. Urban assessors in particular had, since the 1640s, varied these rules to tax landlords directly, as discussed, or exempted additional poor households beyond the statutory provision. There were choices to be made. Because of the good contemporary document survival, these choices can be examined more closely in the post-revolutionary period. Assessors were typically well-known men who knew their locales, because they were selected by London's local ward commissioners or chosen by Bristol's parishes. They were thus well placed to make appropriate choices. They would be answerable to wards and parishes if they failed to assess reasonably, and to the clerk if they erred.

Cities were not static; different parts developed at different rates. Bristol's increasing taxpayer numbers since the Restoration reflected greenfield and brownfield development (Fig. 4.3; Table 4.1). Central

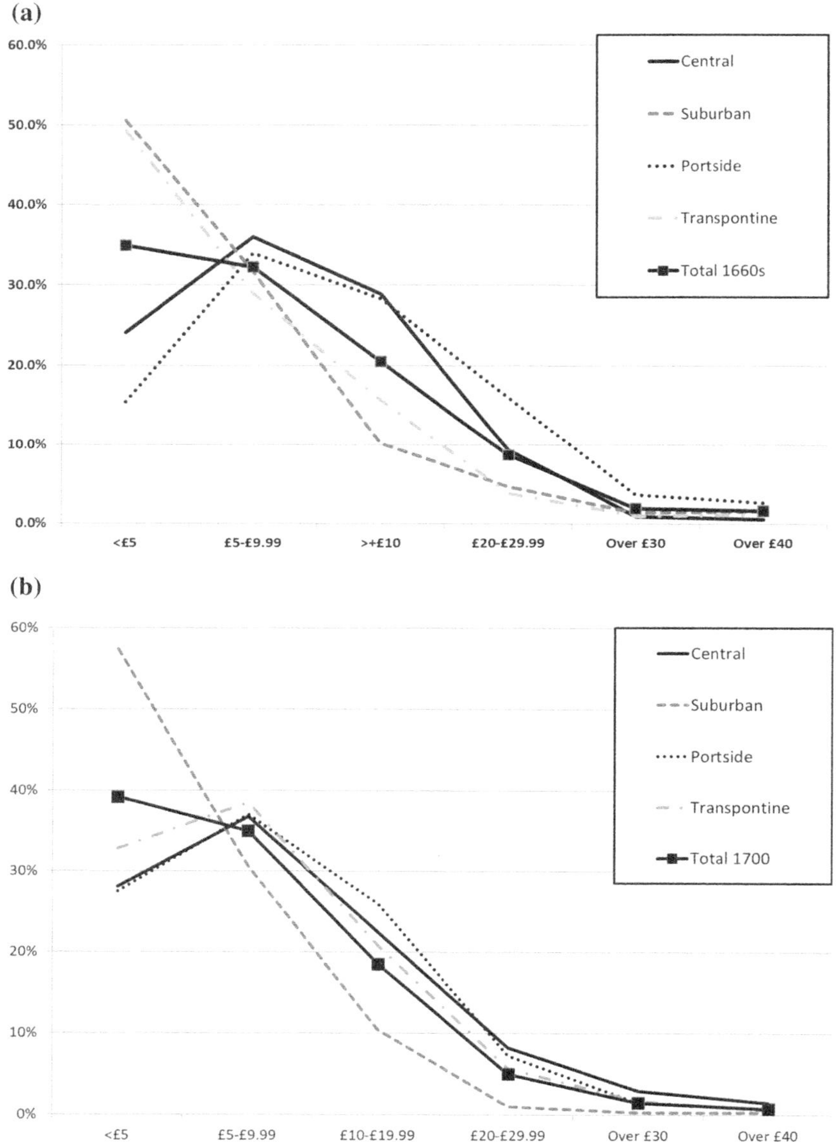

Fig. 4.2 City of Bristol comparison of taxed rent profiles as estimated for (**a**) 1660s and (**b**) early 1700s.[69] *Note* the flattening of the rent profile below £5 in the 1660s and 1700s suggesting exemption of poor households

brownfield development was largely on the old Bristol Castle site, where the City itself held significant lands.[70] This fostered taxpayer growth in Castle Precinct (second in rank in quota growth in Table 3.3). Residential development also occurred in the adjacent suburban parishes of St. James (fifth) and Sts. Phillip & Jacob (third) to the north and east, respectively. Suburban St. Augustine (fourth) and portside St. Stephen (first) also witnessed taxpayer population growth, which probably reflects development of the Marsh by the river. Such growth figures can be deceptive because a single tax charge can mask multiple properties. Castle Precinct is a good example because significantly development had already taken place by the time of the surviving 1666 tax assessments following the 1656 destruction of the Castle itself. A single tax charge for 'City rents'[71] in Castle Precinct's assessment for the 1666 Royal Aid at 16s-8d per month, or £10 per ann., probably equates to total rents of £177.72 in the chamberlain's accounts.[72] In those accounts, the City was receiving some 73 rent payments in respect of over 80 properties, probably collected by John Chock, but with just this single tax charge.[73] By 1693–1694, City rents in Castle Precinct had increased to £202.46,[74] but tax assessment was now significantly on individual residents and landlords and not within a 'City rents' charge.[75] Therefore, much of the taxpayer growth in Castle Precinct (Table 3.3) did not reflect growing numbers of properties, taxpayers or people but a movement in the place of the immediate tax charge from City to inhabitants. This also is visible from the chamberlain's 1690s accounts which show dozens of tax deductions allowed from rents paid to the City in Castle Precinct by tenants, as provided for in the legislation.[76] In other words by the 1690s tenants of the Corporation usually paid the collector directly, but deducted the tax from their rent and thus the tax burden fell on the City. In the 1660s the City probably paid the collector directly with the same result.

Nevertheless, Fig. 4.2 shows a falling away or flattening of the profile of taxed rents below £5, both in the 1660s as well as in 1700. This could of course simply reflect the underlying rent profile in the City. However, it appears much more likely to be because assessors chose to directly tax wealthier landlords for tenants wherever possible at this level, or exempt more of the poorest households completely. In addition, in Bristol, as in many towns and cities, the additional post-revolutionary tax had to be found. Population growth had helped, but at four-shilling tax rates, existing taxpayers would have had to pay considerably more. This was achieved whilst the proportion of tax on land, compared with personal estates increased.

Fig. 4.3 Bristol's changing tax charge numbers between the 1660s and the 1730s[77]

Table 4.1 Bristol's changing tax charge numbers 1660s–1700s

Real estate	*1664–1667*	*1679*	*1693*	*1700s*	*Percentage increase 1660s to 1700s*
Central	674	883	1028	993	47%
Portside	607	605	714	662	9%
Suburban	548	1,097	1,308	1,289	135%
Transpontine	586	614	786	725	24%
Total real estate	2,415	3,199	3,836	3,669	52%
Personal estates	***1664–1667***	***1679***	***1693***	***1700s***	***Percentage increase 1660s to 1700s***
Central	382	391	804	421	10%
Portside	216	238	121	176	−19%
Suburban	174	142	101	114	−34%
Transpontine	241	206	179	143	−41%
Total personal estates	1,013	977	1,205	854	−16%
	1664–1667	*1679*	*1693*	*1700s*	*1730 estimate*
Total real estate	2,415	3,199	3,836	3,669	4,615
Total personal estates	1,013	977	1,205	854	586

Can the increase in tax rate on land in Bristol be estimated? The heaviest Restoration tax burden had been during the mid-1660s to late 1660s, when guide tax rates on land were 3s-10d/£ in Kent and

3s-6d/£ in London. Bristol never stated such a guide rate in the 1660s or at any time during the Restoration, but it can be estimated by comparison with the 1671 subsidy. This had employed land tax methodology and a 1s/£ tax rate and had thus levied £1,165 on land.[78] Assuming that the same land was taxed, the comparable tax for the 1667 assessment was about £2,950, suggesting a tax rate of c. 2s-6d/£, much lower than in contemporary London or Kent.[79] The post-revolutionary increase was therefore proportionately so much greater.

4.1.2 *Estimating Urban Populations and Urban Taxpayer Numbers*

Who paid tax and who did not and why? The arguments advanced here are that assessors were making sensible choices so the local tax quota could be gathered with least trouble. Estimating the proportion of individuals who paid tax, particularly in urban areas, is not a straightforward matter. The populations themselves were shifting and numbers are contested in the historiography. This section will attempt to make some broad estimates of who was taxed and who was not, which individuals were included on the assessor's tax roll and who would escape and why.

In considering the assessors' choice of taxpayers, it is first essential to consider general estimates of urban populations. In London, previous authors have compared populations indicated by the 1690s marriage duty assessments with calculations based on the Bills of Mortality and Birth Records.[80] The marriage duty is often seen as one of the best sources because it attempted to list all individuals. However, there are uncertainties about all these sources and Harding believes the marriage duty understates the population because of 'omissions and the floating population'.[81] Such a floating population was anticipated in the marriage duty legislation which proposed that 'such Persons as shall sojorne or lodge in their respective Houses' should be reported by the householder, but how consistently was this done?[82] Harding's 1690s population figure is 122,089 for the 25 City of London wards based on the marriage duty, but allowing for such omissions she suggests 135,000, and perhaps even 148,000.[83] In Bristol, the 1696 marriage duty records suggest a contemporary population of 20,157 in the 18 City parishes as recorded in the complete set of assessments for that year.[84] Harding argued for 10% as a grossing-up factor for London, but regarded this as something of a guess.[85] Allowing for a similar broad estimation of floating population and omissions in Bristol might suggest an additional 2,000 inhabitants in 1700.[86] There is a difference between 'omissions' and floating or 'transience' following Harding. 'Omissions' suggest error or a deliberate choice on the part of assessors, and by implication, the land tax assessments would probably be similarly deficient. The dwellings and other occupancies of a transient population on the other hand might still be assessed directly on their landlords.

Since the 1640s as discussed, land taxes had been occupier levies on tenants, but with some ability to deduct tax from rent.[87] Taxing landlords directly was the long and widely used practical urban method of taxing multi-occupancy and levying tax on homes occupied by the poor or those less likely to pay. Many city dwellers lived in tenements and other properties where multiple-occupation was common. Secondly, the statutory exemption for the poor in properties below 20s annual rent could be locally extended.[88] In Bristol, c. 4% of taxpayers were deleted from tax lists between 1693–1694 and 1703, and those removed were often paying just above 20s rent (Fig. 4.3, Table 4.1).[89] Local tax assessors, who would have had considerable relevant local knowledge, were probably deliberately omitting homes where people would be least likely to pay or choosing to tax landlords directly. The process would be simpler and collectors' lives made easier. Of course, this could be people moving away in tougher times, but this seems unlikely, and in any case, there are similar patterns in London. In small samples from six varied City of London wards, the corresponding reduction was between 3.8 and 11.1% (Table 4.4).[90] Tenements and houses with named landlords become common in the City of London's extra-mural parish assessments and in alleys, yards and courts across the City. For example, collectors were instructed in 1719 for the First Precinct of Bishopsgate Without Ward that, 'All the Houses until you come to the third house on the left hand in Petty France are rated to Mr Hutchinson ending at John Hills'.[91] Nearby a certain Robert Street was rated at only 18 shillings for two houses behind this. A short distance away, 'The next three houses and Loome ally and all the houses until you come to the 5th house in halfe Moone Street are rated to Mr Street at the White Horse for Mr Claris Landlord at £80 p[er] ann'.

Taxing landlords was not always straightforward as the following example illustrates. A Bristol certificate of uncollected tax amounts for the first and second quarters of the four-shilling land tax was submitted to the Exchequer on 2 July 1694.[92] The document sets out the amounts abated by tax commissioners including some properties belonging to Joshua Cumberbatch in the parish of St. James (Table 4.2).

Table 4.2 City of Bristol, parish of St. James. Certificate of arrears excerpt submitted to the Exchequer on 2 July 1694[93]

Owner	*Location*	*Charged*	*Parish*	*Quarter* (£)	*Arrears written off* (£)		*Rent* (£)
Joshua Cumberbatch	Merchant street	Joseph Baily	St. James	£0.15	£0.15	No distress can be found	£3.00
Joshua Cumberbatch	Merchant street	Henry Stibbs	St. James	£0.10	£0.10	No distress can be found	£2.00
Joshua Cumberbatch	Merchant street	Richard Young	St. James	£0.25	£0.25	No distress can be found	£5.00
Joshua Cumberbatch	Merchant street	Richard Jones	St. James	£0.10	£0.10	No distress can be found	£2.00
Joshua Cumberbatch	Merchant street	Goodwife Paine	St. James	£0.05	£0.05	No distress can be found	£1.00
Joshua Cumberbatch	Merchant street	George Smith	St. James	£0.05	£0.05	No distress can be found	£1.00
Joshua Cumberbatch	Merchant street	Samuel Jones	St. James	£0.15	£0.15	No distress can be found	£3.00
Joshua Cumberbatch	Inner court	Thomas Clarke	St. James	£0.05	£0.10	No distress can be found	£1.00
Joshua Cumberbatch	Inner court	John Fishpool	St. James	£0.08	£0.15	No distress can be found	£1.50
Joshua Cumberbatch	Barrs lane	Nathaniel Pope	St. James	£0.10	£0.10	No distress can be found	£2.00
Joshua Cumberbatch	Broadmead	Mary Thomas	St. James	£0.10	£0.10	No distress can be found	£2.00
Martha Holway?	Bridewell lane	Martha Holway, 2 tenements	St. James	£0.25	£0.25	No distress can be found	£5.00
TOTAL					£1.55		£28.50

Thus, 'Also that another tenem[en]t upp stayrs fronting also to the said [Merchant] street and adjoining to Younges tenem[en]t as we are informed belonging also to the said Comberbatch and the said Hawkins inheritance is rated and charged (by the name Goodwife Paine) at one shilling per quarter & that the said second quarters charge is due unpaid and no distress can there be found for one shilling'. Given such arrears, it would surely have been simplest to tax Cumberbatch directly. Unfortunately, this was impractical as he appears to have been an absentee landlord. There is no Joshua Cumberbatch listed anywhere in Bristol in the 1696 marriage duty assessments nor in the St. James parish land tax assessments for 1693–1694 or 1702.[94] There is a recorded Joshua Cumberbatch residing in St. Nicholas parish in 1684 apprenticed as a 'horner'.[95] However, neither the current author nor contemporary assessors could locate Cumberbatch in the 1690s. The assessors had no choice, given hard-up tenants, but to seek abatement of the tax from the commissioners. Many tenants with small rents in Merchant Street and environs continued to be assessed directly in the early eighteenth century including some in Table 4.2 which indicates that the assessment of landlords was not always possible.[96]

In the City of London, for the 1693–1694 Four Shilling Aid, there is a sharp fall-off in rents below £4–5 as is clear from Fig. 4.1. This could be for one of three reasons; few such rents existed, there was a direct assessment on landlords, or there was an exemption.[97] There is further discussion on this below. Further, across the City, numerous poorer taxpayers disappeared from the assessments by the early 1700s as described above (Table 4.4).[98] In contrast, there is no sign of any reduction in taxpayer numbers in New Romney in Kent.[99] The 1690s was a period of economic downturn and perhaps some taxpayers simply moved away and this may partly explain these city patterns.[100] On the other hand, hard times provided an additional incentive for assessors to remove the poorest from their assessments, which reiterates the importance of sensitivity to local factors.

A further detailed exploration of these possibilities begins in Bristol. A comparison of the 1696 Bristol marriage duty and 1693–1694 land tax assessments suggests numerous occupiers were not taxed directly or at all—but how many? A starting point is Holman who believed that there were 4,560 households based on the detailed marriage duty assessment, which compares with the estimated c. 3,583 land tax charges (Table 4.3).[101] This implies that at least 21% of potential taxpayer occupants were exempt or taxed on their landlords, but this percentage needs to be increased for non-domestic land tax charges (see row F. in Table 4.3). The estimated rent profile, falling away below £5 in Fig. 4.2 suggests exemption or landlord taxation and something similar in the 1660s.[102] Of course, households are notoriously difficult to define and Holman, even on a cursory examination of the data, appears to omit likely tenements and multiple occupiers from his calculation.[103] Two methods are suggested here to adjust Holman's figures for such omissions.

Firstly, taking the example of the central but relatively poor parish of St. John-the-Baptist, Holman believed there were 195 households, using marriage duty data, and the tax assessment shows 161 tax charges.[104] Of these charges, 18 can be identified as non-domestic, being cellars, gardens, a yard, 'brewhouses', warehouses, stables, 'the bowling green' and the 'Taylers Hall', leaving 143 domestic taxpayers (Table 4.3). There were also ten 'alms-people' shown as exempt in the marriage duty assessment but missing from the land tax assessments.[105] Some land tax charges indicate multiple properties with significant numbers of tenements, tenants and one house, all taxed directly on their 27 landlords. The number of such properties was sometimes unstated; for example, the assessment simply mentions 'tenants' or 'tenements', so some estimate must be made. Using the city-wide average tenement rent of two pounds annual rent suggests approximately 100 properties in this parish,[106] or an additional 73 [100, less the 27 already charged].[107] The resulting estimated number of domestic occupiers therefore amounts to 161 – 18 [non-domestic] + 73 [tenements] + 10 [Alms] = 226[108], which is rather higher than Holman's 195 households. Of course, tenements and alms people might overlap, but this is unclear.

The second method uses the marriage duty records for 1696 and deducts from the total number of inhabitants those never or very rarely taxed in their own right: wives, children, other kin, servants, apprentices, lodgers and tablers (Table 4.3).[109] If the remainder are separate households, this gives a higher number in this parish of 245 compared with the 226 of the first method. However, it is possible that some of this 245 may be undemarcated relatives, tablers, or servants in the marriage duty assessment. As the marriage duty itself may contain omissions, the figure may still be a reasonable one.[110] The resulting estimation is shown graphically in Fig. 4.4.

These estimations are rather broad because land tax assessments usually show 'several tenements' or sometimes houses, without further

Table 4.3 City of Bristol parishes with an attempted reconciliation of the number of inhabitants from the 1696 marriage duty and the Four Shilling Aid of 1693–1694[111]

Category	*St. John-the-Baptist*	*Castle Precinct*	*St. Ewen*	*All Saints*	*St. Mary-le-Port*	*St. Werburgh*	*Other parishes*	*Total*
A. Listed inhabitants [1696 marriage duty]	901	1,377	155	274	401	289	16,760	20,157
B. Less non-taxpayers								
—Servants	114	185	42	84	60	78	n/a	
—Children	339	519	57	80	149	92	n/a	
—Other Kin	6	26	1	8	6	2	n/a	
—'Almes people'	10	3	0	8	0	0	293	314
—Wives	153	226	19	36	70	37	n/a	
—Tablers and lodgers	34	76	0	0	10	8	n/a	
C. Revised total	**245**	**342**	**36**	**58**	**106**	**72**	**c. 5,135**	**c. 5,994**
D. Tenements, tenants, etc.	73	37	0	0	1	4	368	483
E. Difference to reconcile C – D–F	29	80	9	5	8	16	c. 1,781	c. 1,928
F. Domestic taxpayers [from Four Shilling Aid 1693–1694]	**143**	**225**	**27**	**53**	**97**	**52**	**2,986**	**3,583**
calculation: charges less non-domestic	161 – 18	226 – 1	27 – 0	53 – 0	99 – 2	55 – 3	3,315 – 229	3,836 – 253
G. Taxed inhabitants ratio A/F	6.3	6.1	5.7	5.2	4.1	5.6	5.6	5.6
H. Holman 'households'	195	289	30	53	91	58	3,844	4,560
—Holman untaxed % (H – F)/H	27	22	10	0	–7	10	22	21
—Untaxed of revised total (%) (C – F)/C	42	34	25	9	8	28	42	40

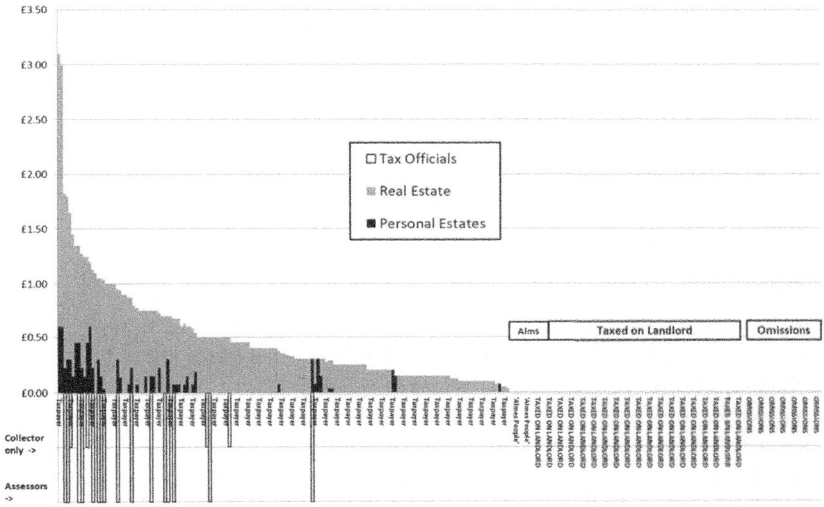

Fig. 4.4 The parish of St. John Bristol 1693–1696. Estimated taxpayer population profile based on a comparison of assessments for the 1696 marriage duty and the 1693–1694 Four Shilling Aid.[112] Quarterly tax vertical scale, taxpayers by weight of land tax (real and personal estates) horizontal scale

qualification, against a single tax charge. Estimation is necessarily based on the few cases where the number of taxed tenements was stated and therefore an average rent can be calculated. Of course, it is possible that a single tenement represented more than a single household. The variation in the parish mean of such numbered tenements was considerable, from £1.29 in suburban St. James to £3.50 in central St. Werburgh. Individual tax charges show annual rents below £1. As many tenements were in poorer suburban parishes, where there are fewer indications as to numbers, the overall average was probably lower than the £2 used here. If the St. James figure of £1.29 is universally applied, the tenements and tenants would increase from 693 (210 charges + 483 additional cases in Table 4.3) to 987, and if the mean was £1 then the figure would be 1,271.

In conclusion, many Bristol occupiers were exempt, or their homes were taxed on landlords (Table 4.3). Female occupiers were less likely to pay tax than their male counterparts.[113] The overall figure for those not directly taxed was at least 21% (after Holman) and could have been as high as 40%.[114] Many who did pay may have deducted this tax from their rent.

These figures seem comparable with Hoppit's national estimation that '30% of the population was judged unable to pay the hearth tax' in 1688 and 15% were in receipt of charity.[115] Although Bristol had at least 314 'Almes people' (Table 4.3) exempted and at least 693 taxed on their landlords, there were many others who cannot be precisely categorised who were not taxed directly (possibly as many as 1,928 in Table 4.3, line E).[116] Assessors had very good reasons not to tax the poorest households. They were less likely to pay and were far less likely to be there when the tax collector called. Such contemporary mobility can be estimated utilising the 1698 poor rate, which used a similar list of taxpayers to the 1693–1694 land tax. Although this was a period of economic decline, the mobility of taxpayers in the parish of St. John over five years was remarkably high, particularly amongst those with the lowest rents (<£5, 57% 'moved'), compared with middling (£5–20, 40%) and higher rents (>£20, 14%).[117] There can be little wonder why assessors made the choices they did.

In London, unlike Bristol, lodgers were often separately charged to land tax, but who else was taxed and who was not? The number of households might be a starting point. Spence has estimated household numbers from 1693 to 1694 Four Shilling Aid and the 1691–1692 Poll, as well as the number of taxed 'wealthy lodgers' (and see Table 4.4).[118] He has compared these figures with the 1695 marriage duty assessments for which 80 of 97 City parishes within the walls survive. Because his figures show the number of households in the marriage duty was only 271 more than the 1693–1694 Four Shilling Aid, a difference of just 1.2%, he argues that the City land tax assessments were fairly comprehensive.[119] The difference he believes could be explained by the statutory exemptions of rents below one pound. There are some difficulties with this. Firstly, Spence has largely equated households with houses, and multi-occupancy has been largely discounted.[120] In the broader sense of household, meaning 'a group of people, often a family, who live together', numerous multiple occupiers and lodgers should probably be added.[121] For example, many of Spence's 1,515 wealthy City lodgers paying land tax might have constituted a separate household, but what of the 8,289 lodgers in the 1692 poll tax assessment?[122] Secondly, as discussed, Harding believed the marriage duty population underestimated the total population by at least 10% and possibly 20%. If so, there must have been omissions for the Four Shilling Aid as well, and following Spence's argument of equivalence, then both the land tax and marriage duty assessments must have understated the City's population.

Table 4.4 City of London. Comparison of 'households' and tax charges in 1693–1694 and 1703 after Spence[123]

		Queenhithe	*Lime street*	*Portsoken*	*Cripplegate without*	*Bassishaw*	*All city*
1690s	Spence 'households' 1692 poll	402	201	740	961	139	17,562
	Lodgers per poll	103	79	83	169	107	8,289
	1692 poll population after Spence						81,812
	1695 marriage duty population estimate						124,000
A	Spence 'households' from 4s database	470	201	1,395	1,711	141	21,095
B	Wealthy lodgers	5	29	42	12	25	1,515
C	Total households and lodgers	475	230	1,437	1,723	166	22,610
D	Real estate tax charges 1693	477	222	1,350	1,626	153	21,013
	Non-domestic	22	26	11	33	13	*546*
E	Tax charges less non-domestic	**455**	**196**	**1,339**	**1,593**	**140**	20,467
	Non-domestic rent 1693	£335	£1,114	£146	£212	£742	
	% non-domestic rent	4%	17%	1%	2%	18%	
	Add known households taxed on their landlord						
F	Multiple houses	8	4	14	77	4	
G	Tenements if average rent is £2.50	8	–	178	208	–	
H	Tenements if average rent is £4	6	–	111	130	–	
J=E+F+G+B	Total A £2.50	476	229	1,573	1,890	169	4,337
K=E+F+H+B	Total B £4	474	229	1,506	1,812	169	4,190
C−J	Difference from Spence @ £2.50	−1	1	−136	−167	−3	
C−K	Difference from Spence @ £4.00	1	1	−69	−89	−3	
1703							
L	1703 tax charges per assessments	453	198	1,196	1,381	146	
	Non-domestic charges	16	2	7	7	6	
M	Tax charges less non-domestic	**437**	**196**	**1,189**	**1,374**	**140**	

(continued)

Table 4.4 (continued)

		Queenhithe	*Lime street*	*Portsoken*	*Cripplegate without*	*Bassishaw*	*All city*
	Add known households taxed on their landlord						
N	Multiple houses	6	–	15	44	4	
O	Tenements if average rent is £2.50	56	–	631	435	–	
P	Tenements if average rent is £4	35	–	395	272	–	
Q = M + N + O + B	Total A £2.50	504	225	1,877	1,865	169	4,640
R = M + N + P + B	Total B £4	483	225	1,641	1,702	169	4,220
S	Personal estates 1693	191	145	373	225	116	
T	Personal estates 1703	0	0	0	0	1	
−(E − M)/D	Movement real estate domestic tax charges 1693–1703	−3.8%	0.0%	−11.1%	−13.5%	0.0%	
−(T − S)/S	Movement personal estates tax charges 1693–1703	−100%	−100%	−100%	−100%	−99%	

Untaxed households or multiple households taxed directly on their landlord are also strongly suggested in Fig. 4.1 by the fall-off in values below £4–5 rents.[124] Further multiple domestic premises were indicated on the face of the 1693–1694 assessments themselves including single tax charges on, 'several tenements', 'two houses' or 'the whole court'. Such phrases are often vague, but estimates of additional households can be made using approximated rental values. Five varied wards were selected for Table 4.4, and estimates were made for any cases indicating such premises in the database, assuming rents were on average £2.50[125] and £4,[126] respectively. Table 4.4 suggests there were more households, at least in extra-mural wards, than Spence has estimated and particularly in Cripplegate Without and Portsoken wards.

In addition, in 1693–1694 Bristol, some individual tax charges demonstrably represented multiple properties even when they were not labelled as such. The same was probably true in London. For examples, some tax charges in the London 1693–1694 database were labelled vaguely as for 'the whole house' which might also suggest multi-occupancy, but no adjustment has been made in Table 4.4. It seems clear that houses and households in their broader sense are probably underestimated by Spence and this takes no account of Harding's 'omissions'. In Bristol households, falling outside direct assessment for land taxes probably comprised 20–40% of the total and in the City of London the figure is probably 10–30% and may have been even higher. Between 1693–1694 and 1703 identifiable multiple occupiers increased in London land tax assessments (Table 4.4).[127] Whereas tax charges decreased, the implied number of households in this sample increased. This latter could be because of an increase in tenement dwelling over this decade or an attempt by assessors to assess landlords directly more often and thus reduce their non-payment risk.

4.2 An Urban Response

The case studies show that urban tax administrators deployed various strategies to maximise reliability to meet their local quota against a fluctuating economic landscape. These included: selecting those taxpayers who were most likely to pay, overassessment, the flexing of local quotas, adjusting property valuation and even modifying the statutory tax rate. All are discussed in this section.

(a) Choosing appropriate taxpayers

Eighteenth-century legislation, echoing that of the 1640s, broadly taxed 'every Person and Persons Bodies Politick and Corporate Guilds Mysteries Fraternities and Brotherhoods whether Corporate or not Corporate having or holding any such Mannors Messuages Lands Tenements Hereditaments or other the Premisses',[128] together with personal estates.[129] In practice, as discussed, many occupiers in London and Bristol were not taxed directly for real estate and decreasingly few were taxed on their personal estates (Tables 4.3, 4.4 and Fig. 4.3). The poorest were least likely to pay, most likely to die, and were also the most mobile, and statute exempted those living in property below 20 shillings annual value. This was a modest figure in urban London and Bristol, therefore the non-payment risk above this level was still very high. Bristol Corporation, which owned a significant real estate portfolio, would have understood this very well. It was landlord to hundreds of dwellings, particularly at the lower value end of the market, and many occupiers struggled to pay their rents. In 1702–1703 Chamberlain Edward Tocknell recognised rent arrears of £503.92 in his accounts for the year in respect of 269 properties with an average rent of £2.55, of which the great majority were well above the land tax exemption threshold.[130] If individuals could not pay their rent on time, they would be unlikely to pay their taxes promptly either. As discussed in the previous section, both London and Bristol therefore taxed landlords directly, wherever this was possible, and in addition extended the 20 shillings statutory land tax exemption of annual rents to minimise non-payment risk.

(b) Overassessment of the tax quota

If all money assessed was not collected there might have to be time-consuming reassessments, so one expedient was to overassess the quota to cover any shortfalls. Unfortunately, though practical, it was not provided for in the legislation as it increased the malfeasance risk. Of course, overassessment could involve either a reassessment of previous arrears which were added to the current year quota, as permitted by statute, or an additional charge to allow for current uncollectable amounts which was not strictly allowed. Most overassessment in London and Bristol was in the second category, according to the assessments themselves, where administrators acted to avoid the considerable delays of reassessment due to non-payment.[131]

Perhaps some overassessment monies were used for doubtful expenses as Ward suggests, but most appear to have been levied to ensure prompt quota delivery without reassessment.[132] In four sample parishes in Bristol between 1701 and 1734, there are no surviving reassessments in St. Nicholas; in Temple there are deficiencies of £5.35 in 1706 and £10 in 1723; there was a larger deficiency in St. Mary-le-Port of £33.55 in 1709; and two reassessments in St. Augustine in 1708 and 1728 of £5.00 and £3.63, respectively. Reassessment therefore appears rare, but modest overassessment, at an average of 0.5% in Table 4.5 was a common practical response if against the letter of the statute. Concerned assessors in the parish of St. Michael thought it best to alert the authorities of their actions:

> The void houses in this parish are charged at the full rate as if they were inhabited and there are so many that the sum charged on them in the Rate amounts to £20-8s-0d in consideration whereof, that the collectors may be able to make the Landlords[133] some allowance in case they should continue void, and also in consideration of the unavoidable deficiencies which allways happen in this Parish by reason of the death and removeall of Many persons and the Poverty and obstinancy of others, this rate is [therefore] made for £9-4s-8½d above the sum charged on the warrant, therefore we thought it proper to acquaint yo[ur] worships therewith that there may be nothing in the rate that has the appearance of Fraud or Clandestine proceeding.[134]

They seem to have got away with their plan. The City of London used overassessment extensively (see Fig. 4.5). In prosperous central wards, virtually full collections were possible and small deficiencies could be recouped by increasing the following year's quota. In central Walbrook Ward in 1710, the acting commissioners, John Moore, David Griel, and Robert Stockdale made provision 'by virtue of another warrant dated the 28th June 1710 for the reassessment of the sum of twenty two pounds 10 shillings [which] was difficient the last year by reason of Empty Houses and cost of stock we have added the aforesaid deficiency to this booke [for 1710] as witness our hands'.[135]

London's poorer extra-mural parishes were more problematic, but overassessment was clearly frowned upon, because of the risk of fraud. Nevertheless, it was a practical expedient. Assessors for the 1691 Aid, Robert Hiscock, Edward Jenkins, and William Harris of the poor precinct of St. Bride-next-Temple-Bar agreed were challenged that there

Table 4.5 Tax overassessment in the City of Bristol. Sums actually assessed from tax assessments 1703–1705 compared with parish quotas[136]

	Sums assessed 1703–1705 (£)	*Parish quota (£)*	*Overassessment (£)*	*Percent overassessed (%)*
Central				
All Saints	£261.80	£261.80	£0.00	0.0%
Castle Precincts	£402.30	£396.98	£5.33	1.3%
Christchurch	£538.50	£536.70	£1.80	0.3%
St. Ewen	£103.55	£103.28	£0.27	0.3%
St. John	£245.80	£245.80	£0.00	0.0%
St. Leonard	£150.20	£149.78	£0.42	0.3%
St. Mary-le-Port	£218.25	£217.71	£0.54	0.2%
St. Peter	£318.45	£317.32	£1.13	0.4%
St. Werburgh	£177.15	£175.15	£2.00	1.1%
Portside				
St. Nicholas	£1,428.55	£1,416.60	£11.95	0.8%
St. Stephen	£712.85	£709.28	£3.57	0.5%
Suburban				
Sts. Phillip & Jacob	£281.10	£277.83	£3.27	1.2%
St. Augustine	£382.80	£382.15	£0.65	0.2%
St. James	£593.50	£588.17	£5.33	0.9%
St. Michael	£253.40	£257.69	−£4.29	−1.7%
Transpontine				
St. Mary Redcliff	£249.00	£245.45	£3.55	1.4%
St. Thomas	£642.85	£636.73	£6.12	1.0%
Temple	£391.65	£391.11	£0.54	0.1%
Average				0.5%

Note Sample parishes in text are shown in bold

had been some failure in overassessing when the proper procedure would have been reassessment. However, they pleaded;

> that wee hope that it will not be judged any great fault seeing that if we saysed [assessed] no more than of just quota wee could not have answered their Majesties their taxe in due tyme …

Without this method, they argued, failure would have been inevitable. This led to an investigation into the overassessment by senior commissioners at Guildhall who sought legal opinion from Sir Bartholomew Shower of the Middle Temple, former City Recorder.[137] He gave

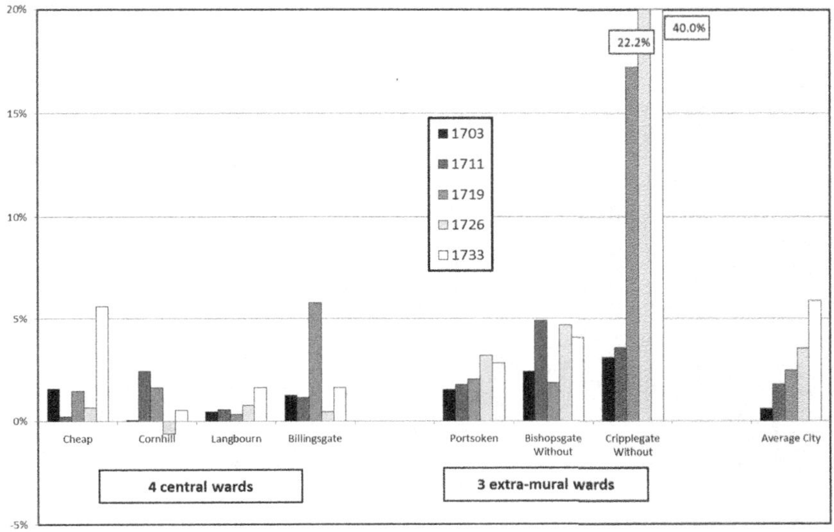

Fig. 4.5 City of London 1703–1733. Patterns of overassessment of land tax quotas comparing central and extra-mural wards[138]

his opinion on 20 August 1693. His opinion *inter alia* was that 'over assessment was irregular & is not justified by any powers in the Act'. Nevertheless, the move to overassessment was unstoppable and quickly became standard City practice. By the beginning of the eighteenth century, it was so well established that ward commissioners contentedly approved such assessments and chief accountant John Smart, who checked almost all of them himself, signed off year in year out, apparently without concern. In the extra-mural wards, overassessment was essential, and commissioners, assessors and others knew it. Over time, it became an increasingly valuable tool (Fig. 4.5).

In rural Kent, with a less mobile population no doubt, strict adherence to the letter of the law was insisted upon. Kentish commissioners set their face against overassessment and it hardly occurred at all in well-documented Wingham. Clerk John Phillips intervened to stop the practice in 1705 (see Sect. 4.3.4) and no further material overassessment was tolerated. In three sample years considered here across 56 parishes, there is one case in 1719, two in 1726 and four in 1732.[139] The total sum overassessed in these seven cases was precisely one pound.

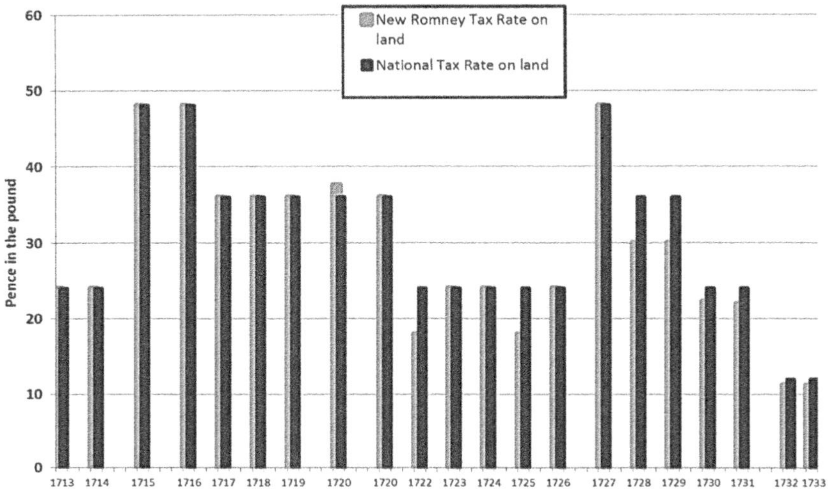

Fig. 4.6 New Romney, Kent 1713–1733 and its flexible tax rate[140]

In New Romney, material overassessment was unknown, but the government officer salaries' element of the tax base was volatile, depending on how many customs and excise men were stationed there in any year. Assessors, according to their warrants, were asked to use their 'utmost care and diligence to assess the full sum' of the proportion or quota at a fixed pound rate and asked to 'fail not at you perill'.[141] Assessors used two main techniques to cope with this volatile tax base. They adjusted the taxed rent element for individuals upwards or downwards, which was standard practice nationally (see section c) below). They then did something unusual. Beginning in 1720, despite the requirement in statute and warrant, they adjusted the tax rate on land to meet the quota (Fig. 4.6). Assessors had found a very practical solution and one that was probably knowingly agreed to by commissioners.

In London, overassessment avoided practical difficulties and some unfairness, as this example illustrates. The town clerk drew up an account for the period 1705–1714 for the City commissioners in a review of the collection and assessment of the precinct of St. Peter Westcheap, Farringdon Within.[142] This was a large relatively prosperous precinct and the assessment in 1705 was for £2,281-3s-0d, or about 1.8% of the City's total, of which all but £4-18s had been collected, but this was still

£71-0s-2d more than the precinct's due quota.[143] This was because the City's overall collection had been short in the previous year and a City-wide reassessment was required, amounting to £47-2s-2d in St. Peter precinct. The precinct also paid £15-8s towards 'deficiencies in the said 4 Divisions [or precincts of Farringdon Within] in that year'. In other words, this relatively successful collectors' round was subsidising other parts of the Ward and the City as a whole.[144] Overassessment by individual wards and precincts meant they did not need others to bail them out.

(c) Adjusting local quotas and the flexibility of tax charges

As is apparent from Fig. 3.13, Bristol administrators regularly adjusted quotas between parishes across the City to spread the land tax burden. There are numerous examples from the commissioners' minute books of the many small adjustments that brought this about. In 1711 in the parish of St. Thomas, it was noted that 'due to the death and removal of several substantial persons, several houses are vacant' and remaining residents would be potentially overcharged.[145] There was a balance to be struck in settling quotas, and commissioners could never satisfy everyone. In 1711, the inhabitants of the wealthy central parish of All Saints complained its 'houses charged at 4s and other parishes pay but 8d'.[146] There was 'like complaint' from two other parishes, Temple and St. Werburgh and these complaints probably led to quota movements shown in the figure. The All Saints complaint seems exaggerated, but Ginter noted in Yorkshire variations 'far greater than any of us might have expected'.[147] All Saints was rewarded in 1712. 'It is ordered that the sum of £40 taken off from the parish of All Saints be payd on the parish of St. Nicholas for the years ensuing'.[148] £5 was also taken off the parishes of St. Mary-le-Port and Castle Precinct. Such minor adjustments from year to year contributed to a broad pattern of change. Bristol benefitted from a historically low tax rate and a rapidly growing urban population with increasing numbers of potential taxpayers, but it had also seen a substantial rise in tax rate.[149]

No doubt there was plenty of special pleading and the extent of consistency achieved is uncertain. If All Saints' complaint above was hyperbole, assessors had the difficult job of property valuation where many properties were not let at rack-rent but had fines, peppercorn rents or other arrangements. This was very often the case in Bristol. Thus, one taxpayer, tobacconist Christopher Patch, held a 99-year lease on three lives dated 25 March 1689 on a messuage known as the Whitehouse with garden and new buildings in Temple Street in Temple Parish, at an annual rent of 24s and a fine of £75.[150] This property was named in the 1694 land tax assessment and valued at nine shillings per quarter or £9 annual value.[151] Similarly, Hugh Turford, a Christchurch parish glover, had a lease dated 9 April 1685 and was paying 40s annual rent and a consideration or fine of £5.[152] He was charged seven shillings quarterly tax in 1693–1694 or £7 rent.[153] In other cases, a single taxed amount can represent multiple properties. Samuel Britten, a land tax assessor himself in 1689 and 1692, was named in a counterpart conveyance in fee-farm dated 24 March 1687 in respect of a tenement or tenements in Castle Street, Castle Precinct, with rent of 42s, and he was assessed in 1693–1694 and 1696 at 19s per quarter or £19 rent and the 1693–1694 charge was presumably on his rent from tenants.[154] John Hudson, another land tax assessor, was charged at 14 shillings land tax per quarter in 1694 or £14 annual rent. He seems to have held four properties in Temple Street and Long Row in Temple parish with a rent totalling £17, suggesting he was slightly undertaxed.[155] Records survive showing Anthony Pickett held two properties in Long Row each with a 30s rent and was taxed at £7 rent in 1694.[156] On the other hand, Francis Barnard's two tenements, mentioned in a conveyance of 15 December 1686, had a rent of £2 and he was charged in 1693–1694 at eight shillings per quarter or precisely £8.[157]

There are several cases where there was no stated indication of multiple properties, but the land tax was higher than the rent. James Powell had a messuage on Long Row, Temple parish for 99 years, determinable on three lives at a rent of 30s per ann., but he was charged 3s-6d/quarter or £3.50 rent in 1694.[158] Samuel Tether held a messuage in Temple Street with garden and backside, and messuage fronting St. Thomas Street for 99 years (in reversion), determinable on two lives at a rent of £3 per ann., but was taxed at 8s per quarter or £8 rent in 1693–1694.[159] Nathaniel Day held a warehouse on a 99-year lease dated 25 March 1690 with a 40s rent, but four years later he was taxed at five shillings per quarter or £5 annual rent.[160] Samuel Whiteing, another tax assessor, also held multiple properties but he specifically held two messuages called The Yellow Anchor on Temple Street, on a 99-year lease dated 10 November 1692 with a rent of £3 per ann. In the Temple parish assessment, he was charged eight shillings or £8. There were several appeals in the commissioners' minute book recorded for 1694 but none for these properties.[161] The likely implication is that these properties were all sublet at a profit.

Table 4.6 Bristol. Real estate taxation of part of Horse Street in the parish of St. Augustine 1716–1723 showing fluctuations in rents assessed for land taxes and the poor rate[162]

Taxpayers	*1716 real estate rent (£)*	*1718 real estate rent (£)*	*1720 real estate rent (£)*	*1721 real estate rent (£)*	*1723 real estate rent (£)*	*Standard deviation as % mean*	*1722 real estate for poor rate assuming 2s/£*
Mr Temple/Singer	7.00	8.22	8.22	8.22	8.08	6	7.00
Edward Price	2.00	1.33	1.33	1.33	1.33	18	
Mr Thomas/Price	6.00	7.00	7.00		7.00	6	5.00
Mr Marks/Capt Way	5.00	6.00	8.00	8.00	8.00	18	2.17
Mr Bradford	5.00	6.00	7.33	7.33	7.33	14	5.00
Mr Morgan/Captain Morgan	5.00	6.00	6.00	6.67	5.50	10	5.00
Robert Williams Tenements	6.00	6.67	6.67	6.67	6.00	5	5.00
Noblett Ruddock Esq.	10.00	12.00	13.33	13.33	12.33	10	13.00
Hugh George/Jones	3.00	4.33	4.33	4.33	2.00	26	3.50
Captain Challoner		4.33	4.33	4.33	4.00	3	3.50
Mr Wm. Lewis Junior/Dowden		4.33	4.33	4.33	4.00	3	3.50
Edward Hopkens	4.00	4.67	4.67	4.67	4.50	6	3.50
Mr Shuttleworth	9.00	10.33	11.33	13.33	12.50	14	11.00
Mrs Wasborough/Blinkhorn	4.00	4.00	4.67	4.67	3.00	15	3.67
Mr Pope	7.00	8.00	8.00	8.00	6.00	11	5.33
Jno Atkins	4.00	4.67	4.67	4.67	4.50	6	4.50
Mr Bayley	6.00	7.00	7.00	7.00	6.67	6	5.33
Mr Jordan/Birkins/Bayly	5.00	5.78	5.78	5.78	6.00	6	4.00
Mr Atwood	10.00	12.00	11.56	11.67	11.50	6	10.00
Wiliam Bull/Blowing/Bandermere	8.00	9.33	9.33	9.33	6.00	16	
John Smith/Lewis/Parnum		9.33	9.33	9.33	9.00	2	6.00
Henry Pritchard/Mr Hort		5.78	5.78	5.33	5.67	3	3.33
Widow Lane/Edward Lane	2.50	3.44	3.33	3.33	3.00	11	2.00

(continued)

Table 4.6 (continued)

Taxpayers	*1716 real estate rent (£)*	*1718 real estate rent (£)*	*1720 real estate rent (£)*	*1721 real estate rent (£)*	*1723 real estate rent (£)*	*Standard deviation as % mean*	*1722 real estate for poor rate assuming 2s/£*
Mrs Brain	4.00		4.67	4.67	2.00	29	
Mr Miles	10.00	10.11	10.22	10.22	10.00	1	9.00
Mrs James/Moors	11.00	12.89	12.89	12.89	12.00	6	9.00
Sam Thomas/Stephens	10.00	10.11	10.11	10.11	10.00	1	8.50
John Hellier	6.00	7.00	8.33	8.33		13	5.00
Constant Jones/Edwards	6.00	7.00	8.33		8.33	13	3.00
Phliip Calloway/Willm Canning/Miles	6.00	7.00	5.67	5.67	5.67	9	4.50
Jos. Josham	6.00	7.00	7.00	7.00	7.00	6	4.50
Mr. Skuse/Bailie/Canning	6.00	7.00	7.00	7.00	7.00	6	4.50
Mr Willsop/Capt Williams/Ruddock	9.00	10.67	11.67	10.67	8.00	13	7.67
William Bowshire	6.00	7.00	7.00	7.00	7.00	6	5.00

Tax assessors would have had to deal with such complexities of property ownership including fines, sub-letting and the ownership of multiple properties when making a reasonable assessment of the annual real estate value. This did not prevent numerous taxpayer appeals and these were copiously recorded in 1690s commissioners' minutes. Good estimation was the best that could be expected with likely modest underassessment to avoid contentious appeals. Bristol took appeals seriously, given the copious records, at least 124 in 1697. However, only 34 of these related to real estate. Assessors compiling their parish assessments had to make up a given quota, even though the parish population fluctuated, those able to pay varied and the amount of tax on personal estates declined. A note on the 1708 reassessment for the parish of St. Augustine reflects this kind of challenge:

> A reassessment on some houses that were not assest in the foregoing rate and are occupied to make good the loss on the Sugar house and other houses which were pull'd down since they were assesst, it being by the approbation & order of the commissioners for the last quarter of the said year 1708.[163]

A further method used by assessors was to slightly vary the real estate tax on properties from year to year. Some differences may reflect property improvement, but most seem an attempt to make the quota add up. An illustration has been compiled here by comparing the imputed rent figure from the real estate tax over a period of time (Table 4.6). The example is from Horse Street in the parish of St. Augustine for 1716–1723.[164] Two resident taxpayers, William Bowshire and Joseph Josham, were charged on the same rent figure of £7.00 every year except 1716 when it was £6.00. On the other hand, Noblett Ruddock, a member of the Society of Merchant Venturers, was taxed at amounts varying from £10.00 in 1716 to £13.34 in 1721.[165] Estimated rent valuation was also used for the new poor rate from 1696, and applying land tax methodology. For example, there is a close correlation between poor rate and land tax, both in the parish of St. John[166] and Castle Precinct.[167] In this example, there was a general tendency for the tax burdens on real estate to rise between 1716 and 1723 by around 7%. This is probably explained by assessors achieving their quota, whilst reducing the tax on personal estates, rather than any underlying change in property value.

4.3 Administration Response

4.3.1 *Delegation, Empowerment and Simplification*

Urban London and Bristol as well as rural Kent faced important administrative challenges in the years after the Glorious Revolution. Tax commissioner numbers increased markedly, and London found ways to keep track of them. It is sometimes suggested that this commissioner expansion was largely a matter of prestige or a demonstration of allegiance for gentlemen listed in statutes, but there was also practical intent to provide additional human resources and facilitate administrative delegation, to parishes, wards, lathes and hundreds.[168] Such practices are clearly demonstrable in London and Kent, glimpsed in Bristol and were probably common across the nation. Local delegation meant that tax could be administered more sensitively and promptly for example in choosing who to tax and in the handling of appeals.

4.3.2 *London*

As London City commissioners expanded in number, keeping track of them became a challenge. Therefore, lists of commissioners were drawn up at Guildhall to appear in the statute and to be handed to the receiver-general as the legislation usually required. The 1700 Act saw a drawing up of several versions of the names of civic officials and others attached to a pre-printed version of the warrant.[169] It was approved by Sir Thomas Trevor the Attorney-General and relevant legislation with blanks left for names and dates.[170] Such toing and froing did not cause delay because the legislation with named commissioners was always in place by the beginning of the tax year, 25 March.[171] Statute demanded that the inaugural commissioners' meeting took place by a specified date in the new tax year. As discussed, commissioners in London, Bristol and Kent almost always achieved this and it would be surprising if this does not epitomise a national effort.[172]

Could relevant officials be located when required? There is a remarkable survival of a 1723 book for the 'Commissioners of the Land Tax' labelled 'Western Walk'.[173] It was certainly drawn up by the town clerk's office and tells where key individuals are located in the western part of the City. The first page contains the names of many familiar tax officials living in Basinghall Street, Bassishaw Ward's significant thoroughfare. Here were Benjamin Burroughs, John Baker, Josiah Shepherd, George

Woodford, Edward Phillips, Jeremiah Sambrooke Esquire, Josiah Diston Esquire, Jonathan Baker, Samuel Ball and Robert Pitman, all tax officials as commissioners, assessors and collectors. The list also includes William Rawstone, an assessor in neighbouring Cheap Ward. Over the page in the same street, we learn that Arthur Bearfoot[174] was a tobacconist, William Monke was against Mr Pitman and that John Knapp and Samuel Williams were against the 'hall gate' presumably Blackwell Hall at the lower end of the road. Levy Ball was 'against Blackwell Hall' and had 'a brass knocker'. The book proceeds voluminously and there is a similar survival for 1738, listing the commissioners' names for each ward and their 'particular place of abode'.[175] It is likely such lists were prepared every year, but most do not survive.[176] If town clerks could keep track in this way, progress could be monitored, and action taken to deal with problems including prompting, cajoling and holding to account. For example, on 17 October 1718, senior City of London commissioners met to review progress for the year. Bread Street commissioners had still not signed the land tax assessment therefore 'the said Book of assessment [should] be returned, and that the Deputy of the said ward be desired to summon the commissioners inhabiting the said ward to meet together at all convenient speed, in order to their signing the same pursuant to the order [?] at the General Meeting of the [City of London] commissioners on the 24th May last'.[177]

The close-knit nature of the tax official community meant that knowledge could be shared and people traced. It was long-standing practice across the country for the appointed tax assessors for a parish or precinct to nominate the collectors for that location and the commissioners would normally approve that choice without a quibble. The assessors of one round in Cornhill Ward were collectors in the other and vice versa. Assessors Daniel Legg and Guilbert Page nominated Timothy Colston and Thomas Payne as collectors for one round and vice versa for the second round for several years in the 1720s. Henry Grant and Thomas Huckell were both assessors and collectors in Aldersgate Within in 1704 for St. Martin's Le Grand. The seven assessors in the ward of Aldgate, which had seven collection rounds, were also the tax collectors on other rounds in that ward, nominated as such by the relevant assessor.

In the City of London, commissioner delegation sharply increased after the Revolution. Despite 1640s experimentation to empower ward officials, pre-Revolutionary common councilmen were rarely tax commissioners themselves. Therefore, few significant tax administrative decisions could be taken in the wards (see Sect. 3.1.3). After the Glorious Revolution, numerous deputies and common councilmen were now appointed, along with significant local taxpayers, as fully-fledged tax commissioners empowered to determine appeals, appoint collectors and approve assessments in local sub-groups with full legislative authority.[178] This is readily apparent from thousands of signed assessments which have been examined in this study.[179] Indeed, this new breed of local commissioners sometimes signed themselves as 'inhabiting the ward'[180] or simply 'the Commissioners of the land tax in [] ward'.[181]

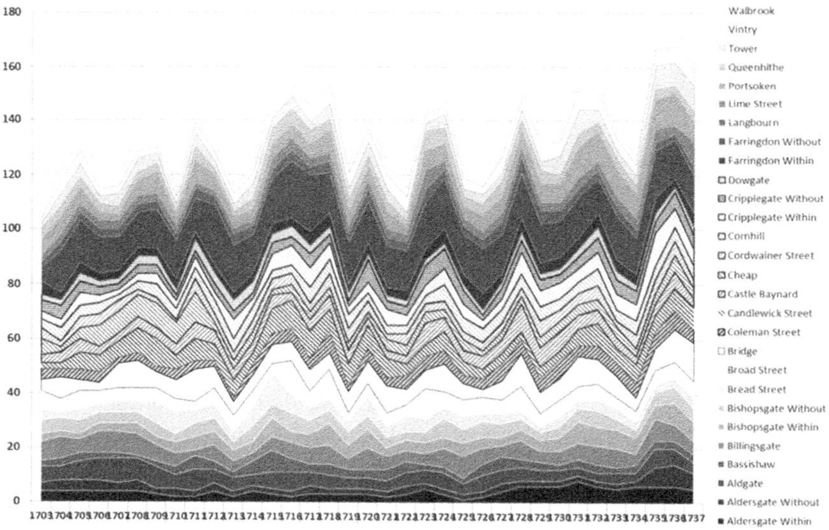

Fig. 4.7 The numbers of City of London tax commissioners approving the ward assessments 1702–1737[182]

Ward commissioners could now directly 'appoint fit and able persons to be Assessors & return their names into the town clerk's office'.[183] These ward commissioners were neither to omit to assess themselves nor the assessors, 'and insert the same in the Books of assessment'. Then, it was for the 'Beadles to summon the commissioners and assessors to meet accordingly' so the latter could be sworn in. Thus, in 1693–1694

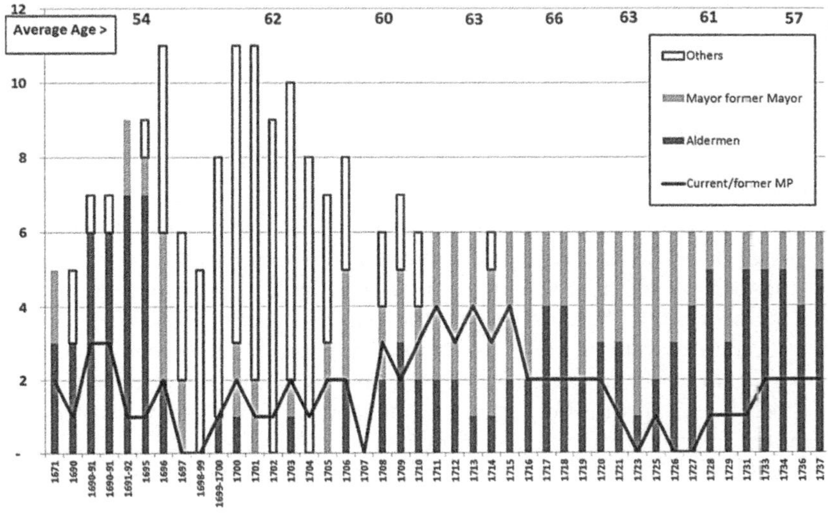

Fig. 4.8 Numbers and identification of signatures on the City of London duplicates 1660–1737[184]

about 78% of commissioners named on the ward assessments operated in just one of the 28 administrative divisions.[185] A few served in two (c. 20%) and a small number in three. The aldermen, MPs and mayor, comprising the traditional commissioner body had far less to do, but retained an executive oversight function, which included signing the City's summary land tax duplicate (Fig. 4.8) and launching the annual process. Some wards and subdivisions worked closely together.[186] Aldersgate had one alderman, serving the Within and Without divisions of the ward and in 1693–1694 a single set of land tax commissioners administered both. On the other hand Cripplegate, both the Within and Without divisions, despite sharing a single alderman, had separate sets of commissioners, but Without also shared some commissioners with nearby Aldersgate. Cordwainer Ward was served by commissioners largely resident in the adjoining Cheap Ward. Portsoken had commissioners living in nearby Aldgate and Vintry from neighbouring Dowgate. The 1693 data is not complete, because the names of commissioners in Langbourn, Lime Street, Queenhithe, Tower and Walbrook wards are missing. However, of the 284 individuals in the statute, at least 123 (46%) were active in approving ward assessments which adjusted pro rata for missing data and suggests 156 (55%) and a further seven senior commissioners approved the City duplicate. The number of commissioners approving assessments fell away slightly in the late 1690s, before increasing again in the 1700s as the sharing of commissioners between Wards and divisions declined. Over the course of the early eighteenth century, typically 110–175 commissioners each year (see Fig. 4.7) were involved in local assessment signing, increasing slightly over time and yet the number of commissioners named in the statute increased dramatically to well over a thousand by the 1730s and most of these played no tangible part in the tax process.[187] It is likely that the remaining commissioners named in the statute were inactive as Brooks suggests, but nevertheless, the post-revolutionary involvement of local men was much greater than ever before.[188] The 'promotion' of common councilmen to be fully-fledged commissioners meant other local men had to be appointed to their former role as tax assessors. There was thus a wider ownership of the tax process.

All Bassishaw's assessment-approving commissioners were local men. Whereas, prior to the Glorious Revolution, only common councilmen and deputies were in charge locally but only as assessors, the new ward commissioner bodies were a more mixed group. Of 32 Bassishaw commissioners signing land tax assessments after the Glorious Revolution, only fifteen were common councilmen, although the latter made up 54% of the signatures. In only one-quarter of cases[189] were the ward assessors themselves deputies or common councilmen, although in the great majority of years 1688–1733 one of the assessors was such.[190] In Bassishaw and elsewhere, the dominance of traditional ward officers in the tax process diminished after 1688. Significant taxpayers appear to have assumed greater authority. No longer was the tax process simply operated by those carrying out their traditional duties in their ward or parish on an occasional basis.

This senior or higher-tier commissioner group controlled the initiation of the annual process and the signing of the City summary tax duplicate. It typically comprised MPs/former MPs, the Lord Mayor/former mayors and senior aldermen (Fig. 4.8).[191] After 1710, there were six signatories every year almost always the mayor and aldermen. The Lord Mayor's was usually the first signature on the duplicate. Virtually all these 'City fathers'[192] had distinguished public careers behind them as justices, aldermen, common councilmen, supporters of charitable institutions and senior figures in the livery companies.[193] This was an exclusively male and largely middle-aged preserve with a mean age of 61 at the time of signing the land tax duplicates.[194] Duplicate signatories were rather younger in the 1690s and in the 1730s (Figs. 4.7, 4.8 and Sect. 4.4).[195] All London MPs of this period were named as City land tax commissioners in statutes, along with numerous MPs living in London but with seats elsewhere.[196] The City elected four MPs, some served for short periods, others for much longer. Of the 74 identified MPs' duplicate signatures, exactly half were by 16 MPs or former MPs for the City, although a few of these individuals also sat elsewhere during their parliamentary careers.[197] Until the 1720s, all types of MPs and former MPs appear as signers, those with Whiggish leanings, waverers, disaffected Whigs and Tory preferences. Well-known MPs Micajah Perry and Sir John Barnard were regular duplicate signatories from the 1720s. These two men were prominent in London politics and during the excise crisis where they were seen as two of the ring-leaders of the City's opposition to the extension of excise whom Walpole dubbed 'sturdy beggars'.

4.3.3 Bristol

If developments in Kent and Bristol seem more pedestrian, there were significant indications of change. Early 1690s Bristol initially saw the Restoration process substantially reintroduced, despite heavier burdens and new taxes, which at commissioner level, resulted in a rather burdensome rigmarole involving endless quarterly meetings *inter alia* to hear appeals (including 31 minuted meetings in 1697), and until 1698 to appoint most of the same assessors as the previous quarter and agree slightly modified parish quotas four times each year.[198] Ward praises their diligence, noting the 'pressure of business' and 'devotion to duty'.[199] To this author, this appears more to be work for its own sake. In meeting the legislative demands in detailed point, had administrators lost focus on the primary objective of effectively gathering Bristol's taxation? Over the following decade, prompted by changing legislation, the process was markedly simplified and improved and exhibited delegation and empowerment similar to London, even if Ward wrongly claims administrators 'did not subdivide their work'.[200] Over this period, more of the process became annual rather than quarterly, including the appointment of assessors and collectors, the completion of the assessments and the agreement of parish quotas as is clear from commissioners' minutes: 'It is ordered that the rates & assessments for every parish be made for one whole year' at a meeting of commissioners 13 June 1707.[201] The four quarterly collections that followed each year then became a matter for paid officials, the clerk, collectors and receiver-general. This is exactly the same pattern that emerged in Kent and the City of London. The receivers' quarterly letters prompted the Bristol clerk to inform the parish collectors when the next payment was due based on the annual assessment. This was only complicated in unusual circumstances such as in 1707 when George Dixon, Bristol's resident receiver died, apparently bankrupt and no letter appeared.[202] Matters were delayed until the new Receiver-General, Bernard Hutchins, and Assistants Robert Baker and Nicholas Jeffery were appointed. A rare example of such clerk's letters survives for three quarters in 1709 from the parish of St. Nicholas, but it probably typifies City administration. It mirrors similar letters in Kent and suggests a standard process nationally. On 21 November receiver Hutchins wrote to Bristol's clerk John Romsey from his home in Hinton St. George some 45 miles distant:

> I desire you to order the severall collectors within the City of Bristoll to make payment of the third quarterly payment of the present Land Tax to Mr Robert Baker and Mr Nicholas Jeffery my deputies or either of them on Wednesday the fourth day of January next at the White Hart Inn – Broad Street Bristoll.[203]

A few days later Romsey no doubt wrote 18 letters to the 18 parish tax collectors including the surviving one to John Brickdale and John Haythorne in St. Nicholas parish[204]:

> This is to give you notice that the Receiver-General hath appointed to receive the third quarterly payments of the present land Tax on Wednesday the fourth day of January next at the White Hart Inn in Broad Street in the said City. And for payment whereof you are not to fayle. Dated at the Tolzey the 3rd day of December 1709.

The first and fourth quarters' correspondence also survive, as does Brickdale's and Haythorne's warrant.[205] Romsey wrote to all parish collectors quarterly in 1709 and in every other year of his service, advising them of such payments. The first quarter was payable on 19 July at the White Hart in Broad Street and this was communicated by letters dated

27 June 1709 at the Tolzey. The fourth quarter was by 10 May 1710 (letters dated 24 March 1710) and the third on 4 January 1710 (letters dated 3 December 1709). In each case, collectors were given about a month's notice of the payment date which was a post-revolutionary norm.[206]

As in London and across the nation, far more Bristol commissioners were now appointed and sworn in than ever before according to the commissioners' minutes. Many of these, as in London, were not otherwise civic officials or would ever be so.[207] There were 35–60 commissioners listed in 1690s statutes and 90–140 in the early eighteenth century. Many were never minuted as sworn in, and others disappear from sight after being sworn.[208] Nevertheless, the number of commissioners sworn in and attending recorded post-revolutionary meetings was still more than twice that of the Restoration. Why was this?

Determining whether and to what extent commissioners named in the statute were active in the tax process is difficult. Potentially, the best source is the commissioners' minute books, but this rather assumes, as Ward[209] appears to do, that these are a complete record of all meetings. They were demonstrably not, because, unlike Wingham in Kent, activities were clearly taking place at times not recorded in the minutes because commissioners were meeting to sign documents at times not documented in those books as will be shown. The commissioners' minutes are nevertheless useful because the clerk seems to have assiduously written down the names of commissioners sworn in. As commissioners were obliged by statute to be sworn, and this tended to happen at the always recorded inaugural meeting of the year, this swearing-in information gives a good sense of the number of commissioners who took some interest in the tax process. After all, this would be the clerk's main record of who had authority to act and who did not. Numerous commissioners are named in statutes who never swear in or take part in any business. Indeed, it might be useful confirmation of the completeness of the clerks' minuting of the swearing in that no unsworn commissioners are ever active according to the minutes and other documents studied.

Most of the most active commissioners, if the minutes are followed, are the aldermen and senior common councilmen. They have been described above in London as the upper tier, but in that city there was also a lower tier of men with duties only in the local Wards. The big question is was there a lower tier of Bristol commissioners active in the parishes? There were indeed many Bristol commissioners who were sworn in at the inaugural meeting, but are never active again according to the minutes. Could these men have acted as a lower tier doing parish work only? There are five strands of supporting evidence, but the situation is not free from doubt. (1) During the 1700s various activities disappear from the commissioners' minutes[210] including the hearing of appeals, the choice of collectors and the settling of disputes. Were these activities delegated to parishes? (2) Over the period 1689–1740, almost half of the recorded sworn-in commissioners did not attend later general meetings as Brooks noted.[211] After 1720, the figure is higher at 65%.[212] There was an adequate resource therefore to carry out additional work. (3) Sub-committee delegation was occasionally referred to in the 1690s commissioners' minute books, but not later. Statute had long encouraged commissioners to subdivide on a regional basis and this clearly happened on 16 March 1692 for the poll: 'The comm[issioners] present proceeded to subdivide themselves … In order for hearing appeals & complaints which shalbe made & then agreed upon'.[213] There was a reference to similar arrangements in the 'Transaction of the Incorporation of the Poor' where aldermen conducted Ward Courts and appointed local Guardians of the Poor.[214] Such sub-committees might determine appeals in the parish simply by annotation on the face of the assessment itself. Ralph and Williams, in respect of the marriage duty, suggest matters may have been left to the assessors themselves to make such decisions, but without proper authority, this seems unlikely.[215] It seems probable then that assessment amendments, following successful appeals, were made with the authority of parish commissioners, but no other record was kept. The alternative would be that the usual general committee of commissioners heard appeals, chose collectors and settled disputes but the clerk kept no minutes of such routine matters.[216] It is difficult to be sure, but this latter seems unlikely. (4) The names of the commissioners often appear separately at the end of the tax assessment for each parish. Could this represent the naming of the local quorum of commissioners who could settle appeals and disputes?

If the question of delegation is not free from doubt, it seems clear that the tax process was simplified during the early 1700s. It became an annual affair with considerably fewer general meetings, and most of the important ones that took place did so at the beginning of the fiscal year: swearing in, setting parish quotas and the appointment of assessors for the whole year. As established in the 1640s (Sect. 2.2.1), the inaugural meeting, with a deadline set by Parliament, was the most important and certainly best attended meeting of the year,[217] because those 'present at such Generall Meeting or Meetings or the major Part of them, are hereby authorized and required to putt this present Act in Execution'.[218] The first business of the day was to launch the tax process and hear correspondence 'under the great seal of England'. So in 1696, a letter was received from the 'Agents Office Westminster' to the mayor's office on 13 February saying they had sent eleven printed copies of the Act and asking him 'to give notice' to the commissioners for a meeting on 20 February 1697.[219] By comparison, in 1694 the statutory deadline was 28 February, and the timely inaugural meeting in Bristol's Tolzey took place on 20 February.[220] At a further meeting on 23 February 1694 it was decided that 'notice and summons be given to all the Commissioners who have not already app[eare]d & taken their oaths to appear Monday next the 26 February' to do so. A total of 35 commissioners eventually took the oaths over the next few days, but others never did so. Numerous minuted eighteenth-century meetings were devoted solely to the swearing-in of commissioners. In 1690 there was even an order requiring that 'an abstract of the head of the act to be publickly read'.[221] This inaugural meeting was usually followed by a further gathering to agree 'Proportions charged on Divisions to be taxed, and to appoint Assessors'.[222]

Matters were simplified further after 1701 when the town clerk also became the tax commissioners' clerk. He could complete the necessary paperwork, the assessments themselves, the duplicate, the assessors' warrants, and the quarterly collectors' warrants and convene a small meeting of senior dignitaries at the Tolzey to sign them, when they were there on civic business or as justices. That such activities took place outside minuted commissioners' meetings is clear from dated documents in a sample analysis from parishes in different parts of the City.[223] Thus, at an unminuted meeting on 5 June 1728 seven commissioners severally signed and dated the parish assessments including Temple, St. Nicholas, St. Mary-le-Port, St. Leonard, and St. Augustine.[224] There were further unminuted assessment signing meetings that year on 31 August and 13 December. The duplicate was similarly signed at an unminuted meeting on 8 July. Numerous other unminuted meetings are identifiable from surviving documents, 62 in this sample study, and many more can be surmised. The signatures from these unminuted meetings all belonged to a narrow group of civic officials. Of 210 signatures on surviving warrants, duplicates and assessments from these unminuted meetings, 153 (73%) were by aldermen, 45 (21%) mayors and the rest by sheriffs (3), town clerks (2) and common councilmen (7).[225] No doubt these leading local dignitaries were quickly pressed into service when it was convenient and as and when required by the clerk.

Much of Bristol's tax administrative burden over the annual cycle, as in London and Kent, now lay with the clerks who were often highly experienced men of standing with a background in the law. From 1697 the clerk's annual poundage had been increased for 1d to 1½d[226] and would remain so and this surely reflects the greater burdens clerks were taking on as the tax process became increasingly annual. After all for most of the year, they were now in charge and their job was no longer simply the Restoration one of 'faire writeing the Assesments Duplicates and Copyes'.[227] They had to liase with collectors, receivers and assessors; receive and send correspondence; correct the mistakes of others; organise meetings; ensure documents were signed; and anything else that came their way. John Romsey Esquire was the first town clerk to take the role in 1701. He was a barrister and served until 1721 when he was replaced by Henry Blaake who had been an MP for his native Calne in the 1690s. He had also been steward of sheriff's court (1712–1721) and port waiter (from 1709). At his death he was replaced by William Cann, later Sir William Cann, baronet, who was a member of a family that had long served Bristol and Gloucestershire in local and national roles. He served until his death in March 1753.

When John Romsey became commissioners' clerk in 1701 he soon focussed his attention on the tax assessments.[228] He noted that in 1702 assessors in Castle Precinct, had made three material errors. There was an arithmetical or 'casting' error of £14-2s-8d, they had double charged one taxpayer £5 for stock and had overcharged another for money at interest by a massive £22-10s-0d.[229] Fortunately, the collectors of Christchurch parish had over-collected for an unspecified reason by £7-17s-4d which recouped some of the shortfalls. The 1702 shortfall was soon made up. The total 'for the land Tax and offices in money £6,619-11s-0d and by Certificate of what was Paid in the fourth yeare of their late Majesties Reign for Personal Estates the sum of £772-9s-7d which makes the full sum'.

4.3.4 *Kent*

In Kent, other than initiating the tax process and agreeing the formulaic lathal and borough quotas, all work had long been delegated to local commissioner groups. Canterbury, Dover, Folkestone, Fordwich, Faversham, Tenterden, Sandwich, New Romney, Lydd and Hythe all had their civic authorities recognised separately as commissioners in statutes since the 1670s (Sect. 2.4.3) and all were given national statutory quotas of taxation to be collected for the first time in 1698. Kent County commissioners had allocated them locally determined quotas long before that.[230] By the early 1700s as in Bristol and London, the tax had become a largely annual event for commissioners, with most of the work then carried out once this approval had been given, by paid clerks, receivers and collectors. Four years after Bristol's town clerk, became commissioners' clerk a new and vigorous clerk was appointed in Wingham in Kent. John Phillips had an immediate impact in reducing errors in 1705.[231] At about the time of an unminuted meeting on 8 May 1705, Phillips carried out detailed checks on 56 Wingham parish assessments and found minor errors, mostly overassessments, in over half the parishes. His notes and initials survive on the face of the assessments themselves. In Coldred parish, Phillips noted that the local parish quota or 'proporcon' [quota] of £24-8s-0d had been met by the assessment, but the calculation was incorrect.[232] It did not 'cast' correctly. £495 rent charged at 1s for the quarter would raise £24-15s-0d—an 'undercast' or overassessment of 7 shillings. In total, the sub-lathe's parishes had been overassessed by about £10. Whatever the case, such overassessment declined sharply thereafter. No minutes and relatively few documents survive for 1690s Kent, so earlier comparison is difficult.

English commissioners' clerks had taken on additional responsibilities since the removal of head-collectors role in 1673–1674, that burden had increased in the 1690s as national processes moved increasingly to an annual basis. Clerks had become exceptionally busy, if the three case studies are anything to go by, for which they received modest additional recompense after 1697. Ensuring the accuracy of tax assessments seems to have become a key task and no doubt contemporary clerks up and down the land were probably carrying out similar checks to those of Smart, Romsey, and Phillips. They had become tax auditors as well as accountants.

4.4 Post-Revolutionary Officialdom

As commissioner numbers increased, parliament made efforts to exert control, by oaths of loyalty and a property qualification. The latter may have been lightly policed, but appears to have changed the commissioner body in both London and Bristol. The profiles of commissioners and other officials can be sketched out via 1690s sources including marriage duties and polls. Receivers and clerks took on most of the day-to-day administration, but there were risks and rewards here.

Although commissioner numbers were increasing, post-revolutionary parliaments tried to control admission to such ranks. Commissioners had to swear the oaths of supremacy and allegiance, subject to a fine of £200, rising briefly to £500 in 1696, but remaining at £200 thereafter.[233] In addition, there were a series of attempts to impose a minimum property qualification on commissioners. The first of these was in respect of the 12d/£ Aid in 1689[234] such that 'Persons be resident, and have Estates to the Value of £1,000; and in such Case they are enabled to execute the said Act, as though they had Real Estates of £100 p[er] ann'.[235] This was somewhat relaxed before being reintroduced at £50 in 1699 and thereafter at £100 in the 1701 Act for commissioners who acted for 'any County at large', implicitly recognising different ranks of commissioner, who paid tax on such property by 'himselfe or his Tennants or Trustees', subject to a penalty of £50.[236] Beckett believes the property qualification was reinforced because Parliament believed successful implementation of land taxes required 'the consent of the landed classes'.[237] However, it is doubtful the extent to which such a qualification was enforced nationally and it seems much more likely that this change was made to ensure appropriate level administrative sign-off. In the cities of both Bristol and London, administrative adjustments were made regarding the signing of the duplicate itself, a document which would have been visible to the Exchequer, and implied authority for the 'County at large'. During the 1690s in both Bristol and London, rather obscure common councilmen had taken an active role in the high-level coordination of land tax matters including the signing of duplicates which had been the pre-Revolutionary preserve of aldermen, MPs, mayors and sheriffs. In London, this relatively youthful group, had an average age of under 50 including Thomas Pitts, Jonathan Mumford, Joseph Wright, Thomas Fyge, Thomas Blackmore, Jonathan Moore, Nicholas Caplin, Joseph Scriven and Daniel Dorville, who signed numerous tax documents, but never achieved high City office (see Fig. 4.8).[238] Alongside them, were some of the usual civic dignitaries including Sir Edward Clarke (alderman and Lord Mayor in 1696 and a member of the Excise Board), Sir Thomas Lane (alderman and Lord Mayor in 1694) and Sir James Collett (alderman and sheriff in 1698). The signatures on duplicates from this period particularly stand out, but traditional aldermanic responsibility was re-established in the early 1700s following the 1701 legislation discussed above (Fig. 4.8). The more youthful commissioners may have lost their position at the higher-tier, but continued to operate in their wards. If the earlier variation to include more youthful officials to perhaps increase operational effectiveness in the executive tier, as seems possible, then the increased importance of the town clerk's office was ample compensation and particularly the employment of John Smart in the City of London from about this time.

4.4.1 Bristol

The pattern is almost identical in Bristol where significant numbers of common councilmen and others, who never reached high civic office, were active in the 1690s tax process, including John Cary, Giles Merrick, George Morgan, Timothy Parker and John Sandford.[239] Of course, it was a particularly busy time for commissioners, with window taxes, marriage duties and polls to administer and these additional hands might have been operationally useful. After 1701, traditional mayoral and aldermanic responsibility was re-established, but here too the town clerk's office assumed a more operation role as commissioners' clerk (Fig. 5.8). It may not be unconnected that only four years later as discussed, John Phillips was appointed in Wingham in Kent.

Most of Bristol's active commissioners were part of the City's wealthy merchant community described by McGrath, who defines a merchant as 'someone who dealt in overseas commerce on a reasonably large scale and for whom such commerce was the main means of livelihood'.[240] About 42% of active post-revolutionary commissioners were members of the Society of Merchant Venturers, but their attendance at minuted commissioners' meetings constituted 52%.[241] Restoration figures were higher still at c. 52 and 59%, respectively.[242] There was much flexibility as McGrath points out. Many men who trained in other trades called themselves merchants and were so called by contemporaries as their businesses developed and diversified.[243] John Cary began as a linen-draper, James Rainsthorpe as a mariner, Sir Richard Crump, as a soap boiler, and Richard Lane a grocer. Whilst merchants were most prominent amongst the ranks of tax commissioners, it was the linen-drapers, grocers, haberdashers, upholsterers, mercers, apothecaries, attorneys, pewterers, brasiers, surgeons, booksellers, tobacco rollers and soap boilers who were most prominent as assessors and collectors (see Fig. 4.9). Of course, though wealthy, 'most of the merchants lived within the narrow limits of the city'.[244] Merchants had many and diverse trading interest, but several such commissioners traded in slaves, including Edward Colston MP, who contemporaries believed had the highest Christian principles and reputation. He was committed to charitable work in Bristol and made a huge fortune, *inter alia*, from 'Negroes shipped off from the coast of Africa'.[245]

Tax officials, whether commissioners, assessors or collectors, paid tax themselves and tended to be at the middle or upper end of the taxpaying profile as already noted for the parish of St. John-the-Baptist (Fig. 4.4).[246] In this parish, only the more significant taxpayers became tax officials. Of these, Francis Plomer, who held various roles as assessor and collector in the 1690s, paid the least tax.[247] The next lowest was tax collector Alexander Fox, who paid £9 annual rent and just above him, Mathias Jones and Edward Blackford, who paid £10. Tax officials generally lived in accommodation rated at above £5, the great majority over £10. In the suburban parish of St. James, 26 of 34 identified officials had rents of £10 or more. The remaining six were spread out down to Richard Baugh shown unusually with a £1 rent. In a small, commercial and central parish like St. Ewen, most male householders paid tax, and given the small size of the population, even the lowliest taxpayer was required to play his part in tax officialdom. Some 83% identifiably did so in the 1690s. The lowliest real estate taxpayer here was Thomas Martin assessed for £7.50 rent in 1693–1694.[248] John Romsey, the then town and commissioners' clerk, and the Chamberlain John Cooke lived here, as did Francis Yeamans, Attorney of the City and sometime assessor for the marriage duty, as well as Richard Yeamans, who earlier served as commissioners' clerk. Many taxpayers here were gentlemen or involved in commerce representing 13 different trades including two upholsterers and two haberdashers.[249]

Most Bristolians did not own their homes, but leased or rented them from institutional or non-resident landlords,[250] and thus, many passed on some of the immediate tax burdens to their landlord by deduction from rent.[251] The commissioners themselves were relatively well-known; the great majority of the most active were familiar civic dignitaries: aldermen, common councilmen and other wealthy individuals.[252] The assessors were local men nominated by their parishes according to numerous references in the commissioners' minutes. In 1704, the 'commissioners ordered notices to issue to the constables and church wardens of every parish within this City to returne the proper persons to be assessors of the tax & to appear before themselves at St. George's chaple upon Friday the 7th day of April next'.[253] Of course, many assessors had been church-wardens themselves.

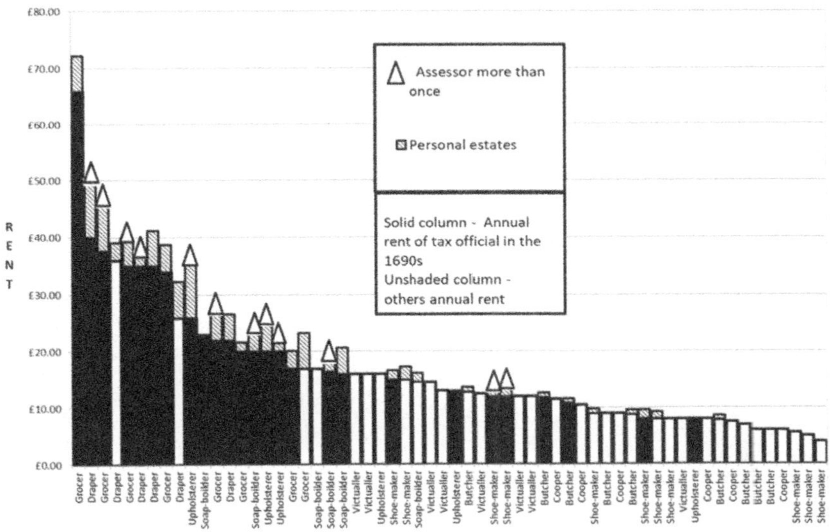

Fig. 4.9 Bristol parishes of St. Nicholas, St. Ewen, and St. Mary-le-Port showing the main trades and professions taken from the 1696 marriage duty assessment and the 1694 poll compared with rental values in the 1693–1694 Four Shilling Aid[254]

Assessors were also commercial men of standing and included merchants, but other wealthy trades were prominent including McGrath's: 'Linen-drapers, woollen-drapers, soap boilers, mercers, clothiers, grocers, vintners, innkeepers' many of whom were also involved in overseas trade and would be included in Sacks' category of the 'major commercial and entrepreneurial occupations'.[255] These were the very trades and professions that dominated the ranks of the assessors in St. Nicholas parish in the 1690s (see Table 4.7) together with surgeons, attorneys and the like. Fortunately, the 1690s was a period when there were polls, marriage

Table 4.7 City of Bristol parishes of St. Nicholas, St. Ewen, and St. Mary-le-Port showing individual trades mentioned in the 1696 marriage duty assessment or the 1694–1695 poll[256]

Normally tax officials. Normally not	*Total St. Nicholas*	*Assessor more than once*	*Other tax officials*	*Not tax official*	*Women in business*	*Total St. Ewen*	*Assessor more than once*	*Other tax officials*	*Not tax official*	*Women in business*	*Total St. Mary-le-Port*	*Assessor more than once*	*Other tax officials*	*Not tax official*	*Women in business*	*% age tax officials*
Apothecary	1	1				1	1				2	1	1			100
Attorney						1		1								100
Baker	2			2							2		2			50
Barber-surgeon or chirugeon						2	2				1	1				100
Bodice maker						1			1	1						0
Book seller						2		2								100
Brasier	2		2								1	1				100
Brewer											1			1	1	0
Butcher	1			1							8	1	1	6		22
Carpenter	2			2												0
Chandler	1			1												0
Coffee seller						1			1	1						0
Corn seller											1			1		0
Confectioner						1		1								100
Cooper	8		1	7												13
Cutler						1	1									100
Feltmaker											1			1		0
Flaxman	1		1													100
Furrier											1	1				100
Glazier	1			1												0
Glover	2	1	1													100
Grocer	5	2	2	1							3	1	2			88
Haberdasher						5	5				1	1				100

(continued)

Table 4.7 (continued)

Normally tax officials. Normally not	*Total St. Nicholas*	*Assessor more than once*	*Other tax officials*	*Not tax official*	*Women in business*	*Total St. Ewen*	*Assessor more than once*	*Other tax officials*	*Not tax official*	*Women in business*	*Total St. Mary-le-Port*	*Assessor more than once*	*Other tax officials*	*Not tax official*	*Women in business*	*% age tax officials*
Hatter	3	1	1	1												67
Hollier?	1			1												0
Iron monger	3	1		2							1			1	1	25
Jeweller						1		1								100
Joiner	3			3							1			1		0
Linen draper	5	2	2	1							1		1			83
Mariner	13		1	12												8
Mercer	4	1	3								1		1			100
Merchant	1			1												0
Milliner	2			2	1	1		1								33
Periwig-maker						1		1								100
Pewterer	3	2	1								1	1				100
Pipe-maker	1			1												0
Plate worker											1			1		0
Rope-maker	1			1												0
Saddler						1		1								100
Saltman	1			1												0
Seamstress	1			1												0
Shoe maker or heelmaker	1			1		1			1		10		4	6		33
Soap bolier or maker	5		3	2							1	1				67
Stationer						1	1									100
Taylor	5		1	4		1			1		1			1		14
Tobacconist	1		1								2			2		33
Turner						1	1									100

(continued)

Table 4.7 (continued)

<u>*Normally tax officials.*</u> Normally not	*Total St. Nicholas*	*Assessor more than once*	*Other tax officials*	*Not tax official*	*Women in business*	*Total St. Ewen*	*Assessor more than once*	*Other tax officials*	*Not tax official*	*Women in business*	*Total St. Mary-le-Port*	*Assessor more than once*	*Other tax officials*	*Not tax official*	*Women in business*	*% age tax officials*
Upholsterer	3	1	1	1		2	1	1			1	1				83
Victualler	16		1	15	3						2			2	1	6
Vintner	2			2	1						1			1		0
Watch man	1			1												0
Watch-maker						1		1								100
Woolen draper	2		2													100
Totals	104	12	24	68	5	26	12	10	4	2	46	10	12	24	3	45

duty as well as land taxes, requiring local men as assessors, presenters and collectors making their activities visible in extant documents. It is also in this period when collectors were most often named in the commissioners' minutes. Therefore, data is available to study these officials in some detail.

Trade and professional information is not universally available, but data from one transpontine, one portside and three central parishes fortuitously survived from the 1690s. This data should be treated with caution. It represents the assessors' judgement at one point in time, when many individuals had a portfolio of interests. Nevertheless, there is some consistency. The 1696 marriage duty lists 104 individuals in St. Nicholas parish with a trade. Of these, 35 served as tax officials in some capacity in the 1690s or early 1700s. Of this group, 12 served as land tax assessor on more than one occasion. By way of comparison, the 1694–1695 poll assessment named trades and professions for the parishes of St. Ewen (26 cases) and St. Mary-le-Port (46) and together this provides details of 53 professions in Table 4.7. It was the wealthier trades of grocer, draper, upholsterer, mercer and soap boiler which clustered in the higher valued properties, contrasting with more lowly trades of butcher, shoemaker, victualler and cooper in the lower valued houses. Many of St. Nicholas parish men used commercial premises on or near the Bridge. On the other hand, just south of the old town wall was King Street, near the 'marsh', which was developed during the Restoration and named after Charles II. In this street clustered some poorer trades: coopers, victuallers, mariners and rope makers. Interestingly, several victuallers named in the marriage duty assessment are not present in the land tax records. Perhaps the explanation is mobility—they had moved away, but more likely that they were exempt because they were too poor to pay. Away from the central and portside areas, there was more space for warehouses and industry and perhaps more opportunity for the industrious to make good.

Over the bridge from the centre, Temple Parish was more industrial (Fig. 2.2). This parish's better-off men were not drapers nor rarely merchants or linen-drapers, but produced soap, sugar, and glass, owned warehouses and some of its coopers were far wealthier than their co-traders in St. Nicholas. One of the wealthiest residents was George Hine, son of former Mayor John Hine, who had inherited a sugar-house, formerly Shuttleworth's brewhouse and warehouse in Temple Street.[257] He was nevertheless not as wealthy as Francis Whitchurch, who with a company of others also owned a sugar-house. He was already a common councilman and was soon to be mayor and an alderman. He had been an active tax commissioner since 1696. Tax assessors here prior to 1703 came from these commercial groups and included three coopers, two sugar-house owners and one each of: linen-draper, clothier, soap boiler, glass maker, brewer, carpenter, mariner, dyer and maltster.

Bristol shared its receivers-general with Somerset. Typically, they also acted for other direct taxes such as the window tax. Few receivers, other than George Dixon, who died in post in 1707, lived in the City. Collectors since 1671 were not usually obliged to travel more than ten miles to deliver their tax monies to receivers. And then there was the small matter of getting money to London and the Exchequer. Dixon's successor, Bernard Hutchins, led a peripatetic existence between London, from where several of his letters to the Bristol commissioners' clerk were addressed, and his county home at Hinton St. George in Somerset.[258] He used deputies to collect money in Bristol and across Somerset. One deputy receiver, Robert Baker, resided in Sutton Montague in Somerset and the other, Nicholas Jefferys, who was also active with the customs, lived in Bridgwater. They visited Bristol on only one named day each quarter for local collectors to deliver cash to them and visited other locations in Somerset similarly for county collectors. Receivers were men of standing and whose sureties would be scrutinised by the Treasury. For example, in 1708 Bernard Hutchins was appointed the new receiver for Bristol and Somerset and as such was responsible for paying £72,473 to the Exchequer for a four-shilling land tax which would give him a salary of about £600 and he provided a 'securities warrant in £45,000'[259] and for similar sums in later years. He must have been trusted by the Treasury, because in 1711 he was appointed 'Paymaster of the £1,500,000 Lottery … with the salary of £500 p[er] ann'.[260] The text of his receiver-general's warrants is preserved as copies in the commissioners' minute books and gives a flavour of what was expected[261]:

> by virtue of his Majesties Letters of Privy-seal bearing the date the sixteenth day of August in the first yeare of his reign, I do hereby certificate and appoint Bernard Hutchins Esq to be his Majestyes Receiver-General for the County of Somerset and City and County of the City of Bristol of and for all sumes of money granted by an Act … and peforme whatsoever shall be requisite as necessary for his Majesties best advantage and service

> in this matter. And to appoint such persons as he shall thinke fit to be his Deputyes for the Receipt of the said monies; for whose performing and discharging their trust, he is to be answerable…that the whole sumes to be Received by him or his Deputyes be paid unto the Receipt of his Majesties Exchequerr in such proportions and at such times as are directed by the said Act …[262]

Where did this local cash come from? A mint had operated at Bristol Castle in medieval times and during the Civil War, but it was closed when parliament took Bristol Castle in 1645. No doubt it aided post-revolutionary cash flow when a provincial mint was set up briefly in Bristol in 1696 during the Great Recoinage, partly at the instigation of MP tax commissioner Robert Yate.[263] By then, there were other ways to transfer monies as Yate realised. He liaised with the Treasury, regarding the scheme for the issue of interest-bearing Exchequer bills, which he actively promoted within the City as the best means of alleviating the chronic shortage of specie and the slump in trade. Although by 1698, the provincial mints were wound up, Yate was paid 200 guineas by the Treasury 'for his adroit management of the recoinage operations in Bristol'.[264] The ability of receivers to transfer money was greatly enhanced by this new 1698 legislation, and further measures in 1705, around Inland Bills of Exchange which ensured such bills were an assignable instrument of credit. So successful was this legislation that soon, Neal believes, the Inland Bill of Exchange 'constituted the bulk of the English money supply in this period'.[265] For Bristol, it meant that money could be transferred to London without the historic need for the secure transfer of cash. The receiver would still require a presence in London, Somerset and Bristol to be successful and there were several examples of partnerships between London and Bristol financiers. After his 1708 appointment as receiver, Bernard Hutchins usually resided in London whilst his deputies, Robert Baker and Nicholas Jefferys, remained in Somerset. Hutchins claimed considerable 'extraordinary expenses' over and above his poundage for this effort including £568-5s-3d 'reported by the late Commissioners for Taxes as due … and £201-9s-0d for his extraordinary allowances for the year 1714'.[266] Such generous allowances were stopped by the Treasury a few years later and receivers would have had to meet their own costs.[267] Similarly, Esquires, Phillip Baker of Somerset and John Derbie of London were joint receivers for Somerset and Bristol for many years after 1731 and no doubt operated in a similar way. Rich rewards came with high risks. Both were involved in a well-known legal case in 1758 involving amounts due to the state after bankruptcy of some of their intermediaries had interrupted payment flows.[268]

4.4.2 London

The mayor and aldermen remained at the heart of City of London tax administration. To them were added the Attorney-General, the Solicitor General and increasingly large numbers of others including deputies, senior common councilmen, lawyers, judges, merchants and financiers as commissioner numbers mushroomed to 284 by 1693 (including the 26 Aldermen) from the mere 93 in 1679 and to well over one thousand by the 1730s.[269] Many of these individuals played similar roles in other taxes including polls, marriage duty and window taxes, as did collectors and assessors. As discussed at Sect. 4.3.1 above, a significant part of this increase in numbers is explained by a delegation of authority to ward level, and for that, additional human resources were required. The database for the 1693–1694 Four Shilling Aid identifies many of these

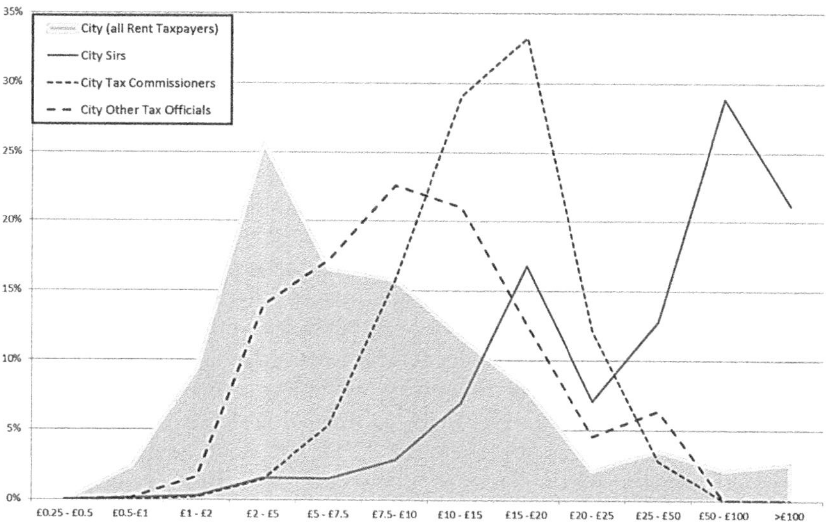

Fig. 4.10 City of London, 1693–1694 Four Shilling Aid. Minor officials (assessors and collectors), commissioners and 'Sirs' compared with the distribution of all taxpayers[270]

individuals and the annual taxed value of their houses (Fig. 4.10). The commissioners had a median taxed value of £15–20 and other officials £7.50–10. Overall, tax officials were predictably living in higher than average rated properties.

Bassishaw Ward illustrates the breadth of tax personnel and the depth of experience available for the land tax.[271] As during the Restoration, most of the middling and higher rated male householders served in ward roles or as tax officials after the Glorious Revolution. Women were of course excluded (and see Sect. 1.4).[272] Now, as commissioner numbers expanded, most well-to-do men appeared to play more of a part at ward level alongside the traditional deputies and common councilmen. So, for the 1706 land tax, the six Bassishaw commissioners approving and warranting the assessors on 23 April included two who would not typically have participated in ward processes during the Restoration. These were the alderman for Lime Street Ward, Sir Robert Beachcroft[273] and a local resident, the MP for Dartmouth and wealthy merchant and financier Nathaniel Herne.[274] In addition, it was signed by the usual ward officials: Deputy Alderman Roger Pococke; Common Councilman Jeremiah Powell[275]; and experienced ward officials, Josiah Diston[276] and Jonathan Shorey.[277] During the Restoration these last four would have been assessors themselves, but now four separate individuals would fulfil this role including two experienced ward officials: William Brown, who had been a collector and assessor since 1692 and active in the ward official since 1688, and Robert Pitman who had also been a collector and assessor since 1697 and active locally since 1686. Along with these seasoned individuals were two assessors with less experience and with no apparent previous tax background: Jonathan Baker (on the wardmote jury since 1696),[278] and Phillip Gibbs (ward scavenger in 1694 and later on the wardmote jury).[279] Later the commissioners would appoint John Taynton and John Verars as collectors. This was the first time for Verars, but Taynton had been a collector in 1699 and continued to serve periodically until 1716. At all levels, there was a significant body of experience.

According to Spence, the recorded population in 1693–1694 Bassishaw was 807, but he believes that total population was at least 100 more at 908.[280] Of the recorded population, 143 (18%) were children and 283 (35%) were servants of various kinds.[281] The poll records show the very mixed nature of Bassishaw's population with one of the highest proportions of private coaches in the City (12 or over 5% of all households).[282] The poll suggests about 131 taxable houses in the ward, two of which were empty, but there are some subdivisions of these and

Spence interprets this as 139 principal households and 107 lodgers.[283] Bassishaw had 153 taxpayers in the 1693–1694 four-shilling database.[284] Beyond these numbers, there would of course be those exempt households and those paid for by their landlord. Comparing these sources, with the Wardmote Inquest minutes, most land taxpayers (78 or 67%) filled one of the wardmote roles at some point in their lives. Thus, 69 (59%) served as jurors, 21 (18%) as constables and two (2%) as beadles. In fact, 17 were current jurors in 1693–1694. There were also as usual, two constables, two scavengers and one beadle in 1694.[285] There were four current common councilmen, but eleven or 9% of the 117 above served as such, at some time in their lives. Sir John Parsons, Knight and MP for Reigate, was then alderman for the ward.

Those who paid most tax were more likely to be involved in tax administration. The three individuals who paid the most tax in the ward (and 9% of all poll and land tax), all had senior tax and finance roles in the City at various points in their lives. They were beyond ward service. They were Sir Salathiel Lovell, an English judge, Recorder of London, sometime tax commissioner, and later a Baron of the Exchequer; Sir Leonard Robinson, Chamberlain of London, and the Receiver-General; and John Goodfellow, City Town Clerk, and clerk to the land tax commissioners. The next five highest taxpayers (11% of all tax) were all land tax commissioners. Of the next 19, ten (83%) were current/former commissioners or assessors or would become such, two were women, excluded from service (see Sect. 1.4), and six, though not tax officials, served other ward roles according to the wardmote minutes. Just seven show no record of any such service.[286] This group paid a further 22% of tax. The next 45 paid a further 31% of the tax bill.[287] Eleven were or became tax officials, 14 performed other ward services, there were 16 men and one female for whom there was no record of tax or ward service. Of the remaining 148, who paid 23% of the tax, only ten were tax officials, 22 were ward officials, but 70 have no record of service.

4.5 The Rise of Experienced Officials

In the three case study areas, post-revolutionary administration at all levels was usually in the hands of highly experienced, capable and long-serving individuals. At commissioner level, wealthy traders and merchants were often in charge with long track records in public service. These were individuals who had the confidence and knowledge to act decisively when called upon, to seek legal advice, to remove failing junior officials and to strive to meet deadlines. Clerks in particular, along with collectors and assessors, played a major part in achieving a regularity of process and significant attention to detail. This was not a system free from difficulty. However, these men often identified problems, wrote down what they were, and dealt with them.

4.5.1 *Tax Commissioners*

Individual commissioners remained in place for years and decades, as is widely recognised and such experience usually aided process efficiency.[288] Post-revolutionary administration relied increasingly on a backbone of these men operating at parish and civic level in all three case study areas. Grover believed in their general honesty and integrity claiming that 'little evidence of the abuses that were alleged to have occurred elsewhere have been found in Kent'.[289] Kent was perhaps not exceptional.

In Bristol, men like Samuel Wallis (30 years of experience, 162 recorded commissioners' meetings), William Jackson (26, 160) and 23 other men like them (Table 4.8) had a huge role in Bristol's commissioner effort, judging by meetings attended and documents signed.[290] In Bristol, 224 identifiable men were named in the commissioners' minutes between 1689 and 1740. Over one-third (84) served ten years or more.[291] Thirty eight served over 20 years, 10 over 30 years and 3 over 40 years as commissioners. Nine had been commissioners for the Restoration assessment and in the case of Alderman John Hickes, as far back as the Royal Aid in 1665. This brought an enormous level of experience to the administration. Most of the highly experienced were aldermen and thus doubled as local justices.

There were thousands like them up and down the land often with considerable capability and experience in local administration, local taxation and the law. In Wingham in Kent: Sir Basil Dixwell, Sir Thomas D'Aeth, Sir Thomas Palmer, Sir Robert Furnese and Hercules Baker, played a similar role and signed hundreds of tax documents between them.[292] They also doubled as the local justices of the peace, as tax commissioners did widely elsewhere.[293] Such men provided a crucial national resource. In Kent, MPs and former MPs bore a heavier share of the administrative burden than others. This group represents 42% of all tax assessment signatures between 1705 and 1733, and 44% of some 1500 assessments were signed by sitting MPs and 92% by current or former

Table 4.8 City of Bristol 1689–1740. List of 25 experienced officials who dominated the attendance at minuted tax commissioners' meetings[294]

Meetings attended	*Period of attendance*	*Name*	*% attended whilst active*	*Alderman*	*Sheriff*	*Mayor*	*Common council*	*Other*
53	1694–1710	John Bacheler	30%	Y	Y	Y	Y	
46	1714–1740	John Becher	30%	Y	Y	Y	Y	
49	1673–1698	Sir Richard Crumpe	30%	Y	Y	Y	Y	MP 1685
59	1696–1724	Sir William Daines	26%	Y	Y	Y	Y	MP 1701–1710; 1715–1722
111	1679–1709	Sir Thomas Day	46%	Y	Y	Y	Y	MP 1695–1701
49	1692–1715	Sir John Duddlestone, bart	20%				Y	
52	1689–1698	Thomas Edwards	32%					Uncertain
41	1696–1712	Sir John Hawkins	19%	Y	Y	Y	Y	
49	1679–1701	Sir William Hayman	28%	Y	Y	Y	Y	
56	1665–1698	John Hickes	34%	Y	Y	Y	Y	
45	1707–1727	Nicholas Hickes	38%	Y	Y	Y	Y	
67	1689–1698	John Hine	41%	Y	Y	Y	Y	
62	1698–1739	James Hollidge	25%	Y	Y	Y	Y	Chamberlain 1710–1739
160	1689–1714	William Jackson	62%	Y	Y	Y	Y	
63	1715–1740	John Jefferis	42%	Y	Y	Y	Y	
91	1689–1704	Sir Richard Lane	43%	Y	Y	Y	Y	
48	1711–1732	Edmond Mountjoy	31%	Y	Y	Y	Y	
52	1696–1721	John Romsey	26% ? understated					Town Clerk 1688–1721
58	1701–1730	Christopher Shuter	29%	Y	Y	Y	Y	
75	1679–1715	William Swymmer	31%	Y	Y	Y	Y	
57	1715–1740	Arthur Taylor	38%	Y	Y	Y	Y	
162	1689–1718	Samuel Wallis	58%	Y	Y	Y	Y	
72	1705–1737	Henry Walter	39%	Y	Y	Y	Y	
42	1696–1711	William Whitehead	28%	Y	Y	Y	Y	
96	1689–1732	Robert Yate	26%	Y	Y	Y	Y	MP 1695–1710
1715 attendances		25 individuals	= 49% of attendances					

MPs.[295] In smaller St. Augustine Lathe, West there are far fewer surviving documents, but John Hardres MP was a regular signatory. Patterns pertaining across the rest of Kent can only be glimpsed from duplicates because little else survives. Kentish duplicates for each sub-lathe normally had three or four signatories and these frequently feature current or former MPs, including cases where several signed a single document.[296] The 1706 tax duplicate for Aylesford South was signed by Philip Boteler (sitting MP for Hythe), John Brewer (sitting MP for New Romney) and Edward Goulston (former MP for New Romney).[297] In a small unscientific sample of 13 sub-lathes for six chosen years, 53% were signed by at least one current or former MP, and 9% by more than one.[298] Although MPs represented less than 10% of contemporary commissioners, they comprised more than 25% of sub-lathal signatories and by implication, a similar proportion of the total commissioner administrative effort, as they ensured coordination and implementation of legislation.[299] Few MPs were duplicate signatories in the boroughs and Cinque Ports, but they had their own local civic authorities.[300]

Many Kentish MP/commissioners in the period 1643–1733 had extensive experience with: the law, sewers, bridge or hospital administration, local rating, finance, other national taxation, the military, militias and civic bodies.[301] MPs usually had industrial, commercial or financial business connections and several had homes in London as well as Kent. Chalklin believed 'the heads of leading country families were usually justices of the peace' and they 'rested their customary control of the administration of the county through their tenure of' this office.[302] Wingham evidence supports Chalklin's view and suggests that in Kent, the tax commissioner role was an adjunct to a portfolio of local government functions.

In Wingham, assessors and collectors were also seasoned and experienced. As in Bristol and London the high rotation of officials common during the Restoration was replaced by the deployment of more experienced individuals for longer terms of service. At this more junior level of 140 parish officials in 1705, 30% were still at work in 1719, and 12.1% of them in 1732. Of the 127 at work in 1719, 28.3% were collecting or assessing the land tax in 1732. These experienced officials were not Ward's 'unwilling' 'grey-beards' but understood what was required by the centre, by Parliament, and personally made sure taxes were gathered.[303] Brooks identified these long continuities in smaller Kent parishes and argues that these men were 'the backbone of local society and parish life, as of national tax administration'.[304] The centre had come to town. Hoppit suggests land taxes 'linked centre and locality directly, involved local sources of authority in the needs of the state, [it] was cheap, and did away with heavy handed State tax collectors'.[305] Hoyle may be right that there was a 'rough and ready' quality[306] to the land tax but it would be wrong to mistake practical efficiency for a careless approach.[307] Many county and borough governors, particularly in the South and East improved administration and achieved highly successful tax collection rates on a par with Kent (Table 1.1). It was essential given the heavy burdens.[308] Neither was Kent unusually supplied with MPs to help its collection effort. With tax at 4s/£, Kent's MPs had a tax: MP ratio of 1MP:£4,636 compared with 1MP:£4,812 in the South-East generally.[309]

Kent commissioners were not dominant landowners, if the tax assessments can be relied upon and bearing in mind Ginter's critique.[310] Nor is there any sign of a potentially corrupt relationship between such landlords and their tenants as assessors or collectors. This also supports Grover's view.[311] From tax assessments in 1705, the 12 named Wingham commissioners owned an estimated 9.1% of the taxable sub-lathe rents, but a tiny 2.1% of the taxable rents involved a relationship between a collector or assessor and any commissioner.[312] In 1732, the estimated figures are only slightly higher at 14.6% and 4%, respectively.[313] For St. Augustine Lathe, West in the same year, it is even less, at 5% and 0.3%, respectively, with many lesser tenants as collectors/assessors, even if this is based on incomplete data. In New Romney, early eighteenth-century commissioners were normally the largest tenants there rather than the landlords.

Ward's notion that '... by 1726 parliament had entrusted the [land tax] administration to a few decaying greybeards' seems far-fetched given the experience, capabilities and skills of many of these individuals.[314] The average age of Wingham's active commissioners was a rather youthful 53.[315] If Kent's 1690s records survive less well than London's or Bristol's, by the early 1700s, Kent's tax processes were a largely annual affair capably in the hands of some vigorously effective clerks, including John Phillips in Wingham, and effective receivers like George Baker. Matters were overseen by competent commissioners, including Sir Basil Dixwell, a former MP for Dover, auditor of excise, Colonel of militia horse, Deputy Lieutenant of Kent, Governor of Dover Castle, court of lodemanage of the Cinque Ports and current justice of the peace.[316] Sir Thomas D'Aeth had travelled widely, had been involved in his father's trading business and had strong London connections. Sir Brook Bridges was a British barrister, admitted to the Middle Temple, and held the office of Auditor of the Imprest of the Treasury, and was a land tax commissioner for Middlesex as well as Kent.

Many commissioners were named in successive statutes and ordinances over decades. In Wingham, Sir Basil Dixwell's career stretched from 1688 to the mid-1730s. Five commissioners served for decades, only ceasing in the year of their death: Sir Henry Palmer 1660–1706,[317] Sir Brook Bridges 1700–1728, John Lynch 1701–1733,[318] John Cason[319] c. 1688–1718,[320] and Sir Thomas D'Aeth c. 1714–1745. All were active commissioners signing hundreds of documents and attending dozens of meetings. In St. Augustine Lathe, West, where document survival is much poorer, Captain Humphrey Pudner[321] and Christopher Milles were both active between the 1690s and 1730s.[322]

There is a similar pattern in New Romney.[323] Richard Baker, John Coates, Robert Mascall, John Norman and John Tookey all served as tax officials for over 30 years and signed and sealed numerous tax documents. Humphrey Wightwicke and many others served for over 20 years, in this case, until his death in 1721. Several progressed to being commissioner after working, perhaps learning the trade, as assessor and/or collector. This was true of Wightwicke, Stephen Brett, Edward Bacheler, Richard Baker, John Bassett, John Coates and Nicolas Durant. Several of the New Romney commissioners appear to be Hipkin's 'successful tenant farmers'. He believes that throughout the early modern period, it was this group, rather than large proprietors, who did most to promote the growth of large farms in Romney Marsh.[324] They especially built up sheep grazing interests. Humphrey Wightwicke left an estate worth £2,434-9s-8d in 1721, half of which consisted of a 1,250-strong sheep flock and 39 cattle.[325] John Coates was regularly referred to in tax assessments as 'grazier'.[326] In many other cases, their lease holdings in New Romney alone increased sharply as their portfolios were built. Edward Bacheler was only paying £7 rent in 1720, but £94 in 1733. This group of agricultural businessmen would implicitly have had significant financial and administrative skills—perhaps an ideal group to administer seventeenth and eighteenth-century land taxes.

Kentish commissioners were experienced men who tried to assure fairness according to rent. Davison quotes from tax commissioner Sir Wyndham Knatchbull's (5th Baronet 1699–1749) diary that on 4 June 1737, he and his fellow commissioners in the Ashford Division, in the

Lathe of Scray, were faced with the usual difficulties of those 'Several complain[ing] of being overrated in their Land Tax'.[327] The only solution with fixed local quotas, as here, would have been to assess others underrated in the parish. Unfortunately, assessors of the relevant parishes '... were asked whether any were underrated. But it appeared they were all rated as near in the same proportion as could well be'.[328] As in Wingham, scrutiny was by justices. '[The Assessments] having been signed [at] last [petty sessions], this was the day for Appeals ...These lists are sworn to by the said Officer who delivers 'em in, and are signed by a Justice; & are to be deliver'd into Court at the next Session by the Constable'.[329]

Experienced men of authority were part of the tax commissioner establishment in Kent, Bristol, London and many other parts of the country. Such authority has an archaic quality to a modern audience, but it empowered such individuals to apply the tax law and operate decisively and effectively. Such local governance structures continued to be at the heart of direct tax-gathering throughout the eighteenth century and beyond and as Daunton has pointed out, supported the success of the early income tax.[330] Such arrangements remained part of modern tax procedures until recently.[331] Often with some grounding in the law themselves, it is striking that these men were comfortable in seeking tax opinions where the law was unclear. 1705 Wingham commissioners would not accept a taxpayer contention that lands owned by the Hospital of Bethlehem should enjoy charitable/tax-exempt status and went on 'to Lay it before Mr ... Phipps a Counsellor in the Court of the Excheq^{r} for his Opinion theron' at a cost of two guineas. It took until 3 December 1706 to receive the opinion, which came back against the contentions of the Hospital, for complex reasons of land ownership. The commissioners therefore resolved to 'directly proceed to raise the arrears ... by the rigour of the law'.[332] In the City of London, opinion was similarly sought from Sir Thomas Trevor, the Attorney-General, who gave such on 17 May 1700 in favour of the tax-exempt status of stock-in-fund or stock-in-trade of the East India Company to the two shilling land tax because, although 'there are general words in the said Act that charge all Bodies Pollitick and Corporate to pay for their Debts and Personall Estates (Except debts and loans to his Majestie), yet I think those Generall words will not be construed to this Company, because this company being [specifically] exempted by Act of Parliament'.[333]

Such actions suggest a sophistication of process and a competence of individuals far beyond that portrayed in much of land tax historiography.

4.5.2 *Discipline, Experience and the Deployment of Officials*

The way commissioners summarily dealt with failing junior officials belies any claim that these men were either in collusion or 'unwilling'.[334] There are numerous examples. Collector William Jarman of Dolphin precinct, Tower Ward suffered painful justice.[335] It is reported that 'under the hands and seals of the commissioners dated 7 day of March [1701] they have seized and secured the personal estate of Wm Jarman … for neglecting or refusing to pay the [collected] sum of 4 and thirteen pounds'. Further, they had called 'a general meeting of all the commissioners at Guildhall on Thursday 3rd [?] of April next at 3 o'clock in the afternoon to sell and dispose of the said estate … in order to pay unto Sir Thomas Cuddon knight his majesty's Receiver-General'.[336] This was not a unique event, indeed this action was part of a general 'policy of sale of estates of collectors failing'[337] to deliver collected sums. In other cases, established collectors were simply dropped. The City warrants from 1702 show most collectors being approved, but in Castle Baynard, although John Halsey and John Young were 'carried in the affirmative', William Territ and John Bateman were not.[338] An unacceptable practice was for officials to commence work without a warrant which legitimised the action of collection. A note on the assessment for Broad Street in 1693 (first quarterly assessment for St. Margaret Lothbury) notes: 'D[?] Hall abated 20s the money being collected before the assessment was made'.[339]

A note of a London commissioners' meeting dated 3 October 1718 states that: 'To order the collectors who are in arrear, to clear their accounts in 14 days, or appear before the commissioners to show cause why they should not be fined for neglect of their duty'.[340] There was a reassessment in Cripplegate Without for 1738 (but attached to the assessment for 1741) for the amount of £309 caused by 'being a deficiency occasioned by the failure of David Jones late one of the collectors'.[341] Recurrent difficulties were caused by a collector's death, their impoverishment, or insolvency (see Table 5.1).[342] A note on the assessment book for Cordwainer reports that 'We return Mr Daniel Phillips to be Collector of the Land Tax of St. Pancras and St. Thomas Apostle Precincts for the remaining part of this year [1729] in the room of Mr

Henry Proctor decd'.[343] On 13 January 1720, the commissioners of St. Michaels East precinct, Candlewick Ward replaced collector 'George Wright that is insolvent' with Thomas Coleman.[344]

Collectors, for various reasons, might fail, even after many years of good performance and commissioners might be forced to act. Samuel Row, who had been a diligent collector in Aldgate Ward for very many years, received summary treatment. He had been reappointed for the fourth Aldgate precinct in 1742, but a draft commissioners' letter suggests that although he 'hath accordingly received of the inhabitants of the said Precinct several moneys for the said tax amounting to [left blank] pounds & upwards which he hath detained in his hands & neglected to pay the same, as in & by the said Act of Parliament is directed'. His 'Goods and chattels & also freehold messuage & premises mentioned in the inventory or schedule underwritten' should therefore become forfeit under the Act and subject to distress. In St. Bartholomew-the-Less, Farringdon Without, less experienced Richard Ryder and Thomas Yeates 'neglected to pay to the receiver-general at the times in and by the said act directed and appointed'.[345] Commissioners Joseph Wright, Richard Pemble and Thomas Fryer signed a warrant dated 9 October 1701 to 'all & every the constables within the City of London and Libertyes thereof … to imprison them … & seize the estates both real and personal which doth belong to them … in order to be sold and disposed of pursuant to this direction of the said act … and you are not to fail'.[346] Neither Yeates nor Ryder appear in the duplicate for 1701, dated 15 December 1702, but Ryder reappears on the duplicate for 1703 suggesting rehabilitation.[347] The foregoing and following accounts are not to chart failure as Ward does, but to demonstrate that with such a large organisation periodic failures and even dishonesty were inevitable. The real issue is whether the commissioners had the appropriate powers and authorities and were prepared to use them. It seems clear that indeed administrative issues and problems that occurred were identified, written down and dealt with to mitigate the impact on tax-flows.[348] It is also to show these instances of failure were exceptional because very many other tax officials were diligent and understood the consequences of failure. The result of such understanding was a remarkable tax-flow year after year (Fig. 5.4).

Wingham commissioners focussed tightly on parliamentary deadlines and particularly the handing into the clerk of the 56 completed parish tax assessments by the deadline they had set so the collectors could get to work.[349] Commissioners were intolerant, and failing assessors had to appear before them to explain themselves (and see detailed account in Sect. 5.4.2).[350]

In Bristol, poorly performing officials would also be fined or removed. If people were absent they would need to be speedily replaced by others. In 1722, 'Mr Richard King & John Brickdale were approved assessors for the parish of St. Nicholas in the roome and stead of Walter Oborne & Mr Williams who were gone out of towne long journey'.[351] At a meeting of 24 May 1703, commissioners demanded that officials be called in next Thursday at 3: 'that those assessors who have neglected to bring in their Bookes to attend & bring them in'.[352]

It was made clear at the outset of each process exactly what was expected of appointed officials in the form of their warrants. It is remarkable from the three case studies that assessors' and collectors' warrants were remarkably consistent in detailed form and indeed it seems likely that this consistency stretched across the country. Although most of these warrants were hand-written by the clerks in some years pre-printed documents were sent out and this must have encouraged that consistency. The warrants themselves certainly give further indication of what was expected of tax officials. The Bristol commissioners' minutes preserve long sequences of such material and some of their flavour comes through from this copy of the letter summoning the assessors for 1733 which states succinctly: 'The Commissioners … do hereby require you and each of you personally to appear at the Council House on Monday next at 11 of the clock in the forenoon to receive your charge as assessors of the said Land Tax …'[353] Similar statements appear repeatedly in the commissioners' minute book. This from 20 April 1698: 'You are by virtue of the powers and authorities of the Act aforesaid appointed presenters and assessors for the parish of [] and are hereby required to be & appear before us and other the commissioners at the Counsell house in the Tolzey of the City on Friday the 29th of April instant by 3 of the clock in the afternoon'. The warrants set out the precise duties and the reasons for performing them. The assessors' warrant of 1701 recalls the Act, the purpose ('for defraying the expence of his [majesty's] navy, guards and Garrisons for one year and other necessary occasions'), the amount due, the period and the taxpayers ['the owners and occupiers of houses and messuages, Lands & Tenemts: and persons possessed of ready money, Debt, personall Estate, annuities, Pensions or Enjoying or possessing any offices or Implo[y]m[e]nts …'], the rates and asking them to make a rate for 'your parish to be fairly written and returned by you to us … at the Tolzey of the said city before [date to insert], and to put down the names of substantiall fit persons to be collectors of the said money'.[354]

Collectors' warrants also quoted from the Act, the amounts to be raised for Bristol and the commissioners' authority. Collectors must visit those assessed 'in your parish and is conteymed in a duplicate [copy] of the said Assessment hereunto annexed and you to whom this warrant is directed being appointed Collectors of the said severall and respective sumes soe rated and assessed … Therefore to require you before [date] to make demand of the sumes rated and assessed of the severall p[er]sons … ought to pay the same'. It pointed out the right of appeal for those 'aggrieved … at the Tolzey' on the specified date. Collectors were also empowered to act in respect of non-payers 'by entering their houses and takeing distresse of the goods of the p^{er}sons neglecting or refuseing' and sold within four days returning any 'overplus' to the taxpayer. Constables could be called to 'break open any trunk, chest, box or other thing'. This was dated 28 July 1701, but similar documents were produced in Kent, London and nationally from the 1650s onwards.[355] Such warrants would no doubt have been shown to taxpayers if they quibbled about their payments.

Experience was important and appreciated as such. When the complex marriage duty was introduced in 1695, Bristol administrators understood the challenges and acted appropriately. Commissioners deployed an unusually large number of 69 assessors or almost four per parish compared with two or three for land taxes. Indeed some of these were indeed fined for non-attendance at the first meeting on 10 May 1695, which was a clear sign of the determination on the part of commissioners to deploy significant numbers of experienced men to make this novel duty work. The Act was read out at that meeting. This was a new tax where the whole population, at least so it was intended, would be assessed. The focus on experience is clear. Assessors were largely drawn from those previously most active as collectors or assessors for polls and land taxes; exactly the right body of men for implementation.[356]

Bristol assessors and collectors were rarely one and the same, based on the sample parishes: St. Mary-le-Port, St. Nicholas, Temple and St. Augustine.[357] As discussed, early Restoration assessors and collectors normally rotated on a quarterly basis with little evidence of continuity. Much greater continuity prevailed after 1672 administrative delayering

(Table 3.5) and this pattern continued into the post-revolutionary period where patterns can be better tracked because of good quality and more continuous documentation. Post-revolutionary tax-gathering remained a largely quarterly process, and in the 1690s officials could still be rotated every three months. The commissioners' minutes for 1691 provide the names of all the collectors and assessors for every quarter and parish.[358] Few assessors were rotated during the year with only eight of 52 replaced. However, in most parishes, collectors were still being changed quarterly. Thus, over 50 of the 87, operating at some time during the year, were replaced. Nevertheless, some parishes were adopting the practice of retaining collectors for the whole year and this is true in: Castle Precinct, Sts. Philip & Jacob, St. James and St. Thomas. These were the populous but poorer parishes where the deployment of more experienced collectors would have been a significant advantage in dealing with more mobile populations. In 1693, for the very first time, all the assessors in every parish kept their job for the whole year, judging from the three surviving quarters. Collector rotation declined sharply in the late 1690s, and during the early eighteenth century, Bristol built up a body of experienced officials, so for most parish collections, at least one and often two of the collectors would have served before.[359]

Restoration City of London collectors were also endlessly rotated (see Sect. 3.3.3), but this changed dramatically after the Revolution and particularly after 1700.[360] The number of collection rounds, where one or more previously serving officers were employed, increased sharply.[361] A large number of highly experienced collectors began to dominate collection in most wards with many individuals serving ten years and more. Across the City after 1703, taxpayers would find at least one of the same collectors operating in their precinct the following year, in four years out of five.[362] Collectors who had served ten years or more at some point in their lives made up 43% of the collection effort.[363] Three hundred and thirty two of such ten-year-serving men can be identified up to 1733. Seventy six of these went on to serve for over 20 years and these men comprised 14% of the collection effort. Every ward in London had a number of such ten-year seasoned individuals. There were just two in Bread Street Ward, but 35 in the much larger Farringdon Without Ward and more impressively, 34 in the much smaller Cripplegate Within Ward. These long-serving collectors worked on average for over 14.7 years and were named in 9.3 duplicates. A group of 70 such served as City collector in 1689–1690 and went on to work for at least a further ten years, providing a backbone for the foundation of post-revolutionary land taxes administration. Least collector continuity is visible in the western and southern wards and subdivisions of Farringdon Within and Without, Bread Street, Queenhithe and Aldersgate Within. The central and northern wards of Dowgate, Langbourn, Cordwainer, Cheap, Coleman Street and Cripplegate Within and Without have the greatest continuity. This is partly explained by ward size because smaller words generally had least rotation. This may then have been a matter of having less people to choose from with appropriate qualifications. Tax collection from 'Waters, etc.' (as discussed corporate taxes), had the greatest collector consistency of all but this is not surprising because collection here required knowledge, skill and good personal networks. The lure of what had become regular income from tax collector poundage tempted some to petition for these posts. Thomas Brearcliffe, a former collector in Cheap Ward, petitioned 'The Lord Mayor and the rest of the commissioners … within the City of London … [to] … grant him the favour of being one of the collectors of the … several taxes laid upon the River water, convex lights and other public stocks' [i.e. 'Waters, etc.'), one of the most lucrative rounds.[364] Unfortunately for Brearcliffe, skilled and capable John Smart (and see Sect. 4.5.3) submitted his own petition that year. He had 'for two years last past … been appointed collector … and hopes he hath discharged the trust reposed in him to your satisfaction'.[365] In fact, Smart was being extremely modest, he had been sole collector for two years, but had been part of the collection group since 1702. Brearcliffe was unsuccessful in his application.

Some London collectors were more fortunate than others in earning poundage. Because average tax charges were higher in central than in extra-mural or riverside wards, collectors in the first could collect the same amount of tax from far less households, with less effort, than their less fortunate colleagues. The tax precinct system meant that most collection rounds involved about 100–200 houses and central ward collectors would obtain more income for the same effort and in shorter time, because average payments were higher. City tax collection was based on traditional ward precincts. There were 25 wards but some 200 tax precincts averaging 120 square yards, many were amalgamated being too small to comprise an effective separate round.[366] Collectors and assessors were allocated to varying precincts, often more than one, although rounds varied (Fig. 4.11).

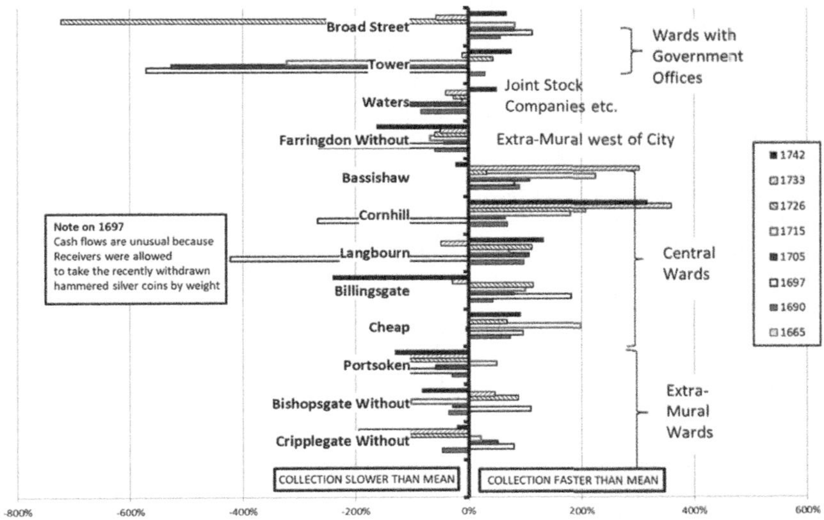

Fig. 4.11 City of London. Speed of tax collection compared 1665–1742[367]

Most post-revolutionary rounds had two collectors, some a few more, but the number of single collectors increased over time and thus the total number of collectors declined. There was a sharp fall in the number of collectors and collection rounds in the early 1700s. The remaining collectors would have a larger share of City poundage. This would have also been an opportunity to select the most effective tax officials and dispense with the services of those less able. It is difficult to demonstrate this from the evidence, but it seems likely. By the mid-1730s over half the rounds had single named collectors. As tax rates fell from four shillings to one in 1732, single-person collection rounds shielded surviving collectors from falling poundage. However, malfeasance risk increased and this was also extra-statutory as legislation still referred to two officials (see Fig. 4.12).[368] There was a mean of 119 City collection rounds between 1699 and 1737, with an average of 190 collectors. In Bassishaw, two tax collectors normally served every year, occasionally more. From c. 1715 to 1716, it became increasingly common in Bassishaw, and elsewhere, for assessors to nominate themselves as collectors as well, thus removing an extra layer of administration.[369] Many experienced individuals progressed to be commissioners themselves and had extremely long

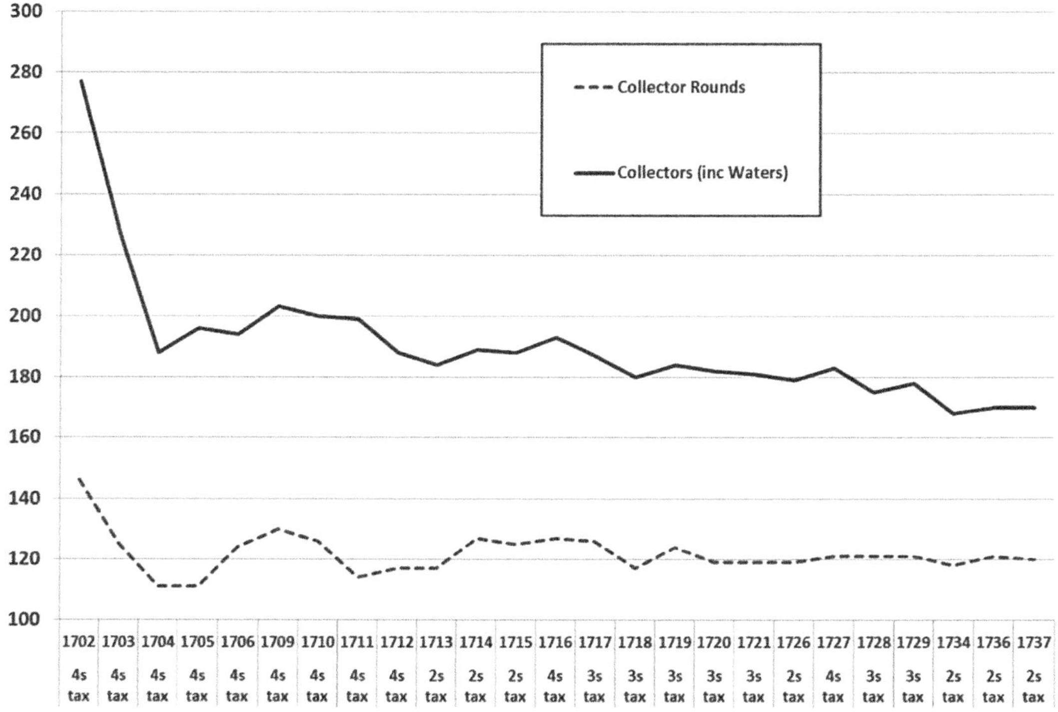

Fig. 4.12 City of London 1702–1737. The number of collectors and collectors' rounds showing a decline in the number of tax-gatherers and rounds over time[370]

careers of up to 30 years. Jonathan Baker began as assessor in 1706 and later served as a commissioner until 1721. William Brown was a serving tax official for at least twenty years from his 1691 appointment as collector. Arthur Barfoot was variously collector, assessor and commissioner between 1714 and 1726, similarly William Coulthurst (1727–1756), Samuel Ellis (1733–1764) and Robert Pitman (1697–1727). In Bassishaw, it should be noted, many traditional ward roles such as scavenger continued to be rotated at this time and individuals sometimes moved on to more senior posts. In Bassishaw, as elsewhere in the City, tax roles had become more stable and consistent and more like the job of Beadle which was rarely rotated.

Senior Bassishaw officials usually progressed through the ranks. William Flewellen was assessor in the 1660s and 1670s[371] and was a common councilman or deputy almost continuously from 1656, at the age of 49, to his death in 1675.[372] All identified assessors held prior ward responsibilities, including Common Councilmen Roger Pocock (assessor in 1663 and 1666 and on the wardmote jury in 1660), Gabriel Whittley (assessor, 1663; wardmote jury, 1661) and Joseph Clutterbuck (assessor, 1673; wardmote jury at least since 1655). Remarkably Sir Thomas Stamp, who was on the wardmote as early as 1657, became an assessor in 1673 and 1678, and an alderman in nearby Cripplegate Ward from 1688 to 1711. Giles Sussex appears as an assessor and commissioner between 1692 and 1694, had been a collector in 1673 and a jury member since 1671. Similarly experienced were: Thomas Bye (assessor, 1694; wardmote jury since 1672); Jonathan Cook, a common councilman (assessor, 1693; wardmote jury from 1672); John Kent (assessor, 1693; wardmote jury since 1674); and John Knapp a commissioner in 1694 (wardmote jury since 1688). Thus, substantial local tax experience had been developed to prevent any process decline through periods when tax was not collected, particularly the long period between 1681 and 1688. Bassishaw officials all had some prior ward experience: collectors (3.7 years after first wardmote jury appearance on average), assessors (10.1 years) and commissioners (14.4 years).[373] Many officials had experience of other taxes as well. For individuals with clerical, basic finance and book-keeping skills, the City provided numerous opportunities for building portfolios of engagements to earn a living, and the job of tax collector became a cornerstone.

4.5.3 *Town Clerk of the City of London*

The City Town Clerk's office had made much administrative progress under William Wagstaffe, as discussed (Sect. 3.3.3), and he was followed by John Goodfellow (elected 17 February 1691–1700) in the immediate Post-revolutionary period who also did much to chase up any slackness.[374] They were followed by Henry Ashurst (1700–1705), James Gibson (1705–1717), Randolph Stracey (1717–1724), but it was one of their clerks John Smart who became the administrative mainstay. Indeed in 1702, he was described simply as 'one of the clerkes in the Town Clerk's office of the City of London & whose business it is to settle & make up the ac[count]s of the collect[or]s of the taxes & subsidies'.[375] He became much more than that.[376] From at least 1702[377] John Smart initialled as 'examined' the vast majority of the tax assessments himself and the good documentary survival of City records after this date probably owes much to him.[378] He advanced quickly. Smart was named eight times between 1702 and 1716 as personally delivering the City duplicate to the Exchequer.[379] He was named as examining the City duplicate in every surviving year from 1715 to 1737,[380] may have briefly been acting town clerk in 1723[381] and was collector for 'Waters, etc.' between 1702 and 1741.[382] Through Smart's tutelage, the town clerks' office became an excellent land tax accounting back office, keeping excellent records, correcting errors, chasing up delays and keeping track of responsible officials. Such checking mitigated varying assessor capability as it had done since the Restoration. Smart lived in Bassishaw Ward, although probably not continuously, from about 1704 until his death in 1743, and appears in tax assessments until his death that year.[383] He published a number of works including groundbreaking tables on interest and discount,[384] and time.[385] He probably also worked at the Exchequer Office at Lincoln's Inn, which explains his work on national tax quotas.[386] The town clerk's role became vital in London, but it was also well remunerated with a poundage of 1½d/£. A four-shilling land tax would thus produce £770.84, but it was a sum only approved for payment once all City tax had been gathered. Thus, the payment for 1705 was only approved on 18 March 1707, and not paid until 24 September 1707.[387] Perhaps Hunt is right when she says, 'Mastery of time-discipline, writing, and accounting gave the seventeenth and eighteenth-century trading classes a new confidence in their ability to comprehend and control the tumultuous world of Commerce' and public administration.[388] John Smart may have been an archetype.

It was not just John Smart who showed an attention to detail. Smart was at the heart of a culture of London City diligence which contradicts Ward's pronouncement that 'London represented the quintessence of the administrative problems of the whole country'.[389] Town clerk's office papers provide ample supporting testimony, but a few examples of error correction must suffice. Valentine Brewis made a note to Smart on 2 October 1735 regarding the tax assessment for Houndsditch in Portsoken Ward that 'our Beadle by a perfect mistake left out sixteen shill[ings] for a y[ea]r Tax … [on] Jno Brooke for his Stables – I pray it may be inserted in the tax books and make the Duplicate comfortable'.[390] Similarly in Tower Ward in 1710, 'Sir William Whetstone knight is through a mistake omitted to be assessed in the Land Tax Book … in respect of his pension payable out of the ordinary of Her Majesties Navy, the sum of sixty eight pounds'. The assessors named 'do desire that the said Sir William Whetstone may be inserted in the said Tax Book'. The note was dated 21 December 1711, more than a year after the original assessment.[391] In 1718, in Tower Ward again, where the assessments of personal estates were highly detailed, the large error of £60-15s-0d was admitted:

> We the Commissioners and Assessors of Tower ward London whose names are under written having through a mistake omitted to assess Dame Elizabeth Hopson and M. Martha Lyddell for their respective pensions payable out of the ordinary of his Majesties' Navy in our Book of assessment … now therefore charge and assess the same …

It was dated 4 November 1718, six weeks after the assessment was approved and brought in on 17 September.[392] Three of the assessors in Tower Ward, Thomas Watterer, Thomas Loveday and Joseph Spearman, wrote to John Smart on 11 November 1704 that;

> by some mistake [we have] omitted a house in Petty Wales precinct, which is now in the possession of Peter Hore, & should have been charged four pounds four shillings, and also omitted one Luke Singleton, being one of the surveyors of the land waiters at the Custom House, and should have been charged twenty seven pounds. We therefore desire they may be inserted into our Booke of Assessment according to their proper places.[393]

Problems could be greatest on large collection rounds as in Farringdon Without ward. The commissioners in St. Bartholomew-the-Great, Farringdon Without wrote to Smart in 1735 that they had 'omitted to add John Whittingham being next after Benj: Bucknall in Folio 11, we do desire he may be Added at the rate of ten pounds p[er] ann'. It was signed by both assessors and two commissioners, Thomas Hunt and Joshua Locke, who had signed the original assessment. Even small errors were spotted. Commissioners in Vintry wrote to Smart on 1 January 1738 about historic omissions of £1 in 1736 and £2 in 1737.

Sometimes Smart prompted corrections himself, which show his own checking was no formality. His note dated 7 November 1728 stated that 'there is a house in St. Martins Vintry Parish in the occupation of John Pemberton which I find is left out in the last years assessment of the Land Tax'.[394] The adjustment was 12s-0d. On 7 October 1730, Smart noted that 'there is a mistake in the present Land Tax booke for Vintry ward in the Three upper precincts. John Parker is charged but Tenn Pounds, should be charged at Twenty Pound p[er] ann.' There are numerous such adjustments amongst Smart's records.[395] Assessors' arithmetical errors were regularly corrected in Smart's office. In Dowgate, in the west division, the five assessors signed off on a total assessment of £542-5s-0d, but this was ten shilling too little. In 1728, the assessors' total for Salisbury Court, Farringdon Without was £1,070-1s-0d, but this was £11 too little, Smart had it right at £1,081-1s-0d.

Smart was directly involved in the assessment and collection of taxes involving the joint-stock companies and particularly important documents survive from 1704 and 1706.[396] In 1706, tax was levied such that 'all and every person and persons, having any share or shares or interests in any fresh stream or Running water brought from the North Parts of London, commonly called the New River'. The assessment names many other waterworks and 'any rents or profits arising thereby'. Similarly taxed were 'any share or interest in any officer or stock for ensuring houses in cases of fire … stock or stock for Printing Books', along with 'all Companies of Merchants in London and the Bank of England', and salaries and pensions in the General Post Office and Excise Office. The companies were rated and paid the tax, but the dividend recipient appears to have suffered the burden because they would have received less dividend because: 'the same shall be paid by the Governors and respective Treasurers or Receivers of the said River Waters & Water Works, & of the said officers & stocks, respectively, & be deducted at &

out of their next Dividend …'[397] Collectors here (Daniel Man, Robert Walker, John Hutton and John Smart) as well as those serving the Navy Office and Custom House in Tower Ward (e.g. Henry Cowdery,[398] John Lewis,[399] and Henry Lomas)[400] were all long-serving but were also responsible for the most substantial tax collection rounds in the City. In fact, across the City, there was a pattern that collector continuity was greatest where tax collection rounds were largest.

England's involvement in continental conflict pushed land tax burdens higher particularly in urban areas and metropolitan London the South and East of England which took more than their fair share of fiscal weight. This did not lead to slack administration or chaos as some historians have suggested. Rather, it has been shown here that local administrators set about improving the effectiveness of the process and a range of solutions were adopted centrally and locally to meet these new demands. There was to be: improved central stakeholder oversight; greater administrative resourcing; the deployment of more experienced personnel; increased delegation; process simplification; flexibility; and a more careful choice of taxpayers. The case studies in Kent, London and Bristol all present post-revolutionary evidence of highly experienced individuals at work at all levels in the tax process. The roles of Commissioner, assessor, collector and clerk all provide excellent examples of long-service, diligence and commitment to successfully delivering tax monies to the Exchequer.

Notes

1. Davison, *The Agrarian Economy of Romney Marsh*, pp. 78–79, lists ten Kentish parishes with customs or excise officers and notes that typically, a riding officer was assessed to the Land Tax at £40, a supervisor of excise at £84. In 1700, two-thirds of all riding officers in England and Wales were stationed in Kent according to Richard Grover, 'The Land Tax in East Kent: A Study in Land Ownership and Occupation with Special Reference to the Methodological Implications of the Land Tax Assessments' (M. Phil. thesis, University of Kent at Canterbury. 1980), p. 204, quoted in Davison, Ibid., p. 79.
2. For example, Ward, *The English Land Tax*, p. 28, claims that taxes were charged to departmental administration.
3. In the Land Tax for 1723 (9 Geo. 1 c. 2.) interest rates fell to 3% and this became the norm.
4. Ward, *The English Land Tax*, p. 15*ff.*

5. For example, HOCJ, vol. 16, 14 December 1710, p. 434.
6. For example, HOCJ, vol. 16, 16 February 1709, p. 111.
7. Ward, *The English Land Tax*, p. 26; David Hayton, Eveline Cruickshanks and Stuart Handley, *The House of Commons, 1690–1715*, vol. 1, The History of Parliament (Cambridge: Cambridge University Press, 2002), p. 403. A special Commons committee was appointed.
8. Ward, *The English, Land Tax*, Chapter IV.
9. For example, HOCJ, vol. 15, 23 February 1708, p. 561, and HOCJ, vol. 13, 3 April 1701, p. 469.
10. For example, HOCJ, vol. 20, 7 February 1724 and 3 December 1724, pp. 255 and 353; HOCJ, vol. 21, 3 March 1731, pp. 651–653.
11. Parenthesis is as per the source. They were receivers in Southampton.
12. CTB, vol. 16, 1 July 1701, p. 83.
13. The City, Westminster, and parts of Middlesex and Surrey within the Bills of Mortality.
14. In fact 15.54%—according to 9 Wm. III, c. 10, £1,484,015 Land Tax, 1698, SoR, vol. 7, pp. 307–364.
15. Based on the marriage duty assessment and the Bills of Mortality c. 150,000, with over 70,000 in Farringdon Without, https://www.locatinglondon.org/static/Population.html#toc3.
16. Roseveare, *The Financial Revolution*, p. 33.
17. Some of the Land Tax Acts refer specifically to 1693 e.g. the 1704 Act [2 & 3 Anne, c. 1. Land Tax for 1704, SoR, vol. 8, pp. 226–245.] states 'and towards the raising and making up the whole sum by this Act charged upon the whole county, city or other places…according to the proportions which were assessed on the same hundreds or divisions respectively, by virtue of an Act of Parliament made and passed in the fourth Year of their late majesties.' City documents show how this was implemented in the City especially, LMA: COL/CHD/LA/03/081/014 [Land Tax and Subsidies Papers re assessment of quotes, liability of excise officers, liability of prize goods which shows how the 1704 quotas were arrived at by adjusting from the 1693 base figures].
18. Leaving some fractional wriggle room at the tax precinct levels within wards.
19. Anon., *Land Tax at 4s in the Pound Paid by England & Wales in 1702, & 1744*.
20. Sources for statutory quotas taken from the various statutes: SoR various. Only one or two including York, saw a fall.
21. Although this was effectively just a change from a locally defined quota to a statutory quota defined centrally.
22. As was recognised by Ward, *The English Land Tax*, Table 1, p. 8.

23. This is perhaps 3,000 or so more than during the Restoration. City population was fairly static according to Harding, 'City, Capital, and Metropolis', p. 124. Harding estimates a population of 135,000–148,000 in the City's 25 wards in 1700, Harding, 'The Population of London, 1550–1700', Table 1. Therefore one in six inhabitants was a taxpayer.
24. After Spence, *London in the 1690s*. The Restoration figure appears to have been c. 20,000 based on counts of tax assessments in the LMA: COL/CHD/LA/03/various.
25. See note 19 above.
26. The 1693–1694 annual value of land for tax purposes in the City of London was c. £450,000 [Spence, *London in the 1690s*, Appendix III], in Bristol £30,000 [BRO: various], and New Romney £1,100 [KHLC: NR/RTL].
27. The 3,800 figure in 1693–1694 is estimated from BRO: F/A/14 and 16 assessments for 1693–1694 and 1694–1695, although taxpayer numbers were not entirely consistent from year to year. This latter is based on estimates from four sample parishes, one from each of the City's division after Sacks, *The Widening Gate*, Fig. 3 (Fig. 2.2): St. Mary-le-port (Central), St. Nicholas (Portside), Temple (Transpontine), and St. Augustine (Suburban); BRO: FL/LT/StN, StMP, StA, and T. Note the taxpayer numbers and the numbers of freemen are similar: Restoration (c. 2,900), 1690s–1700s (c. 3,500), and mid-century (c. 4,500) based on HoP, http://www.historyofparliamentonline.org/volume/1660-1690/constituencies/bristol.
28. With tax of £7,391.53 and 3,800 taxpayers.
29. KHLC: NR/RTL24. The New Romney four shilling/£ tax was £249.85 in 1693 and there were 127 taxpayers, but 171 separate tax charges because some tenants paid for several properties.
30. There were c. 2,400 tax charges in Lathe East and c. 1,450 in West [tax charge counts from the assessments KHLC: Q/CTL/various parishes]. The four shilling tax quotas were approximately £8,023.95 and £3,888.83 respectively [KHLC: Q/C/Tc2 commissioners' Resolves], equivalent to £3.34 and £2.68 or £3.09 on average.
31. For 1703 e.g. £1,997,931.95.
32. E. Anthony Wrigley and Roger S. Schofield, *The Population History of England 1541–1871. A Reconstruction* (Cambridge: Cambridge University Press, 1989).
33. £1,997,931.95/(5.2 m × 1%) = £38.42.
34. He was later Duke of Argyll. Source: *Cobbett's Parliamentary History of England*, vol. 8 (1722–1733). House of Lords Debate on the Salt Duty Bill, 22 March 1732, p. 1055.

35. Davison, *The Agrarian Economy of Romney Marsh*, Appendix 4, Table 4.1.
36. City of London: It varied depending on the amount of taxation on corporate profits. Sources: Duplicates, TNA: SP 28/162–170, London, Middlesex, and metropolitan London; Ancestry.co.uk, London, England; City of Bristol: 81% according to estimates based on BRO: F/Tax/A/14 and 16 1693–1694 and 1694–1695 assessments for the Four Shilling Aid and BRO: F/Tax/M/3 commissioners' minutes.
37. This is an estimate based on the following list of sources. Assessments: from St. Augustine Lathe, East and West, KHLC: Q/CTL/1-213; Thanet (Margate/Broadstairs), KHLC: EK/U1453/01; New Romney, KHLC: NR/RTa9-31 and KHLC: NR/RTL2 (f6-67*ff*).
38. Largely from the Custom House in St. Nicholas parish.
39. Around 7–8% from the Custom House and Navy Office in Tower Ward.
40. Depending on the number of tax officials resident.
41. BRO: 04798 tax commissioners' minutes.
42. (1) As it was termed in contemporary documents. This included the New River Water and (initially) the East India Company. In the special 'Additional Assessment' of 1700 these were much the largest payers. Source: LMA: COL/CHD/LA/03/108/006 [11 Wm. III, c. 2, Aid and Land Tax for 1700, SoR, vol. 7, pp. 545–581. Duplicate assessments of parishes in the City of London, Middlesex, and Westminster under an Act of Parliament]; (2) The tax was on 'all & every persons, having any share or shares or interest in any fresh stream or running water from the north parts of London, commonly called the New Rover or in the Thames Water Works or in Mary[le]bone or Hampstead Waters, or any Rents or profits arising thereby, and all & every person or persons having any share or interest in any office or stock for insuring of houses in cases of fire, or in the convex or other lights or in the stock or stocks for printing of books in or belonging to the House commonly called The Queens Printing House…'. [LMA: COL/CHD/LA/03/019/015 [Land Tax Assessments upon Waters Companies Stocks, Salaries Pensions etc. made by Commissioners of London, dated 30 May 1706]; 3) LMA: COL/CHD/LA/03/019/015 [above] has detailed account for 1704 and 1706 with this breakdown: Corporates including Waters 28–29%, Post Office salaries 7%, Post Office pensions 33–36%, Excise Office salaries 23–28%, Excise Office pensions 4%.
43. TNA: SP 28/162–170, tax duplicates for London and Middlesex at various dates. A maximum 15.9% in 1702 and a minimum of 3.6% in 1704. Between 1704 and 1737 this figure only fell below 10% once in 1715

at 4.76%. Duplicates have not been checked after 1737. LMA: COL/CHD/LA/03/108/006 [above] has a list of the companies.

44. Sources: TNA: E182/594-604, land tax duplicates; LMA: COL/CHD/LA/03/108/006 [above]. Daniel Mann, Jonathan Hutton, Robert Walker, and George Gould were the collectors that year.
45. Cary had been a parish assessor. His most famous work was probably *An Essay on the State of England in Relation to Its Trade, Its Poor, and Its Taxes, for Carrying on the Present War Against France* (Bristol: W. Bonny, 1695), mentioned by Kennedy, *English Taxation*, p. 72.
46. Evidence based on a comparison of Beaven, *Bristol Lists*, and James Johnson, *Transactions of the Incorporation of the Poor in the City of Bristol During a Period of 126 years* (Bristol, 1826).
47. BRO: P. StJB/OP/2b-1672.
48. Cannan, *The History of Local Rates*, p. 105. Cannan's source: 'Directions to Churchwardens for the Faithfull Discharge of their Office', 3rd ed., 1713, p. 51.
49. Based on the 1693–1694 land tax assessment and the 1698 poor rate: BRO: F/PR/StJB/1-1698; BRO: F/Tax/A/14/StJB, assessment 1693–1694. The correlation coefficient of two arrays of 88 numbers using the CORREL correlation coefficient of Microsoft Excel is 0.961264.
50. Sources: TNA: E182/837-842; Johnson, *Transactions of the Incorporation of the Poor*, pp. 26–29.
51. Sources: BRO: F/LSR, Lamp and scavenger rates. Livock, *City Chamberlain's Accounts*, p. xxix, has £13,125 spent over the course of the 1620s.
52. The rate is more formulaic, although the list of payers is virtually identical in 1705.
53. BRO: F/HWR/F/HWR/StMR, Highway rate for 1713.
54. LMA: COL/CHD/LA/03/081/001, Land Tax miscellaneous papers.
55. BRO: F/Tax/M/3, tax commissioners' minutes.
56. LMA: COL/CHD/LA/03/081/014 [above] which shows how the 1704 quotas were arrived at by adjusting from the 1693 base Figs.
57. BRO: 04798 commissioners' minutes. This distraint relates to the window tax.
58. LMA: COL/CHD/LA/03/081/014 [above]. This relates to an appeal against the £478-15s-1 1/2d quota by St. Bartholomew-the-Less precinct in Farringdon Without for 1703 and how certain houses were assessed in the 1693 act.
59. As discussed by Ormrod et al., 'City and Countryside Revisited'.
60. Sources: BRO: F/LT, land tax assessments from various parishes.

61. Wharfage at £100 rent in St. Stephen parish, BRO: F/Tax/A/16/StS, tax assessment.
62. Estimated from properties identified in the assessments and their values: BRO: F/Tax/A/14&16 assessments.
63. BRO: F/Tax/A/15 and 14, tax assessments.
64. Keene, *Metropolitan London in the 1690s* (Database); Spence personal communication; see also Craig Spence, 'Computers, Maps and Metropolitan London in the 1690s', in Matthew Woollard (ed.), *New Windows on London's Past: Information Technology and the Transformation of Metropolitan history* (Glasgow: Association for History and Computing, 2000), pp. 25–46. There were a very small number of cases above £150, 79 in the City (0.36%) and 162 (0.5%) in the rest of London.
65. LMA: COL/CHD/LA/03/062/026 [29 Car. II, c. 1, 17-months' assessment, 1677–1678, SoR, vol. 5, pp. 802–836].
66. BRO: 09374, commissioners' minutes.
67. 12 & 13 Wm. III, c. 10, Land Tax for 1701 SoR, vol. 7. pp. 648–716.
68. Ibid., s. XIV, 'And the severall and respective Tenant and Tenants of all Houses Lands Tenements and Hereditaments which shall be rated by vertue of this Act are hereby required and authorized to pay such Sum and Sums of Money as shall be rated…'.
69. BRO: F/LT, land tax assessments; BRO: F/Tax/A2, tax assessments; with estimations of 17.33d/£ tax rate for the Royal Aid and 27.79d if the Additional Aid is added after 1671 subsidy.
70. BRO: F/Tax/A2, tax assessments, survive for 12 of 18 parishes. Chamberlains' audit papers e.g. BRO: F/AU/1/35 for 1666. The City received rent of £177.72 that year from Castle Precinct. It held significant other City and urban lands much of it more anciently, including some in fee-farm.
71. BRO: F/Tax/A/2 CP, Assessment for the Royal Aid and the Additional Aid. The Additional Aid was an extra 12s-6d per month or £7.50 per ann.
72. Chamberlains' audit papers e.g. BRO: F/AU/1/35 for 1666.
73. (1) Chock's name is on the assessment, next to 'City rents', but he is not specifically identified as a collector. John Chock of St. Thomas parish was identified as a Bodice-maker in the 1668 probate inventories. Edwin and Stella George (assisted by Roget H. Leech), *Bristol Probate Inventories Part 2: 1657–1689* (Bristol: Bristol Record Society Publications LVII, 2005), p. 38; 2) Did the City pay the £10 tax due in 1666? It is not clear from the chamberlain's accounts.
74. Chamberlains' audit papers, e.g. BRO: F/AU/1/62 for 1693, but there are a dozen additional charges.
75. BRO: F/Tax/A/14 CP, tax assessment.

76. The chamberlains' audit papers, e.g. BRO: F/AU/1/72 for 1702–1703 which has a tax deduction of c. £63 on rents of c. £370. However the City was in receipt of rents totalling over £1,300 at this time.
77. Sources for figure and table: BRO: FL/LT, all parishes; BRO: F/Tax/A, various, especially: 1664–1667: BRO: F/Tax/A/2-16 Car. II, c. I and 17 Car. II, c. I, Royal Aid and Additional Aid. Estimates have been made where parish assessments are not available; 1679: BRO: F/Tax/A/4, 30 Car. II, c. 1, 18-months' assessment, 1678–1680, SoR, vol. 5, pp. 867–883. This also includes some estimates; 1693–1694: BRO: F/Tax/A/14, tax assessments, 5 Wm. & Mar., c. 1, Four Shilling Aid, 1693–1694, SoR, vol. 6. pp. 426–442. Estimates have been included; 1700s: BRO: F/LT. No complete run of parish assessments survives from any single year therefore this data is variously taken from 1703 to 1705 assessments; 1730: BRO: F/LT—estimated from the 4 sample parishes.
78. TNA: E179/304/12.
79. Sources: TNA: E179/304/12, 1671 Bristol subsidy; Tax assessments: BRO: F/Tax/A/2-16 and 17 Car. II, c. I and 17 Car. II, c. I. Royal Aid and Royal Additional Aid. The figure of £2,950 includes estimates for missing parishes.
80. For example, Harding, 'The Population of London, 1550–1700'; P. E. Jones and A. V. Judges, 'London Population in the Late Seventeenth Century', *Economic History Review*, vol. 6, 1935, pp. 45–63.
81. Harding, Ibid., p. 117.
82. 6 & 7 Wm. III, c. 6, Marriage Duty Act, 1695, SoR, vol. 6, pp. 568–583, s. XXVI.
83. City wards omitting Bridge Without Ward in Southwark, which was not administered by common councilmen, but had its own alderman.
84. It is 'about 20,000' according to Ralph and Williams, *The Inhabitants of Bristol in 1696*, and John R. Holman, 'Orphans in Pre-industrial Towns—The Case of Bristol in the Late Seventeenth Century', *Local Population Studies*, vol. 15, 1975, pp. 40–44; p. 41 has a population of 20,157 over a third of which were children, 7,356. Original source: BRO: F/Tax/A/17, marriage duty 1696, 6 & 7 Wm. III, c. 6, Marriage Duty Act, 1695, SoR, vol. 6, pp. 568–583.
85. Harding, 'The Population of London, 1550–1700', but she admits the data is inadequate for a 'closer guess', p. 118.
86. There are higher estimates, e.g. Tim Lambert, *A Brief History of Bristol*, http://www.localhistories.org.
87. For example, 'And the severall and respective Tenant and Tenants of all Houses Lands Tenements and Hereditaments which shall be rated by vertue of this Act are hereby required and authorized to pay such

Sum and Sums of Money as shall be rated upon such Houses Lands Tenements and Hereditaments and to deduct out of the Rent so much of the said Rate as in respect of the said Rents of any such Houses Lands Tenements', 12 & 13 Wm. III, c. 10, Land Tax for 1701, SoR, vol. 7. pp. 648–716, s. XIV.

88. For example, 12 & 13 Wm. III, c. 10, Land Tax for 1701, SoR, vol. 7, pp. 648–716, s. LXI has: 'Provided That no Person shall be charged with or liable to the Pound Rate imposed by this Act upon Lands Tenements or Hereditaments whose Lands Tenements or Hereditaments are not of the Yearly Value of Twenty Shillings in the whole.'
89. This estimate is based on a comparison of assessments from BRO: F/Tax/A/14, various tax assessments for 1693–1694 and BRO: F/LT, various tax assessments. The number of assessed £1 rents reduced from 144 to 123 between 1693–1694 and 1703.
90. Two central wards, Bassishaw and Cheap were chosen because of good quality data; two extra-mural wards Portsoken and Cripplegate Without; one riverside ward, Queenhithe; and one other, Lime Street. See e.g. Mark Merry and Philip Baker, 'Family and Household in late 17th Century London', *The Economic History Society Annual Conference, University of Reading, 1st April 2006*. Centre for Metropolitan History/Birkbeck Online, https://core.ac.uk/download/pdf/72487.pdf (Accessed 25 August 2017).
91. Source: Ancestry.co.uk. The online site has wrongly included this first precinct of Bishopsgate Without in Bishopsgate Within so the full online reference is: Ancestry.co.uk, London, England, Bishopsgate Within, 1719, p. 29 of 38.
92. It was approved by Mayor Thomas Day and three other senior commissioners. Source: TNA: E182/838, duplicate papers.
93. Source: TNA: E182/838.
94. Sources: Tax assessments, BRO: F/Tax/A/14 StJ and BRO: F/LT/StJ. Other years have not been checked. Marriage duty, Ralph and Williams, *The Inhabitants of Bristol in 1696*. Neither is there Comberbatch or Comerbatch.
95. On 27 October 1674, a Joshua Cumberbatch became a burgess of Bristol after apprenticeship to his father and payment of 4s 6d according to 'Index to the Bristol Burgess Book. Volumes 1 to 21 1557–1995.' Bristol and Avon Family History Society. *Index to the Bristol Burgess Book Volumes 1 to 21 1557–1995*. www.bafhs.org.uk.' The residence in St. Nicholas parish is according to: old.cumberbatch.org, 'The Descendants of Joshua Cumberbatch', http://old.cumberbatch.org/images/Images/CumberbatchOfBarbados.pdf (Accessed 1 May 2017).

96. Of these 26 were valued at £2 rent and 16 at £1.
97. Source: Keene, *Metropolitan London in the 1690s* (Database). Note that across the metropolis it is only at the £3–4 level that this effect is discernible. Spence, *London in the 1690s*, p. 66. He suggests just 271 exemptions in 1693–1694.
98. People in Place project, *London Marriage Duty Assessment 1695* (London, 2011). British History Online, http://www.british-history.ac.uk/no-series/london-marriage-duty/1695 and a comparison with Keene, *Metropolitan London in the 1690s* (Database).
99. Comparing KHLC: NR/RTL24, for 1692–1693 with NR/RTL32 (1699). There are too few assessments from other parts of Kent between 1693 and 1696 to draw any conclusions.
100. Waddell, 'The Politics of Economic Distress'.
101. Holman, 'Orphans in Pre-industrial Towns', pp. 40–44; Ralph and Williams, *The Inhabitants of Bristol in 1696*. Estimated from incomplete parish assessments: BRO: F/Tax/A/14; 5 Wm. & Mar., c. 1, Four Shilling Aid, 1693–1694, SoR, vol. 6. pp. 426–442; supplemented by F/Tax/A/15 5 & 6 Wm. & Mar., c. 14, Poll 1694, SoR, vol. 6, pp. 472–479.
102. A comparison of real estate taxation from the 1671 subsidy and the Royal Aid suggests a tax rate of 17.33d/£ tax rate for the Royal Aid and 30.32d if the Additional Aid is added (rounded to 2s-6d).
103. And households were increasingly complex and varied in nature according to the People in Place project, http://www.history.ac.uk/cmh/pip/pip.html.
104. This total includes a small number of cases where an individual had been taxed only on personal estates, but not on real estate and therefore they may not have been resident.
105. BRO: F/Tax/A/14 StJB, tax assessment; Ralph and Williams, *The Inhabitants of Bristol in 1696*, p. 96.
106. BRO: F/Tax/A/14 StJB, tax assessment. An annual rent of £2.00 is approximately the average of such rents across the City in cases where there are specified numbers of tenements on the face of the assessment.
107. There are c. 100 tenements identified within 27 tax charges, therefore an additional 73.
108. Given the fact that additional single charges may represent multiple properties, as Ginter recognised in, *A Measure of Wealth*, pp. 31–32, this estimated figure is probably too low.
109. Those rarely taxed were derived from a detailed analysis of parishes in Table 10. A 'tabler' was another form of lodger according to Ralph and Williams, *The Inhabitants of Bristol in 1696*.

110. Harding, 'The Population of London, 1550–1700'; Holman, 'Orphans in Pre-industrial Towns'. The marriage duty assessments made in many parishes, groups individuals named together and linked them by a bracket and Holman has treated these as a single household even where there appear to be multiple family groups. In other cases, there were multiple land tax payers in a single household and in other cases there are names not delineated by a bracket which Holman has not treated as a separate 'household'. If his figure of 195 is adjusted for such anomalies, the revised figure for potential taxpayers would be c. 250 in St. John-the-Baptist parish which is similar to the figure estimated above.
111. Sources: Assessments from: BRO: F/Tax/A/14, tax assessments for the Four Shilling Aid of 1693–1694; marriage duty from Ralph and Williams, *The Inhabitants of Bristol in 1696*; Holman, 'Orphans in pre-industrial towns'.
112. BRO: F/Tax/A/14 StJB, 1693–1694 tax assessment; Ralph and Williams, *The Inhabitants of Bristol in 1696*. Tax officials various: BRO: F/Tax/A, series: BRO: F/LT StJB, tax assessments. Omissions see discussions above.
113. Based on a comparison for Castle Precinct. The figures are male taxed (57%), female (43%) and within the latter: widows (36%), spinsters (25%). The data is from Ralph and Williams, *The Inhabitants of Bristol in 1696*, pp. 5–20; BRO: F/Tax/A/14 CP, tax assessment and F/Tax/A/18 CP, tax assessment, 7 & 8 Wm. III, c. 5, Four Shilling Aid, 1695–1696, SoR, vol. 7, pp. 8–61.
114. Holman 'Orphans in Pre-industrial Towns'.
115. Julian Hoppit, *A Land of Liberty? England 1689–1727* (Oxford: Oxford University Press, 2000), p. 81. The hearth tax provided no further relief by way of deduction.
116. This figure calculated as follows: c. 5,994 (Table 4.3), less 3,583 identified domestic taxpayers less 693 tenants and tenements = c. 1,928 unattributed.
117. Sources: BRO: F/tax/A/14 StJB, 1693–1694 tax assessment and BRO: F/PR/StJB, 1698 Poor Rate. Numbers in each category were 47 (<£%), 88 (£5 – 20) and 14 (>£20).
118. Spence, *London in the 1690s*, Appendix III A & B.
119. Spence, Ibid, p. 66. He cites the much higher exemption rate for the 1692 Poll compared with the 1695 marriage duty.
120. Spence, Ibid., pp. 64–65, '"house" (which are in practice difficult to distinguish from households).'
121. Cambridge English Dictionary: Meanings & Definitions, http://dictionary.cambridge.org/dictionary/english/household.
122. Spence, Ibid., Appendix III B, p. 179. This total includes family members of such wealthy lodgers as well as many other lodgers untaxed.

123. Sources: 1693–1694: Spence, *London in the 1690s*, Appendix III; 1703: Manual counts by the author from Ancestry.co.uk; Keene, *Metropolitan London in the 1690s* (Database).
124. Spence, Ibid., p. 66 hints at this when he says; 'the number of low value rents recorded in poor areas suggest than in some areas…a significant proportion of households may have fallen below the minimum level for assessment'. Ultimately he discounts the notion of significant additional omissions.
125. They were usually labelled: 'tenements' or 'several tenements'. £2.50 is simply the mid-point between £0 and £5, the area in Fig. 4.1 where there is a marked fall-off.
126. This is the average for the small number of cases where the number of tenements is given.
127. Compare J & K (1693–1694) with Q & R (1703).
128. 12 & 13 Wm. III, c. 10, Land Tax for 1701, SoR, vol. 7. pp. 648–716.
129. And with specific reference to 'Mannors Messuages Lands and Tenements and Also All Quarries Mines of Coal Tin and Lead Copper Mundick Iron and Other Mines Iron Works Salt Springs and Salt Works All Allom Mines or Works All Parks Chases Warrens Woods Underwoods Coppices and All Fishings Tithes Tolls Annuities and All Other Yearly Profits and All Hereditaments of What Nature or Kind Soever.'
130. BRO: F/AU/1/72, chamberlains' accounts folios 77–83. These figures exclude arrears by the bailiffs and others not related to individual rented properties—a total of ten such special cases. The total arrears were £733.96, but these special cases amounted to £230.03. The arrears varied from one quarter up to five years, with a mean of just under three-quarters of a year.
131. Sources: Ancestry.co.uk for London and BRO: F/LT for Bristol. The assessment would state that it was for a particular period and amount assessed and this can be compared with the quota stated on the assessments themselves or in the commissioners' minutes. There are occasional examples where the assessment states it was for the current year and previous arrears, but this is very rare.
132. Ward, *The English Land Tax*, p. 99. He cites payment of commissioners' refreshments, clerks' entertainment and similar.
133. Who would have had to pay the tax on empty properties under the statute.
134. BRO: 04798, commissioners' minutes. The note was dated 4 May 1705 and signed by Edward Harford, Richard Gravett, and Benjamin Coole.
135. There were similar cases in 1709, 1711, and 1712 for example.
136. BRO: F/LT, various parish assessments. There are no years for which assessments survive for all parishes therefore extant examples from 1703, 1704, and 1705 have been taken as illustration.

137. LMA: COL/CHD/LA/03/062/026 [above].
138. Sources: LMA: COL/CHD/LA/02/various; TNA: TNA: E182/594 (1689)—E182/604 (1733–1737), land tax duplicates.
139. There are two parish assessments missing for 1719.
140. KHLC: NR/RTL33-67, New Romney land tax assessments. Although not shown in the graph there is no evidence of earlier usage of this method.
141. KHLC: NR/RTL1-15, warrant dated 28 May 1728 for Mr John Cobb and Mr William Gray and signed by Commissioners Edward Bacheler and Richard Elles. This was a 3s/£ land tax and the quota £187-7s-9d.
142. LMA: COL/CHD/LA/03/080/018, Land Tax miscellaneous papers.
143. £2,204-4s-10d—the figure on the 1705 land tax duplicate TNA: E182/599.
144. Although the collection success in this precinct in 1704 is unknown. The remaining £10-14s-18d was paid to the Deputy Thomas Bennet, 'to be applied for expenses of books & of several meetings, differences of assessments for the Water, Orphans tax and other public services of the ward as had been usual.'
145. BRO: 04798, commissioners' minute book.
146. BRO: 04798, the note appears to say 8 shillings, but this must mean 8d.
147. Ginter, *A Measure of Wealth*, p. 116.
148. BRO: 04798, commissioners' minute book.
149. Sources: TNA: E179/304/12, 1671 Bristol subsidy. Tax assessments: BRO: F/Tax/A/2, Various parishes for the Royal Aid and the Additional Aid.
150. BRO: P.St T/D/253.
151. BRO: F/Tax/A/16/T, land tax assessment. 9s per quarter=£1-16s-0d per ann. with a 20% tax rate=£9 annual value.
152. BRO: P.St W/D/4/6.
153. BRO: F/Tax/A/14/Xch, 1693–1694 tax assessment.
154. Sources: BRO: 00351/7. Tax assessments: BRO: F/Tax/A/18/CP, 1696; BRO: F/Tax/A/14/CP, 1693–1694.
155. BRO: P.Tem/Ab/94; 120/1&2; 137; 142; 148/a; 159 including a messuage in Temple Street leased for 99 years in 1666 at £5 rent; a messuage and garden in the same street on 99 year lease in 1678 at £7.50 rent, a shop in the same street for 21 years at £2.50; and a corner messuage in Temple Street and Long Row for 30 years at £2.50.
156. BRO: F/Tax/A/16/T, 1694–1695 tax assessment; BRO: P.Tem/Ab/131, 144/1&2, 153/1.
157. Sources: BRO: 00349/17; BRO: F/Tax/A/18/CP, 1696–1697 tax assessment; BRO: F/Tax/A/14/CP, 1693–1694 tax assessment.

158. Sources: BRO: P.Tem/Ab/134 dated 2 June 1688; BRO: P.Tem/Ab/166/1 of the same date; BRO: F/Tax/A/16/T-1694-5, tax assessment.
159. Sources: BRO: P.Tem/Ab/135 26 July 1688. BRO: F/Tax/A/14/StT-1693-4, tax assessment.
160. BRO: P.Tem/Ab/139; BRO: F/Tax/A/16/T-1694-5. It was described as a messuage or warehouse in the lease, and as a warehouse in the 1694 assessment.
161. BRO: F/Tax/M/3.
162. Sources: Land tax assessments: BRO: F/LT/StA; BRO: F/PR/StA/23a-b; Poor rate: BRO: F/PR/StA/23a-b, 1722 Poor rate for St. Augustine.
163. BRO: F/LT/StA, land tax assessments. The sum was £2-14s-0d. 21 February 1709.
164. Ibid.
165. McGrath, *Merchants and Merchandise*, and Patrick McGrath, *Records Relating to the Society of Merchant Venturers of the City of Bristol in the 17th Century* (Bristol: Bristol Record Society Publications XVII, 1952).
166. The correlation coefficient of two arrays of numbers was calculated using the CORREL function of Microsoft Excel = 0.96 rounded to 2 decimal places for 88 cases. 35 of 88 matched cases had the same value. Sources: BRO: F/Tax/A/14 StJB, 1693–1694 tax assessment; BRO: F/PR/StJB/1, St. John the Baptist 1698 Poor Rate.
167. Correlation coefficient calculated as in previous note = 0.94 rounded to two decimal places for 107 cases. 73 of 107 matched cases had the same value. Sources: BRO: F/PR/CW/1, Castle Precinct 1698 Poor Rate; BRO: F/Tax/A/18, 1696–1697, tax assessment for Castle Precinct.
168. Brooks, 'Public Finance and Political Stability', p. 295 states that: 'These absentees, the irregular attenders, with whom the Commission was padded out, are of importance to the historian of patronage and politics: they barely ruffled the surface of administration.'
169. For example, LMA: COL/CHD/LA/03/081/013, Land Tax miscellaneous papers. 11 Wm. III, c. 2, Aid and Land Tax for 1700, SoR, vol. 7, pp. 545–581.
170. 'Printed for R. Vincent in Clifford-Inn Lane, next St. Dunstan's Church' in Fleet Street and others.
171. The Gregorian calendar of 1752 separated the calendar and tax or legal year.
172. For example the Land Tax for 1704 [2 & 3 Anne, c. 1] required a meeting on or before 6 April 1704 and the City Commissioners had their inaugural meeting on that very day LMA: COL/CHD/LA/03/078/008, Assessments: 12 & 13 Wm. III, c. 10, Land Tax for

1701, SoR, vol. 7, pp. 648–716. Acquittances of receivers-general for sums received from various parishes (Some unsigned).
173. LMA: COL/CHD/LA/03/081/001 [above].
174. Who signs as Barfoott.
175. LMA: COL/CHD/LA/03/081/008, Land Tax miscellaneous papers. There are surviving lists for other years.
176. Some of this is even included in the statute for example the list of commissioners in 1706 refers to 'Joseph Martin in Rood Lane' and 'John Moore in Mincing Lane'.
177. LMA: COL/CHD/LA/03/078/008 [above].
178. As discussed, tax statutes had long involved a commissioners' dividing-up after the inaugural general meeting in a City or County, thus 'That the Commissioners at such Generall Meeting or the major Part of them shall also agree and set down in Writing who and what Number of the said Commissioners shall act in each of the said Divisions or Hundreds and shall deliver true Copies of such Writings to the Receiver Generall', 12 & 13 Wm. III, c. 10, Land Tax for 1701, SoR, vol. 7, pp. 648–716.
179. Sources: Ancestry.co.uk assessments. LMA: COL/CHD/LA/03/various, including warrants and other documents.
180. Ancestry.co.uk, London, England, Bishopsgate, 1703, p. 12 of 60.
181. Ancestry.co.uk, London, England, Lime Street, 1733, p. 6 of 6.
182. Mean ward figures have been taken where data is missing. Sources: Ancestry.co.uk. Numbers compiled from counts of signatures on assessments compiled by this author.
183. LMA: COL/CHD/LA/03/080/001 [above]. The document was probably for the 1699 assessment.
184. Sources: Duplicates, TNA: E182/594 (1689)—E182/604 (1733–1737). LMA: COL/CHD/LA/03/various.
185. There were 25 wards, but three were subdivided = 28. Assessments survive particularly well in 1693 because this was a base year for later assessments. Source: Ancestry.co.uk. There were 25 wards each with a single alderman in the taxable City, but as some wards expanded beyond the ancient walls they were divided into Within and Without subdivisions: Aldersgate, Bishopsgate, and Cripplegate. This created 28 administrative subdivisions in all. Bridge Without was an anomalous "twenty-sixth" ward which still had an alderman, but corresponded to land administered by Southwark authorities, including land taxes. For most tax purposes the subdivided wards were managed separately and so 28 wards and subdivisions are shown on virtually all duplicates and related documents for the seventeenth and eighteenth centuries and each had its own City tax quota.

186. The following based on Keene, *Metropolitan London in the 1690s* (Database); Ancestry.co.uk.
187. Over the period, this amounts to over 14,000 signatures approving parishes, precincts, and wards.
188. Brooks, 'Public Finance and Political Stability', p. 295.
189. And 26% of the signatures compared with 100% during the Restoration.
190. Therefore Deputy John Eyer (or Eyre) was first signer between 1713 and 1719 and similarly William Ellingham in most of the years between 1721 and 1725.
191. Sources: TNA: E182/594 (1689)—E182/604 (1733–1737). There were 6.3 signatures on average per duplicate in the period and each signer on average signs 3.5 duplicates.
192. This term after Alfred P. Beaven, 'Fathers of the City', in *The Aldermen of the City of London Temp. Henry III—1912* (London, 1908), pp. 250–254, http://www.british-history.ac.uk/no-series/london-aldermen/hen3-1912/.
193. Some were directors of the Bank of England including Per Delmé, James Houblon, and John Houblon.
194. Estimated from the cases where there is.
195. Sources: surviving duplicates sent to the Exchequer 1690–1737, TNA/182/592-604. The great majority of individuals can be identified and many of these had a certain or likely birth year.
196. Amongst those MPs representing the City of London, ten did not sign the City duplicate, compared with 19 who did. The former were: Sir John Cass, Sir Francis Dashwood, Peter Godfrey, Robert Heysham, Richard Lockwood, Thomas Papillon, Sir William Pritchard, Sir Thomas Scawen, Samuel Shepheard, and John Ward.
197. The remaining 37 signatures were by 16 identified non-City MPs, including nearby Southwark and Reigate.
198. BRO: F/Tax/M/3, post-revolutionary commissioners' minutes. The meeting numbers include the marriage duty. As discussed later, there probably were additional unminuted meetings.
199. Ward, *The English Land Tax*, p. 39.
200. Ibid., p. 6.
201. BRO: 04798, commissioners' minutes.
202. CTB, vol. 23, 9 December 1709, p. 447. His son, also George, had put up sureties for him but matters were still to be decided and the 'Court of Exchequer having put off judgement till next term upon a cause concerning an extent and commission of bankrupt whereupon they expect to get several thousand £ paid into the Exchequer in part of her Majesty's debt owing by the said Dixon as Receiver General for said

County.' London goldsmith bankers also put up surety which caused them great difficulty. CTB, vol. 22, 18 March 1708, p. 173.
203. BRO: 04798, commissioners' minutes.
204. Unfortunately it is undated.
205. BRO: F/LT/StN. Also pre-printed were warrants from St. Nicholas of c. 17 December 1719 and 1722.
206. BRO: F/LT/StN. The Tolzey or the court and Council House in Corn Street.
207. Sources: BRO: 09374 commissioners' minutes 1721–1748; BRO: 04798 commissioners' minutes 1698–1720; BRO: F/Tax/M/3 post-revolutionary commissioners' minutes.
208. There were no comparable detailed minutes for the City of London.
209. Ward, *The English Land Tax*, p. 39*ff.*
210. Sources: BRO: F/Tax/M/3, BRO: 04798, and BRO: 09374, commissioners' minutes 1689–1748.
211. Brooks, 'Public Finance and Political Stability'. Brooks makes the assumption that all meetings were minuted which as shown here was not the case.
212. Sources: see previous note.
213. BRO: F/Tax/M/3 commissioners' minutes 1689–1698.
214. Johnson, *Transactions of the Incorporation of the Poor*. Thus, for example, in 1728 some 33 commissioners were sworn-in but only four were present at the meeting to nominate assessors and six at the meeting to agree parish quotas. In that year the parish assessment for St. Nicholas names and assesses the commissioners Peter Day, Henry Walter, Arthur Taylor, and Henry Blaake. Peter Day was not shown as attending any general meeting and was not sworn-in so would have been unable to act, but the other three were all sworn-in and could have acted as a small sub-committee to determine appeals and agree assessments. Similarly, Mayor Henry Nash, John Becher, and Joseph Jefferis were all sworn-in for St. Mary-le-Port parish in the same year.
215. Ralph and Williams, *The Inhabitants of Bristol in 1696*, in respect of the marriage duty.
216. Ibid., p. xiv. In respect of 1695, but the land tax appeals at this time seem exhaustively minuted so this also seems unlikely.
217. Sources: BRO: F/Tax/M/3, BRO: 04798, and BRO: 09374, commissioners' minutes 1689–1748.
218. 11 Wm. III, c. 2, Aid and Land Tax for 1700, SoR, vol. 7, pp. 545–581.
219. This seems about the normal number of printed copies from several references in the minutes e.g. on 3 January 1690 ten copies of the Act of parliament 'by special messenger' and on 22 January ten copies of the Act for an Additional Aid.

220. 6 & 7 Wm. & Mar., c. 3, Four Shilling Aid, 1694–1695, SoR, vol. 6. pp. 510–563.
221. BRO: F/Tax/M/3, commissioners' minutes.
222. Ibid.
223. Warrants were usually pre-printed and sent out by the Exchequer. The clerk would simply need to fill in some basic details for each pair of parish collectors (each pair only received one warrant between them) and organise a small quorum of commissioners to sign them.
224. Only these parishes in the sample check.
225. Sources: BRO: F/LT various; TNA: E182/838-842 tax duplicates; BRO: F/Tax/M/3, BRO: 04798, and BRO: 09374, commissioners' minutes 1689–1748.
226. 8 & 9 Wm. III, c. 6, Land Tax & subsidies, 1696–1697, SoR, vol. 7, pp. 166–189, s. XX.
227. Thirty Car. II, c. 1, 18-months' assessment, 1678–1680, SoR, vol. 5, pp. 867–883, s. XXXIX.
228. BRO: 04798.
229. The two overcharged amounts were probably both for Joseph Vigor junior (or possibly senior as both appear on the assessment). The Vigors were both involved in land tax gathering as assessors, collectors or commissioners. Knowing the tax system may have helped to achieve this tax reduction.
230. Previously all had had locally defined quotas.
231. Meeting 7 August 1705 KHLC: Sa/ZO3, commissioners' minutes.
232. Sources: KHLC: Q/CTL/52, 1705 tax assessment for Coldred parish. Commissioners' meeting 7 August 1705 record from KHLC: Sa/ZO3.
233. (1) 1 Wm. & Mar., Sess. 1, c. 8, 'An Act for the Abrogating of the Oathes of Supremacy and Allegiance and Appointing other Oathes', SoR, vol. 6, pp. 57–60; (2) 7 & 8 Wm. III, c. 5, Four Shilling Aid, 1696, SoR, vol. 7, pp. 8–61.
234. 1 Wm. & Mar., c. 20, twelve pence Aid, 1689–1690, SoR, vol. 6, pp. 77–85.
235. There was a proviso in an amending Act that 'Their Majesties [were] enabled to appoint such Persons in Counties, Cities, &c. to be Commissioners, as they shall find necessary; Proviso, that such Persons be resident, and have Estates to the Value of £1,000; and in such Case they are enabled to execute the said Act, as though they had Real Estates of £100 p[er] ann.' 1 Wm. & Mar., c. 31, twelve pence aid addition, 1689–1690, SoR, vol. 6, p. 95.
236. 12 & 13 Wm. III, c. 10, Land Tax for 1701, SoR, vol. 7. pp. 648–716, s. LXXII.
237. Beckett, 'Land Tax Administration at the Local Level', p. 163.

238. Sources: TNA: E182/594 (1689)—E182/604 (1733–1737), tax duplicates.
239. BRO: F/Tax/M/3, commissioners' minutes 1689–1698: Morgan, 15 meetings, 1689–1696 (sheriff 1686–1687, common councilman 1678–1688); Merrick, 12, 1689–1696 (sheriff 1684–1685, Master and Treasurer SMV, common councilman 1680–1688); Parker, 8, 1692–1698 (?); Sandford, 32, 1689–1696 (sheriff 1687–1688, common councilman 1680–1688); Cary, 29, 1692–1688 (common councilman 1688, Warden SMV).
240. McGrath, *Merchants and Merchandise*, p. ix. Sources for this paragraph: Comparison of named officials in the statutes (SoR) and signing commissioners in the minute books (BRO: 04798 and 09374, BRO: F/Tax/M/3) with Beaven, *Bristol Lists.*
241. Calculations made from Sources: BRO: F/Tax/M/3, BRO: 04798, and BRO: 09374, tax commissioners' minutes 1689–1748 and Beaven, *Bristol Lists.*
242. BRO: F/Tax/M/2, Restoration tax commissioners' minutes and Beaven, *Bristol Lists.*
243. McGrath, *Merchants Merchandise*, and McGrath, *Records Relating to the Society of Merchant Venturers.*
244. McGrath, *Merchants and Merchandise*, p. xxxi.
245. Eight of 19 leading managers of Bristol slaving voyages were tax commissioners in David Richardson, *Eighteenth-Century Slave Trade to America, Vol 1 1698–1729* (Bristol: Bristol Record Society Publications XXXVIII, 1986), p. xxi.
246. Based on a comparison of the 1693–1694 Four Shilling Aid, the 1696 marriage duty, and contemporary polls. Sources: BRO: F/Tax/10, 2 Wm. & Mar., c. 2, Poll, 1689–1690, SoR, vol. 6, pp. 156–164; F/Tax/A/12, 3 Wm. & Mar., c. 6, Poll, 1691–1692, SoR, vol. 6, pp. 302–310; BRO: F/Tax/A/14, tax assessments, 5 Wm. & Mar., c. 1, Four Shilling Aid, 1693–1694, SoR, vol. 6. pp. 426–442; F/Tax/A/15, 5 & 6 Wm. & Mar., c. 14, Poll, 1694–1695, SoR, vol. 6, pp. 472–479; F/Tax/21, 9 Wm. III, c. 38, Poll, 1697–1698, SoR, vol. 7, pp. 411–420; Ralph and Williams, *The Inhabitants of Bristol in 1696.*
247. And only on his personal estate not on real estate tax.
248. Thomas Milton paid less, but only paid personal taxation.
249. According to BRO: F/Tax/A/15, 5 & 6 Wm. & Mar., c. 14, Poll, 1694–1695, SoR, vol. 6, pp. 472–479.
250. For example, Sacks, *The Widening Gate* and personal email communication.
251. As discussed, since the Restoration landlords and tenants could agree not to deduct tax from rent.

252. Identified from Beaven, *Bristol Lists.*
253. BRO: 04798, commissioners' minutes.
254. Ralph and Williams, *The Inhabitants of Bristol in 1696*; BRO: F/Tax/A/15 StE, 5 & 6 Wm. & Mar., c. 14, Poll, 1694–1695, ScR, vol. 6, pp. 472–479.
255. McGrath, *Merchants and Merchandise*, p. ix. Sacks, *The Widening Gate*, p. 114. A number of assessors and collectors were members of the SMV including, for example: Restoration officials such as Shershaw Cary and William Swymmer in the parish of St. Augustine, and post-revolutionary Christopher Willoughby and Michael White in St. Stephen parish.
256. BRO: F/Tax/A/15 StE, 1994–1995 Poll; BRO: F/Tax/A/14 StE and StN, 1693–1694 Four Shilling Aid; Ralph and Williams, *The Inhabitants of Bristol in 1696.*
257. BRO: 13325/35.
258. He was also a tenant farmer there and later freeholder. A. P. Baggs and R. J. E. Bush, 'Parishes: Hinton St. George', in R. W Dunning (ed.), *A History of the County of Somerset: Vol. 4* (London, 1978), pp. 38–52, British History Online, http://www.british-history.ac.uk/vch/som/vol4/pp38-52. He had increased his farm to 100 acres by 1715.
259. CTB, vol. 22, 27 January 1708, p. 98. Securities by way of surety.
260. CTB, vol. 26, 5 April 1712, p. 229.
261. BRO: 09374, commissioners' minutes 1721–1748.
262. Signed by Lord Shrewsbury then Lord High Treasurer.
263. Robert Yate (1643–1737), of Wine Street and The Red Lodge, Bristol; and Charlton House, Wraxall, Somerset. Source: HoP. Bristol was the local centre for turning old money into new. See CTB, vol. 32, 16 December 1718, p. 654. Nicholas Baker had been the Receiver-General of Taxes for the county of Worcester and was rewarded, according to this source, for 'the great expense he was at in 1696 and 1697 in carrying the old money to Bristol [for Recoinage] and bringing the new money [coined at Bristol] to London, together with the loss of the old money.'
264. Ibid.
265. Larry Neal, 'The Finance of Business During the Industrial Revolution", in Roderick Floud and Deirdre Nansen McCloskey (eds.), *The Economic History of Britain Since 1700: 1700–1860* (Cambridge: Cambridge University Press, 1994), pp. 151–181; 162.
266. CTB, vol. 29, 15 December 1715, p. 851.
267. Ward, *The English Land Tax*, p. 68.
268. T. B. Hughes, *A Report of the Case of the King Against Bebb and Others, Assignees of Castell and Powell, Bankrupts, on an Extent; with Explanatory Notes* (London: A. Strahan for J. Butterworth, 1811).

269. 4 Wm. & Mar., c. 1, Four Shilling Aid, 1692–1693, SoR, vol. 6, pp. 323–372. Aldermen including Bridge Without Ward.
270. Data from Keene, *Metropolitan London in the 1690s* (Database).
271. LMA: COL/CHD/LA/03/111/006 [above]. One of the earliest duties of ward commissioners was to appoint and warrant the assessors to commence their work and some summary records of this appointment process survive.
272. However, they often paid significant tax. Bassishaw widows alone in 1693–1694 paid 7.2% of the tax on rent and 2.9% of personal tax.
273. Knighted in 1700, he had been a common councilman for Tower 1699–1701. He was the then current alderman for Lime Street and became Lord Mayor in 1711.
274. Herne, Nathaniel (1668–1722), of St. Michael Bassishaw, London. Herne was involved with the Merchant Adventurers to N.W. America in 1691, the Royal African Co. 1701–1702, and the Old East India Company 1699–1702 according to HoP (Accessed 4 May 2017).
275. Who had previously been a collector and assessor (1692–1704) in the ward and a member of the wardmote jury since 1688. Sources for these paragraphs: Bassishaw Wardmote Inquest minutes 1655–1752, LMA: CLC/W/GA/002; City of London duplicates naming collectors, TNA: E182/594 (1689)—E182/604 (1733–1737); Tax assessments from Ancestry.co.uk. London, England, Bassishaw, various; Other sources: LMA: COL/CHD/LA/03/various.
276. At least since 1698.
277. At least since 1693 and a former collector.
278. He served several times more as assessor and commissioner until 1721.
279. All four assessors signed the 1706 assessment. Baker, though inexperienced in 1706, continued to serve as a tax and ward official until 1728.
280. Spence, *London in the 1690s*, p. 14.
281. Servant was a very broad term embracing not only household servants, but those assisting in businesses and others.
282. Spence, *London in the 1690s*, p. 14 and CLRO Assessment Box 40, no. 61. The poll tax was assessed for a modest £110.55 in 1692 whereas the annual assessment for the 4s tax came to £1,153.20 of which £845.60 (73%) was related to rent.
283. Spence, *London in the 1690s*, Appendix III B. There are some small differences between different assessments in Spence, for example he lists one apprentice in the *Metropolitan London in the 1690s* database when the poll shows four. The poll assessment divides houses by a horizontal line and this produces the 131 figure, but there are subdivisions and it is not always clear if some named were lodgers in the household or a separate household which explains the minor difference between my figure and Spence's.

284. Spence, *London in the 1690s*, Appendix III, has 141 households.
285. After Stow, *A Survey of London*.
286. Excluding the three non-domestic company halls.
287. Excluding one company hall and one empty property.
288. Ward, *The English Land Tax*, p. 4. He quotes the case of Oxfordshire and claims one quarter of commissioners of 1660 were still operating in 1693. Brooks, 'Public Finance and Political Stability', p. 295. He looks at the parish of St. Margaret, Westminster in detail and briefly refers to Bristol.
289. Richard Grover, The Land Tax in East Kent, Chapter 2, and especially p. 189. This was an investigation of the administration of assessed taxes in Kent from 1692. His alleged abuses refer to Ward, *The English Land Tax*.
290. Sources for these paragraphs: Ibid. These are compared with Beaven, *Bristol Lists*. Other sources: BRO: F/LT, various land tax assessments.
291. Including periods before 1688. There are very few illegible names.
292. Sources throughout this section: Wingham tax commissioners' minutes, KHLC: Sa/ZO3; Wingham Justices Minutes, KHLC: PS/W/M; Tax assessments: St. Augustine Lathe, East and West, KHLC: Q/CTL/1-213, and New Romney, KHLC: NR/RTL.
293. Norma Landau, *The Justices of the Peace, 1679–1760* (Berkeley: University of California Press, 1984), pp. 27 and 219; Grover, *The Land Tax in East Kent*, p. 145; both these sources are quoted in Davison, *The Agrarian Economy of Romney Marsh*, p. 58. London and Bristol aldermen were all justices as they were widely across the country.
294. Sources: BRO: F/Tax/M/2, Restoration commissioners' minutes; BRO: F/Tax/M/3, post-revolutionary minutes; BRO: 09374, minutes 1721–1748; BRO: 04798, minutes 1698–1720. As discussed, there were additional unminuted meetings. Records are incomplete and information stated is as surviving records show.
295. And 31% of those attending meetings, according to the minute book, were current or former MPs. Additional Sources: HoP.
296. TNA: E182/430 (1694–1697)-E182/436 (1731–1733), Kent duplicates.
297. TNA: E182/432.
298. Years: 1695, 1706, 1709, 1718, 1726, and 1733. The choice was based on good survival and reasonable spacing. Sub-lathes: Upper Scray; Lower Scray; Sutton-at-Hone upper (Blackheath); Sutton-at-Hone lower; Aylesford East; Aylesford South; Aylesford North; Wingham; St. Augustine Lathe, West; Shepway; Shepway West; Sutton-at-Hone (1) Bexley, Bromley, and Beckenham and (2) Axton, Dartford, Wilmington.

299. Including 'Whigs' like Thomas D'Aeth and 'Tories' such as John Hardres both active commissioners in St. Augustine Lathe. Sources: HoP.
300. Historically these were: Hastings, New Romney, Hythe, Dover, Sandwich, but they were linked with other towns and ports.
301. Sources: HoP.
302. Christopher W. Chalklin, *Seventeenth-Century Kent: A Social and Economic History* (London: Longmans, 1965), pp. 210 and 46.
303. Ward, *The Early English Tax*, p. 175.
304. Brooks, 'Public Finance and Political Stability', p. 290.
305. Hoppit, *A Land of Liberty?* p. 125.
306. Richard Hoyle, 'Who Owned Earls Colne at the End of the Eighteenth Century? Or, How to Squeeze More Value Out of the Land Tax', *The Local Historian*, vol. 41, 2011, pp. 267–277.
307. For example, in Cumberland, Beckett, 'Local Custom and the "New Taxation"' or Ginter's Yorkshire, *A Measure of Wealth*.
308. Commonwealth Exchequer Papers, TNA: SP 28/various.
309. Kent had the 13th highest MPs per square mile ratio according to contemporary sources: Anon., *Land Tax at 4s in the Pound Paid by England & Wales in 1702, & 1744*.
310. See Grover, 'Early Assessments for Kent and Sussex Explored', p. 216 and his comparisons with marriage duty for 1705 which show residents owning 15% of taxed land. Sources: Wingham Tax assessments, KHLC: Q/CTL/1-213. Sources: Based on the amount of rent stated on tax assessments, KHLC: Q/CTL, various parishes. These may be owners as well as occupiers but great caution must be exercised following Ginter, *A Measure of Wealth*. There is no data for St. Augustine Lathe, West in 1705.
311. Grover, *The Land Tax in East Kent*, Chapter 2, and especially p. 189.
312. Sources: KHLC: Q/CTL, various parishes. There are some difficulties with common names particularly as the assessments do not always provide first names.
313. Estimated because there is no list of commissioners for the year, so the net has been cast slightly wider to include all those commissioners appearing in the minutes in recent years.
314. Ward, *The English Land Tax*, p. 91.
315. There is limited information concerning six of these 26 commissioners. Sources for the remainder: HoP for MPs; Edward Hasted, *The History and Topographical Survey of the County of Kent*. Vol. 10 (1800), pp. 121–144, http://www.british-history.ac.uk; Justices' Minutes, KHLC: PS/W/M; Three Decks—Warships in the Age of Sail, naval

history web resource, http://www.threedecks.org; KASMI, Churchyard Monumental Inscriptions, http://www.kentarchaeology.org.uk.

316. Dixwell, Sir Basil, 2nd Bt. (1665–1750), of Broom House, Barham, Kent. Source: HoP (Accessed 4 May 2017).
317. Actively signing documents from at least 1673 to 1706 [TNA: E179/129/745].
318. John Lynch of Groves buried in Staple churchyard. KASMI, Churchyard Memorial Inscriptions, http://www.kentarchaeology.org.uk.
319. And probably the unsuccessful parliamentary candidate for Sandwich in 1685.
320. Edward Hasted, *The History and Topographical Survey of the County of Kent*. Vol. 10 (1800), p. 140.
321. Three Decks—Warships in the Age of Sail, naval history web resource, http://www.threedecks.org.
322. Sources: Commissioners' lists in legislation and signed and sealed documents from St. Augustine Lathe, West; KHLC: Q/C/Tc/2, commissioners' resolves.
323. Sources: Commissioners' lists in legislation and signed and sealed documents from New Romney.
324. Hipkin, *The Structure of Land Ownership*, p. 89, where he provides several examples.
325. Davison, *The Agrarian Economy of Romney Marsh*, p. 9. Livestock were kept at home and on the Marsh. CKS PRC27/41/104.
326. For example, KHLC: NR/RTL36-38, 1703–1705.
327. Davison, *The Agrarian Economy of Romney Marsh*, p. 59 and personal email communication 12 August 2017. TNA: E182, various.
328. Davison, Ibid., p. 59.
329. Ibid., p. 58. This does not sound entirely accurate, because the tax process was outside the sessions and court process, but no doubt took place at the same building and on the same day.
330. Daunton, *State and Market in Victorian Britain*, p. 83 and Martin Daunton, 'The Politics of British Taxation, from the Glorious Revolution to the Great War', in Yun-Casalilla and O'Brien, with Comín (eds.), *The Rise of Fiscal States*, pp. 111–144.
331. Department for Constitutional Affairs. General Commissioners, http://webarchive.nationalarchives.gov.uk/20060820083451/hmrc.gov.uk/leaflets/tax-appeals.pdf. The General Commissioners have now been subsumed into HM Courts & Tribunals Service.
332. KHLC: Sa/ZO3 1705–1706, commissioners' minute book.
333. LMA: COL/CHD/LA/03/080/004, Land Tax miscellaneous papers. In other words, although the land taxes normally taxed corporates, this company was specifically exempt.

334. Ward, *The English Land Tax*, p. 122.
335. LMA: COL/CHD/LA/03/081/013 [above], signed 19 March 1701 by 'Ashurst'. This case is also mentioned in Spence, *London in the 1690s*, p. 12.
336. LMA: COL/CHD/LA/03/081/013 [above].
337. Ibid.
338. LMA: COL/CHD/LA/03/078/008 [above].
339. Ancestry.co.uk, London, England, Broad Street, 1692, p. 14. If there was no assessment, there could be no collector's warrant and therefore no authority to collect.
340. LMA: COL/CHD/LA/03/080/011[above].
341. Sources: Ancestry.co.uk, London, England, Cripplegate Without, 1741, p. 41 of 204.
342. Sources: Ancestry.co.uk, London, England, various.
343. Sources: Ancestry.co.uk, London, England, Cordwainer, 1729, p. 12 of 20.
344. Sources: Ancestry.co.uk, London, England, Candlewick, 1719, p. 13 of 14.
345. In relation to 11 Wm. III, c. 2, Aid and Land Tax for 1700, SoR, vol. 7, pp. 545–581.
346. LMA: COL/CHD/LA/03/081/013 [above].
347. TNA: E182/598, duplicate.
348. Ward, *The English Land Tax*, numerous instances.
349. As discussed, this deadline became less important in London and Bristol.
350. KHLC: Sa/ZO3. For example, the 1732 assessors for Buckland and Charlton, Wootton & Giddings, Lydden, River, and Poulton parishes discussed at Example 4 below.
351. BRO: 04798, commissioners' minutes.
352. BRO: 04798, commissioners' minutes.
353. BRO: 09374, commissioners' minutes.
354. BRO: 04798, commissioners' minutes.
355. Ibid.
356. Sources: BRO: 09374 and BRO: 04798 commissioners' minutes.
357. Sources: Land tax assessments, BRO: FL/LT: StN, StMP, StA, and T.
358. BRO: F/Tax/M/3, commissioners' minutes.
359. Ibid. In Central parishes (one collector served before in 87% of cases, two collectors in 50%), Portside (79% and 43%), Suburban (93% and 51%), and Transpontine (85% and 58%).
360. Sources: Ancestry.co.uk. Document survival is much poorer in the 1690s, so continuity of officials is less clear.
361. Collectors responsible for each round were named in the land tax duplicates sent to the Exchequer and retained in the National Archives.

Sources: Tax duplicates, TNA: E182/594 (1689)—E182/604 (1733–1737).

362. Sources: Duplicates TNA: SP 28/162-170. 65% of collectors appeared the following year, but there was doubling up, so one of two or more collectors on each round would be the same the following year hence the much higher figure. In 1709 for example, 91% of the 127 collection rounds had one or more collectors who were the same as the previous year, but because such 'repeaters' tended to have had slightly larger rounds they made up for 93% of the total tax collected.
363. (1) Many others fell just short of this ten-year figure, serving seven, eight or nine years; (2) This analysis does not imply that collectors necessarily served each and every year, although many did, just that their names appear at least twice, ten years or more apart. This figure also includes their early years as well as later ones. So, a long-serving collector would still be relatively inexperienced in his first and second years for example.
364. LMA: COL/CHD/LA/03/081/001 [above].
365. Ibid.
366. After Roy Porter, *London A Social History* (London: Hamish Hamilton, 1994), p. 72.
367. Source: LMA: COL/CHD/LA/02/various.
368. Land Tax Acts specified 'two more able and sufficient persons…to be collectors' for each subdivision.
369. The Restoration model was to have assessors and collectors only at ward level with some decision referred to the Centre. In the 1690s, there were commissioners, assessors and collectors all busy at ward level. From 1715 it was most common to have just ward commissioners and ward assessor/collectors.
370. Sources: TNA: SP 28/162–170, duplicates.
371. 1663, 1666, and 1673.
372. Woodhead, *The Rulers of London*. He may and probably did have ward roles earlier than this, but there are no available records.
373. Although more experienced than during the Restoration.
374. LMA: COL/CHD/LA/03/015/024 [3 Wm. & Mar., c. 5, £1,651,702 Aid, 1691–1692, SoR, vol. 6, pp. 259–301. Over Assessments in the parish of St. Brides. Accounts, reports, affidavits, opinions and in relation to the over assessing of the inhabitants of St. Brides and defaults of the collectors]. He writes regarding the aid raised from 25 December 1691 for one year dated 4 January 1693 at £8583-2s-8d per month which was charged on the City and £565-5s-5d was charged on Cripplegate Within and Without, but £34-5s-8d per month 'is due and unpayd' for the first quarter, £17-2s-10d in respect

of Cripplegate Within. Commissioners and assessors of the ward were to assess for arrears within six days.

375. LMA: COL/CHD/LA/03/081/014 [above].
376. Doolittle calls him 'another important City official', I. G. Doolittle, 'Government Interference in City Elections 1714–1716.', *Historical Journal*, vol. 24, no. 4, 1981, pp. 945–948; 946.
377. The earliest initials on the 1702 assessment from Coleman Street Ward. Source: Ancestry.co.uk, London, England, Coleman Street, 1702, p. 17 of 17.
378. There are few assessments surviving between 1692–1694 and 1702. Sources: LMA: various—Ancestry.co.uk. Every surviving assessment, and there are thousands of these, has been checked from 1702 (when good assessment survival commences) to 1733. The great majority of assessments survive after 1703, but the Ancestry website has significant misclassification, so patience is required to find all of them.
379. Matched by William Dobinson over the next 20 years. Source: TNA: E182/594. The town clerk's office was apparently responsible for passing the duplicate to the Exchequer. Most of the duplicates amongst the Exchequer papers were marked with the name of the person handing the duplicate over and the date.
380. 1737 is the latest year checked.
381. LMA:/COL/CHD/LA/03/080/006, Land Tax miscellaneous papers.
382. After 1717 he appears to have been carrying out this duty on his own; 1712–1716 with Robert Walker and before that with two or three others. As the tax on these sources amounted to over £8,000 per year and sometimes much more, this would have been very lucrative at 3d/£. Even with a two shilling tax rate in 1731, he would have received £109 and it was not taxed according to the assessment, probably because it was not a government office.
383. Permanently from 1719–1743. In 1743 Charles Bainbridge occupies his former house according to the tax assessment. Source: Ancestry.co.uk, London, England, Bassishaw, 1743, p. 5 of 6.
384. (1) John Smart of Guildhall, *Tables of Simple Interest and Discount at 3, 4, 5, 6, 7, 8, 9, and 10l. per cent. per ann. Also Tables of Compound Interest at the Same Rates* (London, 1707, ECCO. It was reprinted in 1719; 2) John Smart of Guildhall, *Tables of Interest, Discount, Annuities, &c: First Published in the Year 1724* (London, 1726), ECCO. It was reprinted again in 1780; 3) John Smart at the Town-Clerk's-Office, London, *Tables of Compound Interest at the Same Rates. Whereby the Amount or Present Value of Any Sum of Money, or Any Annuity, or*

Other Yearly Payment, &c. for Any Number of Years, Not Exceeding One Hundred, is Readily Found (London. Publisher: printed by H. Meere, at the Black-Fryar in Black Fryars, and sold by S. Crouch, at the Corner of Popes-Head-Alley in Cornhill, 1707), ECCO.

385. John Smart of Guildhall, *Tables of Time Calculated for Two Hundred Years Vizt. The XVII. and XVIII. Centuries: To Which Are Added Mr. Flamsteed's Table of the Equation of Natural Days, and Other Usefull Tables* (London, 1702). An abridged version was used in schools.
386. (1) Edward Jones, *Index To Records Called, the Originalia and Memoranda on the Lord Treasurer's Remembrancer's Side of the Exchequer*, by Edward Jones of the Inner Temple (London, 1743; Gale ECCO, Print Editions, 16 June 2010); (2) John Smart, of Guildhall London, *A Scheme of the Proportions the Several Counties in England Paid to the Land Tax in 1693, and to the Subsidies in 1697, Compared with the Number of Members They Send to Parliament* (London, 1698).
387. Sources: LMA: COL/CHD/LA/03/111/006 [Warrants of Commissioners for payment of Clerks etc.], 1702 (1 August 1704), 1704 (19 October 1706), 1706 (6 July 1708), 1707–1710 (all 17 July 1712), 1711 (31 December 1713).
388. Margaret Hunt, 'Time-Management, Writing, and Accounting in the Eighteenth-Century English Trading Family: A Bourgeois Enlightenment', *Business and Economic History* (2nd ser.), vol. 18, 1989, pp. 150–159.
389. Ward, *The English Land Tax*, p. 93.
390. This is wrongly catalogued in Ancestry.co.uk. The source is: Ancestry.co.uk, London, England, Portsoken, 1710, p. 119 of 119. Brewis had been Master of the Worshipful Company of Distillers in 1732.
391. This is wrongly catalogued in Ancestry.co.uk. The source is: Ancestry.co.uk, London, England, Portsoken, 1718, p. 101 of 101.
392. Indeed, there was an unspecified further adjustment of £85.
393. LMA: COL/CHD/LA/03/080/008, Land Tax miscellaneous papers. Below they indicated that by 'proper places' they meant folio 26 of the assessment for Peter Hore and folio 62 for Singleton.
394. Source: Ancestry.co.uk, London, England, Vintry, 1728, p. 9 of 18.
395. For example, LMA: COL/CHD/LA/03/080/009, Land Tax miscellaneous papers. Below they indicated that by 'proper places' they meant folio 26 for Peter Hore and folio 62 for Singleton.
396. LMA: COL/CHD/LA/03/019/015 [above], 2 & 3 Anne, c. 1. Land Tax for 1704, SoR, vol. 8, pp. 226–245; 4 & 5 Anne, c. 1, Land Tax for 1706, SoR, vol. 8, pp. 382–451.

397. LMA: COL/CHD/LA/03/019/015 [above]. Daniel Man, Robert Walker, John Hutton, and John Smart were appointed as collectors in 1706 and the sum assessed was £14,188-19s-0d and this same amount appears in the duplicate, TNA: E182-599.
398. Served 1690–1729.
399. Served 1704–1717.
400. Served 1721–1737*ff*.

CHAPTER 5

Four Detailed Examples of Post-Revolutionary Administrative Improvement and Resilience

The period after the Revolution is seen by some commentators as one of land tax administrative decline. This chapter rebuts that judgement. It provides fresh data and analysis that contradicts some established historiological narratives and questions the evidence presented in traditional texts around the effectiveness of early eighteenth-century land tax. Ward makes much of the inevitable decay or 'unchecked decline' of eighteenth-century land tax administration and complains of the 'inadequate … assessments' and the 'amateurish … collecting machine'.[1] Brewer decries the 'hodge-podge of amateur and local officials …'.[2] The evidence presented in Chapter 4 provides quite a different picture. This evidence is supplemented here by four detailed examples showing how administrators: established reliable tax-gathering machinery, adjusted to political volatility in the second decade of the century, amended the statutory process to meet local needs and everywhere established regular process routines. Early eighteenth-century Kent, London and Bristol developed effective tax administrations, inevitably mirrored across the highly taxed, if less well-documented, South-East and urban areas, because of the comparable collection rates.

S. Pierpoint, *The Success of English Land Tax Administration 1643–1733*, Palgrave Studies in the History of Finance,
https://doi.org/10.1007/978-3-319-90260-9_5

5.1 Example 1. Post-Revolutionary Administration and Tax Revenue Flows in the City of London

This section highlights the remarkable consistency of tax revenue flows in early eighteenth-century London and the importance of biannual financial cycles to the fiscal process. Evidence presented contradicts traditional narratives of an early eighteenth-century London administrative decline.

> In many ways London represented the quintessence of the administrative problems of the whole country ... If there were abuses from collectors elsewhere, habitual standards in London were shocking. London arrears were always on a gigantic scale.[3]
>
> For the next twenty years [after 1742] the Chamberlains [as receivers] performed as well as ever.[4]

It is difficult to reconcile Ward's two contradictory statements above, but the latter opinion appears to be supported by the evidence presented here, whilst the former is not. Ward is right to recognise that once national and local quotas were fixed, differential metropolitan economic and social development created inconsistency and local challenges in meeting quotas—but elsewhere his observations miss the mark.[5] Because of its size, metropolitan London's tax collection was under constant Treasury scrutiny.[6] The City's tax processes appear extremely orderly and resulted in the extraordinary regularity of annual payments shown in Fig. 5.2. London was inevitably behind statutory deadline in its tax delivery because of the way City administrators operated around City seasonal financial cycles and annual fiscal cycles. This was not a matter of bumbling City officials unable to cajole reluctant assessors and collectors to do their jobs, it was the result of what the City bureaucracy chose to do, and had long chosen to do, to transform legislatory requirements and demands into a workable, stable and efficient process across the City and broader metropolis.[7] Eighteenth-century statute usually required annual tax payments to the Exchequer by the four traditional quarter days: 24 June, 29 September, 25 December and 25 March.[8] In years when tax rates were lower, this was sometimes reduced to two half-yearly payments at Michaelmasand Lady Day. Across most of the country, including Bristol and Kent, collectors would, as discussed above (Sect. 3.3.3), usually only deliver quarterly tax monies when the receiver or deputy visited their locale.[9] However, as described, post-revolutionary metropolitan London was never really troubled by this because collectors could pay up from 'time to time' whenever they had monies, usually directly to the City Chamberlain at the nearby Guildhall.[10] Funds were most readily available in twice-yearly City seasonal financial cycles as had been the case at least since the Restoration.[11] These cycles were centred upon the two main traditional settlement dates of Lady Day (25 March) and Michaelmas (29 September) when money would naturally be freed up, people settled their debts, and collectors could move in.[12] The City's annual 'seasonal business cycle' was probably linked to these important dates.[13] The result, from contemporary account books, was a remarkable regularity of payments year after year, up the tax-gathering chain from collector to receiver-general and on to the Exchequer.[14] This was true of both the City of London and the broader metropolis (Fig. 5.2). It was true over decades and of most of the receivers including Sir Leonard Robinson (receiver and chamberlain until his death in 1696), Sir Thomas Cuddon (receiver and chamberlain to 1701), Mr Jonathan Harris (1702), Sir William Fazakerley (chamberlain to 1718), Sir Harcourt Master (receiver to 1719),[15] Sir George Ludlam (receiver and chamberlain to 1727), Sir Robert Baylis (to 1728), Samuel Robinson (to 1732 and chamberlain to 1734), Richard Milan (1733) and William Selwin.

Ward claimed that 'repeated admonitions could not prevent the rate of payment around London ... from declining faster than in the country as a whole'.[16] There is no evidence to support this claim (and see Sect. 1.2). To his credit, Ward goes on to propose that 'the achievements of the land-tax administration in these years [c. 1689–1699] must not be forgotten. The following tables [Tables IV–VI] have been compiled to illustrate these achievements'.[17] Unfortunately, his supporting footnote evidence presented provides examples of arrears and not any worsening or improvement.[18] His Tables IV–VI on page 57 appear to show only a general decline in receipts across the nation from 1693, and particularly in London, and no obvious achievement (1693 receipts: 73.7% by year end; 1701: 54.4%; 1704–1710: 38.4%; and 1713–1715: 37.5%).[19] These tables purport to show the percentage of taxes collected within 12 months of the various acts coming into force. If so, the tables themselves are entirely misleading because these data are not comparable for the selected years. In 1693, the first tax payment nationally was due on 25 March and the last on 25 December and the commissioners would have commenced the tax process in February. However, the statutory process began much later on 17 June in 1701 and tax payments from 1701–1710 all began three or more months later than in 1693 on 24 June and ended on 25 March. Therefore, less tax would be collected by year end. During the period 1713–1715, because there were only two rather than four tax payments in those years, the first payment was due even later on 29 September and processes would be even further behind 1693 as is clear from Fig. 5.11 (Bristol), and Fig. 5.12 (Kent). There is an exception. The London receivers' accounts suggest that funds came in initially much more quickly from the first statutory payment date in 1697 than in comparative years in Fig. 5.1, but this is because of the special case of Recoinage (see Fig. 5.4).[20] There is a further difficulty for Ward's argument. Because of the London seasonal financial cycles discussed (Fig. 5.2), the earlier start to collection in 1693 would mean that collection could take the benefit of the Lady Day seasonal financial cycle when money was freed up in the City. In the years from 1701, when processes commenced much later, this was never possible. In 1713–1715, the tax process started even later and would severely restrict collection in the Michaelmascycle as well (Figs. 5.11, 5.12). Lady Dayand Michaelmas financial cycles were not unique to London, and this may well explain further variability in Ward's tables elsewhere. Ward's 'decline' between 1701 and 1704–1710 cannot be readily explained by these arguments, but there is no material deterioration visible based on the receivers' accounts shown in Fig. 5.1.[21] The evidence presented above is important because Ward believes that in 1693, despite 'amateurish' administration, willing taxpayers 'paid promptly … and the Receivers delivered the money to the Exchequer as efficiently as any bureaucracy'[22] and decline set in as war progressed. No such decline is in fact apparent for the period considered here or demonstrated by his evidence.[23]

In statutory terms, metropolitan London would always be late, if consistently late, in delivering monies to the Exchequer, but was nevertheless remarkably regular. As in Bristol, where there were occasional difficulties, it was often the receiver to blame, but London receivers were not sticky-fingered and paid money on quickly to the Exchequer (Fig. 5.3b). The sometime unreliability of a few receivers was precisely why Parliament protected itself through sureties, as it did successfully in the case of Bristol's two failed receivers John Bowdidge and George Dixon (see Sect. 5.2). In London, receiver-general and alderman, Sir Harcourt Master, was the sole comparable example. He was a director of the South Sea Company and was removed from office leaving incomplete records and sums missing.[24] Remarkably, he remained an alderman. It is important to note that despite the 'somewhat improvised governmental institutions of the rest of the metropolis' outside the City, tax-gathering speed in the former was almost as good as the latter judging by cashflow (Fig. 5.3a).[25]

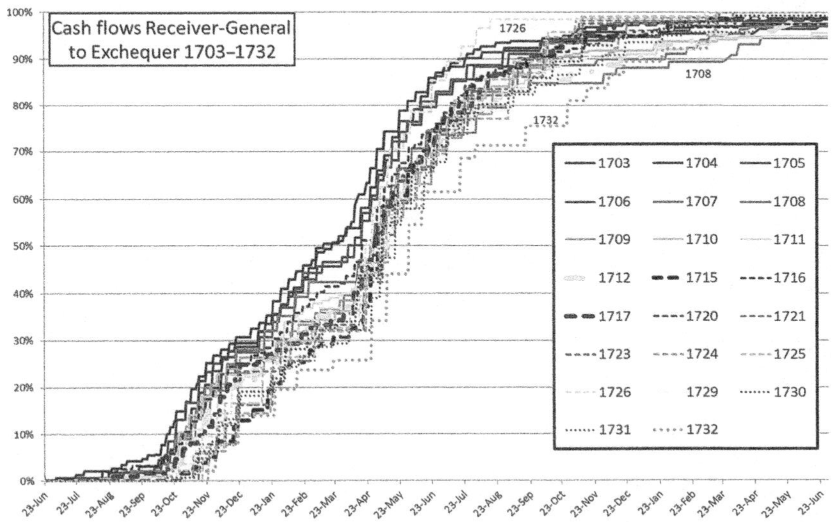

Fig. 5.1 City of London cumulative annual tax cashflows by the receiver to the Exchequer 1703–1732 showing their consistency.[26] *Note* Data from years where accounts are complete or nearly so

In most years where accounts survive, City tax-gathering began in June, or slightly later, but it might take a further two years for all cash to be remitted. The following example from 1705 illustrates the administrative process in relation to seasonal financial cycles. According to the Land Tax Act for that year,[27] commissioners should hold their inaugural meetingby 6 April to instigate the tax process allowing first-quarter payments to be made to the receiver by 24 June. By the time officials were appointed and assessments completed, the Lady Day cycle (Fig. 5.2) was long passed, so this first payment deadlinewould inevitably be missed. In fact, given that the next deadline was 29 September and the next main collection season did not start until October, there would be restricted

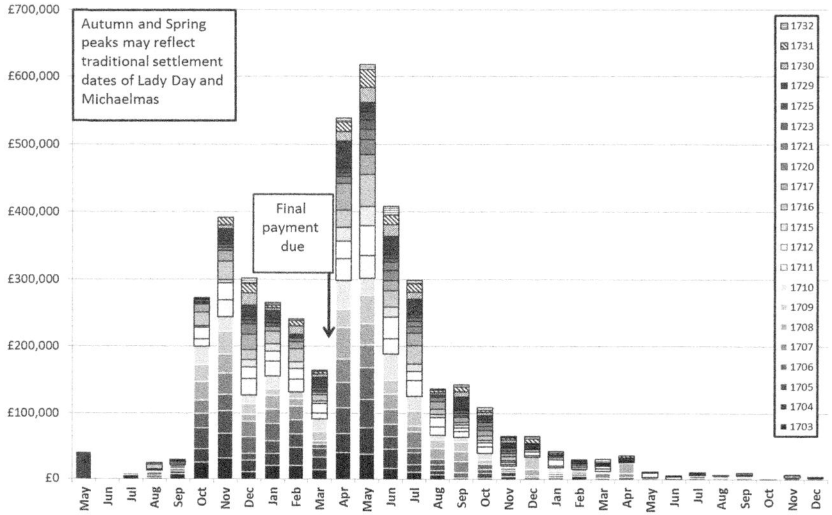

Fig. 5.2 Metropolitan London's land tax collection cycle of payments from receiver to the Exchequer 1703–1732 by month[28]

payments made by this later date. This would of course be true of all years in the eighteenth century because of the juxtaposition of tax cycles and financial cycles.

Tax assessment in the wards could only start work once local officials knew their quota after senior officials in the 'upper tier' of City administration had 'set down in writing the several [ward] proportions which ought to be charged'.[29] Although the proportion of tax to be paid by each City ward had become static by 1700, the actual tax to be paid could only be calculated after the 'upper tier' commissioners had agreed the deduction from the City total of the considerably varying amounts of tax charged on companies and government salaries ('Waters, etc.'). So, in 1706 the City charge at a four-shilling rate was exactly £123,334.13 but £14,188.95 was deducted leaving £109,145.18 for the wards.[30] In 1711, the deduction was much larger at £18,759.15 leaving only £104,575.00.

There might be further delays in ascertaining the government salary data for the Excise Office in Broad Street Ward and the Custom House and Navy Office in Tower Ward as City commissioners complained in 1704, because there had been unusually long delays.[31] That year, a tax

(a)

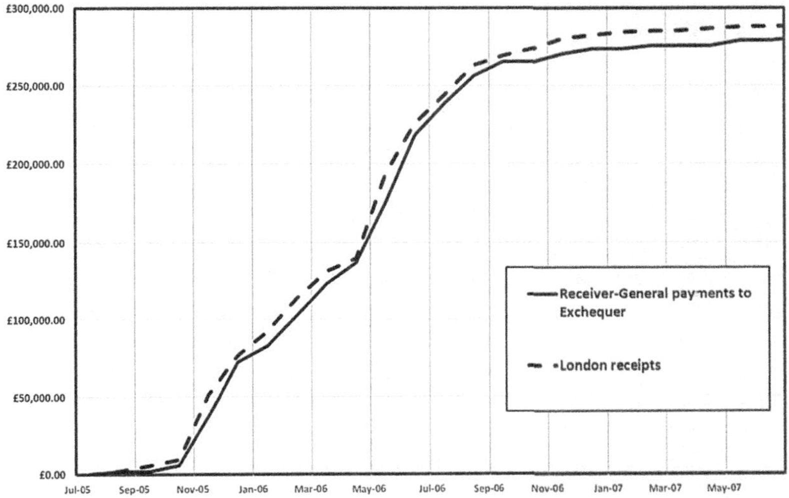

(b)

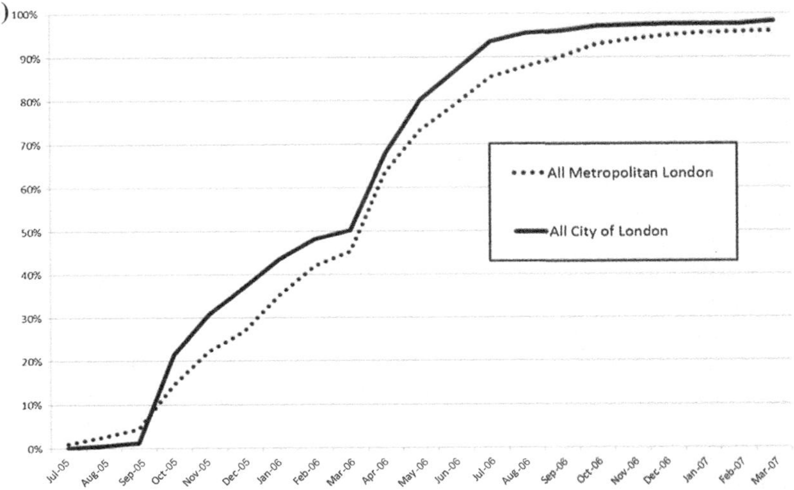

Fig. 5.3 **a** Comparison of City and metropolitan London cumulative payments by the receiver to the Exchequer for 1705. **b** Comparison of payments to and by the receiver for the same year[32]

opinion was required from the Attorney-General, and the quota was not agreed until 3 August and the final assessors' warrantswere signed five days later. In fact, lessons were learnt from this and such exceptional delays were not repeated. Nevertheless, by 19 October 1704, commissioners were chasing collectors for payment arrears presumably because they understood the importance of the Michaelmas financial cycle.

With local quota decided, ward commissioners would then meet to appoint assessors. According to surviving warrants, assessors were normally appointed in April or May.[33] Assessors would then bring in their assessments and collectors, once appointed and warranted, could commence their work. The consequence was that the first payments to the receiver were not made until the summer. In 1705, the first such collectors' payment was made on 27 July, but significant amounts were not delivered until October during the Michaelmas financial cycle. Of course, in the Lady Daycycle of 1705 (April/May), it was tax monies from the previous year 1704 that were still being gathered. The consequence was that tax collection would always be predictably behind statutory deadlines (Fig. 5.2). For 1705, it was unlikely that more than half of the tax money could be delivered before 25 March 1706 when all should have been paid.

As is clear from Fig. 5.2, this policy and practice changed little over decades. City officials clearly believed that this was sufficient for Exchequer purposes, and was all they could reasonably achieve, even if on occasion Treasury might protest.[34] In 1709, Chamberlain Sir William Fazakerley had to attend the Treasury to explain metropolitan land tax and window tax arrears.[35] He was asked to 'write to the Aldermen of each Ward therein to hasten the raising of said arrears within their respective wards'.[36] On 24 December 1711, Treasury again raised the matter of arrears with the High Bailiff of Westminster, the High-Sheriff of Middlesex and the Lord Mayor of London and letters were written to the commissioners on 5 September 1712.[37] Similar questions concerning arrears arose in 1713. Town Clerk James Gibson wrote on behalf of the City Commissioners to Robert Harley 'Earl of Oxford & Mortimer, Lord High Treasurer of Great Britain' on 10 June 1713[38] responding to such complaints. Harley himself was under pressure as an instigator of lower land taxation to bring monies in after the rate had been reduced to two shillings. In 1711, he had also been appointed to the committee to consider the arrears of parliamentary funds, so he had many reasons to chase London's delay. By 23 March 1713, there were still arrears of £70,709 out of £123,334 of the Four Shilling Aid for 1712 or 57%. As explained, this was in no way surprising or unusual. In their June letter, the commissioners pleaded that since that latter date 'the sum of £44,300 or thereabouts' had been paid (following the Lady Day cycle)and 'we assure your lordship, That we shall use such diligence for raising and paying in the residue of the said arrear, that we hope your lordship will have no further cause of complaint'. These were weasel words, but then excuses in terms of London's annual financial cycles would have hardly been placatory to Harley. The 1712 collection had been fractionally worse than the average, possibly because of the deployment of more inexperienced collectors as discussed below, but after the date of Gibson's letter, collection performance declined further and certainly did not improve (Fig. 5.2). Unsurprisingly, further questions were asked the following year and Fazakerley had to report to Treasury again and promise reassessments of wards.[39] Neither was any clear attempt made to improve or upgrade the City's remarkably regular and effective tax process thereafter. It was effective enough, and contrary to Ward and others, showed no sign of 'decay' at least during the first half of the eighteenth century.[40]

This process success actually required vigilance, intervention and management on the part of the receiver-general, commissioners and particularly the town clerk as discussed. There are numerous examples from the receivers-general's accounts showing clusters of payments within a multiple-precinct ward suggesting local collectors were being encouraged to deliver to local deadlines. In Walbrook Ward in 1733, collectors in all seven precincts appear to have had a 31 October deadline. Six collectors made payments on this date: Thomas Mason in St. Mary Abchurch, John Barsby in St. Mary Bothaw, Hezekiah Walker in St. John's, Henry Latané in St. Stephen Walbrook, Thomas Honitt[?] in the second precinct of St. Swithin and Isaac Ferris in the first. Matthew Fuller in St. Mary Woolchurch precinct had even paid exactly a week earlier. The point of this significant detail is to demonstrate that the regularity achieved in the accounts shown in Fig. 5.1 was achieved by a general culture of diligence and vigilance, and the hard work of many officials who were committed to a highly effective tax process.

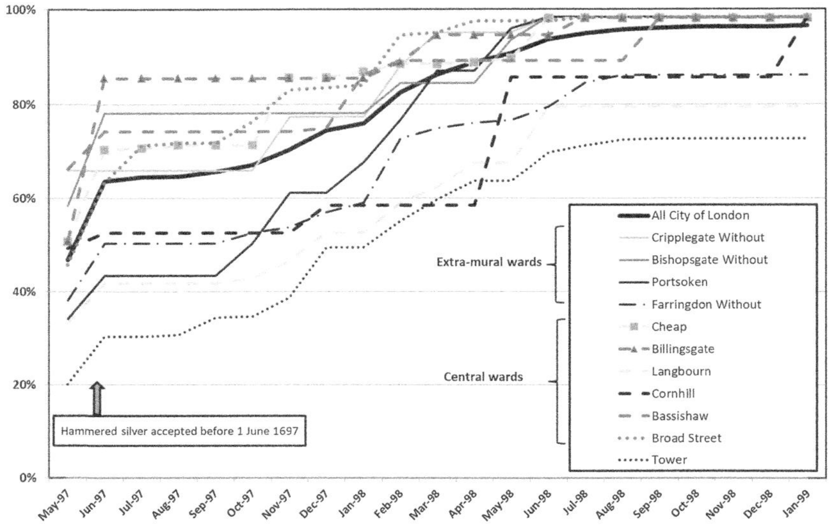

Fig. 5.4 City of London 1697. Flows of land tax money from receiver-general to Exchequer, including selected wards. *Note* Receivers could accept hammered silver coins 'att the Rate of Five Shillings and Eight Pence an Ounce', if delivered to the collector by 1 June 1697[41]

5.1.1 The Great Recoinage and Paper Money

As discussed in the foregoing and Sect. 2.5, if annual seasonal financial cycles might explain the normal tax-flows to the Exchequer, the Great Recoinage had a very distinctive impact. Parliament set deadlines in both 1697[42] and 1696[43] as to when receivers could continue to accept tax payments in old hammered silver. In 1696, receivers could 'receive in Payment Clipt Money, being Sterling Silver, &c. or of coarser Alloy, before 4th May 1696, at the same Rate as if unclipt'[44] and for the following year 'att the Rate of Five Shillings and Eight Pence an Ounce', if delivered to the collector by 1 June 1697. In London, the latter produced a response in the form of early payment to the receiver particularly from commercial wards including Cheap, Billingsgate and Bishopsgate, with streets lined with shops and businesses (Fig. 5.4). How much of this cash was tax money already collected and how much the recycling of old money by collectors from their friends, family and acquaintances, to be made up later from tax receipts, is impossible to ascertain.

5.1.2 Round Sum Flows 1645–1742

The City of London's development as a financial centre did much to support tax revenue flows in the metropolis and no doubt surrounding counties. The importance of the role of London's goldsmith-bankers from the late seventeenth century in issuing tradeable bearer instruments was probably important. There was nothing new about banking, but as Roseveare notes by the 1620s there was a burgeoning literature in England seeking the foundation of banks, common elsewhere in Europe at the time, partly in response to the lack of coinage.[45] Kim argues that: 'After the Civil War, and especially after the Restoration of 1660, goldsmith-bankerswere transformed from creditors into the biggest debtors in London, and soon afterwards in all of England, as they started massively taking deposits and issuing paper debts'.[46] Of course, bills of exchange and other paper instruments were also favoured by some. The Additional Aid of 1665 as mentioned had been collateralised by the issue of tradeable receipts payable at 6%. A few taxpayers may have settled their debts with paper in the capital, and collectors may have paid some monies to the receiver in paper form. By 1697, receivers were statutorily obliged to accept bills of exchange (Sect. 2.5) and collectors could profit if they could buy bills at a discount. Some such payments can certainly be identified in the chamberlain's accounts for 1708 and 1709.[47] During the Restoration and in the Interregnum, most payments collectors made to receivers were in precise round sums as crudely shown in Fig. 5.5. For the reasons discussed in Sect. 3.1.5 regarding Interregnum Kent (and see Fig. 3.10), it is tentatively proposed that many of these amounts were settled in paper not coin.

Of course, other non-round sumpayments may have been in paper form. For example, Henry Grant and Thomas Huckle, the collectors for the St. Martin's Le Grand precinct of Aldersgate Within Ward, made five payments in settlement of their quota of exactly £536, between 20 October 1705 and 31 July 1706 of: £100, £100, £100, £120 and £109 7s 9d, and they retained £6-12s-3d as poundage.[48] The first four of these payments would appear in the table above and figure as round sums in Fig. 5.5. The fifth payment, as can be readily imagined, might have involved part round sums and part coin, but would not figure. Therefore, although Fig. 5.5 suggests that only 56% of the payments in 1705 were in round sums, the actual paper element could have been larger. As discussed, 1697 was an exceptional year at the time of the Great Recoinage and here only 7% of payments were round sums as defined because collectors and receivers had every incentive to pay in physical cash form. In other years, in a country starved of gold and silver coins, the importance of paper transactions to the success of metropolitan tax collection appears significant.[49]

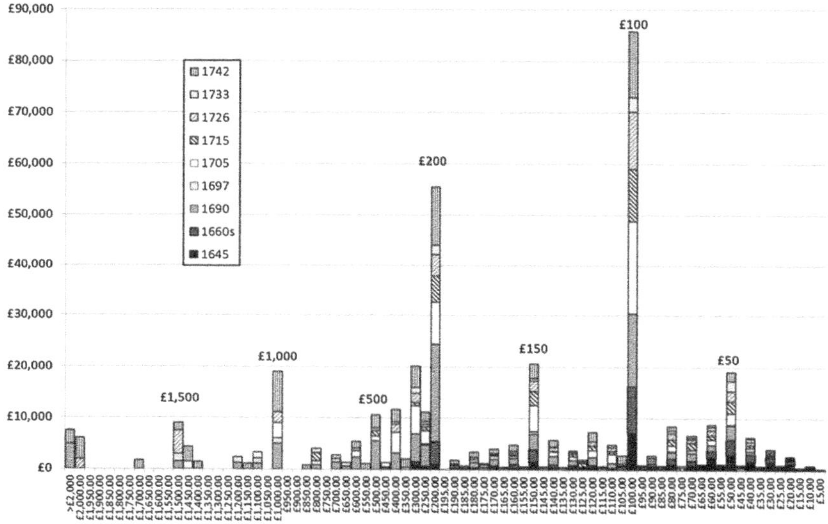

Fig. 5.5 City of London round sum payments to the receiver-general from collectors 1640s–1742 in selected years[50]

5.2 Example 2. Political Volatilities 1710–1720

Political instability in the second decade of the eighteenth century, which increased the rotation of administrative personnel in London and Bristol, did not lead to a material reduction in tax receipts or process failure as some established texts have argued. Indeed, there is some clear indication of emerging process improvement. Little stirred in contemporary Kent as tax processes continued untroubled.

The volatility and sometime violence of national and local politics in the second decade of the eighteenth century saw successive Whig, Tory and Whig administrations reflected in the parliamentary representatives from Bristol, London and Kent as well as in civic politics.[51] War had become unpopular and Henry Sacheverell's High Church anti-dissenting views became a political touchstone. His personal presence and his 'progress' in the West Country ignited Coronation riots in 1714, and Bristol crowd shouted 'Sacheverell and Ormond, and damn all foreigners!'[52] Sacheverell's presence was particularly contentious in Bristol with its substantial dissenting minority. The following year saw the 1715 Rising. There was also some overspill impact of such political traumas on tax administration, although Ward's exaggerates all the 'havoc wrought' which resulted in 'a great purge' in central administration.[53] There was indeed a particularly high turnover of receivers in 1711 (17) and 1715 (24) compared with an average of 6.5 between 1700 and 1716, and additional parliamentary pressures were placed on these men at a time of political strain.[54] This turnover is also reflected in greater rotation in tax officialdom in the cities of London (see Fig. 5.6 and an investigation see Table 5.1) and Bristol (Fig. 5.8), but precise mechanisms are uncertain. In Bristol, this period ultimately led to process improvements and the same is true of Kent, where George Baker was receiver.

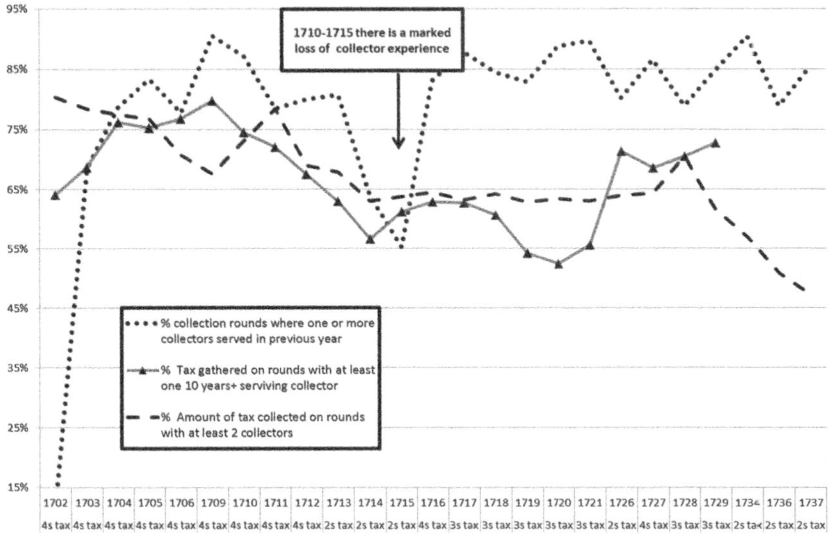

Fig. 5.6 The City of London 1702–1737. The eighteenth-century continuity of collectors and experienced collectors[55]

Table 5.1 City of London. Summary of 1710–1716 tax accounts for the wards of Bassishaw, Cripplegate Without and Cheap forming part of a contemporary exercise investigating tax balances in the City[56]

Bassishaw	*Assessed (£)*	*Quota (£)*	*Surpluses (£)*	*Deficiencies [non-payers and costs] (£)*	*Surplus-deficiency (£)*	*Deficiency/ Quota (%)*	*Notes*
1710	1,051.80	1,028.45	23.35	22.05	1.30	2.1%	
1711	1,044.40	1,016.04	28.36	24.26	4.10	2.3%	
1712	1,086.10	1,060.51	25.59	33.89	−8.30	3.1%	
1713	581.70	570.64	11.06	8.76	2.30	1.5%	
1714	571.25	532.25	39.00	42.50	−3.50	7.4%	
1715	559.65	525.98	33.67	25.73	7.95	4.6%	
1716	1,063.70	1,049.87	13.83	15.75	−1.92	1.5%	
Total	5,958.60	5,783.73	174.87	172.94	1.93	2.9%	'The balance … remains in the hands of Mr Deputy Eyre to help towards making good the present year's deficiencies'

Cripplegate Without	*Assessed (£)*	*Quota (£)*	*Surpluses (£)*	*Deficiencies [non-payers and costs] (£)*	*Surplus-deficiency (£)*	*Deficiency/ Quota (%)*	*Notes*
1710 and 1711							'John Clark dyed and his books cannot be come at'
1710 and 1711				267.75			'John Buckmaster broak and went beyond sea & carried his Books with him' but leaving an unpaid deficit of £267 14s 11d
1712	2,868.20	2,796.55	71.65	124.78	−53.13	4.4%	
1713	1,551.30	1,504.77	46.53	102.95	−56.41	6.6%	

(continued)

Table 5.1 (continued)

Cripplegate Without	*Assessed (£)*	*Quota (£)*	*Surpluses (£)*	*Deficiencies [non-payers and costs] (£)*	*Surplus-deficiency (£)*	*Deficiency/ Quota (%)*	*Notes*
1714 including re-assessment	1,936.55	1,403.55	533.00	172.89	360.11	8.9%	
1715	1,545.00	1,387.00	158.00	138.19	19.81	8.9%	
1716	3,062.45	2,768.49	293.96	267.90	26.06	8.7%	
Total	10,963.50	9,860.35	1,103.15	1,074.45	28.70	9.8%	

Cheap	*Assessed (£)*	*Quota (£)*	*Surpluses (£)*	*Deficiencies [non-payers and costs] (£)*	*Surplus-deficiency (£)*	*Deficiency/ Quota (%)*	*Notes*
1710	3,668.10	3,660.74	7.36				£70 14s 0d 'Deficient in the said Ward, by reason of appeals, empty houses and persons who have become insolvent during the said seven years'
1711	3,624.50	3,616.56	7.94				
1712	3,775.20	3,774.85	0.35				
1713	2,033.93	2,031.17	2.75				
1714	1,902.05	1,894.55	7.50				
1715	1,881.20	1,872.21	8.99				
1716	3,747.65	3,736.98	10.67				
Total	20,632.63	20,587.06	45.56	70.70	−25.14	0.3%	
Adjustments					22.48		'Paid by Mr Oswald Hoskins, one of the collectors...more than the amount of his book'
					2.66		'Paid by Mr Robert Makmorran one of the present collectors, more than' was collected
					0.0		

Note Percentage deficiencies added

There was marked contemporary disruption in City of London collector continuity and the appearance of some less-experienced individuals (see Fig. 5.6), but the average collection rates are barely impacted. The years 1712 and 1715, for example, in Fig. 5.1 do not markedly stand out from the rest.[57] Military and civil mobilisation around the time of the Rising might be partly responsible, as some individuals were called into service elsewhere. City tax commissioners ordered the wards to carry out a review on 2 August 1717, although their precise purpose is unstated.[58] The review showed that despite disruption there were no material City arrears overall despite the difficulties outlined and some sharp local challenges. In Cripplegate Without Ward in 1711, one collector John Clarke had died, and the other 'John Buckmaster broak and went beyond sea [leaving] £267-14s-11d deficient' (Table 5.1).[59] Because the Ward had been overassessed in other years, it was nevertheless in surplus by £28.70. The review documented no specific outcomes, but might well have come to the conclusion that this disruption was in fact much ado about nothing.

There was disruption in Bristol as well. The period 1709–1711 showed a sharp change in the continuity of both assessors and commissioners. Much less experienced commissioners were pressed into service, as senior aldermen disappeared from the tax process (Fig. 5.8). Matters were exacerbated by the death or incapacity of some faithful and capable old hands including Sir Thomas Day (122 identified prior commissioners' meetings), John Bacheler (55), William Whitehead (42) as well as the City Chamberlain Edward Tocknell (38). Others left soon afterwards, including Sir John Duddlestone (1715, 49 meetings), Sir John Hawkins (1712, 42), William Jackson (1714, 172), George Stephens (1718, 36), William Swymmer (1714, 76) and the long-serving and diligent Samuel Wallis (1718, 176).

Parliament became concerned and local administrators and receivers doubtless felt additional pressure placed on them. There were local issues as well. Somerset and Bristol Receiver-General George Dixon (Sect. 4.3.3) died bankrupt in 1707 with sums unpaid. Although he had cleared his 1706 accounts, he ran into difficulty the following year and sureties had to be called into settle his account after his death.[60] His successor Bernard Hutchins was reliable, but there were then two new receivers in quick succession: John Bowdidge who acted from 19 July 1715[61] and John Rodbard from 30 April 1717.[62] The former had written to the Treasury on 30 September 1715 expressing his concerns about 'insurrection' and threats to his receipts.[63] In fact in 1717, Bowdidge in his periwig fled, possibly via Dover or Harwich, chased by the authorities 'with a great sum of the public moneys in his hands' and his sureties were called in.[64] Perhaps the most important lesson from these episodes is that the established process was resilient. If some receivers were unreliable, the surety system could substantially protect the state from financial loss.

Whatever the detailed rationale, Bristol's tax administrators made two significant contemporary changes. Mirroring London and the legislation itself, Bristol had, by the start of the century, moved to a largely annual process with a single land tax assessment, but quarterly collection.[65] From 1716, this changed to a largely twice-yearly assessment basis.[66] Why was this? Firstly, there may be some practical tax reasons. Semi-annual assessments had particular advantages in keeping track of a mobile taxpayer population, permitting more flexible parish quotas and reducing the legally dubious measure of overassessment (Sect. 4.2b refers). Even in a small parish like St. Mary-le-Port, the second half-yearly assessment in 1730 saw about 15% of tax charges changed from the first half-year assessment to the second, either because of the movement of people or the adjustment of tax charges to make up the half-yearly quota.[67] Overassessment also declined with biannual assessment. Secondly, from 1717 newly appointed Receiver John Rodbard began rigorously checking and pointing out the albeit rather modest tax arrears in all his quarterly letters to experienced clerk John Romsey. Rodbard's successors continued this improved tracking practice thereafter. It seems probable that this same process applied across the county of Somerset given their shared receiver.

Prior to Rodbard, there was only occasional mention of arrears in receivers' letters and it was usually unspecific, reminding collectors to 'pay in their arrears at the same time' as the current quarterly payment.[68] From 1717 onwards, the receiver set out every quarter the precise amounts of arrears by parish and all these letters or copies survive.[69] Clerks no doubt quickly informed relevant collectors. When tax assessments were annual, as they were between 1700 and 1717, it might have been reasonable to expect that arrears from one quarter could be caught up later, so there was no need to flag a problem unless amounts were sizeable as occasionally happened (Fig. 5.7). Therefore, immaterial arrears probably went unflagged in receivers' letters before Rodbard. It is impossible to be certain that Rodbard and his successors included all arrears in their more detailed letters, but it seems very likely they tried to do so for two reasons. Firstly, receivers also acted for the contemporary window tax and these more frequent arrears were stated in the same letters, even though this was a much lighter tax. Secondly, where parish arrears persisted, which was rare, receivers would write to the clerk demanding that the recalcitrant collectors deliver the outstanding tax monies to him at a location convenient for him rather than locally within Bristol.[70] For example, Rodbard wrote to the clerk from his home in Taunton on 30 April 1722 pointing out that Temple parish was in arrears for £150 for the final quarterly payment of the tax year 1721 due on 25 April 1722.[71] These slow collectors were required to deliver this sum 'to me or my deputy at the Lamb Coffee house on Tuesday the fifteenth day of May next', in Taunton some 37 miles distant.[72] Rodbard would not be inconvenienced by the failure of Bristol's tax officials—they would come to him.

Yet Bristol arrears were unusual. For the period 1716–1748, total land tax was £175,548.92, compared with stated arrears, according to the receiver at any point in time, of £8,015.77. Thus, just 4.7% of tax was behind its required deadline. In the great majority of cases, parish

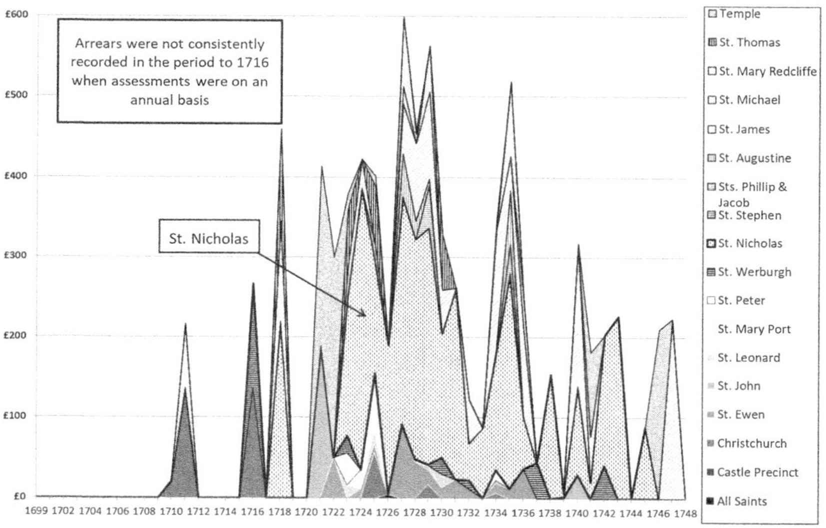

Fig. 5.7 Bristol land tax arrears 1700–1748 as recorded in the receivers' quarterly letters[73]

arrears do not appear again in the following quarter, strongly suggesting they were quickly paid off. Arrears peaked in c. 1728–1730, and in 1728 there was a brief temporary reversion to quarterly assessments (Fig. 5.7). This new assiduousness in tracking arrears is a clear example of process improvement and one which was continued by later receivers following Rodbard's innovation. All this evidence runs counter to Ward's view that during the eighteenth-century land tax was in a state of continual decline.

St. Nicholas was by far the worst performing of the parishes for land tax arrears according to the receivers at £3,695.01 for 1716–1748 or 46% of the total (Fig. 5.7). However, the parish's window tax arrears were unexceptional. Why was this? St. Nicholas was a very large commercial parish paying 15–19% of the City's quota.[74] It also contained the Custom House and almost half of its tax was on government salaries. It seems most likely that, as in London (Sect. 5.1), it was the government salaries' tax that caused this problem. The only other parish with significant arrearswas suburban St. James at £1,199.79 or 15% of the total (and 8–9% of the total tax). It had the lowest average rent and one of the lowest figures of tax per acre, suggesting it may have been more difficult to collect from poorer taxpayers here.

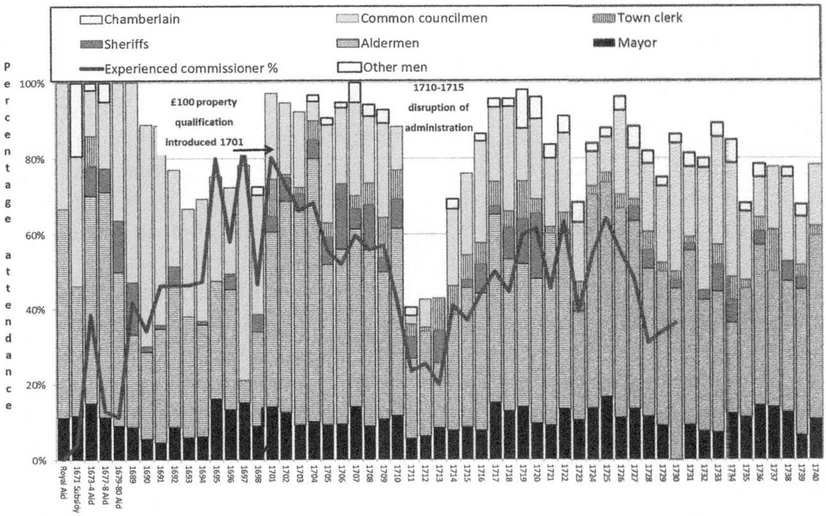

Fig. 5.8 City of Bristol. Administrative composition from the commissioners' minutes showing the annual percentage of commissioners who were civic officials 1665–1740[75]

In Kent little stirred at this time. Here, there is no evidence of increased rotation of tax officials or worsening of the tax process (see Figs. 5.12 and 5.13).

5.3 Example 3. Post-Revolutionary Duplicates in London and Bristol

The tax duplicate—a summary of locally assessed taxation—was one of the few documents regional tax administrators shared with state officials. It is clear that this document was sent to the Treasury much later in the eighteenth century than ever before. This has traditionally been seen as evidence of process decay or administrative slackness. It is argued here that this view is entirely mistaken. The duplicate was in fact invented in the 1640–1650s and by the turn of the century had long outlived its traditional role as a budget statement, that is an itemised statement of expected future income to be used at the start of the tax process. In the mid-seventeenth century, statutory quotas and local quotas varied, but they had become far more static by 1700. The budget, so to speak, was already clear and settled. Instead, at least in London and Bristol, administrators turned it into an outturn statement at process closeout and this was probably happening elsewhere.

Duplicates summarised the locally determined tax quotas demanded from contributing parishes, wards or townships to make up the county or city total specified in the statutes. Such duplicate*s* had been part of tax administration since the 1640s. Post-revolutionary statute continued to require them to be delivered to the Exchequer early in the tax process, usually by 8 August of the tax year.[76] With fixed post-revolutionary national quotas after 1698, the accounting value of duplicate*s* was severely diminished. Ward makes much of eighteenth-century delays in duplicate delivery against deadline, but he greatly exaggerates their importance for eighteenth-century national accounting.[77] Whereas in Kent, administrators still used the duplicate delivery date as an important milestone in the annual tax cycle, City of London administrators ignored this deadline throughout the post-revolutionary period and Bristol did the same after 1716 (Fig. 5.10).[78] If minor variations in local quotas remained, the Exchequer, Treasury and Parliament were largely interested in county or city totals actually paid by the receiver.[79] Traditional duplicates had become irrelevant and most commissioners knew it.

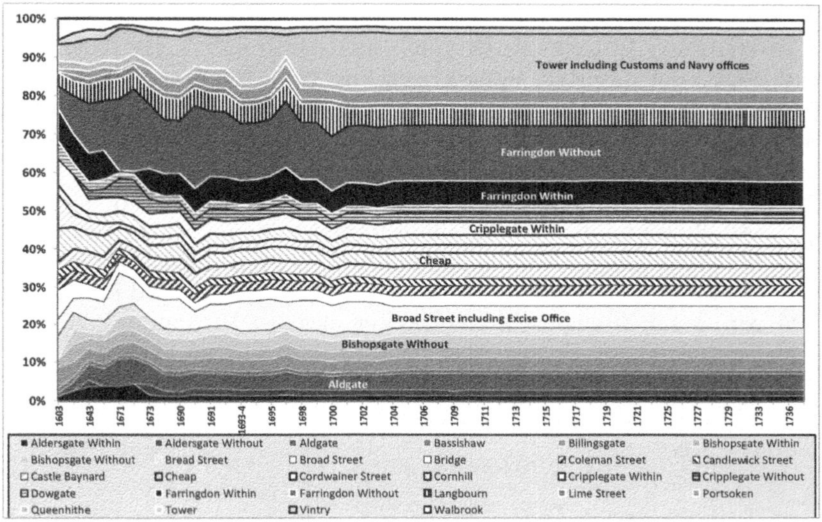

Fig. 5.9 London 1603–1737. City ward tax quota proportions after deduction of corporate taxes or 'Waters, etc.' Note that quotas became fixed in the early 1700s[80]

Post-revolutionary London administrators viewed the duplicate as having little value in its historic form after City ward quotas were made static by early 1700s administration (Fig. 5.9). Instead, City administrators turned the duplicate into something useful for themselves, as an outturn statement of income received signalling the end of the tax process. Its delivery to the 'Kings' Remembrancers Office of the Exchequer'was consequently always and inevitably extremely late in statutory terms. For Ward, late duplicate*s* were a further sign of decay and an 'abuse' of the system, because they were 'essential for accounting and the Exchequer'. However, this was simply not the case.[81] The part the duplicate played in the City of London tax process every year, from at least 1699, is described below with 1705 as an exemplar. Between 1689 and 1699, delivery dates are rarely preserved, but that of 1689 already follows the later outturn statement pattern.[82] In 1705, the City duplicate was due by 8 August 1705 according to statute,[83] but was actually signed on 8 March 1707 and delivered to the Exchequer on 28 March 1707 by John Smart at process end.[84] By 8 March 1707, all monies had been paid to the receiver less collectors' poundage of 3d/£ save for £552-8s-7d in respect of tax on salaries at the Navy Office in Tower Ward. As the salaries were effectively a state liability, this sum could be safely ignored for the purposes of clearing the City's land tax books.[85] The final payment triggering duplicate-signing was one of £704-19s-6d in respect of tax on 'Waters, etc.' made on 7 March 1707.[86] The City duplicate was signed the following day and on 18 March commissioners signed a warrant approving the poundage payment of £770-16s-9d[87] to the town clerk, 'Imployed as Clerke to attend the Execution of the said Act who hath carefully transcribed the several warrants, *estreats* and Duplicates'.[88] This effectively confirmed process closeout. As might be expected, collectors had long cleared their books with 79% of wards settled by August 1706 with some stragglers in the poorer parts of Farringdon Without Ward.

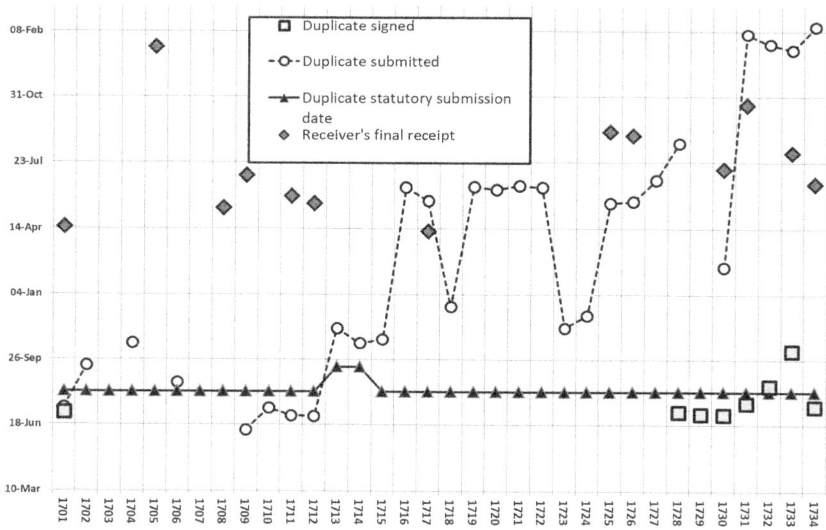

Fig. 5.10 City of Bristol 1701–1734. A comparison of the signing and submission of tax duplicates to the Exchequer with statutory deadlines and receiver's confirming receipt. *Note* (1) Much later submission starts in 1716; (2) 1728–1734, even though duplicates are signed closed to deadline they are not submitted until much later[89]

Bristol probably recognised the redundancy of duplicate*s* when it switched to biannual assessments in c. 1716 (see Sect. 5.2 above). Because there could be amendments between each half year, statutory duplicate deadlines could no longer be met. Evidence is scarce here because far fewer duplicate*s* were dated compared with London, and there are no surviving receivers' cash books. The receivers-general's receipt, which should statutorily have been issued within a month after receipt of all tax monies, as it was in Kent, shows little regularity. Nevertheless, it is clear from Fig. 5.10 that after many years of duplicate submissions to the Exchequer before or just after the statutory deadline, the process was changed in 1716 and submission pushed back much later in the tax process. It is suggested here that submission as in London marked process closeout. This speculative suggestion is largely made because although duplicate-signing appears to have been taking place by the statutory date (signing dates are only available for 1728–1734 to show this), submission to the Exchequer was much later. Abandonment of duplicate deadlines was not true everywhere. Kentish officials continued to endeavour to submit duplicate*s* by deadline 'as by the Act of Parliament is dictated'.[90] Nevertheless, evidence of delayed duplicate*s* should not be taken as evidence of failing processes as Ward proposes, because they had long lost their historic accounting value as budget statements.

5.4 Example 4. Establishing Regular Process Routine

Land tax processes did not work because they were complicated, requiring constant adjustment and intervention, they worked because they were sufficiently simplified and adequately resourced by local administrations to create an annually repeatable routine. Further evidence is presented here from the three case study areas of ways in which processes were simplified and improved in the early eighteenth century.

5.4.1 Bristol

In the immediate post-revolutionary aftermath, Bristol's tax process showed observance of the new governing order. The detailed recording of swearing-in and minuting of meetings suggests something of the ritualised nature of proceedings. During the 1690s, direct taxation was experimental, often with additional complexities inserted into the old land tax or new taxes such as the marriage duty introduced. For example, the Act of 1696–1697, although a traditional land tax, was also encumbered by a poll.[91] There were many different rates and special rules. Administrators in Bristol diligently attempted to enact this by providing assessors with a template marked out in columns.[92] When land tax quotas were temporarily discarded in the period to 1698, commissioners were inundated with appeals and this is best exemplified by surviving documents in Bristol which include the commissioners' minutes, but also return certificates sent to the Exchequer, including that of 2 July 1694.[93] This complexity mirrors Ward's description of the contemporary Westminstercommissioners.[94] From the 1694 Act,[95] appeals had to be heard under oath and taxpayers might bring in evidence of debts owed, mortgages and the like or simply swear that the amount taxed was too high or they had other debts to set off against these charges, and to have an 'allowance in respect thereof'.[96] Taxpayers were far more likely to appeal in respect of personal estates, as Ward has pointed out, or where the tax rules were complicated.[97] There were serial appellants. In the parish of St. Peter, 'Mr Edward Hackett charged at £44 p[er] ann. appears to be let at but £42 p[er] ann. out of which £3-2s p ann. is paid to the poor of St. Peters Almshouse is reduced to £39 p[er] ann.'[98] The 1693–1694 Four Shilling Aidassessment of the parish does not survive, but Hackett was present on the 1694–1695 assessment, charged £1-17s-0d tax per quarter or £7 per year on himself and his warehouse, indicating £35 per year rental value.[99] After further appeals, by 1703, this was only £6-2s-0d or £30-10s-0d.[100] With multiple levies and numerous

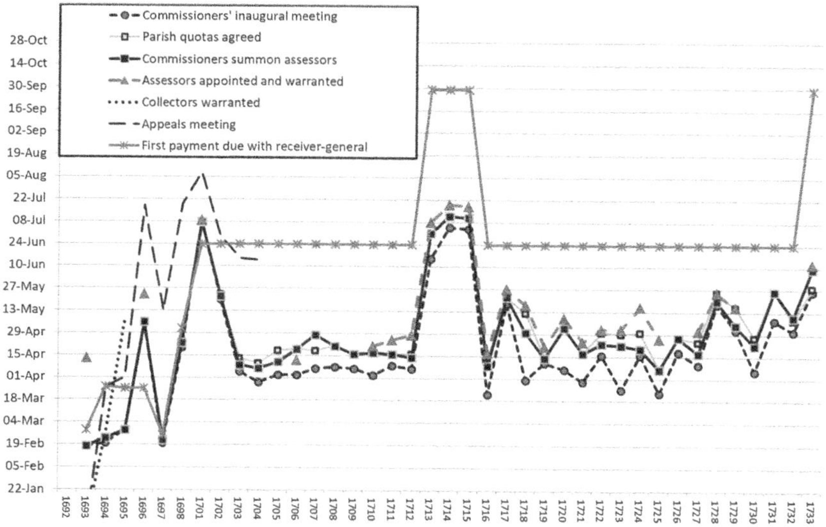

Fig. 5.11 Bristol 1693–1733. The regularity of the tax process compared with first payment deadline. *Note* Compare Fig. 5.12 from Kent[101]

such appeals, the 1690s process was burdensome to operate and required a host of commissioners' meetings.

It was the appeals against those difficult to evaluate personal estates that were the most problematic. There were almost twice as many personal estate appeals (52%) as real estate appeals (27%) recorded in 1697 even though taxed amounts were much less for the former than the latter.[102] By reducing the personal tax element and delegating some tasks to parish officials (Sect. 4.3.3), Bristol administration became much simpler. The eighteenth-century process was remarkably regular, with the Treasury letter informing commissioners to launch their local process. The inaugural meeting almost always met the statutory date or in three cases within three days of that in 1717, 1719 and 1728. Figure 5.11 shows this regular routine year after year from 1692 to 1733. Once commissioners' business was out of the way, there was still plenty of time to complete tax collection before the first payment date. This probably explains the very modest recorded tax arrears. The one exception was 1701. This was the year that John Romsey was appointed commissioners' clerk on 20 May, so the delay was probably related to this handover, but there was also a problem with quotas because of customs' salaries that year.[103] These issues probably explain the long gap between the delayed inaugural meeting and the agreement of parish quotas. Comparable documentation is not available for the City of London. However, Kent shows similar patterns to Bristol hinting at something of a national pattern.

5.4.2 Kent

There is evidence throughout the early eighteenth century that commissioners in Kent, supported by the receiver-general and their clerks, steadfastly endeavoured to carry out the tax process closely adhering to legislation. The commissioners regularly proclaim such adherence in their minutes, but this was no idle boast. They were largely successful as is shown in Wingham which was one of the largest sub-lathes with 56 collection rounds and 11% of Kent's tax quota throughout.[104] Early eighteenth-century Wingham administrators established a highly organised tax process with a keen focus on legislative deadlines. There is evidence here for the commissioners' application of disciplinary powers for failing officials, the calling of constables to successfully levy fines and resort to legal opinion to check the interpretation of legislation in a highly effective by-the-book tax-gathering operation. Commissioners met several times each year to fulfil their duties. There would have been an initial Kent-wide meeting, usually in Maidstone, to agree or 'resolve' the local sub-lathe quotas, before 'dividing up'.[105] By the 1720s, when documentation survived, these meetings were a sparsely attended formality because quotas were substantially fixed. Wingham commissioners (and elsewhere) then required four key annual, but routine, meetings to carry out their specific tasks, almost always at the Dog or Red Lion in Wingham: (1) to be sworn in and summon the assessors; (2) to appoint and warrant the assessors and set a deadline for return of the parish assessments; (3) to approve/amend the completed assessments and appoint collectors and arm them with assessments and warrants; and (4) to hear appeals.[106] The twelve 1705 Wingham commissioners were named in the minute book as Sir Henry Palmer, Sir James Oxenden, Sir Basil Dixwell, Sir Richard Sandys and esquires: Henry Oxenden, John Cason, John Lynch, Charles Bargrave, Nordash Rand, Thomas Marsh, Thomas Turner and William Hammond. Sandys, Turner, Rand, Bargrave and the two Oxendens were rather less active than the others (and see Sect. 4.5.1).[107]

The routine but deadline-focussed nature of the process is clear from the commissioners' minutes, which are more detailed than Bristol's. The clerk seems to have minuted all meetings here. Although there were 56 parish assessments to be agreed by the commissioners' specified date, virtually all assessments were completed to commissioners' stated deadline every year. For instance, at the 8 May 1705 meeting, all parish assessments were approved or 'seen and allowed' by the commissioners evidenced by signing and sealing by three or more of those present as required by the Act.[108] Dixwell, Lynch, Cason and Palmer were signatories in 1705. Dixwell signed almost every document that year and three quarters of all 1,500 surviving assessments in the period 1705–1733; Lynch over half in this longer period. Lynch actually attended slightly more meetings than Dixwell. These two men and six others were the backbone of the local process, most living within ten kms of Wingham where they usually met.[109] Three assessments were dated after the 8 May meeting, but this was possibly not tardiness by assessors but because they required amendment following the clerk's review. In the following year, 1706, two parishes missed the 3 May assessment deadline for that year and recalcitrant assessors had to appear before the commissioners to explain themselves. They claimed under oath not to have been informed by the constable of the deadline and were apparently exonerated.

Assessments dated later than the deadline were rare, certainly less than one a year on average.[110] However, in 1732, a record five parishes missed the 20 June deadlineand were signed late at the appeals meeting on 4 July as is shown in Fig. 5.14.[111] This default, of course, did not go unnoticed by the commissioners who ordered that the assessors 'incurred the penalty of 40 shillings'.[112] When the missing assessments were delivered by the following meeting, the penalty was 'discharged'. Needless to say, no assessors missed their deadline in 1733. Some excuses can be made for officials in 1732, even if assessors were not paid themselves, the collectors, receivers and clerks around them had seen their poundage reduced that year because the tax rate was only 1s/£.

Figure 5.14 shows the assessment delivery routine for this worst year 1732, partly because it also allows a comparison with St. Augustine Lathe, West, for the same year which had just one late assessment. In this sub-lathe, significant earlier documentation has not survived. Other than these late deliveries, the pattern of assessment submission to the commissioners looks much like any other year with a clustering of deliveries on deadline day or in the day or two just before. The figure also says something about local coordination. Local assessors were being informed what to do and when and in these two sub-lathes most of the time they were delivering to a deadline. They knew the consequence of failure. Of course, the point of the commissioners' insistent actions was to meet two locally important statutory deadlines: the delivery of the duplicate to the Exchequer by 8 August [+20 days] in the case of 1705 and to enable collectors to make the first quarterly payment to the receiver by 24 June.[113] Earlier documentation does not survive well so it is difficult to be sure about the detailed processes of the seventeenth century, but similar clusterings of assessment delivery to those described are visible in 1698 and 1699 for Wingham. Therefore although Clerk John Phillips was certainly a new efficient broom in 1705, good processes were probably operating earlier than that. Indeed, as described in earlier chapters Kent could operate effective processes at least by the 1650s.

Figure 5.12 shows the regular pattern of meetings and deadlines and perhaps a growing confidence that the process could be delivered in shorter order, even if Ward might view this as failure.[114] Normally, the receiver-general gave additional time in any case.[115] His deadlines were set out in his annual standard letters providing a time and place of delivery of monies addressed to all commissioners' clerks in the sub-lathes and boroughs. Deadlines and places were then copied onto the warrants for assessors and collectors.[116] At a final meeting as that of 1 August 1732, the commissioners confirmed all duplicates and required them to be sent to the Exchequer by 8 August 'as by the Act of Parliament is dictated', confirming the focus on Parliament's process.

A New Romney assessors' warrant dated 24 May 1725 gives a further flavour of this desire to comply (and see Table 5.2).[117] It appointed John Dray and Edward Bacheler as assessors and was signed by commissioners Mayor John Whitcomb, Robert Mascal and John Gray. The warrant, like others of the period, was long and detailed on process. *Inter alia,* it asks the assessors 'to use your utmost care and diligence to assess the full specified sum of £124-18s-6d' and 'to bring Two Copies thereof fairly written and exactly cast up in every column … to the Sign of the George in New Romney on Monday the Seventh Day of June' by ' four of the Clock'. They were also to nominate 'two able and sufficient persons' to act as collectors. This latter phrase was of course copied directly from the legislation. Did the process ensure timely payment to the receiver-general? Delays could occur and it might have been tempting for some collectors to hang on to monies overly long. At their meeting on 2 October 1705, Wingham commissioners noted that 'severall collectors … have collected severall sums of monies with the intent to apply the same to their own uses Contrary to the Law'. They were ordered to pay all such monies to John Phillips, the clerk within a week. They probably did so, because there were no further minuted references. As might be expected, hardly any of the receipts given by the receiver-general to individual parish collectors have survived in Kent.[118] However, once all monies for the year had been received, receivers had been statutorily obliged to give a final overall receipt to commissioners since the 1690s.[119] These receipts survive in St. Augustine Lathe, East from 1706*ff*, West from 1723*ff* and from 1708*ff* in New Romney. According to statute, the receiver should receive the final tax instalment by 25 March of the tax year and issue a final receipt within 'one month', so by 25 April. Were these issued promptly? It is difficult to say, but given the Kentish focus on statutory deadlines it seems likely (Table 5.2). No receiver would surely issue them before full payment had been made. New Romney, with its hundred or so tax charges, usually achieved this 25 April deadline (Fig. 5.13), but it was hardly ever met in St. Augustine Lathe, East or West, with their c.2,450 and c.1,650 charges, respectively, although under receiver George Baker results improved after 1715.[120] Nevertheless, these receipts would confirm that all monies had been paid from numerous parishes and collectors and no monies were ever more than six months overdue throughout this period. This quite remarkable result posits the question whether collectors were dipping into their own pockets to meet deadlines, particularly as receiver-general George Bakerwas threatening 'no salary for arrears'[121] and the commissioners stated in warrants that, 'you are not to fail as you will answer the contrary at your perills?'[122] This was no idle threat given their summary treatment of assessors recorded in the minutes. Were officials in St. Augustine Lathe , East and West, and New Romney exceptional for Kent? The evidence is limited, but suggests only modestly so.

Duplicates survive well, and Exchequer delivery deadlines retained an importance in Kent if not in Bristol or London. In the early eighteenth century, this was normally 8 August [+20 days]. How did the other Kentish lathes perform? Whereas in the sample, dated duplicates from St. Augustine Lathe, East and West, together with Upper and Lower Scray, Sutton-at-HoneLower, Aylesford East and South never missed a deadline: Shepway missed just once (2 October 1732) and Sutton-at-Hone Upper three times (6 December 1709, 13 September 1726 and 11 September 1732).[123] This general efficiency just hints that similarly effective processes were indeed occurring across Kent. There is also some indication that Kent was one of the most efficient counties in its tax-gathering based on evidence from the House of Commons Journal. In 1701, Kent had the fifth least arrears, out of 43,[124] and in 1708 it had collected the tenth highest proportion of land tax for the year.[125]

Many other south-eastern counties, with heavy tax burdens similar to Kent's (Table 1.1), had effective administrations in terms of delivering cash to the Exchequer from the evidence of Treasury Books[126] and reports to parliament. Kent may have been one of the most effective county's, but many others were not far behind and some had even heavier burdens than Kent's to contend with. Ward believed the Home Counties performed better than most other parts of the country, and despite the flaws described in his tables IV-VI on page 57, his average rank order of his selected counties from best to worst would be Bedfordshire, Norfolk, Buckinghamshire, Essex, Devon, Lancashire, Oxfordshire, metropolitan London, Yorkshire, Worcestershire, Cumberland & Westmorland, Cornwall and Sussex.[127] In other words, Ward's evidence generally shows that the counties that had long had the heaviest tax burdens were often the most efficient. This is no surprise. Heavily burdened counties had developed effective tax processes, well-targeted taxation and had bodies of committed officials to meet parliamentary demands (Table 5.2).

Table 5.2 Land tax legislatory requirements compared with surviving compliance evidence from Kent[128]

b	*Broad evidence*	*Types of Kent evidence*
'Commissioners to meet on or before 6th Apr, 1705…for the putting of this Act in Execution'	General Pan-Kent Commissioners' meetings took place and where documented, Kent commissioners always met on or before Parliament's deadline	Commissioners' General Meeting Resolves 1720*ff*[1]
'..and set down in writing the several proportions which ought to be charged upon every hundred, lathe, … etc'	All surviving '*resolves*' set out the detailed allocation to county subdivisions	Commissioners' Resolves 1720*ff*
Commissioners to '..subdivide and distribute themselves…as three or more … appointed for the service of each hundred, lathe…'	Regular group of commissioners were appointed and operating in all parts of Kent	Commissioners' Resolves, St. Augustine Lathe, East Commissioners' minute book[2]; Signed assessments[3]; Pan-Kent duplicates[4]
'..to direct their several or joint Precept or Precepts to such [persons] …to be … assessors.' [and instruct] 'how and in what manner they should and ought to make their assessments'	Detailed instructions and deadlines are contained in all the surviving assessors' warrants	Assessors' warrants[5]
'..to appoint and prefix a certain Day and Place for the said assessors to appear before them and to bring in their Assessments in writing …'	Warrants contain details of where and when assessments are to be delivered and the quality of what is required	Minute book. Assessors' warrants
Assessors are also to 'Return the Names of two or more able and Sufficient persons, … to be collectors of the Monies'	Collectors are always named either by assessors in the assessments themselves—and/or in the minute book	Collectors' warrants[6] Minute book
Commissioners 'or any three or more of them are hereby ordered to Sign and Seal two Duplicates'	Virtually all Kent duplicates examined are signed and sealed as required. Very few have only 2 names and occasional duplicates are unsigned presumably in error	Assessment duplicate

(continued)

Table 5.2 (continued)

b	*Broad evidence*	*Types of Kent evidence*
The commissioners are to 'nominate and appoint for each Parish … with warrant to the said collectors'	Collector's warrants survive in Kent from the 1640s through to the 1730s	Collectors' warrants[7]
Collectors are 'hereby required and Enjoyned to Pay the respective Receiver-General … the said rates and assessments by them respectively Collected …'	Receipts or acquittances were signed by the receiver. Timetables sent out by receiver-general saying what has to be paid, when and where	Commissioners' receipt from the receiver-general[8] Collectors' receipt[9]
'..every Receiver-General…within the space of one month after he shall have received the full sum..[from any 'hundred or division']…to such Commissioners'	Surviving in St. Augustine Lathe, East and West, and New Romney but receipts are limited in number	Commissioners' receipts from the receiver-general

[1] KHLC: Q/C/Tc2 Kent commissioners' resolves
[2] KHLC: Sa/Zo3, KHLC: Q/C/Tc1/1 (Post 1740) St. Augustine Lathe East
[3]Assessments: St. Augustine Lathe East and West KHLC: CKS/Q/CTL/1-213; Thanet (Margate/Broadstairs), KHLC: EK/1453/01; New Romney KHLC: NR/RTa9-31 & KHLC: NR/RTL6-67
[4] Duplicates for Kent: TNA: E182/430(1694–1697)-E182/436(1731–1733)
[5] For example, New Romney assessors KHLC: NR/RTL1 1723–1748
[6] Minute books: KHLC: Sa/Zo3, KHLC: Q/C/Tc1/1 (Post 1740) St. Augustine Lathe East
[7] Collectors warrants: KHLC: NR/RTL1-5
[8] Numerous examples across Kent
[9] TNA: 182/430-436ff, 1692-1733ff
[10] St. Augustine East, lathe KHLC: Q/C/Tc11, St. Augustine Lathe West KHLC: Q/C/Tc12, New Romney. KHLC: NR/RTL4 (f1-37ff)
[11] New Romney usually on collectors' warrants reverse, e.g. KHLC:NR/RTL1 (f19) 7 October 1724

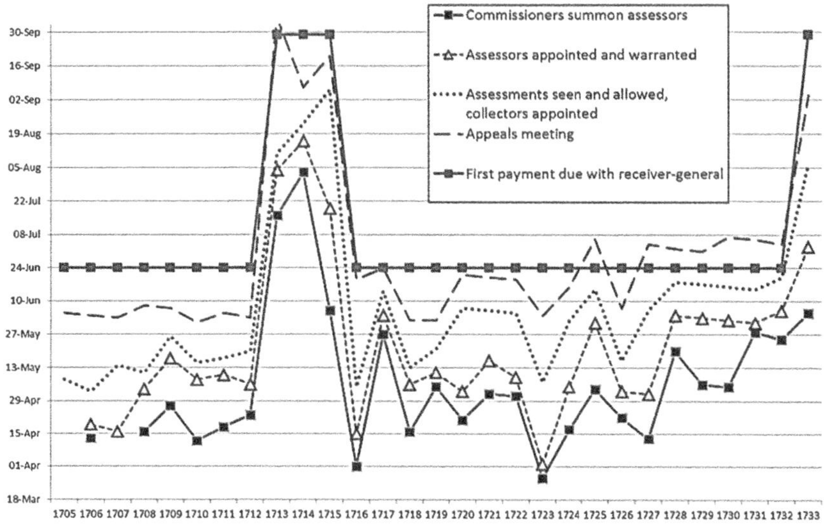

Fig. 5.12 Kent, St. Augustine Lathe, East, timetable of meetings for the land tax administration 1705–1733 showing a regularity of process and a shortening of timetable. *Note* The due date peaks in 1713–1715 and 1733 result from a reduction in the tax rate allowing a later payment date[129]

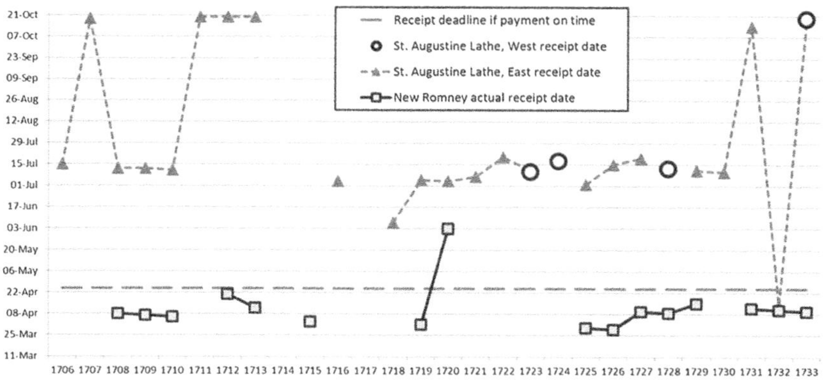

Fig. 5.13 Kent 1706–1732. Dates of commissioners' surviving tax receipts and deadlines, St. Augustine Lathe, East and West sub-lathes and New Romney. *Note* Monies should be paid by 25 March, and the receipt deadline was set within a further month, thus 25 April[130]

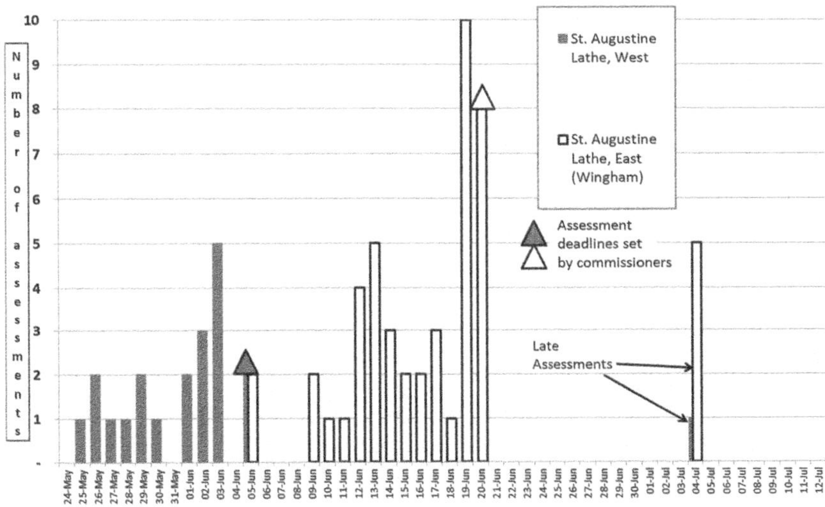

Fig. 5.14 St. Augustine Lathe, Kent, 1732. Timely delivery of dated tax assessments to the commissioners

5.4.3 *London*

The year in and year out effectiveness of London's receivers, the town clerk's office under John Smart (Sect. 4.5.3) and the collection flows around seasonal financial cycles (Sect. 5.2) have already been discussed.[131] Effectiveness was both City and broader metropolitan.[132] Although there was some post-revolutionary reduction in the variation between rich and poor wards in the production of tax assessments, tax collection still took longer in poorer wards, but cash was ultimately delivered (Fig. 4.11).[133] Tax processes in smaller urban contexts, whether Bristol or New Romney, could be generally faster and slicker and in rural Kent, effective by following the statute.[134] The vastness of City and metropolitan London was more of a grind requiring diligence, management and some level of oversight, and cajoling and prompting at all levels. This quality is apparent from Fig. 5.1. The process ground on year after year delivering tax on a regular and predictable basis. The delegation to ward commissioners certainly assisted. Most post-revolutionary wards organised their affairs so that newly completed assessments, for all ward sub-precincts, were signed off by their assessors on the same day as a meeting of the local ward commissioners took place to approve them.[135] Shortly after that meeting, they would be 'brought in' to John Smart's Guildhalloffice for scrutiny where an acknowledgement date might be added.[136] Similarly, taxpayers had the right of appeal and exercised that right where they believed assessments were too high or they were assessed elsewhere. There are few surviving commissioners' minutes for the City, but notes of London appeals sometimes survive,[137] which indicate that the process might continue into the winter months long after the collection process had begun.[138] Appeals, since the Restoration, had been signed off at ward level, originally by common councilmen, and after the Glorious Revolution, by local commissioners.[139] Sometimes, the town clerk had to order the already submitted assessment book to be amended when this occurred.[140]

Were Bristol, London and Kent exceptional? The answer is that they were probably not. Process, deadlinesand targets were set out clearly in the legislation with some scope for variability and some acceptable leeway. Quotas gave receivers and commissioners clear success criteria. Nationally in the early decades of the eighteenth century, if tax was not always delivered to deadline, then 85–90% of it was in the hands of the Treasury within six months of the yearly deadline, normally 25 March of the following year, according to Treasury Books.[141] This result was very much on a par with London, and seasonal financial cycles may partly explain delays, but these figures are worse than in Kent, where virtually all tax was paid within six months, and Bristol. In urban areas and the rural South-East, where burdens were heavy, there would inevitably have been greater focus on process effectiveness and simplification. The case study administrations' punctilious record-keeping might also indicate a similar attention to collecting taxes making these areas exceptional. However, survival of local material appears something of a haphazard matter because there was no particular legal requirement to keep such material long term at this time. The similarity of process in three quite differing contexts, whether in the detailed form and wording of warrants or receivers' quarterly letters, the keenness of commissioners to meet inaugural meetingdeadlines, the summary treatment of failing officers, makes it likely that this was a national process not just a local one, and one that administrators felt obliged to follow. This was a national tax, reliable because it was in local hands, not in spite of it.

Notes

1. Ward, *The English Land Tax*, pp. 37, 38, and 58.
2. Brewer, *The Sinews of Power*, pp. 100–101.
3. Ward, *The English Land Tax*, p. 93, referring to the period after 1715.
4. Ibid., p. 112.
5. Ibid., pp. 94–99.
6. For example, Ibid., p. 93 quotes CTB, vol. 30, 26 June 1716, p. 302. His 'gigantic' arrears comment come from William Lowndes letter to Chamberlain Sir William Fazakerley of 26 June 1716, which referred to 'My Lords observe that great arrears are standing out and unpaid in the several places [of London, Westminster, etc.] whereof you are Receiver'.
7. As early as 1702, John Smart drew up comparisons of due dates and paid dates. So the first two quarters of 1702 were due by 29 September on the City timetable but paid on 11 February 1703, and for the last two quarters the due date was 25 March 1703 but payment was not until 9 June 1703 and results were similar for later years LMA: /COL/CHD/LA/03/081/014 [above].
8. At least until 1752.
9. The exception being when the receiver demanded arrears to be paid as in the case of Bristol.
10. LMA: COL/CHD/LA/03/066/025[above], 1666 Warrant attached to the collectors' copy of the assessment.
11. Receivers' accounts survive for most post-revolutionary years to the end of the period considered with ward books and day books and the payment made by him to the Exchequer and often include the wider metropolitan area as well as the City. LMA: COL/CHD/LA/02/037-170, 1689–1733.
12. For example, 'when the Michaelmas rents came due', according to Jacob Price, 'Sheffeild v. Starke: Institutional Experimentation in the London Maryland Trade c.1696–1706', in R. P. T. Davenport-Hines and Jonathan Liebenau (eds.), *Business in the Age of Reason* (London: Frank Cass & Company, 1987), pp. 19–39, 42.
13. The term 'seasonal business cycle' is used by Robert B. Barsky and Jeffrey A. Miron, 'The Seasonal Cycle and the Business Cycle', *Journal of Political Economy*, vol. 97, 1989, pp. 503–534.
14. LMA: COL/CHD/LA/02/037-170, City accounts, 1689–1733.
15. But see pages 179–181 regarding Sir Harcourt Master. The chamberlain was not receiver every year, so there are some gaps in Figure 32 because no records survive.
16. Ward, *The English Land Tax*, p. 41.
17. Ibid., p. 56.

18. Ibid., p. 41, fn5 which cites CTB, vol. 27, 18 November 1713, pp. 436–437; CTB, vol. 28, 28 January 1714, pp. 114–115; and CTB, vol. 29, 16 July 1715, pp. 639–640. Ward's references have been expanded and slightly amended here.
19. Ward's stated source: TNA: E181/1 and E181-2. He claims to have averaged the figures in each period.
20. LMA: COL/CHD/LA/02/040 (1690); /080 (1697).
21. This was the year when the tax rate fell to one shilling/£ and no payment was due until Michaelmas. The loss of poundage as tax rates fell may also partially explain the slowness.
22. Ward, *The English Land Tax*, p. 58.
23. Based on years in Figure 32 at 95% and 50% collected. Trend lines are, respectively, improving or flat.
24. Ward, *The English Land Tax*, pp. 102–103.
25. Vanessa Harding, 'Controlling a Complex Metropolis, 1650–1750: Politics, Parishes and Powers', *London Journal*, vol. 26.1, 2001, pp. 29–37, and abstract.
26. Showing only those years where the data are complete. Sources: LMA: COL/CHD/LA/02/various.
27. 3 & 4 Anne, c.1, Land Tax for 1705.
28. LMA: COL/CHD/LA/02/various.
29. Ibid., but similar wording occurs every year.
30. TNA: 182/599 signed 16 March 1708. The four-shilling quota was £123,334-2s-7d
31. LMA: COL/CHD/LA/03/080/008, land tax miscellaneous papers. The dates for initial commissioners' meeting survive 1702–1771 and were usually in April or May, sometimes as early as March and as late as 2 July in 1713.
32. LMA: COL/CHD/LA/02/119 and 120, City Receipts book—Land Tax 1705.
33. LMA: COL/CHD/LA/03/various. For example, in 1704 between 12 April and 11 May (6 surviving wards), in 1705 between 19 April and 30 April (10 cases), and in 1706 between 19 and 22 April (two cases).
34. There are various other references to London arrears in CTB.
35. CTB, vol. 24, 18 and 24 August 1710, pp. 38 and 41. This demand also referred to the Inns of Court, Middlesex and Westminster.
36. CTB, vol. 24, 25 August 1710, p. 424.
37. CTB, vol. 26, 5 September 1712, p. 70. Further questions were asked on CTB, vol. 28, 15 January 1714, p. 6.
38. LMA: COL/CHD/LA/03/080/011, land tax miscellaneous papers; Harley, Robert (1661–1724), of Brampton Bryan, Herefordshire, Source: HoP (accessed 1 May 2017).

39. CTB, vol. 28, 3 March 1714, p. 22.
40. Ward, *The English Land Tax*.
41. 1) Sources: LMA: COL/CHD/LA/02/080, City Receipts book (Wards) Land Tax 1697; 2) 8 & 9 Wm. III, c. 6, Land Tax & subsidies, 1696–1697, SoR, vol. 7, pp. 166–189; 3) Notes: TNA: E182/596 includes a receipt dated 3 July 1697 for £2,964-6s-1d from Thomas Cuddon Receiver-General of Middlesex (and London) for 10,462 ounces five pennyweights of 'hammered silver'. Receivers could accept hammered silver coins 'att the Rate of Five Shillings and Eight Pence an Ounce', if delivered to the collector by 1 June 1697. Commercial wards such as Cheap, Bishopsgate and Billingsgate made particular use of the facility. This was less the case in Tower Ward perhaps because much of its tax came from government salaries.
42. Ibid.
43. 7 & 8, Wm. III, c. 1, Recoinage, 1695–1696, SoR, vol. 7, pp. 1–4.
44. Ibid., 'Provided they do not appear to be base Metal.'
45. Roseveare, *The Financial Revolution*.
46. Kim, 'How Modern Banking Originated', p. 942. Also, Horsefield, 'The Beginnings of Paper Money in England'.
47. LMA: COL/CHD/LA/02/125 City Receipts Book (Cash) Land Tax 1708. LMA: COL/CHD/LA/02/129 City Receipts Book (Cash) Land Tax 1709.
48. LMA: COL/CHD/LA/02/119-120, 1705, chamberlains' account books.
49. Paper transactions were used to transfer tax receipts at least since the 1590s. See Kerridge, *Trade and Banking* p. 55.
50. LMA: COL/CHD/LA/02/001 – 172, City and Metropolitan Receipts Books. Round sums are taken at £5 intervals up to £200 (so £5, £10, £15…£195, £200) and at £50 intervals above that. 1645 represents payments to the Treasurers at War.
51. Before greater stability as The Septennial Act 1716 replaced the Triennial Act of 1694.
52. Paul K. Monod, *Jacobitism and the English People, 1688–1788* (Cambridge: Cambridge University Press, 1983), p. 174.
53. Ward, *The English Land Tax*, pp. 55 and 64.
54. It is not clear if this was just the cajoling of receivers to pay up more quickly in politically difficult times. There were some threats of dismissal (CTB, vol. 25, 25 August 1711, p. 421), and Conway the receiver for Chester was so threatened. There was also a threatened 10% charge on receivers' unpaid balances (Ward, *The English land Tax*, p. 100; 1 Geo. I, st. 2, c. 36.; CTB, vol. 31, 6 November 1717, p. 59; HOCJ, vol. 18, 23 March 1716, p. 410, 'for the more effectually obliging the Receivers

General of the land Tax, and other duties to make speedy payment of the money in their hands into the Exchequer').

55. Sources: London & Middlesex: TNA: E182/594 (1689) – TNA: E182/604 (1733–1737), land tax duplicates.
56. Sources: LMA: COL/CHD/LA/03/016/004 [Land Tax Deficiencies Returns of Collectors of the several wards of the total of their assessment as compared with their quota, showing the surplus and the deficiency for each year].
57. LMA: COL/CHD/LA/02/ various account books. The longest delays matched by a short period in the late 1720s.
58. LMA: COL/CHD/LA/02/37A collectors' returns of 'overpluses' and deficiencies 1710–1716. The review may have focussed on surpluses and deficits in fact and the review identified both.
59. Sources: LMA: COL/CHD/LA/03/016/004.
60. CTB, vol. 22, 16 Jan 1708, p. 87.
61. CTB, vol. 29, 22 July 1715, p. 649; BRO: 04798. His warrant was copied into commissioners' minutes.
62. BRO: 04798. His warrant was copied into commissioners' minutes.
63. CTB, vol. 29, 30 September 1715, p. 292. The response from Treasury was only 'to use all diligence to get returns for their money as fast as it can be collected'.
64. CTB, vol. 31, 21 June 1717, p.380. Treasury wrote to the customs office at Dover and Harwich: 'it is probable he may be at your port and will come thither in order to his passage beyond sea to defraud and injure the public and his sureties. In case you find him you are to stop him and secure him and immediately send notice by special messenger to my Lords. He is a tall man about six feet high, well set, of a light brown complexion and wears a periwig; aged about 35 years'. The amount seems to have been £13,183. CTB, vol. 29, 3 July 1717, p. 394. See also CTB, vol. 31, 3 May 1717, p. 14 and CTB, vol. 31, 8 July 1717, p. 397. £10,000 seems to have been paid up from sureties with some reduction in the total for allowances.
65. Collectors were warranted quarterly, matching the receivers' letters.
66. Evidence here is based on the four parish stratified sample, St. Mary-le-Port (Central), St. Nicholas(Portside), Temple (Transpontine) and St. Augustine (Suburban). Sources: BRO: F/LT/ various.
67. BRO: F/LT/StMP, land tax assessments.
68. BRO: 04798, commissioners' minutes, 23 November 1703 from Edward Raymond.
69. BRO: 04798 and BRO: 09374, commissioners' minute books 1698–1748.

70. Under the statute, collectors were not obliged to travel more than ten miles. The demand to travel further was extra-statutory but reasonable given that the collector was obliged to deliver tax on time under the Act.
71. The usual date in the statute was 25 March, but most receivers gave collectors additional time to pay up as familiar in both Kent and Bristol. As well as for two parishes, St. Stephen and St. John, for the window tax. BRO: 09374, commissioners' minute book 1721–1748. The amount was not stated, but the arrears were for three quarters x £50.
72. Edward Whitchurch, John Baker and Thomas Millard.
73. BRO: 09374 and 04798, F/Tax/M/3, commissioners' minutes.
74. Sources: BRO: F/Tax/M/3, BRO: 04798 and BRO: 09374, tax commissioners' minutes 1689–1748.
75. BRO: 09374 and 04798, F/Tax/M/3, commissioners' minutes.
76. Later, if there were two rather than four collections scheduled in the statute.
77. Ward, *The English Land Tax*, p. 37.
78. Sources: Kent duplicates, TNA: E182/430(1694–1697)-E182/436(1731–1733); Commissioners' minute book, KHLC: Sa/ZO3. Here, there are numerous references to the importance of the duplicate delivery date.
79. For example, CTB confirm this county or City focus of Treasury.
80. Sources: TNA: E182/594 (1689) – E182/604 (1733–1737). London & Middlesex duplicates. 'Waters, etc.' includes tax on companies and government salaries. Legend to be read horizontally, then vertically.
81. Ward, *The English Land Tax*, p. 37.
82. For years after 1699, the date was given on the reverse of the duplicate itself along with the name of the person delivering it to the Exchequer.
83. 3 & 4 Anne, c.1, Land Tax for 1705, SoR, vol. 8, pp. 304–326. 8 August was the normal date for all commissioners for most years.
84. TNA: E182/599 1705, duplicate.
85. It was not cleared until 4 September 1707.
86. LMA: COL/CHD/LA/02/119 and 120, City Receipts book Land Tax 1705.
87. LMA: COL/CHD/LA/03/111/006 [above]. It was paid to both the new clerk James Gibson and Elizabeth Ashurst widow of former clerk Henry Ashurst on 24 September 1707.
88. A phrase very similar to in the Act itself.
89. Sources: TNA: E182/839 [1701] – E182/842 [1734]; Bristol tax duplicates. Receipts: BRO: 09374 and 04798 commissioners' minute books 1698–1748.

90. Source: Commissioners' minute book, KHLC: Sa/ZO3.
91. 8 & 9 Wm. III, c. 6, Land Tax & subsidies, 1696–1697, SoR, vol. 7, pp. 166–189. It *inter alia* taxed servants, barristers, attorneys, farmers and graziers.
92. BRO: F/Tax/M/3 Bristol commissioners' minutes.
93. TNA: E182/838, Bristol duplicate and returns of deficiencies of payment.
94. Ward, *The English Land Tax*, p. 39. He mentions '*hearing appeals which poured in immense numbers.*' From May 1693 to March 1694 the commissioners for the parish of St. Margaret held 56 busy meetings and 44 the next year.
95. 6 & 7 Wm. & Mar., c. 3, Four Shilling Aid, 1694–1695, SoR, vol. 6. pp. 510–563.
96. 'Persons delivering in Specification, to give Commissioners an Account on Oath of the Debts owing by them at Interest', 8 & 9 Wm. III, c. 6, s. LXXX, Land Tax & subsidies, 1696–1697, SoR, vol. 7, pp. 166–189.
97. Ward, *The English Land Tax*, p. 39.
98. BRO: 04798, commissioners' minutes. Hackett appears in Ralph and Williams, *The Inhabitants of Bristol in 1696*, p. 164, where he had £600 of personal estates.
99. And 12s-6d on personal estates per quarter, BRO: F/Tax/A/16 StP, tax assessment.
100. BRO: F/LT/StP, land tax assessment.
101. BRO: 04798 & 09374, commissioners' minutes.
102. BRO: F/Tax/M/3, Bristol commissioners' minutes. Central: personal (54%), real (20%) and other (26%); portside: 52%, 31% and 17%; suburban: 45%, 39% and 16%; and transpontine: 57%, 19% and 24%.
103. BRO: 04798, Bristol commissioners' minutes; Ralph and Williams, *The Inhabitants of Bristol in 1696*, p. xvi.
104. The rounds varied very slightly over the period.
105. KHLC: Q/C/Tc2 has commissioners' 'resolves' from these meetings from 1720*ff.*
106. 1) The Inns in Wingham were also where the same men met as justices of the peace until the twentieth century (KHLC: PS/W); 2). Additional meetings might also be required if there were particular matters to be dealt with.
107. KHLC: Sa/ZO3 and Q/C/Tc/1/1*ff*, commissioners' meeting minutes.
108. 3.75 signatures on average.
109. Percentages of all assessments signed 1705–1733: Major Richard Harvey (43%), Sir Thomas D'Aeth (35%), Sir Brook Bridges (25%), Vice-Admiral Salmon Morrice (22%), Thomas Marsh (21%) and William

Hammond (18%). This group comprised 74% of the key meeting attendances 1705–1733.

110. About 20% of assessments were not dated, but virtually all were probably signed at the designated meeting because of (1) the consistency of signatories and (2) the lack of reference to lateness in the minute book.
111. Admiral Salmon Morrice was present at this later meeting, but not at the earlier one, according to the minute book and he signed each of these five assessments presumably at that later date.
112. KHLC: Sa/ZO3, Buckland and Charlton, Wootton & Giddings, Lydden, River, and Poulton parishes.
113. Twenty days was the normal period of grace.
114. *The English Land Tax*, p. 90, cites the reducing numbers of meetings in the Wingham division as evidence of decline.
115. For example, St. Augustine Lathe, West, KHLC: Q/C/Tc/2, received 25 April 1719; New Romney, KHLC: NR/RTL2 (f6-17), 1725*ff*.
116. For example, New Romney assessor, KHLC: NR/RTL1 (f3-18) 1724*ff*; collectors KHLC: NR/RTL1 (f19-21).
117. NR/RTL1 (f18) New Romney land tax assessors' warrant 24 May 1725.
118. Some have survived in New Romney, e.g. NR/RTL1 (f19).
119. Suggested in legislation from the 1670s and a requirement from the 1690s.
120. A single individual might pay multiple charges. 1705 taxpayer counts from St. Augustine Lathe, East (2,461 taxpayers = 10.7% of Kent quota), and St. Augustine Lathe, West (c. 1,667 taxpayers = 5.5% of Kent quota).
121. KHLC: NR/RTL2 (f16) New Romney 25 April 1725. George Baker's letter to the Commissioners for New Romney from his house at Hawkhurst Lodge.
122. New Romney 5 June 1724. KHLC: NR/RTL1 (f19). Warrant signed on the reverse by Baker by way of receipt, precisely on the deadline set by him. The 'at your perills' phrase has a long pedigree, e.g. a warrant of 21 March 1645 from Milton near Gravesend uses identical language TNA: SP 28/158.
123. KHLC: Q/C/Tc/11 and 12 and sample from TNA: E182/430-436: 1706, 1709, 1719, 1726, 1732.
124. HOCJ, vol. 13, 3 April 1701, p. 469, behind Gloucester, Norfolk, Bedfordshire and Berkshire of 43 counties.
125. HOCJ, vol. 15, 23 February 1708, p. 561, after the Queen's household, Gloucester, Berkshire, Cambridgeshire, Bedfordshire, Essex, Lincoln, the County of Southampton and Warwick.
126. CTB various.

127. Ward, *The English Land Tax*, p. 58 and Tables IV–VI.
128. Sources: [1] Resolves: KHLC: Q/C/Tc2 Kent commissioners' resolves; [2] Wingham commissioners' minute books: KHLC: Sa/Zo3 (1705–1740], KHLC: Q/C/Tc1/1 (Post 1740); [3] Assessments: St. Augustine Lathe, East and West KHLC: CKS/Q/CTL/1-213; Thanet (Margate/Broadstairs), KHLC: EK/1453/01; New Romney KHLC: NR/RTa9-31 and KHLC: NR/RTL6-67; [4] Duplicates for Kent: TNA: E182/430 (1694–1697)-E182/436 (1731–1733); [5] Assessors' warrants: For example, New Romney assessors, KHLC: NR/RTL1, 1723–1748; [6] Collectors warrants: New Romney, KHLC: NR/RTL1-5; [7] Commissioners' receipts from receiver-general: St. Augustine Lathe, East, KHLC: Q/C/Tc11, St. Augustine Lathe, West, KHLC: Q/C/Tc12, New Romney, KHLC: NR/RTL4 (f1-37*ff*); [8] 3 & 4 Anne, c.1, Land Tax for 1705, SoR, vol. 8, pp. 304–326; [9] New Romney only usually on the reverse of collectors' warrants, e.g. KHLC:NR/RTL1 (f19) 7 October 1724.
129. Sources: Commissioners' minute book, KHLC: Sa/ZO3.
130. Sources: Receiver-general receipts: Wingham, KHLC: Q/C/Tc/11; St. Augustine Lathe, West, KHLC: Q/C/Tc/12; New Romney, KHLC: NR/RTL4 (f1-37*ff*).
131. Sources: LMA: COL/CHD/LA/02/037-170 1689-1733, City accounts. With the exception of Sir Harcourt Master.
132. Ward, *The English Land Tax*, Chapter VII often cites Westminster's failings in his 'decay' narrative but metropolitan London compares well with the City throughout the period considered here.
133. Source: Dated assessments provide evidence of variation between areas. Source: Ancestry.co.uk, London, England.
134. St. Augustine Lathe, East, KHLC: Q/C/Tc11; St. Augustine Lathe, West, KHLC: Q/C/Tc12; New Romney, KHLC: NR/RTL4 (f1-37*ff*).
135. As noted above, this was not true of Farringdon Without, the largest ward, where multiple teams of commissioners and other tax officials operated. Neither was it true in Aldersgate Within where two separate teams operated in St. Martin's Le Grand and the Freedom part.
136. Source: Ancestry.co.uk. Quite often the term 'brought in' was used, but in many cases there was simply a date shown on the bottom edge of the final or penultimate page of the assessment. The author has taken all these dates as 'brought in' dates, as seems most likely, because the location and often the hand of the date is the same as that of other office text.
137. LMA: COL/CHD/LA/03/078/008 [above].
138. In 1704, the dated appeals were in November and December.

139. There may have been some later approval by commissioners, but this is unclear.
140. Town Clerk John Goodfellow signed many such in the 1690s, e.g. LMA: COL/CHD/LA/03/080/001, Land Tax miscellaneous papers. Many of these were pre-printed with details to be inserted later.
141. CTB various. CTB reported outcomes at Michaelmas (29 September) for 1703–1717. The 85–90% figure is the normal range for these years.

CHAPTER 6

Conclusion

It is time to rethink land taxes and their successful contribution to the English state. They were invented in the 1640s and not after the Revolution. They were the most significant of all early modern English taxes until the early eighteenth century and remained prominent for decades thereafter, and yet they have been unappreciated and overlooked. The breadth and weight of tax were revolutionary in the mid-seventeenth century as was their effective process design targeted at cashflows in the English economy. It is time that land tax's regular ability to successfully engage tens of thousands of Englishmen in a coordinated national tax-gathering effort was properly understood and appreciated. This is not simply a matter of appreciating an effective tax, it is also about understanding the nature of the contemporary English state.

This neglect is no small part because land tax success runs counter to models of an English state successful in war and at home because it was becoming more institutionalised and bureaucratic. And yet, English bureaucracy was modest in size and capability and its institutions hardly developed. These same narratives have also significantly undervalued the role of local governance in the English state and the development of the economy. Local governance had been and continues to be an intrinsic part of the English and British state. The analysis presented here has also highlighted the flawed nature of some well-known texts and the confusion they have caused. There is also a recurrent problem throughout the historiography of inappropriate, disparaging and anachronistic

S. Pierpoint, *The Success of English Land Tax Administration 1643–1733*, Palgrave Studies in the History of Finance,
https://doi.org/10.1007/978-3-319-90260-9_6

terminology including use of the term 'amateur' to descry land tax administration. Land taxes were successful because they were well designed to exploit cashflows from England's growing wealth within a developing Atlantic economy. They had sound tax processes and could rely on the services of tens of thousands of willing and committed men up and down the land, many with skills and capabilities to gather in tax monies.

It is time for a reassessment. Even the notion that the fiscal-military nature of the English state at this time was its defining characteristic should be questioned. The seventeenth-century state could gather taxes and fight wars, but it could also dispense justice, provide welfare provision, repair and build highways, supply water and light and clean the streets, and most of these actions were administered locally through collective action, often within a national framework. This was an English state which could coordinate the actions of its men in a remarkable way. There are numerous examples in this text including: Kentish assessors' timely delivery of their tax assessments to the clerk in Wingham; the Bristol collectors' annual delivery of gathered taxes to the deputy receiver at the White Hart Inn; commissioners across the nation hurrying to their annual inaugural meeting by parliamentary deadline; and the regular checking and correcting of tax assessments by clerks. It was a flawed state made of flawed individuals; of course it was. Tax administrators were patriarchal, some were happy to evade other taxes, officials were prepared to profit from tax cashflows, and a few traded in slaves. But it was a state that could fund itself and the land tax was the largest part of that for decades.

Powerful institutional state-building narratives have relegated economic factors, the mechanics and form of taxation and local governance to secondary roles in fiscal growth. The evidence presented here supports the notion that all three were vital factors. Institutional narratives have also led to a misinterpretation of land tax development. Eighteenth-century land taxes would never have been established without 1640s innovations which created a distinctly new tax and process, which, if rooted in traditional administration, had quite different purpose and application in many parts of the country. The new assessment or land tax took the point of taxation close to monetary flows and commercial cycles in the developing English economy when cash was scarce. Economic development was a necessary condition for such fiscal growth, but it required prolonged adaption of tax form and process to find a workable solution. Protracted supply needs of the extended crisis of the Civil War and its aftermath provided the opportunity for this development to take place. Old-fashioned subsidies, aimed at the reluctant wealthy few, were unable to reliably deliver sufficiency of resources for such conflicts. They were displaced by broadly based taxes directly targeting the occupiers of land which would be paid out of what farms produced, shops sold, businesses manufactured, residents earned and sometimes what tenants paid. The more commercialised urban and rural land markets, particularly in the South and East, were a prime target, where occupiers could deduct the tax they had paid from their landlords' rent. By the mid-seventeenth century, more people than ever before had something to lose, whether personal assets that could be seized by powers of distraint for non-payment of taxes, or personal prestige. Most, but far from all of such taxpayers, were men. English land tax administration usually employed traditional and patriarchal local authority figures including mayors, aldermen and justices. By the mid-seventeenth century, many such traditional male roles were filled by successful farmers, merchants and local businessmen who were benefitting from the developing economy. Many had strong portfolios of skills, knowledge and capabilities developed by new opportunities in state service and commerce. If they now paid more by way of land taxes, by becoming administrators they would at least have some level of control. Many places, particularly in the South and East, benefitted from state investment in dockyards, military facilities and administration, and it was in the interest of these local men to participate in the state for the sake of their personal interests and the local economy. State legislators, in partnership with such capable local governors, created administrative processes capable of timely and coordinated tax-gathering actions, locally and nationwide. The tax fostered local collective actions to national plans and deadlines. The bargain between state and locale was that as long as a fixed quota was met, local governors could allocate it as they saw fit. This created a level of trust. Commissioners, assessors and collectors as well as taxpayers therefore gained some process ownership and responded with collective action as Daunton observes.[1] Thus, many were involved in the state, some were rewarded, and if many paid tax, some of this immediate burden was shifted to the better off.

This collective action had a very public face, and there was a transparent reasonableness about this land tax. It was levied chiefly on visible real property; the visiting collector was probably someone known to the taxpayer; and the legislation, assessments and warrants were available to read. This book has focussed on southern and urban contexts because they were heavily taxed and mostly likely to develop new tax forms and processes. Elsewhere, in lightly taxed regions, traditional assessment methods clung on, but it would be a mistake to regard these areas as typical or central to land tax success. Despite negative historiography, this book has shown that innovation continued as Restoration and post-revolutionary national and local administrations developed improved processes including more regular and better paid officers, simplification, delegation and improved stakeholder oversight. Thinner contemporary records of what was happening locally, as the eighteenth century progressed, were not a matter of breakdown, but of delegation to capable clerks and administrators, and simplification of process.

The historiography has long mistaken contemporary accounts of the individual failure of tax officials as evidence of general administrative breakdown. Rather, these accounts, as shown here, demonstrate that problems were being identified, documented and tackled. State bureaucrats might flatter themselves and keep excellent records of their achievements for posterity, to be treasured in national archives. However, the great fiscal achievement of the late seventeenth and early eighteenth-century state was not the appointment of a few hundred bureaucrats of mixed integrity and capability, but the delegation of state authority, through oaths, signatures and seals, greatly assisted by printed written instructions, to hundreds of thousands of Englishmen in taxing themselves and their neighbours in a coordinated national effort. Negotiation, coercion and consent perhaps all played some part, but the ownership of process by local commissioners, assessors, collectors and even taxpayers (through complaint and appeal) was vital. Accident should not be ignored. A levy devised during the Civil War to target the unwilling, including absentee royalist and neutral landlords through their tenants, proved mightily effective thereafter. The brilliant notion of a tax where occupiers could be forced to pay, but pass some immediate burdens to wealthier landlords, was a 1640s masterstroke. Officials' success criteria were straightforward whatever the individual's politics—deliver the monarch's quota. Such land tax success also meant that standing and honour were visibly maintained whilst perhaps the less-transparent avoidance and evasion of other taxes were tacitly tolerated. In 1733, if the land tax was not loved, it was owned and somewhat tamed by many, countrywide. This fostered a rare defeat for the inexorable rise of the 'monstrous' and bureaucratic excise, perhaps as Graham remarks, 'precisely because it gave extensive oversight to local political interests rather than unpopular bureaucratic officials'.[2] This was about building not just a state, but also a nation. Notions that society, politics or war made the state are too broad.[3] Taxes played a part, and crucially, the land tax involved hundreds of thousands of people as payers or as officials assuming state authority and responsibility in coordinated action.

There is much more work to do on land taxes. Developments beyond the three case study areas have only been glimpsed in these studies. How far did the new forms of Interregnum land taxes extend and how far did traditional forms persist in time and space? Documentary survival is poor, but there is more to learn from the Commonwealth Exchequer Papers and indeed in local archives. There is much more to do on tax incidence; where did the real burdens lie? How many were able to effectively deduct tax from their rent? Did women play such a very small part in tax administration, or would other sources reveal more? There are also valuable side issues to be explored concerning tax payments by paper bills which can usefully be pursued. Links with Dutch land taxes have only been touched upon here, but merit further research.

Why did the significance of land taxes decline in the later eighteenth century and why did tax-gathering slow down as Ward maintains. There are a number of areas which would merit further work regarding the latter, but two stand out. Firstly, the role of receiver was increasingly filled by general financiers or bankers.[4] For example, the City of London Chamberlain was less likely to be the London receiver as the eighteenth century wore on. The Baker family sometime receivers in Kent were heavily involved in banking. Were such individuals more likely to hold on to cash to deploy in their banking activities rather than hand it over to the state as has been suggested by several authors? Secondly, the value of poundage had declined in real terms as inflation reduced the value of money in the second half of the eighteenth century to little more than 35–40% of its 1700 value.[5] The real value of poundage earned by collectors', receivers' and clerks' would all have been reduced as a result. Why would tax officials work as hard for effectively less money? Would officials try less hard or strive to create value from the tax monies in other ways?

6.1 Overview

Successful deployment of land taxes after 1643 owed much to the early development of effective legislation and the local response of well-established local administrations, to exploit commercialised land ownership. In a radical departure from the past, a broadly based and substantial occupier tax was created which gave tenants some ability to pass the immediate fiscal burden to their generally wealthier landlords (Sect. 2.2).[6] These taxes also possessed other invaluable fiscal attributes including clear deadlines and processes, powers of distraint, clear success criteria in fixed tax quotas and the ability to reassess if the quota was short (Table 2.1). Real estate was increasingly commercialised in many areas as contemporaries understood (see Sect. 3.1)[7] and metropolitan London's growth was a major cause of this change as 'the city drove the countryside'.[8] In 1643, there was an obvious fiscal opportunity for a parliament desperate for supply. Mid-1640s officials across metropolitan London with their tax on out-landlords (Sect. 3.1.3), in Kent with their 'rent-tax' (Sect. 3.1.1), and in other south-eastern counties quickly embraced this new tax and developed their own local solutions, as is clear from hundreds of surviving tax documents. If traditional forms of tax-gathering were permitted, this largely applied to the North and West where burdens were always much lighter (Fig. 1.2). In the South and East, contemporary assessments, warrants and letters demonstrate that officials thoroughly understood how the new tax should operate (Sect. 2.5 and Sect. 3.2.2) and strove to apply it locally. Regular legislative tinkering in the first decade after 1643 suggests regular feedback from locality to centre. Early legislators knowingly targeted flows of economic value and cash around the increasingly commercial enjoyment of land (Sect. 3.1), just as the contemporary excise tapped product supply chains, in a period when there were severe constraints on coinage supply (Sect. 2.5). These developments permitted higher tax burdens than ever before when monarch and parliament worked together to face trade and continental conflicts. It was the South and East of England which bore the fiscal brunt throughout the ninety-year study period, and the chosen case studies of rural Kent and the cities of London and Bristol provided an opportunity to consider this fiscal challenge through good archival survival.

In a break from earlier taxes, officials ensured these new levies were tied to Kent's rural acreage (Fig. 3.2) and to the 'true yearly value' of urban properties (Sect. 3.1.3) in London, through a county-wide rate (Sect. 2.2.2) and a real estate revaluation, respectively. Despite much heavier burdens (e.g. Fig. 3.4), there is clear evidence of early effective tax-gathering in London and Kent with highly coordinated actions across county (Fig. 3.8) and City (Fig. 3.12). The timing of tax payments themselves was linked to periods when cash became available through farming cycles and seasonal produce (Fig. 3.9) or City seasonal financial cycles (Fig. 5.2) and this sometimes constrained the ability of collectors to meet tax deadlines (discussed in Sect. 5.1).

English local governance had developed over hundreds of years, but had become increasingly effective since the late sixteenth century in the administration of justice and the poor law as local communities were increasingly 'bound … into a national society and economy'.[9] Many of the middling male sorts had widening skill sets built in the spheres of law, finance, international trade, administration and taxation. The prior development of such a cadre of able and experienced officials was an important enabler for the new tax, and competencies were enhanced by work on county committees.[10] Kent was well supplied with such men including Members of Parliament and local justices of the peace. Meanwhile, Bristol and London had long-established civic administrations even if parliamentary interference was required to ensure appropriate support in the 1640s and at the Restoration (Sects. 3.2.3–3.2.4). Because of the City's importance to supply, the 1640s parliament constantly intervened in London's civic administration and was perhaps most effective in empowering common councilmen in local wards (Sect. 3.1.3).

Assessments and excise proved indispensable during the Restoration, despite previous damning royalist rhetoric, and land taxes reached record levels during the Second Anglo-Dutch War and were particularly heavy in Kent (Sect. 3.3.2). Land taxes, though tainted by Commonwealth associations, were retained because they were hugely effective in reliably and predictably delivering supply (Fig. 1.1). Fiscal success created problems in transferring unprecedented tax receipts in coin to London. This could be done by guarded wagons, but use had been made of paper transactions, at least since the 1590s, using methods developed in the world of commerce (Sect. 2.5) and this increased in response to heavier 1660s taxation when a London Exchange Office was created contemporary with improved London banking facilities

(Sect. 2.5 and Fig. 3.10), which did much to 'to lessen the charge and clamour of the waggons'. The cash transfer problem nevertheless persisted.[11]

The 1670s was also a period of administrative innovation. The 1671 assessment-style subsidy prompted revaluation of real property in many parts of the country and provided a basis for future land taxes, especially in the post-Fire City (Sect. 3.3.2). The administrative delayeringand better rewarding of officialdom, provided for in 1670s legislation (Sect. 3.3.3), prompted a move away from the traditional rotation of inexperienced tax-collectors whereby every man of all but the poorest means was expected to do his duty to parish, town or borough. In Bristol, the rotation of collectors and assessors slowed markedly (Table 3.5), a little less so in Kent. In the City of London, although rotation of collectors continued, only individuals with greater local administrative experience could now take such roles (Fig. 3.14). Similar changes probably led to improved collection nationally.

The Revolution led to major European engagements with ambitious supply needs, which required excise, customs and land taxes as well as several fiscal expedients and considerable debt to meet them. Land taxes were often much heavier at 4s/£ than before, and they became effectively permanent, at least until their 1963 abolition. The Financial Revolution boosted the state's ability to fund itself, but the locally administered land tax remained the largest levy until 1714 and a major supply source thereafter.[12] Considerable attention is given to this period because despite their success, land taxes are tainted in the literature by widespread and unjust descriptions of amateurism (Sect. 1.2) and their 'hodge-podge of amateur and local officials.'[13] Such views are misplaced and similar governance structures continued to be essential throughout the eighteenth century and indeed to recent times.[14] Post-revolutionary promptings from Commons and Treasury stakeholders were more regular than ever before, and officials in London and elsewhere were held to account (Sect. 4—preamble and Sect. 5.1) and were criticised in the most candid terms. It is argued here that such criticism and promptings far from indicating failure, as some authors have argued, indicated success.[15] This was a sound assuranceprocess where remote stakeholders had good intelligence and could challenge failure. However, much of the innovation to handle the challenges of the heavy post-revolutionary tax burdens took place locally.

In the 1690s, new national taxes were added to local administrative workloads. In urban areas in particular, there were higher fiscal burdens for both taxpayers and administrators with: poor rates, scavenger rates, highway rates and other local taxes (Sect. 4—preamble). Uncertainties around the quota-less land tax of the mid-1690s generated numerous taxpayer appeals and reduced tax effectiveness. Urban areas were notorious for taxpayer morbidity, mobility, mortality and poverty, and the problems of tax collection with so many of such 'poor, dead, and gone' had been identified in the metropolis since the 1640s (Sect. 3.1.3). The 1690s presented an even greater urban challenge than elsewhere (Sect. 4.1) particularly as the growth of tax on cities had increased faster than in most rural areas. Ward's account of the period after 1688 is one of administrative decay once initial taxpayer enthusiasm for the Revolution had subsided.[16] Unfortunately, Ward's arguments are substantially flawed because they are based on non-comparable data (Sect. 5.1), and he mistakes problem identification and solution for systems collapse. What has been identified in this study is that the years after 1688 witnessed administrative improvement involving delegation, empowerment, process simplification (Sect. 4.3), the deployment of more experienced officials (particularly at collector level—see Sect. 4.4 and in the clerk's office Sect. 4.5.3), a practical choice of taxpayer (Sect. 4.2a) and a further move away from personal to real estate taxation. Personal taxation was bedevilled by legitimate volatility and illegitimate concealment, both of which led to constant appeal. Real estate taxation provided a much more reliable basis of charge for a quota tax (Sect. 3.1). To avoid missing the local tax quota because of problems of the non-paying 'poor, dead, and gone', the simple if 'irregular' expedient of quota overassessmentwas adopted in Bristol and London (Sect. 4.2b). Another simple expedient was not to risk missing the quota, because of non-payment risk, by omitting from charge those least likely to pay. The poorest occupiers would either be exempted or their landlords would be taxed directly (London: Fig. 4.1 and Table 4.4; Bristol: Fig. 4.3, Fig. 4.4 and Table 4.3). Obsolete parts of legislative demands, including the supply of duplicates to the Exchequer, were dispensed with or adapted in London and Bristol to meet contemporary needs (Sect. 5.3). Increasing numbers of government staff and corporate earnings could be taxed to relieve burdens elsewhere (Sect. 4—preamble). Eighteenth-century administration coped with disruption during the second decade (Sect. 5.2) and established effective and regular process routines in all case study areas (Sect. 5.4) capable of delivering predictable supply, even if the ambitious quarterly deadlines required by statute could not always be met because of seasonal financial cycles.

The seventeenth century saw considerable fiscal experimentation to support a militarised state, but it was the taxes that could best exploit flows of economic value or cashflows in a measured way, which were most successful. The ancient customs, the new excises and land taxes triumphed, whereas: polls, subsidies, the fifteenth and tenth and hearth taxes all fell away. If the tax base of the subsidy was far too narrow and too optional to capture incomes from new forms of wealth, the fifteenth and tenth too slight, then the hearth tax was too arbitrary and insensitive. Land tax survived crisis in 1733, but it was the excise which became the major fiscal force of the later eighteenth century because it could readily be adjusted to best tap commercial supply chains. As lightly taxed non-landed forms of wealth increased, there was simply no political will to increase land taxes by a further revaluation or increase from a four-shilling rate, to capture the large increase in land values of the late eighteenth century and beyond.[17] Nevertheless, land taxes still represented a hefty 13% of national taxation at Redemption in 1798, when landowners could buy out future liability for a hefty lump sum.[18] Kent, London and Bristol had all benefitted hugely from urbanisation, trade and commercial growth, as well as the development of a militarised state including Medway naval facilities and opportunities for employment in their majesties' service, but had paid their full share of taxation in the huge expansion of the revenues of the English and British state.

Until the 1640s, England's taxation punched below its economic weight in Europe. It had a commercialised economy but few effective fiscal tools capable of exploiting it. Because of England's isolation from European conflict, there was insufficient revenue need and its ancient tax forms remained static, difficult to reform and ineffectually targeted the wealthy few who could effectively self-assess. They would never raise significant supply. Civil War provided the substantial and urgent supply need, and a sufficiently protracted period, to develop new workable tax structures that could target commercial value flows, not rich individuals, and could spread the burden, in the case of the excise, or spread the charge in the case of the land tax. Parliament required significant sums of money and needed supporters, enemies and neutrals alike to pay up and developed fiscal forms to achieve that. Such forms once developed were ideally suited to funding the post-Restoration state's trade wars and post-revolutionary continental conflicts. Excises, land taxes and a revitalised customs were simply far better targeted taxes than anything before them. Customs and land taxes were the two primary levies between 1643 and 1714 when excise overtook them both.[19] International commercial competition, assisted by a growing population and rising consumer demand, created the very fiscal opportunities to supply and maintain sea and land forces.

It has been argued here that the main drivers of successful English taxation in the seventeenth century were not, as some have claimed, a more willing people or a more coercive government, although Parliamentary authority was an essential prerequisite. Parliamentary authority was useless without effective means of supply. The mid-century critical success factors for the land taxes were the development of competent local governance, which had developed since the late sixteenth century, a commercialised economy, which generated taxable cashflows, and a protracted period for legislative development. The commercialisation of land meant that in many parts of the country annual real estate values could be readily appraised and tax levied by capable people with local knowledge and sensitivity. Such taxing opportunities were more widely available in the South and East, both in terms of land ownership structures and skills, which partly explains the skewed quotas of land taxation.[20] If rent was paid, tax could be deducted, thus shifting the immediate burden from taxpayer to landlord, somewhat diffusing any fiscal discomfort. Most tax would be paid by the middling or better sort of occupier, whose location was known, who were less mobile and whose possessions could be seized in case of non-payment. By the mid-seventeenth century, people had more valuable goods in their homes, stock in their shops and warehouses, and stock or crop in their fields, which made ancient tax powers of distraint more powerful than ever, particularly when such seizure was often a public act and meant social disgrace. Improved wagon technology and better roads allowed the considerable sums raised in coin to be remitted to London, a process which in itself could be partly replaced by the development of paper transaction facilities. Good local governance had been developing for decades before 1643, but could now be applied to great effect in raising national taxation which through intelligent legislation, distributed in printed form, provided local administrators with clear deadlines and targets. The state's stakeholder role in the process could be exercised through elected MPs or more straightforwardly by Treasury or Parliament, calling commissioners and receivers to account.

Local tax administration was part of a remarkable coordinated national effort stretching across ten thousand parishes and was reliant on 'the delegation of central authority to men of quite humble status across thousands of parishes'.[21] Officials often understood the tax business extremely well and were demonstrably intolerant of error and failure. If the post-1688 fiscal-military state had more bureaucrats than before, it was wholly reliant for its success on the delegation of authority to and participation of such men, who far outnumbered them. They were supported by increasingly experienced and capable clerks, receivers and collectors particularly after 1700. Their effective tax-gathering in reliably delivering supply gave confidence to investors in government debt. The scale of the post-revolutionary effort and the success achieved should not be underestimated, as thousands of local governors authorised, by signatures, and seals, tens of thousands of officials to assess and gather weighty taxes from hundreds of thousands of citizens year in and year out. Just a few of them are commemorated in the text and index here. A coordinated national effort was required and expected from every official involved with the knowledge that many others, known and unknown, near and far, up and down the land would also play their part for the state. During their inaugural meeting each and every tax year, on a date set by statute, thousands of punctual and capable commissioners up and down the land received their copies of the statute and laid their local plans, as collectively they set out to tax the nation.[22]

Notes

1. Martin Daunton, *Trusting Leviathan: The Politics of Taxation in Britain, 1799–1914* (Cambridge: Cambridge University Press, 2007), 'Chapter I, Trust, collective action and the state', p. 1*ff.* See also Blanton and Fargher, *Collective Action in the Formation of Pre-modern States.*
2. Graham, *Corruption Party and Government*, p. 21, which follows Brooks, 'Public Finance and Political Stability', p. 284: 'The Land Tax thus stands as the antithesis of the Excise'.
3. Tilly, 'Reflections on the History of European State Making', p. 42; See Graham, '*Corruption, Party and Government*', p. 229.
4. See Ward, *The English Land Tax*, p. 164ff.

5. There are various methods of calculation. The National Archives Currency converter would suggest 37% (accessed 16 February 2018).
6. Noting Ginter's doubts that not all named as tenants or occupiers were anything of the kind, *A Measure of Wealth*, pp. 46–47.
7. E.g. 1671 Kentish land tax commissioner and future Chancellor Heneage Finch comments already cited above.
8. Ormrod et al., 'City and Countryside Revisited', Figs. 3 and 5, p. 15*ff.*
9. Wrightson, *English Society*, p. 21; Hindle, *The State and Social Change*; Innes, 'The Domestic Face of the Military-Fiscal State'.
10. E.g. Everitt, *The Community of Kent*, Chapter 5.
11. CTB, vol. 2, 5 June 1667, p. 8.
12. Rolling basis for the period after the Glorious Revolution after Beckett, 'Land Tax or Excise', Table 2. In some individual years land tax was not the largest tax.
13. Brewer, *The Sinews of Power*, pp. 100–101.
14. Daunton, *State and Market in Victorian Britain*, p. 83.
15. Ward, *The English Land Tax*, especially Chapters 3–5.
16. *The English Land Tax*, Chapter 4.
17. Although, it is noteworthy that after 1745, freeholders would only be entitled to vote if they were assessed for the Land Tax.
18. Lee Soltow, 'The Land Tax Redemption Records, 1798–1963', *The Economic History Review*, vol. 35, 1982, pp. 427–433.
19. Beckett, 'Land Tax or Excise', Table 2.
20. Gerald E. Aylmer, *The Crown's Servants: Government and Civil Service Under Charles II, 1660–1685* (Oxford: Oxford University Press, 2002). Table 4.2 shows both a Restoration and 1625–1642 civil service drawn 50%+ from the South-East and c. 75% residing there.
21. Hindle, *The State and Social Change*, p. 16.
22. With intentional allusion to Benedict Anderson, *Imagined Communities: Reflections on the Origin and Spread of Nationalism* (London: Verso, 1983).

Bibliography

Archives

Kent History and Library Centre (KHLC), London Metropolitan Archives (LMA), Bristol Record Office (BRO), and The National Archives (TNA).

Primary Manuscript Sources

The National Archives

SP 28—Commonwealth Exchequer Papers:

SP 28/157–160 and 234, Kent, Various Dates; SP 28/162–170, London, Middlesex, and Metropolitan London, Various Dates; SP 28/192, Hampshire, Hertfordshire, Huntingdonshire; SP 28/193, Leicestershire, Lincolnshire, London, Middlesex 1642–1643; SP 28/197, Derbyshire—Kent, with Strays from Buckinghamshire, Lancashire, Lincolnshire, and Surrey, Various Dates.

High-Collectors Records of the Commonwealth and Protectorate (Kent):

1. Upper Scray: Anthony Webb, TNA: E179/128/678; Joshua Pix, TNA: E179/128/679; William Catlett, TNA: E179/128/685;
2. Aylesford South: William Polehill, TNA: E179/128/681-2 and E179/249/20;
3. Aylesford North: Edward Whitton, TNA: E179/128/672;
4. Lower Scray: John Rabson, TNA: 179/128/680;
5. Shepway: Thomas Rooke, TNA: E179/249/16 and SP 28/158-60;
6. Sutton-at-Hone: Robert Joseph, TNA: SP 28/159 and 259.

Land Tax Duplicates

S. Pierpoint, *The Success of English Land Tax Administration 1643–1733*, Palgrave Studies in the History of Finance,
https://doi.org/10.1007/978-3-319-90260-9

Kent: E182/430 (1694–1697)-E182/436 (1731–1733); London and Middlesex: E182/594 (1689)-E182/604 (1733–1737); Bristol TNA: E182/837 (1689–1692)-E182/842 (1730–1734).

E179 Database at TNA. http://www.nationalarchives.gov.uk/e179/, Various Material.

Kent History and Library Centre

Kent Commissioners' Resolves, KHLC: Q/C/Tc2.

Wingham Commissioners' Minute Books, KHLC: Sa/ZO3 and KHLC: Q/C/Tc1/1.

New Romney

- Assessments: KHLC: NR/RTi1 12/7/1648; KHLC: NR/RTa/9-28; 1662–1690.
- Land Tax Assessments: KHLC: NR/RTa/2.

Lydd

- Assessments: KHLC: Ly/9/3-15 and KHLC: NR/ZLy1 (1663–1680).

Land Tax, Assessments and Related Material.

- St. Augustine Lathe, East and West: KHLC: CKS/Q/CT1-213.
- Thanet (Margate/Broadstairs): KHLC: EK/1453/01.
- New Romney Land Tax Assessments: KHLC: NR/RTa9-31 and KHLC: NR/RTL/2/6-67ff; Assessors' Warrants: KHLC: NR/RTL/1/3-18 1724ff; Collectors' Warrants: KHLC: NR/RTL/1/19-21.

Land Tax Commissioners' Receipts

- St. Augustine Lathe, East: KHLC: Q/C/Tc11.
- St. Augustine Lathe, West: KHLC: Q/C/Tc12.
- New Romney: KHLC: NR/RTL/4/1-37ff.

London Metropolitan Archives

Chamberlain's Audit Papers: LMA: COL/CHD/LA/02/various.

Parish and Ward Assessments and Related Material: LMA: COL/CHD/LA/03/various.

Bristol Record Office

Commissioners' Minutes: BRO: F/Tax/M/2 (Restoration); BRO: F/Tax/M/3 (1689–1698); BRO: 04798 (1696–1720); BRO: 09374 (1721–1748).

Tax Assessments: BRO: F/Tax/A/1-4/ Various Parishes (Restoration Assessments); BRO: F/Tax/A/7-25/ Various Parishes (Post-revolutionary Taxes to 1702); BRO: F/LT/ Various Parishes (Post-revolutionary Land Tax).

Other Taxes: BRO: HWR—Highway Rate; BRO: LSR—Lamp and Scavenger Rates; BRO: PR/ Various Parishes—Poor Rates; BRO: WT—Window and House Tax.
Audit Papers: BRO: F/AU/1.

Databases

Keene, Derek. *Metropolitan London in the 1690s: Four Shillings in the Pound Aid, 1693–1694; for the City of London, the City of Westminster, and Metropolitan Middlesex.* 1966. Database. The UK Data Service. Persistent Identifier: 10.5255/UKDA-SN-3497-1. https://discover.ukdataservice.ac.uk.

Primary Online Sources

Ancestry.co.uk. *London, England, Land Tax Records 1692–1932* [Database Online]. London: Printed in Association with the London Metropolitan Archives. 2011. https://www.ancestry.co.uk/.

Bristol and Avon Family History Society. *Index to the Bristol Burgess Book Volumes 1 to 21 1557–1995.* www.bafhs.org.uk.

Hearth Tax Online. Centre for Hearth Tax Research, University of Roehampton, London. http://www.hearthtax.org.uk/communities/kent/.

History of Parliament (HoP)—British Political, Social & Local History. http://www.historyofparliamentonline.org/.

KASMI, Kent Archaeological Society Monumental Inscriptions. Churchyard Monumental Inscriptions. http://www.kentarchaeology.org.uk.

Kent Archaeological Society Database of Individuals. http://www.kentarchaeology.org.uk.

Lang, R.G. (ed.). *Two Tudor Subsidy Rolls for the City of London, 1541 and 1582.* London, 1993, pp. xv–lxxvii. British History Online. http://www.british-history.ac.uk/london-record-soc/vol29/xv-lxxvii.

O'Brien, Patrick K. and Hunt, Philip A. 'Data Prepared on English Revenues, 1485–1815.' European State Finance Database. http://www.esfdb.org/.

old.cumberbatch.org, 'The Descendants of Joshua Cumberbatch'. http://old.cumberbatch.org/images/Images/CumberbatchOfBarbados.pdf.

Old Maps—The Online Repository of Historic Maps. http://www.old-maps.co.uk.

People in Place Project. *London Marriage Duty Assessment 1695.* London, 2011. British History Online. http://www.british-history.ac.uk/no-series/london-marriage-duty/1695.

Three Decks—Warships in the Age of Sail, Naval History Web Resource. http://www.threedecks.org.

Printed Primary Sources

Anon. *A Letter to a Freeholder on the Late Reduction of the Land Tax to One Shilling in the Pound, by a Member of the House of Commons*. London: Printed for J. Peele, 1732.

Anon. *Land Tax at 4s in the Pound Paid by England & Wales in 1702, & 1744, Proportion'd and Compar'd by 513 Parts, According to ye No. of Members of Parliament, and ye Square Miles in Each County: Also ye Members Sent, & Land Tax Paid by Scotland*. London, 1745. Eighteenth Century Collections Online. Gale. Cambridge University Library, BL. Harleian 4226ff. 15–16.

Cary, John. *An Essay on the State of England in Relation to Its Trade, Its Poor, and Its Taxes, for Carrying on the Present War Against France*. Bristol: W. Bonny, 1695.

Cobbett, William. *Cobbett's Parliamentary History of England: From the Norman Conquest, in 1066 to the Year 1803*, vols. 1–12. London: T.C. Hansard, 1806–1820.

Corporation of London Records Office. *London Rate Assessments and Inhabitants Lists in Guildhall Library and the Corporation of London Records Office*. London: Library Committee, Corporation of London, 1968.

Department for Constitutional Affairs. *Tax Appeals: A Guide to Appealing Against Decisions of the Inland Revenue on Tax and Other Matters*. http://webarchive.nationalarchives.gov.uk/20060820083451/hmrc.gov.uk/leaflets/tax-appeals.pdf.

Graunt, John. *Natural and Political Observations Mentioned in a Following Index, and Made Upon the Bills of Mortality*. Printed by Tho: Roycroft, for John Martin, James Allestry, and Tho: Dicas, at the Sign of the Bell in St. Paul's Church-yard, 1662.

Owen, Robert, and Robert Dale Owen. *Letterpress The Crisis; or, The Change from Error and Misery to Truth and Happiness*. London, J. Eamonson, Gray's Inn Road, 1833.

Parliamentary Select Committee of 1821, Session 23 January to 11 July 1821, vol. viii, pp. 5–169, *Reports from Committees (5). Militias; Receivers General; Malt; Royal Burghs; Ireland: etc.* 'Report from the Select Committee of the Duties of the Receivers General of Land and Assessed Taxes.'

Petty, William. *A Treatise of Taxes & Contributions, Shewing the Nature and Measures of Crown Lands, Assessments, Customs, Poll-Money, Lotteries, Benevolence, Penalties, Monopolies, Offices, Tythes, Raising of Coins, Harth-Money, Excize, etc*... Printed for N. Brooke, at the Angel in Cornhill, 1662.

Smart, John at the Town-Clerk's-Office, London. *Tables of Compound Interest at the Same Rates. Whereby the Amount or Present Value of Any Sum of Money, or Any Annuity, or Other Yearly Payment, &c. for Any Number of Years, Not Exceeding One Hundred, Is Readily Found*. London. Publisher: Printed by

H. Meere, at the Black-Fryar in Black Fryars, and Sold by S. Crouch, at the Corner of Popes-Head-Alley in Cornhill, 1707.

Smart, John of Guildhall. *A Scheme of the Proportions the Several Counties in England Paid to the Land Tax in 1693, and to the Subsidies in 1697, Compared with the Number of Members They Send to Parliament*. London, 1698.

Smart, John of Guildhall. *Tables of Time Calculated for Two Hundred Years Vizt. The XVII. and XVIII. Centuries: To which are Added Mr. Flamsteed's Table of the Equation of Natural Days, and Other Usefull Tables*. London, 1702. Eighteenth Century Collections Online. Gale. Cambridge University Library.

Smart, John of Guildhall. *Tables of Interest, Discount, Annuities, &c: First Published in the Year 1724*. London, 1726. Eighteenth Century Collections Online. Gale. Cambridge University Library.

Smart, John of Guildhall. *A Short Account of the Several Wards, Precincts, Parishes, &c. in London*. London, 1742. Eighteenth Century Collections Online. Gale. Cambridge University Library.

Smart, John of Guildhall. *Tables of Simple Interest and Discount at 3, 4, 5, 6, 7, 8, 9, and 10l. Per Cent. Per Ann. Also Tables of Compound Interest at the Same Rates*. London, 1707. Eighteenth Century Collections Online. Gale. Cambridge University Library.

Stow, John. *A Survey of London. Reprinted from the Text of 1603*. Edited by C.L. Kingsford. John Stow's Survey, Reprinted from the 1603 Edition. British History Online. http://www.british-history.ac.uk/no-series/survey-of-london-stow/1603.

Strype, John. *A Survey of the Cities of London and Westminster*. London, 1720. Published Online November 2007 by hriOnline. https://www.hrionline.ac.uk/strype/figures.shtml.

Secondary Sources

Acemoglu, Daron. 'Politics and Economics in Weak and Strong States', *Journal of Monetary Economics*, vol. 52, 2005, pp. 1199–1226.

Acemoglu, Daron, and James A. Robinson. *Why Nations Fail: The Origins of Power, Prosperity and Poverty*. London: Profile Books, 2012.

Alexander, James M.B. 'The Economic and Social Structure of the City of London, c.1700.' PhD Thesis, London School of Economics, 1989.

Allen, Robert C. *Enclosure and the Yeoman*. Oxford: Clarendon Press, 1992.

Allen, Robert C. 'Economic Structure and Agricultural Productivity in England', *European Review of Economic History*, vol. 3, 2000, pp. 1–25.

Allen, Robert C. 'Progress and Poverty in Early Modern Europe', *Economic History Review*, vol. 56, 2003, pp. 403–443.

Allen, Robert C. *The British Industrial Revolution in Global Perspective, New Approaches to Economic and Social History*. Cambridge: Cambridge University Press, 2009.

Allen, Robert C. 'Why the Industrial Revolution was British: Commerce, Induced Invention, and the Scientific Revolution', *Economic History Review*, vol. 64, 2011, pp. 357–384.

Allen, Robert C., and Jacob Weisdorf. 'Was There an "Industrious Revolution" Before the Industrial Revolution? An Empirical Exercise for England, c.1300–1800', *Economic History Review*, vol. 64, 2011, pp. 715–729.

Anderson, Benedict. *Imagined Communities: Reflections on the Origin and Spread of Nationalism*. London: Verso, 1983.

Andrewes, Jane. 'Industries in Kent', in Michael Zell (ed.). *Early Modern Kent 1540–1640*. Kent County Council. Woodbridge: Boydell Press, 2000, pp. 105–140.

Archer, Ian W. 'The Burden of Taxation on Sixteenth-Century London', *Historical Journal*, vol. 44, 2001, pp. 599–627.

Archer, Ian W. 'The Government of London, 1500–1650', *London Journal*, vol. 26, 2001, pp. 19–28.

Ashley, Maurice. *Financial and Commercial Policy Under the Cromwellian Protectorate*. Oxford: Oxford University Press, 1934.

Aylmer, Gerald E. *The State's Servants: The Civil Service of the English Republic, 1649–1660*. London: Routledge & Kegan Paul, 1973.

Aylmer, Gerald E. *The Crown's Servants: Government and Civil Service Under Charles II, 1660–1685*. Oxford: Oxford University Press, 2002.

Baggs, A.P., and R.J.E. Bush. 'Parishes: Hinton St. George', in R.W. Dunning (ed.). *A History of the County of Somerset: Volume 4*. London, 1978, pp. 38–52, British History Online. http://www.british-history.ac.uk/vch/som/vol4/.

Bailey, Joanne. 'Favoured or Oppressed? Married Women, Property and 'Coverture' in England, 1660–1800', *Continuity and Change*, vol. 17, no. 3, 2002, pp. 351–372, 352

Barsky, Robert B., and Jeffrey A. Miron. 'The Seasonal Cycle and the Business Cycle', *Journal of Political Economy*, vol. 97, 1989, pp. 503–534.

Beaven, Alfred B. *Bristol Lists. Municipal and Miscellaneous. Compiled by the Rev. A.B. Beaven*. British Library, Historical Print Edition, 1899.

Beaven, Alfred P. 'Fathers of the City', in *The Aldermen of the City of London Temp. Henry III—1912*. London, 1908, pp. 250–254. British History Online. http://www.british-history.ac.uk/no-series/london-aldermen/hen3-1912/.

Beckett, John V. 'Local Custom and the "New Taxation" in the Seventeenth and Eighteenth Centuries: The Example of Cumberland', *Northern History*, vol. 12, 1976, pp. 105–126.

Beckett, John V. *Local Taxation National Legislation and the Problems of Enforcement*. Dorchester: Bedford Square Press, 1980.

Beckett, John V. *Coal and Tobacco: The Lowthers and the Economic Development of West Cumberland, 1660–1760*. Cambridge: Cambridge University Press, 1981.

Beckett, John V. 'Land Tax or Excise: The Levying of Taxation in Seventeenth- and Eighteenth-Century England', *English Historical Review*, vol. 100, 1985, pp. 285–308.

Beckett, John V. 'Land Tax Administration at the Local Level 1693–1798', in Michael Turner and Dennis Mills (eds.). *Land and Property: The English Land Tax 1692–1832*. Gloucester: Alan Sutton, 1986, pp. 161–179.

Blanton, Richard, and Lane Fargher. *Collective Action in the Formation of Pre-modern States*. New York: Springer, 2008.

Bonney, Richard (ed.). *Economic Systems and State Finance*. Oxford: Oxford University Press, 1995.

Bonney, Richard (ed.). *Rise of the Fiscal State in Europe, c.1200–1815*. Oxford: Oxford University Press, 1999.

Boulton, Jeremy. *Neighbourhood and Society: A London Suburb in the Seventeenth Century*. Cambridge Studies in Population, Economy and Society in Past Time. Cambridge: Cambridge University Press, 1987.

Bower, Jacqueline. 'The Kent Yeoman in the Seventeenth Century', *Archaeologia Cantiana*, vol. 14, 1994, pp. 149–163.

Boxer, Charles Ralph. 'Brazilian Gold and British Traders in the First Half of the Eighteenth Century', *Hispanic American Historical Review*, vol. 49, 1969, pp. 454–472.

Braddick, Michael J. *Parliamentary Taxation in 17th-Century England. Local Administration and Response*. The Royal Historical Society Studies in History. Woodbridge: Boydell Press, 1994.

Braddick, Michael J. *The Nerves of the State: Taxation and the Financing of the English State 1558–1714*. Manchester: Manchester University Press, 1996.

Braddick, Michael J. 'The Early Modern English State and the Question of Differentiation from 1550 to 1700', *Comparative Studies in Society and History*, vol. 38, 1996, pp. 92–111.

Braddick, Michael J. *State Formation and Social Change in Early Modern England, c.1550–1700*. Cambridge: Cambridge University Press, 2000.

Braddick, Michael J. 'Fiscal Transformation and Political Compliance: England, 1550–1700', *Illes I Imperis*, vol. 13, 2010, pp. 21–37.

Brewer, John. *The Sinews of Power: War, Money and the English State*. London: Unwin Hayman, 1989.

Brewer, John. 'Revisiting "The Sinews of Power"', in Aaron Graham and Patrick Walsh (eds.). *The British Fiscal-Military States, 1660–c.1783*. Abingdon: Routledge, 2016, pp. 27–34.

Brewer, John, and Eckhart Hellmuth (eds.). *Rethinking Leviathan: The Eighteenth-Century State in Britain and Germany*. Oxford: Oxford University Press, 1999.

Broadberry, Stephen, Bruce M.S. Campbell, Alexander Klein, Mark Overton, and Bas van Leeuwen. *British Economic Growth, 1270–1870*. Cambridge: Cambridge University Press, 2015.

Broadberry, Stephen, Bruce M.S. Campbell, Alexander Klein, Mark Overton, and Bas van Leeuwen. *Rethinking England's Economic Past*.https://www2.warwick.ac.uk/fac/soc/economics/research/centres/eri/bulletin/2010-11-1/broadberry/, *Warwick University, 15 November 2010. Accessed 12 January 2017*.

Brooks, Christopher. 'The Agrarian Problem in Revolutionary England', in Jane Whittle (ed.). *Landlords and Tenants in Britain, 1440–1660, Tawney's Agrarian Revolution Revisited*. Woodbridge: Boydell Press, 2013, pp. 183–199.

Brooks, Colin. 'Public Finance and Political Stability: The Administration of the Land Tax, 1688–1720', *Historical Journal*, vol. 17, 1974, pp. 281–300.

Brunton, Douglas, and Donald H. Pennington. *Members of the Long Parliament*. London: Allen & Unwin, 1954.

Bush, Henry. *Bristol Town Duties: A Collection of Original and Interesting Documents*. Bristol, 1828. British History Online. http://www.british-history.ac.uk/no-series/bristol-duties.

Cannan, Edwin. *The History of Local Rates in England*. London: Longmans, Green, and Co., 1896.

Carlos, Ann M., and Larry Neal. 'Women in the City: London 1720–1725', 200 XIV International Economic History Congress, 21–25 August 2006, Helsinki, Finland. http://www.helsinki.fi/iehc2006/papers3/Carlos.pdf. Accessed 24 April 2017.

Chalklin, Christopher W. *Seventeenth-Century Kent: A Social and Economic History*. London: Longmans, 1965.

Champion, Justin A. *London's Dreaded Visitation: The Social Geography of the Great Plague in 1665*, no. 31. London: Historical Geography Research Monograph, 1995.

Chandaman, Cecil D. *English Public Revenue 1660–1688*. Oxford: Clarendon Press, 1975.

Clark, Gregory. A Review of Leandro Prados de la Escosura (ed.). *Exceptionalism and Industrialization: Britain and Its European Rivals, 1688–1815*. Cambridge: Cambridge University Press, 2004. *Journal of Economic History*, vol. 66, 2006, pp. 833–834.

Clark, Gregory. *A Farewell to Alms: A Brief Economic History of the World*. Princeton: Princeton University Press, 2007.

Clement, Catharina. 'Political and Religious Reactions in the Medway Towns of Rochester and Chatham During the English Revolution, 1640–1660.' PhD Thesis, Canterbury Christchurch University, 2013.

Cnossen, Sijbren. *Excise Systems: A Global Study of the Selective Taxation of Goods and Services*. Baltimore: John Hopkins University Press, 1977.

Coates, Ben. 'The Impact of the English Civil War on the Economy of London, 1642–1650.' PhD Thesis, University of Leicester, 1997.

Coates, Ben. *The Impact of the English Civil War on the Economy of London, 1642–50*. Farnham, Surrey: Ashgate Publishing, 2004.

Coffman, D'Maris. 'The Fiscal Revolution of the Interregnum: Excise Taxation in the British Isles, 1643–1663.' PhD Thesis, University of Pennsylvania, 2008.

Coffman, D'Maris. 'Towards a New Jerusalem: The Committee for Regulating the Excise, 1649–1653', *English Historical Review*, vol. 128, 2013, pp. 1418–1450.

Coffman, D'Maris. *Excise Taxation and the Origins of Public Debt*, Palgrave Studies in the History of Finance. Basingstoke: Palgrave Macmillan, 2013.

Coffman, D'Maris, Adrian Leonard, and Larry Neal (eds.). *Questioning Credible Commitment: Perspectives on the Rise of Financial Capitalism*. Cambridge: Cambridge University Press, 2013.

Coleby, Andrew M. *Central Government and the Localities: Hampshire 1649–1689*. Cambridge: Cambridge University Press, 1987.

Colley, Linda. *Britons: Forging the Nation 1707–1837*. New Haven: Yale University Press, 1992.

Conway, Stephen, and Rafael Torres Sanchez (eds.). *The Spending of States; Military Expenditure During the Long Eighteenth Century: Patterns, Organisations and Consequences, 1650–1815*. Saarbrucken: LIT Verlag, 2011.

Coxe, William. *Memoirs of the Life and Administration of Sir Robert Walpole, Earl of Orford*, vol. 2. London, 1800.

Crafts, Nicholas F.R. *British Economic Growth During the Industrial Revolution*. Oxford: Oxford University Press, 1985.

Cummins, Neil, Morgan Kelly, and Cormac Ó Gráda. 'Living Standards and Plague in London, 1560–1665', *Economic History Review*, vol. 69, 2016, pp. 3–34.

Dale, Thomas Cyril. *The Inhabitants of London in 1638*. London: Centre for Metropolitan History, 1931. British History Online. http://www.british-history.ac.uk/no-series/london-inhabitants/1638/.

Daunton, Martin. *Trusting Leviathan: The Politics of Taxation in Britain, 1799–1914*. Cambridge: Cambridge University Press, 2007.

Daunton, Martin. *State and Market in Victorian Britain: War, Welfare and Capitalism*. Woodbridge: Boydell Press, 2008.

Daunton, Martin. 'The Politics of British Taxation, from the Glorious Revolution to the Great War', in Bartolomé Yun-Casalilla and Patrick K. O'Brien, with Francisco Comín Comín (eds.). *The Rise of Fiscal States: A*

Global History, 1500–1914. Cambridge: Cambridge University Press, 2012, pp. 111–144.

Davison, Anne. 'The Agrarian Economy of Romney Marsh and Its Hinterland, with Special Reference to the Knatchbull Estate, c.1730–90.' PhD Thesis, Canterbury Christchurch University, 2011.

De Krey, Gary S. *A Fractured Society, The Politics of London in the First Age of Party, 1688–1715*. Oxford: Clarendon Press, 1985.

De Krey, Gary S. 'Player, Sir Thomas (d. 1672)', *Oxford Dictionary of National Biography*. Oxford University Press, 2004; Online Edition, January 2008. http://www.oxforddnb.com/view/article/22363.

De Vries, Jan. *The Industrious Revolution: Consumer Behavior and the Household Economy, 1650 to the Present*. New York: Cambridge University Press, 2008.

De Vries, Jan, and Ad van der Woude. *The First Modern Economy. Success, Failure, and Perseverance of the Dutch Economy, 1500–1815*. Cambridge: Cambridge University Press, 1997.

Dickson, Peter G.M. *The Financial Revolution in England. A Study in the Development of Public Credit 1688–1756*. London: Macmillan, 1967.

Dietz, Frederick C. *English Public Finance 1558–1641*. London: Cass, 1964.

Doolittle, I.G. 'Government Interference in City Elections 1714–1716', *Historical Journal*, vol. 24, no. 4, 1981, pp. 945–948.

Dowell, Stephen. *A History of Taxation and Taxes in England*, vol. II. London: Longmans, Green & Co., 1884.

Eales, Jacqueline, and Andrew Hopper (eds.). *The County Community in Seventeenth-Century England and Wales*. Hatfield: University of Hertfordshire Press, 2012.

Erickson, Amy Louise. 'Married Women's Occupations in Eighteenth-Century London', *Continuity and Change*, vol. 23, no. 2, 2008, pp. 267–307.

Evans, John T. *Seventeenth-Century Norwich: Politics, Religion and Government, 1620–1690*. Oxford: Clarendon Press, 1979.

Everitt, Alan. *The Community of Kent and the Great Rebellion 1640–1660*. Leicester: Leicester University Press, 1966.

Fine, Selma Evelyn. 'Production and Excise in England, 1643–1825.' Unpublished PhD Dissertation, Radcliffe College, 1937.

Finlay, Roger. *Population and Metropolis: The Demography of London 1580–1650, Cambridge Geographical Studies*. Cambridge: Cambridge University Press, 2009.

Finlay, Roger and Beatrice Shearer. 'Population Growth and Suburban Expansion', in A.L. Beier and Roger Finlay (eds.). *London 1500–1700: The Making of the Metropolis*. London: Longman, 1986, pp. 37–59.

Fletcher, Anthony. *A County Community in Peace and War: Sussex 1600–1660*. London and New York: Longman, 1975.

Fletcher, Anthony. *Reform in the Provinces: The Government of Stuart England.* London: Yale University Press, 1986.

Floud, Roderick, and Deirdre Nansen McCloskey (eds.). *The Economic History of Britain Since 1700: 1700–1860.* Cambridge: Cambridge University Press, 1994.

Fox, Christine M. *A History of Bassishaw Ward: c.1200–c.1600.* London: eBook Partnetrship.com, 2014.

Fritschy, Wantje. *Public Finance of the Dutch Republic in Comparative Perspective. The Viability of an Early Modern Federal State (1570s–1795).* Leiden: Koninklijke Brill, 2017.

Gauci, Perry. *Emporium of the World: The Merchants of London 1660–1800.* London: Hambledon Continuum, 2007.

Gentles, Ian. *The English Revolution and the Wars in the Three Kingdoms, 1638–1652.* Harlow: Pearson Longman, 2007.

George, Edwin, and Stella (Assisted by Roger H. Leech). *Bristol Probate Inventories Part 2: 1657–1689*, vol. LVII. Bristol: Bristol Record Society Publications, 2005.

Gibson, Jeremy. *The Hearth Tax and Other Later Stuart Tax Lists and the Associated Oath Rolls.* Birmingham: Federation of Family History Societies, 1985.

Gibson, Jeremy, Mervyn Medlycott, and Dennis Mills. *Land and Window Tax Assessments*, Second Edition. Birmingham: Federation of Family History Societies, 1998.

Ginter, Donald E. *A Measure of Wealth, The English Land Tax in Historical Analysis.* London: Hambledon Press, 1992.

Glass, David V. 'Introduction', *London Inhabitants Within the Walls 1695.* London Records Society, 1966. British History Online. http://www.british-history.ac.uk.

Goldie, Mark. 'The Unacknowledged Republic: Officeholding in Early Modern England', in Tim Harris (ed.). *The Politics of the Excluded, c.1500–1850.* Basingstoke: Palgrave, 2007, pp. 153–194.

Graham, Aaron. *Corruption, Party, and Government in Britain, 1702–1713.* Oxford: Oxford University Press, 2015.

Graham, Aaron, and Patrick Walsh. 'Introduction', in Aaron Graham and Patrick Walsh (eds.). *The British Fiscal-Military States, 1660–c.1783.* Abingdon: Routledge, 2016, pp. 3–25.

Graham, Aaron, and Patrick Walsh (eds.). *The British Fiscal-Military States, 1660–c.1783.* Abingdon: Routledge, 2016.

Grigg, David B. 'The Land Tax Returns', *Agricultural History Review*, vol. 11, 1963, pp. 82–94.

Grover, Richard. 'The Land Tax in East Kent: A Study in Land Ownership and Occupation with Special Reference to the Methodological Implications of the

Land Tax Assessments.' M.Phil. Thesis, University of Kent at Canterbury, 1980.

Grover, Richard. 'Early Land Tax Assessments Explored (2) Kent and Sussex', in Michael Turner and Dennis Mills (eds.). *Land and Property: The English Land Tax 1692–1832*. Gloucester: Alan Sutton, 1986, pp. 204–218.

Habakkuk, H. John. 'English Landownership, 1680–1740', *Economic History Review*, vol. 10, 1940, pp. 2–17.

Hammer, Michael, and James Champy. *Reengineering the Corporation: A Manifesto for Business Revolution*. London: Nicholas Brealey Publishing, 1993.

Harding, Vanessa. 'The Population of London, 1550–1700: A Review of the Published Evidence', *London Journal*, vol. 15, 1990, pp. 111–128.

Harding, Vanessa. 'City, Capital, and Metropolis: The Changing Shape of Seventeenth-Century London', in Julia F. Merritt, (ed.). *Imagining Early Modern London: Perceptions and Portrayals of the City from Stow to Strype, 1598–1720*. Cambridge: Cambridge University Press, 2001, pp. 117–143.

Harding, Vanessa. 'Controlling a Complex Metropolis, 1650–1750: Politics, Parishes and Powers', *London Journal*, vol. 26, no. 1, 2001, pp. 29–37.

Harris, Peter. *Income Tax in Common law Jurisdictions. From the Origins to 1820*. Cambridge: Cambridge University Press, 2006.

Hart, Marjolein 't. 'The Devil or the Dutch? Holland's Impact on the Financial Revolution in England, 1643–1694', *Parliaments, Estates and Representation*, vol. 11, 1991, pp. 39–52.

Hasted, Edward. *A Historical and Topographical Survey of the County of Kent*, 12 vols. Canterbury, 1797–1801. British History Online. http://www.british-history.ac.uk/search/series/survey-kent.

Hayton, David, Eveline Cruickshanks, and Stuart Handley. *The House of Commons, 1690–1715*, vol. 1, The History of Parliament. Cambridge: Cambridge University Press, 2002.

Hill, Christopher. *Some Intellectual Consequences of the English Revolution*. London: Weidenfeld and Nicolson, 1980.

Hindle, Stephen. *The State and Social Change in Early Modern England c.1550–1640*. Basingstoke: Palgrave, 2000.

Hipkin, Stephen. 'Tenant Farming and Short-Term Leasing on Romney Marsh, 1587–1705', *Economic History Review*, vol. 53, 2000, pp. 646–676.

Hipkin, Stephen. 'Property, Economic Interest and the Configuration of Rural Conflict in Sixteenth and Seventeenth-Century England', *Socialist History*, vol. 23, 2003, pp. 67–88.

Hipkin, Stephen. 'The Structure of Landownership and Land Occupation in the Romney Marsh Region, 1646–1834', *Agricultural History Review*, vol. 51, 2003, pp. 69–94.

Hoffman, Philip T., and Kathryn Norberg (eds.). *Fiscal Crises, Liberty, and Representative Government 1450–1789*. Stanford: Stanford University Press, 1994.

Holman, John R. 'Orphans in Pre-industrial Towns—The Case of Bristol in the Late Seventeenth Century', *Local Population Studies*, vol. 15, 1975, pp. 40–44.

Holmes, Clive. Review of Anthony Fletcher, *A County Community in Peace and War: Sussex 1600–1660*. London and New York: Longman, in *American Historical Review*, vol. 82, 1977, pp. 632–633.

Hoppit, Julian. 'Review of the Sinews of Power: War Money and the English State by John Brewer and War and the Economy in the Age of William III and Marlborough by D.W. Jones', *Historical Journal*, vol. 33, 1990, pp. 248–250.

Hoppit, Julian. 'Patterns of Parliamentary Legislation, 1660–1800', *Historical Journal*, vol. 39, 1996, pp. 109–131.

Hoppit, Julian. *A Land of Liberty: England 1689–1727*. Oxford: Oxford University Press, 2000.

Hoppit, Julian. 'Compulsion, Compensation and Property Rights in Britain, 1688–1833', *Past and Present*, vol. 210, 2011, pp. 93–128.

Hoppit, Julian. Unpublished Paper Given at the British Fiscal States Conference, Oxford, 2013, Cited in Graham and Walsh, *The British Fiscal-Military Sates*, p. 9.

Hoppit, Julian. 'Political Power and British Economic Life, 1650–1870', in Roderick Floud, Jane Humphries, and Paul Johnson (eds.). *The Cambridge Economic History of Modern Britain, volume 1, 1700–1870*. Cambridge: Cambridge University Press, 2014, pp. 344–367.

Horsefield, J. Keith. 'The Beginnings of Paper Money in England', *Journal of European Economic History*, vol. 6, 1977, pp. 117–133.

Hoskins, William G. 'The Rebuilding of Rural England, 1570–1640', *Past and Present*, vol. 4, 1953, pp. 44–59.

Hoyle, Richard. 'Tenure and the Land Market in Early Modern England: Or a Late Contribution to the Brenner Debate', *Economic History Review*, vol. 43, 1990, pp. 1–20.

Hoyle, Richard. 'Who Owned Earls Colne at the End of the Eighteenth Century? Or, How to Squeeze More Value Out of the Land Tax', *The Local Historian*, vol. 41, 2011, pp. 267–277.

Hughes, Edward. *Studies in Administration and Finance, 1558–1825 with Special Reference to Salt Taxation in England*. Manchester: Manchester University Press, 1934.

Hughes, T.B. *A Report of the Case of the King Against Bebb and Others, Assignees of Castell and Powell, Bankrupts, on an Extent; with Explanatory Notes*. London: A. Strahan for J. Butterworth, 1811.

Hull, Felix. *Guide to the Kent County Archive Office*. Maidstone: Kent County Council, 1958.

Hunt, Margaret. 'Time-Management, Writing, and Accounting in the Eighteenth-Century English Trading Family: A Bourgeois Enlightenment', *Business and Economic History* (2nd ser.), vol. 18, 1989, pp. 150–159.

Hutton, Ronald. *The Restoration: A Political and Religious History of England and Wales 1658–1667*. Oxford: Clarendon Press, 1985.

Innes, Joanna. 'The Domestic Face of the Military-Fiscal State: State and Society in Eighteenth-Century Britain', in Lawrence Stone (ed.). *An Imperial State at War: Britain 1688–1815*. Abingdon: Routledge, 1994, pp. 96–127.

Johnson, James. *Transactions of the Incorporation of the Poor in the City of Bristol During a Period of 126 Years*. Bristol, 1826.

Jones, Edward. 'Index to Records Called, the Originalia and Memoranda on the Lord Treasurer's Remembrancer's Side of the Exchequer', by Edward Jones of the Inner Temple. London 1743. Gale ECCO, Print Editions, 16 June 2010.

Jones, P.E., and A.V. Judges. 'London Population in the Late Seventeenth Century', *Economic History Review*, vol. 6, 1935, pp. 45–63.

Keene, Derek. 'A New Study of London Before the Great Fire', *Urban History Yearbook*, 1984, pp. 11–21.

Keene, Derek. 'Changes in London's Economic Hinterland as Indicated by Debt Cases in the Court of Common Pleas', in James A. Galloway (ed.). *Trade, Urban Hinterlands and Market Integration c.1300–1600*. London: Centre for Metropolitan History Working Papers Series No. 3, 2000, pp. 59–81.

Kennedy, William. *English Taxation 1640–1799*. London: G. Bell & Sons Ltd, 1913; Elibron Classics Edition, 2007.

Kent, Joan. 'The Centre and the Localities: State Formation and Parish Government in England, Circa 1640–1740', *Historical Journal*, vol. 38, 1995, pp. 363–404.

Kerridge, Eric. *Trade and Banking in Early Modern England*. Manchester: Manchester University Press, 1988.

Kim, Jongchul. 'How Modern Banking Originated: The London Goldsmith-Bankers' Institutionalisation of Trust', *Business History*, vol. 53, 2011, pp. 939–959.

Lambert, Tim. *A Brief History of Bristol*. http://www.localhistories.org.

Landau, Norma. *The Justices of the Peace, 1679–1760*. Berkeley: University of California Press, 1984.

Langelüddecke, Henrik. '"I finde all men & my officers all soe unwilling": The Collection of Ship Money, 1635–1640', *Journal of British Studies*, vol. 46, 2007, pp. 509–542.

Langford, Paul. *The Excise Crisis: Society and Politics in the Age of Walpole*. Oxford: Clarendon Press, 1975.

Langford, Paul. *Walpole and the Robinocracy*. Cambridge: Chadwyck-Healey, 1986.

Livock, D.M. (ed.). *City Chamberlain's Accounts in the Sixteenth and Seventeenth Centuries*, vol. XXIV. Bristol: Bristol Record Society Publications, 1966.

Loft, Philip. 'Political Arithmetic and the English Land Tax in Reign of William III', *Historical Journal*, vol. 56, 2013, pp. 321–343.

Mann, Michael. *The Sources of Social Power, 1, of a History of Power from the Beginning to AD 1760*. Cambridge: Cambridge University Press, 1986.

Martin, Isaac W., Ajay K. Mehrotra, and Monica Prasad. 'The Thunder of History: The Origins and Development of the New Fiscal Sociology', in Isaac W. Martin, Ajay K. Mehrotra, and Monica Prasad (eds.). *The New Fiscal Sociology: Taxation in Comparative and Historical Perspective*. Cambridge: Cambridge University Press, 2009, pp. 1–27.

Martin, J.M. 'Landownership and the Land Tax Returns', *Agricultural History Review*, vol. 14, 1966, pp. 96–103.

McCusker, John J., and Kenneth Morgan (eds.). *The Early Modern Atlantic Economy*. Cambridge: Cambridge University Press, 2000.

McGrath, Patrick. *Records Relating to the Society of Merchant Venturers of the City of Bristol in the 17th Century*, vol. XVII. Bristol: Bristol Record Society Publications, 1952.

McGrath, Patrick. *Merchants and Merchandise in Seventeenth-Century Bristol*, vol. XIX. Bristol: Bristol Record Society Publications, 1955.

McK Clough, T.H. (ed.). *The 1712 Land Tax Assessments and the 1710 Poll Book for Rutland*, no. 7. Rutland: RLHRS Occasional Publication, 2005.

Merritt, Julia F. (ed.). *Imagining Early Modern London: Perceptions and Portrayals of the City from Stow to Strype, 1598–1720*. Cambridge: Cambridge University Press, 2001.

Merry, Mark, and Philip Baker. 'Family and Household in Late 17th Century London', The Economic History Society Annual Conference, University of Reading, 1 April 2006. Centre for Metropolitan History/Birkbeck. Online. https://core.ac.uk/download/pdf/72487.pdf.

Mills, Dennis. 'Appendix. Survival of Early Land Tax Assessments', in Michael Turner and Dennis Mills (eds.). *Land and Property: The English Land Tax 1692–1832*. Gloucester: Alan Sutton, 1986, pp. 219–234.

Minchinton, Walter E. 'Bristol: Metropolis of the West in the Eighteenth Century: The Alexander Prize Essay', *Transactions of the Royal Historical Society*, vol. 4, 1954, pp. 69–89.

Mingay, Gordon E. 'The Land Tax Assessments and the Small Landowner', *Economic History Review*, vol. 17, 1964, pp. 381–388.

Monod, Paul K. *Jacobitism and the English People, 1688–1788*. Cambridge: Cambridge University Press, 1983.

Monson, Andrew, and Walter Scheidel. *Fiscal Regimes and the Political Economy of Early States.* An International Conference Sponsored by the Department of Classics, Stanford University, and the Alexander Hamilton Center, New York University, 2010.

Monson, Andrew, and Walter Scheidel (eds.). *Fiscal Regimes and the Political Economy of Premodern States.* Cambridge: Cambridge University Press, 2015.

Muldrew, Craig. *The Economy of Obligation: The Culture of Credit and Social Relations in Early Modern England.* Basingstoke: Palgrave, 1998.

Muldrew, Craig. 'Wages and the Problem of Monetary Scarcity in Early Modern England', in Jan Lucassen (ed.). *Wages and Currency: Global Comparisons from Antiquity to the Twentieth Century.* Bern: Peter Lang, 2007, pp. 391–410.

Musgrave, Richard A. 'Schumpeter's Crisis of the Tax State: An Essay in Fiscal Sociology', *Journal of Evolutionary Economics*, vol. 2, 1992, pp. 89–113.

Neal, Larry. 'The Finance of Business During the Industrial Revolution', in Roderick Floud and Deirdre Nansen McCloskey (eds.). *The Economic History of Britain Since 1700: 1700–1860.* Cambridge: Cambridge University Press, 1994, pp. 151–181.

North, Douglass, and Barry Weingast. 'Constitutions and Commitment: The Evolution of Institutions Governing Public Choice in Seventeenth-Century England', *Journal of Economic History*, vol. 49, 1989, pp. 803–832.

O'Brien, Patrick K. 'The Political Economy of British Taxation, 1660–1815', *Economic History Review*, vol. 41, 1988, pp. 1–32.

O'Brien, Patrick K. 'The Nature and Historical Evolution of an Exceptional Fiscal State and Its Possible Significance for the Precocious Commercialization and Industrialization of the British Economy from Cromwell to Nelson', *Economic History Review*, vol. 64, 2011, pp. 408–446.

O'Brien, Patrick K., and Philip A. Hunt. 'The Rise of a Fiscal State in England, 1485–1815', *Historical Research*, vol. 66, 1993, pp. 129–176.

O'Brien, Patrick K., and Philip A. Hunt. 'The Emergence and Consolidation of Excises in the English Fiscal System Before the Glorious Revolution', *British Tax Review*, vol. 1, 1997, pp. 35–58.

Ormrod, David. *The Rise of Commercial Empires England and the Netherlands in the Age of Mercantilism, 1650–1770.* Cambridge: Cambridge University Press, 2003.

Ormrod, David, James M. Gibson, and Owen Lyne. *City and Countryside Revisited. Comparative Rent Movements in London and the South-East, 1580–1914.* Studies in Economics 1117, Working Paper. Department of Economics, University of Kent, 2011.

Ormrod, Mark, Margaret Bonney, and Richard Bonney (eds.). *Crises, Revolutions and Self-sustained Growth in European Fiscal History, 1130–1830.* Stamford: Paul Watkins Publishing, 1999.

Overton, Mark, Jane Whittle, Darron Dean, and Andrew Hann. *Production and Consumption in English Households 1600–1750*. London: Routledge, 2004.

Palma, Nuno. 'Anglo-Portuguese Trade and Monetary Transmission During the Eighteenth Century, Nova School of Business and Economics'. Current Draft (Incomplete, Not for Circulation): October 21, 2012. http://www.histproj.org/completed/PALMA_Anglo-Portuguese%20Trade%20And%20Monetary%20Transmission%20During%20the%20Eighteenth%20Century.pdfBoxer.

Peacey, Jason T. 'Livesay, Sir Michael, First Baronet (1614–1665?)', *Oxford Dictionary of National Biography*. Oxford University Press, 2004.

Pearl, Valerie. *London and the Outbreak of the Puritan Revolution. City Government and National Politics 1625–1643*. Oxford: Oxford University Press, 1964.

Pearl, Valerie. 'Change and Stability in Seventeenth-Century London', *London Journal*, vol. 5, 1979, pp. 3–34.

Petersen, E. Ladewig. 'From Domain State to Tax State, Synthesis and Interpretation', *Scandinavian Economic History Review*, vol. 23, 1975, pp. 115–148.

Phelps Brown, Henry, and Sheila V. Hopkins. *A Perspective of Wages and Prices*. London: Methuen, 1981.

Pierpoint, Stephen J. 'The Importance of Direct Taxation to the Fiscal-Military State in Early Modern Britain', *Structural Change and Economic Dynamics*, vol. 40, 2017, pp. 13–28.

Pierpoint, Stephen J. 'The Administration of the Land Tax in England 1643–1733.' PhD Thesis, University of Cambridge, 2017

Pincus, Stephen, and James A. Robinson. 'What Really Happened During the Glorious Revolution?' in Sebastian Galiani and Itai Sened (eds.). *Institutions, Property Rights and Economic Growth: The Legacy of Douglass North*. Cambridge: Cambridge University Press, 2014.

Pincus, Stephen, and James A. Robinson. 'Challenging the Fiscal-Military Hegemony: The British Case', in Aaron Graham and Patrick Walsh (eds.). *The British Fiscal-Military States*, 2016, pp. 229–261.

Porter, Roy. *London a Social History*. London: Hamish Hamilton, 1994.

Prak, Maarten, and Jan Luiten van Zanden. 'Tax Morale and Citizenship in the Dutch Republic', in Oscar Gelderblom (ed.). *The Political Economy of the Dutch Republic*. Farnham: Ashgate, 2009, pp. 143–166.

Pressnell, Leslie S. 'Public Monies and the Development of English Banking', *Economic History Review*, vol. 5, 1953, pp. 378–397.

Price, Jacob. 'Sheffeild v. Starke: Institutional Experimentation in the London Maryland Trade c.1696–1706', in R.P.T. Davenport-Hines and Jonathan Liebenau (eds.). *Business in the Age of Reason*. London: Frank Cass & Company, 1987, pp. 19–39.

Ralph, Elizabeth. *Guide to the Bristol Archives Office*. Bristol: Bristol Corporation, 1971.

Ralph, Elizabeth, and Mary E. Williams. *The Inhabitants of Bristol in 1696*, vol. XXV. Bristol: Bristol Record Society Publications, 1968.

Rappaport, Steve. *Worlds Within Worlds: Structures of Life in Sixteenth-Century London*. Cambridge: Cambridge University Press, 1989.

Reddaway, Thomas Fiddian. *The Rebuilding of London After the Great Fire*. London: Jonathan Cape, 1940.

Richardson, David. *Eighteenth-Century Slave Trade to America, Vol. 1 1698–1729*. Bristol: Bristol Record Society Publications XXXVIII, 1986.

Roberts, Stephen K. 'State and Society in the English Revolution', in Michael J. Braddick (ed.). *The Oxford Handbook of the English Revolution*. Oxford: Oxford University Press, 2015, pp. 294–311.

Roseveare, Henry. *The Financial Revolution, 1660–1760*. London: Longman, 1991.

Russell, Conrad. Review of Michael J. Braddick. *Parliamentary Taxation in 17th-Century England. Local Administration and Response*. Woodbridge: Boydell Press, 1994. *Economic History Review*, vol. 110, 1995, pp. 1215–1216.

Sacks, David H. *The Widening Gate: Bristol and the Atlantic Economy, 1450–1700*. Berkeley: University of California Press, 1991.

Sandford, Cedric. *Why Tax Systems Differ; A Comparative Study of the Political Economy of Taxation*. Bath: Fiscal Publications, 2000.

Schumpeter, Joseph A. 'The Crisis of the Tax State', *International Economic Papers*, vol. IV, 1954, pp. 5–38. http://www.scribd.com/doc/36871535/Schumpeter-The-Crisis-of-the-Tax-State.

Sharpe, Kevin. *The Personal Rule of Charles I*. London: Yale University Press, 1992.

Shaw-Taylor, Leigh. 'The Rise of Agrarian Capitalism and the Decline of Family Farming in England in England', *Economic History Review*, vol. 65, 2012, pp. 26–60.

Shaw-Taylor, Leigh, and E. Anthony Wrigley. 'Occupational Structure and Population Change', in Roderick Floud, Jane Humphries, and Paul Johnson (eds.). *The Cambridge Economic History of Modern Britain, Volume I, 1700–1870*. Cambridge: Cambridge University Press, 2014, pp. 53–88.

Slack, Paul. 'Government and Information in Seventeenth-Century England', *Past and Present*, vol. 184, 2004, pp. 33–68.

Sng, Tuan-Hwee. Review of Bartolomé Yun-Casalilla and Patrick K. O'Brien, with Francisco Comín Comín (eds.). *The Rise of Fiscal States a Global History 1500–1914*. Cambridge: Cambridge University Press, 2012; *Economic History Review*, vol. 67, 2014, pp. 310–311.

Soltow, Lee. 'The Land Tax Redemption Records, 1798–1963', *Economic History Review*, vol. 35, 1982, pp. 427–433.

Spence, Craig. *London in the 1690s: A Social Atlas.* London: Centre for Metropolitan History, 2000.

Spence, Craig. 'Computers, Maps and Metropolitan London in the 1690s', in Matthew Woollard (ed.). *New Windows on London's Past: Information Technology and the Transformation of Metropolitan History.* Glasgow: Association for History and Computing, 2000.

Stephens, William B. *The Seventeenth-Century Customs Surveyed. William Culliford's Investigation of the Western Ports 1682–84.* Farnham: Ashgate, 2012.

Stephenson, Judy Z. '"Real" Wages? Contractors, Workers, and Pay in London Building Trades, 1650–1800', *Economic History Review*, 2017. http://dx.doi.org/10.1111/ehr.12491.

St. John Adcock, Arthur (ed.). *Wonderful London*, vol. I. London: Amalgamated Press, 1926–1927.

Stone, Lawrence. *An Imperial State at War: Britain 1688–1815.* Abingdon: Routledge, 1994.

Storrs, Christopher. *War, Diplomacy and the Rise of Savoy, 1690–1720.* Cambridge: Cambridge University Press, 2000.

Storrs, Christopher (ed.). *The Fiscal-Military State in Eighteenth-Century Europe, Essays in Honour of P.G.M. Dickson*. Farnham: Ashgate, 2009.

Supple, Barry. *Commercial Crisis and Change in England, 1600–42: A Study in the Instability of a Mercantile Economy.* Cambridge: Cambridge University Press, 1959.

Sussman, Nathan, and Yishay Yafeh. 'Institutional Reforms, Financial Development and Sovereign Debt: Britain 1690–1790', *Journal of Economic History*, vol. 66, 2006, pp. 906–935.

Thirsk, Joan, and John P. Cooper (eds.). *Seventeenth-Century Economic Documents.* Oxford: Clarendon Press, 1972.

Tilly, Charles. 'Reflections on the History of European State Making', in Charles Tilly (ed.). *The Formation of National States in Western Europe*. Princeton: Princeton University Press, 1975, pp. 3–83.

Tracy, James D. *The Founding of the Dutch Republic. War, Finance, and Politics in Holland 1572–1588.* Oxford: Oxford University Press, 2008.

Turner, Michael. 'The Land Tax, Land and Property: Old Debates and New Horizons', in Michael Turner and Dennis Mills (eds.). *Land and Property: The English Land Tax 1692–1832. Gloucester: Alan Sutton, 1986*, pp. 1–35.

Turner, Michael, and Dennis Mills (eds.). *Land and Property: The English Land Tax 1692–1832.* Gloucester: Alan Sutton, 1986.

Turner, Michael, John V. Beckett, and Bethanie Afton. *Agricultural Rent in England, 1690–1914.* Cambridge: Cambridge University Press, 1997.

Unwin, Robert W. *Search Guide to the English Land Tax.* Wakefield: West Yorkshire County Records Office, 1986.

Van Bavel, Bas J.P. 'The Organization and Rise of Land and Lease Markets in Northwestern Europe and Italy, c.1000–1800', *Continuity and Change*, vol. 23, no. 1, 2008, pp. 13–53.

Van Zanden, Jan Luiten. 'Early Modern Economic Growth: A Survey of the European Economy 1500–1800', in Maarten Prak (ed.). *Early Modern Capitalism, Economic and Social Change in Europe 1400–1800.* London: Routledge, 2001.

Waddell, Brodie. 'The Politics of Economic Distress in the Aftermath of the Glorious Revolution, 1689–1702', *English Historical Review*, vol. 130, 2015, pp. 318–351.

Ward, William R. 'The Office of Taxes 1665–1798', *Bulletin of the Institute of Historical Research*, vol. 25, 1952, pp. 204–212.

Ward, William R. *The English Land Tax in the Eighteenth Century.* London: Oxford University Press, 1953.

Wennerlind, Carl. *Casualties of Credit: The English Financial Revolution, 1620–1720.* Cambridge, MA: Harvard University Press, 2011.

Whittle, Jane (ed.). *Landlords and Tenants in Britain, 1440–1660, Tawney's Agrarian Revolution Revisited.* Woodbridge: Boydell Press, 2013.

Woodhead, J.R. *The Rulers of London 1660–1689 a Biographical Record of the Aldermen and Common Councilmen of the City of London.* London, 1966. British History Online. http://www.british-history.ac.uk/no-series/london-rulers/1660.

Woollard, Matthew (ed.). *New Windows on London's Past: Information Technology and the Transformation of Metropolitan History.* Glasgow: Association for History and Computing, 2000.

Woolrych, Austin. 'Historical Introduction', in Don M. Wolfe (ed.). *Complete Prose Works of John Milton*, 8 vols. New Haven, CT: Yale University Press, 1953–1958.

Wrightson, Keith. *English Society 1580–1680.* London: Hutchinson, 1982.

Wrigley, E. Anthony. 'A Simple Model of London's Importance in Changing English Society and Economy, 1650–1750', *Past & Present*, vol. 37, 1967, pp. 44–70.

Wrigley, E. Anthony. 'Urban Growth and Agricultural Change: England and the Continent in the Early Modern Period', in E. Anthony Wrigley (ed.). *People, Cities and Wealth: The Transformation of Traditional Society.* Oxford: Blackwell, 1987, pp. 157–193.

Wrigley, E. Anthony, and Roger S. Schofield. *The Population History of England 1541–1871. A Reconstruction.* Cambridge: Cambridge University Press, 1989.

Yun-Casalilla, Bartolomé, and Patrick K. O'Brien With Francisco Comín Comín (eds.). *The Rise of Fiscal States a Global History 1500–1914*. Cambridge: Cambridge University Press, 2012.

Zahedieh, Nuala. *The Capital and the Colonies: London and the Atlantic Economy 1660–1700*. Cambridge: Cambridge University Press, 2010.

Zell, Michael (ed.). *Early Modern Kent 1540–1640*. Kent County Council. Woodbridge: Boydell Press, 2000.

Index

S. Pierpoint, *The Success of English Land Tax Administration 1643–1733*, Palgrave Studies in the History of Finance,
https://doi.org/10.1007/978-3-319-90260-9

C

K

L

M

N

O

U

W

EcoJustice Education for Elementary Classrooms

EcoJustice Education for Elementary Classrooms

Real-World Lessons for a Sustainable Future

Greer Burroughs
Marissa E. Bellino

BLOOMSBURY ACADEMIC
NEW YORK • LONDON • OXFORD • NEW DELHI • SYDNEY

BLOOMSBURY ACADEMIC
Bloomsbury Publishing Inc, 1359 Broadway, New York, NY 10018, USA
Bloomsbury Publishing Plc, 50 Bedford Square, London, WC1B 3DP, UK
Bloomsbury Publishing Ireland, 29 Earlsfort Terrace, Dublin 2, D02 AY28, Ireland

BLOOMSBURY, BLOOMSBURY ACADEMIC and the Diana logo are trademarks of Bloomsbury Publishing Plc

First published in the United States of America 2026

Cover design by Kathi Ha
Cover image © iStock.com/skynesher

Library of Congress Cataloging-in-Publication Data is available

ISBN: HB: 978-1-5381-9753-0
PBK: 978-1-5381-9754-7
ePDF: 979-8-8818-6625-9
eBook: 978-1-5381-9755-4

Typeset by Deanta Global Publishing Services, Chennai, India

For product safety related questions contact productsafety@bloomsbury.com.

To find out more about our authors and books visit www.bloomsbury.com and sign up for our newsletters.

I dedicate this book to the two young men who compel me to keep doing this work, my sons Grant and Garrett, because they deserve a future that allows all people to prosper and live in harmony with the earth.

Greer

To all the teachers, family, and friends who have supported this project and to the future generations that will hopefully benefit from its impact.

Marissa

Companion Website Resources

bloomsbury.pub/ecojustice

There were more materials than we could fit into this book, so please visit our companion website for additional resources, links, and lesson activities. We hope this site aids you in digitally accessing instructional materials presented in the book, building your critical lens on topics and case studies presented, and helps you create engaging EcoJustice lessons for your own classrooms.

Specific resources include:

- Digital versions of K-2 and 3-5 Instructional Materials for each chapter theme
- Mentor texts on EcoJustice topics for K-5 students
- Cloud Institute Education for Sustainability Standards
- United Nations Sustainable Development Goals
- Chapter resources for expanding teaching knowledge
- Pedagogical strategies that support student-centered learning

Contents

Preface

*The ground begins beneath **my** feet*

—Emma, Early Childhood Teacher

The above statement was made by one of our former students during a weekend spent exploring EcoJustice topics and place-based learning. We stood in a circle, barefoot in the grass, acknowledging the people who walked that land before us and celebrating our connection to the Earth when she made the declaration. On its surface it sounds so obvious, of course the ground begins beneath one's feet! But as she elaborated it became clear it was so much more. It was her recognition that she was part of nature and connected to the Earth in ways that also made her responsible. For us, this sentiment became a sort of call to action. The ground does begin beneath our feet, but first we must understand that connection, then we must be willing to take action, to step forward and walk the walk, as stewards for the environment and social justice.

Witnessing the transformation of this young woman, and many others we have worked with over the years, is why we do the work we do. We know that all of us are connected to the Earth, but for many, modern life has led to a loss of this innate understanding. Awareness of our deep connections to nature is the first step in caring for our planet and all living beings. However, valuing this connection is not enough. If we are to protect our Earth and nurture systems that will bring a better quality of life, measured in terms of health and justice, then there is much to be learned. We also understand that our current models of education and teacher preparation don't do enough to foster the connections and develop the knowledge and skills to take action in our own lives and collectively so that we can reach these goals.

Our experience as professors of education in a teacher preparation program has allowed us to see the kinds of courses students are exposed to in our elementary education program. Students take methods courses that reinforce the disciplined nature of learning. They take science and math methods classes together, as if this is the only way to pair these content areas. Social studies is usually addressed in a separate course, disconnected from the other content areas, and students take most of their courses in literacy. And while this is not problematic in and of itself, it is problematic that we never have a space that allows the integrative thinking and synthesis of these subjects. Environmental and social justice issues are at the margins of the content instead of being integrated into all methods and theory courses. Our program is not unique. Most teacher preparation programs follow a similar model and in this way the belief that learning these subjects should happen in isolation is reinforced.

This is part of the problem we are hoping to address with this text. We want to help teachers see beyond the separation of content toward the interconnectedness of content, modeling the way realities of our world show up for people. We also see the need to demonstrate how science and social studies content and learning experiences are places where an education that fosters knowledge, skills, and values to meaningfully care for the Earth and others is possible. A survey we conducted in Spring 2024 with students in our school of education around EcoJustice Education revealed that students don't have well-developed values around social and environmental issues and therefore lack a personal and professional worldview that encompasses a deeper understanding of issues driving environmental degradation and social inequities. However, they did express a deep interest and desire to learn more about how to bring EcoJustice topics into their future classrooms.

Many well-intentioned educators have come before us who have tried and sometimes succeeded in awakening an environmental consciousness in young people through various forms of environmental and place-based education. However, there are a multitude of challenges with the ways environmental education has been introduced to children in schools. First and foremost, because "the environment" is not a subject we think of as a traditional school subject, it is often relegated to science classrooms where the focus becomes only about learning the scientific knowledge that is needed to understand specific environmental phenomena. For example, the climate crisis is typically diagnosed scientifically by looking at carbon emissions, sea levels rising, frequency and intensity of storms, and other indicators we can observe, measure, and track. However, this knowledge must be built upon with an understanding of the inequitable social implications this crisis will bring, a critique of the economic policies that are being offered as solutions, and the ways we are socialized into our role as consumers in a throwaway society, topics typically associated with social studies classrooms. In this brief overview, you can see how the climate crisis subverts the boundaries of the traditional disciplinary structure of school, and so teachers are unsure where it even belongs and thus either teach about it in isolation or don't teach about it at all.

Another shortcoming of formal environmental education is that, as a result of not having a true home in schools, it is often reduced to Earth Day activities or other one-off days that reinforce the message "You can save the Earth if you just . . ." When we fill in the blank with our common-sense answers to this question, recycle, change a lightbulb, ride a bike, plant a tree, reduce plastic—we are not going deep enough to develop an ethic of care and responsibility among young children and we are oftentimes equating environmental care with a form of consumption. Bill Bigelow writes in his powerful essay *How My Schooling Taught Me Contempt for the Earth,*[1] "Recently, I've been questioning what I learned in school about the environment. I've concluded that although there was no explicit ecological curriculum, there was a profound hidden ecological curriculum that taught my classmates and me neglect and even contempt for the Earth." He goes on to acknowledge the lack of place-conscious education his school offered, the way school sent messages that work is only done indoors, an acceptance that the degradation and development of the land are forms of progress, and notes the overall lack of ecological interdependency that was taught—how any notion that our very livelihood is connected to healthy soil, plants, waters, and people was rendered invisible. He ends with this powerful statement:

> The hidden ecological curriculum at Bel-Aire School encouraged students to not-think about the Earth, to not question the system of commodification that turns the world, including the land, into things to be bought and sold. These are not merely curricular omissions, but active processes of moral anesthesia. Poet Adrienne Rich writes in a penetrating line that "lying is done with words, and also with silence." When the curriculum is silent about aspects of life—racism, sexism, global inequality, or the degradation of the Earth—that silence normalizes these patterns, implicitly telling kids, "Hey, nothing to worry about; that's just the way things are, the way they ought to be." And that's the lie.

The silence, mistruths and disconnection that schools have perpetrated on young people when it comes to their relationship with the environment are what compelled us to do more inside and outside of our methods courses. We strongly believe that critical thinking and community and place-based pedagogies play a large role in the development of an EcoJustice consciousness. So, in 2017 we took a group of five pre-service teachers to Lesvos, Greece to learn and serve alongside Lighthouse Relief, an organization working to support refugees fleeing from Syria via Turkey and landing (not always safely) on the shores of the island. Our students met with staff and volunteers learning about their on-the-ground efforts to respond to the dynamic situation by supplying emergency food, water, clothing, and medicine to new arrivals while these now "refugees" navigated the complex road to their transition home at refugee camps.

Lighthouse Relief was simultaneously responding to the ecological impact of the influx of people and material waste that was littering the shores of the island during these years. Everything from clothing, shoes, life jackets, and rafts was washing up on the beaches of Lesvos and needed to be dealt with. Cleanups and upcycling efforts were a part of the response, and our students participated in these tasks, as well as water rescue training and packing backpacks for new arrivals. Documenting the experience through reflective journals and critical dialogues, our students' understanding of the interconnectedness of the systems that caused this socio-environmental crisis to happen in the first place, as well as the international response to the refugee crisis, was expanded. They saw firsthand the relationship between the social and ecological impacts and the role they each played, via their assumptions and the media coverage, in perpetuating the othering of people escaping violence who were labeled "refugees."[2]

After we returned from this experience, we worked with our pre-service teachers on translating their transformative experiences and insights into lessons for young children. They developed lessons alongside the expertise of in-service educators and together created instructional materials that challenged the dominant narratives about refugees, addressed food access and security, and deepened the often surface teaching of reduce, reuse, recycle. It was clear throughout the experience working with just a small group of students that there was a passion in them for EcoJustice lesson development opportunities that had not been ignited in their other learning contexts.

These early experiences provided us with powerful insights and inspired us to develop a comparable model for groups of pre-service teachers. For two years we brought small groups of students to Ecuador where they learned from local food producers and activists, Indigenous communities, and eco-tourism entrepreneurs. The goals for our students were similar to our initial Lesvos experience—to challenge existing assumptions about others by seeing themselves in relationship with the diversity of people and places we learned from, to critically reflect on notions of progress as a result of exporting global capitalist ideologies, and to listen and learn from local experts. Again, we captured our students' experiences via reflection journals and critical dialogue circles, centering their experiences and connections to what we were seeing and learning, and ultimately translated their ideas into elementary classroom lessons.

In 2020, COVID-19 put an abrupt end to our abroad experiences, which proved an opportunity as we were able to create a critical place-based learning experience more locally. We hosted an EcoJustice Professional Development weekend for twelve in-service and pre-service teachers and again incorporated place-based learning experiences with opportunities for critical reflection, meaning-making dialogues, and lesson development. All of the experiences we organized and co-created with our students and teachers have been met with tremendous enthusiasm. These relevant learning experiences challenge assumptions and connect often disparate ideas together to make greater sense of both the social-environmental issues themselves and our role and responsibilities to these issues. We have witnessed the personal transformation in their thinking and engaged them as they asked more complex and critical questions about what they had been taught to believe. They have felt deeper connections to one another, their fellow humans, and the Earth. This has filled them up, given them a stronger sense of purpose as a human and a teacher, and set them on a path toward being the critical educator that children need.

This book is an outgrowth of this collection of experiences, honoring the deep hunger teachers have for this kind of meaningful teaching and learning and the support they seek to integrate socio-environmental topics into their classrooms. We align our work to others who call for education that is grounded in Ecoliteracy, Ecopedagogy, EcoJustice, Environmental Citizenship, Eco-consciousness, Environmental Justice, and Environmental Sustainability Education. In name, what we are offering is not new. What is new is the distillation of critical, interconnected, diverse ways of thinking about common topics—economics, food, water, and land—that are rooted in justice and equity (that we know all teachers value) and then helping teachers align these topics to current social studies and science standards in their elementary classrooms.

What we are offering is in some ways radical. In many places today this type of learning is labeled "indoctrination" and even prohibited. We currently have an administration that is dismantling policies and practices to address environmental protections. In addition, closing the Office of Environmental Justice and External Civil Rights (OEJECR) essentially ends federal government protections or interest for communities that are disproportionately impacted by environmental hazards. Add to this, the Executive Order Ending Racial Indoctrination in K–12 Schooling which denies, "Federal funding sources and streams, including grants or contracts, that directly or indirectly support or subsidize the instruction, advancement, or promotion of gender ideology or discriminatory equity ideology: A) in K–12 curriculum, instruction, programs, or activities."[3] It is understandable that school districts might shy away from learning experiences where students are allowed to question systems that unequally favor some while harming others. However, we have seen how teachers we work with find creative ways to integrate EcoJustice concepts and learning into their teaching while following national and/or state standards.[4] Eventually there will be a new administration in power, with new goals and commitments, and teachers might be freed to address salient issues that impact our nation and prepare the next-generation of students to be part of caring for the Earth, people, and animals that inhabit it. But we cannot sit back and wait for that time. We must begin now, however one's teaching situation allows for.

This book is offered as guidance and a roadmap for in-service and pre-service teachers. By introducing them to EcoJustice Education goals, topics, practices, and support, regardless of where they currently are in their professional journey, we believe this kind of education can be transformative for all.

In this work, it has been our students first, and then the teachers we have worked with, who have confirmed what we thought possible. While there are literally hundreds of students we have taught, we want to thank those who have been part of the journey we began in 2017 and came to call, Learn Globally, Teach Locally. They continue to inspire us as they go into classrooms or adjacent professions and walk the walk.

Notes

1 Bill Bigelow, "How My Schooling Taught Me Contempt for the Earth," *Rethinking Schools* 11, no. 1 (1996): 14–17.

2 Greer C. Burroughs and Marissa E. Bellino, "Nurturing a Global EcoJustice Consciousness among Preservice Teachers through Critical Place-Based Learning," *Journal of Global Education and Research* 8, no. 1 (2024): 34–48.

3 "Ending Radical Indoctrination in K-12 Schooling," *Executive Order, The White House*, January 20, 2025, https://www.whitehouse.gov/presidential-actions/2025/01/ending-radical-indoctrination-in-k-12-schooling/.

4 Marissa E. Bellino and Greer Burroughs, "Developing an EcoJustice Consciousness for Classroom Teachers and their Students," in *Climate Change Education Across Disciplines K-12: New Jersey and Beyond*, ed. L. Madden (New York: Rowman & Littlefield, 2025).

Thank you to:
Serina
Paige
Shannon
Shannon
Marcie

Ellen
Briana
Gaby
Emma
Alex
Hannah
Arabella

Introduction

Chapter Outline

Los Angeles is on fire as we write the opening to this book. The unthinkable has happened as hundreds of thousands of people are displaced, whole communities have been obliterated, and lives have been lost among people and animals. Current damages and economic losses are estimated to be a quarter of a trillion dollars or more as a result of the fast-moving wildfires. How did this happen in the land of eternal sunshine? How did one of the wealthiest states in the richest nation, where some of the most brilliant minds of engineering and technology are found, fall prey to this disaster?

Wildfires such as the California fires of January 2025 are one of the results of a rapidly changing climate. Experts explain that wildfires in the twenty-first century are fundamentally different due to climate changes that have led to drought conditions, high winds, and rising temperatures. John Vaillant, author of *Fire Weather*, explained in an interview with the *Guardian*, "Climate science ain't rocket science. When you make things hotter and drier, they burn more easily."[1]

According to the National Centers for Environmental Information (NCEI), a division of the National Oceanic and Atmospheric Administration (NOAA), there were twenty-seven confirmed weather/climate disaster events in the United States in 2024. Flooding, droughts, severe storms, and wildfires are among the events that cost the United States billions of dollars in 2024 and have been steadily increasing over the last 30 years. The National Centers for Environmental Information, a part of the National Oceanic and Atmospheric Administration, has created an interactive website that tracks the cost of weather and climate-related disasters.[2] The figure below shows weather and climate disaster events that cost over a billion dollars during the past five years.

Shifting patterns in weather brought on by climate change are not the only explanation for the level of destruction seen in California. Some of the phenomena are due to building and land management practices and policies designed to deal with wildfires. As conditions have changed, so too must actions change. Some of this will require new policies based on

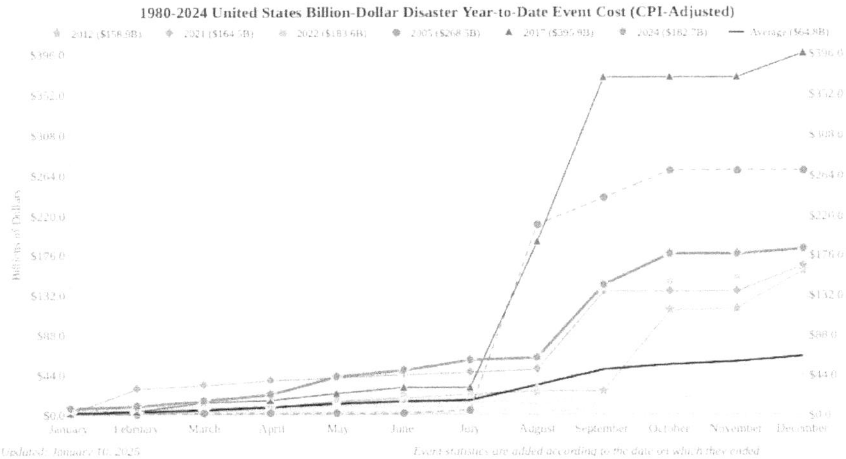

Figure I.1. US billion-dollar weather and climate disaster date (1980–2024). https://www.ncei.noaa.gov/access/billions/

what has been learned, but some of the answers might already exist and are rooted in thousands of years of cultural knowledge and practices among Indigenous communities. Indigenous peoples have used intentional fires, "cultural burns" as a form of land management for thousands of years. The burns have been used to cultivate biodiversity and sustainable growth that make landscapes more resilient.[3] The idea to apply Indigenous knowledge to the wildfire threat has been validated through studies such as one from Stanford University in 2019 that was conducted in conjunction with the US Forest Service and the Yurok and Karuk Tribes. The study found that incorporating traditional techniques into current fire suppression practices could help reduce wildfire risks.[4] It seems that we need to look in new and unexpected places for potential solutions to the climate crisis.

The California fires made headlines due to the large scale of destruction and suffering; however, smaller scale socio-environmental tragedies are playing out all over the country and world. A predominantly Black elementary school in Louisiana is shutting down for the entire 2025–6 school year due to unsafe toxic emission levels released from an adjacent petrochemical factory.[5] The District of Columbia is suing the federal government for allowing decades of sewage, trash, industrial waste, and chemicals to be dumped in the Anacostia River, causing harm to mostly poor and minority communities living near the river.[6] Each of these situations and many others mentioned will need creative responses from civil society, as well as the business and government sectors.

Additionally, data shows that one in every five children in the United States (with Black and Hispanic children at almost twice the risk) lives with food insecurity, unsure where they will get their next meal.[7] Remedies to improve childhood nutrition and to combat hunger must address limited access to healthy and affordable food for all. Addressing this will require innovative solutions that are not likely to come from an administration that worked to restrict access to food assistance programs like the Supplemental Nutrition Assistance Program (SNAP, formerly food stamps) and school meal programs during their first term.[8] Rather, answers might need to come from civil society and the business sector and through the work of creative leaders.

All of these problems are occurring in the midst of another national crisis, which is a crisis of how we receive and process information. As we write today, a good percentage of the American people believe that the new president has restored their freedoms from a government mandate that never actually existed. In his inauguration speech of January 20, 2025, President Trump said, "With my actions today, we will end the Green New Deal, and we will revoke the electric vehicle mandate. . . . In other words, you'll be able to buy the car of your choice." However, there never was a mandate to manufacture or buy electric cars. Rather, the Biden Administration's March 2024 standards called for reductions in auto emissions by setting new guidelines for tailpipes and allowed for varied pathways for auto manufacturers to comply, such as improvements in internal combustion engine vehicles, hybrids, plug-in hybrids, and battery electric vehicles.

The goal of the Biden Administration standards was to reduce US greenhouse gas emissions by 7.2 billion metric tons through 2055, which is about four times the total emissions of the transportation sector as of 2021.[9] Not only would this go a long way toward reducing greenhouse gas emissions in the United States, there were expected public health impacts such as a reduction in heart attacks, aggravated asthma, and decreased lung function. These are health problems that disproportionately impact lower-income Americans who are more likely to live in congested cities,[10] thus making this a social justice issue as well.

Many Americans, however, will never consider these facts. Instead, what they will believe is that their freedom from an intrusive government mandate has been lifted (many will also believe that climate change is not caused by an increase in carbon emissions). We don't fault people for this belief, after all, this is what many news sources will state, and the nation's leader has also told them this is true. This is what concerns us most, that this will become truth and will not be contested through individual actions or demands for policy changes. This inaction will contribute to the continued production of greenhouse gases, the worsening impact of global climate change, and the disproportionate burdens felt by those of lower socioeconomic status and power here in the United States and across the world.

When thinking about the conditions outlined above, the question for us is, what role can and should education play? We believe it is imperative that we teach children to think critically so that they can reach informed decisions. We must teach them that they cannot rely on a single news source (or even worse, social media) to provide the information needed to make those informed decisions. Rather, we need to develop critical literacy skills among young people so that their first reaction to *any* news or information is to conduct a fact-checking investigation of their own. Students need to learn how to detect bias, to evaluate the credibility of a source, to seek out and analyze multiple sources, and to draw conclusions based on the synthesis of credible information.

We must also develop a sense of possibility among young people to think outside the box and look for answers in unexpected places. We believe that the pedagogical practices and Pillars for EcoJustice Education that we lay out in the next chapter of this book are part of the answer for what education can and must do to lay the groundwork for new solutions. Without this, we are in danger of ignoring the famous warning by Albert Einstein "We cannot solve our problems with the same thinking we used when we created them."[11] Therefore we are also advocating for an education that questions the status quo from an informed and critical perspective. Before we can move forward, though, it is important to look at how we got to where we are today and how practices and policy have impacted classrooms for centuries, and in turn society.

A Historical Overview of Trends in Education and the Impacts

The way that the American story is learned contributes to the development of individual identity, as well as the nature of the dominant culture. Sociologists recognize education as one of the major agents of socialization into one's society, and educators and lawmakers have long understood this role and thus trends in our schools reflect goals for society. Throughout the book, we explore how content in social studies and science is typically taught in elementary school and what the implications of this are. For now, though, we offer a brief overview of some of the major shifts in order to demonstrate how education has been used in the United States to meet goals defined by those in power, and thus changed the nature of schooling for the masses.

In the very beginning, education in the colonies was focused on preserving and spreading Christianity. The Massachusetts Colony passed The Law of 1647, also known as the Old Deluder Satan Act, to ensure that public education would exist to prevent "old deluder, Satan, to keep men from the knowledge of the Scriptures."[12] The Common School Movement of the 1800s called for free, universal, nonsectarian public schools; however, throughout the nineteenth century schooling continued to focus on basic literacy and moral development. In the largely agrarian society, no further learning was required for the vast majority of the population.

The late nineteenth and early twentieth century saw a shift in societal needs as cities grew and immigration surged. The goal of education in much of the country then became to "Americanize" the children of new immigrants. The most extreme manifestation of the "Americanization" goal was the residential schools that Native American children were forced to attend in order to be assimilated into the dominant culture. During the Progressive Era (1901–29), many sought to bring change to American society, which was expressed in reforms to labor laws, treatment of prisoners, and of course, education. During this period, John Dewey introduced the notion that schools are laboratories of democracy and therefore students should be active participants in their learning. Dewey also believed that schools should prepare students for real life and therefore be relevant to their lives. In this way, elements of a traditional system of memorization, recitation, or writing were replaced with more hands-on and experiential learning.

In 1957 when the Soviet Union launched Sputnik, a panic was felt in the United States that the Soviets were winning in the space and arms race. This led to calls for math and science education to be strengthened in order to keep up with the Soviet Union. The US Congress responded by passing the National Defense Education Act, which provided funding for more science and technical education, as well as low-interest loans for university studies. These actions once again dramatically changed the focus of American education with more individuals pursuing higher education and the primacy of math and science as a form of national defense against Cold War enemies.

The Civil Rights Movement of the 1960s and 1970s led to further changes to American schools with calls for more equity in education. This led to laws requiring funding to schools in low-income communities, better access for persons with disabilities, gender equality, and the rise of ethnic studies and multicultural approaches in education.

Since 2002, the 21st Century Skills Movement in the United States has called on schools to "align classroom environments and core subjects with 21st century skills. . . . To successfully face rigorous higher-education coursework and a globally competitive work environment. By combining both skills and content, educators can impart the expertise required for success in today's world."[13] In essence, the current goal of education in the United States is to prepare the next workforce for the competitive global market. This can also be understood as a means to grow the US economy and theoretically raise the standard of living for workers and increase the purchasing power of the consumer.

In the last decade, American education has experienced another wave of pressure in the form of culture wars. Battles over the inclusion of creationism in science texts have re-emerged alongside attacks on teaching about climate change. In states such as Florida, the words "climate change" don't even appear in the elementary or middle school education standards.[14] In 2021, a focus on the teaching of Critical Race Theory in K-12 schools took center stage. The fear, it seemed, was that schools were teaching children (white children) to feel bad about their race and to stir up discord in society. Politicians and activists quickly jumped in and in June of 2021, Texas became the first state to enact a law restricting teaching about race in the state's public schools.[15] Parent groups such as Moms for Liberty have also joined the fray, making demands for topics and books to be removed from schools with a particular focus on LGBTQ+ issues and books detailing racism. School boards and state legislatures across the country have enacted policies restricting topics, and thousands of individual administrators and teachers now avoid "controversial topics" out of fear, thereby succumbing to these pressures.

Author and activist Paulo Freire explained in his landmark book, *Pedagogy of the Oppressed*, that education can be a tool to maintain the status quo or be a catalyst for change. What that change looks like depends on *what is taught* and *how it is taught*. Freire wrote that when discourse is absent and the teacher or school is seen as the holder of knowledge and the students passive recipients of information, "the more they [the student] tend simply to adapt to the world as it is and to the fragmented view of reality deposited in them."[16] Therefore, if climate change is not taught, it ceases to be a problem. Similarly, if underlying conditions that lead to inequality are never examined, the myth of meritocracy remains intact. In this way, knowledge and the potential to act on that knowledge is suppressed and many become unwitting participants in the destruction of our Earth and injustice. However, education can also be a liberating force. Freire wrote that, "To surmount the situation of oppression, people must first critically recognize its causes, so that through transforming action they can create a new situation, one which makes possible the pursuit of a fuller humanity." A history of education is not the purpose of this book, but knowing this brief account of our historical arc in education is useful to understand that what is taught in schools doesn't necessarily reflect what is best for individuals, society, or our planet.

What We See in Schools Today

We are each content specialists. Greer has taught social studies and social studies methods of teaching for over 30 years, and Marissa has taught science and science methods of teaching for over 20 years. Additionally, we both have taught courses on sustainability education, urban education, social foundations of education, teacher action research, and critical pedagogy. Our experiences in schools span decades and across K-16 classrooms. Over this time, we have witnessed a narrowing of the elementary school curriculum, with math and language arts dominating. What many teachers are currently required to spend most of the day teaching is often counterintuitive to the needs of the children and is not moving us closer to addressing issues of inequality or climate change. This has left many teachers feeling alienated from their work.

We have spent a lot of time in schools, both as classroom teachers and now as supervisors for pre-service teachers, and we have seen this firsthand. Over and over, we visit schools where our students are placed for practicum and student teaching experiences, in the hopes of seeing a social studies lesson that truly engages a group of learners, or a science lesson that activates the wonder and curiosity of children, and most of the time, we leave with deep disappointment. We often discuss these observations with sadness and frustration, not blaming our pre-service and in-service teachers, but rather the curricular choices being offered, or lack of choice that are foisted upon teachers in schools today. Anecdotally, we have both heard from many students in the last few years that they are afraid to address social justice and climate change topics as new teachers or that they have explicitly been told in field placements by cooperating teachers that it is best not to get caught in the controversy.

When we began teaching, we had a form of academic freedom to create lessons that were developmentally appropriate and culturally responsive to the community of learners in our classrooms. While we know today's teachers are mindful of who is in the room and what their needs are, the outcomes that are being asked of teachers are often limited to reading, writing, and math proficiencies. Outcomes are monitored and measured by technological software that students are engaging with and quantified by standardized tests. As a result, teachers spend much of their time doing uncreative work in the form of drill and kill teaching, practice tests, and other forms of rote teaching in order to prepare students for high-stakes exams.

As a result, K-5 classroom teachers are not often supported in engaging students in the kinds of complex decision-making and critical thinking that we know are good teaching. Social studies and science are often pushed to the margins. On the positive end of the spectrum, students might receive social studies and science instruction for 30–40 minutes a day; however, in many cases this is reduced to once or twice a week, and sometimes an entire marking period (typically 10 weeks) passes with the focus on only one of the subjects, leading to science instruction one marking period and social studies the next. What do we sacrifice in the learning and development of children's hearts, bodies, and minds when we diminish these subjects, disembodying them from interdisciplinary connections and instead focusing on mechanized practice of skills in math and language arts. And what connections to one another and their environments are we severing in young children when we dismember our teaching and their learning experiences from the realities facing their communities?

Let us be clear, we are teachers, we love working with teachers and know that teachers are not to blame for these disconnections. We would never assume that teachers do not know and believe in the ideas we are presenting in this book, or that they do not care about their students' learning and their local communities. But what we do know, from our years of observing classrooms, is that teachers are not given the space and time to bring to life the kind of learning that will lead to sustainable change for the diversity of life on this planet, and that includes humans. Over and over again when we talk to teachers, they speak to us about the ways their time and knowledge are restricted, not valued, and told that the goal of education is to make sure their students do well on tests. Restricting the creativity that teachers can exercise can also lead to teachers restricting their own pursuit of knowledge, especially around critical topics that impact them and their students. In this book, we hope to support teachers in building some of that critical knowledge that is not obviously showing up in existing curriculum and how to align that knowledge to existing national social studies and science standards.

Social Studies and Science Standards

What is the need to consider standards in a book about EcoJustice Education, a field where no standards exist? The simple answer is that we want to make EcoJustice Education accessible and relevant to you in your teaching contexts by aligning instructional materials to national standards for social studies and science. This gives you the rationale with parents, administrators, and other teachers for why you are teaching the topics that you are. The national standards for science and social studies make clear content that should be addressed in elementary school. They also can be used to give teachers confidence that they are still teaching "science" and "social studies." The authors of *Understanding by Design*

Guide to Advanced Concepts in Creating and Reviewing Units[17] Jay McTighe and Grant Wiggins explained their view of standards as

> they focus on outcomes, not curriculum or instruction . . . **educators must translate the Standards into an engaging and effective curriculum** (our emphasis). So, what is the proper relationship between the Standards and curriculum? Consider another analogy with home building and renovation: The standards are like the building code. Architects and builders must attend to them but they are not the purpose of the design. The house to be built or renovated is designed to meet the needs of the client in a functional and pleasing manner—while also meeting the building code along the way.[18]

In this way, we urge teachers to see the standards as the "codes" which must be attended to when planning for student learning, which must be designed to meet the needs of today's students and society. Clearly, the need to save our planet and protect the people and living beings on it should be paramount in planning. Fortunately, the National Council for the Social Studies (NCSS) and Next-Generation Science Standards (NGSS), the national standards for each field, provide the building codes for this type of education, as we will explore next.

Social Studies in Elementary Education

Social Studies is the place in the elementary school curriculum where children learn about the social nature of the communities, state, nation, and world they inhabit. High-quality social studies education should help students obtain the knowledge, skills, attitudes, and perspectives needed to become active, informed, and contributing members of local, state, national, and global communities. The National Council for Social Studies defines the discipline as "the study of individuals, communities, systems, and their interactions across time and place that prepares students for local, national, and global civic life."[19]

Elementary Social Studies covers four main content areas: History and Culture, Geography, Economics, and Government and Civics. State standards across the United States incorporate these four content areas, and most state standards also include the need to develop certain skills among students. Although the field of social studies has become a battleground for what is taught, with arguments over the inclusion of racial or social topics that can make children "uncomfortable" or engender a worldview that is not representative of a child's parents, there is a lot of agreement about the broad content areas of social studies. A brief comparison of a sample from grade 1 standards from the two most populous states in the United States, Texas and California, makes this point. It is noteworthy that these two states also represent differing political ideologies, with majorities in Texas voting Republican in statewide and federal elections, while in California, majorities vote Democratic. It very well may be these political leanings that account for some of the differences stressed under the broad themes. *Note these differences as you examine the table and consider how they might impact the children in classrooms where the standards are applied.*

Table I.1. Comparison of Social Studies Standards in Texas and California for Grade 1

Texas Social Studies Standards for Grade 1[a]	California Social Studies Standards for Grade 1[b]
Students study their relationship to the classroom, school, and community to establish the foundation for responsible citizenship in society.	Students describe the rights and individual responsibilities of citizenship. [Students] understand the rule-making process in a direct democracy and in a representative democracy, giving examples of both systems in their classroom, school, and community.
Students develop concepts of time and chronology by distinguishing among past, present, and future events.	Students know and understand the symbols, icons, and traditions of the United States that provide continuity and a sense of community across time.
Students identify anthems and mottoes of the United States and Texas.	[Students] Identify American symbols, landmarks, and essential documents, such as the flag, bald eagle, Statue of Liberty, US Constitution, and Declaration of Independence, and know the people and events associated with them.
Students create simple maps to identify the location of places in the classroom, school, and community.	Students compare and contrast the absolute and relative locations of places and people and describe the physical and/or human characteristics of places.
Students explore the concepts of goods and services and the value of work.	Students understand basic economic concepts and the role of individual choice in a free-market economy.
Students describe the importance of family customs and traditions and identify how technology has changed family life.	Students describe the human characteristics of familiar places and the varied backgrounds of American citizens and residents in those places.

[a] TEKS Resource System, "Browse Standards," accessed July 2024, https://www.teksresourcesystem.net/module/standards/Tools/Browse?StandardId=237594.

[b] IXL, "California Social Studies Standards—Grade 1," accessed July 2024, https://www.ixl.com/standards/california/social-studies/grade-1.

National Council for the Social Studies

As the largest association of social studies educators in the United States and a provider of curriculum materials and professional development programs, as well as the publisher of four journals and numerous books, the National Council for the Social Studies (NCSS) has a lot of influence over the field. The four main content areas found in state standards for social studies are embedded throughout the NCSS standards. For this reason and the fact that this book is designed to be accessible to teachers throughout the United States, the NCSS standards are used to guide content discussions and lesson plans in this text. Therefore, the NCSS standards will be cited throughout this book to illustrate how naturally the lessons align with the goals of social studies education and build on topics that teachers should already be addressing.

Beyond the content knowledge embedded in the NCSS standards are goals grounded in an inquiry stance. To guide teachers in this process, in 2013 NCSS created the *The College, Career, and Civic Life (C3) Framework for Social Studies State Standards*. In the opening page of the book, the authors make clear the goal for social studies education with the following:

> Students need the intellectual power to recognize societal problems; ask good questions and develop robust investigations into them; consider possible solutions and consequences; separate evidence-based claims from parochial opinions; and communicate and act upon what they learn. And most importantly, they must possess the capability and commitment to repeat that process as long as is necessary.[20]

The C3 Framework proposes four dimensions for teachers to follow to reach the goals stated. The C3 Framework illustrates the emphasis on building skills and a mindset among young learners, such as the need to evaluate evidence in order to develop claims. It should be clear from a review of the C3 Framework Dimensions that students need learning experiences that provide for critical thinking, active and relevant learning experiences.

Science in Elementary Education

Science is the human endeavor to understand how the world works. It is a process, typically nonlinear, where the answer to one scientific inquiry typically leads to another. Where collaboration is at the heart of the endeavor, and scientific knowledge is both stable and dynamic, changing and evolving as new techniques and technologies are invented to study phenomena. It is this very nature of science that makes it challenging to teach in schools and why, in K-12 settings, it is often reduced to a "scientific method" where scientific facts are presented as stable knowledge.

The American Association for the Advancement of Science (AAAS), an international nonprofit organization dedicated to "promoting cooperation among scientists, defending

Table I.2. The NCSS C3 Framework[a]

Dimension 1: Developing Questions and Planning Inquiries	**Dimension 2: Applying Disciplinary Tools and Concepts**	**Dimension 3: Evaluating Sources and Using Evidence**	**Dimension 4: Communicating Conclusions and Taking Informed Action**
Developing Questions and Planning Inquiries	Civics Economics	Gathering and Evaluating Sources	Communicating and Critiquing Conclusions
	Geography History	Developing Claims and Using Evidence	Taking Informed Action

[a] National Council for the Social Studies, College, Career, and Civic Life (C3) Framework for Social Studies State Standards (NCSS Bulletin 113, 2013), https://www.socialstudies.org/standards/c3.

scientific freedom, encouraging scientific responsibility, and supporting science education and outreach" is the world's largest general scientific society. In 1993, they laid the foundation for systemic science education reform with their *Benchmarks for Science Literacy*, organizing knowledge and skills of science literacy that have been influential in shaping K-12 state science standards. According to the AAAS Benchmarks, by the end of their time in school, students should be able to understand and engage in discussions of science issues in the news from a place of deep understanding rather than rote memorization. They also wanted the teaching and learning about science to impart on students an appreciation of the ways that science influences policy as well as foster a critical eye toward public perceptions and support of scientific issues. Finally, the Benchmarks, in honoring the social nature of science, encouraged students to question who historically had power to engage in science endeavors and who has been denied access because of their gender, race, and other identities.[21]

Building off of the work done by AAAS publications like *Science for All* (1989) and the *Benchmarks for Science Literacy* (1993), the Next-Generation Science Standards[22] once again pushed science educators to more intentionally incorporate both the skills and practices that scientists engage in (e.g., asking questions, using models, constructing explanations from evidence) as well as universal concepts that cut across disciplines (e.g., cause and effect, structure and function, patterns). The hope of the NGSS was to transform science education by integrating disciplinary knowledge with applications of scientific concepts in order to enhance science literacy for all students, highlight the real-world applications of science, and develop a lifelong curiosity and wonder about the world around us. Science pedagogy that is aligned with these standards draws heavily on phenomena-based instruction and creates opportunities for students to build upon existing mental models with new information. An integration of the practices, cross-cutting concepts, and disciplinary core ideas (physical science, life science, Earth and space science) are part of the NGSS learning standards and an array of curricular materials have been developed to support these three dimensions of science learning. Thus, most K-5 science classrooms ought to introduce students to core science disciplinary content while developing the habits of mind needed for scientific inquiry through hands-on, relevant, equitable, and accessible science experiences. While the NGSS have not been adopted by all fifty states, twenty states, and the District of Columbia use these standards.[23] Many other states have created their standards in a similar fashion to the NGSS and it is for this reason that we will use these standards throughout the instructional materials presented in the book.[24]

Alignment Across NCSS and NGCC

In this section, we will look at how naturally the discipline of elementary social studies and science complement one another and, frankly, need each other in EcoJustice Education. We will also provide an example of a natural alignment between the two using climate

Table I.3. Comparison of NCSS C3 Framework and the Next-Generation Science Standards Science and Engineering Practices

4 Dimensions of the NCSS C3 Framework	NGSS 8 Science and Engineering Practices
1. **Developing questions** and **planning inquiries**	1. **Asking Questions**
2. Applying **disciplinary concepts** and **tools**	2. Developing and Using **Models** 3. **Planning** and Carrying Out **Investigations** 4. **Analyzing** and **Interpreting Data**
3. **Evaluating sources** and using **evidence**;	5. Using **Mathematics** and **Computational** Thinking 6. **Constructing Explanations** 7. Engaging in Argument from **Evidence**.
4. **Communicating** conclusions and **taking informed action**.	8. Obtaining, Evaluating, and **Communicating** Information.

change as our topic. In the table below, we compare the social studies essential skills and competencies as outlined in the NCSS C3 Framework and the Next-Generation Science Standards Science and Engineering Practices. When looking across the two content areas, we can see the overlap in skills we are working to develop in our students (see Table I.3).

When thinking about science as a discipline that strives to explain and understand phenomena in the natural world and social studies as a discipline that strives to explain and understand phenomena in the social world, we can see how each is but one part of a larger whole that leads to a more complete picture of the diverse experiences of life on Earth. When looking at the science standards in isolation, it is obvious that the human impacts of scientific and technological decisions have not been given a space for critical consideration, and we don't often talk about taking action (something we learn in social studies) in science. And when we look at social studies in isolation, while not intentional, we obscure the ways that the scientific revolution led to a way of thinking, seeing, and being in the world that created the economic, social, and political systems that have evolved in the United States over time. By honoring the interplay of science and social studies, we have expanded the skills in the table above into an overall set of skills that we know are foundational for the development of an informed, reasoned, and responsible citizen.

1. Collaboration with one another and their communities
2. Developing and Using Models
3. Asking Questions
4. Planning for Inquiry/Investigations
5. Evaluate Sources
6. Consider, analyze, and seek out diverse perspectives
7. Collecting Data/Research

8. Analyze and interpret data (patterns, etc.)
9. Making Evidence-based arguments
10. Deliberation, civil discourse, building consensus
11. Communication Information
12. Taking informed action

Climate change education is a great example that highlights the natural synergy across the two disciplines. An education needed to mitigate the impacts of climate change will need to draw on the combined skills we listed above. When, in 2020, New Jersey became the first state in the nation to include climate change learning standards across content areas, it called for multidisciplinary efforts toward teaching the topic. According to the NJ Department of Education, "These standards are designed to prepare students to understand how and why climate change happens, the impact it has on our local and global communities and to act in informed and sustainable ways."[25] From this statement, you can see how science literacy helps us to understand how and why climate change is happening, that both science and social studies will help students develop a sense of the impacts climate change has on our local and global communities, and that social studies teaches us the skills to act in informed and sustainable ways. Therefore, it is clear that both disciplines play an important role and can work together to effectively provide students with knowledge and skills needed to address climate change.

Honoring the complexity of the task in the above standards statement, the NJDOE encourages school districts to use the standards to create interdisciplinary units focused on climate change "that include authentic learning experiences, integrate a range of perspectives and are action oriented" including relevant ELA and Math content. This is an invitation to teachers to see the multidisciplinary nature of the climate crisis and to create learning opportunities for students to access both the knowledge and the skills to address climate change in the state. Below we show an example of aligning the standards across social studies and science to develop the skills that will foster an EcoJustice consciousness and empower students to be change agents for issues like climate change as well as other socio-environmental issues impacting communities today.

In Table I.4 we compare three NCSS standards that students learn about under the heading People, Places and Environments and three NGSS performance expectations suggested for students to reach by the end of grade 2. Additionally, we highlight the relevance the combined understanding of each has toward a more complex and holistic understanding of climate change on both people and the environments they occupy.

In classroom practice, this can be done by guiding students in questions that help young children see the connections between seasonal patterns of temperature and precipitation and broadly discussing ways climate impacts where and how we live (D2. Geo.4.K-2/1-ESS1-2). Students can be engaged in looking at evidence to support that human activities do affect the cultural and environmental characteristics of a place (D2. Geo.5.K-2) while exploring scientific, technological, social, economic, and political solutions that can reduce human impact on places (K-ESS3-3). Current events can be used to look at how catastrophic events (floods, fires, landslides) have affected people

Table I.4. Comparison of NCSS and NGSS Climate Change Relevant Standards

NCSS	NGSS	Relevance
D2.Geo.4.K-2. Explain how weather, climate, and other environmental characteristics affect people's lives in a place or region.	1-ESS1-2—Make observations at different times of the year to relate the amount of daylight to the time of year.	Helps students understand seasonal patterns, which are connected to human decision-making and evidence for climate change.
D2.Geo.5.K-2. Describe how human activities affect the cultural and environmental characteristics of places or regions.	K-ESS3-3—Communicate solutions that will reduce the impact of humans on the land, water, air, and other living things in the local environment.	Encourages students to think about how human actions affect the cultural and environmental characteristics of places, engaging students in climate impacts and solutions.
D2.Geo.12.K-2. Identify ways that a catastrophic disaster may affect people living in a place.	2-ESS2-1—Compare multiple solutions designed to slow or prevent wind or water from changing the shape of the land.	Helps students identify the social and environmental impacts from climate change and how communities of people can mitigate and adapt to climate impacts.

(D2.Geo.12.K-2). Students might then explore factors that contributed to the catastrophic events and what actions might have mitigated the situation (2-ESS2-1). The last step could be for students, even very young students, to engage in awareness-raising campaigns to educate others about actions that all can take to help remedy damage to the environment and the social and economic consequences. This is just one small example of how teachers can use what they are already being asked to do and bring in new opportunities for students' learning and development with an EcoJustice lens. *We do want to add the caveat that while much of what we offer in this book is meant to illuminate opportunities for interdisciplinary lessons, we know sometimes there is disciplinary knowledge that might need to be standalone.* This makes sense considering the deep disciplinary divides already present in schools. However, our work as EcoJustice Educators should always be toward helping students uncover the connections they are seeing across the disciplines. It is for this reason that we move a little beyond our respective disciplines to highlight two additional frameworks for thinking about sustainability education that have guided our work.

Beyond Standards

While this book aligns with the national social studies and science standards, we also introduce the Cloud Institute Standards for Sustainability Education and the United Nations Sustainable Development Goals (SDGs). We believe both of these resources enrich the conversation on what counts as a standard for learning for young children in schools and provide valuable inspiration for teachers. With this in mind, we align our work with more inclusive and multidisciplinary standards that promote and address multicultural literacies, human rights and peace, social-emotional learning, and justice, equity, and inclusive education.

The Cloud Institute Standards for Sustainability Education

The Cloud Institute developed a set of nine standards and associated performance indicators for educating for sustainability. The work of the Institute has been to push formal education toward education for sustainability, and the standards and benchmarks capture the complexity of the socio-environmental issues that are part of sustainability conversations. The developers drew upon learning theories including social-emotional learning and mindfulness, social studies concepts including global citizenship and sustainable economics, and science concepts including systems, dynamic change, and ecological principles. All of the Cloud standards are aligned to EcoJustice Education and will be referenced in the thematic chapters where they apply. You can read the nine standards on the Cloud Institute website,[26] but we highlight two here and their connection to chapters in this book.

Cloud Standard: Sustainable Economics

One of the most foundational systems influencing and interacting with our social, political, and ecological spheres is our model of free-market economy. Our first two thematic chapters of the book are dedicated to expanding understanding of the free-market economic system known as ***capitalism***. Economic topics are not often explicitly taught in elementary schools, and the role economics plays in science and technology is not discussed at all. The sustainable economics standard reads, "The evolving set of theories and practices of economics that integrates the economic, and social systems with the ecological systems required to support and maintain life on the planet. Students will know and understand 21st century economic practices and will produce and consume in ways that contribute to the health of the financial, social, and natural capital."[27] This idea of an economic model that integrates and honors that ecological principles shape the very survival of the planet and all of her organisms is novel and revolutionary at this moment in time. However, it is exactly what is required of us if we want to live on a thriving and sustainable Earth.

Cloud Standard: Healthy Commons

Throughout the book we will make reference to the ***Commons***. The Cloud Institute recognizes the need for a Healthy Commons—"that upon which we all depend and for which we are all responsible (i.e., air, trust, biodiversity, climate regulation, our collective future, water, libraries, public health, heritage sites, top soil, etc.)."[28] As you can see from the examples given, the commons are both material/physical/tangible resources that lend themselves to our very survival on the planet, as well as social and cultural norms on which we depend for a thriving healthy society. What all of the Commons have in common is that they are collectively owned, shared, and managed in community, rather than privately held or government controlled. An EcoJustice consciousness allows students to recognize their interdependence with the commons but also our shared responsibility to take actions that care for the Commons.

United Nations Sustainable Development Goals

In June of 1992, at the Earth Summit in Rio de Janeiro, Brazil, 178 countries adopted a comprehensive plan to build a global partnership for sustainable development that focused on improving human lives and protecting the environment. This began decades of work that culminated in 2015 with the adoption of the *2030 Agenda for Sustainable Development*. The *Preamble for Transforming our World: the 2030 Agenda for Sustainable Development*, is a great resource for lesson inspiration. Some of the Preamble is presented below. As you read each of the principles, consider the impact of an education that incorporated these ideas into lessons for children of all ages.

From the Preamble:

This Agenda is a plan of action for people, planet, and prosperity. It also seeks to strengthen universal peace in larger freedom . . . We are determined to take the bold and transformative steps that are urgently needed to shift the world onto a sustainable and resilient path . . . The Goals and targets will stimulate action over the next fifteen years in areas of critical importance for humanity and the planet:

People: To ensure that all human beings can fulfill their potential in dignity and equality and **in a healthy environment.**

Planet: To protect the planet from degradation, including through **sustainable consumption and production, sustainably managing its natural resources and taking urgent action on climate change**, so that it can support the needs of the present and future generations.

Prosperity: To ensure that all human beings can enjoy prosperous and fulfilling lives and **that economic, social, and technological progress occurs in harmony with nature.**[29]

There are 17 Sustainable Development Goals (SDGs) outlined in the Agenda 2030. Full descriptions of each SDG, along with specific targets, actions taken, resources, and publications, are available at the Department of Economic and Social Affairs homepage.[30]

Below is a brief description of each goal. Although the goals are intertwined and we believe all are important, some are more relevant to this text than others and will therefore be referenced in specific chapters.

- Goal 1 End poverty in all its forms everywhere
- Goal 2 End hunger, achieve food security and improved nutrition and promote sustainable agriculture
- Goal 3 Ensure healthy lives and promote well-being for all at all ages
- Goal 4 Ensure inclusive and equitable quality education and promote lifelong learning opportunities for all
- Goal 5 Achieve gender equality and empower all women and girls
- Goal 6 Ensure availability and sustainable management of water and sanitation for all
- Goal 7 Ensure access to affordable, reliable, sustainable, and modern energy for all
- Goal 8 Promote sustained, inclusive, and sustainable economic growth, full and productive employment, and decent work for all
- Goal 9 Build resilient infrastructure, promote inclusive and sustainable industrialization, and foster innovation
- Goal 10 Reduce inequality within and among countries
- Goal 11 Make cities and human settlements inclusive, safe, resilient, and sustainable
- Goal 12 Ensure sustainable consumption and production patterns
- Goal 13 Take urgent action to combat climate change and its impacts
- Goal 14 Conserve and sustainably use the oceans, seas, and marine resources for sustainable
- Goal 15 Protect, restore, and promote sustainable use of terrestrial ecosystems, sustainably manage forests, combat desertification, and halt and reverse land degradation and halt biodiversity loss
- Goal 16 Promote peaceful and inclusive societies for sustainable development, provide access to justice for all, and build effective, accountable, and inclusive institutions at all levels
- Goal 17 Strengthen the means of implementation and revitalize the Global Partnership for Sustainable Development

Knowledge of science and social studies topics is needed to understand the goals of the SDGs, as well as to assess actions taken to reach the goals. Therefore, incorporating the goals into elementary education provides opportunities for students to see real-world applications of the concepts they are learning. The SDGs can also be used to draw inspiration for lessons and have a wealth of information to educate oneself and build lessons around, as we have done. We also use a resource specifically designed for educators called Teach SDGs.[31] A message on the Teach SDGs homepage by Irina Bokova, a former director-general of the United Nations Educational, Scientific and Cultural Organization (UNESCO) is a powerful reminder of why this work is so important:

> There is no more powerful transformative force than **education**—to promote human rights and dignity, to **eradicate poverty** and **deepen sustainability**, to build a better future for all, founded on equal rights and social justice, respect for cultural diversity, and international solidarity and shared responsibility, all of which are fundamental aspects of our common humanity.

How to Use This Book

In this final section, we share how the chapters in the book are organized. We have embedded EcoJustice instructional materials into thematically based chapters on ***Economic Foundations, The Materials Economy, Land, Water, and Food.*** Each chapter begins with an example of how social studies and sometimes science is conventionally taught and a critical analysis and reimagining through an EcoJustice orientation. Then we focus on building teacher knowledge by including information and resources for teachers to deepen their own understandings of related socio-environmental issues. Two sets of standards-aligned instructional materials are offered, designed for K-2 and 3–5 audiences, and organized utilizing a modified 6E learning model (see Table I.5).[32] We end each chapter by offering community and place-based learning opportunities to engage students as members of their local communities and an invitation for teachers to build their own lessons from all the resources presented.

While each thematic chapter offers K-2 and 3–5 instructional materials, we encourage teachers to utilize their knowledge and expertise of their students to guide their planning process. All materials are aligned to NCSS standards and NGSS, Cloud Standards for Sustainability Education, one or more UN SDG, and of course our EcoJustice Education Pillars. The 6E learning model was chosen as it is popular in elementary science classrooms and includes a mix of learning activities for individuals, small groups, and whole class instruction. This learning theory informs our instructional materials as the 6E model guides students to build on early conceptions through explorations and explanations into action-oriented activities that extend and evaluate student learning. In most cases, if instructional materials are more heavily geared toward one disciplinary content, the extension activity will be used as a place to make cross-curricular connections to the other content area. For example, in the **Economic Foundations** chapter, the K-2 instructional materials are heavily geared toward the social studies content. Therefore, the extension activity was designed to engage science literacies that accompany the topic. We want to acknowledge that the 6E learning model is simply a way to help organize instructional materials for student learning, but we understand that each stage may extend beyond the

Table I.5. The 6E Learning Model Used for Lesson Development of Instructional Materials

ENGAGE	**Establish connection to prior knowledge, generates interest, wonder, and curiosity**
EXPLORE	Active investigation of new topic to collectively build understandings about new topic
EXPLAIN	Share findings from exploration, clarification of concepts, introduction to new vocabulary
ELABORATE	Build deeper understandings and applications of knowledge
EXTEND	Apply knowledge across contexts to diverse situations
EVALUATE	Assess student learning and understandings

allotted time you have in your day to teach. We encourage you to pick and choose aspects of the instructional materials based on your expertise, time, and material constraints. It is also possible to break any materials provided into multiple sessions if that works better in your teaching context.

It is our hope that through the diversity of resources presented, you can both expand your understanding of socio-environmental issues as well as develop your own instructional materials beyond what is offered in this text. We want to empower you to move beyond the examples shown and share with us examples you have created to engage your students with EcoJustice topics. At the end of the book and on our companion website, you will find additional resources for expanding your own knowledge base and resources to engage young children in critical thinking and pedagogies. These are more universal strategies that we have utilized in our own teaching and methods courses and include activities, questioning techniques, lesson design, and more. At various points in the book, we will reference these Appendix activities and website resources as possible ways to build and expand instructional materials.

We are excited that you are reading this book and hope it offers you guidance on your path to becoming an EcoJustice Educator. Teachers are invited to engage at whatever level they feel most comfortable. For some teachers, that might be reframing a traditional lesson in social studies to include more of an EcoJustice perspective. For others, it might be utilizing the EcoJustice instructional materials in ways that work best for you and your teaching contexts. And for others, it might be planning a community or place-based learning experience for your class. Embedded in every chapter are references to multiple resources for teachers to access in order to build their EcoJustice consciousness, including readings, podcasts, interviews, and other visual and print media. By inviting teachers to build a deeper well of knowledge on a few topics, we hope the skills of critical thinking—questioning, research, analysis, reflection—become a reflexive part of teacher practice. Creating exciting opportunities for new ways of thinking about and engaging with your current teaching curriculum and practices and how they align with EcoJustice Education is our primary goal. The next chapter presents an overview of EcoJustice Education, our EcoJustice Education Pillars, and the pedagogical traditions that have informed our work.

Notes

1 Victoria Namkung, "How the Climate Crisis Fuels Devastating Wildfires: 'We have Tweaked Nature and Pissed it Off,'" *The Guardian*, January 11, 2025, https://www.theguardian.com/us-news/2025/jan/11/wildfires-los-angeles-climate-crisis-john-vaillant.

2 "Billion Dollar Weather and Climate Disasters," *National Centers for Environmental Information website*, January 10, 2025, https://www.ncei.noaa.gov/access/billions/.

3 Robyn Schelenz, "How the Indigenous Practice of 'Good Fire' can Help Our Forests Thrive," *University of California*, April 6, 2022, https://www.universityofcalifornia.edu/news/how-Indigenous-practice-good-fire-can-help-our-forests-thrive.

4 Stanford Report, "Native Approaches to Fire Management Could Revitalize Communities, Stanford Researchers Find," August 27, 2019, https://news.stanford.edu/stories/2019/08/traditional-fire-management-help-revitalize-american-indian-cultures.
5 Josie Abugov, "Elementary School Next to Controversial Louisiana Chemical Plant to Shut Down Next Year," *NOLA.com,* November 7, 2024, https://www.nola.com/news/environment/louisiana-cancer-alley-pollution-environmental-justice-school/article_ea759872-9d33-11ef-95a3-3faf44318ad9.html.
6 Michael Casey, "DC Sues Federal Government Over Pollution in Anacostia River," *The Associated Press*, January 10, 2025, https://apnews.com/article/washington-dc-anacostia-pollution-environmental-cleanup-lawsuit-e00b90f883cfc83aeed341f43f69b7dc.
7 Feeding America, "Facts About Child Hunger," https://www.feedingamerica.org/hunger-in-america/child-hunger-facts.
8 Karen Perry Stillerman, "What a Second Trump Administration Means for Food and Farms," *Union of Concerned Scientists*, November 6, 2024, https://blog.ucsusa.org/karen-perry-stillerman/what-a-second-trump-administration-means-for-food-and-farms/.
9 Kelly Livingston, "New EPA Vehicle Standards Would Cut US Emissions, Ramp up Pressure for more EVs," *ABC News*, March 20, 2024, https://abcnews.go.com/Politics/new-epa-vehicle-standards-cut-us-emissions-ramp/story?id=108728.
10 Asthma and Allergy Foundation of America, "Asthma Disparities in America: A Roadmap to Reducing Burden on Racial and Ethnic Minorities," 2020, aafa.org/asthmadisparities.
11 Albert Einstein as quoted in Alice Caprice, *The Ultimate Quotable Einstein* (Princeton, NJ: Princeton University Press, 2010).
12 Old Deluder Satan Law of 1647, Free Speech Center, https://firstamendment.mtsu.edu/article/old-deluder-satan-act-of-1647/.
13 "The 21st Century Skills Movement," *ACSD* 67, no. 1 (September 1, 2009), https://ascd.org/el/articles/the-21st-century-skills-movement.
14 Winston Choi-Schagrin, "Many States Omit Climate Education. These Teachers Are Trying to Slip it in," *NY Times*, Updated Nov. 10, 2022, https://www.nytimes.com/2022/11/01/climate/middle-school-education-climate-change.html.
15 Jelani Cobb, "The Man Behind Critical Race Theory," *The New Yorker*, September 13, 2021, https://www.newyorker.com/magazine/2021/09/20/the-man-behind-critical-race-theory.
16 Paulo Freire, *Pedagogy of the Oppressed*, trans. Myra Bergman Ramos (New York: Herder and Herder, 1970), 73.
17 Jay McTighe and Grant Wiggins, *Understanding by Design Guide to Advanced Concepts in Creating and Reviewing Units* (Alexandria, VA: ASCD, 2012).
18 Wiggins and McTighe, *From Common Core Standards to Curriculum: Five Big Ideas* (2012), https://exemplars.com/sites/default/files/inline-files/McTighe%20Wiggins%20From%20Common%20Core%20Standards%28129.pdf.
19 National Council for the Social Studies, "Definition of Social Studies," accessed July 2024, https://www.socialstudies.org/about/definition-social-studies.
20 National Council for the Social Studies (NCSS), *The College, Career, and Civic Life (C3) Framework for Social Studies State Standards: Guidance for Enhancing the Rigor of K-12 Civics, Economics, Geography, and History* (Silver Spring, MD: NCSS, 2013).

21 American Association for the Advancement of Science (AAAS), *Benchmarks for Science Literacy. Project 2061* (New York: Oxford University Press, 1993).

22 National Research Council, *A Framework for K-12 Science Education: Practices, Crosscutting Concepts, and Core Ideas* (Washington, DC: The National Academies Press, 2012).

23 Next-Generation Science Standards, accessed July 2024, https://www.nextgenscience.org/.

24 National Science Teaching Association, "Science Standards," accessed July 2024, https://www.nsta.org/science-standards.

25 New Jersey Department of Education, "Climate Change Education by Grade Band," accessed July 2024, https://www.nj.gov/education/climate/learning/gradeband/.

26 The Cloud Institute for Sustainability Education, "The EfS Benchmarks," accessed July 2024, https://cloudinstitute.org/efs-benchmarks.

27 The Cloud Institute for Sustainability Education, "The EfS Benchmarks," accessed July 2024, https://cloudinstitute.org/efs-benchmarks.

28 The Cloud Institute for Sustainability Education, "The EfS Benchmarks," accessed July 2024, https://cloudinstitute.org/efs-benchmarks.

29 United Nations General Assembly, "Transforming Our World: The 2030 Agenda for Sustainable Development," *preamble*, October 21, 2015, https://sdgs.un.org/2030agenda.

30 United Nations, Department of Economic and Social Affairs, "The 17 Goals," accessed August 5, 2025, https://sdgs.un.org/goals.

31 TEACH SDGs, accessed July 2024, http://www.teachsdgs.org/.

32 Şeyma Şahin and Abdurrahman Kiliç, "Effectiveness of the Project-based 6E Learning Model," *European Journal of Open, Distance and E-Learning* 25, no. 1 (2023): 31–48.

1

EcoJustice Education and Pedagogical Influences

Chapter Outline

EcoJustice Education teaches students to understand their impact on the environment, the social and political implications of these issues, and how they can work towards making change.

—Arabella, Elementary Pre-service Teacher

Introduction

Who is the young person we want to emerge from elementary school? In the Introduction, we highlight several environmental, social, and economic crises that need immediate and ongoing attention. According to Piaget, "The principal goals of education is to create [people] who are capable of doing new things, not simply repeating what other generations have done; [people] who are creative, inventive, and discoverer. The second goal of education is to form minds which can be critical, can verify, and not accept everything they are offered.[1] Progressive educators have long believed schools can and should be embedded in communities and places where children and youth are nurtured beyond academics, but as whole, curious, creative human beings. To combat the multitude of social and environmental challenges we currently face, we need a system of education that is fulfilling these goals of progressive education.[2] When we ask ourselves whether the education typically offered to today's elementary school children is fulfilling this goal, we sadly conclude that it is not.

We don't believe this is from a lack of good teaching. We see so much good teaching in the classrooms we visit, as teachers are abundantly aware of the diverse needs of their students and have deep respect for and honor the whole child that arrives each day to their classroom. What we do not see are opportunities for teachers to teach curricular materials that enable young people to learn meaningful content, question what they are learning, analyze new information, form conclusions, and share connections they are making to their own lives. Good curriculum, when taught by good teachers, creates space to explore ideas across multiple disciplines, leverages the social nature of human beings, and honors that all students bring knowledge through their experiences in the world. Good curriculum also empowers students to love and care for themselves, one another, and the Earth by equipping them with the knowledge and skills they need to be successful actors in this endeavor. This isn't just what we believe, we draw on years of experience, educational research, and the work of leading theorists that speak to the transformational power of education. In this chapter, we introduce EcoJustice Education and our Ecojustice Educational Pillars, as well as present an overview of the theories and educational philosophies that have influenced our teaching and served to guide us in the construction of instructional materials shared throughout the book.

Teaching for Active Engagement in Our Society

To address the challenges ahead, we need individuals who are knowledgeable in many areas of both science and social studies, and fortunately, there are national standards (which we shared in the Introduction and will be referenced throughout the book) and other educational materials to provide guidance on content selection. However, knowledge will not be enough. We need a generation of individuals who understand the complexities of environmental degradation and climate change, *and* who possess the skills to take reasoned, informed, and responsible actions, *and* who are concerned with the welfare of the people and the planet and feel a responsibility to take action. The Venn diagram below illustrates the interconnectedness of three domains: knowledge, skills, and attitudes. It is equal attention to all three domains that leads to the intersection and development of young people who are prepared to be responsible, reasoned, and informed decision-makers. It is a basic premise of this book and an EcoJustice Education that all three domains must be addressed in order to prepare young people to be the *actors* we need.

The proposition that we must teach in order to develop all three domains might seem daunting and even out of reach at first. However, what we are proposing is actually rooted in many mainstream learning theories, the science of how the brain works, and accepted

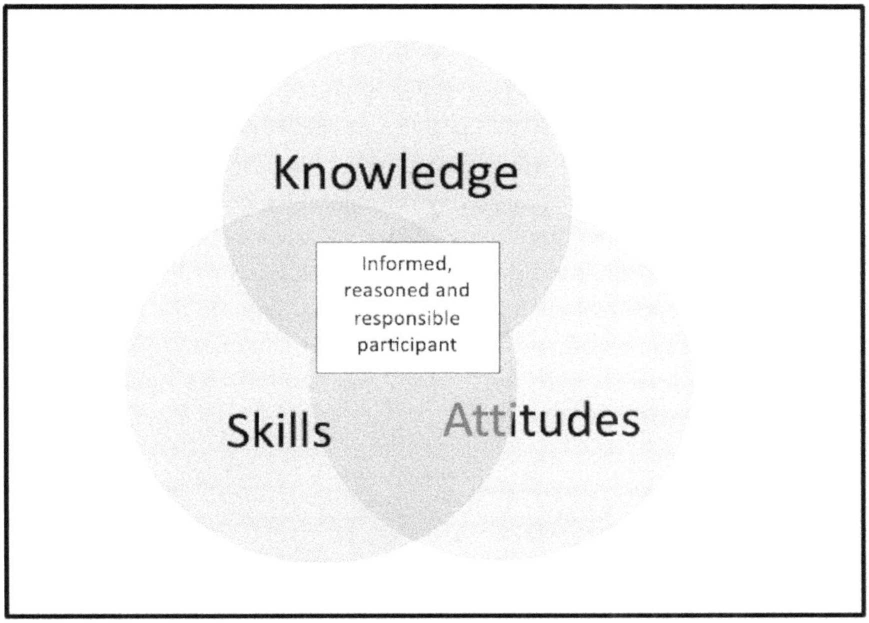

Figure 1.1. Venn diagram showing the intersection of knowledge, skills, and attitudes to develop into an informed, reasoned, and responsible participant. Author created.

educational standards, as well as articulated in the goals of many national and transnational organizations, including the American Association for the Advancement of Science and the United Nations. It is our goal to make clear how EcoJustice Education is in line with existing practices and standards, how instructional materials that align with EcoJustice goals can be brought into elementary classrooms, and how doing so can lead to a sustainable future that benefits people and the planet.

EcoJustice Education

As we shared in the Preface, our conceptualization of EcoJustice Education and its impact on teachers came from the place-based learning experiences and reflective critical pedagogies we directly engaged in with our students and the teachers we worked with. When we first began our work, we didn't call it EcoJustice Education and have since come to appreciate this term as a way of situating the kinds of thinking we engage teachers in and, in turn, they engage their students. EcoJustice Education is not simply teaching about the environment; it's a holistic approach that addresses environmental issues alongside social injustices and recognizes that marginalized communities often bear the brunt of environmental degradation and are least economically and politically positioned to deal with the consequences.

We have thought and written extensively about how we view our work as a form of EcoJustice Education[3] and so we will make clear in this section the principles we drew on for our prior projects and share the EcoJustice Pillars that we developed to frame this book. EcoJustice Education engages broadly with the social and material conditions that have led to diverse forms of environmental and social degradations—issues like pollution, poverty, food insecurity—as well as the social and political processes needed to eliminate them.[4] It aligns with Environmental Justice principles calling for the education of present and future generations which emphasizes social and environmental issues, based on experience and an appreciation of diverse cultural perspectives.[5] EcoJustice Education requires the development of habits and skills to critique cultural norms and structures that create and sustain unjust and unsustainable practices and attitudes.[6] We see the principles and our EcoJustice Education Pillars (outlined below) as a means to this end. *As you engage with the ideas presented, we invite you to reflect on the ways they resonate with you and your comfort, familiarity, and understanding of each.*

EcoJustice Principles

Interdependence with systems: The EcoJustice principle of interdependence with systems highlights an acceptance and valuing of the interconnectedness of all systems that influence how society functions and how individuals interact with the world.[7] These systems include the complex networks of structures, institutions, and frameworks, including political, economic, sociocultural, and ecological. This principle prompts individuals to not only uncover, understand, and accept their role and participation within systems, but also how systems interact with one another in complex, often invisible ways. By making these connections more visible, individuals and communities can advocate for meaningful change. For example, when coal is burned to make electricity, it emits carbon dioxide as well as other pollutants into the air. These emissions harm our shared atmosphere, harming the health of many living organisms. When the health of organisms, including humans, is negatively impacted, this can impact the capacity people have to work, which in turn has an impact on the economy. An understanding of this relationship can help local communities advocate for policy that protects both the health and economic well-being of those most impacted.

Recognition of hierarchical systems: We have all been socialized into the world today via our individual and group experiences in the contexts in which we were raised. Where we are raised is shaped by a history of valuing some beings over others. In developing an EcoJustice consciousness, we seek to recognize the dominant narratives that made us believe that hierarchical systems that position humans over nature, and some humans as superior to others, are normal and just. We can see this in the case of settler colonialism, where European settlers claimed land and resources that were stewarded by Indigenous people because they believed they possessed cultural superiority. If we are to critically examine and transform the cultural assumptions that underpin ecological and social injustices, we must acknowledge and challenge systems that lead to and perpetuate unjust hierarchies.[8] We must recognize that **all** living beings hold inherent value and deserve equal consideration and respect within our ecosystem.

Analysis of unjust systems: This principle highlights the ability to critically analyze the cultural, political, and economic forces that create and sustain unjust and unsustainable practices and beliefs.[9] For example: Capitalist economies often prioritize profit over environmental and social concerns, leading to exploitation of natural resources and labor. The case of Flint, Michigan, where cost-saving measures led to the contamination of the city's water supply with lead, disproportionately affected low-income and predominantly Black communities, is an example. This crisis highlighted the intersection of environmental injustice, economic inequality, and systemic racism.

Uncovering dominant narratives: This principle asks us to recognize that individuals participate in systems of domination and therefore must uncover the forces that have unknowingly shaped deficit views and participation in damaging practices toward people and the environment.[10] Realizing this can help us see how we might unknowingly contribute to unfair systems and how we can do things differently. For example, if we buy products that are made in ways that harm the environment or exploit workers, we are indirectly supporting those harmful practices. It's important to recognize our role in these systems so we can change them.

Contextualized learning: This principle speaks to the need for an approach to learning that is contextualized and real world. EcoJustice Educators do this by engaging students in researching problems in communities and seeking solutions, while also deconstructing the cultural roots of the problems.[11] Connecting what we learn in the classroom to real-life situations helps students broaden their own perspectives and helps build empathy. For example, instead of just reading about problems like pollution or poverty, students might go out into their communities to research these issues firsthand. This helps them understand the problems better and come up with practical solutions that are rooted in community relationships.

Local engagement and partnerships: EcoJustice Education emphasizes the need to work within local systems, form partnerships and value the knowledge and traditions held by locals. Developing and honoring these relationships is vital in the problem-solving process.[12] This involves focusing on issues and solutions within our own communities. For example, by working together with local organizations, businesses, and residents, we can better understand the specific challenges faced and come up with tailored solutions that take into account local knowledge, traditions, and needs. This approach values the expertise and experiences of people who live in the community.

EcoJustice Education Pillars

These combined principles represent thinking from diverse EcoJustice Educators and have laid the groundwork for our own EcoJustice Education Pillars that guide the thinking and materials populating the rest of this book. Our EcoJustice Pillars bring the knowledge, skills, and dispositions embedded in the EcoJustice principles to life in an EcoJustice Education framework. We want students to understand the crosscutting concepts that shape science and social studies literacies (as presented in the Introduction), have them apply critical thinking skills across levels (individual, group, systems), and nurture the dispositions that will lead to a sense of care and responsibility for one another and the Earth. Our Pillars, outlined below, bring all of this into conversation. Each Pillar includes "components" that serve as guides for creating and evaluating EcoJustice Education materials. This ideas will be expanded on and applied as you encounter them in the thematic chapters that follow.

Our EcoJustice Education Pillars

We seek a system of education that develops:

- **Pillar I:** An **understanding** and valuing of the interconnectedness of all living beings and systems. This includes students developing the knowledge, skills, and dispositions to:
  - Acknowledge that our well-being is interconnected with the well-being of our planet
  - Accept responsibility for the part we play in the ecological web of life
  - Care for the welfare of all beings
  - Protect and nurture the health and well-being of our Earth
  - Become conscious consumers and producers in all areas of existence
  - Understand that all actions have multiple consequences
  - Think globally and act locally
  - Evaluate choices and decisions at multiple levels (self, community, state, country) through a systems lens
- **Pillar II:** An **orientation** toward innovative, action-oriented, and collaborative problem-solving. This includes students developing the knowledge, skills, and dispositions to:
  - Accept our power as change agents, take risks, and fail forward
  - Value diverse knowledge and honor that knowledge is constructed from many and sometimes unexpected sources
  - Imagine new ideas and ways of being that challenge our socialized norms
  - Recognize the need and power of working in solidarity with others, across perceived difference, to achieve common goals
  - Become comfortable with ambiguity
  - Build skills of proactive citizenship
  - Advocate for changes that focus on environmentally sustainable and just solutions and policies
- **Pillar III:** A **commitment** to investigating socio-environmental issues through the lens of power and justice. This includes students developing the knowledge, skills, and dispositions to:
  - Critically read the world[13]—uncovering and questioning the social, political, and economic forces that shape our lives
  - Ongoing self-education and information seeking that mines contradictions and tensions

  - Reflect and evaluate the ongoing process of our socialization and the mechanisms that shape our ways of being
  - Change direction and/or one's mind when evidence suggests it is warranted
  - Accept that there may not be right answers, but we are all healthier and suffer less by choices that are aligned to environmental sustainability and social justice
- **Pillar IV: Transdisciplinary approaches** that focus on cross-curricular knowledge and connections rather than siloed thinking that leads to incomplete understandings. This includes students developing the knowledge, skills, and dispositions to:
  - Connect ideas across disciplinary boundaries
  - Apply content knowledge in real world, interconnected contexts
  - Understand the relevance and value of why they are learning what they are learning
  - Draw on knowledge from multiple disciplines in order to form educated understandings and take informed **actions**

You may be starting to see how the EcoJustice principles and Pillars outlined above center the knowledge, skills, and dispositions that students develop through both science and social studies content and thought processes. This is a great starting point for the justification of bringing this teaching into your classroom. And theoretically, you may be thinking, yes, I love this, it makes sense to me! This is something we hear over and over again from pre-service teachers—until they become teachers and find that truly integrating this into the classroom is more difficult than they expected. In this next section, we explore a few of the reasons that make this work difficult and also hope to help you see why, despite these challenges and even because of these challenges, EcoJustice Education is more important than ever.

Why Is This Work So Difficult?

We have been collaborating on engendering an EcoJustice consciousness in pre-service teachers for over 8 years and have discussed at length why doing this work in schools is so difficult to enact. Theoretically, pre-service and in-service teachers are drawn to the ideas inherent in EcoJustice Education, but in practice, they have expressed difficulty in bringing it alive in the classroom. One of the largest reasons for this is that there just aren't many examples of EcoJustice Education in practice. The theoretical work that underpins the pedagogical principles outlined above often comes from work in community organizations and higher education. We have been hard-pressed to find concrete examples happening in K-12 classrooms although we have found some. An additional challenge is the amount of time spent on ELA and Math in elementary classrooms at the expense of science and social studies. Much of the curriculum in schools is paced, scripted curriculum, with little freedom for teachers to bring in their own ideas. When social studies and science are taught, they are often for short periods of time, one-off lessons, and often curriculum and teaching practices that feel irrelevant to children. Teachers we have heard from also fear that parents will not see the value in this kind of education and push back on time dedicated to EcoJustice content. These are very real constraints placed on teachers, and they have led us to ask some important questions about our own purpose in writing this book.

In lengthy conversations we wrestle with big questions like, "*Why this book and who is it for*?" More specifically we ask ourselves questions like, "Is this book for preservice teachers or in-service teachers or both? Where would this book make the most impact? What do teachers today need and want in a book about education? Are we too idealistic to believe that people care about this kind of stuff? Do teachers inherently care about social and environmental issues and justice? Does being in a blue state or a red state impact how you will read this work? Is it more important to speak to an audience of people who already value social and environmental justice ethics and see the value in teaching this to children? Or should we be trying to speak to people who don't see value in this kind of justice-oriented teaching? Or should we be trying to speak to folks who are somewhere in between? Are we living in bubbles that make us believe and see things so vastly different from one another? Where can we have an impact? What kind of impact do we seek to make as human beings? As educators of young children? How do we fit this book into the existing structure of school while also challenging that structure? Do we all have the same values when it comes to educating young children? If not, why not? If yes, what are some of these shared values?"

These questions illuminate the challenge and difficulty of presenting a book on EcoJustice, and yet we know from our work with teachers that we have something to offer them and the children they teach. Young children are full of possibilities and potential. One of the most powerful responsibilities we have as educators, especially of young children, is to guide them as they become an embodied person in the world and witness and support them as they seek and learn what is possible for themselves and for our world. Throughout the elementary school years, children are learning about their rights, what they are entitled to want and dream and believe and expect. To meet this charge, educators must ask what is the role of the teacher, the curriculum, the classroom, and the school community in guiding students on their human journey, and how are schools complicit in reducing and diminishing the possibilities that young people imagine and their access to a just and sustainable future?

In her book *EcoMind: Changing the Way We Think, To Create the World We Want*, Frances Moore Lappé[14] asks the question, "If humans are all this—cooperative, empathetic, and sensitive to fairness—if we need to feel efficacious, seek meaning, and are naturally imaginative and creative, then why in the world do we mindlessly participate every day in a social ecology that generates so much destruction and misery for so many?" She identifies these six essential traits that humans have evolved a deep capacity for (cooperation, empathy, fairness, efficacy, meaning, and creativity) and acknowledges our readiness to tap into them. But every day we each mindlessly participate in a social process of schooling that does damage to both teachers and students. Lappé suggests three conditions that have been shown throughout history to elicit the worst parts of us because they deny our very expression of our positive traits. These conditions are extreme power inequalities, secrecy/lack of accountability, and scapegoating. As teachers we can see how these conditions are part of the undercurrent of schools and sometimes our classrooms, with mindsets of lack, scarcity, and rivalry. Cobb and Krownapple write, "Belonging has been neglected in the name of achievement, which is an environment where only the achieving belong. Due to the lack of focus on belonging, we have harmed the health and well-being of our young people, our schools, and our democracy"[15]

We believe in these innate human traits, for all beings, and yet we also know that schools do much harm to young children by denying them the time, space, and right to exercise these in our classrooms. Carla Shalaby writes,

> For the most part, schools value quiet children over loud ones and operate as though adults are the only teachers in the room. The adults get to speak while the young people listen. Questions are answered rather than asked. Our schools are designed to prepare children to take their assumed place in the social order rather than to question and challenge that order. Because we train youth in the image of capitalism instead of a vision of freedom—for lives as individual workers rather than solidary human beings—young people are taught academic content that can be drilled and tested rather than understanding literacies and numeracies as forms of power, tools for organizing, fodder for the development of their own original ideas.[16]

Scripted curriculum that lacks the development of critical literacies is a very real constraint for teachers, especially new teachers, and yet *this book is asking you to resist the urge to reproduce the status quo that you know restricts the potential and possibilities of your students' innate positive human traits*. The challenges presented by schools are structural and do not say anything about who we are as human beings or our capacity to overcome the limitations imposed upon us to do what we know is good and right for our own well-being and that of others and the planet. These constraints are deeply embedded in our system of public education and they are only going to get worse as the conservative agenda continues to drain the pool of public funding in schools in favor of school choice. And rest assured, when this happens, history will be rewritten, climate change education will disappear, and the safety of all students will no longer be guaranteed. This is why we ground our work in a diversity of educational pedagogies that nurture the critical thinking that we are seeking to foster in this book. By aligning EcoJustice Education to learning and pedagogical theory and instructional materials to content standards, we hope to support you in finding the space in your classrooms to enact the teaching and learning presented in this book.

Our Pedagogical Influences

We all develop a philosophy of teaching and learning that is the foundation of our practice. These philosophies emerge and coalesce over time and include years of classroom teaching, years of advanced education and research (that of others and our own), and countless hours of reflection on what we have learned. Here we share the most influential thinking that shaped our philosophy of teaching and learning and include brief overviews of some of the leading theories and practices that have guided us as educators and researchers. It is these pedagogical influences that serve as the foundation of our EcoJustice Pillars and for this book. You will notice that there are commonalities among the theories and practices; however, each theory also offers unique elements that are essential to this book. *As you read through this overview, consider which theories and associated practices you have experienced as a learner, teacher, or both and what the outcomes were?*

Constructivism

The lynchpin of Constructivist Learning Theory is the belief that individuals construct meaning by integrating new knowledge into an existing schema of knowledge drawn from prior experiences. According to this learning theory, individuals learn best when they are able to make connections between new information and existing knowledge through active engagement in their learning. This learning theory counters the idea that individuals are "blank slates" when they enter schools, or empty vessels waiting to be filled with the knowledge imparted by the teacher. In this latter, more traditional approach, students receive information as factual, through lectures or text, and demonstrate mastery by regurgitating the desired information on assessments that usually require identification of the right answer through multiple choice, true or false, matching or fill-in-the-blank prompts. Little room is left for student interpretations based on lived experiences or different ways of thinking.

Another important element of constructivist theory is the social nature of meaningful learning. It is when we grapple with new information through a task, share our ideas with others, and reflect on what we have learned that we are most likely to achieve deeper levels of understanding. In this instance, the teacher facilitates learning by providing opportunities for social interaction and collaborative learning. Another feature of constructivist learning is considering a concept or problem from multiple perspectives, pursuing inquiry and/or experimentation before drawing conclusions. In other words, students apply critical thinking to evaluate new and diverse sources of information and evidence as part of their learning. Lastly, assessments are designed to understand what students have learned through their own voice or demonstrations of learning, therefore they tend to be authentic tasks ranging from essays to presentations to real-life actions. You will notice throughout the instructional materials (presented in Chapters 2–6) an emphasis on student connections to their own life experiences and the social nature of the teaching and learning process.

Experiential Learning

In simple terms, experiential learning is learning by doing, but in reality, it is much more. It is a systematic approach to learning that is intended to deepen students' knowledge, build skills, and shift or clarify attitudes. Experiences, particularly when tied to emotions, tend to be remembered far longer than traditional lectures. However, to bring about the desired results, teachers must be intentional in planning for experiential learning. The Association for Experiential Education website explains that "educators purposefully engage with learners in direct experience and focused reflection in order to increase knowledge, develop skills, clarify values, and develop people's capacity to contribute to their communities."[17] It is important that educators who employ this model engage students throughout the learning process to apply knowledge to tasks, ask questions, draw conclusions, make decisions, reflect on their learning, and make adjustments to conclusions when appropriate. This is a cyclical process that can continually be built on as new learning occurs, which is authentic to how we process new information throughout our lives. Experiential learning can be challenging to bring into our classrooms, so we end each chapter with opportunities for *community and place-based learning opportunities* you can draw inspiration from.

Active Learning Theory

Experiential learning is closely aligned to Active Learning Theory, where the emphasis is for students to participate in their own learning. There are many ways to engage students in their learning that range from thinking, practicing skills, discussing, investigating, solving problems, making decisions, and creating. Studies show that students are not only more likely to be motivated to learn when they are actively engaged, but they retain information longer.[18] Table 1.1 shows examples of active learning tasks and passive learning tasks. Consider which are most effective in your own learning, keeping in mind that a combination of each can work well!

Table 1.1. Comparison of Active and Passive Learning and Example Classroom Tasks

Examples of Active Learning	Examples of Passive Learning
Group Problem-solving	Lectures and presentation
Simulations, role plays and games	Reading text
Think-pair-share	Completing worksheets
Learning labs	Note-taking
Peer-to-peer instruction	Watching a powerpoint
Debates, discussions	Watching videos
Readers Theater, dramatic presentations	
Project-based learning	

Bloom's Taxonomy and Teaching for Critical Thinking

Although the work of Benjamin Bloom (American educational psychologist, 1913–1999), and the taxonomy of cognitive behaviors that he identified (and the updated version), is not actually a learning theory, it is integral to many of the other theories presented here and to our work: therefore an understanding of the cognitive taxonomy is important.

In 1956, Benjamin Bloom created a taxonomy of cognitive tasks, and he identified learning experiences that coincide with each level on the taxonomy. This became known as Bloom's Taxonomy and has been used to provide guidance for teachers globally for the last six plus decades. In 2001, Lorin Anderson and David Krathwohl (one a former student and the other a colleague of Bloom) made revisions to the original taxonomy and created "Bloom's Revised Taxonomy."[19] While the two taxonomies only differ slightly, a major shift is the use of verbs to identify each level, rather than nouns. For example, the level of knowledge became "Remembering" to state what it is students are doing at this level. The other major difference is that in the revised taxonomy, "Creating" is placed at the highest cognitive level and "Evaluating" is the second highest. What is most useful to educators is to understand that different learning tasks elicit different cognitive actions and that these cognitive actions have been further classified into the categories of *lower-order thinking* and *higher-order thinking*. When teachers use Bloom's revised framework in their planning, they can be intentional about when and how they are moving students to higher-order thinking or critical thinking tasks. Table 1.2 highlights tasks associated with each level of

Table 1.2. Bloom's Revised Taxonomy Showing Movement from Lower- to Higher-Order Thinking Tasks

Level on Taxonomy	What Students Will Do	Action Verbs to Guide Students' Work
Remember	Recall facts and basic concepts	define, duplicate, list, memorize, repeat, state
Understand	Explain ideas or concepts	classify, describe, discuss, explain, locate, recognize, report, select, translate
Apply	Use information in new situations	execute, implement, solve, use, demonstrate, interpret, operate, schedule, sketch
Analyze	Examine, methodically and in detail, in order to explain and interpret it and or make connections among ideas	differentiate, organize, relate, compare, contrast, distinguish, examine, experiment, question, test
Evaluate	Develop a stand or decision based on analysis	appraise, argue, defend, judge, select, support, value, critique, weigh
Create	Produce new or original work	design, assemble, construct, conjecture, develop, formulate, author investigate

the revised taxonomy, as well as when students are engaged with lower-level cognitive tasks (Remember, Understand) to higher-order thinking tasks (Analyze, Evaluate, Create). *Keep this information in mind as you read on, particularly when reading about brain-based learning and the implications.*

Social-Emotional Learning

Children are whole beings who are developing intellectually, socially, and emotionally as they progress through their schooling. How schools recognize and respond to this reality has been shown to greatly impact students. From this awareness, many schools have adopted practices aligned with Social-Emotional Learning theory (SEL). SEL is broadly defined as "the process through which individuals learn and apply a set of social, emotional, and related skills, attitudes, behaviors, and values that help direct students. This includes thoughts, feelings, and actions in ways that enable them to succeed in school."[20] SEL focuses on the development of children in five areas: self-awareness, self-management, social awareness, responsible decision-making, and relationship skills. The five dimensions of SEL and the goals for each are presented in Table 1.3. Note how many of the goals overlap with the goals of a responsible decision-maker, who relies on critical thinking to form conclusions, as well as assess their own welfare and that of others.

Table 1.3. Goals of Social and Emotional Learning (SEL)

Self-Awareness	Self-Management	Social Awareness	Responsible Decision-Making	Relationship Skills
Recognize one's emotions, values, strengths, and weaknesses	Manage emotions and behaviors to achieve one's goals	The ability to put yourself in the shoes of another person	Make ethical, constructive choices about personal and social behavior	Form positive relationships with people from diverse backgrounds
Understand how one's emotions, thoughts, and values influence behavior	To take control and ownership of one's thoughts, emotions, and actions in various situations to achieve one's goals	To act with empathy and in an ethical manner within your home, school, and community	Weigh the consequences for your well-being and others when making decisions	Learn to listen to and be able to communicate effectively
				Know when to ask for or offer help.
				Deal with conflict constructively

Mindfulness in Education

Similar to SEL, educators understand that children experience stress and have emotional needs that impact their well-being and learning. Many schools have come to see mindfulness practices as a valuable tool to better serve children. Jon Kabat-Zinn, an American professor emeritus of medicine, a mindfulness teacher and the creator of the Stress Reduction Clinic and the Center for Mindfulness in Medicine, Health Care, and Society at the University of Massachusetts Medical School, describes mindfulness as "the awareness that emerges through paying attention on purpose, in the present moment, non-judgmentally."[21] He and many other researchers and practitioners have found that mindfulness practices in education can reduce levels of stress and anxiety among children, help to increase focus and self-regulation, and improve academic performance.[22]

The late Thich Nhat Hanh, Buddhist monk, Zen teacher, and co-author of *Happy Teachers Change the World*, explains,

> Even very young children can often be the victims of their strong emotions and painful feelings. If they do not know how to handle these painful feelings and emotions, they will suffer. We can, as teachers . . . help our students suffer less. . . . When students are happy and relaxed, the work of teaching and learning becomes much easier.[23]

Through focused breathing and movement exercises, journaling, coloring, connecting to nature and themselves, students are taught how to use mindfulness practices to achieve more calm and focus, as well as a greater sense of connectedness, to be more receptive to learning, as the next section on brain-based learning will make clear.

Brain-Based Learning

In recent decades educators have benefited from new scientific knowledge about how the brain works. Brain researchers have learned that certain stimuli ignite parts of the brain that help the brain to be more receptive to receiving and retaining new information. When educators understand the process of how information is moved from short-term to long-term memory, they can use this knowledge to create learning experiences that have a higher likelihood of engaging students and stimulating long-term memory centers in the brain. This has become known as brain-based teaching and learning.

Brain-based learning involves teachers creating conditions that increase student motivation, engagement, and long-term retention by tapping into the natural ways the brain receives, processes, and stores information. In *Understanding a Brain-Based Approach to Learning and Teaching*, Geoffrey Caine and Renate Nummela Caine proposed that educators leverage neuroscience to improve students' knowledge retention and performance.[24] The Caines found that students had better comprehension and retention in a collaborative, hands-on, brain-based learning environment than those in a traditional lecture-based classroom. Scientifically speaking, active learning leads to the growth of dendrites, nerve cell extensions in the brain that influence how neurons collect and process information.

Author of *Teaching with Superpowers: Instructing Through Brain-Informed Practices*, Dr. Bobbi Hansen, shared a list of practices that leverage what is known about brain-based learning. Here is a list of some of the principles that are relevant for elementary schools and classrooms.[25] *As you read through the principles consider how many can be achieved through active learning and attention to SEL and mindfulness.*

Textbox 1.1. Nine Key Principles of Brain-Based Learning by Dr. C. Bobbi Hansen

1. **Activity and movement.** Physical activity isn't only for the gym. When students are able to take stretch breaks, go for short walks, or otherwise move their bodies during lessons, the more engaged they will be when they come back. Energize and revitalize students (and teachers)
2. **Group work.** When learning new material, it can be highly valuable to hear other students' reactions or experience how they take in new information. Group activities help students learn from one another and may even help them understand information better than they would have from their teachers' presentations.
3. **Peer teaching.** Teaching others is the most effective way to learn, and this applies to students as well. If a handful of students grasp a concept right away, they can then turn around and teach their peers, thereby strengthening their own understanding and delivering this new information in a way that resonates with their classmates.
4. **Practice.** Repetition, experimentation, and productive failure [developing through reflection of learning and integrating feedback and self-evaluation] are all more effective than simple memorization of facts or vocabulary. Students should have an opportunity to practice new skills and retrieve new knowledge.
5. **Limiting lectures.** Traditional lecture-based teaching has been proven not to be as effective as active learning. Making lessons more active rather than passive promotes students' knowledge retention.
6. **Meaningful information.** Academic concepts can often feel disconnected from students' actual lives. Finding ways to connect course materials to the real world improves student engagement and gives relevant meaning to abstract concepts.
7. **Written and verbal information.** Lessons and assignments that incorporate varied modes of delivery give students a better chance of moving information from short-term to their long-term memory.
8. **Stimulation.** Incorporating movement, humor, games, or current events that are of interest to their age group can increase students' participation, processing abilities, and the likelihood that they will remember the course content.
9. **Stress mitigation.** In general, stress negatively impacts our brains' neuroplasticity [Stress chemically changes the brain], preventing us from retaining information. Students learn and perform better in a classroom environment that is calm, safe, supportive, and positive.

Critical Place-Based Learning

David Greenwood (formerly Gruenewald) unites critical pedagogy and place-based education into an educational framework for research and practice referred to as a critical pedagogy of place. By fusing the theoretical roots of critical pedagogy and the ecological focus of place-based education, Greenwood argues that a critical pedagogy of place aims to (a) identify, recover, and create material spaces and places that teach us how to live well in our total environments (reinhabitation); and (b) identify and change ways of thinking that injure and exploit other people and places (decolonization).[26] He further states what we really need are "structures and practices that help rethink classrooms as the fundamental site of teaching learning."[27] A critical pedagogy of place highlights how "places are social constructions filled with ideologies, and the experience of places . . . shapes cultural identities."[28] Thus, a critical pedagogy of place encourages educators to advocate for a pedagogy that "relates directly to student experience of the world, and that improves the quality of life for people and communities."[29]

This style of learning seeks to empower students to critically examine the social, economic, and political dynamics that influence their local communities and environments. Greenwood states, "A focus on the lived experience of place puts culture in context, demonstrates the interconnection of culture and environment, and provides a locally relevant pathway for multidisciplinary inquiry and democratic participation."[30] As such, a critical pedagogy of place raises questions about why certain conditions exist and challenges the unequal power dynamics that continue to mask and perpetuate dominant conditions that exploit people, communities, and resources. By connecting people with places outside of their familiar classroom space, critical place-based pedagogies afford opportunities to more deeply investigate and understand local socio-environmental issues, and recognize that people hold deep knowledge about their lives and experiences. Again, we will point readers to the *community and place-based learning opportunities* sections of each chapter to see how diverse place-based pedagogies can be enacted.

Conclusion

It is important to us that we clearly show how the philosophies of teaching and learning that we present in this book and undergird our understanding of EcoJustice Education evolved from pedagogical and learning theory that is rooted in multiple areas of educational research. From new insights coming out of the brain-based learning sciences to transformative learning traditions like critical place-based pedagogies, all of these ideas, theories, concepts, and practices have pushed our thinking and the ways we engage with the work we do with teachers. In the chapters that follow we offer instructional materials that bring our EcoJustice Pillars into classrooms using multiple learning theories and pedagogies. It is our hope that by introducing EcoJustice Education as an expanded lens through which to view socio-environmental issues, you and your students recognize and intentionally foster a renewed relationship to the Earth, her resources, and people. This book is both an effort to tap into the enthusiasm we know teachers have for meaningful, place-based, critical, reflective pedagogies while simultaneously scaling up these efforts so that more teachers find the capacity to regain their autonomy. The cost of not trying to develop an EcoJustice consciousness among teachers and students will leave us stuck in the cycle of trying to solve our problems with the same thinking that got us here, and we simply can't afford that.

Notes

1 Duckworth, E. (1964). Piaget rediscovered. The Arithmetic Teacher, 11(7), p. 499.
2 Jean-Claude Bringuier, *Conversations with Jean Piaget* (Chicago, IL: University of Chicago Press, 1980).
3 M. E. Bellino and G. Burroughs, "Learn Globally, Teach Locally: Developing an EcoJustice Stance among Preservice Teachers through a Critical Place-Based Pedagogical Model," in *Ecocritical Perspectives in Teacher Education*, ed. J. Lupinacci, A. Happel-Parkins, and R. Turner, Constructing Knowledge: Curriculum Studies in Action (Leiden: Brill, 2023).
4 C. A. Bowers, *Educating for Eco-Justice and Community* (Athens: University of Georgia Press, 2001).
5 People of Color Environmental Leadership Summit, *Principles of Environmental Justice* (Washington, DC: People of Color Environmental Leadership Summit, 1991).
6 R. Turner and R. Donnelly, "Case Studies in Critical Ecoliteracy: A Curriculum for Analyzing the Social Foundations of Environmental Problems," *Educational Studies* 49, no. 5 (2013): 387–408; J. Lupinacci and A. Happel-Parkins, "Ecocritical Foundations: Toward Social Justice and Sustainability," in *The Social and Cultural Foundations of Education: A Reader*, ed. J. D. Diem (New York: Peter Lang, 2016): 34–56.
7 J. A. Henderson, "Out of Sight, Out of Mind: Global Connection, Environmental Discourse and the Emerging Field of Sustainability Education," *Cultural Studies of Science Education* 10, no. 3 (2015): 593–601.
8 Rebecca A. Martusewicz, "EcoJustice for Teacher Education Policy and Practice: The Way of Love," *Issues in Teacher Education* 27, no. 2 (2018): 17–35.
9 R. Turner and R. Donnelly, "Case Studies in Critical Ecoliteracy: A Curriculum for Analyzing the Social Foundations of Environmental Problems," *Educational Studies* 49, no. 5 (2013): 387–408.
10 J. Lupinacci and A. Happel-Parkins, "Ecocritical Foundations: Toward Social Justice and Sustainability," in *The Social and Cultural Foundations of Education: A Reader*, ed. J. D. Diem (New York: Peter Lang, 2016): 34–56.
11 Ethan Lowenstein, Rebecca Martusewicz, and Lloyd Voelker, "Developing Teachers' Capacity for Ecojustice Education and Community-Based Learning," *Teacher Education Quarterly* 37, no. 4 (2010): 99–118.

12 C. Bowers and R. Martusewicz, "Ecojustice and Social Justice," in *Encyclopedia of the Social and Cultural Foundations of Education*, ed. E. Provenzo and A. Provenzo (Thousand Oaks, CA: SAGE Publications, Inc., 2009).

13 Paulo Freire, *Pedagogy of the Oppressed* (New York: Bloomsbury Publishing USA, 2018).

14 Frances Moore Lappé, *EcoMind: Changing the Way We Think, to Create the World We Want* (New York: Nation Books, 2011), 101.

15 Floyd Cobb and John Krownapple, *Belonging Through a Culture of Dignity: The Keys to Successful Equity Implementation* (San Francisco: Mimi & Todd Press, 2019), 41.

16 Carla Shalaby, *Troublemakers: Lessons in Freedom from Young Children at School* (New York: The New Press, 2017), xvi.

17 Association for Experiential Education, "What Is Experiential Education?" accessed August 6, 2025, https://www.aee.org/what-is-experiential-education.

18 Louis Deslauriers, Logan S. McCarty, Kelly Miller, Kristina Callaghan, and Greg Kestin, "Measuring Actual Learning versus Feeling of Learning in Response to Being Actively Engaged in the Classroom," *Proceedings of the National Academy of Sciences* 116, no. 39 (2019): 19251–7.

19 Lorin W. Anderson and David R. Krathwohl, eds., A *Taxonomy for Learning, Teaching, and Assessing: A Revision of Bloom's Taxonomy of Educational Objectives* (New York: Longman, 2001).

20 National University, "What is Social Emotional Learning (SEL): Why It Matters," accessed August 6, 2025, https://www.nu.edu/blog/social-emotional-learning-sel-why-it-matters-for-educators/.

21 Jon Kabat-Zinn, *Wherever You Go, There You Are: Mindfulness Meditation in Everyday Life* (New York: Hyperion, 1994), 4.

22 Kimberly A. Schonert-Reichl, Eva Oberle, M. S. Lawlor, Diane Abbott, Kimberly Thomson, Tim F. Oberlander, and Adele Diamond, "Enhancing Cognitive and Social-Emotional Development through a Simple-to-Administer Mindfulness-Based School Program for Elementary School Children: A Randomized Controlled Trial," *Developmental Psychology* 51, no. 1 (2015): 52–66.

23 Thich Nhat Hanh and Katherine Weare, *Happy Teachers Change the World: A Guide for Cultivating Mindfulness in Education* (Berkeley: Parallax Press, 2017), 3.

24 Renate Nummela Caine and Geoffrey Caine, "Understanding a Brain-Based Approach to Learning and Teaching," *Educational Leadership* 48, no. 2 (October 1990): 66–70.

25 C. Bobbi Hansen, *Teaching with Superpowers: Ten Brain-Informed Practices* (Thousand Oaks, CA: Corwin Press, 2024).

26 David A. Gruenewald, "The Best of Both Worlds: A Critical Pedagogy of Place," *Educational Researcher* 32, no. 4 (May 2003): 3–12.

27 David A. Gruenewald, "The Best of Both Worlds: A Critical Pedagogy of Place," *Educational Researcher* 32, no. 4 (May 2003): 10.

28 David A. Gruenewald, "The Best of Both Worlds: A Critical Pedagogy of Place," *Educational Researcher* 32, no. 4 (May 2003): 5.

29 David A. Gruenewald, "The Best of Both Worlds: A Critical Pedagogy of Place," *Educational Researcher* 32, no. 4 (May 2003): 7.

30 David A. Gruenewald and Gregory A. Smith, eds., *Place-Based Education in the Global Age: Local Diversity* (New York: Lawrence Erlbaum Associates, 2008), 148.

lesson or taught about Jamestown yourself? How was the experience similar to what we share here? Keep these questions in mind as you read on.

Typical lessons on Jamestown that focus on the economic aspects of the colony include objectives such as:

- Students will be able to explain why the English wanted to colonize America
- Students will be able to explain why the Jamestown settlers came to America
- Students will be able to locate Jamestown on a map and explain why that site was selected to be settled

What knowledge will students need to meet these objectives? It might seem obvious that students will learn reasons why the British wanted to colonize in America, where Jamestown was located and why, and reasons why colonists went to Jamestown. They will learn that England wanted to expand its empire into North America and there were economic opportunities in the American colonies. Spain had colonies in South America where silver mines were found and native people were a source of cheap labor, and England wanted to reap similar rewards. Thus, students will typically be able to explain that England also wanted colonies in the "New World" and that many of the first settlers came in search of gold. Students will be required to *recall* and *comprehend* information, both lower-level cognitive actions on Bloom's taxonomy (see Chapter 2). Students will also learn some basic map reading skills when locating Jamestown and applying the map legend to understand the geographic features of the area, some of which are significant to why the site was selected. This will require the *application* of a skill and knowledge, which is slightly higher on the cognitive taxonomy.

Students usually learn next about the daily life and struggles of the settlers and the role that John Smith played in providing leadership. They typically learn that there were already people living in the area where the settlement was and that these native people were called the Powhatan. Some lessons still include the fictionalized story of a love affair between John Smith and Pocahontas (popularized by Disney, but not historically accurate). An example of common learning objectives for lessons on the relationship between the settlers and the Powhatan are:

- Students will be able to compare/contrast the settlers and native people
- Students will be able to explain the relationship between the settlers and the native people, and how it changed.

In order for students to describe ways the settlers and native people were similar and different, they will need some content knowledge of each group. This typically includes information on how the Powhatan people dressed, obtained food, the types of homes they lived in, and that their leader was a chief. Little to no information is usually offered to describe the relationship of the Powhatan people to the land and the sustainable practices they employed to access food and live in harmony with the Earth. However, students will have some basic knowledge of each group that they can *analyze* (which is the beginning of critical thinking) in order to draw comparisons. The students are also expected to understand how and why the relationship between the two groups changed over time, which requires *recall* of facts and *comprehension* when explaining the reasons. At the conclusion of a sequence of lessons built around the sample objectives, we can see that students will learn about the first permanent settlement by the English in what would become the United States. They will learn why England wanted to colonize there, what led to settlers coming, what life was like for them, and what kind of relationships they had with the Powhatan people who were Indigenous to the land. They will also develop some skills of critical thinking and working with maps. When considering this learning, some questions to ask are, what sense will students make of this? How will they come to understand the significance of Jamestown? How might that shape their worldview? Another question to ask is, what didn't the students learn? Let's unpack the lesson through an EcoJustice approach.

An EcoJustice Critique of the Conventional Approaches

An EcoJustice Education calls for a study of history and the present day that recognizes how some benefited from actions at the expense of both human and ecological systems. Students are encouraged to consider these realities, as well as ecological principles, as part of individual and collective decision-making. With these goals in mind, let us consider some of the consequences of continuing to teach children lessons like the example above.

To begin with, let's look at the lesson ideas again and ask some questions such as, from whose perspective are students exploring this history? Will the perspective of Native people be considered? Will students consider how the settlement and practices of the English impacted the environment? What are the consequences of the Powhatan people's experience, or the impact on the environment, not being addressed? The Powhatan people are usually part of the settlement story; however, only in relation to the English settlers. Students might learn that they initially helped the settlers or traded with them, later they will learn of tensions and warring among the groups. In the end, they will learn that the English settlers triumphed. This story reinforces a view of European dominance over people and the environment without a critique of settler colonialism.

An alternative way to learn about the Jamestown colony would include the reality that settlement of the territory caused an interruption to the way of life of those who already lived there, as well as alterations to the ecosystem. An overarching question to lead the students' study could be, "Should the Europeans have settled at Jamestown?" As students learn many aspects of the Jamestown settlement, such as the geography of the land, the people who lived there, the economic goals of the settlers and the London Company (the company of investors who sponsored the trip), the use of and competition over resources, and the hardships faced by the settlers and Powhatan people, this question could be revisited. Students could engage in problem-solving activities to consider alternatives that could have been more beneficial to all of the parties. Presenting the lesson this way allows for students to consider how competition over resources was a driving factor in the settlement of Jamestown that came at a cost to the Indigenous people, the environment, and even the many settlers who died. Although we cannot change history, questioning the past may help us make future decisions that are more conscious of environmental and human costs.

An extension to the study could be for students to learn about displacement of people and the disruption to culture and ecosystems in the Amazon today by big oil companies.[1] The unit could end with students considering how they could take action on an EcoJustice issue, as the women of the Amazon have. This could lead to a single lesson brainstorming actions, or to projects where students create awareness campaigns on EcoJustice issues, and even to students taking actions to support the people of the Amazon whose homes and way of life are under threat.

This re-envisioning of how to teach this seminal topic in US History reflects the Pillars we have identified to guide our work (see **Chapter 1** for a review of EcoJustice Pillars). *Pillar I An understanding and valuing of the interconnectedness of all living beings and systems* is developed as students come to recognize that the actions of one group impact others and the environment. Several of the components of Pillar I can also be developed: *Accept responsibility for the part we play in the ecological web of life; Care for the welfare of all beings;* and *Evaluate choices and decisions at multiple levels (self, community, state, country) through a systems lens.* When students engage in problem-solving tasks such as seeking alternative ways to share limited resources with the Powhatan, *Pillar II An orientation toward innovative, action-oriented, and collaborative problem-sol*ving is addressed. Similarly, *Pillar III A commitment to investigating socio-environmental issues through the lens of power and justice* can be explored when the students question if the English should have settled on the land.

Our final *Pillar IV Transdisciplinary Approaches*, can help students see cross-curricular connections rather than siloed thinking about content that leads to incomplete understandings. In the Jamestown example, we can easily find cross-curricular connections to elementary science concepts including natural resources, renewable and nonrenewable materials, energy, and ecosystem scarcity and competition. These topics are commonly taught to students devoid of any historical, social, or economic connection, but we can see how the Jamestown colony lesson could be enhanced and even understood through an ecological lens if these conceptual connections were made explicit. Students might ask questions about what resources were abundant in the specific climate and what Indigenous knowledge guided the ways of being of the Powhatan people. They might also question the practices of the settlers, comparing the impact on the environment of the settlers and the Powhatan, and have deeper dialogues about how each viewed nature and the resources it provided. While most conversations in science are about competition within and across species for resources, an inclusion of humans and social groups of humans (the settlers and the Powhatan) raises additional questions of justice, equity, and power. Adding this discussion and applying this scientific knowledge to the Jamestown example shows the natural opportunities and synergies between these content areas.

Expanding Teacher Content Knowledge

By reframing how we teach about the Jamestown colony through an EcoJustice lens, we hope you can begin to see how conventional approaches have the potential to reproduce colonizer perspectives. This happens via the reinforced notions of hierarchical valuing of some beings over others (European settlers over Indigenous people) and an uncritical acceptance that competition over resources is inevitable, leading to "winners" and "losers." Additionally, without making any cross-curricular connections between social studies and science, we make invisible the ecological context that shaped the experiences of humans and their diverse ways of relating to their environment. This may have been your experience when learning about topics like colonization and ecology in school. But we hope through this example you are able to see that by glossing over the socio-environmental impacts of the European colonizers, we miss a unique and powerful opportunity to expand young people's understanding of ecological principles that connect humans to the Earth and help develop the ethic of care and responsibility for the Earth that we need to survive. In this section, we want to push your own critical thinking capacities around the relationship between economics and ecology. First, we will look at a few economic principles, policies, and measures of success that guide the dominant economic view in our country and predominantly across the globe, free-market capitalism. Then we examine some of the fundamental ecological concepts that dictate how ecosystems function, sustain life, and maintain balance. Finally, we will discuss the tensions and contradictions that exist between economics and ecology and offer some critical questions for reflection.

Basic Economic Principles

What do you know about our current economic system? Where did you learn about our current economic system? School? Home? Work? What principles guide your economic decision-making? How has your understanding of economics prepared you for the realities you currently face? Has the dominant belief about equality of opportunity and that hard work leads to prosperity borne out in practice for you or in the lives of others in your community? What gaps in your knowledge do you have about how our economic system operates? We are assuming the answer to this last question is many, since so much about the rules and regulations that mediate the economy is written in language that obscures how the economy actually operates. While this section is not going to fill in all of those gaps, we hope it offers some guiding ideas to better understand and critique free-market capitalism, especially from an EcoJustice perspective. Many authors and resources are referenced throughout this section, and we encourage you to look into the writings of authors whose ideas resonate with you.

An *economic system* can be defined as encompassing the activities and rules of production, consumption, and the exchanging of material goods and services. Free-market capitalism evolved over centuries and today has become established in the human psyche as normal, natural, and an accepted way of thinking about the economy. Because of this, most of us do not recognize that our current economic system is a social system (this is why it is taught in the social studies content) that evolved from early trade systems, expanded during the industrial revolution, and emerged as the dominant economic model most exported across the globe.

Today's free-market capitalism is guided by principles of individual freedom, competition, profit-seeking, minimal government regulation, and a belief in the self-regulating "nature" of markets. Even this language implies that there is something "natural" about our economic system even though it is a human-constructed system. These principles are upheld by government policies of deregulation, tax cuts for the wealthy (a.k.a. Trickle-Down economics), privatization and commodification of many commons, free trade and globalization, and reductions of government funding for social safety nets (e.g., Social Security, Medicare, food and housing assistance, unemployment). However, we must recognize that all of these policies are forms of government intervention that organize and enforce the rules of the free market. In reality, the free market and government are intertwined so deeply and the people making the rules in government are heavily influenced by corporations and wealthy individuals via campaign financing and lobbying influences. In free-market capitalism, economic success is often defined by growth, efficiency, and profitability. Measures like an increase in Gross Domestic Product (GDP), low unemployment, and rising consumer spending are seen as signs of a thriving economy in free-market capitalism.

Our cultural norm is not to question free-market capitalism as the dominant economic model, but Robert Reich, former secretary of labor from 1993 to 1997, has been raising the alarms about income inequality stemming from capitalism and its threats to democracy for over 40 years. His strong advocacy work led him to start *Inequality Media*, a nonprofit digital media organization, creating accessible content about the intersection of economics and democracy.[2] In a video from late 2024, he identifies ten of the biggest myths about our economy, and he discusses the history of how the economic system has been rigged to benefit some and harm others.[3] Beginning with the interrelated myths that economics is an objective science and that government is an obstruction to the free market, he moves through many of the assumptions, policies, and measures of success associated with capitalism, debunking each and asking us to see the moral underpinnings, role of power, and the social and environmental costs of our economy.

Our free-market capitalist economic system is not the only economic model that we can look to for guidance on how to produce, consume, and distribute goods and services. Indigenous economics, exemplified by gift economies, are grounded in sustainability, interconnectedness, reciprocity, and respect for the natural environment. Robin Wall Kimmerer, a Potawatomi botanist, author, and the director of the *Center for Native Peoples and the Environment*, asks in her book, *The Serviceberry: Abundance and reciprocity in the natural world* a very simple question: "What is economics for anyway?"[4] She goes on to critically acknowledge that the answer depends largely on who you ask and then contrasts our capitalist economic model with a gift economy. She writes that a gift economy is

> an antecedent alternative to market economies, another way of "organizing ourselves to sustain life." In a gift economy, wealth is understood as having enough to share, and the practice for dealing with abundance is to give it away. In fact, status is determined not by how much one accumulates, but by how much one gives away. The currency in a gift economy is relationship, which is expressed as gratitude, as interdependence and the ongoing cycles of reciprocity. A gift economy nurtures the community bonds that enhance mutual well-being; the economic unit is "we" rather than "I," as all flourishing is mutual.[5]

Charles Eisenstein in his text, *Sacred Economics: Money, Gift & Society in the Age of Transition* reminds us that while scarcity is one of the central axioms of modern economics, it is not the truth of our whole reality. He writes, "So immersed in scarcity are we that we take it to be the nature of reality. But in fact, we live in a world of abundance. The omnipresent scarcity we experience is an artifact: of our money system, of our politics, and of our perceptions."[6] There are many schools of economic thought reimagining alternative and sustainable economic models including circular economics,[7] donut economics,[8] and ecological economics.[9] While each of these represents a unique school of thought beyond what can be included here, collectively, they are more aligned to ecological principles, address environmental and social concerns, and prioritize equity and long-term well-being over traditional profit-driven capitalism. Now let's look more closely at some of the principles of ecology that present limits and constraints to free-market economics.

Basic Ecological Principles

Reflect on your understanding of ecology. What do you remember from school about ecology and the environment? Do you remember having many wonderings about the natural world as a child and making observations of your environment that blew your mind? When did you feel most connected or disconnected from the natural environment? Did your experiences with ecology impact your relationship with the Earth? What questions are you still curious about when it comes to how ecosystems function? Similar to our discussion of economics, this section will review some of the major ecological concepts that inform an EcoJustice perspective.

Ecology is the study of the interactions between all living things and their living (***biotic***) and nonliving (***abiotic***) environment. You probably remember hearing all of these terms in school. Essentially, the field of ecology seeks to investigate and understand relationships and natural processes that support life on Earth. Familiarity with the principles of ecology can help us understand how nature operates and offers guidance for sustainable interactions between humans and the environment. Unlike our economic systems, which are socially constructed, ecological systems are governed by natural and biological processes that cannot be reshaped and reimagined to fit human desired outcomes.

Some of the very EcoJustice principles and Pillars that we have outlined in Chapter 1 are aligned to ecology. Here we will highlight a few that are significant to our understanding of the relationship between ecology and economics. ***Interdependence***, the idea that all living things are dependent upon one another and their environment for their survival, is something that we often study as food webs. But humans are often missing from these webs, and our invisibility has led to a separation of humans from nature that plagues much of our modern ways of thinking. As an interconnected system, any disturbance that disrupts a part of the system can have consequential outcomes for other parts and the whole. Another important ecological principle is ***conservation of matter and energy***. The natural world does not waste matter or energy—matter is cycled and recycled back into usable forms, and energy is moved and transformed via a diversity of processes (i.e., photosynthesis, digestion). Each organism plays its crucial role in the processes of nutrient cycling and energy transformation, even humans, and our activities as humans can disrupt these processes. Finally, the ecological principle of ***biodiversity*** is what gives ecosystems and our planet stability and resilience to disturbances. The more diverse an ecosystem, the more stable it is. The principle of diversity applies to all environments, from our forest and ocean health to how we grow our foods to our social environments.

The availability of ***natural resources***, the material substances found in nature needed for survival, also determines the health and well-being of ecosystems and species. As a human construct and means to our own survival, natural resources include all the requirements for humans and other living things, including water, air, soil, forests, minerals, fossil fuels, and the biodiversity present on the planet. Natural resource availability limits species' capacity to grow and thrive on the planet. There are finite resources on Earth, and while this does not directly mean that all resources are scarce, it does mean that the amount and distribution of resources limits and shapes the populations of all living things (including humans) that can be supported. This is one of the biggest laws of nature that we tend to forget when living our day-to-day lives. It is imperative to remember that the resources on Earth are not for human consumption alone. We are but one species on this planet, and the services that are provided by a healthy and thriving ecosystem (e.g., clean air, clean water, pollination, healthy soils) are shared benefits for all. In the opposite vein, damage we do and have done to the healthy balance of our ecosystems has had, and will continue to have, social, economic, and health impacts that touch all of our lives.

Implications of Current Economics on Our Social and Ecological Systems

Our current economic model premised on limitless profits and intensive resource extraction works against the science of ecology. Robin Wall Kimmerer reminds us of this when she wrote, "We continue to embrace economic systems that prescribe infinite growth on a finite planet, as if somehow the universe had repealed the laws of thermodynamics on our behalf."[10] Ecology shows us that nothing in nature is infinite, everything is finite, that natural systems have limits, and it takes time to regenerate resources once they have been extracted. If we overexploit both our ecological and social resources, we will destabilize systems which, if not given time to recover, can lead to collapse. Ecology also shows us that nature does not waste but works in cycles, constantly recycling materials and energy through complex nutrient cycling processes and decomposition. Just look at the footprint of plastic waste on our planet to see how we are using and taking at much greater rates than our planet can assimilate.

The global economy is heavily dependent on fossil fuel consumption, which is directly impacting our carbon and water cycles. Our industrialized food system is based almost exclusively upon principles of monoculture, growing a single crop, and is dependent on heavy amounts of energy, water, and chemical fertilizer inputs. Ecology teaches us that greater biodiversity leads to more stable and resilient ecosystems that can resist catastrophic events, and growing our food with these regenerative principles in mind can sustain soil, water, and access to healthy foods (see Chapter 6: Food). As a result of free-market capitalism, privatization and commodification have led to overexploitation and extraction of natural resources and record profits for transnational corporations. Ecology teaches us that these natural resources work in concert with one another, and Indigenous wisdom shows us that when we keep resources as public commons, we are all invested in caring for them.

Unlike economic systems, there are no alternatives to how we organize or "do" ecology. Therefore, a deeper understanding of our current economic system illuminates the way it violates principles of ecology. Being able to see this and feel the impacts of this violation can produce profound shifts in our relationship with people and the planet. Integrating social studies and science teaching and learning around these topics can help us better see the ways that corporate profits are privileged over the well-being and sustainability of the environment, and we can begin to imagine and create new possibilities.

Look at the current situation in the United States as but one example of corporate power converging with government power to grab, privatize, and commodify resources, sometimes without us even knowing. Other times, coercive and militarized tactics have been used to undemocratically impose an unjust and unsustainable agenda on people and the planet. Here are some examples to illustrate how the economic policies and practices that dictate the "rules" of free-market capitalism, predicated on corporate greed, are playing out, contributing to the social and ecological consequences that permeate our current social landscape.

- Over the past three years, Tesla reported $10.8 billion in US income but paid only $48 million in federal taxes, resulting in an effective tax rate of 0.4 percent, significantly below the statutory corporate tax rate of 21 percent.[11]
- According to a report by the Institute for Policy Studies (IPS), US billionaires added $2.1 trillion to their wealth during the first 19 months of the pandemic, between March 2020 and September 2021. This surge in wealth is attributed to rising stock markets, booming tech sectors, and other factors that disproportionately benefited the ultra-wealthy during the crisis.[12]
- In 1979, the wealthiest 1 percent owned about 20 percent of the nation's wealth. By 2021, that share had risen to over 35 percent, reflecting the growing inequality in wealth distribution in the United States.[13]

- Between 1979 and 2020, real wages for the median US worker grew by just 11 percent—a slow increase considering that productivity during this period rose much faster, by about 70 percent.[14]
- As of 2021, the top 1 percent of households in the United States hold about 32 percent of all wealth in the country, and 40 percent of US wealth is inherited. This highlights how wealth is increasingly concentrated in families that already have substantial resources, perpetuating dynastic wealth over generations.[15]
- In 2019, the median net worth of white families was $188,200, while the median net worth of Black families was $24,100 and the median net worth of Latino families was $36,100. This indicates that the median wealth of Black families was only 12.8 percent of white families' wealth, and Latino families' median wealth was about 19.2 percent of white families.[16]
- As of 2023, poverty rates in the United States were reported to be approximately 11.6 percent of the population, which translates to about thirty-seven million people living in poverty. About 50 percent of people in poverty live in households with incomes less than $25,000 per year.[17]
- Research from Oxford University suggests that shocks to the global economy related to biodiversity loss and ecosystem damage could cost upward of $5 trillion.[18]
- Over the past 50 years, the global economic cost of invasive species has been estimated at $1.288 trillion.[19]
- In 2024, the United States experienced twenty-seven weather and climate disaster events, each causing losses exceeding $1 billion.[20]

Honing Your Critical Lens

As you can see, the interconnected landscape of economics and ecology has had an immense impact on our social and environmental health and well-being in the form of massive economic inequality, environmental degradation, concentration and influence of corporate power, and economic instability. The social and environmental impacts of constant and endless economic growth call into question the sustainability of this economic model and beg for systemic reform. You and your students have a part to play in reimagining an economic system that does not exploit people and the environment for the profit of a few. You have power as a teacher of young people. All children and youth today are dependent on us for their future.

This section merely scratches the surface in highlighting the multitude of ways that our current economic system comes up against the science of ecology. With this new understanding, we offer some questions below as a way to critically analyze the impacts and contradictions inherent in our current economic system. Remember that most of our systems are massive and interconnected, which means there are many parts that are intentionally and unintentionally obscured and rendered invisible. Our work, as we hone our EcoJustice and critical consciousness, is to wrestle with embedded assumptions that appear normal. Noam Chomsky writes, "I try to encourage people to think for themselves, to question standard assumptions . . . don't take assumptions for granted. Begin by taking a skeptical attitude toward anything that is conventional wisdom. Make it justify itself. It usually can't. Be willing to ask questions about what is taken for granted. Try to think things through for yourself."[21] It is okay to not know the answers yet. The book will continue to explore these questions, and we know you will be coming up with your own questions as well. By engaging in these reflective exercises, you will be better equipped to meaningfully and powerfully engage your classroom with the instructional materials we are offering and be more inspired to create your own EcoJustice lessons

- Who are the winners in our current economic model and what are the outcomes for the winners?
- Who are the losers in our current economic model and what are the outcomes for the losers?
- How does your understanding of the ecological principles as described above influence your daily decision-making?
- In what ways are you receiving economic messages that conflict with what you know is sustainable and ecological?

Free Write and Research Activity: Choose any question posed above and do a quick free write. Try to find a piece of writing or thinking that is related to your question. Our website resources have a table of suggested texts for you to engage with to push your thinking about some economic topics. Find an excerpt from any resources (e.g., book, essay, video, or podcasts) and share some connections you are making on this topic. Be mindful of the resources that you engage in your search for answers as these will inform the views that are presented.

Standards and Goals for Teaching and Learning

Now that you have more background knowledge and context about the relationship between economics and ecology, we hope you feel a greater sense of urgency to teach these topics in your own classroom. This section broadly outlines the standards for social studies and science teaching at the elementary level that relate to these topics of study. The study of economics and ecology is central to understanding the problem of scarcity (i.e., the fact that we do have limited resources), which has led to a mindset of competition for resources, exploitative production of goods and services, and many other practices that contribute to socio-environmental problems. Fortunately, the study of economics and ecology is considered important for all students to understand and therefore both are embedded in national and state standards. Not surprisingly, both the Cloud Standards and the UN Sustainable Development Goals also include guidance for how to address economics as part of educating for sustainability. We will highlight relevant standards in this section that connect across social studies, science, and sustainability.

Social Studies Standards from NCSS

Within the NCSS Themes and C3 Framework, fundamental concepts of economics described so far are directly stated and therefore are easy to align to lessons that explore economic topics related to socio-environmental issues. This alignment provides inroads to teaching that supports our Pillars. Below, guidance for Social Studies from NCSS is presented.

NCSS Theme VII. Production, Distribution, and Consumption: The study of how goods and services are produced, distributed, and consumed. This theme calls for learning experiences that help children understand and explore the ideas:

> People have wants that often exceed the limited resources available to them. The unequal distribution of resources necessitates systems of exchange, including trade, to improve the well-being of the economy, while the role of government in economic policy-making varies over time and from place to place. Increasingly, economic decisions are global in scope and require systematic study of an interdependent world economy and the role of technology in economic growth. As a result, a variety of ways have been invented to decide upon answers to four fundamental questions: What is to be produced? How is production to be organized? How are goods and services to be distributed and to whom? What is the most effective allocation of the factors of production (land, labor, capital, and entrepreneurship)?[22]

Theme VII articulates the goals to develop students' knowledge, skills and attitudes related to economic activity by the end of grade 12. The NCSS C3 Inquiry Framework provides more specific guidance by offering progress indicators by grade bands in elementary education. A full list of the relevant social studies indicators that can be used to anchor EcoJustice lessons is provided in the Appendix. Below we share a sampling of NCSS C3 indicators for economics to see how they align to topics discussed in this chapter.

Textbox 2.1. NCSS C3 Inquiry Framework Indicators for Grades K-2

D2.Eco.1.K-2. Explain how scarcity necessitates decision-making.
D2.Eco.2.K-2. Identify the benefits and costs of making various personal decisions.
D2.Eco.4.K-2. Describe the goods and services that people in the local community produce and those that are produced in other communities.
D2.Eco.5.K-2. Identify prices of products in a local market.
D2.Eco.6.K-2. Explain how people earn income.
D2.Eco.7.K-2. Describe examples of costs of production.
D2.Eco.10.K-2. Explain why people save.
D2.Eco.12.K-2. Describe examples of the goods and services that governments provide.
D2.Eco.13.K-2. Describe examples of capital goods and human capital.

Textbox 2.2. NCSS C3 Inquiry Framework Indicators for Grades 3–5

D2.Eco.1.3–5. Compare the benefits and costs of individual choices.
D2.Eco.2.3–5. Identify positive and negative incentives that influence the decisions people make.
D2.Eco.3.3–5. Identify examples of the variety of resources (human capital, physical capital, and natural resources) that are used to produce goods and services.
D2.Eco.7.3–5. Explain how profits influence sellers in markets.
D2.Eco.8.3–5. Identify examples of external benefits and costs.

Next-Generation Science Standards

While the NGSS do not explicitly address economic foundations like money, goods, and services, a scientifically literate citizen will understand the ecological principles outlined earlier as well as some basics of material science and the distinction between renewable and nonrenewable resources in order to better see how access to resources has shaped the economic realities of humans. Drawing on scientific literacy from the AAAS Benchmarks[23] and NGSS,[24] we can see the following progression of thinking for children from grades K-5. From the science perspective, additional practices and cross-cutting concepts help us better understand the science of ecology, including making and using models, asking questions and defining problems, and engaging in argument from evidence.

Textbox 2.3. Next-Generation Science Standards for Grades K-2

By grade 2 students understand:

- Some materials come directly from nature while some materials are made with resources that originally came from nature but are man-made/manufactured. (2-PS1-2)
- Some materials can be used over again (reused) and some materials can be recycled (parts of the materials can be made into new materials). (K-ESS3-3)
- All living things require resources to survive, and they require them from the land, air, and water (e.g., land = food, nutrients from soil, air, and water, fire = wood). (K-LS1-1, K-ESS3-1)
- Animals and plants rely on one another for survival. (2-LS2-2, 2-LS4-1)
- Living things and nonliving things are both part of an ecosystem. (K-ESS3-1, 2-LS4-1)
- Matter is required by organisms and they get this from their environment. (K-LS1-1)
- Plants and animals require things from their environment. When their environment changes that can damage/kill plants and animals in the area. (K-ESS3-1, K-ESS2-2)

Textbox 2.4. Next-Generation Science Standards for Grades 3–5

By grade 5 students understand:

- All the resources we need to live must come from our planet. (3-ESS3-1, 5-ESS3-1)
- Some resources are naturally occurring on Earth and are called natural resources (e.g., air, water, soil, minerals, metals, plants, animals, energy)—all come from the environment. (5-ESS3-1)
- Some resources come back during our lifetime (renewable). Some renewable resources are only renewable at great costs. (5-ESS3-1)
- Some resources will not come back during our lifetime (nonrenewable). (5-ESS3-1)
- Natural materials can be processed and combined with other materials to change their properties. (5-PS1-3, 5-PS1-4)
- Discarded products contribute to problems of waste, some materials are easier to recycle than others. Some nonrenewable resources can be reused (like metal, plastic). (5-ESS3-1)
- Plants/Phytoplankton are the base for food for all life on Earth. (5-PS3-1, 5-LS2-1)
- Organisms move energy and matter by eating one another. (5-LS2-1)
- When living things die, they are decomposed and their matter is recycled back into the environment. (5-LS2-1)
- Healthy ecosystems have many relationships. (3-LS4-4, 5-LS2-1)
- When the environment changes (lack of food, temperature), it may allow some species to survive, migrate, or die. (3-LS4-4)
- Plants grow from getting matter from the air and the soil that helps them grow (nutrients and oxygen)—Amount of matter is conserved. (5-LS1-1)
- Decomposers move matter back to the air and the soil. (5-LS2-1)

Cloud Institutes Education for Sustainability Content Standards

Standard F from the **Cloud Standards** describes the relationship between individuals and communities and the natural and ecological principles that guide and sustain life on our planet. By honoring that our livelihoods are governed by these natural laws, students can see how they are deeply connected to the planet and they are responsible for making sustainable choices that honor and serve one another and the Earth. Below is the description of Standard F from the Cloud Institute.

> Natural Laws & Ecological Principles—The laws of nature and science principles of sustainability. Students will see themselves as interdependent with each other, all living

things, and natural systems. They will be able to put their knowledge and understanding to use in the service of their lives, their communities, and the places in which they live.[25]

UN Sustainable Development Goals

The United Nations Sustainability Goals are another resource that provides guidance for educators. Many of the SDGs speak directly to issues of the environment, climate change, and inequitable burdens. Many of the SDGs will be addressed in future sections of this book, however for this chapter, the SDG that is most relevant is SDG *Goal 12 Ensure Sustainable Consumption and Production Patterns.* On the U.N. website, the case for enacting SDG 12 is made with the statement, "Our planet is running out of resources, but populations are continuing to grow. If the global population reaches 9.8 billion by 2050, the equivalent of almost three planets will be required to provide the natural resources needed to sustain current lifestyles."[26] Goal 12 reads as follows:

> The goal is to make sure resources are not wasted when things are made and used. Important ways of achieving this include halving food waste worldwide; monitoring harmful chemicals that are discharged when making things to prevent water, air, and soil contamination; and adopting the Three R's (reduce, reuse, recycle) to minimize waste.

How can education help to foster a mindset among children that considers all three aspects of People, Planet, and Prosperity, as outlined in the *Preamble for Transforming our World: the 2030 Agenda for Sustainable Development* discussed in Chapter 1? Much of the guidance under Sustainability Goal 12 calls for actions by governments and the business sector, however, children can learn about actions individuals can take to help reach the goal of sustainable consumption and production patterns and to consider the Triple Bottom Line of People, Planet (Place), and Prosperity (Profit).

Applying EcoJustice Pillars to Chapter Instructional Materials

So where do we begin? We need to find places to build EcoJustice Education from the beginning of children's formal schooling experiences. As early as kindergarten we can introduce lessons that integrate our EcoJustice Education Pillars. In this section we will detail how we believe that this can be accomplished and provide examples of instructional materials related to foundational understandings of economics for K-5 classrooms.

An EcoJustice approach to education prepares students to think critically about the impact of decisions, practices, and policies on the degradation or sustainability of systems. On a personal level, students are encouraged to look at multiple perspectives and weigh options when making decisions and to value that the health and welfare of people, animals, and the Earth should be driving considerations. Thus, this chapter lays the foundation for rational decision-making that takes into account the economic realities of scarcity and limited and renewable resources as well as ecological principles of abundance, connection, and diversity. Students are further encouraged to understand that access to resources is not the same for all people and populations and that burdens of decisions are not shared equally either. We are not advocating for equality of condition, but rather for decision-making that weighs burdens and consequences, individual and collective well-being, and the health of the planet in the process.

We have employed somewhat of a "Backwards Design"[27] approach when creating examples of instructional materials. We start with the question, where do we want to end? We first identified the desired outcome we seek when a student completes elementary school. From there we worked backwards to identify developmentally appropriate goals by grade level bands. In this way we offer the instructional materials for grades K-2 as appropriate for building foundational knowledge, skills and attitudes that can then be further explored and added to in upper elementary school years. Figure 2.1 shows the progression by grade bands, K-2 and 3–5 and the goals at each level in order to reach the level of understanding and consciousness regarding economic issues from an EcoJustice Education perspective. The final column represents the goal for an adolescent completing K-5 education. Review the progression and consider the types of learning experiences students will require to reach the stated goals for each grade band and for the end of elementary school.

The goals of the instructional materials for elementary classrooms offer simple places to start thinking about how we are participating in the current economic system, the social

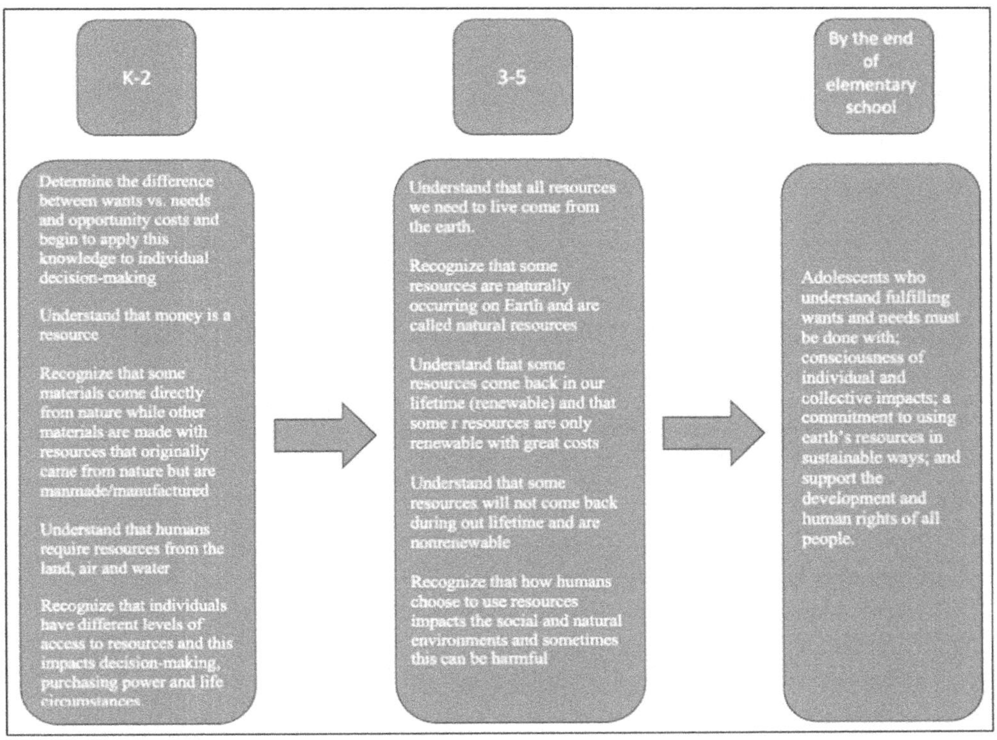

Figure 2.1. Flow chart K-5 to achieve an emerging EcoJustice consciousness related to economics. Author created.

and ecological impacts of participation, and how we might make different choices with a more critical lens. Instructional materials were designed to help reach the goals articulated in Figure 2.1 for each grade band. Materials can be used as they are presented here, modified to meet your classroom needs, or as inspiration to draw on for new classroom learning opportunities.

We suggest that before you teach the concepts presented, refresh your comfort with the following terms: *Scarcity*, *Consumers*, *Opportunity Cost*, *Incentives*, *Money*, *Decision-Making*, *Cost-Benefit Analysis*, *Savings*, and *Investing*. These terms are not often viewed through critical lenses, and so it is our work as teachers to invite that critical perspective when reviewing these concepts. Remember that exploring economics through a critical lens will question common-sense assumptions embedded in economic theories and practices, including power dynamics, potential negative impacts on society, and will often highlight issues like income inequality, environmental damage, the concentration of wealth, and the exploitation of workers. Below we offer a teacher perspective on the Economic Foundations instructional materials for grades 3–5 followed by the instructional materials for grades K-2 and 3–5.

Economic Foundations Instructional Materials

The value I see throughout these lessons, both for teachers and students is how each lesson is intentionally planned for experiential learning. Students are given the opportunity to reflect, apply knowledge, and draw conclusions. The lessons are also strong examples of Social Emotional Learning—where students are asked to make responsible decision-making based on their learnings and reflections. There is no doubt that students would appreciate these types of lessons, as they are engaging and mindful. Teachers are given the space to bring the objectives to life through active discussion rather than telling students what they need to do.

—*Briana, Elementary Teacher*

Textbox 2.5. K-2 EcoJustice Instructional Materials Economic Foundations

Essential Question(s): How can your awareness of wants versus needs impact the things you buy?

Objectives: Students will be able to:

- **Understand** the difference between wants and needs
- **Recognize** money is a (limited) resource.
- **Understand** that due to scarcity, we can't fill all of our wants and therefore need to make responsible choices.
- **Recognize** that people have different access to resources.
- **Describe** how individual and collective actions can lead to change

Standards:

Social Studies

- **D2.Eco.1.K-2.** Explain how scarcity necessitates decision-making.
- **D2.Eco.2.K-2.** Identify the benefits and costs of making various personal decisions.
- **D2.Eco.10.K-2.** Explain why people save.
- **D2.Civ.6.K-2.** Describe how communities work to accomplish common tasks, establish responsibilities, and fulfill roles of authority.
- **D2.Civ.2.K-2.** Explain how all people, not just official leaders, play important roles in a community.

Science

- **K-ESS3-1:** Use a model to represent the relationship between the needs of different plants or animals (including humans) and the places they live.
- **K-PS3-1:** Use observations to describe that different kinds of materials are needed by different human-made products.
- **K-ESS3-3:** Communicate solutions that will reduce the impact of humans on the land, water, air, and/or other living things in the local environment.

Materials:

Lesson 1

- Needs and Wants Explained video
- Pictures of wants and needs items
- Needs versus Wants Bingo Cards

Lesson 2

- *A Boy, a Budget, and a Dream* Read aloud available at https://www.youtube.com/watch?v=DPAj6WWiKJ4&t=2s

Lesson 3

- *A Chair for My Mother* Read aloud available at https://www.youtube.com/watch?v=DEoEEWEnool&t=1s

Important Vocabulary/Concepts:

- Want
- Need
- Scarcity
- Savings
- Spending
- Economic decision-making
- Incentives
- Natural Resources versus Man-made

Instructional Materials Description and Overview:
In this set of instructional materials for grades K-2, students are first introduced to the concept of wants and needs through dialogue, video, and games.

Note to Teacher:
The focus of the K-2 instructional materials presented here is more aligned to a social studies classroom, but we will offer examples in the EXTEND sections of lessons to engage students with science literacies.

A Boy, a Budget, and a Dream is a great book to illustrate how even children can be faced with making economic decisions and why savings can be powerful. The book, *A Chair for My Mother*, can be used to help students explore the idea that people have different economic conditions which lead to access to different resources.

Lesson 1: Wants Versus Needs
ENGAGE: Lesson Introduction

- Show the students two images, one of a need such as water or food and the other of a toy. Ask the students if the items are both important to them? Then ask if they want both? Then ask if they need both
- Explain that today they will learn the difference between needs and wants and point to the terms on the anchor chart as you say each term
- Explain that they will now watch a video that will help explain the difference between a need and a want https://www.youtube.com/watch?v=TP1gPF6e3UM
- During the video:
    - Stop the video at 1:20 and review the terms "want" and "need" with the class
    - Tell the students that they will see many examples of needs and wants and watch the rest of the video

EXPLORE: Shared practice and reinforcement of terms

- Return to the anchor chart and tell the students you will show them some images of items, and they will need to decide if each is a need or a want
- Show the students some pictures and allow them to call out if it is a need or a want, or you can use symbols to represent the terms and have students raise the symbol for their choice for each image
- After all of the students have shared their answers, tape the image next to the correct term. Be sure to listen to the responses to determine if all of the students understand the difference between the concepts

EXPLAIN: Defining Terms

- As a class, develop a definition for want and need in students' own language and understanding

ELABORATE: Application activity

- Needs versus Wants Bingo (See Sample Bingo Card)
    - For this activity, students can work independently or with a partner depending on their ability and comfort level

- Pass out the bingo card included or use the card generator at https://bingobaker.com/?bingo_id=6216876 to create several different versions of the card.[28] This is best for older students (second grade)
- Tell the students that you will flip a coin (or you can use a coin toss generator) and one side will represent the word, "Want" and the other side will represent the word, "Need"
- Explain that when you call out the term "Want" everyone should place a marker, or draw a line through the box with an image of something that would be considered a "Want", and that when you call out the term "Need" they should place a marker or draw a line through the box with the image of a need
- Explain when they have a row of boxes marked off (across, up/down, or diagonally) they should call out bingo
- Let the student with bingo come to the front of the class and explain if each item in the row is a need or a want and ask the class each time if they think the answer is correct. This will serve as an additional reinforcement of the terms and check for understanding

https://bingobaker .com/ ?bingo _id =6216876

EXTEND: Activity and Critical Dialogue

- Have students cut up their bingo card and sort the items into two new categories—natural and man-made
- Have students move around the room and see how other groups categorized their items and then return to their home group to make any changes
- Have groups share out (Science and Engineering Practice: Engaging in argument from evidence) which items they think are natural and which are man-made and why
- Get to a final agreement about which items belong in each category
- Facilitate a dialogue with students to co-create a definition for each based on their observations and evidence
- Critical Dialogue: Discuss why knowing the difference between natural resources and man-made resources matters. Try to get students to make connections that highlight their understanding that almost everything we need comes from nature and that knowing this will allow them to make responsible decisions based on a sense of interdependence, conservation, and sustainability (that things will be available for future generations)

EVALUATE: Wrap-Up Activity/Assessment

- Have each student write the words Want and Need on a piece of paper and then tell them to write or draw an example of a want and a need under each term

Lesson 2: Spending and Saving
ENGAGE: Lesson Introduction

- Ask students if they have ever wanted something that costs too much money for them to buy?
- Then ask if they have ever saved their money to buy something they really want and allow a few to share their examples.
- Tell them they will listen to a story of a boy who was in this situation, and they will learn what he did.

EXPLORE: Read Aloud

- Pause to ask questions and discuss the following points:
    - Why does Joey's sister have more money saved than Joey?
    - Is Joey making a good decision about spending his money?
    - Is Cass making good decisions? How do you know?
    - What can Joey do to get the money to go to STEM camp?
    - Do you think Joey should buy the video camera now or save money for STEM camp?

EXPLAIN: Text Analysis

- Discuss what Joey did to get the money he needed for STEM camp
- Make a list with the students and discuss what Joey had to give up to get what he really wanted (Opportunity Cost, Savings, Incentives, and Economic Decision-making)

ELABORATE: **Writing Reflection**

- Ask the students if they think Joey made a good decision. Have students turn and talk to a partner about why they think Joey made a good decision or not.

EXTEND: Activity and Critical Dialogue

- Think about a recent decision you made about something you wanted. Draw a picture of it or write it down on a piece of paper.
- Turn and talk with a partner about why you wanted this particular thing and how you came to make the decision that it was something you wanted.
- What impact did the thing you wanted have on the environment? For example, did you want a new toy and the toy came in plastic packaging?
- Did you think about the environmental impact when you made your decision? Why or why not? Could you have thought more about this when making your decision?
- Critical Dialogue: In small groups, have students discuss the questions:

- Why is it important to think about the impacts on the environment when we make economic decisions?
- Is there a way to make sure everyone has what they need without hurting the Earth?
- Bring students together as a class for a whole class discussion.

EVALUATE: **Wrap-Up/Assessment**

- Students complete the writing prompt below
  - I think Joey did/didn't make a good decision because . . .

Lesson 3: Access to Resources
ENGAGE: **Lesson Introduction**

- Ask the students who can remember how Joey was able to get the money he needed for STEM camp. Reinforce that he was given an allowance from his parents.
- Explain that they will hear a story about another child who wants to buy something very much, but she doesn't have an allowance and that they will learn what she does about this.

EXPLORE: During the Read Aloud

- Pause to ask questions and discuss the following points:
  - How was the family trying to save money?

- What does the family plan to do when they have enough money?
- Why can't the family simply buy a new chair?
- How did the family get items they needed for their home after the fire? (These items can be written on an anchor chart and students can discuss if the items are needs or wants. The students might change their views as more of the story is read.)
- How was the family able to finally buy the chair?

EXPLAIN: Text Connections

- Ask the students to brainstorm a list of other items they think the little girl in the story would have liked to buy with the money she earned?
- Ask the students why they think the main character wanted to help buy the chair?

ELABORATE: Perspective Building

- Ask the students if they would make a similar decision if they were in her position?

EXTEND: Collage Models and Critical Dialogue

- What kinds of materials make this? Review the concept of natural resources and discuss how some can be used over and over again (reused) while some materials can be recycled (parts of the materials can be made into new materials), and some materials are thrown out. Students will make a model collage of the materials that make up a common household item.

  - Have each student choose one item from the list of items made during the EXPLAIN that they want to investigate further or make groups of students for specific items from the class list.
  - Have students create a collage that has an image of the item on big paper (or have this already prepared) and have them collage the materials that make up the item. For example, if the item is a chair, what is the chair made of? Wood, a cushion. Continue to push students to get more detailed. For example, what is a cushion made of? Fabric and filling. Have students engage in some research/discussion to find out at least three materials that make up each item and add images of these to their collage.
  - Have students build their collage model (write/draw/show/tell) where each of the materials came from if they are able to figure that out. Example: Wood comes from a tree.
  - Have students share their final collage with the class. During the sharing of the collages, construct a table as a class of all the materials that students learned about, where they come from, and ask whether they can be reused, recycled, or thrown away when they are no longer needed.

- **Critical Dialogue:** Engage the class in a discussion about why the ideas on the table are important to consider in making decisions. Encourage students to think about how they know when something is ready to be reused, recycled, or thrown away.

EVALUATE: Wrap-Up/Assessment

- Each student responds to the prompt either orally or in writing.
- Prompt: I think the girl in the story did/didn't make a good decision because . . .

Textbox 2.6. 3–5 EcoJustice Instructional Materials Economic Foundations

Essential Questions:

How can your awareness of wants versus needs impact the things you buy?

How can you make choices that are beneficial to you, your community, and the environment?

Objectives: Students will be able to:

- **Describe** the value of natural resources
- **Explain** how competition over natural resources can be problematic for the Earth and all living beings
- **Explain** the significance of "the commons"
- **Evaluate** ways to protect the commons to maximize benefits to the Earth and all living beings
- **Describe** individual and collective actions that can be taken to bring about positive change

Standards:

Social Studies

- **D2.Eco.1.3–5.** Compare the benefits and costs of individual choices
- **D2.Eco.2.3–5.** Identify positive and negative incentives that influence the decisions people make
- **D2.Eco.3.3–5.** Identify examples of the variety of resources (human capital, physical capital, and natural resources) that are used to produce goods and services
- **D2.Geo.5.3–5.** Explain how the cultural and environmental characteristics of places change over time
- **D2.Geo.9.3–5.** Analyze the effects of catastrophic environmental and technologicalevents on human settlements and migration

- **D2.Civ.6.3–5.** Describe ways in which people benefit from and are challenged by working together, including through government, workplaces, voluntary organizations, and families
- **D2.Civ.12.3–5.** Explain how rules and laws change society and how people change rules and laws
- **D2.Civ.13.3–5.** Explain how policies are developed to address public problems
- **D2.Civ.14.3–5.** Illustrate historical and contemporary means of changing society

Science

- **4-ESS3-1:** Obtain and combine information to describe that energy and fuels are derived from natural resources and that their uses affect the environment
- **5-ESS3-1:** Obtain and combine information about ways individual communities use science ideas to protect Earth's resources and environment
- **5-LS2-1:** Develop a model to describe the movement of matter among plants, animals, decomposers, and the environment

Materials:

Lesson 1

- Tragedy of the Commons Activity from The State of Rhode Island, Department of Environmental Management[29] https://dem.ri.gov/sites/g/files/xkgbur861/files/programs/bnatres/fishwild/outreach/critter-kits/balance-lesson01-tragedy-commons.pdf

Lesson 2

- *Wangari's Trees of Peace: A True Story from Africa* Read aloud available at https://www.youtube.com/watch?v=08PbLwOtZJA&t=1s

Lesson 3

- TED Talk Video: What is a gift economy? at https://ed.ted.com/lessons/what-is-a-gift-economy-alex-gendler

Important Vocabulary/Concepts:

- Natural resources
- Competition
- Policymaking
- Advocacy
- The Commons
- Gift Economy

Instructional Materials Description and Overview:

In this set of instructional materials for grades 3–5, students learn about how scarcity can impact the larger community when access to resources is not equal. Both individual and collective decision-making are explored and how each can impact the lives of others is analyzed. Students then read *Wangari's Trees of Peace: A True Story from Africa*, which uses the real-life story of activist Wangari Maathai to explore how overconsumption of trees in Kenya had a devastating impact on the land and the role that an individual can play. This series ends with an exploration of the difference between a market economy and a gift economy.

Note to Teacher:
If your students don't have the background knowledge about Wants versus Needs, Goods and Services, and Consumption—see the K-2 instructional materials and the resources available to teach these concepts.

Lesson 1: Scarcity and the Community
ENGAGE: Lesson Introduction

- Show students images of natural resources such as: soil, trees, bodies of water and ask students to discuss with a partner what they have in common (images below can be used for this task)
- Listen to a few responses and then clarify that these are all natural resources that humans rely on for all kinds of things
- Ask students to list some ways that humans use these resources
- Explain to students that they will play a game to consider how people make decisions about using natural resources

https://www.flickr.com/photos/usfsregion5/page2

https://www.flickr.com/photos/50976304@N07/33798168846

https://www.flickr.com/photos/18161271@N00/6019675073

https://www.flickr.com/photos/67430875@N03/16752715921

EXPLORE: Game

The Tragedy of the Commons is a great activity for students to recognize that even natural resources can become depleted due to human actions and that the actions of individuals impact others.

- We suggest playing several rounds of the game (as described at the resource) with some rounds silent and others where the students can talk to one another.

EXPLAIN: Discussion

After the game concludes, lead the students in a discussion with questions such as:

- How many of you were satisfied with the outcome of the game?
- Why were you satisfied/not satisfied?
- What did you learn about competition over resources?
- What could your group do differently to ensure that all members have enough food and that the fish would continue to survive and renew? (this could lead into a follow-up lesson where students draft plans and present them).
- Explain to students that in reality, competition over resources has led to many problems in how the Earth, animals, and people have been treated, and ask if anyone knows of examples of this.

ELABORATE: Commons in our classroom.

- Where are commons in our classroom, our school, and our community?
- How do you feel our classroom and school commons are shared?
- How can we set up a system to share the commons equitably?

EXTEND: Interview a community member

- Interview someone who is responsible for caring for commons. Examples might be the custodian in your school, a librarian, park maintenance staff, and so on.
- As a class, come up with a series of questions.
- Learn about how these people work to protect the commons they are responsible for.

EVALUATE: One-minute sketch

- Have students take one minute to draw a big idea from the lesson that they are taking with them.

Lesson 2: Competition over Resources

ENGAGE: Lesson Introduction

- Show the students the first three pictures in the book. Begin with the images that depict Wangari in Kenya when she was growing up and prompt them to make observations about the environment and how Wangari and her family interacted with and benefited from nature.
- Next, show the picture of Kenya after Wangari returned from studying in the United States and to instruct the students to note how the environment changed.

- Then ask the students to make predictions about what they think happened and how these changes might have impacted the lives of people in Kenya.

EXPLORE: During the Read Aloud

- Ask the students questions such as:
  - What problems did Wangari see after she returned to Kenya?
  - Who suffered from the deforestation in Kenya? Who benefited? (Lists of the students' answers can be made)
  - Before reading the entire book, stop and ask the students to consider actions Wangari could take to help improve conditions in Kenya. This could be extended into a small group activity where students create proposals and reasons to defend their plan. The proposals could be presented to the class before the rest of the book is read.
  - Read the rest of the book.

EXPLAIN: Text Analysis and Discussion

- Ask the students to recall the actions Wangari took and the challenges she faced.
- Ask the students to consider why they think Wangari was treated so poorly?
- Ask them if they think they would be as brave or persistent as Wangari was if they saw something that really needed to be improved in their environment. Why/why not?

ELABORATE: Advocacy Discussion to Uncover a Local Issue

Announce to the students that they will consider local issues that they think need to be changed in some way.

- Have individual students brainstorm ideas.
- Have students share in small groups and choose one issue to present to the whole class that they feel is important.
- Whole class discussion to choose one or more issues to advocate for.

This can be a single discussion where students list ideas and discuss ideas for how they could help make change in their communities.

EXTEND: Project Ideas

- Students participate in a photovoice project where they are instructed to take pictures of environmental or community issues that they think need to be improved. (Directions for Photovoice are in the Appendix.)
- Students can select one of the topics presented in the photovoice projects and join together with others to conduct research on the topic, propose an action plan, and possibly implement the plan or parts of it.

EVALUATE: Share Photovoice Topic

- Create a short pitch for your topic that you share with the class
- Allow students time to take photos and use additional days for students to share photos using Photovoice Protocols in Appendix

Lesson 3: Exploring a Gift Economy

ENGAGE: Lesson Introduction

Have students discuss the following questions in small groups:

- Ask students if they've ever given or received a gift without expecting anything in return.
- What do people usually do when they need something? (Buy it, trade it, make it)
- Have you ever given something to someone just because they needed it? (Examples: sharing snacks, lending a toy)
- What do you think would happen if people shared things instead of buying them?

As a whole class, discuss how these experiences made them feel and why people give gifts. Explain that in a market economy, people use money to buy things. In a gift economy, people share, give, and exchange freely without expecting direct payment. Indigenous communities use gift economies to meet their needs and build relationships. In a gift economy, the stronger the relationship, the stronger the economy.

EXPLORE: Research Gift Economies

Have small groups of students research the following examples of gift economy and share findings with the class:

- Koha: Koha is a custom of the Māori people in New Zealand, which involves visitors donating or giving gifts such as food, valuable items, or money to a tribal meeting house to support the cost of hosting a community gathering.
- Kula exchange: Kula (also known as the kula exchange or kula ring) is a ceremonial gift exchange between villages and islands in Papua New Guinea.
- Potlatch: In a potlatch, a leader strengthens their community bond by giving away valuables to their supporters and gets rewarded with attribution of honor, respect, and social status. Indigenous cultures of the Pacific Northwest practice potlatch rituals.
- !Kung (Ju/'hoansi) people of the Kalahari Desert in southern Africa are a group of hunter-gatherers who exchange materials and food using principles of gift economy.
- Donating blood: A blood donation given on a volunteer basis is a form of gift-giving in a gift economy.

EXPLAIN: TED Talk Video

Watch the TED Talk Video: What is a gift economy? Share the following discussion questions/prompts with students prior to watching the video:

- What did you notice was the biggest difference between a gift economy and a market economy?
- What are the most important elements of a gift economy?
- Have you ever participated in a gift economy in your own life? Be prepared to share.

Have small group and whole class discussions after the video using the above prompts.

ELABORATE: Create a Gift for a Giving Ceremony.

- Give students time to think of or create a small gift to offer the entire class/classroom. A gift could be material (a drawing), verbal (kind words or sentiment), experiential (a dance or song), a skill (fixing something), or anything else that students would like to share with the class.
- Have students sit in a circle and offer their gifts to the class in a giving ceremony.
- Discuss how students felt participating in the gift-giving ceremony.

EXTEND: Develop a Gift Share Project

- Have the class brainstorm a gift-sharing project that they can do for their community. Examples might include a free library, free toy store, free food pantry, free plant garden, free pet supplies, and free clothing.
- Set this up in your classroom or school as an ongoing resource. Check out https://littlefreelibrary.org/ to learn more about setting up a free library.

EVALUATE: Create a Short Video

In small groups, have students create a short video that explains their understanding of a gift economy.

Community and Place-Based Learning Opportunities

This section is an invitation to teachers and parents to engage community members, outside school experts, and other local knowledge resources to extend the EcoJustice learning experiences that students are engaging with in classrooms.

For this first theme of economics and ecology, we suggest any of the following community and place-based learning experiences for you and your students:

- Visit a local cooperatively owned business to learn more about how a cooperative model works (e.g., agriculture stores, food cooperatives).
- Visit a local park and discuss the benefits of the park. Discuss the ways we value the benefits of what parks provide for us. How is the park maintained and supported? Explore how national and state parks generate revenue while protecting biodiversity. Study the economic benefits of conservation, tourism, and ecosystem services. Discuss the ethics of entrance fees and access to public lands.
- Visit a local business that is focused on sustainability. Discuss how they balance people and profits and how they make other economic decisions that intersect with the environment.

- Visit an Indigenous community to learn about land stewardship, reciprocal economies, and sustainable harvesting. Discuss the impacts colonization had on Indigenous communities and the ways that colonization disrupted Indigenous economies and ecosystems. Compare Indigenous conservation practices with modern conservation practices.
- Visit a local renewable energy project and discuss the costs and benefits of renewable energy versus fossil fuels. Explore the role of government and corporations on your local energy options. Examine the social and environmental trade-offs of a local renewable energy or other sustainability-related project.
- Meet with your local green team or other local officials who make decisions about sustainability in your community. Learn more about how they are making choices that impact you and your community and discuss what more you would like to see being done.

Teacher Turn

Now it is your turn. Here we offer next steps for you to develop your own EcoJustice instructional materials that meet the needs of your school curriculum and your students' interests. There are many EcoJustice issues that are linked to our current economic model of free-market capitalism even for children. We invite teachers to dig deeper into any of these issues with your class by utilizing the resources provided here to create your own lessons. We offer resources for teachers to further expand their own knowledge base and understanding of issues as well as pedagogical resources for teachers to engage in lesson development with their students.

We first invite you to answer the following questions:

- Which standard fits with your school curriculum? (See the list in the Appendix of NCSS and NGSS standards we have identified as offering opportunities to incorporate our Pillars). Also look at the Cloud Standards and the SDGs for further connections to your curriculum and ideas.
- Which concepts are you and your students interested in learning more about? (e.g., resource exploitation and depletion, labor exploitation, commodification of resources, local economies, etc.)
- Which resources (suggested or your own) would you like to use to expand your own understanding of these concepts?
- What pedagogical activities are most appropriate for your teaching context? (Many instructional strategies are available in the Appendix and our website resources.)

Remember that EcoJustice issues are often related to issues of access and equity since those with the most resources have the greatest access and those with the least material resources have the least access. Additionally, in the United States, those who are most marginalized are also the most vulnerable to exploitation. We have put together many resources in this chapter, and the Appendices and our companion website offer resources for you to build an EcoJustice lesson including a lesson plan template, relevant national social studies and science standards, resources to expand your own thinking about EcoJustice issues, and common teaching strategies we have used in our own classrooms. You don't have to do this alone either. Include your students in the process of creating relevant and meaningful lessons for them. Tap other teachers who are aligned to EcoJustice for ideas and accountability. We are eager to support you on your journey toward becoming an EcoJustice Educator!

Notes

1 Amazon Frontlines, "Indigenous Women Put Their Bodies On the Line to Defend the Amazon," accessed August 6, 2025, https://amazonfrontlines.org/chronicles/Indigenous-women-put-their-bodies-on-the-line-to-defend-the-amazon/.
2 Inequality Media, "About," accessed August 7, 2025, https://www.inequalitymedia.org/about.
3 Inequality Media, "The 10 Biggest Myths About Our Economy," YouTube video, 8:28, posted December 23, 2024, https://www.youtube.com/watch?v=HZ3j4hHMO5E.
4 Robin Wall Kimmerer, *The Serviceberry: Abundance and Reciprocity in the Natural World* (New York: Scribner, 2024), ebook, chapter 3.
5 Robin Wall Kimmerer, *The Serviceberry: Abundance and Reciprocity in the Natural World* (New York: Scribner, 2024), ebook, chapter 3.
6 Charles Eisenstein, *Sacred Economics: Money, Gift, and Society in the Age of Transition* (Berkeley, CA: Evolver Editions, 2011), ebook, chapter 2: The Illusion of Scarcity.
7 Ellen MacArthur Foundation, *Towards the Circular Economy Vol. 1: An Economic and Business Rationale for an Accelerated Transition* (Ellen MacArthur Foundation, 2013).
8 Kate Raworth, *Doughnut Economics: Seven Ways to Think Like a 21st-Century Economist* (London: Penguin Random House, 2017).
9 Robert Costanza, Richard B. Howarth, Ida Kubiszewski, Shuang Liu, Chunbo Ma, Gaël Plumecocq, and David I. Stern, "Influential Publications in Ecological Economics Revisited," *Ecological Economics* 123 (2016), 68–76, https://www.robertcostanza.com/wp-content/uploads/2017/02/2016_J_Costanza_InfluentialPublications.pdf.
10 Robin Wall Kimmerer, *Braiding Sweetgrass* (Minneapolis, MN: Milkweed Editions, 2013), ebook, Chapter: Windigo Footprints.
11 Truthout, "Tesla Paid Zero Federal Income Tax in 2024, Despite $2.3 Billion in Income," August 6, 2025, https://truthout.org/articles/tesla-paid-zero-federal-income-tax-in-2024-despite-2-3-billion-in-income/.
12 Institute for Policy Studies, "Billionaire Bonanza 2021: Wealth Windfalls, Tumbling Taxes, and Pandemic Profiteers," December 2021.
13 Federal Reserve, "Distribution of Household Wealth in the U.S. since 1962," *Survey of Consumer Finances*, 2021.
14 Economic Policy Institute, "The Productivity–Pay Gap," 2021, https://www.epi.org/productivity-pay-gap/.

15 Institute for Policy Studies, "Wealth Transfer Report: How America's Wealthiest Families Use Inherited Wealth to Further Concentrate Power," 2021.
16 Institute for Policy Studies, "The Road to Economic Justice: Addressing the Racial Wealth Gap," 2020.
17 U.S. Census Bureau, "Income and Poverty in the United States: 2023," September 10, 2024, https://www.census.gov/library/publications/2024/demo/p60-283.html.
18 University of Oxford, "$5 Trillion of Nature-Related Economic Risks Will Amplify Climate Change, Says Oxford Study," December 14, 2023, https://www.ox.ac.uk/news/2023-12-14-5-trillion-nature-related-economic-risks-will-amplify-climate-change-says-oxford.
19 National Invasive Species Information Center, "Economic and Social Impacts," accessed August 7, 2025, https://www.invasivespeciesinfo.gov/subject/economic-and-social-impacts.
20 NOAA Climate.gov, "2024: An Active Year of U.S. Billion-Dollar Weather and Climate Disasters," accessed August 7, 2025, https://www.climate.gov/news-features/blogs/beyond-data/2024-active-year-us-billion-dollar-weather-and-climate-disasters.
21 Chris Hedges, "Noam Chomsky Has 'Never Seen Anything Like This,'" interview with Noam Chomsky, Common Dreams, April 19, 2010, https://www.commondreams.org/views/2010/04/19/noam-chomsky-has-never-seen-anything.
22 National Council for the Social Studies, "National Curriculum Standards for Social Studies: Chapter 2—The Themes of Social Studies," accessed January 17, 2025, https://www.socialstudies.org/national-curriculum-standards-social-studies-chapter-2-themes-social-studies?check_logged_in=1#7.
23 American Association for the Advancement of Science, *Benchmarks for Science Literacy* (New York: Oxford University Press, 1993).
24 NGSS Lead States, *Next-Generation Science Standards: For States, By States* (Washington, DC: The National Academies Press, 2013), https://www.nextgenscience.org.
25 The Cloud Institute for Sustainability Education, "EfS Standards and Performance Indicators," accessed August 7, 2025, https://cloudinstitute.org/cloud-efs-standards-performanceindicators.
26 United Nations, "Sustainable Development Goals, Goal 12: Ensure Sustainable Consumption and Production Patterns," accessed January 27, 2025, https://www.un.org/sustainabledevelopment/sustainable-consumption-production/.
27 Jay McTighe and Grant Wiggins, *Understanding by Design Framework* (Alexandria, VA: Association for Supervision and Curriculum Development, 2012), https://files.ascd.org/staticfiles/ascd/pdf/siteASCD/publications/UbD_WhitePaper0312.pdf.
28 Produced by Bingo Baker at https://bingobaker.com/?bingo_id=6216876.
29 The State of Rhode Island, Department of Environmental Management, "Tragedy of the Commons," accessed January 27, 2025, https://dem.ri.gov/sites/g/files/xkgbur861/files/programs/bnatres/fishwild/outreach/critter-kits/balance-lesson01-tragedy-commons.pdf.

3

Production and Consumption

Chapter Outline

This topic will clearly reinforce the concepts of needs vs wants which I feel is so important in our excessively materialistic society. Bringing awareness to this excess and the damage that it is doing to the natural world is vital.

—*Marcie, Early Childhood Teacher*

Introduction

In 1925, President Calvin Coolidge stated, "After all, the chief business of the American people is business. They are profoundly concerned with producing, buying, selling, investing and prospering in the world."[1] This statement sums up a reality of American culture that has existed from the beginning of European settlement to today. It is true that for many, migration to the American colonies meant religious freedom, escape from the limits of social class, and opportunities to start over, and this is the version of the "American Dream" that is most often taught. However, another parallel reality is that the United States is a nation that was founded for profit motives. The rich resources of the country, coupled with seemingly endless opportunities (for some) led to an ethos of growth and prosperity. In essence, the chief business of American culture has been, and still is, business.

Policy decisions, the rhetoric of leaders such as President Coolidge, and messages sent to the American people have all played a role in the evolution of the economy. In many ways, consumerism has been conflated with patriotism. For example, during the Second World War, citizens were asked to show their patriotism by purchasing war bonds. The government engaged Madison Avenue advertising agencies to create posters urging consumers "to do their part" in fighting the Nazis and supporting the troops. Another example was following the attacks on the United States on 9/11/2001, President George W. Bush spoke to the American people and told them that in order to beat the terrorists, they should go to Disney World and take their "families and enjoy life the way we want it to be enjoyed."[2] These comments came to be understood to mean that Americans should get out and spend. In 2008, following the Great Recession, President Bush once again recognized the importance of the American consumer when he signed into law a stimulus bill which he called, "a booster shot for our economy"[3] by putting $300–$1,200 in the hands of consumers. Through policy and persuasion, the American identity became cemented to the system of capitalism, which called on citizens to consume as much and as often as possible.

How do we learn our role as workers, producers, and consumers in the United States? In many ways, both explicit and implicit, American education leads students to form conceptions about the US economic system, their role in it, and the role of government in shaping economic policy. A primary role of public education is to prepare individuals for adult life. This explicit goal is reflected in actions such as the creation in 2010 of the College Career and Readiness Skills (formulated as part of the Common Core Standards), adopted by forty-one states in the United States.[4] However, the preparation of future economic citizens is often less overt. Social scientist and educator Jean Anyon researched and wrote about the role that schools play in social reproduction based on the "type" of schooling one receives in *Social Class and School Knowledge.*[5] In essence, Anyon's research demonstrated schools prepare students for different roles in the United States, labor market, with lower-income students traditionally prepared to be the "workers," while those who attend elite schools are prepared to be the executives of corporate America. The *hidden curriculum*, the unintentional and implicit lessons, values, and behaviors that students learn in a school, often through interactions and the environment, rather than formal instruction, is also ever present in education.[6] The hidden curriculum sends messages to students through what is taught/not taught and how it is taught. All of these factors contribute to how one comes to view the world and their place in it, and in this instance, how the economy should function.

In this chapter we explore how elementary school education, particularly in social studies, reinforces a perspective that the United States and its inhabitants are meant to prosper economically. The notion of the American Dream is embedded in the sentiment, "The Land of Opportunity," and this narrative is reinforced in the way that many topics are taught. We will begin this chapter with a discussion of the ways students are taught some common topics in US History and how typical narratives contribute to individual and collective identities as consumers and producers. We then offer a critique through an EcoJustice lens, followed by a section to build teacher background knowledge specifically as it relates to the production and consumption of material goods. In the next section of the chapter, we share instructional materials designed to help young people understand many current patterns of production and consumption and the pros and cons for the individual, society, and the environment. The final sections of the chapter offer resources and guidance to support teachers if they choose to create their own materials for EcoJustice Education in their classrooms.

The Conventional Approach

Most elementary social studies standards call for students to learn fundamental concepts of economics. These are represented in state and national standards. The Council for Economic Education (which received funding from the United States Department of Education) published Voluntary National Standards in Economics to serve as a guide to teachers on what should be taught in the elementary school years to ensure a financially literate citizenry. Table 3.1 highlights some of the benchmarks suggested for students to reach by the end of grade 4.[7]

If students are able to acquire and apply the knowledge presented in the Council for Economic Education benchmarks, they will certainly have a basic understanding that as a consumer they will need to make choices and that some of these choices will be limited by available resources and influenced by their wants. However, there is little reason to assume that the students would be taught to examine the use of resources from the perspective of

Table 3.1. Fourth Grade Voluntary National Content Standards in Economics

At the Completion of Grade 4, Students Will Know That:	At the Completion of Grade 4, Students Will Use This Knowledge To:
People's choices about what goods and services to buy and consume determine how resources will be used.	Explain why a choice must be made, when a land owner has alternative uses for the property.
Whenever a choice is made, something is given up because resources are limited.	From a list of four toys, ask students to rank, order their preferences, state their first choice and identify the second toy as what is given up.
Productive resources are the natural resources, human resources, and capital goods available to make goods and services.	Identify examples of natural resources, human resources, and capital goods.
Most people produce and consume. As producers they help make goods and services; As consumers they use goods and services to satisfy their wants.	Identify people who are consumers and provide examples in which students were consumers of goods and services. Identify people who are producers and provide examples of situations in which students helped produce goods and services.

harms done to the planet, people, and animals, or how consumers can make choices that contribute to environmental sustainability. Clearly, for the goals of EcoJustice to be met, more would be needed to supplement these standards.

Although economics is an integral subject of social studies, there is no guarantee that it is taught in elementary school. Typically, social studies in elementary school focuses on the teaching of US History. Social studies lessons in elementary school most often focus on a series of events without consideration of economic factors and analysis of the impact on peoples of the time and the present day, as well as the costs to the environment. In the following paragraphs, we will explore how a few topics in US History are typically presented and how this contributes to a cultural and individual economic identity. *As you read the section below, consider these questions:*

1. How do you think these narratives have likely impacted how we understand our economic system and the role consumers are expected to play?
2. Remember when you learned about these events, were you taught this was just the way it was, or were you encouraged to consider the impact on people of the time period and how you were making sense of the events?
3. What might be the outcome if students were regularly asked to consider the impacts of economic actions on different groups of people and the environment?
4. What if students were challenged to consider short- and long-term outcomes and alternative actions and empowered to think of themselves as conscious actors in the system?

The First "Americans"

When students learn about the Americas before European settlement, they typically learn that there were many Indigenous nations who inhabited the region. This study usually focuses on aspects of culture such as types of housing including pueblos, tepees, and longhouses. A typical elementary school project includes building a longhouse from popsicle sticks. In this way, we claim to pay homage to the people who are native to the land of the United States. *What if we went beyond housing, dress, and means of food collection and learned more about the relationship many Indigenous cultures had to the Earth?*

In our home state of N.J. elementary school students learn that the Lenni Lenape people inhabited the land before European settlers arrived. This is an opportunity to learn not only about the Lenape, but to learn *from* the Lenape, particularly about their relationship to the Earth. A descendant of the Lenape and member of the Delaware Tribe of Indians, Curtis Zunigha, explained the connection to the Earth as "Lenapehoking [the land of the Lenape] is the land, it's the waters, the rivers, the lakes, even the ocean, all of the cosmos, all of our connection with the Earth, the waters, the sky, the animals, all life, the mountains, the ancient ones, the ones that have the ancient memory, all of these things, to the Lenape have a spirit."[8]

A quick Google search on how to teach about the Lenni Lenape turned up this description of a third grade field trip:

> *Students explored the historic coastal way of life of the Lenape through interactive activities such as making fire by rubbing sticks together, practicing their hunting skills playing a game called "Spear the Deer," and trying their hand at fishing with a seine net. This day filled with hands-on experiences not only enhanced the students' understanding of Lenape traditions but also tied perfectly into the Third Grade's annual in-depth study of New Jersey, which begins with lessons on the Lenni Lenape.*[9]

Field trips are great opportunities for place-based learning, but that doesn't ensure that values of EcoJustice Education will be present in the learning. Consider what lessons students can take away from a field trip such as the example shared. They will learn that the Leni Lenape lived off of the land by hunting and fishing, but will the reverence for the land come through? Will students learn the philosophy of many Indigenous nations that the Earth and its resources should be used only as needed and be given ample time to rejuvenate? Students should be exposed to these aspects of Native American cultures so they can reflect on their own views of past and present use of resources and consumption.

Colonization

From the very beginning, the American colonies were established so that the British could have access to natural resources not readily available in England. This economic relationship led to the shipping of natural resources across the Atlantic to England to be turned into manufactured products. Manufactured goods were then sent back to the colonies to be purchased, creating the need for a perennial consumer. When this aspect of colonial settlement is taught, it is typically boiled down to the term, *mercantilism*—a system where a nation seeks to gain wealth and power by maximizing exports and minimizing imports. Students learn that the British government regulated trade in the colonies in order to protect this relationship, and eventually this was a factor leading to tension with England and ultimately the American Revolution.

What is taught less often is that this arrangement also created a system where some did the hard work of producing and/or extracting resources through voluntary and involuntary labor, while others benefited from the profits of this labor through trade. When European colonization is taught, it is usually a story of success rather than an exploration of how use of the Earth's resources and human labor served to benefit few at the expense of many. Applying an EcoJustice lens, students would be encouraged to consider what the impact of the economic decisions were for the Indigenous people, those who labored, those who profited and the environment. In this way students can begin to explore history through the lens of a *Triple Bottom Line* approach where People, Place, and Profit are all considered in a decision-making model for economically and environmentally sustainable options.

The Consumer

When the colonists began to resent the control that England had over them, they used the role of consumer as a form of protest. As students learn about the lead up to the Revolutionary War, they are usually required to memorize a series of events. The Stamp Act Congress of 1765, which along with colonial boycotts eventually led to the repeal of taxes by the British Parliament, is one such event. Almost every elementary school child can probably recount that a group of men dressed like "Indians" dumped tea overboard at the Boston Tea Party. But are children encouraged to understand these events in the context of public protest and the power of the consumer over government actions, or that sometimes individuals make choices that can cause some personal loss or discomfort but benefit the whole? There is an opportunity to teach students about trade-offs when making economic decisions. Concepts like *opportunity cost* and how economic decision-making should include *cost/benefit analysis* of the impacts on the individual and society can be included. Younger students can learn these concepts through examples from their own lives and the stories of others. Upper elementary children can draw parallels to more recent economic acts of protest, both individual and collective. All students can be taught to consider consequences of economic decisions and learn to make informed, conscious choices.

The Rise of American Economic Independence and Prosperity

As the American economic identity continued to take shape in the early years of the nineteenth century, some leaders believed that independence could only be fully realized when the young United States achieved self-sufficiency in the production of their own goods. In the 1820s, Senator Henry Clay from Kentucky called for Congress to adopt the "American System" plan, which would lead to the production and movement of goods in the country through investments in infrastructure.[10] Through the nation's early years, the desire for economic growth and independence became a national goal and part of the national ethos. A bit later in the nineteenth century, the concept of Manifest Destiny entered into the American psyche. The idea that the United States was destined by God to "expand its dominion and spread democracy and capitalism across the entire North American continent,"[11] led to policies of expansion, the displacement of Indigenous people, and even war. Students can be asked to consider what the consequences, good and bad, were for the people and land. Older students can explore how a belief in Manifest Destiny is still shaping a worldview that believes laying claims over a sovereign nation for the benefit of American national security seems just. Problem-solving tasks to consider alternative solutions could be a worthwhile class activity where students consider multiple perspectives and outcomes.

The American Dream

The Oxford English Dictionary defines the *American Dream* as "the ideal that every citizen of the United States should have an equal opportunity to achieve success and prosperity through hard work, determination, and initiative." This narrative is typically introduced in elementary education through the teaching of immigration. The immigration story typically begins with a review of "push" and "pull" factors. The push factors include realities such as religious or political persecution, poverty, war, or a general lack of opportunity. On the other hand, pull factors to immigrate to the United States are most commonly understood as financial opportunities and freedoms not experienced in one's home country. In this narrative, personal gain and opportunity become the accepted reasons for migration to the United States. Rarely are the perspectives of those who "involuntarily" were brought to the United States or assumed into the population through conquest considered as part of the immigration story. If students instead studied the expansion of the US population through a more inclusive approach, they might come to understand that prosperity and freedom have not been available to all. Students could learn that for some, opportunity was readily available, but how resources, including human labor, were used did not lead to equal opportunities for all. This presentation of history would challenge the narrative that hard work is a path to economic success and therefore the American Dream.

An EcoJustice Perspective on Conventional Approaches

While there are many other moments and trends in American history that can be added to the above overview, the goal of the review is to explore how what is typically taught contributes to national and individual conceptions of how resources should be used, the "rightness" of US economic supremacy and the role that the consumer plays in the process. When we apply the principles of EcoJustice, it becomes clear that more needs to be taught if we hope to produce consumers who understand the dynamics of production and consumption in terms of not just wants, needs, and profit, but extends to a consciousness of the impacts on people and the planet. It also becomes clear that this can be done with modifications to what and how common topics called for in curriculum standards are taught.

When the EcoJustice Education Pillars are used as guides, these commonly taught topics can be transformed. When students learn about Indigenous Peoples and European settlement, teaching about the interconnectedness of all living beings and systems (Pillar I) is possible. Students could analyze Native American prayers to explore the relationship of many Indigenous People to the Earth. The excerpt below is from the Lakota Sioux, translated in 1887 by chief Yellow Lark.[12]

Great Spirit Prayer

Oh, Great Spirit,
Whose voice I hear in the winds
and whose breath gives life to all the world.
Hear me! I need your strength and wisdom.
Let me walk in beauty, and make my eyes
ever hold the red and purple sunset.
Make my hands respect the things you have made
and my ears sharp to hear your voice.
Make me wise so that I may understand
the things you have taught my people.
Let me learn the lessons you have hidden
in every leaf and rock.

By reading the prayer, students could come to understand how important all of nature was to the Lakota Sioux and their belief that nature was a teacher to be respected. In this way students can see how the human and ecological systems are interconnected. Students might also be inspired to *care for the welfare of the Earth and all beings,* which is a component of Pillar I. Students could then compare and contrast the lifestyles of Indigenous People living on the east coast with that of the European settlers and consider the implications for the different populations and the local ecosystems. An activity such as this would address other components of Pillar I: *Understand that all actions have multiple consequences*, and *Evaluate choices and decisions at multiple levels through a systems lens.*

An EcoJustice perspective calls for a study of European settlement to review how some profited, while many faced hardships and losses in the pursuit of wealth—theirs and others. *Pillar III, A commitment to investigating socio-environmental issues through the lens of power and justice* can be incorporated into this study. Students can be assigned to research the experience of different groups present during early settlement, such as enslaved Indigenous People and Africans, indentured servants, women, relocated criminals, investors in the London Company and members of the Gentlemen class. Students can rank the groups in terms of power and economic status and then explore who benefited through the lens of power and wealth and draw conclusions. This type of learning helps to develop the practice *to critically read the world—uncovering and questioning the social, political, and economic forces that shape our lives*, a component of Pillar III.

When studying the actions taken by ordinary colonists who participated in boycotts of British goods, *Pillar II An* ***orientation*** *toward innovative, action-oriented, and collaborative problem-solving* can be developed. As students study the collective actions of the colonists, another component of Pillar II is incorporated: *recognize the need and power of working in solidarity with others, across perceived difference, to achieve common goals.* When students are encouraged to see the actions of the colonists in the context of the time and to learn about the personal risks and sacrifices made, they can begin to see that all individuals have agency. This idea can help to develop additional components of Pillar II: *Accept our power* *as change agents, take risks, and fail forward*, and *Imagine new ideas and ways of being that challenge our socialized norms.*

When we call on students to explore the role that consumers have played in shaping the American economy in the past and present, there are many ways to include our Pillars of EcoJustice Education. If students explore consumer and government actions and are asked to consider alternative choices and models, *Pillar II An orientation toward innovative, action-oriented, and collaborative problem-solving* can be developed. Older students can consider where and how the consumer has been manipulated, where the consumer had power, and how the consumer has used that power to influence outcomes. Students can reflect on their own economic decision-making and potential consequences. Such an investigation could further the goals of *Pillar III Reflect and evaluate the ongoing process of our socialization and the mechanisms that shape our ways of being* and many components of Pillar I: *Accept responsibility for the part we play in the ecological web of life*; *Become conscious consumers and producers in all areas of existence; Understand that all actions have multiple consequences*; and *Evaluate choices and decisions at multiple levels through a systems lens*

A fuller understanding of the factors leading to and creating barriers to the American Dream can lead to questioning about systems that have historically led to this. A next step might be to explore the experiences of immigrants in their community. Students could conduct interviews and analyze the responses in light of the American Dream. In this way, components of *Pillar III* are addressed: *Critically reads the world—uncovering and questioning the social, political, and economic forces that shape our lives* and *Ongoing self-education and information seeking that mines contradictions and tensions.* Components of Pillar IV are also present as students, *Apply content knowledge in real world, interconnected contexts* and *Understand the relevance and value of why they are learning what they are learning.*

There are many other possibilities to address concepts of EcoJustice while studying US History. As one becomes more familiar with the Pillars and concepts of EcoJustice Education, the openings become more and more evident. Continuing to build one's pedagogical and content knowledge will be necessary for most educators due to gaps in our educational experiences. The next section is meant to expand your knowledge about production and consumption, also known as the materials economy, so you can feel more confident engaging your students in the sample lessons offered and imagine building your own lessons for your class.

Expanding Teacher Content Knowledge

Conceptions of progress, government actions and policies, and the marketing and advertising industry have driven production and consumption and shaped the American consumer identity. Post Second World War, and increasingly more in the digital age, American life has been deeply defined by consumer culture. As a result, a large part of the identity we shape in our lives is through our consumption of and relationship to material goods. Naomi Klein, a prominent author and social activist, reminds us in her seminal text on corporate power and consumer culture, *No Logo*, that corporate branding is not about selling products, it's about selling an idea of belonging, of community, of personal identity. In a world where traditional sources of identity—religion, community, even family—are being eroded, brands step in to fill the void.[13]

Consumer spending has increased since 1940 from 50 percent of GDP to approximately 70 percent of GDP.[14] The post-Second World War era has been heavily shaped by our consumption of material goods and the identity these material objects have created for us individually and culturally. But many of us are not taught to think about the socio-environmental impacts of our consumption. In this section on expanding your knowledge, we dive deeper into the materials economy and look more closely at the role marketing and advertising have played in fueling this era of hyper consumerism. We then highlight the environmental impacts of this level of consumption by introducing the concepts of ecological footprint, planetary boundaries, and ecosystem services. We end by supporting you in rethinking your relationship with consumption from a more critically conscious perspective by first discussing some of the social and environmental implications of this model of materials production and offering opportunities for you to reflect on your own relationship and engagement in consumer culture.

The Materials Economy: An Overview

The ***materials economy*** describes the way material products are created from start to finish. This process includes resource extraction, production, distribution, consumption, and disposal. As we shared in Chapter 2, the policies and measures of success for our economy are predicated on a false assumption of infinite growth and infinite resources. Our common model for materials production operates under similar assumptions as it is primarily a linear system with waste and exploitation of people and the planet at every level. One of the most widely viewed and accessible videos on the materials economy, *The Story of Stuff*, released in 2007 by Annie Leonard, is a 22-minute video that showcases the social and environmental impacts of the material economy by following an iPod as it moves through this system.[15] She went on to write the book, *The Story of Stuff* and create other videos about the materials economy specifically related to plastic water bottles, electronic waste, and corporate influence on democracy.[16] We highly recommend watching the videos as they are more relevant now than ever before, but we will also summarize the key aspects of the materials economy from resource extraction to disposal.

The Materials Economy: Resource Extraction

Resource extraction is the first step in producing any material good. This is the process whereby the raw materials needed to create a product are extracted from the environment. This is often done with force and violence to achieve the scale of production to meet consumer demand. It is hard to imagine when you think about the level of resource extraction happening to produce all of the products we see, so we will use a low-tech product, the reusable Giant Stanley Cup, to demonstrate the process of resource extraction through disposal. We are choosing to use the Stanley Cup for a few reasons. As a low-tech product, it still requires an extensive number of raw materials to be made. Imagine the materials input of all the higher-tech items that we have in our lives! Additionally, it is trendy and has become an internet phenomenon and collector's item, with marketing and advertising targeting influencers, women, and teenagers. Stanley saw their annual sales soar from $70 million before 2020 to a projected $750 million in 2023.[17] Finally, the Stanley Cup is a great symbol of *green consumerism*, a phenomenon and strategy employed by companies, where consumers are made to feel like their purchase is helping the environment. In reality, as is the case with the Stanley Cup and many other products marketed as "green," the product becomes over-consumed, with individuals owning multiple Stanley Cups, thus reducing the sustainable impact of the product in the first place.

As a low technology product, a Stanley Cup is made primarily from stainless steel and plastic. But neither stainless steel nor plastic are natural resources. So where do each of these come from? Stainless steel, a common alloy metal, is made from iron ore, chromium, nickel, and sometimes other elements depending on the properties of the final product.[18] Extractions for all of the above are often done by strip and pit mining, which has significant impacts on the workers and the environment. Miner's physical and mental health is often compromised by exposure to dangerous and unhealthy mining situations.[19] Toxic chemicals like sulfuric acid and cyanide, known carcinogens, are used in the extraction process (this is the case for chromium and nickel extraction), impacting both laborers and the environment. Plastic also requires similar extractive processes of raw materials, but in the case of plastic, the predominant material is crude oil which requires a lot of energy and water to extract.[20]

The environmental impacts of mining for metals and other rare minerals include pollution to the surrounding air, water, and soil, further impacting the health of human and non-human communities. The United States, via the creation of the Environmental Protection Agency, created regulations that would control and hold responsible those polluters; however, within his first weeks in office, President Trump signed executive orders reducing regulations for multiple industries' release of mercury, toxic air pollutants, soot, wastewater, workplace chemicals, and greenhouse gas emissions.[21] Much of the mining of metals and rare minerals is controlled by a handful of multinational corporations who are exploiting natural resources in more and more remote locations (as we use up the more easily accessible raw materials) and oftentimes offer low wages and unsafe working conditions, especially in countries with less strict labor laws.[22] All of these factors also have geopolitical implications, including economic competition, trade wars and tariffs, national security and political tension, as well as the environmental ethics of mining for rare minerals in ecologically sensitive regions. Similar to stainless steel, the environmental and social implications of crude oil extraction to make plastics include air and water pollution, loss of biodiversity and habitat destruction, dangerous and unhealthy working conditions, and displacement of communities.[23]

The Materials Economy: Production

Production is similar to manufacturing, and this is the step in the materials economy where the actual products get made from raw materials. Manufacturing typically occurs in factories or plants that are oftentimes overseas as it is typically cheaper to make goods in places like China, India, Japan, and Brazil. It is important to note that all of the raw materials that are extracted for the production of most goods need to be brought to the manufacturing facility, which requires fossil fuels for transportation. Again, using the Stanley Cup as an example, the company does use recycled stainless steel in their production, reducing their need for new raw materials. The stainless-steel industry is an energy-intensive industry, accounting for roughly 7 percent of carbon emissions worldwide.[24] Additionally, during the manufacturing process, there are toxic emissions released in the form of heavy metals, hazardous acids produced, as well as other wastes that are usually added to landfills. These environmental impacts affect the health of the people who work in stainless steel manufacturing plants? and workers are exposed to toxic fumes that can lead to respiratory diseases.[25] Stanley does not use recycled plastic for the lids of water bottles. The refining of crude oil and the manufacturing of plastic are also energy- and water-intensive processes. It is important to ask the question of why anyone would want to work in a toxic environment like a manufacturing plant. The answer ties back to the exploitation of resources and raw materials. As we intensify the extraction process, we are displacing communities and severing ties that people had to the land and water as a way of sustaining their livelihoods. Examples of this are abundant, but a recent example from Argentina involves the mining of lithium for batteries that is taking place in the biodiverse salt flat ecosystem. Indigenous communities are fighting to protect the water from excessive consumption and contamination from multiple mining companies' extraction of lithium.[26] Inevitably, as local environments are eroded along with their associated local economies, we leave people with little choice but to move to urban areas looking for work. The UN reports that nearly one million people per week move from rural to urban areas[27] leading to poor and overcrowded living conditions exacerbating poverty and inequality, as well as significant strains on natural resources like water, energy, and land.

The Materials Economy: Distribution

Distribution is the part of the materials economy where the newly manufactured products are brought to the global market. Stanley Cups are primarily made in China and Brazil, and so in order for you to get your Stanley Cup at a local brick-and-mortar store or online requires transportation, storage, and distribution. Most products are shipped via ocean on giant container ships that carry upward of a million products on one ship. The shipping industry is also a large carbon emitter and releases toxic pollution into the air and water via fuel usage.[28] Once container ships arrive at US ports the containers are loaded onto trucks and brought to regional warehouses and distribution centers. Typically located along the east and west coasts as well as in the Midwest, these distribution centers and warehouses also have environmental and social impacts. In the past ten years, we have seen a 25 percent increase in total warehouse space reflecting the rise of e-commerce and the growing demand for faster shipping times.[29] We will explore warehouses in more detail in Chapter 4, but keep in mind that warehouses take up large amounts of space, often leading to urban sprawl, the loss of agricultural land, and an increase in the amount of impervious surface for water runoff. There are also social consequences related to working in a warehouse or distribution center in the United States. As e-commerce and online shopping grow, there is more of a demand for laborers in this sector. Approximately 1.5 million people work in this industry[30] that is predominantly characterized by low-wage, insecure jobs that have led to mental and physical health impacts on workers. Distribution also involves the selling of goods at retail markets to consumers. Oftentimes, prices of goods do not reflect all of the environmental and social costs we have discussed so far. This is called ***externalizing the cost of production***. By externalizing the costs of products, it obscures the realities of environmental destruction from raw material extraction, toxic chemical pollution to air, land, and water, displacement and exploitation of people, carbon emissions from transportation, and poor working conditions.

The Materials Economy: Consumption and Advertising

Consumption involves the decision-making about how we spend our money. This is the part of the materials economy that most of us are directly connected to as it is the choices we make about how we spend our money that we are constantly faced with. The primary way we are influenced to spend our money is through marketing and advertising campaigns. Author, activist, and feminist, Jean Kilbourne states, "Advertising is our environment. It's our culture. It's the air we breathe," in her influential work, *Killing Us Softly*, a powerful documentary series critiquing the advertising industry and its impact on identity and culture.[31] One of the most insidious aspects of modern advertising is that it creates an artificial need for more and links purchasing with happiness, success, or social acceptance. This has become more damaging with the rise of digital marketing, making advertising hyper-personalized and increasing impulse buying as links are directly accessible through social media and other online platforms.[32] In the United States we see the highest levels of advertisements per person at $1,246 per person in 2024.[33] The psychosocial impact of advertising has led people to participate in a treadmill-like grind of working to earn enough money to spend. In a 2023 report 61 percent of Americans reported living paycheck to paycheck, with millennials reporting 73 percent.[34]

Advertising is one way that corporations incentivize purchasing. Another way they do this is through the tactic of planned obsolescence. Have you had the experience where you just bought something and it breaks after a short period of time and use? I know we can think of multiple examples of this in our own lives. Most of us don't think about why this is the case but rather toss the broken object and jump on Amazon and purchase a new one, with a quick one-day delivery promise. This is *planned obsolescence*, the practice of designing products to intentionally have a limited lifespan. This tactic is utilized by manufacturers and reinforced by retailers and companies to get consumers to continue to throw away, replace, and upgrade products that are still useful. Apple is one of the most complicit in this strategy as it often makes minor design changes but promotes them as essential, compelling consumers to buy the most recent product. They also do this in how they constantly change the chargers for the iPhone. Planned obsolescence and the normalization by companies and their advertisers have shifted our culture toward more disposable products while keeping the materials economy constantly in motion.

The Materials Economy: Disposal

Disposal is the final step in the materials economy and references what happens to products that are no longer in use by consumers. Our dominant linear materials flow typically ends with products being hauled and dumped in a landfill or incinerated. There are many categories of waste produced by the typical household including organic waste like food and yard waste (30–40 percent), recyclables like paper, cardboard, glass, and metal (25–30 percent), non-recyclable waste like single-use plastic packaging, Styrofoam, and other mixed materials items like juice boxes (20–25 percent), and hazardous waste which accounts for a small percentage of household waste and includes batteries, paint, electronics, and other chemicals.[35] What is interesting about this breakdown is that the majority of our waste can be composted or recycled and yet 95 percent of food waste ends up in landfills or incinerators and only 5–6 percent of total plastics consumed are recycled with the rest ending up in landfills.[36]

Many materials can be recycled, upcycled, reused, and composted, but this is typically not the way most materials are discarded in the United States. We generate a lot of waste, 292.4 million tons reported in a 2018 EPA report, and more than 50 percent of that waste ends up in landfills.[37] Landfills take up valuable space in communities, are often sited near low-income neighborhoods, release methane (a potent greenhouse gas) into the atmosphere, as well as toxic leachate into the soil and water. About 12 percent of waste ends up being incinerated or burned in facilities that transform solid waste into electricity. This process, while attempting to create electricity from a renewable source, adds carbon dioxide and other dangerous pollutants into the atmosphere. Additionally, the fine solids that remain after the burning process are also toxic substances that must be disposed of in special landfills for hazardous waste. There are only seventy-two municipal solid waste incinerators left in the United States and 85 percent of them are located within a 3-mile radius of lower-income communities and/or communities of color. This translates to nearly 4.5 million people in the United States who are exposed to pollution from waste incinerators.[38]

Our Ecological Footprint, Planetary Boundaries, and Ecosystem Services

Scientific frameworks and tools have been designed to measure our impact on the Earth and her resources. Here we introduce the idea of ecological or carbon footprint and the Planetary Boundaries Framework. Our *ecological* or *carbon footprint* is a way of quantifying our individual and collective impact on the Earth and her resources in relation to the Earth's capacity to regenerate those resources. There are many online calculators that measure your ecological footprint.[39] Some have baseline data built into the calculation based on the regional and cultural differences of the country you live in. For example, in the United States we are heavily dependent on car and air travel, we live in large homes, we eat more energy-intensive foods like meat, and our food travels great distances to get to our plate. These, along with other lifestyle choices common to US households, have resulted in the average person in the United States having an ecological impact of 7.5–8.0 global hectares compared to the global average of 3.7 global hectares per person.[40] Ecological footprints often compare human demands of the Earth to her biocapacity (ability to regenerate resources). When the ecological footprint exceeds the biocapacity, it means we are overshooting the Earth's natural limits and depleting resources faster than the Earth can replenish them.

Planetary Boundaries are another way of seeing humanity's impact on the Earth. The Planetary Boundary scientific framework identifies nine key Earth system processes that regulate the stability and resilience of the planet, including climate change, land system change, and freshwater change. If these boundaries are crossed, there is an increased risk of destabilizing an Earth system, which can have consequences for the human and more-than-human world. The nine planetary boundaries are best visualized, so study Figure 3.1 and visit the *Stockholm Resilience Center* to learn how the planetary boundaries framework has evolved and where we are as a planet in terms of having crossed them. According to their work on planetary boundaries, six of the boundaries have been exceeded, which signals heavy pressure on the Earth's systems and a need for action.[41]

Ecosystem Services was a concept popularized in the 1990s as a way to highlight the economic value of the diversity of benefits humans derive from healthy ecosystems. A paper published in 1997 was the first to attempt to quantify the value of the Earth's natural resources, estimating the natural capital of the Earth at 33 trillion dollars per year.[42] A few examples of ecosystem services and their approximate value to mankind are as follows:

- Pollination by bees and other insects is valued at \$235–\$577 billion annually.[43]
- Wetlands filter water and remove pollutants, which is valued at \$56,803 per acre per year.[44]
- Forest capture and sequestration of carbon to help regulate climate and mitigate climate change is valued at \$4.7 trillion per year.[45]

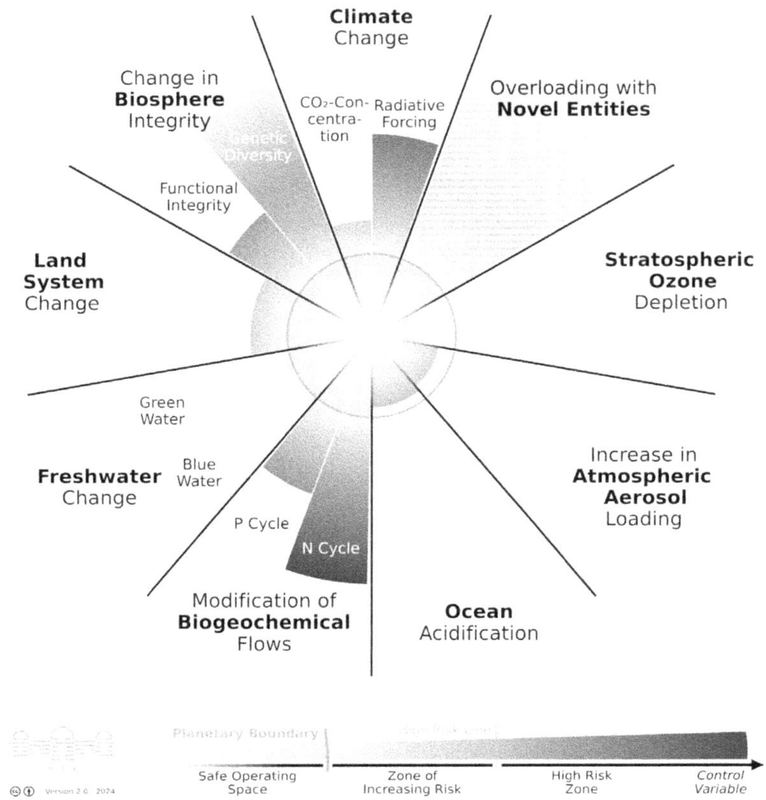

Figure 3.1. Planetary Boundaries 2024 based on the planetary health check.

There are many sources of data that calculate the value to humanity of soil health and fertility, natural coastal buffers from storms, freshwater resources, tourism and recreation, and the spiritual value provided by nature.

Implications of Current Production and Consumption Practices on our Social and Ecological Systems

Trying to put all of this together can feel daunting, and it is easier to not know how the materials economy, advertising, and green consumerism all contribute to the damage we have done to the planet and the resources it provides to all life. The materials economy is something that really exists outside of our immediate view, and we are not asked to think about the ways we have been targets of corporate marketing and advertising. We rarely have time to reflect on our consumption behaviors, and credit cards, mortgages, student loans, and other borrowing practices have normalized debt as a cultural phenomenon. For both adults and children, an opportunity to reflect on our spending habits might reveal to us that we have not prioritized responsible and sustainable consumption. According to Do Good People, a company that specializes in sharing sustainable solutions with organizations, some of the characteristics of a responsible and sustainable consumer include making conscious and critical choices informed by an ethical and ecological set of values.[46] Below we highlight some data about consumption habits in the United States and its related environmental and social impacts of our materials economy.

- Consumer spending on services has increased compared to goods. In 1950, roughly 40 percent of total consumer spending was on services, while 60 percent was spent on goods. By 2020, nearly 70 percent of consumer spending was on services, with categories like healthcare, housing, and leisure activities seeing substantial growth.[47]
- In 2022, 19 percent of all food at the retail or consumption stage was wasted, totaling 1.05 billion metric tons. Households contributed 60 percent of this waste, averaging 79 kilograms per person annually.[48]
- Since the 1970s, consumer spending has been more reliant on credit. By the early 2000s, the average American household had over $8,000 in credit card debt.[49]
- In 2022, consumer spending on bottled water in the United States was approximately $19 billion.[50]
- According to the Global Footprint Network, as of 2023, humanity's ecological footprint was estimated to be **1.7 Earths**, indicating that our resource consumption was 71 percent higher than the planet's capacity to regenerate those resources.[51]
- According to the 2022 Toxics Release Inventory (TRI) report by the US Environmental Protection Agency (EPA), approximately 4.1 billion pounds of toxic chemicals were released into the environment by reporting facilities in 2022.[52]
- The waste generation rate in 1960 was just 2.68 pounds per person per day. It increased to 3.66 pounds per person per day in 1980. In 2000, it reached 4.74 pounds per person per day and then decreased to 4.69 pounds per person per day in 2005. The generation rate was 4.9 pounds per person per day in 2018.[53]
- 1.4 million hectares of tree loss: Between 2001 and 2020, mining activities led to the loss of nearly 1.4 million hectares of trees, predominantly in tropical primary rainforests and protected areas. This deforestation released approximately 36 million tons of carbon dioxide annually.[54]
- The Great Pacific Garbage Patch, a large area of primarily plastic debris, is estimated to range in size from 270,000 square miles to 620,000 square miles, an area about the size of Texas.[55]
- 73 percent Decline Over 50 Years: Wild vertebrate populations have experienced a 73 percent decline from 1970 to 2020, indicating a severe erosion of biodiversity.[56]
- Land degradation has reduced productivity in 23 percent of the global terrestrial area, and between $235 billion and $577 billion in annual global crop output is at risk as a result of pollinator loss.[57]
- A survey conducted by the National Institute for Occupational Safety and Health (NIOSH) found that 40 percent of warehouse workers reported feeling "very stressed" due to the physical demands and pressure to meet performance quotas.[58]
- Globally, nearly two billion workers are engaged in informal employment, accounting for close to 70 percent of workers in developing and low-income countries, and 18

percent in high-income countries. This prevalence indicates a significant portion of the global workforce operates without formal labor protections or benefits.[59]

- Between 1998 and 2019, the United States experienced the elimination of nearly five million manufacturing jobs, primarily due to increased global competition and shifts in trade policies. This decline in manufacturing employment has had cascading effects on communities reliant on these jobs.[60]
- Worldwide eighty billion pieces of clothing are consumed every year, a 400 percent increase from only twenty years ago. However, approximately 85 percent of these textiles end up in a landfill every year. The production of fast fashion clothing employs the use of 8,000 synthetic chemicals. Some of these chemicals have been shown to cause cancer, and factory workers are regularly exposed to and breathing in these chemicals.[61]

Honing Your Critical Lens

As you can see, the materials economy, as it operates at a global scale, has clear social and environmental impacts across the planet. From deforestation and mountaintop removal and other extractive mining methods to the exploitation of vulnerable populations of people, our materials economy has wreaked havoc on our planetary systems as well as our bodies and spirits. But always remember that you have choices, even if unclear and difficult, in how you spend your money. By expanding your understanding of the materials economy and engaging your students in critical discussions about how the materials economy works, you can raise the consciousness of young children so they are more informed and committed to collective care and responsibility to one another and our planet. This section serves as merely an introduction to the social and environmental impacts of production and consumption, and we hope you continue to educate yourself more on the topics presented above. Our hope is that you become inspired to infuse EcoJustice perspectives into your own classroom by rethinking how we teach conventional social studies topics, incorporating the **Instructional Materials** we present in this chapter, and utilizing the Appendices and website resources to create your own EcoJustice lessons for your elementary classroom.

We end this section with several questions that offer opportunities for critical reflection and dialogue. If this is the first time you have really considered how all the products that surround you were born into existence, you are not alone. We are not taught in school or more broadly in our lives to ask questions about our consumption behaviors and their impacts. Our hope is that this book will continue to support you as you wrestle with and explore these questions and that you engage your students in the active learning process of asking their own questions.

- Who are the winners in the materials economy and what are the outcomes for the winners?
- Who are the losers in the materials economy and what are the outcomes for the losers?

- **D2.Civ.2.K-2.** Explain how all people, not just official leaders, play important roles in a community.
- **D2.Civ.5.K-2.** Explain what governments are and some of their functions.
- **D2.Civ.6.K-2.** Describe how communities work to accomplish common tasks, establish responsibilities, and fulfill roles of authority.
- **D2.Civ.8.K-2.** Describe democratic principles such as equality, fairness, and respect for legitimate authority and rules.
- attentively to others when addressing ideas and making decisions as a group.
- **D2.Civ.10.K-2.** Compare their own point of view with others' perspectives.
- **D2.Civ.14.K-2.** Describe how people have tried to improve their communities over time

Textbox 3.2. NCSS C3 Inquiry Framework Indicators for Grades 3–5

- **D2.Eco.1.3–5.** Compare the benefits and costs of individual choices.
- **D2.Eco.2.3–5.** Identify positive and negative incentives that influence the decisions people make.
- **D2.Eco.3.3–5.** Identify examples of the variety of resources (human capital, physical capital, and natural resources) that are used to produce goods and services.
- **D2.Geo.4.3–5.** Explain how culture influences the way people modify and adapt to their environments.
- **D2.Geo.7.3–5.** Explain how cultural and environmental characteristics affect the distribution and movement of people, goods, and ideas.
- **D2.Geo.8.3–5.** Explain how human settlements and movements relate to the locations and use of various natural resources.
- **D2.Geo.9.3–5.** Analyze the effects of catastrophic environmental and technological events on human settlements and migration.
- **D2.Civ.1.3–5.** Distinguish the responsibilities and powers of government officials at various levels and branches of government and in different times and places.
- **D2.Civ.2.3–5.** Explain how a democracy relies on people's responsible participation, and draw implications for how individuals should participate.
- **D2.Civ.6.3–5.** Describe ways in which people benefit from and are challenged by working together, including through government, workplaces, voluntary organizations, and families.
- **D2.Civ.8.3–5.** Identify core civic virtues and democratic principles that guide government, society, and communities.

Next-Generation Science Standards

The materials economy, consumerism, and responsible and sustainable decision-making are tied to Next-Generation Science Standards that address human and environmental interactions, resource use, and informed decision-making associated with the engineering design process. Primarily associated with the physical sciences where students learn about matter, the conservation of matter, and the different properties of materials, a look at the materials economy highlights the different properties of materials used in common products as well as the choices we make in product creation. Broadly speaking, for the elementary grades, students learn about the properties of objects, that some can be used again, and that there are trade-offs when choosing particular materials to make things.

Additionally, topics in this chapter on production and consumption reinforce the Earth and space science disciplinary core ideas about human impact on the Earth, the importance of natural resources, and that we need to be conscious of how we utilize these resources. The disposal process of the materials economy is directly linked to these standards and to the very popular elementary school topic, the 3Rs—reduce, reuse, recycle. It is our hope that classes engage in deeper and more critical discussions about reducing consumption as well as reusing, recycling, and even upcycling. *Upcycling*, transforming materials that are considered "waste" into new materials or products, is a great way to repurpose materials in products in new and novel ways. There is a lot of opportunity in classrooms to engage students in upcycling projects by having them bring in different products that are still useful but no longer needed and finding ways to repurpose them. Life science topics are related to the materials economy as students can make connections between the impacts of the materials economy (i.e., pollution, climate change, urbanization) on biodiversity and local and global habitats. Finally, the materials economy lends itself to lessons that engage with the engineering design principles embedded in the NGSS as students are asked to apply scientific ideas to design solutions taking into consideration the constraints and costs of available resources. Once again, integrating the science and engineering practices and cross-cutting concepts explicated in the NGSS allows students to see how scientific knowledge is generated from the processes scientists engage in and better understand the phenomena that shape the natural world.

Textbox 3.3. Next-Generation Science Standards for Grades K-2

By grade 2 students understand:[65]

- Humans affect the environment with our choices, and our impact can be reduced through certain actions. (K-ESS3-3, K-ESS2-2)
- How objects are made, what materials they are made from, and how to solve simple problems related to materials and waste. (2-PS1-1, 2-PS1-2)
- How to make observations of matter—texture, visual, aural. (K-PS1-1, 2-PS1-1)
- Matter is made of small particles that combine together to form larger matter. If we cut things into smaller and smaller pieces, they become invisible but that doesn't mean that matter has disappeared or is no longer there. (2-PS1-3)

- Everything is made up of small particles even if the individual particles are invisible.
- Some kinds of materials are better than others for making particular things, and there is usually a tradeoff. (2-PS1-2)
- It takes many steps to make things, tools are used to make things, and tools have special purposes. (K-2-ETS1-1, K-2-ETS1-2, K-2-ETS1-3)

Textbox 3.4. Next-Generation Science Standards for Grades 3–5

By grade 5 students understand:[66]

- The specific impacts humans are having on the air, water, land, and biosphere (life on the planet) and that through our choices we can reduce our impact. (Note: this is not specifically related to individual choices but also choices made by corporations throughout the materials economy). (5-ESS3-1, 5-ESS3.C)
- The specific ways that resource use is linked to sustainability and the environmental impacts of choices made to meet human needs. (4-ESS3-1)
- The growth of technology has led to an increased use of resources. (5-PS1-3, 5-PS1-4)
- Through science and technology, materials that do not appear in nature have become available (i.e., plastic, steel, synthetic fibers). (5-PS1-3, 5-PS1-4)
- Mass production has reduced the amount of time and cost to make a product. Automatic machines make most products in the industrialized world and few things are made by hand. (3-5-ETS1-1, 3-5-ETS1-2, 3-5-ETS1-3)

Cloud Institutes Education for Sustainability Content Standards

The Cloud Institute for Sustainability Education offers resources specifically for teachers, including standards and indicators to guide lesson planning. **Standard D, Sustainable Economics**, is described as "The evolving set of theories and practices of economics that integrates the economic and social systems with the ecological systems required to support and maintain life on the planet."[67] This standard calls for students to know and understand the practices and policies that shape our economic system, including the production and consumption of materials. It asks that students recognize the environmental and social constraints that exist on our planet and make choices aligned with and that contribute to a sustainable future for all. These twenty-first century economic practices will produce and consume in ways that contribute to the health of the financial, social, and natural capital.

United Nations Sustainable Development Goals

UN Sustainability Goals, Goal 8—Promote sustained, inclusive and sustainable economic growth, full and productive employment and decent work for all,[68] is another resource for guidance. A quick search of this sustainability goal will highlight a range of data that inform why this goal is included in a deeper call for sustainable development. Unemployment rates, educational attainment, and number of workers in jobs with no social protection are part of the goal as well as topics including green economy and sustainable tourism.

A note about the green economy is important here. The idea of a green economy is a sort of catchall term for economic growth that also takes into account environmental sustainability. Language that incorporates buzzwords like "green" should make your critical antenna wiggle. You may have noticed how the word "green" has become synonymous with "eco-friendly." Both terms are used in corporate advertising and marketing to sell all kinds of products and services (e.g., green dry cleaning, green fashion collections, eco-friendly cups, bags, energy, etc.). However, many argue that it is a wolf in sheep's clothing, not addressing the deeper systemic issues with free-market capitalism. Utilizing this kind of language can incentivize more individual sustainable behaviors, *but* they emphasize individual consumption, obscuring systemic inequalities inherent in capitalism.[69]

As consumers, we are made to believe that if you just buy that Stanley Cup *you* will help save the planet. If this feels familiar to you, do a little digging of your own into greenwashing, green consumerism, and green economy to learn more about how corporations have taken the word "green" and used it to create new avenues for profits.

Applying EcoJustice Pillars to Chapter Instructional Materials

Below we provide instructional materials that can be used for elementary classrooms to help students understand the materials economy and the role that consumers and producers play. The instructional materials reflect our EcoJustice Education Pillars and are aligned to social studies and science standards. Employing the Backwards Design Model, we present the flowchart below to illustrate the knowledge, skills, and attitudes that we hope a student possesses upon completion of elementary school and the goals for the K-2 and 3–5 grade bands in order to reach the end goal (Figure 3.2).

The instructional materials we share as models focus on teaching students to understand factors that motivate us as consumers, to recognize the power that consumers have in a market economy, and to become more conscious consumers by considering the impact of production and consumption on the Earth, people, and animals. The goals of the materials we introduce for elementary classrooms offer simple places to start thinking about how we are participating in the current economic system, the social and ecological impacts of

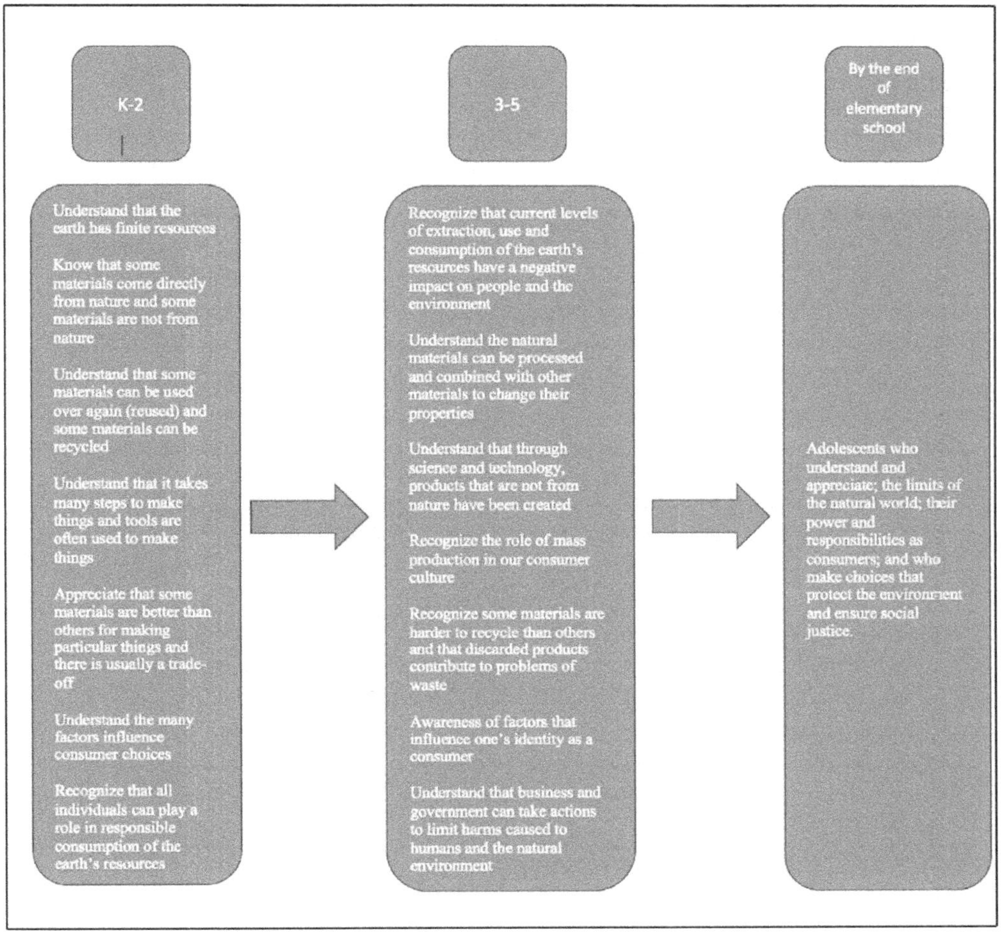

Figure 3.2. Flow chart K-5 to achieve an emerging EcoJustice consciousness related to the materials economy. Author created.

participation, and how we might make different choices with a more critical lens. We offer these materials to be used as they are designed, to be modified to meet your classroom needs and draw on your background knowledge, or as inspiration to draw on.

We suggest that before you teach the concepts presented, refresh your comfortability with the following terms: *Goods, Services, Triple Bottom Line, Externalities, Opportunity Costs, Marketing, Production, Consumption,* and *Consumer.* These terms are not often viewed through critical lenses, and so it is our work as teachers to invite that critical perspective when reviewing these concepts. Remember that exploring the production and consumption through a critical lens will question common-sense assumptions embedded in economic theories and practices, including power dynamics, potential negative impacts on society, and will often highlight issues like waste disposal, exposure to toxic pollutants, loss of ecosystem services, and exploitation of workers in the materials economy. This is the most important work you can do to best prepare yourself to teach your students about these topics.

Production and Consumption Instructional Materials

I love that this lesson inspires me as a teacher to think deeply about goods and the impact that consumerism is having on the environment before introducing the topic to children. The example of the Multipet Company and showing where these pet toys are made in China on a map brings a whole other dimension into the discussion. It is not just the materials used from the natural world, but it is also the pollution created in transporting the goods that harms the environment. I think that teachers need to be educated as much as the children on this extremely timely topic so that lessons about environmental concerns do not become surface. This series of lessons lends to discussions that encourage some deep critical thinking. Kids are competent learners. We should not sell them short with our teaching and we have so much to learn from their thinking if we provide them the opportunities to discuss real world concerns such as this one.

—Marcie, Early Childhood Teacher

Students will gain tremendous value from these lessons, both academically and personally. Students will (possibly for the first time) begin to see the hidden story behind everyday items that they are very connected to (their clothes). Students are also going to reflect on the choices that have to be made for "fast fashion" to occur, and encourage their peers to take action. There's no doubt that students will build empathy during these lessons and foster a sense of global responsibility. As an educator, I'm excited to see students provided with the opportunity to TAKE ACTION. The lessons within this mini unit create the space for students to take ownership of their learning. They are able to make connections before knowledge transfer occurs, conduct research based on that connection, and then take action. This topic is one that all students can feel connected to and will feel passionate about.

—Briana, Elementary Teacher

Textbox 3.5. K-2 EcoJustice Instructional Materials: Production and Consumption

Essential Question(s):

- Can individuals help to reduce negative impacts of production and consumption on the Earth and people and still get their needs and wants met?

Objectives: Students will be able to:

- **Define** and give examples of *goods* (things you can touch and use) and *services* (things people do for others)
- **Sort** examples of goods and services in their community
- **Describe** the resources that are used to make common goods
- **Explain** what it means to "act green" and give examples
- **Analyze** how their choices (like throwing away trash or using less water) can help take care of the planet
- **Reflect** on their own habits and decide one thing they can do to "act green" at home or at school

- **Analyze** influences on their own decision-making
- **Identify** choices people make based on limited resources

Standards:

Social Studies

- **D2.Geo.5.K-2.** Describe how human activities affect the cultural and environmental characteristics of places or regions.
- **D2.Eco.7.K-2.** Describe examples of costs of production.
- **D2.Geo.2.K-2.** Use maps, graphs, photographs, and other representations to describe places and the relationships and interactions that shape them.
- **D3.Geo.7.K-2.** Explain why and how people, goods and ideas move from place to place.

Science

- **K-ESS3-3:** Communicate solutions that will reduce the impact of humans on land, water, air, and other living things in the local environment.
- **2-PS1-1:** Plan and conduct an investigation to describe and classify different kinds of materials by their observable properties.
- **2-PS1-3:** Make observations to construct an evidence-based account of how an object made of a small set of pieces can be disassembled and made into a new object.

Materials:

Lesson 1

- Intro video on Goods and Services for young children—https://www.youtube.com/watch?v=laKl9VRjaw0
- Have the following terms on an anchor chart: Good, Product, Service
- Images for School Sort Activity
- Images of Pet Store showing large quantities of pet toys for sale

Lesson 2

- Images of pet toys from Multipet
- World Map that can be displayed and marked up
- Images of ways companies help and harm the environment

Lesson 3

- Images of "Going Green, Thinking Green, Acting Green"
- *Not for Me, Please! I Choose to Act Green* by Maria Godsey at https://www.youtube.com/watch?v=Uh8Mtswua2w
- Handout: Choices I can make that are good for the environment:
- Images of community engagement to help the environment

Lesson 4

- *Those Shoes* by Maribeth Boelts at https://www.youtube.com/watch?v=TcMSz1Okob8

Important Vocabulary/Concepts:

- Goods
- Services
- Natural Resources
- Renewable Resource versus Nonrenewable Resource
- Production
- Consumption
- Consumer
- Reduce, Reuse, Recycle, Upcycle

Instructional Materials Description and Overview:
In this set of instructional materials for grades K-2, students learn how to distinguish between goods and services. From here, they explore how goods are transported to our store shelves through a case study of pet toys. Students are then encouraged to consider actions they can take in their own lives to support a healthier environment.

Note to Teacher:
Students will need to know the concepts: scarcity, want, need, incentives, and costs, which are all covered in the lessons in Chapter 3. If they don't have this background, see the K-2 lesson in Chapter 3.

We include a fourth day using the book, *Those Shoes*. This book lets students explore the issue of scarcity and making tough economic decisions through the eyes of a young boy. The focus of this lesson is on the reality of scarcity in the lives of individuals and how this can impact decision-making.

The instructional materials are designed sequentially, but depending on where your class is, feel free to use them in your own way. The Extend activities are designed to enrich understanding of the topics but can be used as you see best, for example, on another day or as an assignment for early finishers.

Lesson 1: Goods and Services

ENGAGE: Lesson Introduction

- Show two pictures like the ones below and ask students how they are the same or different. Allow the students to share a few responses and then explain that while both pictures have shoes in them, the pictures are about different concepts. Explain that the class will watch a short video on the new concepts and point to the anchor chart and read the terms, "Good," "Product," and "Service."

By Brooke Fishwick—I Brooke Fishwick created this work entirely by myself, CC BY-SA 3.0, https://commons.wikimedia.org/w/index.php?curid=9555912

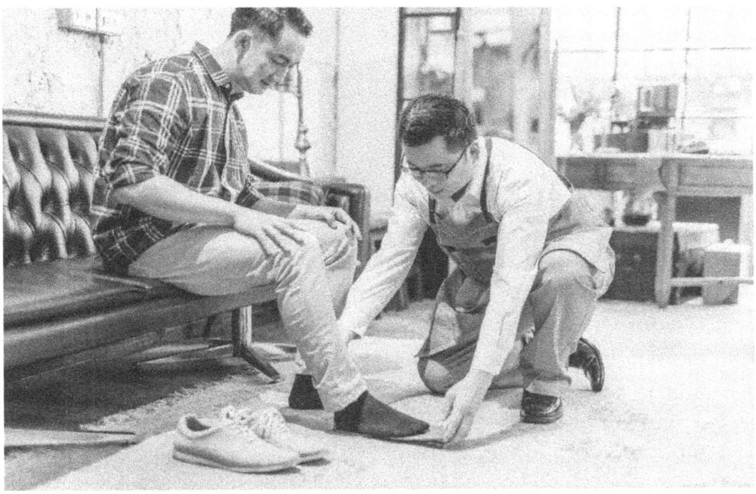

https://www.istockphoto.com/photo/luxury-shoe-shopping-in-taipei-gm1165953194-321001363

EXPLORE: Sorting Goods and Services

- Have several sets of images with examples of goods and services that students use in school (Examples: School Nurse, Books, Playground, Cafeteria Staff, Crayons, etc.). Give each small group of students a set of images and have students analyze and sort the images into categories (students might not yet recognize the differences between a good or a service).
- Have the students share their sorted list—moving across the groups one image at a time to get strong participation and class feedback.

EXPLAIN: Video Explanation

- Play the video *What are GOODS and SERVICES? Educational Fun Facts for Kids*
- Stop the video at 2:50 and review with the students what the terms "good" and "product" mean.
- Stop the video at 5:12 and review with the students what the term "service" is, then ask students to make any revisions to their previous sorted images.. Listen to the students' responses to be sure they understand the concept. After 30 seconds, you can allow a few students to share their example.
- Explain to the students that next they will see examples in the video and they should decide each time if it is an example of a good or a service. Tell the students they can say their answer out loud, or you can use symbols to mean good and service and have students raise the symbol to represent their choice for each example.

ELABORATE: Application activity

- Tell students to think of a pet they have or would like. Tell them to write the name of the pet on a handout or other paper. Students can also draw a picture of the pet if they finish early or there is enough time.
- Have students write the terms "Goods" and "Services" across the top of the paper, or provide a handout with the terms already written. Having an anchor chart or whiteboard with the terms written is helpful and can be used to guide younger students through the activity.
- For students who can write: Tell the students to consider what goods/products they would need to buy for their pet and list those under the term "goods" and then list "services" the pet might need in the other column.
- For developing writers: The teacher can sit with a small group of students or with the class and be the scribe as the students share ideas of goods and services required for a pet.
- Let students share one good and one service from their list with a partner.

EXTEND: Photo Elicitation and Critical Dialogue

- Show students a picture of a big box or local pet store that highlights the amount of product, including toys, that is available to purchase for your pet (example below).

https://www.flickr.com/photos/13194817@N00/49795058841

- Engage students in a critical dialogue about the toys a pet "needs" including:
  - What do you notice in these pictures?
  - How many toys do you think a pet "needs"?
  - How are pet toys marketed to the consumer/pet owner when they go to the pet store?
  - What are toys usually made out of? Are these materials renewable or nonrenewable?
  - What happens to these toys over time? Where do they go when the pet no longer uses the toy?

EVALUATE: Wrap-Up Activity/Assessment

- Have students do a think-pair-share activity discussing one good and one service they purchased recently.
- Have all pairs share one idea from their discussion.

Lesson 2: Production and Distribution

ENGAGE: Lesson Introduction

- Begin the lesson by asking the students to explain the difference between a good and a service. Then show the images below (or ones similar made by Multipet, a company that designs, produces, and sells animal toy products.)
- Ask the students if the images are goods or services.
- Ask the students if they had similar items on their lists from yesterday, or for a pet at home. Let a few share their answers.

Lambchop Dog Toy. Author created.

Cat Toys. https://www.flickr.com/photos/29001414@N00/5501646682

EXPLORE: Mapping Activity

- Explain to the students that the pet toys are made in China and then shipped to a warehouse in Rutherford, NJ. From there they are sent to stores or to people's homes.
- Next, show the students where China is on the displayed map and mark it with a pin. Then mark the location of Rutherford, NJ, with a pin.
- Ask the students how they think the toys get from one location to the other. Let the children share ideas with a partner or discuss as a class.
- Teacher note, this lesson can also include math by letting the children estimate and compare how many miles it would take to transport the toys by air and sea.
- Let the children share their thoughts about how the toys can be transported to the United States.

EXPLAIN: Teacher Explanation and Class Discussion

- Explain to the children that many goods are manufactured in other countries and that this can lead to lower prices, but it can also cause pollution to the air and sea when transported.
- Next, explain that the company that makes the toys is concerned about the environment, so they try to help in different ways. Share the image from the website at https://www.multipet.com/sustainability/ and explain what it means to recycle and repurpose materials.
- Engage students in a brief discussion about their experiences with recycling and repurposing materials at home/school.

ELABORATE: **Application activity**

- Assign the students to work in partners or small groups.
- Explain to the students that they should make a list of ways that companies like Multipet both help protect the environment and also harm the environment.
- Provide students time to work in small groups.

EXTEND: Photo Elicitation and Critical Dialogue

- Share images of the ways that companies both hurt and help the environment (examples below).

Twenty-four Students' photo, licensed as CC BY-SA 2.0 https://www.flickr.com/photos/53771866@N05/6350418468

https://www.flickr.com/photos/88123769@N02/15947941600

https://www.flickr.com/photos/8176740@N05/2919607754

- Ask students what they notice in these pictures and how they relate to the discussion of how companies can both hurt and help the environment.
- Using the list created by students during the ELABORATE activity, see if students had the ideas from photos on their list. Ask them to share why they included them.
- Have groups share additional ideas they had, and as a class, try to find images of their ideas.

EVALUATE: Wrap-Up Activity/Assessment

- Have students respond to the following prompt orally or in writing:
    - Why would you want to buy from a company that helps the environment?

Lesson 3: Consumption
ENGAGE: Lesson Introduction

Show the students images, symbols, and signs that represent care for the environment—images that say "think green" or "act green," and ask them to think about what the message might be. Remind the students to look for "clues" in the picture and think about what they might already know about the words or images.

- After a minute, let the students take turns telling a partner their thoughts.
- Then let a few students share their responses with the class.
- Explain to the students what it means to "Think" or "Act" Green and tell them they will listen to a book about a boy who wants to act green.

EXPLORE: Read Aloud

- Read aloud or listen to the video of the book, *Not for Me, Please! I Choose to Act Green* by Maria Godsey
- Stop at various points to allow students to discuss with their partner different decisions the boy is making and allow a few students to share their responses.
- Tell the students to pay careful attention to all the choices the boy makes in the book.
    - Older students can write down examples as they hear them.
    - For younger students. Stop after each example to discuss how the boy will make a decision to help protect the environment. Ask the students what the boy did and write the action on a flipchart or whiteboard. Examples should include: recycle, turn lights out, turn off water, bring reusable containers for food to school.

EXPLAIN: Text Analysis

Lead the class in a discussion of the following questions:

- Why did the boy in the story change some of his behaviors?
- Which of his actions do you think were useful to help the environment?
- Which of the actions do you think you could take?
- Why is it important for individuals to take action?

ELABORATE: Writing Reflection

- Provide students with a handout that states at the top of the page, "Choices I can make that are good for the environment":
    - Tell students to individually write down a list of behaviors they would like to adopt (or continue). Encourage them to go beyond what was introduced in the book.
        - Older students should include a few sentences explaining how these choices will be good for the environment.
        - Younger students can draw a picture of an action they will take.

EXTEND: Photo Elicitation and Critical Dialogue

- Share images of the ways that individuals work in community to also help the environment.

https://www.flickr.com/photos/63294405@N06/41972135020

https://www.flickr.com/photos/41464593@N02/37919110622

- Engage students in a critical dialogue about how to move beyond individual action and into community engagement projects including:
  - What do you notice in these pictures?
  - Have you ever engaged in a community project like making a community garden or doing a community cleanup?
  - What is the difference between individual action and community actions?
  - Why do you think it is important to do both?
  - What is a community action we can do as a class to help the environment?

EVALUATE: Wrap-Up/Assessment

- Have students complete an exit ticket sharing one individual action they will commit to doing this week.

Lesson 4: Economic Decision-Making
ENGAGE: Lesson Introduction

- Ask students if they have ever wanted something that is too much money for them to buy?
- Ask the students to share some items they would like to buy and ask them to consider if the items are wants or needs? And to explain why they want these things.

EXPLORE: Read Aloud

- Review the terms (written on an anchor chart) Wants, Needs, Scarcity
- Read the book, *Those Shoes,* pausing to ask the questions below:
  - What does the main character want?
  - Why isn't he able to get it? (prompt the students to make the connection to scarcity)
  - Why does he want the shoes so much?
  - What does the character do to try to get the shoes he wants?

EXPLAIN: Economic Decision-Making

- Lead the students in a discussion, or let them discuss the questions with a partner first.
- Do you think the boy made good decisions when he bought the new shoes he wanted?
- Why do you think he gave his shoes to Antonio?

ELABORATE: Pro/Con Activity

- Explain that when we make economic decisions, we should consider the pros and cons of options.
- Introduce the cost/benefit (or Pro/Con) T-chart to the students. The chart should be labeled "Reasons to buy/not buy the shoes" across the top. On one side of the T-chart the word "Pros" should be written and on the other side "Cons"

should be written. Providing a visual model on an anchor chart is helpful. For younger children, the anchor chart can be used to guide a class discussion of the pros and cons, with the teacher acting as the scribe.

- For children who can write, tell them to list reasons under each heading. This can be done individually or with a partner.
- Once the lists are complete, ask the students to decide if they would buy the shoes if they were the main character.
- Students write out their reasons or this can be discussed as a class.
- Ask students if they think the character in the story might have made a different decision if he had used an economic decision-making model like the class did? Allow students to discuss this idea.

Another variant is to designate one spot in the room for students to gather if they would buy the shoes and another spot for students who wouldn't. Allow students to move to the spot that reflects their choice and tell them to explain their reasons to others in the same spot.

After several minutes, tell each side to list several reasons to support their position and then let each side state their reasons. After both sides have shared their reasons, you can ask if anyone has changed their decision based on what they heard.

EXTEND: Photo Elicitation and Critical Dialogue

- Share images of closets of shoes or sneakers that have many shoes or sneakers.

https://www.istockphoto.com/photo/shoe-shelf-in-preschool-gm1198281429-342409725

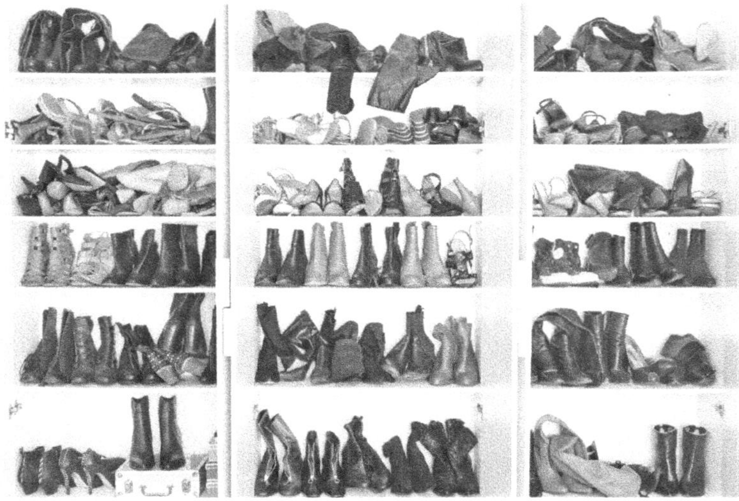

https://www.istockphoto.com/photo/empty-messy-shoes-closet-gm1216603282-354822506

- Engage students in a critical dialogue about wants, needs, and excess, including:
  - What do you notice in these pictures?
  - Do you connect with this picture? Why or why not?
  - Why do you think someone would choose to have this many shoes?
  - Do you think having this many shoes is a good thing or a bad thing? Why?
  - What does having this many shoes say about the person and their economic choices?

EVALUATE: Wrap-Up/Assessment
Students should be instructed to write a sentence explaining why it is useful to use an economic decision-making model.

Textbox 3.6. 3–5 EcoJustice Instructional Materials Production and Consumption

Essential Questions:
How can your awareness of the social and environmental impacts of fast fashion impact your relationship to how you consume?

Objectives: Students will be able to:

- **Identify** the steps in the materials economy (extraction, production, distribution, consumption, and disposal) and describe how they relate to the fast fashion industry.
- **Explain** how clothing is made, including the raw materials used (e.g., cotton, polyester) and the environmental impact of textile production.
- **Illustrate** the journey of a piece of clothing from raw material to disposal, highlighting key environmental and social issues along the way.

- **Analyze** the social impacts of fast fashion by describing working conditions in garment factories and how they affect workers' lives.
- **Evaluate** their own clothing choices and propose ways to reduce waste and make more sustainable fashion decisions.

Standards:

Social Studies

- **D2.Eco.1.3–5.** Compare the benefits and costs of individual choices
- **D2.Eco.2.3–5.** Identify positive and negative incentives that influence the decisions people make
- **D2.Eco.3.3–5.** Identify examples of the variety of resources (human capital, physical capital, and natural resources) that are used to produce goods and services

Science

- **4-ESS3-1:** Obtain and combine information to describe that energy and fuels are derived from natural resources and their uses affect the environment
- **5-ESS3-1:** Obtain and combine information about ways individual communities use science ideas to protect the Earth's resources and environment
- **5-PS1-3:** Make observations and measurements to identify materials based on their properties
- **5-ETS1-2:** Generate and compare multiple possible solutions to a problem based on how well each is likely to meet the criteria and constraints of the problem

Materials:

- Homework: Students will bring in their favorite piece of clothing for Day 1. Have students write a short story about their favorite piece of clothing and why it is meaningful to them. (ELA connection)
- 6 Interesting Facts About Fast Fashion for Kids https://kids.earth.org/climate-change/6-interesting-facts-about-fast-fashion-for-kids/
- Maps of the world
- Images of the social and environmental impacts of fast fashion. See examples from Mountains of clothes washed up on Ghana beach show cost of fast fashion | The Independent https://www.independent.co.uk/climate-change/news/fast-fashion-ghana-clothes-waste-b2132399.html[70]
- Computers to conduct research and create presentations
- The Story of Stuff video: the story of stuff youtube

Important Vocabulary/Concepts:

- Fast fashion

Instructional Materials Description and Overview:

In this set of instructional materials for grades 3–5, students are introduced to the social and environmental consequences of fast fashion. Students use their favorite clothing to learn more about the materials economy. They conduct research into an ecological or social consequence of fast fashion and develop an action to help raise awareness of what they have learned.

Note to Teacher:

This series of instructional materials deviates from others presented throughout the book in that it moves through all six of the Es over the course of 3 days. As always, modify as needed, inserting formative evaluations at the end of each day.

Lesson 1: Exploring Phenomena and Model Building
ENGAGE: Photo Elicitation and small group discussions

- Show images/slideshow of images that show fast fashion. Both relatable images for 3–5 graders (stores, racks of clothing) as well as images that show some of the social and environmental impacts of fast fashion. Select about ten images (the resources listed in lesson materials can be used as sources for images). Show each for about a minute and ask students to record their questions, thoughts, feelings, connections to each image. (See photo elicitation protocol in Appendix)
- Have students turn and talk, sharing one idea from their handout—ask students to find consensus on one image to share with the class
- Gather a few ideas from student groups and record them on a t-chart—image|f eeling/questions/connection

EXPLORE: Research and Collaborative Model Building

- In small groups, have each student share their favorite piece of clothing and why it is their favorite. Allow them to share the story of their clothing.
- Ask students to guess where their favorite clothing was made.
- Have them look at the labels and see where their clothing was made and mark on the group map.
- Have students look up the marketing and advertising campaign for their favorite clothing.
- Have students choose one piece of clothing and ask them to create a model or visual representation about how they think their piece of clothing was made and found its way to their closet. What materials were needed to make it, who made it, by what process, and how did it get to their closet?
- Wrap up: Students share some of their models or visuals and collect questions about gaps in their thinking.
- Tell students tomorrow they will learn more about the production-to-consumption cycle.

Lesson 2: Model Revision and Research
EXPLAIN: Video and Model Revision

- Students watch the *Story of Stuff* or another film about the supply chain and learn about the supply chain from raw material to consumption to waste.
- Ask students to modify their model/visual with new information that they have learned from film.
- Have students share their new models with the class.

ELABORATE: Small Group Research and Presentation Building

- Have students work in groups using the resource, 6 *Interesting Facts About Fast Fashion for Kids*. Assign each group one of the interesting facts.
- Have groups read their facts and go deeper. Ask each group to research more about their fast fashion fact and create a two- to three-slide presentation to share with the class. Presentations should include both words and images, and each student should be prepared to present something from one of the slides.

Lesson 3: Taking Action
EXTEND: Actions Brainstorm

- Students share their presentations.
- Brainstorm **actionable** ways students can help raise awareness of the problems and impacts of fast fashion and what they can do about it!
  - Ideas can include live or video PSAs, create a bulletin board for the school, create a picture book for the classroom or lower grade classrooms, host a clothing drive for a local organization, and so on.
- Choose one or more of the actions from the EXTEND brainstorm and make it come to life. Have students document the process of implementing their action.

EVALUATE: Action Implementation and Reflection

- Have students engage in a final reflection about fast fashion by completing the following prompts:
  - I used to think_______
  - Now I think ________
  - Something I might change now is _____________
  - A way I can help others in my community is _____________

Community and Place-Based Learning Opportunities

This section invites teachers and parents to engage community members, outside school experts, and other local knowledge resources to extend the EcoJustice learning experiences that students are engaging with in classrooms. We know taking trips with students can be difficult, so sending these suggestions home to families might be a good idea. Additionally, we included inviting some speakers to visit your classroom to discuss in more detail their work as it relates to the materials economy.

For this theme of production and consumption, we suggest any of the following community and place-based learning experiences for you and your students:

- Visit a local landfill or waste transfer station. Many towns have waste collection facilities that might be open to visitors. If not, invite a speaker from your town, city, or municipality dedicated to waste management to visit your classroom and discuss where the waste goes in your community.
- Visit a recycling facility or other upcycling space in your community. For example, Terracycle, a mission-driven business with a nonprofit arm dedicated to recycling, upcycling, and eliminating the idea of "waste," has a location in Trenton, NJ, that welcomes visitors.[71] If visiting a facility is not possible, invite a speaker who is involved in recycling or upcycling efforts in your community to visit the class and speak about the process of reducing waste.
- Visit a local composting facility at a farm or other space in your community. If visiting a farm is not possible, invite a farmer or other person who is engaging in composting to come and speak to your class about how organic waste (like food and other yard waste) can be taken out of the municipal waste stream and transformed into compost.
- Engage in a cleanup at a local park or beach. If unable to get to a space outside of school, consider doing a cleanup around your school. Have students discuss the diversity of materials they collect and sort them into categories—waste, recyclable, reusable, upcyclable, or compostable. Share your findings with the school and host monthly or seasonal cleanups at the school, continuing to collect data about waste collected. Create a campaign to raise awareness about reducing waste and litter around the school.
- Visit a local factory or business that is making products from raw materials. Students can see in real time the materials economy come to life and engage in critical conversations about the social and environmental impacts of the local factory. If it is not possible to visit a factory, consider a virtual tour of a factory and engage in a similar discussion about the social and environmental impacts of the factory. Lego, Coca-Cola, and Patagonia are a few examples of companies that have information about their supply chain, and some have virtual tours.
- Visit a local store that sells sustainably produced products. Have students observe the products, ask questions about the products, and interview the owner. Ask students to make observations about the materials used, where products were made, the packaging of the products, and prices. Engage in a discussion where students compare their observations with observations made of products from a big box store.
- Host a school-wide swap. Have students bring in products that they no longer use and gift and trade with other students. The swap can be around a single type of product (i.e., clothing, toys, etc.) or more general. Include your students in the planning and decision-making process for even more buy-in.

Teacher Turn

Now it is your turn. Here we offer next steps for you to develop your own EcoJustice instructional materials that meet the needs of your school curriculum and your students' interests. As you have learned throughout this chapter, there are many EcoJustice issues that are linked to our current materials economy and our roles as consumers. Perhaps most important is for children to begin to understand the power of sustainable and conscious choices when it comes to consumption and that our choices have environmental and social impacts that expand far beyond what we are able to perceive. We invite teachers to dig deeper into any of these issues with your class by utilizing resources provided in this chapter and in our Appendices and website to create your own lessons.

A good place to start is to answer the following questions:

- Which standard fits with your school curriculum? (See the list in the Appendix of NCSS and NGSS standards we have identified as offering opportunities to incorporate our Pillars.) Also look at the Cloud Standards and the SDGs for further connections to your curriculum and ideas.
- Which concepts are you and your students interested in learning more about? (e.g., resource exploitation and depletion, labor exploitation, commodification of resources, local economies, etc.)
- Which resources (suggested or your own) would you like to use to expand your own understanding of these concepts?
- What pedagogical activities are most appropriate for your teaching context?

Remember that EcoJustice issues are often related to issues of access and equity since those with the most resources have the greatest access and those with the least material resources have the least access. Additionally, in the United States, those who are most marginalized are also the most vulnerable to exploitation. We have put together many resources in this chapter, the Appendices, and on our website for you to build out an EcoJustice lesson including a lesson plan template, national social studies and science standards, resources to expand your own thinking about EcoJustice issues, and common teaching strategies we have used in our own classrooms. You don't have to do this alone either. Include your students in the process of creating relevant and meaningful lessons for them. Tap other teachers who are aligned to EcoJustice for ideas and accountability. We are eager to support you on your journey toward becoming an EcoJustice Educator!

Notes

1 Calvin Coolidge, "The Press Under a Free Government," speech, American Society of Newspaper Editors, Washington, DC, January 17, 1925.

2 George W. Bush, "Remarks by the President to Airline Employees," *O'Hare International Airport*, Chicago, IL, September 27, 2001, The White House Archives.

3 "Bush Signs Stimulus Package into Law," *NBC News*, February 13, 2008, https://www.nbcnews.com/id/wbna23143814.
4 National Governors Association Center for Best Practices and Council of Chief State School Officers, *Common Core State Standards* (Washington, DC: National Governors Association Center for Best Practices, Council of Chief State School Officers, 2010), https://corestandards.org. "Common Core States 2025," *World Population Review*, accessed August 7, 2025, https://worldpopulationreview.com/state-rankings/common-core-states.
5 Jean Anyon, "Social Class and School Knowledge," *Curriculum Inquiry* 11, no. 1 (1981): 3–42, https://doi.org/10.2307/1179509.
6 Henry A. Giroux and Anthony N. Penna, "Social Education in the Classroom: The Dynamics of the Hidden Curriculum," *Theory & Research in Social Education* 7, no. 1 (1979): 21–42.
7 Council for Economic Education, *Voluntary National Content Standards in Economics*, 2nd ed. (New York: Council for Economic Education, 2010), https://www.councilforeconed.org/wp-content/uploads/2012/03/voluntary-national-content-standards-2010.pdf.
8 "Plants as Medicine: Lenape Healing Traditions Continue Today," *Columbia University School of Nursing*, April 20, 2021, https://www.nursing.columbia.edu/news/plants-medicine-lenape-healing-traditions-continue-today.
9 "Lenape and the Jersey Shore," *New Jersey Sea Grant Consortium*, accessed August 7, 2025.
10 Henry Clay, "Speech on American Industry, 1824," *Bill of Rights Institute*, accessed August 7, 2025, https://billofrightsinstitute.org/activities/henry-clay-speech-on-american-industry-1824.
11 History.com Editors, "Manifest Destiny," *History*, last modified December 1, 2017, https://www.history.com/topics/19th-century/manifest-destiny.
12 "Great Spirit Prayer," *Native American Prayers*, Jesuit Resource, Xavier University, accessed January 27, 2025, https://www.xavier.edu/jesuitresource/online-resources/prayer-index/native-american.
13 Naomi Klein, *No Logo: Taking Aim at the Brand Bullies* (Toronto: Knopf Canada, 1999).
14 Mike Patton, "A Historical Look at The Components of U.S. GDP: 1929 to 2011," *Forbes*, December 30, 2014, https://www.forbes.com/sites/mikepatton/2014/12/30/a-historical-look-at-the-components-of-u-s-gdp-1929-to-2011/.
15 Annie Leonard, *The Story of Stuff*, directed by Louis Fox (Berkeley, CA: Free Range Studios, 2007), video.
16 The Story of Stuff Project, "The Story of Stuff," accessed August 7, 2025, https://www.storyofstuff.org/movies/story-of-stuff/.
17 Heidi Groover, "Seattle-based Stanley Rides the Wave of Water Bottle, Tumbler Addiction," *The Seattle Times*, January 12, 2024, https://www.seattletimes.com/business/seattle-based-stanley-rides-the-wave-of-water-bottle-tumbler-addiction/.
18 "What Is the Composition of Stainless Steel? Full Guide & Key Components," *Jindal Stainless*, September 30, 2024, https://www.jindalstainless.com/blog/a-complete-guide-to-stainless-steel-compositions/.
19 Kala Bhattar, "A Wonderful World Withering Away: The Malignant Industry of Mining for Minerals," *UAB Institute for Human Rights Blog*, May 2, 2022, https://sites.uab.edu/

humanrights/2022/05/02/a-wonderful-world-withering-away-the-malignant-industry-of-mining-for-minerals/.

20 "The Global Plastics Crisis," *Eco-Cycle*, accessed August 7, 2025, https://ecocycle.org/our-programs/reducing-plastics/global-plastics-crisis/.

21 Justine Calma, "The Trump Administration Faces a Fight Over "Biggest" Environmental Deregulatory Action in US History," *The Verge*, July 10, 2024, https://www.theverge.com/news/629128/trump-environmental-deregulation-epa.

22 Gracelin Baskaran, "Why Responsible Mining Is a Human Rights Imperative," *Center for Strategic and International Studies*, December 1, 2023, https://www.csis.org/analysis/why-responsible-mining-human-rights-imperative.

23 "Plastics—Fueling Oil Demand, Climate Change and Pollution," *United Nations*, accessed August 7, 2025, https://www.un.org/en/climatechange/science/climate-issues/plastics.

24 "Big Steelmakers Failing to Make the Switch to Renewables, Survey Shows," *Reuters*, November 29, 2024, https://www.reuters.com/business/big-steelmakers-failing-make-switch-renewables-survey-shows-2024-11-29/.

25 Sajjad Mozaffari et al., "Effects of Occupational Exposures on Respiratory Health in Steel Factory Workers," *Frontiers in Public Health* 11 (2023): 1082874, https://pmc.ncbi.nlm.nih.gov/articles/PMC9971494/.

26 Fred Pearce, "Why the Rush to Mine Lithium Could Dry Up the High Andes," *Yale Environment 360*, September 21, 2022, https://e360.yale.edu/features/lithium-mining-water-andes-argentina.

27 United Nations, *Department of Economic and Social Affairs, Population Division, World Urbanization Prospects: The 2018 Revision* (New York: United Nations, 2018), https://www.un.org/development/desa/en/news/population/2018-revision-of-world-urbanization-prospects.html.

28 "Climate Impact of Shipping," *Transport & Environment*, accessed August 7, 2025, https://www.transportenvironment.org/topics/ships/climate-impact-shipping.

29 "CBRE Group, Inc. Reports Financial Results for Second-Quarter 2021," *CBRE Investor Relations*, July 29, 2021, https://ir.cbre.com/press-releases/detail/57/cbre-group-inc-reports-financial-results-for.

30 U.S. Bureau of Labor Statistics, "Warehousing and Storage: NAICS 493," last modified August 1, 2025, https://www.bls.gov/iag/tgs/iag493.htm.

31 Jean Kilbourne, *Killing Us Softly 4: Advertising's Image of Women*, directed by Sut Jhally (Northampton, MA: Media Education Foundation, 2010), DVD.

32 Lorraine Song, "How Social Media Fuels Impulse Purchasing," *SU Social*, accessed August 7, 2025, https://susocial.com/how-social-media-fuels-impulse-purchasing/.

33 "Digital 2025: Global Advertising Trends," *DataReportal*, accessed August 7, 2025, https://datareportal.com/reports/digital-2025-sub-section-global-advertising-trends.

34 PYMNTS and LendingClub, *New Reality Check: The Paycheck-to-Paycheck Report: The Generational Divide Edition* (Boston: PYMNTS.com, 2023), https://www.pymnts.com/study/reality-check-paycheck-to-paycheck-consumer-planning-financial-emergency/.

35 U.S. Environmental Protection Agency, "Guide to the Facts and Figures Report about Materials, Waste and Recycling," *EPA*, accessed August 7, 2025, https://www.epa.gov/facts-and-figures-about-materials-waste-and-recycling/guide-facts-and-figures-report-about.

36 Judith Enck, Jan Dell, and Jennifer Congdon, "The Real Truth About the U.S. Plastics Recycling Rate: 2021 Facts and Figures," *Beyond Plastics and The Last Beach Cleanup*,

May 4, 2022, accessed August 7, 2025, https://static1.squarespace.com/static/5eda91260bbb7e7a4bf528d8/t/62b2238152acae761414d698/1655841666913/The-Real-Truth-about-the-US-Plastic-Recycling-Rate-2021-Facts-and-Figures-_5-4-22.pdf.

37 U.S. Environmental Protection Agency, "Frequent Questions Regarding EPA's Facts and Figures about Materials, Waste and Recycling," *EPA*, accessed August 7, 2025, https://www.epa.gov/facts-and-figures-about-materials-waste-and-recycling/frequent-questions-regarding-epas-facts-and.

38 Tishman Environment and Design Center, The New School, "New School Map Reveals Most Incinerators Pollute Low-Income and Communities of Color, Worsen Climate Change," *The New School*, accessed August 7, 2025, https://www.newschool.edu/pressroom/pressreleases/2022/TishmanCenterIncineratorMap.htm.

39 "Footprint Calculator—Measure Your Impact," *Global Footprint Network*, accessed August 7, 2025, https://www.footprintnetwork.org/resources/footprint-calculator/.

40 Treehugger, "What Is Ecological Footprint? Definition and How to Calculate It," *Treehugger*, accessed August 7, 2025, https://www.treehugger.com/what-is-ecological-footprint-4580244.

41 Stockholm Resilience Centre, "Planetary Boundaries," *Stockholm Resilience Centre*, accessed August 9, 2025, https://www.stockholmresilience.org/research/planetary-boundaries.html.

42 Robert Costanza, Ralph d'Arge, Rudolf de Groot, Stephen Farber, Monica Grasso, Bruce Hannon, et al., "The Value of the World's Ecosystem Services and Natural Capital," *Nature* 387, no. 6630 (May 15, 1997): 253–60, https://doi.org/10.1038/387253a0.

43 Intergovernmental Science-Policy Platform on Biodiversity and Ecosystem Services (IPBES), *Global Assessment Report on Biodiversity and Ecosystem Services,* ed. E. S. Brondízio, J. Settele, S. Díaz, and H. T. Ngo. Bonn (Germany: IPBES Secretariat, 2019), accessed August 9, 2025, https://ipbes.net/global-assessment.

44 Turner, R. Kerry, W. J. Mitsch, and S. E. Jorgensen, "The Economic Value of Wetlands: A Global Perspective," *Wetlands Ecology and Management* 13, no. 1 (2005): 5–23.

45 M. E. Sierra, S. N. Stephenson, and others. "The Value of Forests in Carbon Sequestration," *Nature* 507, no. 7492 (January 2014): 153–5, accessed August 9, 2025, https://www.nature.com/articles/506153a.

46 DoGoodPeople, "Responsible and Sustainable Consumption for Children: How Can You Teach Them?" *DoGoodPeople*, accessed August 9, 2025, https://www.dogoodpeople.com/csr-trends/responsible-and-sustainable-consumption-for-children-how-can-you-teach-them/.

47 U.S. Bureau of Economic Analysis (BEA), "Personal Consumption Expenditures by Type of Product," accessed August 9, 2025, https://apps.bea.gov/iTable/?reqid=19&step=3&isuri=1&nipa_table_list=2017&categories=underlying.

48 United Nations, "Goal 12: Ensure Sustainable Consumption and Production Patterns," *United Nations Sustainable Development Goals*, accessed August 9, 2025, https://www.un.org/sustainabledevelopment/sustainable-consumption-production/.

49 Board of Governors of the Federal Reserve System, *Report on the Economic Well-Being of U.S. Households in 2019* (Washington, DC: Federal Reserve, May 2020), accessed August 9, 2025, https://www.federalreserve.gov/publications/files/2019-report-economic-well-being-us-households-202005.pdf.

50 Beverage Marketing Corporation, *US Bottled Water Market—2022: Key Trends and Forecasts* (New York: Beverage Marketing Corporation, 2022).
51 Global Footprint Network, "How Many Earths? How Many Countries?" *Earth Overshoot Day*, accessed January 23, 2026, https://overshoot.footprintnetwork.org/how-many-earths-or-countries-do-we-need/.
52 U.S. Environmental Protection Agency (EPA), "New Toxics Release Inventory Data Reported," *EPA*, accessed August 9, 2025, https://www.epa.gov/newsreleases/new-toxics-release-inventory-data-reported.
53 U.S. Environmental Protection Agency (EPA), "National Overview: Facts and Figures on Materials, Wastes and Recycling," *EPA*, accessed August 9, 2025, https://www.epa.gov/facts-and-figures-about-materials-waste-and-recycling/national-overview-facts-and-figures-materials.
54 Associated Press, "Miners Are Razing Forests to Meet Surging Demand for Metals and Minerals, Worsening Climate Emissions in Indonesia," *AP News*, accessed August 9, 2025, https://apnews.com/article/mining-deforestation-indonesia-climate-emissions-3bf4395f4a16d6097727da0793e311e4.
55 The Ocean Cleanup, "The Ocean Cleanup Project: Annual Report 2020," *The Ocean Cleanup Foundation*, 2020, accessed August 9, 2025, https://theoceancleanup.com.
56 World Wildlife Fund, "Living Planet Report 2024," *World Wildlife Fund*, October 10, 2024, accessed August 9, 2025, https://www.worldwildlife.org/publications/2024-living-planet-report.
57 Intergovernmental Science-Policy Platform on Biodiversity and Ecosystem Services (IPBES), *Summary for Policymakers of the Global Assessment Report on Biodiversity and Ecosystem Services of the Intergovernmental Science-Policy Platform on Biodiversity and Ecosystem Services*, ed. S. Díaz, J. Settele, E. S. Brondízio, H. T. Ngo, and others (Bonn, Germany: IPBES secretariat, 2019), accessed August 9, 2025, https://doi.org/10.5281/zenodo.3553579.
58 National Institute for Occupational Safety and Health (NIOSH), "Stress and Mental Health of Warehouse Workers," *NIOSH*, 2020, accessed August 9, 2025, https://www.cdc.gov/niosh/.
59 World Economic Forum, "The Future of Jobs Report 2023: Introduction—The Global Labour Market Landscape in 2023," *World Economic Forum*, 2023, accessed August 9, 2025, https://www.weforum.org/publications/the-future-of-jobs-report-2023/in-full/1-introduction-the-global-labour-market-landscape-in-2023/.
60 Robert E. Scott, Valerie Wilson, Jori Kandra, and Daniel Perez, "Botched Policy Responses to Globalization Have Decimated Manufacturing Employment with Often Overlooked Costs for Black, Brown, and Other Workers of Color: Investing in Infrastructure and Rebalancing Trade Can Create Good Jobs for All," *Economic Policy Institute*, January 31, 2022, accessed August 9, 2025, https://files.epi.org/uploads/239189.pdf.
61 Emma Ross, "Fast Fashion Getting Faster: A Look at the Unethical Labor Practices Sustaining a Growing Industry," *GW International Law and Policy Brief*, October 28, 2021, accessed August 9, 2025, https://studentbriefs.law.gwu.edu/ilpb/2021/10/28/fast-fashion-getting-faster-a-look-at-the-unethical-labor-practices-sustaining-a-growing-industry/.

62 National Council for the Social Studies (NCSS), "Chapter 2—The Themes of Social Studies," in *National Curriculum Standards for Social Studies, Theme VII: Production, Distribution, and Consumption*. NCSS, accessed August 9, 2025, https://www.socialstudies.org/national-curriculum-standards-social-studies-chapter-2-themes-social-studies.

63 National Council for the Social Studies (NCSS), "Chapter 2—The Themes of Social Studies," in *National Curriculum Standards for Social Studies, Theme III: People, Places, and Environments*. NCSS, accessed August 9, 2025, https://www.socialstudies.org/national-curriculum-standards-social-studies-chapter-2-themes-social-studies#3.

64 National Council for the Social Studies (NCSS), "The College, Career, and Civic Life (C3) Framework for Social Studies State Standards: Guidance for Enhancing the Rigor of K–12 Civics, Economics, Geography, and History," *NCSS*, 2013, accessed August 9, 2025, https://www.socialstudies.org/sites/default/files/c3/C3-Framework-for-Social-Studies.pdf.

65 Next-Generation Science Standards (NGSS), "Elementary Standards: Kindergarten Through Grade Five Disciplinary Core Ideas," *NGSS Lead States*, September 2017, accessed August 9, 2025, https://www.nextgenscience.org/sites/default/files/K-2DCI.pdf.

66 Next-Generation Science Standards (NGSS), "Elementary Standards: Third Through Fifth Grade Performance Expectations by Topic," *NGSS Lead States*, September 2017, accessed August 9, 2025, https://www.nextgenscience.org/sites/default/files/3-5Topic.pdf.

67 The Cloud Institute for Sustainability Education, "The Benchmarks by The Cloud Institute. Version 1.2," *The Cloud Institute for Sustainability Education*, 2017, accessed August 9, 2025, https://cloud-institute.squarespace.com/s/EfS-Benchmarks_ver1x2.pdf.

68 United Nations, "Goal 8: Promote Sustained, Inclusive and Sustainable Economic Growth, Full and Productive Employment and Decent Work for All," *United Nations Sustainable Development Goals*, accessed August 9, 2025, https://www.un.org/sustainabledevelopment/economic-growth/.

69 Richard Kahn, "Producing Crisis: Green Consumerism as an Ecopedagogical Issue," *Green Theory & Praxis: The Journal of Ecopedagogy* 5, no. 1 (2010): i–iv.

70 Tom Batchelor, "Mountains of Clothes Washed Up on Ghana Beach Show Cost of Fast Fashion," *The Independent*, August 3, 2022, https://www.independent.co.uk/climate-change/news/fast-fashion-ghana-clothes-waste-b2132399.html.

71 TerraCycle, Inc, *TerraCycle Official Website* (Trenton, NJ: TerraCycle, Inc., 2025), accessed August 9, 2025, https://www.terracycle.com/en-US/.

4
Land

Chapter Outline

So much of life is fast-paced and go, go, go. It's very rare that we as humans stop to consider the ways in which the Earth has been molded to fit the needs of the current social and economic climate.

—*Elementary Teacher*

Introduction

"I discovered many islands inhabited by numerous people. I took possession of all of them for our most fortunate King by making public proclamation and unfurling his standard," Christopher Columbus's letter to the King and Queen of Spain in 1493 regarding his "discovery" and claiming of lands in the New World.[1]

How is it that conceptions of land use and ownership are formed? In the UK hikers can roam freely on land known as "open access land" or "access land," which includes mountains, moors, and paths that are *privately owned*.[2] Many Indigenous cultures in North America believe one cannot "own" land, they may only live with the land. Members of the Cambodian

Hill tribes believe their ancestors live in nature and therefore to leave the land of their ancestors would be to betray them. At least twenty-eight states of the United States have some form of a "Stand Your Ground" law, which removes the duty to retreat from an intruder to your private property and instead allows one to defend themselves if they feel an imminent threat. How is it that there are so many conceptions of land and land rights?

Questions of land ownership/stewardship become even more complex when we consider concepts like "Eminent Domain." Under the doctrine of Eminent Domain, the government may take private property and convert it into public use as long as the owner(s) are compensated. In the United States this is true even if the landowner does not wish to sell their land. This calls into question whose land is it then? Should the good of the many override the individual's interest? Who determines if the interests of the Cambodian Hill[3] people are less important than the larger community of Cambodia? How land has been viewed, used, abused, taken and controlled, and how we teach this, is at the heart of this chapter.

In this chapter, we begin by exploring how elementary education helps to shape dominant views of how land should be viewed and used in the United States. A discussion of Social Studies topics will explore how typical narratives contribute to understandings of what seems "normal" and "right" when it comes to how we view access to land and land use. We will continue to build on the economic foundations laid in Chapters 2 and 3; therefore, references will be made to economic concepts such as: wants, needs, scarcity, production, consumption, distribution, opportunity cost, the Triple Bottom Line, renewable and nonrenewable resources, and externalities. We will continue with offering an EcoJustice perspective on how to approach traditional topics, followed by a section designed to build the reader's knowledge base and resources, instructional materials, and guidance on how to implement concepts in elementary school classrooms.

The Conventional Approach

The voluntary National Standards for Geography, *Geography for Life*, provide a definition of geography as "the study of the physical and human systems across Earth's surface."[4] There are eighteen Geography for Life standards that are organized under six Essential Elements: (1) The World in Spatial Terms, (2) Places and Regions, (3) Physical Systems, (4) Human Systems, (5) Environment and Society, and (6) The Uses of Geography. For our purposes, we will highlight just a few of the Essential Elements for students K-4 (fifth grade is grouped with the middle school standards up to grade 8 and therefore will not be presented in this discussion).

As you review the selections from the standards and desired outcomes for students in Table 4.1, consider what knowledge, skills and attitudes can be developed among students in grades K-4 through the inclusion of these standards. Also, ask yourself if the standards, as they are written, will guide teachers to infuse aspects of the EcoJustice Education Pillars?

Table 4.1. A Selection of the Voluntary National Standards for Geography

Essential Element: The World in Spatial Terms	Essential Element: Human Systems	Essential Element: Human Systems
Standard 1 contains these themes: Properties and Functions of Geographic Representations, Using Geospatial Data to Construct Geographic Representations.	**Standard 9** contains these themes: Characteristics of Population, Spatial Distribution of Population, and Migration.	**Standard 13** contains these themes: Territorial Divisions, Cooperation, and Conflict.
1. Properties and functions of geographic representations A. Identify and describe the properties (position and orientation, symbols, scale, perspective, coordinate systems) and functions of geographic representations, as exemplified by being able to: • Identify and describe the properties of a variety of maps and globes and purposes. • Identify and describe the functions of a variety of geographic rep-resentations. • Identify and describe the properties and functions of maps students collect from magazines, news articles, and tourist brochures. B. Describe how properties of geographic representations determine the purposes they can be used for, as exemplified by being able to: • Identify the maps or types of maps most appropriate for specific purposes. • Describe how a variety of geographic representations (maps, globes, graphs, diagrams, aerial and other photographs, GPS) are used to communicate different types of information. • Describe how maps are created for a specific purpose.	2. Spatial Distribution of Population—People live in many different places on Earth A. Describe how the number of people varies from place to place, as exemplified by being able to: • Identify and describe the locations of types of places where different numbers of people live in the local area • Describe how ways of making a living influence how many people live in a certain place. • Identify and describe places in the state where the greatest and few-est numbers of people live. B. Explain why people live in different types of places, as exemplified by being able to: • Describe and explain why the founders of the local community elected to settle there (e.g., easily accessible or defensible, acceptable climatic conditions, proximity to other resources or transportation routes). • Explain why people sometimes settle in inhospitable environments (e.g., availability of valuable resources, economic opportunities, diminishing availability of more desirable locations).	2. The role cooperation has in managing Earth's surface A. Explain how people cooperate in managing and using Earth's surface, as exemplified by being able to: • Explain how international water boundaries are examples of people cooperating in dividing and using Earth's surface • Analyze activities in the local community to describe ways in which people solve problems by cooperating (e.g., working in groups to pick up trash along a road, participating in community house-building projects). • Describe how communities and states cooperate in providing relief efforts during and after natural disasters (e.g., donations of money and food aid, sending medical teams and supplies, construction workers and equipment).

(Continued)

Table 4.1. (Continued)

Essential Element: The World in Spatial Terms	Essential Element: Human Systems	Essential Element: Human Systems
2. Geospatial data are connected to locations on Earth's surface	3. Migration—People move for a variety of reasons	3. Conflicts arise when there is disagreement over the division, control, and management of Earth's surface
A. Identify examples of geospatial data, as exemplified by being able to: • Identify landmarks on the school grounds and describe their size, shape, and location. • Identify the spatial location of each student's assigned seat in the classroom. • Identify the locations and types of trees in the neighborhood of the school.	A. Describe examples of different human migrations, as exemplified by being able to: • Describe why and how people moved west during the California Gold Rush. • Describe why and how the Pilgrims moved from England to the US colonies. • Describe why and how Native Americans moved to federally designated reservations.	A. Analyze examples of disagreements over land uses in their community, as exemplified by being able to: • Identify and describe the reasons for disputes over play space on the playground or lunchroom, analyzing the situation from the perspectives of the key stakeholders. • Identify local land use issues in which there are disagreements and analyze the perspectives of the key stakeholders (e.g., protection of environmentally sensitive areas, land use for commercial purposes, locating waste disposal sites). • Describe the means by which communities resolve disputes over land use issues (e.g., decisions by planning commissions, by elected officials, by judges, by community voting).
B. Construct maps and graphs to display geospatial data, as exemplified by being able to: • Construct a map that displays geospatial data using symbols explained in a key (e.g., a classroom map showing different types of tables, desks, and chairs). • Describe the results of a survey of classmates about a geographic question concerning their school (e.g., where to add another swing set, where to place more drinking fountains) using graphs and maps. • Construct a map of the United States using symbols to show quan-tities by state (e.g., population, professional sports teams, mountain peaks over a certain elevation).	B. Explain why people move from one place to another, as exemplified by being able to: • Explain the reasons why people might be willing to move to a new location (e.g., for more or better jobs, for better living conditions). • Explain reasons why people may feel forced to leave their current homes to go to a new location. • Explain how groups of people may be forced to move against their wills (e.g., African slave trade, Cherokee Trail of Tears, Japanese in-ternment camps in the Second World War).	

The standards can be viewed in their entirety at the National Council for Geographic Education website.

Let's consider the implications of the standards presented. Standard 1 is fairly easy to implement in Social Studies lessons and represents typical concepts, skills, and activities already in use. Students need this foundational knowledge and the skills in order to develop spatial awareness, to understand how spatial patterns are represented, and the value of these representations. Maps are important tools to help students make visual connections to history, such as mapping where the colonists settled at Jamestown and how the location was relative to geographic and social features in the area. However, if we stop at standard 1 and the associated activities, students might never be prompted to ask the questions representative of an EcoJustice perspective, such as what happened to the ecology of the area where the colonists settled?

Standard 9 calls for knowledge and skills that offer many opportunities to expand students' awareness of EcoJustice concepts. The content and activities addressed under *Spatial Distribution of Population—People live in many different places on Earth*, are helpful to once again build foundational knowledge about population movement and are easily addressed in stand-alone geography lessons or infused into Social Studies lessons. For example, the bullet point, *Explain why people sometimes settle in inhospitable environments (e.g., availability of valuable resources, economic opportunities, diminishing availability of more desirable locations)* can and should be part of a study of Jamestown and settlement in many parts of the United States. An opportunity to bring EcoJustice perspectives comes with subtopic B. *Explain why people move from one place to another*, as students can be prompted to think deeply about how people respond to geographic features in making decisions and how these decisions can alter relationships among people and with the Earth. However, it would be up to the individual teacher to help facilitate these connections. Similarly, the bullet point, *Explain how groups of people may be forced to move against their wills* (e.g., African slave trade, Cherokee Trail of Tears) does not explicitly require that teachers focus on the underlying economic, resource, and land issues that led to the displacement of these people.

Standard 13 addresses the important reality that competition over resources leads to conflicts among people, which is in alignment with EcoJustice Education. The bullet point, *Analyze activities in the local community to describe ways in which people solve problems by cooperating (e.g., working in groups to pick up trash along a road, participating in community house-building projects)* hints at the idea that human behavior can negatively impact the environment, as in the case of trash, and that humans can work together to ameliorate problems. Subtopic 3, *Conflicts arise when there is disagreement over the division, control, and management of Earth's surface,* directly addresses that management of the Earth's surface leads to conflict, although issues of power imbalances in decision-making are still left up to the teacher to elucidate. In general, the standards presented offer starting points for teachers to extend geography lessons or to integrate geography into teaching US History in ways that can bring the goals of EcoJustice to light. However, this requires awareness of the issues and commitment by the teacher to do so. Hopefully, as you continue to read this chapter, you will build confidence in your ability to do so, as well as the desire to.

Teaching US History and Developing Conceptions of Land Use

In the last section we illustrated that standards exist to guide the teaching of geography and that these standards can be used to build on and implement EcoJustice Education. However, similar to the issue with economics, geography does not get much attention, beyond basic map reading and making skills and the study of landforms in elementary education. It is primarily through learning the "American" story in history that we are socialized into views of how land should be used and by whom. Therefore, we will now explore how commonly taught topics contribute to this socialization process.

Beginning with Columbus

For much of the twentieth and into the twenty-first century, American school children learned that in 1492 Christopher Columbus discovered America. Although it is now taught that his role was more to make European powers aware of the existence of North America, which then spurred on exploration and settlement of North America and the Columbian Exchange. However, the typical narrative usually overlooks that this was also the beginning of widespread European exploitation of the land and people there.

According to The Capitulations of Santa Fe, the agreement signed between Columbus and the Spanish Monarchy in 1492, Columbus received many incentives to explore and claim lands for Spain. Among these, he was granted the title of Governor of the lands he discovered and 10 percent of the riches and profits the new lands yielded, the remainder would go to the Spanish Crown. In a very real way, Columbus felt justified through this agreement to claim the lands inhabited by others for himself and Spain. During Columbus's very first journey, he captured native people and brought them back to Spain to show them at the Spanish Court. Thus, it was clear that Columbus believed his rights to the land extended to conquering the people who already lived there.

A simple Google search for materials and lessons to teach about Christopher Columbus revealed that there is a growing trend to question the celebration of Columbus and increasing interest to discuss Indigenous Peoples Day. However, many of the lessons found still present Columbus and the significance of his expeditions in a neutral manner. For example, one of the first sites to pop-up in a Google search listed these activities.

Columbus Day Art Activities

Ship Art

Have children create ships with construction paper or draw on paper. Then use blue fingerpaint to create the ocean around the ship.

Egg Carton Ships

Give children three individual egg holders from an egg carton. Let them decorate or paint their egg cartons. Stick a toothpick with paper flag taped or glued into each egg carton, so the children will have three ships.

Puffy Paint Boat

Using a black marker, have children draw a boat on water, or print out the boat template. Make puffy paint by having the children mix together equal amounts of shaving cream and glue, along food coloring to the mixture. Using the Puffy Paint mixture, have the children paint the boat and water.

Boat in a Jar

Give each child a walnut shell half, a small piece of playdough, a toothpick and a small square of white paper for a sail. Let the kids decorate their sails. Take the lid of a baby food jar and squish blue playdough for water. Place the walnut boat into the playdough and screw on the baby food jar so that it stands lid-side down.

Integrating art into the curriculum has many wonderful benefits such as developing fine motor skills, spatial reasoning, visual literacy, and creativity; however, implementing tasks such as these as part of a Columbus Day lesson creates false notions about his role in the history of North America, the suffering experienced by millions of people, and the legacy still felt today.

Two other lessons easily found in my search represent what is often seen in elementary school classrooms. Each of the lessons is partially shared below. Review the goals and tasks of each lesson and consider:

1. What knowledge and skills can students develop through the lessons?
2. What is implied and what is left out?
3. How might these messages impact students' understanding of the significance of Columbus?

Lesson 1: Chart Columbus's Voyages[5]

Objectives

- Students will be able to map out Columbus's four voyages.
- Students will create a key for a map.

Procedures

1. Distribute the world maps and colored pencils to each student.
   - Have students plot each of Columbus's voyages in a different color.
   - Students can make a key to indicate the meaning of each color.

- For extra credit, ask students to calculate the distance (using the scale) that Columbus traveled on each voyage.

2. Distribute the Just Where Was Columbus? and Columbus's Voyages handouts, go over them with the students, and have a short class discussion using the following questions:
   - What were Columbus's *intended* destinations for each voyage?
   - *Why* was he trying to get to each destination?

Lesson 2: Who Writes History? Rethinking Columbus Day[6]

Objectives

- Students will explore why certain historical figures get credit for their accomplishments while others are forgotten.
- Students will think about historical accuracy.

Procedures

1. Begin a class discussion using the following questions. Write student comments on the chart paper during the discussion to facilitate drawing conclusions at the end.
   - If Columbus was not the first person to discover America, why do most people think he did?
   - Can you name several reasons why you might have thought Columbus discovered America before you learned about other explorers such as Leif Ericson?
   - How does history get remembered?
   - Who decides which historical figure gets credit for a discovery?
   - What does this tell you about the way history is written?
2. As a concluding activity, ask the following question, review the comments written down during the discussion, and ask students to use them to draw conclusions about the nature of history.
   - Is history a permanent, unchanging story of the past or is it something that changes over time? (Think about the story of Columbus)

When lessons such as those shared above are experienced by students year after year, as Columbus Day is a yearly event, it is easy to understand how European exploration and settlement seems to be a natural occurrence and without much baggage. Turning the narrative on its head by including perspectives of Indigenous people or questioning the rightness of taking or claiming land of others, would enable students to not only have a more truthful understanding of history but also learn what mistakes we might not want to repeat. Consider how upper elementary students' understanding of the Columbus expedition might change if they learned that, on May 4, 1493, Pope Alexander VI issued an edict establishing the Doctrine of Discovery, which declared that any lands not inhabited by Christians were available to be "discovered" and claimed by Christian rulers. What if they also learned that this doctrine stated that "the Catholic faith and the Christian religion be exalted and be everywhere increased and spread, that the health of souls be cared for and that barbarous nations be overthrown and brought to the faith itself,"[7] and that it was later used to justify the seizure of land, as well as the enslavement, torture, and killing of millions of Indigenous peoples by Europeans who followed Columbus? Perhaps an equally important question is: What happens to young people's understanding of history, power, and justice when they never learn this information at all?

Plymouth Settlement

After students learn about the Jamestown settlement, they soon learn about the plight of the Pilgrims who fled religious persecution and came to settle at Plymouth, Massachusetts. Students typically learn that the small group who sailed on the Mayflower made an agreement to abide by group decisions when they signed the Mayflower Compact, and this action helped establish a system of self-government in the new colony. Sometimes students create a class compact, modeled after the Mayflower Compact, which all students agree to follow. In this way, students are experiencing the spirit of self-governance.

What is rarely taught is how the Plymouth colonists viewed their role in settling on the land of several Indigenous nations. In the second line of the Compact it states, *Having undertaken for the Glory of God and advancement of the Christian Faith and Honor of our King and Country, a Voyage to plant the First Colony in the Northern Parts of Virginia* (Virginia was the original destination planned for the new settlement). If students analyzed this portion of the Compact, they might understand that the colonists at Plymouth felt justified in their actions since they were taken for the *Glory of God.* Perhaps to learn this point in isolation students would merely be reminded that the group came for religious purposes; however, if this was viewed in the context of the Doctrine of Discovery, a pattern begins to emerge concerning the belief among European settlers that taking the land of non-Christians was just.

The story of the Plymouth Colony is always tied to the story of the "first" Thanksgiving. Usually, students learn about a period of great suffering and hunger and how the colonists were aided by a friendly Indigenous man named Squanto. Students learn that Squanto taught the colonists farming methods that helped lead to an abundant crop the following fall. It is not mentioned, or simply brushed aside, that Squanto learned to speak English while held captive and taken to Europe as a slave in two separate instances. Another fact often not addressed is that large swaths of land had already been cleared by Indigenous Peoples who had previously farmed the land. A widespread epidemic in New England (1616–19) brought on by European diseases and resulted in the death of up to 90 percent of the population by most estimates,[8] left the land free to be taken and farmed by the colonists. This fact was not lost on the English and seen as a sign from God of the rightness of their mission. Even before the Mayflower sailed, King James of England gave thanks to "Almighty God in his great goodness and bounty towards us," for sending "this wonderful plague among the savages."[9] Death among the Indigenous people also meant that some of their food source was left for the Plymouth settlers to enjoy. One settler wrote in his journal during the early days at Plymouth,

> We marched to the place we called Cornhill, where we had found the corn before. At another place we had seen before, we dug and found some more corn, two or three baskets full, and a bag of beans.... In all we had about ten bushels, which will be enough for seed. It was with God's help that we found this corn.[10]

Students typically learn that through hard work and perseverance, the settlers reaped a large crop and therefore held a celebratory feast in 1621, which is known as the "First Thanksgiving" and that they invited individuals from the local Indigenous community to join them. This version forms the impression that it was the settlers' success that was being celebrated. How would students hear the settlement story of Plymouth if they learned that in a very real way, the Pilgrims survived not due to the help of one or a few English-speaking native men, but from the hard labor of likely 1000s who cleared land and prepared the fields for crops?

The Louisiana Purchase

In 1803 the United States doubled in size when the European ruler, Napoleon Bonaparte, sold the Louisiana Territory to the United States for $15 million. One online resource that provides educators with social studies lessons and materials described the sale as:

> The Louisiana Purchase was one of Thomas Jefferson's greatest contributions to the United States. Doubling the size of the United States without losing any American lives paved the way for purchasing other territory. As you will soon learn, the Louisiana Purchase also opened the way for Americans to travel West. It wouldn't take long for the United States to grow and become the most powerful nation in the world.[11]

The use of the term "Americans" is interesting to note. Who was included in this designation in 1803 and who wasn't? Both African Americans and Native Americans were not considered citizens at that time. African Americans would not be granted citizenship until the passage of the 14th Amendment in 1868, and Native Americans did not receive citizenship until 1924; therefore, neither group was considered in this statement. When the acquisition of the LA Territory is taught, students typically complete maps, identify the modern states that make up the territory, and make comparisons of the size of the country before and after the purchase. Older students might be called on to analyze how the geography of the territory, particularly the Mississippi River and Port of New Orleans, offered opportunities to the United States. The experience for Native Americans is usually distilled down to another figure, Sacagawea, the Indigenous woman who served as a guide for the Lewis and Clark expedition of the territory in 1804–6. Students typically learn that the team was charged by President Thomas Jefferson to map the territory and make records of all the plant and animal life encountered. They learn that Sacagawea was their guide and interpreter. The Monticello Organization provides a list of activities[12] that can be done with students when learning about the expedition. Some of the ideas are:

- Ask students the question: "If you had been chosen to join the Expedition, what would you have thought essential to pack?" Have students compare Lewis's list with their own. Refer to Capt. Lewis's packing list (available at the website).
- Have students research the importance of buffalo to Native American people and have students create masks of buffalo or other animals of the Great Plains.
- Lead a discussion with students about the challenges encountered by the members of the Expedition. Possible topics might be: physical and mental strain, long arduous journey, separation from family and friends, geographical challenges, extreme weather conditions, wild animals, prickly pear cactus underfoot, lots of mosquitoes.

Although the presence of Native peoples is recognized in one of the tasks, the focus is only on the importance of the buffalo to the people. It is also worth noting that Sacagawea is not mentioned in any of the activities. The expedition is packaged as an adventure with challenges that the explorers had to overcome. Nowhere is there a consideration of the meaning of the expedition for the future of the hundreds of thousands of Native people who already lived there. Once again, the narrative taught suggests that this was another step in the successful rise of the United States and its *citizens*, and the Native American story is largely missing.

Cherokee Removal

In the state where we live and teach, the two standards listed below are part of the grades 3–5 Social Studies Standards:

- Describe how the migration and settlement patterns of Native American groups impacted different regions of the Western Hemisphere.
- Compare and contrast the voluntary and involuntary migratory experiences of different groups of people and explain why their experiences differed.

Neither of these mention the battles, treaties, laws, and processes of Indian removal that occurred on the east coast of the United States from colonization to the 1830s. As already discussed, schoolchildren all over the country learn that Native People were present during colonial times and played a role in the Thanksgiving celebration at Plymouth. Living on the east coast, we do not see many Native Americans, yet we live with the presence of Native American history. We grew up next to cities and towns with names like Lake Hiawatha and Manhasset. We said these names easily, probably not associating them with the history that had come before us, or questioning where did these people go?

The complete lack of mention of Cherokee Removal and the Trail of Tears could be in part due to the time periods most typically covered in elementary school social studies classes. However, what impressions do we leave children with when we tell them on the one hand that Native People populated the land where we live, but we don't offer explanations for what happened to them? While this might seem particularly relevant to the east coast, most people in the United States today do not live among Native People, in part because they only represent 2–3 percent of the US population. Yet we all live with the stories of

Thanksgiving and the names of rivers, parks, towns, etc. Maybe we owe it to not only the Native People and their ancestors, but to all Americans to learn what happened to these people and their land?

An EcoJustice Perspective on Conventional Approaches

The examples above represent common themes in US History and how the topics are taught in elementary school. There are many other topics that include a study of land, such as the geography of an area, landforms that dominate different regions of the United States (think mesas and plateaus) or the agrarian nature of American culture pre-twentieth century or the rise of cities. Some of these topics offer opportunities to infuse the EcoJustice Education Pillars as well, such as, why were the poor so often forced to live in overcrowded tenement housing? The topics we presented above were selected primarily due to the fact that they tell a story of how land use and ownership have been viewed as the rightful purview of European Americans in this country.

This narrative begins in elementary school classrooms and continues through secondary schooling and most likely shapes views we hold as adults. We contend that the dominant narrative teaches us to accept private ownership and use of land for profit as "normal" and that some "deserve" land ownership and the most desirable land more than others. This in turn leads to acceptance of many actions and policies that disproportionately benefit some at the expense of many. For example, why do we see land ownership that led to generational wealth amassed on the backs of others as fair? Why do we accept gentrification in urban communities as a natural process when largely poor people and people of color are those displaced? Whole communities are torn apart by gentrification in the name of capitalism and progress, rather than pursuing economic policies that could help people remain in their communities and build sustainable economies. How is it that in the face of climate change we are preparing to cut down more forests in the United States when trees are vital to absorbing carbon dioxide and producing oxygen? Under a 2025 Executive Order, *Immediate Expansion of American Timber Production*, the Trump Administration has opened the door to increases in timber production, deviating from the policy of forest conservation on public lands. What if we looked at land use differently when we teach American history? Could this help change some of these unjust and unsustainable practices?

Some ways to integrate EcoJustice Education into topics that are already taught were presented above. When we bring in different experiences, such as that of the Taino people Columbus first encountered, Squanto's prior enslavements, and the impact of westward expansion on the Plains Nations, children might better appreciate aspects of Pillar I, *An understanding and valuing of the interconnectedness of all living beings and systems*, particularly that *all actions have multiple consequences*. Ultimately, we want to nurture a habit of mind that *evaluates choices and decisions at multiple levels through a systems lens*.

As children learn about the presence of Native People, they should also learn why and how they were displaced. Books such as *Only the Names Remain; the Cherokees and the Trail of Tears*, written for children ages eight to eleven can be used to help children critically examine what happened to Native People. As a passage in the book explains:

> Now, no man alive in Georgia remembers the Cherokee Nation. . . . All that is left are the names. Some towns and rivers in North Georgia have names which sound like music and make one think of a time when the Cherokee ruled this land. There is a small town named Hiawassee and another named Ellijay. Such names sound like the wind whispering in the mountain pines. Other towns are called Rising Fawn and Talking Rock and Ball Ground.[13]

The book tells the story of Cherokee Removal in an accessible and truthful way for elementary school children. Although this history is hard to learn, what is the alternative? To leave blank spaces in our understanding or lack of American history? To be left with an awareness that these people were here, but no clear answers to what happened to them? Especially when we are looking at a history of land use and how the teaching of topics is part of how we form conceptions of land use, it seems negligent not to address Indian Removal.

In the early grades, children can reflect on decisions over land use close to home and with topics more accessible to them. They could learn to recognize how limited resources and competing wants can create conflicts. They could also apply the Triple Bottom Line approach in considering potential options. Many aspects of the EcoJustice Education Pillars can be addressed in learning experiences such as this, in particular, from *Pillar III: A commitment to investigating socio-environmental issues through the lens of power and justice: Critically reads the world—uncovering and questioning the social, political, and economic forces that shape our lives.* Science topics are also easily and naturally integrated into the study of local land use. For example, if children are studying competing proposals on how to use local land, for example, build a parking garage versus a park, they are addressing *K-ESS3-3: Communicate solutions that will reduce the impact of humans on the land, water, air, and/or other living things in the local environment.* Related topics might address the ways that humans have changed the landscape through various practices (i.e., development, agriculture) and investigate how this impacts the living and nonliving things. When interdisciplinary connections are made explicit, *Pillar IV: Transdisciplinary approaches that focus on cross-curricular knowledge and connections rather than siloed thinking that leads to incomplete understandings*, is brought to life and creates opportunities for all of the Pillar IV components to be incorporated: *Connect ideas across disciplinary boundaries; Apply content knowledge in real world, interconnected contexts; Understand the relevance and value of why they are learning what they are learning;* and *Draw on knowledge from multiple disciplines in order to form educated understandings and take informed actions.*

In the upper elementary grades, the same can be done with more complex issues. Children could also read the book *Only the Names Remain; the Cherokees and the Trail of Tears* and be guided to consider competing views on the Cherokee Removal. A problem-solving activity could engage students in cost-benefit analysis of the different wants and brainstorming alternative solutions. Students might then look at current land use issues as case studies (many topics are shared in the section on building your knowledge). This could be a jumping-off point for mini-research, problem-solving, or advocacy projects. Learning experiences such as this help to reach many of the goals of Pillar II *An orientation toward innovative, action-oriented, and collaborative problem-solving: Value diverse knowledge and honor that knowledge is constructed from many and sometimes unexpected sources; Imagine new ideas and ways of being that challenge our socialized norms;* and *Recognize the need and power of working in solidarity with others, across perceived difference, to achieve common goals.*

Integrating the Pillars into all of the topics listed above can be accomplished with simple modifications of existing lessons. When teaching about the Columbus voyages and exploration, a book that can be used with elementary school students is *Encounter* by Jane Yolen, which describes the arrival of European explorers through the eyes of a Tiano[14] child who fears the strangers' presence. Understanding the reality that people were already in the "New World" and they might not have viewed the arrival of Columbus as positive connects to the goals of *Pillar I: An understanding and valuing of the interconnectedness of all living beings and systems*, and the components: *Understand that all actions have multiple consequences* and *Evaluate choices and decisions at multiple levels through a systems lens.* Similar connections can be achieved when students consider the series of occurrences which led to survival at Plymouth. As they understand that natural disasters like the plague that devastated the local people, the labor of the people who had already cleared the land and grew crops, and the belief among many settlers that they were divinely just in settling the land, all played a part in the formation and continuance of the Plymouth Colony, students can begin to understand how interconnected we are with others and nature, which are aspects of Pillar I.

When the Louisiana Purchase is only taught as a benefit to the United States, so many opportunities are lost. If students were asked to consider what they think will happen beyond the Lewis and Clark expedition, they can engage in critical thinking that can foster systems thinking, understandings of interdependence and the consequences of actions—all embedded in Pillar I. They can also extend this to a review of population distribution in the region today, including exploring maps of Native American reservations. This can lead to integrating Pillar III: *A commitment to investigating socio-environmental issues through the lens of power and justice.*

We hope it is clear how integrating EcoJustice education can be done within existing curricula, and that we have made a case for the benefits of this approach. We also believe that stand-alone lessons that build understandings of land use issues historically and today are important. However, we know that many teachers will still have concerns about their own gaps in knowledge about land use, so in the next sections we will attempt to alleviate some of these apprehensions. First, we will provide information to expand one's own knowledge and then we will share some examples of instructional materials that can be used.

Expanding Teacher Content Knowledge

We begin this section on expanding teacher knowledge regarding land by broadly contrasting Indigenous and colonizer views of public and private land. Included is a discussion of 40 acres and a mule and the legacy of *redlining*, a means of controlling and dispossessing Black and brown communities from access to homeownership. A discussion of the ecological impacts of settler colonialism illuminates the scale of habitat and biodiversity loss, erosion and degradation of soil, and contamination and alterations of watersheds. We then use case studies to highlight some land use issues communities have faced historically and today. In discussion of each case, we include the impact these decisions have on local communities and ecosystems. Cases presented cover the increasing number of warehouses being built across the United States, the concentration and impacts of excessive levels of pollutants in Cancer Alley in Louisiana, the expansion of the interstate highways system and the impact on Black communities, and the creation and work of a community land trust in Puerto Rico organized to resist the impacts of gentrification. We highlight some environmental and social impacts of land use decisions and end this section with an opportunity for you to hone your critical lens by connecting the dots across topics introduced.

Before we begin however, we wanted to take a moment to unpack the term *settler colonialism* and explain how and why we are choosing to use this term. Wolfe states, "Settler colonialism destroys to replace."[15] This simple statement captures the systemic oppression of settler colonialism in that the purpose was to subjugate and oppress, with the outcome of cultural eradication and elimination of a pre-existing population, often Indigenous or native to an area, in order to replace it with the colonizing and settler-like ways of being. The use in this section of settler colonialism is meant to capture the breadth and depth of ways that settlers attempted to subjugate the Native American populations not just in body (through killing) but also through mind and cultural assimilation, via the American Indian Boarding Schools, and through spirit, by destroying the sacred lands and waters, the plants and animals, and the ways of being that sustained Indigenous communities for centuries. It is for these reasons that we seek to emphasize the systematic ways that European settlers attempted to oppress, exploit, and destroy Native American culture in order to gain access to the land, knowledge, and resources that were present on the continent, often with violent outcomes. We contend that this ideology still exists today in the actions of how land is used, how marginalized populations are disproportionately harmed by practices and even displaced.

Historical and Political Traditions of Land Ownership

In order to understand the complicated relationships we have with land today, we must first start by exploring how land became real estate, a form of privately held property, in this country. Ownership of land is directly tied to colonization, as the concept of land ownership did not exist for Indigenous communities. Europeans, upon their arrival, brought with them the idea of private land. They saw land as a commodity, something to be bought, owned, and sold, and with this came the erasure of Indigenous notions of land stewardship and collective/communal/shared ownership. This shift signified a transition to private ownership of land, the creation of a real estate market, and investment in and profiting from land for agriculture, housing, and development. This shift toward private land ownership was legitimized by laws, policy decisions, and treaties that justified Indigenous land grabs leading to the removal of Native Americans from newly privatized land. The era marked by colonial expansion led to the creation of systems of wealth accumulation through land ownership, the legacy of which is still felt today in wealth injustice and inequitable land access.

A historic land redistribution effort followed the Civil War in 1865 known as the "40 acres and a mule" policy which stated, "The islands from Charleston. South Carolina, the abandoned rice fields along the rivers for thirty miles back from the sea, and the country bordering the St. Johns River, Florida, are reserved and set apart for the settlement of the Negroes [*sic*] now made freely the acts of war and the proclamation of the President of the United States."[16] This promise, made to enslaved people, was a result of a discussion between twenty Black community leaders and Union General William T. Sherman. The community leaders sought reparations by asking that each family receive 40 acres of tillable land and that the lands would be governed by Black people themselves. With this order 400,000 acres would be redistributed to newly freed slaves and Sherman added that the army could lend their mules to new landowners.[17] By summer of 1865, however, after the assassination of President Lincoln, his successor, Andrew Johnson, quickly reversed this decision and returned the land to the original owners. The NAACP, to this day, is still calling for reparations in the form of land redistribution.[18]

The power that comes with land access and ownership has shaped every aspect of how we live on the land today. While land grabs reshaped much of the access Native Americans had to their ancestral lands, redlining and housing and lending policies historically shaped land access for Black and immigrant communities in the United States. Beginning in the 1930s, *redlining*, a discriminatory housing practice used by government agencies and banks in which maps were used to identify areas with high Black and immigrant populations, outlined in red (hence the name), was used as a tool to uphold and reinforce segregation in most urban communities. People who lived in areas within the red lines were not approved for mortgages and other loans to secure housing. Even if financially qualified, Black families were systematically denied access to loans and movement to newly expanding suburbs, and as a result, today we still see the legacy of these policies in the concentrated poverty in Black and brown communities, segregated predominantly white suburban communities, and wealth accumulation of white families through homeownership.

The Fair Housing Act of 1968 made redlining illegal; however, the implications of racially motivated housing and lending policies are evident in the disparities in homeownership rates, wealth accumulation, educational opportunities, and access to community resources. New Jersey State Senator Cory Booker's story is an example of the continued discrimination that permeated the housing lending sector even after redlining policies were revoked. In 1970, his family worked with the Fair Housing Council to help them acquire a home in Harrington Park, NJ. The Booker family was told the home was sold, but a white couple, sent by the Fair Housing Council, was told it was not and began contract negotiations for the home purchase. The day of the closing, the Booker family showed up and informed the real estate agent he was in violation of NJ state laws on fair housing and would be reported unless he went through with the sale to the Bookers.[19] This example showcases how historic policies continued to impact land access and the associated wealth that comes with land and homeownership.

Today in the United States, most land, approximately 60 percent, is privately owned by individuals, corporations, or other organizations with restricted access. Public land constitutes about 28 percent of land in the United States and is "owned" by federal, state, and local governments. The federal government manages this public land through the National Park Service, the Bureau of Land Management, and the Fish and Wildlife Service. While this land is considered public land, access is sometimes restricted and most national parks have an entrance fee of $30 per vehicle. Finally, Tribal Land constitutes a little over 2 percent of land in the United States and is held in trust by the federal government with access limited to tribal members. It is important to reflect on the ways history and policies have shaped the outcomes of land distribution. Today, the top twenty largest landowners in the United States own over 21 million acres of land.[20]

Ecological Impacts of Settler Colonialism

We often focus on the social impacts of settler colonialism; however, it is just as impactful to understand the ecological impacts during the time of European colonization in the United States. The ecological impacts are typically associated with natural resource extraction and exploitation, disruption and destruction of habitats, and introduction of invasive species. All of these impacts led to changes in and stability of ecosystems, leading to loss of biodiversity, erosion and degradation of soil, and loss of ecological resilience. In their book, *Endangered Ecosystems: A Status Report on America's Vanishing Habitat and Wildlife*, Noss and Peters open by stating,

> Since the time of European colonization, millions of acres of North America's natural ecosystems have been destroyed, degraded and replaced by agriculture and concrete. Iowa's tallgrass prairies, once habitat for wolves and buffalo, are now fields of corn. California's golden bear, a subspecies of grizzly, can now be found only on the state flag. The native wildflowers and bunchgrasses of California have dwindled and the hills are now covered with wild wheat, thistles and mustard from Europe and Asia. The entire south Florida landscape, including the Everglades and pine rockland habitat for endangered Key deer, is so seriously degraded that we have identified this entire area as the most endangered ecosystem in the nation.[21]

They continue by sharing that the nation has lost 117 million acres of wetlands—more than 50 percent of what was here when Europeans arrived; the Northwest has lost 25 million acres—90 percent—of its ancient forest, and forests in the Northeast were reduced to less than 10 percent of their original extent by the end of the nineteenth century.[22] The forests of the Northeast used to be thick with organic material multiple feet deep. The health of the forest and soil integrity was stewarded by Indigenous Traditional Ecological Knowledge; however, colonizer practices of deforestation, tilling land for crops, grazing animals, and reducing the use of fire to manage land led to degradation in the soil quality and soil health.[23] Today, due to the cutting down of the majority of old growth forests for timber and agriculture, the organic layer in many Northeast forests is only a few inches deep.

The extinction of species is also intertwined with settler colonialism. Since the arrival of European settlers, extinction and threats to species of animals and plants have increased. The Passenger pigeon has gone extinct and bison, a species that was significant to many Native American Tribes including the Lakota, Sioux, Blackfeet, and other Tribes of the Great Plains, were nearly wiped out due to hunting and intentional killing by settlers.[24] Prairie grasses and the species of insects and birds dependent upon them for nesting and food sources have also been severely degraded, replaced by monocultures of soy and corn. According to Samson and Knopf, more than 97 percent of US tallgrass prairie has been converted to monoculture.[25] This legacy of ecological destruction that our nation is founded upon continues to mediate the land use decisions we make today. In the next section, we highlight a few case studies that showcase the social and ecological tensions of land use decisions.

Land Use Case Studies Today: A Settler-Colonizing Legacy

Today, land use decisions are tied to local zoning laws and city and town planning boards. These local policies shape who lives where and what land can be used for. Most land is used for residential housing, commercial and industrial uses, agriculture and food production, energy production, infrastructure, and conservation. Each of these land uses comes with multiple decisions that must be made, and it is important to consider who has the power to make decisions, how communities can participate in the decision-making process, and what the short- and long-term impacts of decisions are. Discussing all of the nuances of land use decision-making is beyond the scope of this chapter; however, we wanted to outline a few cases to help you think through the ways that decisions about land have impacted people and places. We encourage you to read these brief descriptions, learn more about each case using our website resources and your research skills, and imagine ways to adapt these cases for your elementary classroom. While presented as case studies in this chapter on land, these issues also intersect with water and food, topics that will be further explicated in Chapters 5 and 6.

Case Study 1: The Amazonification of New Jersey

As we read about in Chapter 3, distribution is a crucial part of the materials economy, and our increasing consumption habits require ever more space to store, sort, and distribute goods. In the Delaware River Watershed in New Jersey, there are almost 150 proposed, approved, or newly built warehouses totaling 88 million square feet of space.[26] Automation is driving the demand for new, larger, and higher-tech warehouses, and consumer demand for fast delivery is causing warehouses to be built in areas near population centers. New Jersey is ideal for warehouse development as it is located near major urban centers with interstate highway access via the New Jersey Turnpike. New York, Philadelphia, Washington D.C., Wilmington, and Baltimore are all on this route. Twelve percent of jobs in New Jersey are related to distribution (also known as logistics) and warehousing, and the addition of new warehouses is promising local economic and job growth. However, this kind of expansion comes with environmental impacts, and in some cases, decision-makers are not enforcing the ecological mitigation and remediation warehouse developers are required to complete.[27]

Regulations surrounding the development of warehouses attempt to account for increased light, water, and air pollution—all resulting from higher amounts of truck traffic, which itself adds more strain to local roads. Additionally, warehouses can be large and unsightly, which impacts community aesthetics. Often, warehouses are sited on undeveloped agricultural land that could be used for local food production. This increases impervious surfaces, which leads to increased water runoff and flooding. As rain falls on these asphalt surfaces, there is less water infiltration and recharge of underground aquifers. Surface water runs off quickly, picking up pollutants like oil and salts along the way, contaminating local tributaries and ultimately nearby rivers and lakes. Warehouses are not being built without a fight, and local communities are organizing to push back against the increase of warehouses. A local New Jersey group called Stop Warehouses And Trucks (SWAT) listed multiple impacts on their community for just one proposed warehouse.

> The building would be the size of nine football fields. Noise/air pollution will be 24/7 and trucks could be idling overnight. 80,000-pound tractor trailers will drive over the gas lines hundreds of times per day. Homestead Road is only two lanes with no shoulders. This is the main access road from the east side of town for the high school. You will have inexperienced drivers sharing the road with tractor trailer trucks; Tractor trailers will be driving on our residential roads. Hillsborough tax payers will be responsible for maintaining these roads. Tractor trailers will affect the traffic in Hillsborough, Manville, Montgomery, Princeton. Traffic will be increased throughout all the neighborhoods. Increased flooding danger.[28]

In New Jersey one in three residents lives within a half mile of a mega warehouse,[29] but New Jersey is not alone in experiencing this level of increased warehouse development. Since 2007, there has been a rise of warehouses from 14,600 to 22,000 across the country, with many states including neighboring Pennsylvania, Georgia, Texas, and Arizona all experiencing similar warehouse expansion to New Jersey.[30] The case of warehouse expansion in New Jersey and across the country is interesting as it crosses social class and communities. The next case illuminates the environmental injustice of land use decisions and the legacy of these decisions on low-income communities and communities of color.

Case Study 2: Cancer Alley: Sacrifice Zones and Low-Income Communities

An 85-mile stretch along the Mississippi River in Louisiana that connects Baton Rouge and New Orleans is known as "Cancer Alley." Nicknamed Cancer Alley in 1988, this area is home to over 200 fossil fuel and petrochemical refineries, a population of approximately 40,000 people, and folks with the highest cancer risk in the country. In the last 10 years, over 850 cases of cancer have been connected to exposure to toxic air pollution in the region.[31] Demographically, the area has a much higher proportion of Black residents and a lower average income than both Louisiana and the United States as a whole. A report released by the Tulane Environmental Law Center found a relationship between air pollution and neighborhood cancer rates. The study cited differences between poor and affluent communities, noting that Black and low-income neighborhoods are disproportionately located near petrochemical plants and therefore bear the brunt of environmental and health risks.[32]

The story of Cancer Alley is a familiar one where economic growth was prioritized over the health and well-being of the community. At the end of the Civil War, former plantations became defunct and were bought up by petrochemical giants like Standard Oil and Shell upon new oil discoveries in the area. Simultaneously, newly freed Blacks were establishing communities along the river, and the industry was welcomed by Black people seeking work in the region. Post-Second World War, the oil and gas boom became the driver of Louisiana's economic development, and global corporations bought more land along the Mississippi to expand refineries and petrochemical plants. Petrochemical plants take fossil fuel byproducts and convert them into ethylene, propylene, methanol, and other petrochemicals for use in the manufacture of products such as single-use plastics, rubber, synthetic fertilizers, and pesticides.[33] The abundance of these refineries for manufacturing is directly linked to discussions of the materials economy from Chapter 3.

The petrochemical industry made economic promises to the communities in the form of jobs, meant to justify the high health and environmental costs. However, most of the high-paying jobs went to white workers even in predominantly Black communities.[34] A Tulane study found "that between 2010 and 2022, the petroleum industry in St. John the Baptist Parish got $19 million in first-year tax credits but created no new direct jobs."[35] Despite almost one billion dollars in tax breaks and government incentives to attract petrochemical investments, there has been little to no oversight by state and local governments to ensure job access and community reinvestment.[36] Community activists are fighting against the expansion and construction of new petrochemical refineries through grassroots organizing and legal channels.[37] As of April 2025, the fifth US Circuit Court of Appeals upheld a lawsuit that is requiring a moratorium on new petrochemical construction in the region.[38]

The NGO Human Rights Watch has created a 135-page report outlining the social, ecological, and regulatory impacts of the petrochemical industry along Cancer Alley. This report uses the term *sacrifice zone* to describe an area that has been deeply damaged by environmental pollution and industry in the name of economic prosperity. The full document outlines so much more than we can discuss in this section; however, it is important to read the strength of the language in the opening summary:

> In 2022, the UN Special Rapporteur on Human Rights and the Environment identified Cancer Alley as one of several global "sacrifice zones," among the most polluted and hazardous places on Earth, illustrating egregious human rights violations. "The continued existence of sacrifice zones is a stain upon the collective conscience of humanity," the special rapporteur wrote, representing "the worst imaginable dereliction of a State's obligation to respect, protect and fulfill the right to a clean, healthy and sustainable environment."[39]

The report details the high rates of cancers, autoimmune diseases, reproductive harms, and respiratory illnesses that plague the residents of the multiple parishes in the region. Images throughout the report highlight resident experiences, generations of families with multiple cancer diagnoses within neighborhoods, schools, and playgrounds in close proximity to the petrochemical facilities, and communities suffering from poverty with limited means to move out of the area.

While the human health and community impacts are tragic, the ecological impacts are also staggering. Air pollution in the form of climate disruptive carbon dioxide emissions from petrochemical facilities, along with emissions of carcinogenic chemicals far exceeding EPA emission limits, pollutes the air local residents breathe. Chemical emissions include chloroprene, ethylene oxide, benzene, and vinyl chloride, all chemicals deemed hazardous air pollutants and regulated under the EPA.[40] Additionally, all of these refineries are regularly dumping water pollutants directly and indirectly into the Mississippi River, including hazardous chemicals like vinyl chloride, ammonia, nitrates, formaldehyde, and sulfuric acid.[41] All of the toxic chemicals being dumped into the Mississippi River flow downstream to the Gulf of Mexico, which contributes to the already existing dead zone at the river delta, where low-oxygen levels in the water make it difficult for life to survive. The wetland ecosystems along the banks of the river, abundant with biodiversity and offering protection from floods and storms, are also vulnerable, and much has been destroyed by the continued expansion of construction of buildings.[42]

Cancer Alley contains multiple ***superfund sites***, areas of excessive contamination by hazardous waste that require long-term remediation to be made habitable again. As is the case with this region of Louisiana, superfund sites are often located near low-income communities where nearly half of all people living within three miles of superfund sites are people of color.[43] While the history of Cancer Alley is complex, it reveals a stark reality: the very systems designed to protect people and regulate emissions are failing, with limited enforcement allowing clear violations of the Clean Air Act and Clean Water Act to persist. Cancer Alley represents one of the most public and researched environmental justice issues in the country; however, these kinds of socio-environmental injustices are happening across many other low-income communities of color. The next case, exploring the expansion of the interstate highway network, continues to explore this theme.

Case Study 3: Expansion of Interstate Highways Through Black Communities

Many people don't know the history of the expansion of the interstate highway system in the United States, the impact it had on Black communities, and the health and environmental impacts of its construction. The National Interstate and Defense Highway Act signed by President Dwight D. Eisenhower in 1956 paved the way for the expansion of the interstate highway system and was designed to improve access to transportation routes across the country. From 1958 to 1966 the expansion of the interstate highway system was the largest source of federal funding to the states and displaced upward of one million people. *The Washington Post* article, *We mythologize highways, but they've damaged communities of color*, reveals that planners knew about the threats to communities of color but proceeded anyway. Citing the Sagamore Conference in 1958, where the Highway Research Board and top federal, state, and municipal officials, academics, and civic leaders issued a report that clearly noted the perils of highway construction warning "widespread displacement, with low-income, non-White and elderly residents facing the greatest potential injury."[44]

During the 1960s into the 1970s, more than 40,000 miles of highway were planned and built. An ACLU report, *Racism by Design: The Building of Interstate 81*, notes the relationship between the highway expansion and the civil rights movement, writing:

> As the civil rights movement was gaining momentum, the highway system became a way to enforce segregation through other, quite literal, means. So-called slum clearance destroyed under-resourced but thriving working-class Black neighborhoods while enhancing the flow of white commutes and tax dollars to the suburbs. Communities of color were cut off from developing downtown centers, and not just freeways but also refineries, landfills, and power plants were dumped in non-white areas labeled "sacrifice communities."[45]

The construction of highways like I-81 explicitly targeted Black neighborhoods, perpetuating patterns of displacement, segregation, and economic marginalization that persist today. Demolition of communities and the resulting isolation of communities from major urban centers with no access to transportation were forms of both de facto (in practice) and de jure (by law) segregation.

One example is Overtown, Miami. Overtown was a vibrant Black community with 40,000 residents, Black-owned businesses, Black homeownership, and a thriving cultural and entertainment scene which gave rise to its nickname, The Harlem of the South. The article, *Rethinking Highway Construction as De Jure Segregation: A Case Study for Equal Protection Lawsuits*, makes explicit the connection between housing policy and transportation policy, as well as the intentionality of using the 1956 Interstate Highway Act as a way to remove Black Overtown residents to a newly constructed, segregated, all-Black housing development five miles away from the city center. Under the guise of "slum-clearance" and "urban-renewal" local and state administrators decided to run I-95 right through Overtown, eliminating forty square blocks of the community and removing 10,000 homes from the neighborhood. The article states that "by 1968, only 8,000 of Overtown's 40,000 residents remained. Black homes, businesses, churches, and other institutions were condemned and replaced by parking lots, industrial and commercial spaces, performance venues directed at white suburbanites, and city, state, and federal office buildings."[46] All of this was done without one single public hearing with Overtown residents. This example highlights the ways that policies, like the Interstate Highway Act, while not explicitly designed to segregate communities, were used by many city and state officials to entrench existing segregation patterns and exacerbate racial injustice.

Across the country, countless Black communities had little to no opportunity to participate in decision-making or resist the outcome of discriminatory decisions. Washington D.C., New Orleans, San Francisco, and Greenwich Village in New York City offer only a few examples of where organizing efforts were successful in fighting a highway route. Success for these resistance efforts has been attributed to coalition building among stakeholders—interracial alliances of community members, environmentalists, historians—with aligned interests, working together to stop highway expansion efforts.[47] Some of the tactics that were most successful were attendance at public hearings, petitions, protests, media campaigns, and other forms of direct community actions.

Environmental and social impacts from the construction and expansion of the interstate highway system often intersected, leading to significant ecological damage to wildlife habitat and people. In addition to targeting Black neighborhoods, transportation projects were also built through wetlands and other wildlife habitat, leading to loss of biodiversity and the dissecting of habitat and wildlife migration corridors.[48] The construction process often involved clearing land, which led to soil erosion and pollution, affecting local ecosystems and water quality. The increased impervious surface as a result of the expansion of paved roads also created substantial water runoff, with pollutants like oils, metals, salts, and other chemicals being added into the water.[49]

Environmental Protection Agency air quality research shows that people living near highways and freeways are more likely to be exposed to air pollution, as well as noise and water pollution, all increasing the potential for illnesses like asthma and cardiovascular diseases from increased exposure to poor air quality. The EPA research specifically states that "people living in low socioeconomic communities are among those at higher risk for health impacts."[50] The human health impacts from the structural racism embedded in the interstate highway expansion can be seen most starkly when looking at the legacy of the Cross Bronx Expressway, which displaced upward of 60,000 people, the largest displacement of any infrastructure project in history. The highway project created an impenetrable barrier between the Bronx and the rest of Manhattan and has made the Bronx the county with some of the highest asthma rates in the country. The op-ed: *Let the Bronx Breathe—Address the Cross Bronx Expressway's Impact on Asthma*, written by two medical residents in the Bronx, states, "Research has shown that growing up near highways like the Cross Bronx Expressway is linked to poor lung development, increased asthma incidence, and more frequent asthma attacks. Amongst the pediatric population in the Bronx, asthma rates have been found to be as high as 17 percent, almost three times higher than rates nationally"[51] with African American and Latino patients accounting for more than 80 percent of the cases.[52]

The systemic racial injustices embedded in highway planning are not a thing of the past. The ACLU report highlights the legacy of the Interstate Highway Act of 1956 noting, "the I-81 project was completed in 1968—and Syracuse remains one of the most segregated cities in the country, with the highest concentration of poverty among communities of color and one of the highest rates of lead poisoning in children. The viaduct still physically separates the poorest and wealthiest communities, and the city's Black population has been harmed for generations."[53] Recent projects, such as the proposed widening of highways in Chicago,[54] California,[55] and Houston[56] threaten to demolish or displace Black and Latino neighborhoods, perpetuating a cycle of environmental and social injustice. These expansions often prioritize commutability over community well-being, leading to increased air pollution, noise, and further land loss in vulnerable areas. The legacy of the interstate system reveals a pattern of racial bias, where infrastructure development was used as a tool to displace Black communities, reinforce segregation, and prioritize suburban white mobility—an impact that continues to shape urban landscapes and environmental and community health today.

While there is a lot to digest in the above overview and cases on land, we know this is not the entire story. Communities have come together and continue to work in solidarity to push back on notions of private, individual, and unsustainable land use and reclaim and protect sacred and ecologically significant and vulnerable land. Movements like *land back*, where land is being returned to First Nations people, *land cooperatives*, where land is collectively owned and shared, and *rewilding efforts*, where land is brought back to an uncultivated form in the hopes of restoring ecology and biodiversity, are all examples of ways that humans are attempting to repair and restore relationships with the land. We present one final case that looks at the way a community in Puerto Rico resisted gentrification efforts and took control of community decision-making through participatory and democratic efforts.

Case Study 4: Community Land Trusts and the Fideicomiso de la Tierra Caño Martín Peña

It is not common that the residents of an area that has been slated for "revitalization," "renaissance," or "urban renewal," all coded language for gentrification, are able to stay and participate in revitalization efforts. More often than not, residents are removed, relocated, and priced out of their neighborhoods. However, residents of the Caño Martín Peña community, a neighborhood in San Juan, Puerto Rico, were able to do just that by creating a land trust where 2,000 families collectively own 200 acres of land that cannot be sold off for development.

The canal neighborhood of Caño Martín Peña had been established informally over many generations and was home to businesses, schools, churches, and other community resources. The eight communities that live along both sides of this tidal canal experienced frequent flooding with water that was heavily polluted from sewage overflow. Many residents did not have official land titles to land that had been in families for generations, making them vulnerable to removal. When the city announced plans to dredge the canal, current residents knew this was a sign of impending gentrification and increased cost of living in the area.

It took two decades of organizing residents, hundreds of meetings, and lobbying the Puerto Rican government, but finally a special act of the Puerto Rican legislature permitted the forming of a community land trust and a transfer of all 200 acres into the trust.[57] The current land trust structure is through three organizations: "The G-8, a grassroots organization that represents the Caño's eight communities; Fideicomiso de la Tierra, the organization that holds the land title and manages it on behalf of residents; and the ENLACE Project, a public company that carries out, plans, develops and coordinates the district's comprehensive development plan together with residents."[58] Today the 2,000 families who were without legal rights to the land now have legal access to their generational land, guaranteeing affordable and safe housing remains accessible.[59]

The Caño Martín Peña Community Land Trust collectively makes decisions that have had transformative social and environmental impacts. The trust has not only legalized the rights to land tenure, but it has been committed to the fair resettlement of families living in the most flood-prone areas where future dredging will occur.[60] Additionally, the trust has worked toward the remediation and dredging of the canal channel, the development of basic infrastructure that has reduced flooding and improved public health, and generated income via rental properties and the development of new projects. The Caño Martín Peña Community Land Trust serves as a model for alternative forms of land ownership that honor collectivity and community engagement and local control over decision-making—all powerful tools for sustainable development and community resilience.

Implications of Current Land Issues on Our Ecological and Social Systems

Enhancing your background knowledge can feel daunting, especially when it comes to issues of land use and land justice. There are so many avenues to explore that connect to EcoJustice issues but once again, most of these issues are often out of sight, out of mind. We don't often make the connections between highways and structural racism, and yet so many of our urban areas have been bisected by interstate highways that run directly through low-income communities of color. Take a look for yourself the next time you are driving through New York, Philadelphia, Boston, Syracuse, Chicago, Houston, Los Angeles, or Portland, Oregon. Even faster, conducting a quick Google search (search terms: City Name and Interstate Highway Act and Segregation) will most often reveal the name of a low-income community, probably a Black, Latinx, or other non-white neighborhood that was destroyed in the name of "progress." Below we add a few more statistics related to home and land ownership in the United States, as well as some statistics related to environmental justice and ecological degradation in the United States. Read these with a sense of curiosity and desire to understand better how our history and policies have shaped so many outcomes often rendered invisible.

- White (non-Hispanic) homeownership rate: 74.4 percent; Black homeownership rate: 44.1 percent.[61]
- Black Americans owned around 14 million acres of land by 1910, considered the peak of Black land ownership in the United States. But by 2022, that number had dropped to 1.1 million acres—a 90 percent decline, with a cumulative loss of about $326 billion in value.[62]
- Black household median wealth ($24,520) was about one-tenth the median wealth of households with a White householder ($250,400). [63]
- Zoning laws and land use policies have historically clustered polluting industries and hazardous land uses in low-income and minority communities, creating "sacrifice zones" and perpetuating health and quality-of-life disparities.[64]
- In the United States, people of color make up 42 percent of the total population but represent 52 percent of residents in counties with unhealthy air pollution and 63 percent in counties with the worst air quality, highlighting ongoing environmental inequities despite justice movements.[65]
- Across the United States, people of color are consistently exposed to higher levels of fine particulate matter (PM2.5) than white populations, regardless of income or region. This pollutant is linked to serious health issues, including asthma and heart disease.[66]
- Communities of color are more likely to live near hazardous waste facilities. For instance, 26 percent of Black Americans and 29 percent of Hispanics live within 3 miles of such sites, compared to 20 percent of the overall US population.[67]
- Since 1970, grassland bird populations in North America have declined by 43 percent, primarily due to habitat loss from agricultural expansion and urban development.[68]
- Land provides the principal basis for human livelihoods and well-being, including the supply of food, freshwater, and multiple other ecosystem services, including biodiversity. Human use directly affects more than 70 percent (likely 69–76 percent) of the global, ice-free land surface (high confidence). Land also plays an important role in the climate system.[69]
- Loss of 221,000 acres of wetlands, primarily to uplands, between 2009 and 2019. These losses disproportionately affected vegetated wetlands (forested, scrub-shrub, and/or emergent), resulting in a net loss of 670,000 acres of these wetlands, more than the land area of Rhode Island.[70]
- In upstate New York, the Onondaga Nation recovered 1,000 acres of ancestral land, including the headwaters of Onondaga Creek, as part of a federal Superfund settlement.[71]
- Between 2021 and 2023, over 3,000 volunteers dedicated more than 7,000 hours to plant 100,000 native trees, shrubs, and grasses across 5 key sites, including Rancho Sierra Vista and Paramount Ranch. This effort was part of a collaborative project led by the National Park Service, Re:wild, Snap Inc., and the Santa Monica Mountains Fund.[72]

Honing Your Critical Lens

Land issues are complex, localized, and have far-reaching environmental and social impacts. They bring communities together, but they also can divide them. It is the local land use decisions that allow us to exercise our power, as individual citizens and as collective members of our communities. The issues are vast and encompass so much: the relationship between homeownership and wealth injustice, decision-making power about where warehouses, petrochemical plants, and highways will be sited and who is most disposable, replaceable, and vulnerable to the social and environmental outcomes. But there are also land justice projects across the United States and beyond that are rooted in solidarity, reparations, and healing the people and the land. By expanding your understanding of the history of land ownership in this country and exploring the diversity of cases presented above, we hope you feel empowered to engage your students in critical discussions about land use and environmental justice issues facing your community.

This section serves as merely an introduction to the history and policy that have shaped land issues and the associated social and environmental impacts of the few specific cases presented in this section. Remember to use the website resources for references to expand your own understanding of topics presented here, specifically the Chapter 4 website resource includes articles and additional information for each case study. We end this section with several questions that offer opportunities for critical reflection and dialogue. If after reading these opening sections you feel overwhelmed, a little frustrated, angry, and sad, you are not alone—writing this section brought up a lot of feelings and important conversations for us. So much of the way we teach topics in our schools obscures the connections of history and science to the lives of real people experiencing tangible outcomes from land use decisions. It continues to be our hope that this book offers a space for personal growth as well as support and guidance in how you can expand your own awareness on topics presented and, in turn, engage your students in similar learning opportunities.

Free Write and Research Activity: Think back to when you were in school and learned about the Indigenous communities that were the original caretakers and spiritual keepers of the land where your school is located. Reflect on what you were taught about and do a free write using the following questions as possible prompts. If you don't know the answers to some of these questions, use them as jumping-off points to educate yourself more deeply about the Indigenous communities in your region.

- Whose traditional land am I living/teaching on?
- What do I know about the original Indigenous communities in my region?
- What do I know about the ecosystem, ecological diversity, and traditional ecological knowledge in my region prior to colonization?
- What do I know about the cultural traditions of the Indigenous communities in my region?
- What do I know about the treaties, agreements, or acts of dispossession that shaped my region?
- What are the grand narratives that I remember being taught about Indigenous peoples and communities? Whose voices were centered?

- What has been the fate of the native Indigenous peoples that were in my region? How do I still see impacts from settler colonialism today?
- Have any reparations, new treaties, or other agreements been made with my local/regional Indigenous communities to make amends for the impacts of settler colonialism?
- Do I have relationships with Indigenous people and communities today?
- What responsibility do I have to educate children and youth about the historical and current impacts of settler colonialism on Indigenous communities and the original ecosystems that were here?

Standards and Goals for Teaching and Learning

With new knowledge about the historical impact settler colonialism had on Indigenous communities, the ecological diversity of the United States and an understanding of some of the social and environmental impacts of current land use decisions, we hope you are making connections to what you can teach in your elementary classrooms. This section broadly outlines the standards for social studies and science teaching at the elementary level that relate to these topics of study, as well as how the Cloud Institute's Education for Sustainability Content Standards and the UN Sustainable Development Goals can also be addressed and provide guidance to teachers.

Social Studies Standards from NCSS

Issues of land are relevant for several of the NCSS National Standards for Social Studies; however, the two that are most closely related are *Theme 2 Time Continuity and Change* and *Theme 3 People, Places and Environments.*

Under Theme 2, students are directed to study past events to understand the context in which events took place and make connections to life today. The importance of this theme is explained as, "Historical analysis enables us to identify continuities over time in core institutions, values, ideals, and traditions, as well as processes that lead to change within societies and institutions, and that result in innovation and the development of new ideas, values, and ways of life."[73] To fully understand the nature and implications of land use in the United States today, we look to the past to see how we got here. The study of colonization and European settlement should be pivotal in learning how European values and desires influenced actions and conflicts with the Indigenous People. One of the goals for elementary education under this Theme is to use stories of the past to "help children develop their understanding of ethical and moral issues as they learn about important events and developments. . . . They begin to understand the linkages between human decisions and consequences."[74]

The second NCSS theme that is most relevant is *Theme 3 People, Places and Environments.* Although this includes learning about the physical environment and the location and nature of geographic features, studies related to this theme extend to understanding human interactions with the environment and the implications. The need for this type of learning is explained as, "Today's social, cultural, economic and civic issues demand that students apply knowledge, skills, and understandings as they address questions such as: Why do people decide to live where they do or move to other places? Why is location important? How do people interact with the environment and what are some of the consequences of those interactions?"[75]

Relevant Indicators for Student Learning from the NCSS C3 Inquiry are presented below. Beyond Themes 2 and 3, concepts from economics and civics are also important to integrate into a study of land use and land justice. As you read over the list of indicators for student learning, consider the many ways these goals can be incorporated into learning experiences that reflect the goals and Pillars of EcoJustice Education.

Textbox 4.1. Relevant NCSS C3 Inquiry Framework Indicators for Grades K-2

D2.His.1.K-2. Create a chronological sequence of multiple events
D2.His.2.K-2. Compare life in the past to life today
D2.His.3.K-2. Generate questions about individuals and groups who have shaped a significant historical change
D2.His.4.K-2. Compare perspectives of people in the past to those of people in the present
D2.Geo.1.K-2. Construct maps, graphs, and other representations of familiar places.
D2.Geo.2.K-2. Use maps, graphs, photographs, and other representations to describe places and the relationships and interactions that shape them.
D2.Geo.3.K-2. Use maps, globes, and other simple geographic models to identify cultural and environmental characteristics of places.
D2.Geo.4.K-2. Explain how weather, climate, and other environmental characteristics affect people's lives in a place or region.
D2.Geo.5.K-2. Describe how human activities affect the cultural and environmental characteristics of places or regions.
D2.Geo.6.K-2. Identify some cultural and environmental characteristics or specific places.
D2.Geo.7.K-2. Explain why and how people, goods, and ideas move from place to place.
D2.Geo.8.K-2. Compare how people in different types of communities use local and distant environments to meet their daily needs.
D2.Geo.9.K-2. Describe the connections between the physical environment of a place and the economic activities found there.
D2.Eco.1.K-2. Explain how scarcity necessitates decision-making.
D2.Eco.2.K-2. Identify the benefits and costs of making various personal decisions.

D2.Eco.4.K-2. Describe the goods and services that people in the local community produce and those that are produced in other places.
D2.Civ.1.K-2. Describe roles and responsibilities of people in authority.
D2.Civ.2.K-2. Explain how all people, not just official leaders, play important roles in a community.
D2.Civ.5.K-2. Explain what governments are and some of their functions.
D2.Civ.6.K-2. Describe how communities work to accomplish common tasks, establish responsibilities, and fulfill roles of authority.
D2.Civ.8.K-2. Describe democratic principles such as equality, fairness, and respect for legitimate authority and rules.
D2.Civ.9.K-2. Follow agreed-upon rules for discussions while responding attentively to others when addressing ideas and making decisions as a group.

Textbox 4.2. Relevant NCSS C3 Inquiry Framework Indicators for Grades 3–5

D2.Civ.1.3-5. Distinguish the responsibilities and powers of government officials at various levels and branches of government and in different times and places.
D2.Civ.2.3-5. Explain how a democracy relies on people's responsible participation, and draw implications for how individuals should participate.
D2.Civ.6.3-5. Describe ways in which people benefit from and are challenged by working together, including through government, workplaces, voluntary organizations, and families.
D2.Civ.8.3-5. Identify core civic virtues and democratic principles that guide government, society, and communities.
D2.Civ.9.3-5. Use deliberative processes when making decisions or reaching judgments as a group.
D2.Civ.10.3-5. Identify the beliefs, experiences, perspectives, and values that underlie their own and others' points of view about civic issues.
D2.Civ.12.3-5. Explain how rules and laws change society and how people change rules and laws.
D2.Civ.13.3-5. Explain how policies are developed to address public problems.
D2.Civ.14.3-5. Illustrate historical and contemporary means of changing society.

Next-Generation Science Standards

Land primarily connects to NGSS disciplinary core ideas in Life Science and Earth Sciences. These standards address the needs of all living things for survival and that there is a direct relationship between where organisms (including humans) live and the resources provided by the land. These standards also honor that humans have had a differential impact on the land and that, once again, our choices can have consequences. Elementary students can also engage in engineering design challenges to design simple solutions to land use challenges (i.e., pollution, lack of access to green space, where to put a school garden) or, more broadly, sketch a land use design for a community where the diverse needs of all living things are balanced. Below is a textbox of K-2 and 3–5 NGSS standards modified for land use teaching.

Textbox 4.3. Next-Generation Science Standards for Grades K-2

By grade 2 students understand:[76]

- All living things, including humans, have survival needs (water, air, and resources from the land) and their needs are related to the places they live. (K-ESS3-1, K-LS1-1)
- As a result of the survival needs of humans, we have had an impact on the land, water, air, and other living systems in our local environments, and our choices can minimize/maximize that impact. (K-ESS3-3)
- Seasonal changes can affect decisions about how land is used. (1-ESS1-2)
- Human land use decisions and development have changed the shape of the land. Humans can design solutions to protect land. (2-ESS2-1)
- Over time, humans have changed their relationship with land, and not all humans have equal access to land. (2-ESS2-2)
- Different land use practices have different impacts on biodiversity. (2-LS4-1)

Textbox 4.4. Next-Generation Science Standards for Grades 3–5

By grade 5 students understand:[77]

- Land use decisions impact community resilience to natural disasters, and more often than not, marginalized communities are disproportionately impacted by land use decisions that harm the environment and people. (3-ESS3-1)
- Land use decisions have impacts that can be observed/measured on the stability of the land and biodiversity. (4-ESS2-1)
- Land is impacted by human energy and fuel needs, and our extraction practices and choices have environmental and social consequences. (4-ESS3-1)

- Diverse communities have managed land differently over time, and this has led to exploitation and protection of the Earth's resources and environment. (5-ESS3-1)
- Land use decisions have impacted the health of ecosystems, including the diversity of plants and animals and the movement of matter among organisms (nutrient cycling). (3-LS4-4, 5-LS2-1)

Cloud Institutes Education for Sustainability Content Standards

We look to the Cloud Institute's Education for a Sustainable Future Benchmarks and Standards to see beyond our content standards and draw upon the transdisciplinary frameworks they present. When we engage with topics and themes that relate to land use and land justice, we are drawing upon multiple benchmarks and standards. To begin, we draw upon the **Cultural Preservation and Transformation** standard that reads:

> The preservation of cultural histories, heritages and knowledge of place, and the evolution of cultural identities and practices that contribute to sustainable communities over time. Students will understand the inextricable link between the health of the biosphere and the health of the "ethnosphere", and with the help of the arts and social sciences, will develop the ability to continuously discern with others what to preserve and what to change in order for future generations of cultures and communities to thrive over time.[78]

This standard ties to the First Nations people, the cultural, historical, spiritual, and ecological knowledge they embodied and the ways that we seek to return to the forms of traditional ecological knowledge as a guide for how to navigate the present and future in sustainable ways. The Cultural Preservation and Transformation standard reminds us that there are many ways of knowing and that our modern and Western ways of knowing are but one way that can inform land use decisions as we co-create a more sustainable future.

A second core content standard developed by the Cloud Institute is **Responsible Local and Global Citizenship**. This standard is embedded in the civics education work associated with social studies; however, it is often underemphasized in the sciences. This standard reminds us that it is through diverse knowledge that we engage with through our learning of, with, and in the living world that we develop our sense of responsibility and are called to action. Our learning experiences should never be far from action, and this standard calls upon all of us as individuals and communities to participate in the shared creation of sustainable ways of being.

A third Cloud Institute standard that is particularly important across many of the chapters, but is illuminated in various ways throughout the land use and land justice chapter is the notion of a **Healthy Commons.** The standard for Healthy Commons reads:

> The necessary reconciliation of individual rights with collective responsibilities for the tenure and welfare of the Commons as society progresses towards sustainability. Students will be able to recognize and value the vital importance of the Commons in our lives and for

our future. They will understand and assume the rights, responsibilities and actions to care for the health of the Commons, and to hold them in trust for future generations.[79]

As you read this you may hear the similarity to our EcoJustice Pillars. The sense of collective responsibility to care for and protect the resources, visible and invisible, that are ours like air, democracy, trust, biodiversity, climate regulation, our collective future, water, libraries, public health, heritage sites, and so many more, is not the job of any one person alone and must be done through individual and collective action as well as legal and policy channels.

The final standard that informs land use and land justice topics is a **Strong Sense of Place**. While this standard is significant and relevant across all of the themes we present in this text, it feels particularly important for this topic as it asks us to reflect upon and more deeply recognize the relationship and connections we have with the places we live. This standard reminds us that we are both shaped by and shape place, that place is connected to "the social, economic, ecological, geological, and architectural history and current condition of the place"[80] and that we have a responsibility to the health and well-being of where we live.

United Nations Sustainable Development Goals

This chapter draws inspiration from two United Nations Sustainable Development Goals (SDG). The first is **Goal 11** which seeks to **make cities and human settlements inclusive, safe, resilient, and sustainable**. Goal 11 addresses many of the topics discussed in our case studies, including access to affordable housing (1.1 billion people live in urban slums[81]), access to sustainable and affordable transportation, a commitment to include communities in more participatory decision-making processes, and to increase access to open and public space. The second SDG that is relevant to land use and land justice is **Goal 15** which aims to **protect, restore and promote sustainable use of terrestrial ecosystems, sustainably manage forests, combat desertification, and halt and reverse land degradation and halt biodiversity loss.**[82] This goal seeks to challenge and reimagine the relationship between humans and nature, identifying loss of species, loss of forests, and land degradation as part of our shared responsibility. Targets for this goal include implementing sustainable forest management policies that reduce deforestation and protect species in order to reduce biodiversity loss by including ecosystem values in local planning efforts. Together, these SDGs speak to a range of issues that young people can become advocates for, especially as we engage them in EcoJustice issues as presented in the chapter.

Applying EcoJustice Pillars to Chapter Instructional Materials

The provided instructional materials are models of the type of elementary instruction that can help students understand land use and land justice issues. The instructional materials reflect our EcoJustice Education Pillars and are aligned to NCSS and Next-Generation Science Standards, as well as to Cloud Standards and the UN SDG goals. The flowchart below illustrates the knowledge, skills and attitudes that we hope for a student to have upon completion of elementary school and the goals for the K-2 and 3–5 grade bands in order to reach the end goal. The instructional materials we model are designed with these goals in mind and are offered as examples of how they can be addressed in elementary education.

The instructional materials we offer for this topic are focused on teaching students to reflect upon their relationship with land, the history of the land, and the complexity of land use decisions. However, the lessons also encourage students to acknowledge that no matter how complex these issues might seem, there are typically issues of power at play where either certain people or corporations seem to matter more than others. The lessons we share as models focus on teaching students to first learn about, honor, and develop respect for the Indigenous people who took care of the Earth before the arrival of Europeans. We then encourage students to wrestle with land use decisions using real and fictional examples and allow them to see how they can be part of actions that influence land use decisions. The goals of the lessons we offer for K-2 and 3–5 classrooms offer one place to start thinking about how we can more critically introduce EcoJustice land use issues to our students. Each lesson was designed to help reach the goals articulated in Figure 4.1 for each grade band. We offer these materials to be used as you see fit. You may use them as we have designed them, mix and match parts of lessons together to create your own lessons, or simply as inspiration to create your own lessons for your teaching context.

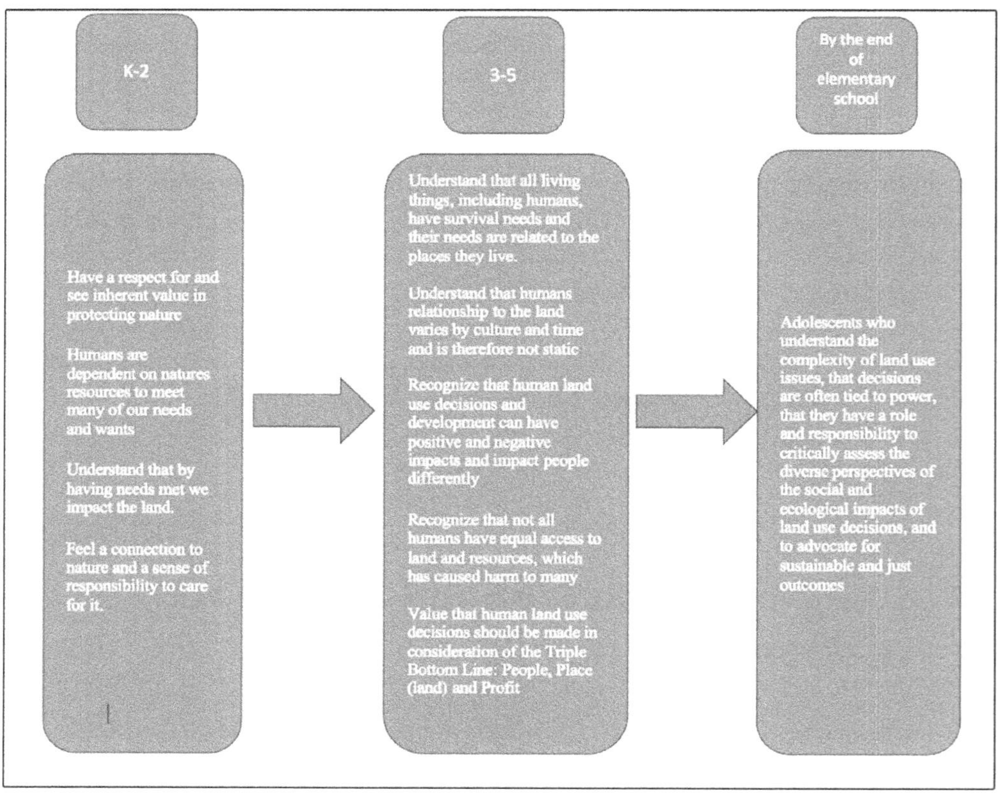

Figure 4.1. Flow chart K-5 to achieve an emerging EcoJustice consciousness related to land use. Author created.

We suggest that before you teach the concepts presented, refresh your own content knowledge by reviewing the historical topics in the **Introduction** and **Expanding Teacher Knowledge** sections and educate yourself more deeply about the Indigenous people who inhabit/ed your region (see the **Free Write and Research Activity** above for more guidance). This will prepare you to see the lessons through a more critical lens. Remember that exploring all of the topics we present through a critical lens will force you to question common-sense assumptions embedded in society today like home and land ownership, the legacy of segregation in urban areas as a result of redlining and the Interstate Highways Act, and why in so many parts of the country there is little tangible evidence of the original Native peoples beyond their names. We also hope it empowers you to seek alternatives to that which we take for granted as "normal" and see examples like community land trusts and other grassroots movements, rooted in justice and equity, as signs of hope and possibility.

Land Instructional Materials

I would use these lessons in my classroom. Students will explore diverse perspectives in a way that lets them think beyond themselves. How cool is it to research the land your house might live on to see "our home on native land"? Not only are they researching something very close to them, (their homes), they are then thinking about who lived there before them. This creates the space for them to build empathy and understand the complexity of land and justice. As an educator, this type of human-centered learning is deeply powerful, and oftentimes lacking in scripted curriculums.

—*Briana, Elementary Teacher*

Textbox 4.5. K-2 EcoJustice Instructional Materials Land

Essential Question(s):

- How do human choices, economic interests, and government actions shape our environment?
- What can we do to create positive change in our community and beyond?

Objectives:
At the conclusion of the lessons, students will be able to:

- **Describe** how climate impacts the local ecology and lives of people
- **Explain** economic incentives for altering the environment
- **Discuss** actions that humans can take to change the local environment
- **Discuss** the role that government can play in protecting the environment
- **Advocate** for a land use issue that they care about and brainstorm methods to make a positive change in their environment

Standards:
Social Studies

- **D2.Geo.4.K-2.** Explain how weather, climate, and other environmental characteristics affect people's lives in a place or region.

- **D2.Geo.5.K-2.** Describe how human activities affect the cultural and environmental characteristics of places or regions.
- **D2.Geo.7.K-2.** Explain why and how people, goods, and ideas move from place to place.
- **D2.Geo.8.K-2.** Compare how people in different types of communities use local and distant environments to meet their daily needs.
- **D2.Civ.2.K-2**. Explain how all people, not just official leaders, play important roles in a community.
- **D2.Civ.14.K-2**. Describe how people have tried to improve their communities over time.
- **D2.His.1.K-2.** Create a chronological sequence of multiple events.
- **D2.His.2.K-2.** Compare life in the past to life today.

Science

- **K-ESS3-1:** Use a model to represent the relationship between the needs of different plants or animals (including humans) and the places they live.
- **K-ESS3-3:** Communicate solutions that will reduce the impact of humans on the land, water, air, and/or other living things in the local environment.
- **2-ESS2-1:** Compare multiple solutions designed to slow or prevent wind or water from changing the shape of the land.
- **2-LS4-1:** Make observations of plants and animals to compare the diversity of life in different habitats.

Materials:
Lesson 1

- *The Tree Lady*
- Video of read aloud https://www.youtube.com/watch?v=xQM1Um0AME8
- Images of urban areas with and without greenspaces

Lesson 2

- *The Lorax*
- Video of read aloud https://www.youtube.com/watch?v=sJ0BvL5ELko
- Images of landscapes that have been cleared of trees

Lesson 3

- Images of people working together on a variety of community project
- Our School Community Project worksheet
- Images of before and after pictures of community projects

Important Vocabulary/Concepts:

- Desert
- Greenspace
- Deforestation
- Community Engagement

Instructional Materials Description and Overview:
In this series of lessons, students are introduced to ways that humans can impact the local ecology in positive and negative ways. They also explore the power that individuals can have on their own and working with others. Ultimately, the children are encouraged to think about their own environment and how they can improve it.

Lesson 1: *The Tree Lady*
ENGAGE: Lesson Introduction

- Show the children the picture of Kate lying among the trees on the cover of the book, *The Tree Lady* (the video link for the read aloud can be used to display the picture from the cover if you don't have access to the book) and ask the following questions:
  - What do you think is happening in this picture?
  - Is there something in nature that you enjoy doing?
  - How would you feel if you couldn't do that anymore?

EXPLORE: Read Aloud: *The Tree Lady*
At several points, it is recommended that the teacher pause the video or reading the book to ask the children questions. This can lead to a class discussion with a show of hands, or students can turn and talk to a buddy. Using a turn and talk increases opportunities to engage all students in the conversation!

- Tell the students they will now listen to a story about the girl in the picture. Explain that she lived more than 100 years ago in California.
- You can do a read aloud or use the video https://www.youtube.com/watch?v=xQM1Um0AME8
- Stop the video at 2:49 (the picture with Kate in the classroom and the window shows the bare landscape) ask the students:
- How do they think Kate feels? Be sure to ask them to share details from the story and the picture to explain their response.
- What would you do if you were Kate?
- Stop the video at 3:55 and ask the students what actions was Kate taking and why?
- Stop at 5:03 and ask the students how they think Kate can get thousands of more trees to plant in Balboa Park?

EXPLAIN: Reading Comprehension and Analysis

- When the book is finished, ask the students to list in sequence the actions Kate took to bring trees to San Diego. For younger children, the class can make a list of the actions she took together, and the teacher can list on a whiteboard. Then students can put them into sequence order, or you can give the students the five steps below. For younger children, the steps can be written out on strips of paper, and the children can put them in the correct order.

1. Kate left her job to become a gardener
2. Kate asked people from all over the world for seeds for trees that could grow in San Diego
3. Kate's trees were planted around streets, schools, parks, and homes in San Diego
4. Many people volunteered to plant trees in Balboa Park
5. Kate planted trees and gardened for the rest of her life

ELABORATE: Brainstorm

- Have students brainstorm a list of things they care about in their community or school the way that Kate cared about trees.
- Record their answers.

EXTEND: Photo Elicitation and Critical Dialogue

- Explain to the students that many cities have created green spaces where there are trees, grass, and plants, for people to enjoy.
- Show some images of city neighborhoods with green spaces and without.

Bdx, CC BY-SA 4.0 <https://creativecommons.org/licenses/by-sa/4.0>, via Wikimedia Commons

EXPLORE: Read Aloud: *The Lorax*

- Tell the students you are going to read the book, *The Lorax,* to find out what happened.
- The book is usually easily accessible, so it can be read aloud, or the video with a read aloud can be used https://www.youtube.com/watch?v=sJ0BvL5ELko

EXPLAIN: Reading Comprehension and Analysis

- Lead the children in a discussion about why they think the Once-ler wanted to make Thneeds
- Remind the children to think about wants versus needs
- Ask them if the Once-ler needed to make the Thneeds
- Ask the children what were the consequences of the Once-ler's actions, both positive and negative? (These points can be listed on a whiteboard)
- Explain that sometimes when people take from nature to make goods, there can be harm to nature

ELABORATE: Problem-Solving Activity

- Tell the children that they will now have an opportunity to brainstorm actions that the Once-ler and the Lorax could take to help restore the environment
- Let the children work in small groups to brainstorm ideas
- As a class, listen to the ideas and then let children choose the action that they think is best
- Each child can draw a picture of the action and write a statement about why they chose this action

EXTEND: Photo Elicitation and Critical Dialogue

- Explain to the students that while *The Lorax* is a fictional story, in real life trees are often cut down for many reasons. Share images similar to the ones here that highlight deforestation.

https://www.flickr.com/photos/76771610@N00/10094847976

https://www.flickr.com/photos/119707083@N02/14729321605

https://www.flickr.com/photos/72482589@N07/30626466567

- Engage students in a critical dialogue about deforestation on Earth:
  - What do you notice in these pictures?
  - Why do you think this situation exists?
  - Why is it important to have healthy forests?
  - What happens when we don't have access to healthy forests?
  - What can be done about this situation?

EVALUATE: **Wrap-Up Activity/Assessment**
- Read the students' statements from the Problem-Solving Activity to assess if they understand that actions by individuals can make a difference in caring for the environment.

Lesson 3: An Issue *You* care about
ENGAGE: Lesson Introduction
- Show children images that represent different forms of community engagement. Ask them to describe what they see. Try to find images that are local to your context and include children if possible.

EXPLORE: Photo Elicitation
- Ask the children why they think the people are doing what they are doing in the pictures. Allow them time to share their ideas with a partner and discuss as a class.

EXPLAIN: **Defining Terms**
- Ask the children if they know what is meant by *Community Engagement*
- Explain that this means working together with others to achieve a common goal in your community
- Explain that the children all belong to the school community and that means they all have a responsibility to care for the community to make it a positive space for everyone

ELABORATE: **Brainstorm**
- Ask the children to list one action they can take with others to help make their school community a positive place.
- List the ideas the children share on a whiteboard.
- After several ideas have been shared, ask the children which issue is most important to them and then group students with others who care about the same issue (if many students care about the same issue, they can be divided into smaller groups of 3–4 students).
- Explain to students that with their group mates, they will complete the Our School Community Project worksheet (before giving the students time to work, it could be useful to move to the Extend Activity so the children can view the before and after pictures). The worksheet can be found in the Appendix, or a version from the image below can be replicated for use.
- For younger students, the teacher can facilitate this task as a group and act as the scribe if needed.

Our School Community Project	
Something we want to change in our school community to make it a positive place for everyone is . . .	Our plan to work with others to make this change is . . .
Before Picture (how we see the problem now)	After Picture (what we would like to see change)

EXTEND: Photo Elicitation

Explain to the students that it takes a lot of effort and strong community relationships to complete a community project for the school. Show images of before and after pictures of some community projects.

- Engage students in a critical dialogue about community projects:
    - What do you notice in these pictures?
    - Why do you think these situations exist in the before pictures?
    - How do you think they came to be in the after pictures?
    - Why is it important to do community projects?

EVALUATE: **Wrap-Up Activity/Assessment** (this can take place at another time after the children have completed their worksheets)

- Students present their plans to the class

Textbox 4.7. 3–5 EcoJustice Instructional Materials Land

Essential Question(s):

- Is it important to respect those who have cared for the land in the past?
- How should we care for the land today?

Objectives

At the conclusion of the lessons, students will be able to:

- **Identify** the original Indigenous peoples of their local region and describe aspects of their relationship to the land.
- **Explain** the purpose of a land acknowledgment and why it matters today.
- **Describe** how government policies impact land use.
- **Understand** how current land use (e.g., development, agriculture, conservation) affects the environment and communities, including Indigenous communities.
- **Evaluate** land use decisions and actions to draw individual conclusions.

Standards:

Social Studies

- **D2.Eco.2.3-5.** Identify positive and negative incentives that influence the decisions people make.

- **D2.Eco.3.3-5.** Identify examples of the variety of resources (human capital, physical capital, and natural resources) that are used to produce goods and services.
- **D2.Eco.7.3-5.** Explain how profits influence sellers in markets.
- **D2.Eco.8.3-5.** Identify examples of external benefits and costs.
- **D2.Geo.12.3-5.** Explain how natural and human-made catastrophic events in one place affect people living in other places.
- **D2.Civ.1.3-5.** Distinguish the responsibilities and powers of government officials at various levels and branches of government and in different times and places.
- **D2.Civ.2.3-5.** Explain how a democracy relies on people's responsible participation, and draw implications for how individuals should participate.
- **D2.Civ.6.3-5.** Describe ways in which people benefit from and are challenged by working together, including through government, workplaces, voluntary organizations, and families.

Science

- **3-ESS3-1:** Make a claim about the merit of a design solution that reduces the impacts of a weather-related hazard.
- **5-ESS3-1:** Obtain and combine information about ways individual communities use science ideas to protect the Earth's resources and environment.
- **3-LS4-4:** Make a claim about the merit of a solution to a problem caused when the environment changes and the types of plants and animals that live there may change.
- **3-5-ETS1-2:** Generate and compare multiple possible solutions to a problem based on how well each is likely to meet the criteria and constraints of the problem.

Materials:

Lesson 1

- Local Land Acknowledgment
- Laptops/Chromebooks and access to website Native-Land.ca
- Video: Indigenous land acknowledgments, their purpose, and how to make them meaningful | CBC Kids News https://www.youtube.com/watch?v=i7juFo9nKmM&t=211s
- Video: Treaties with Indigenous peoples in Canada, explained | CBC Kids News https://www.youtube.com/watch?v=SVaK9rAV32A

Lesson 2

- Laptops/Chromebooks for research

Lesson 3

- 2 Executive Orders on Forests (See Lesson for Links)
- Laptops/Chromebooks for research

- Trump's plan to boost timber in national forests faces backlash at https://www.youtube.com/watch?v=ohZPNdgzDmI
- Town Hall Instructions (Optional Activity—available in the Appendix)

Important Vocabulary/Concepts:

- Land Acknowledgment
- Treaties
- Executive Order
- Timber
- Town Hall Meeting

Lesson Overview: This 3-lesson sequence begins with students exploring land acknowledgments and why they are important. Students are introduced to a website that shows where Indigenous communities live and have lived as well as native languages and treaties. In the second lesson, students conduct their own research about the local Indigenous community practices and culture and share their new knowledge with the class. In the third lesson, students discuss the executive order released by President Trump in March 2025, which allows timber harvesting in National Forests, evaluate the potential impacts of the order, and write an op-ed piece about how they feel about the issue.

Lesson 1: Land Acknowledgments
ENGAGE: Lesson Introduction

- Read or share a video of a land acknowledgment that is local to your region. If you are unsure, use the following video: https://www.youtube.com/watch?v=I8Gu2sO7C4I
- Ask students to think-pair-share about what a land acknowledgment might be for, what is included, and why we might do one.

EXPLORE: Explore Website of Native Lands and Territories

- Give students 5–10 minutes to explore the website, Native-Land.ca. This site allows students to explore the Indigenous communities across the Earth, including their names, languages, and any relevant treaties.
- Have students make general observations about what they notice in the map.
- Have students spend a little time exploring broadly and then ask them to hone in on the specific geographic location of the town/school and record the name(s) of the Indigenous territory/territories where they are living.

EXPLAIN: Video Analysis

- Watch the following video: Indigenous land acknowledgments, their purpose, and how to make them meaningful | CBC Kids News at https://www.youtube.com/watch?v=i7juFo9nKmM&t=211s

- Engage students in a dialogue about their thoughts and ideas related to what they learned about in the video.

ELABORATE: **Application activity**

- Watch the video: Treaties with Indigenous peoples in Canada, explained | CBC Kids News at https://www.youtube.com/watch?v=SVaK9rAV32A
- Have students use Native-Land.ca to see if any treaties exist in their area.
- Engage students in a discussion about what they learned from the video and their research on treaties. (Note: If no treaties exist in your area, encourage them to visit another area but also engage in a discussion about why this is the case).

EXTEND: Photo elicitation and Critical Dialogue

- Show students pictures of Indigenous people resisting environmental damage from governments or corporations. For example:

https://www.flickr.com/photos/44550450@N04/29630653446

https://www.flickr.com/photos/44550450@N04/15510370827

- Engage students in a critical dialogue about the forms of activism they see:
    - What do you notice in these pictures?
    - How do you think this connects to land acknowledgments and treaties?
    - Why do you think Indigenous people are responding in these ways?
    - What do you think they are fighting for and how does this relate to you/us?
    - Are these issues you also care about and impact our community?
    - What questions would you ask a person who was involved in this kind of activism?
    - Do you think only Indigenous people are involved in these protests? Why or why not?
    - What is a form of protest that we might want to do if we or our neighbors and communities are also impacted by government or corporate decisions?

EVALUATE: **Wrap-Up Activity/Assessment:**

- Have students work in small groups to write their own land acknowledgment that honors the Indigenous territory and people who lived on the land before Europeans arrived.
- Have students come up with one action they can do to further acknowledge the Indigenous communities that inhabited the land they are on today.
- Have students share their acknowledgments and actions with the class.

Lesson 2: Research on Local Indigenous Communities
ENGAGE: Lesson Introduction

- Show images of Indigenous communities in your region. Include a variety of images that show what the ecosystem looked like prior to settler colonization and images of cultural and ecological Indigenous traditions and practices. Some examples might include:

https://www.flickr.com/photos/73645804@N00/5907692738

https://openverse.org/image/c89f6b2e-b125-4cb4-a693-75d29f926dc1?q=native+american+blanket&p=2

https://www.flickr.com/photos/50693818@N08/8590394025

EXPLORE: Making Observations and Asking Questions

- Have students begin to document their observations of the images, paying particular attention to the ecosystems they see, the practices they notice, and have them keep track of observations and what they think they are seeing in a T-chart (observations|wondering, ideas, questions).
- Facilitate a brief discussion about their observations and ideas and connect their ideas to the land acknowledgment.
    - For example, students may observe that the Indigenous people of the area did a lot of fishing, and they might also notice that included in the land acknowledgment is a recognition of the local waters and how they fed and sustained communities.

EXPLAIN: Research Local Indigenous Community

- Make small groups of students and explain that each group will research a different aspect of Indigenous life from before settler colonization to present day. Have groups document their research in your preferred way or in a shared Google Slides presentation.
- Some possible groupings and questions might include:
    - Land and History:
        - Who were the first people to live on the land where our school (or town) is now?
        - What is the name of the Native nation(s) that live or lived in our region?
        - How did Indigenous people care for the land before settler colonization?

- Cultural Traditions
  - What is the native language spoken? What are a few words in the native language that you can find?
  - What are some of the important traditions, ceremonies, and stories of the native community that lived in our region? Try to find one story that you would like to share with the class.
  - What did the Native people in your region believe in?
  - What are some of the tools, dress, styles of art, and homes of the Indigenous community that lived here?
- Ecology and Ecological Practices
  - What did the ecosystem look like prior to settler colonization?
  - What were some significant ecological practices utilized by Indigenous communities and why did they use these practices?
  - What were some plants used by Indigenous people for healing and medicinal uses?
  - What type of food production was utilized by the Indigenous community?
  - What plants were most important for food to the Indigenous people?
  - What animals were significant for the Indigenous people?
- Indigenous and Settler Relations
  - When did settlers arrive in the region and what happened to the Indigenous community in your area when they did?
  - Are there still native communities/reservations in our area? If so, where? If not, why not?
  - What historical or current treaties were made between settler colonizers and the Indigenous people in your region?
- Current Events and Issues
  - How are the Native Indigenous communities being impacted today by the legacy of settler colonialism?
  - Where do we see mention of our local Indigenous communities in the news and other media outlets?
  - Who are current Native artists, scientists, educators, activists working locally in our community?

ELABORATE: **Sharing Knowledge**

- Have each group share their research with the class.
- While students are presenting, have other students document their notes, ask questions, and make connections to their topics.

EXTEND: Photo Elicitation and Critical Dialogue

- Ask each group of students to select one image that they believe is powerful and would engage the class in a good discussion. Use student images to co-facilitate (with each group) the photo elicitation activity and critical dialogue.
- As students share their image, have them ask the class the following questions:

- What do you notice in this image?
- How do you connect to this image?
- What feelings does this image evoke?
- Why do you think we chose this image?
- What can we learn from this image?
- How does this image connect to our thinking today?

EVALUATE: Wrap-Up Activity/Assessment

- Have students record in their notebook/exit ticket the most impactful new piece of information they learned from their research and the class presentations.

Lesson 3: Indigenous Communities and Land Use Today
ENGAGE: Lesson Introduction

- Have students read (or read to them) Section 1 of the Executive Order: Federal Register: Strengthening the Nation's Forests, Communities, and Local Economies—https://www.federalregister.gov/documents/2022/04/27/2022-09138/strengthening-the-nations-forests-communities-and-local-economies
    - Explain to the students this was written by former President Biden in April 2022
- Have the students read (or read to them) Section 1 of the Executive Order: Immediate Expansion of American Timber Production—https://www.whitehouse.gov/presidential-actions/2025/03/immediate-expansion-of-american-timber-production/
    - Explain to the students this was written in March 2025 by President Trump
- Engage students in a brief discussion about their reactions to each of the executive orders
    - What do they notice about each one?
    - How are they similar? How are they different?
    - What questions do you have to better understand current policy and the impacts of it?

EXPLORE: Student Question Research

- Have students take some of their questions and learn more about them through research. Depending on the questions, this might look like internet research or using maps, books, and other texts to explore their questions and ideas.
- Give opportunities for students to share their new learning with the class.

EXPLAIN: Video Analysis

- Watch the following videos (feel free to include more that highlight other perspectives).

- Video 1: Trump's plan to boost timber in national forests faces backlash at https://www.youtube.com/watch?v=ohZPNdgzDmI
- Video 2: Trump executive orders to ramp up domestic timber production welcomed by logging industry | Fox News Video at https://www.foxnews.com/video/6369585891112
- Video 3: Beyond the Forest. Indigenous Rights in Forestry at https://www.youtube.com/watch?v=yI5cI9Nw6ng

- Have students discuss the diverse perspectives being represented in each video.
- Guide them to create a list of all the beings that are impacted by this new executive order and how.
- Record the class list on the board or chart paper.

ELABORATE: **Application activity**

- Discuss with students what value they believe the forest offers to them. Record their ideas on the board or chart paper.

EXTEND: Town Hall Activity (see Appendix for further explanation of how to facilitate)

- Have students/student groups take on different roles in the community representing the diverse interests of the timber industry, Indigenous communities, locals, environmental activists, developers, a logger, national parks ranger, and so on..
- Have students research more deeply about how this new executive order will impact them in their role and their community.
- Have students engage in a town hall meeting (see Appendix I for how to conduct a Town Hall Meeting) where they advocate for their position on the new executive order expanding timber production in National Forests.

EVALUATE: **Wrap-Up Activity/Assessment**

- Have students write an op-ed piece that showcases their opinion about the new executive order. Use the following sentence starters as needed.
  - I believe that . . .
  - I care about this because . . .
  - Other people should care about this because . . .
  - One reason I believe this is because . . .
  - Others may think that . . .
  - I hope people will . . .
  - This is why I believe . . .

Community and Place-Based Learning Opportunities

This section invites teachers and parents to engage community members, outside school experts, and other local knowledge resources to extend the EcoJustice learning experiences that students are engaging with in classrooms. We know taking trips with students can be difficult, so sending these suggestions home to families might be a good option. We included whole class community projects and explorations as well as inviting speakers with relevant knowledge about land use/justice to visit your classroom.

For this theme of land use and land justice, we suggest any of the following place-based learning experiences for you and your students:

- Community Mapping and Storytelling—Have students explore the school community or other parts of their community (in groups, as a class, as a family) and record places that are meaningful to them. Have them create maps, interview one another about their maps, and write stories about the places that are meaningful to them.
- Neighborhood Walk and Observations—Have students explore the school community or other parts of their community (in groups, as a class, as a family) and create a map showing the different kinds of land uses. Have students take pictures and write captions for their observations of their photos.
- Bring in a local planning board member—Have students write interview questions for a planning board member. Allow space to discuss the kinds of work they do, what decisions they are responsible for making, and how community members can be involved.
- Visit a local Indigenous Museum or other Indigenous space—See our website resources for a brief list of Indigenous Museums, Cultural and Heritage Centers, and Historical Sites.
- Invite an Indigenous community member to visit the class—Have students write interview questions for an Indigenous community member visiting the class.
- Visit a Housing Cooperative, Community Land Trust, or other Land Cooperative Model in your community or invite someone in to discuss this in more detail.
- Invite a community activist to visit the class to discuss ways they are organizing around land use decisions in your community.

Teacher Turn

Now it is your turn. Here we offer next steps for you to develop your own EcoJustice instructional materials that meet the needs of your school curriculum and your students' interests. As you have learned throughout this chapter, there are many EcoJustice issues that are linked to our current policies and practices of land use. Perhaps most important is for children to critically analyze who makes decisions about land ownership and land use and whether this is a fair, just, and sustainable model for land access. Additionally, children should learn how some communities bear a larger burden of the environmental and social impacts of land use decisions than others and what the implications of that are. We invite teachers to dig deeper into any of these issues with your class by utilizing resources provided in this chapter, on our website, and in our appendices to create your own lessons.

A good place to start is to answer the following questions:

- Which standard fits with your school curriculum? (See the list in the Appendix of NCSS and NGSS standards we have identified as offering opportunities to incorporate our Pillars). Also look at the Cloud Standards and the SDGs on our website resources for further connections to your curriculum and ideas.
- Which concepts are you and your students interested in learning more about? (e.g., access to green space, cost of living/housing in the local community, present and historical presence of Indigenous communities, etc.)
- Which resources (suggested or your own) would you like to use to expand your own understanding of these concepts?
- What pedagogical activities are most appropriate for your teaching context?

As reinforced by the case studies in this chapter, EcoJustice issues are often related to issues of access and equity, displacing the most vulnerable populations and privileging those with the most power. We have put together many resources in our Appendices and on our website for you to build out an EcoJustice lesson including a lesson plan template, national social studies and science standards, resources to expand your own thinking about EcoJustice issues, and common teaching strategies we have used in our own classrooms. You don't have to do this alone either. Include your students in the process of creating relevant and meaningful lessons for them. Tap other teachers who are aligned to EcoJustice for ideas and accountability. We are eager to support you on your journey toward becoming an EcoJustice Educator!

Notes

1 Christopher Columbus, "Letter on the First Voyage," March 1493. In Columbus reports on his first voyage, 1493. Translated and published by the Gilder Lehrman Institute of American History, accessed August 9, 2025, https://www.gilderlehrman.org/history-resources/spotlight-primary-source/columbus-reports-his-first-voyage-1493.

2 GOV.UK, "Rights of Way and Accessing Land: Use Your Right to Roam," *GOV.UK*, accessed August 10, 2025, https://www.gov.uk/right-of-way-open-access-land/use-your-right-to-roam.

3 Sun Narin, "'Our Ancestors' Graves have been Drowned': Cambodian Dam Wipes Out Hill Tribe Way of Life," *Indigenous Peoples Major Group for Sustainable Development (IPMG)*, November 29, 2018, accessed August 10, 2025, https://Indigenouspeoples-sdg

.org/index.php/english/ttt/927-our-ancestors-graves-have-been-drowned-cambodian-dam-wipes-out-hill-tribe-way-of-life.

4 National Council for Geographic Education (NCGE), "Empowering Educators & Connecting Classrooms to the World," *NCGE*, 2025, accessed August 10, 2025, https://ncge.org/.

5 TeacherVision, "Chart Columbus's Voyages," *Columbus Day Full Lesson, TeacherVision*, accessed August 10, 2025, https://www.teachervision.com/columbus-day/chart-columbuss-voyages.

6 TeacherVision, "Who Writes History? Rethinking Columbus Day," *Full Lesson, TeacherVision*, accessed August 10, 2025, https://www.teachervision.com/social-studies-history/who-writes-history-rethinking-columbus-day.

7 The Gilder Lehrman Institute of American History, "The Doctrine of Discovery, 1493," accessed August 10, 2025, https://www.gilderlehrman.org/history-resources/spotlight-primary-source/doctrine-discovery-1493.

8 John S. Marr and John T. Cathey, "New Hypothesis for Cause of Epidemic among Native Americans, New England, 1616–1619," *Emerging Infectious Diseases* 16, no. 2 (2010): 281–6, accessed August 10, 2025, https://pmc.ncbi.nlm.nih.gov/articles/PMC2957993/.

9 Feenie Ziner, *Squanto* (Hamden, CT: Linnet Books, 1988 [1965]), 147.

10 James W. Loewen, "The Truth About the First Thanksgiving," *Monthly Review* 44, no. 6 (November 1992), accessed August 10, 2025, https://monthlyreview.org/1992/11/01/the-truth-about-the-first-thanksgiving/.

11 Splash Publications, *Westward Expansion & Manifest Destiny*, https://splashpublications.com/product/westward-expansion-manifest-destiny-interactive-notebook-unit-louisiana-purchase-lewis-clark-gold-rush-digital-download/.

12 Monticello Organization, "List of Suggested Activities for Lewis and Clark Studies," *Monticello*, accessed August 10, 2025, https://www.monticello.org/research-education/for-educators/lewis-clark-study-resources/suggested-study-activities/.

13 Alex W. Bealer and William Sauts Bock, *Only the Names Remain: The Cherokees and the Trail of Tears* (Boston: Little, Brown and Company, 1972), 5.

14 The Taíno were the Indigenous people who inhabited the Caribbean islands and the Bahamas when Christopher Columbus arrived in the late fifteenth century.

15 P. Wolfe, "Settler Colonialism and the Elimination of the Native," *Journal of Genocide Research* 8, no. 4 (2006): 387–409, p. 388.

16 General William T. Sherman, "Special Field Orders, No. 15," January 16, 1865, in Special Field Orders No. 15, BlackPast, accessed August 10, 2025, https://www.blackpast.org/african-american-history/special-field-orders-no-15/.

17 PBS, "The Truth Behind '40 Acres and a Mule,'" *The African Americans: Many Rivers to Cross, PBS*, accessed August 10, 2025, https://www.pbs.org/wnet/african-americans-many-rivers-to-cross/history/the-truth-behind-40-acres-and-a-mule/.

18 NAACP, "Reparations," *NAACP*, 2025, accessed August 10, 2025, https://naacp.org/resources/reparations.

19 Cory Booker, "A Conspiracy of Love," *Global Leadership Network*, accessed August 10, 2025, https://www.globalleadership.org/article/conspiracy-love-cory-booker.

20 Jim Dobson, "The Top 20 Landowners In America, According To A New Report," *Forbes*, January 20, 2024, accessed August 10, 2025, https://www.forbes.com/sites/jimdobson/2024/01/20/the-top-20-landowners-in-america-according-to-a-new-report/.

21 Reed F. Noss and Robert L. Peters, *Endangered Ecosystems: A Status Report on America's Vanishing Habitat and Wildlife* (Washington, DC: Defenders of Wildlife, 1995).

22 Noss and Peters, *Endangered Ecosystems: A Status Report on America's Vanishing Habitat and Wildlife*.

23 William Cronon, *Changes in the Land: Indians, Colonists, and the Ecology of New England* (New York: Hill and Wang, 2011).

24 William T. Hornaday, *The Extermination of the American Bison* (DigiCat, 2022).

25 Fred Samson and Fritz Knopf, "Prairie Conservation in North America," *BioScience* 44, no. 6 (1994): 418–21.

26 Delaware Currents, "A Guide to Fighting Warehouses in Your Community from a New Jersey Resident," August 9, 2024, accessed August 10, 2025, https://delawarecurrents.org/2024/08/09/warehouses-new-jersey/.

27 Chris Mele, "How did the 'Amazonification' of New Jersey happen?" *Delaware Currents*, May 2, 2023, accessed August 10, 2025, https://delawarecurrents.org/2023/05/02/new-jersey-warehouses/.

28 Stop Warehouses And Trucking (S.W.A.T.), *Stop Warehouses And Trucking Official Website* (Hillsborough, NJ: Stop Warehouses And Trucking, 2025), accessed August 10, 2025, https://www.swat-hb.org/.

29 Environmental Defense Fund, "New Report Finds Roughly 1 in 3 New Jersey Residents Lives Near a Mega-warehouse," *Environmental Defense Fund*, June 18, 2024, accessed august 10, 2025, https://www.edf.org/media/new-report-finds-roughly-1-3-new-jersey-residents-lives-near-mega-warehouse.

30 Retail Brew, "Here's Where Experts Say the Next Warehouse Hotspots Will be," *Retail Brew*, November 1, 2022, accessed August 10, 2025, https://www.retailbrew.com/stories/2022/11/01/here-s-where-experts-say-the-next-warehouse-hotspots-will-be.

31 64 Parishes, "Cancer Alley," *64 Parishes*, accessed August 10, 2025, https://64parishes.org/entry/cancer-alley.

32 Tulane Environmental Law Clinic, "Tulane Study: Louisiana's Severe Air Pollution Linked to Dozens of Cancer Cases Each Year," *Environmental Research Letters*, June 21, 2021, accessed August 10, 2025, https://law.tulane.edu/news/tulane-study-louisianas-severe-air-pollution-linked-dozens-cancer-cases-each-year.

33 Center for International Environmental Law (CIEL), *Fossils, Fertilizers, and False Solutions: How Laundering Fossil Fuels in Agrochemicals Puts the Climate and the Planet at Risk* (Washington, DC: CIEL, October 6, 2022), accessed August 10, 2025, https://www.ciel.org/reports/fossil-fertilizers/.

34 WWNO, "In Louisiana's 'Cancer Alley,' Most Oil and Gas Jobs Go to White Workers, New Research Says," *WWNO*, October 6, 2023, accessed August 10, 2025, https://www.wwno.org/coastal-desk/2023-10-06/in-louisianas-cancer-alley-most-oil-and-gas-jobs-go-to-white-workers-new-research-says.

35 Gianna St. Julien and Kimberley Terrell, Tulane Environmental Law Clinic, "A Horror Story—How the Law Simultaneously Addresses and Perpetuates Environmental Racism in Cancer Alley," *Global Network for Human Rights and the Environment*, September 9, 2024, accessed August 10, 2025, https://gnhre.org/?p=18198.

36 Tristan Baurick, "Petrochemical Jobs Bypass Black Communities in Louisiana, Study Finds," *Environmental Health News*, August 2, 2023, accessed August 10, 2025, https://www.ehn.org/petrochemical-jobs-bypass-black-communities-in-louisiana-study-finds.

37 Earthjustice, "Cancer Alley Rises Up," *Earthjustice*, accessed August 10, 2025, https://Earthjustice.org/feature/cancer-alley-rises-up.

38 Reuters, "Lawsuit Alleging Racism in Louisiana's Cancer Alley Revived on Appeal," *Reuters*, April 10, 2025, accessed August 10, 2025, https://www.reuters.com/legal/government/lawsuit-alleging-racism-louisianas-cancer-alley-revived-appeal-2025-04-10/.

39 Human Rights Watch, "We're Dying Here: The Fight for Life in Louisiana's Fossil Fuel Sacrifice Zone," *Human Rights Watch*, January 25, 2024, accessed August 10, 2025, https://www.hrw.org/report/2024/01/25/were-dying-here/fight-life-louisiana-fossil-fuel-sacrifice-zone.

40 Lowlander Center, "EPA Passes Air Quality Protection in 'Cancer Alley' and Beyond . . . but Federal Judge Overturns Decision," *Lowlander Center*, April 11, 2024, accessed August 10, 2025, https://www.lowlandercenter.org/news-and-updates/2024/4/11/epa-passes-air-quality-protection-in-cancer-alley-and-beyond.

41 Environmental Working Group, "Releases of Carcinogens and Other Toxic Chemicals from Industrial Facilities in Louisiana's Cancer Alley," *Environmental Working Group*, 2020, accessed August 10, 2025, https://www.ewg.org/research/releases-carcinogens-cancer-alley.

42 Samantha Layden, "Land of the Free? Environmental Racism and Its Impact on Cancer Alley, Louisiana," *Keele University Extinction Project*, accessed August 10, 2025, https://www.keele.ac.uk/extinction/controversy/canceralley/.

43 Juan Declet-Barreto and Jacob Carter, "Superfund Site Cleanups Ignore Communities of Color," *Union of Concerned Scientists Blog*, September 21, 2020, accessed August 10, 2025, https://blog.ucs.org/juan-declet-barreto/superfund-site-cleanups-ignore-communities-of-color/.

44 Washington Post, "We Mythologize Highways, But They've Damaged Communities of Color," *Made By History*, January 19, 2023, accessed August 10, 2025, https://www.washingtonpost.com/made-by-history/2023/01/19/interstate-highways-black-neighborhoods/.

45 ACLU, "Racism by Design: The Building of Interstate 81," *ACLU*, August 10, 2025, accessed August 10, 2025, https://www.aclu.org/news/racial-justice/racism-by-design-the-building-of-interstate-81.

46 Teddy Rube, "Rethinking Highway Construction as De Jure Segregation: A Case Study for Equal Protection Lawsuits," *NYU Journal of Legislation & Public Policy Quorum*, October 9, 2023, accessed August 10, 2025, https://nyujlpp.org/quorum/rube-rethinking-highway-construction-as-de-jure-segregation/.

47 NPR, "A Brief History Of How Racism Shaped Interstate Highways," *NPR*, April 7, 2021, accessed August 10, 2025, https://www.npr.org/2021/04/07/984784455/a-brief-history-of-how-racism-shaped-interstate-highways.

48 U.S. Environmental Protection Agency (EPA), "Rethinking Highways for Healthy Communities," *EPA*, 2024, accessed August 10, 2025, https://www.epa.gov/smartgrowth/rethinking-highways-healthy-communities.

49 Federal Highway Administration, "Chapter 2: Effects of Roads on Wildlife Populations," in *Wildlife Crossing Structures Handbook: Design and Evaluation in North America* (Washington, DC: Federal Highway Administration, 2025), accessed August 10, 2025, https://www.fhwa.dot.gov/clas/ctip/wildlife_crossing_structures/ch_2.aspx.

50 U.S. Environmental Protection Agency (EPA), "Research on Near Roadway and Other Near Source Air Pollution," *EPA*, 2025, accessed August 10, 2025, https://www.epa.gov/air-research/research-near-roadway-and-other-near-source-air-pollution.

51 Ananna Kazi and Sarah Shidid, "Opinion: Let the Bronx Breathe—Address the Cross Bronx Expressway's Impact on Asthma," *City Limits*, October 6, 2023, accessed August 10, 2025, https://citylimits.org/opinion-let-the-bronx-breathe-address-the-cross-bronx-expressways-impact-on-asthma/.

52 Columbia Center for Children's Environmental Health, "Asthma," *Columbia University Public Health*, accessed August 10, 2025, https://www.publichealth.columbia.edu/research/centers/columbia-center-childrens-environmental-health/our-research/health-effects/asthma.

53 ACLU, "Racism by Design: The Building of Interstate 81," August 10, 2025, https://www.aclu.org/news/racial-justice/racism-by-design-the-building-of-interstate-81.

54 Aydali Campa and Brett Chase, "Plans for I-55 Expansion in Chicago Raise Concerns Over Air Quality and Community Health," *Inside Climate News*, May 23, 2023, accessed August 10, 2025, https://insideclimatenews.org/news/23052023/plans-for-i-55-expansion-in-chicago-raise-concerns-over-air-quality-and-community-health/.

55 Coalition for Clean Air, "The Hidden Legacy of Highway Expansions," *Coalition for Clean Air*, September 28, 2023, accessed August 10, 2025, https://www.ccair.org/the-hidden-legacy-of-highway-expansions/.

56 *The Guardian*, "Plan to Expand Texas Highway Stalled Over Environmental Racism Concerns," *The Guardian*, March 23, 2021, accessed August 10, 2025, https://www.theguardian.com/us-news/2021/mar/23/plan-to-expand-texas-highway-stalled-over-environmental-racism-concerns.

57 ENLACE Caño Martín Peña, "Fideicomiso de la Tierra del Caño Martín Peña," *ENLACE*, accessed August 10, 2025, https://martinpena.org/fideicomiso/.

58 RioOnWatch, "Community Land Trusts in Latin America: Dialogues Between Brazil and Puerto Rico," *RioOnWatch*, October 26, 2021, accessed August 10, 2025, https://rioonwatch.org/?p=68482.

59 Centro de Estudios de la Realidad Puertorriqueña (CEREP), *The Caño Martín Peña Community Land Trust: A Tool for Equitable Development in Informal Settlements* (San Juan, PR: CEREP, 2015), https://martinpena.org/wp-content/uploads/2015/09/CMPLT_Report.pdf.

60 Lorena Zárate, "By the People, For the People: Social and Environmental Revitalisation of the Caño Martín Peña, Puerto Rico," *Urbanet*, June 7, 2022, accessed August 10, 2025, https://www.urbanet.info/cano-martin-pena/.

61 U.S. Census Bureau, "Housing Vacancies and Homeownership, 2023 Q4," *US Census Bureau*, January 30, 2024, accessed August 10, 2025, https://www.census.gov/housing/hvs/.

62 American Bar Association, "The Contemporary Relevance of Historic Black Land Loss," *ABA*, January 6, 2023, accessed August 10, 2025, https://www.americanbar.org/groups/crsj/resources/human-rights/archive/contemporary-relevance-historic-black-land-loss/.

63 Economic Policy Institute, "Housing Discrimination Underpins the Staggering Wealth Gap Between Blacks and Whites," *EPI*, December 12, 2017, accessed August 10, 2025, https://www.epi.org/blog/housing-discrimination-underpins-the-staggering-wealth-gap-between-blacks-and-whites/.

64 Christine Quattro, "Environmental Justice and Zoning Reform," P*AS Report 608. American Planning Association*, 2023, accessed August 10, 2025, https://www.planning.org/publications/report/9295614/.

65 Center for Sustainable Systems, University of Michigan, "Environmental Justice Factsheet," CSS Pub. No. CSS17-16, 2024, accessed August 10, 2025, https://css.umich.edu/publications/factsheets/sustainability-indicators/environmental-justice-factsheet.

66 U.S. Environmental Protection Agency (EPA), "Study Finds Exposure to Air Pollution Higher for People of Color Regardless of Region or Income," *EPA*, September 20, 2021, accessed August 10, 2025, https://www.epa.gov/sciencematters/study-finds-exposure-air-pollution-higher-people-color-regardless-region-or-income.

67 U.S. Environmental Protection Agency (EPA), Office of Land and Emergency Management, "Population Surrounding 1,857 Superfund Remedial Sites," September 2020, accessed August 10, 2025, https://www.epa.gov/sites/default/files/2015-09/documents/webpopulationrsuperfundsites9.28.15.pdf.

68 Associated Press, "North American Grassland Birds in Peril, Spurring All-out Effort to . . .," *AP News*, August 25, 2023, accessed August 10, 2025, https://apnews.com/article/grassland-birds-decline-endangered-species-climate-ce14337f33e77f190e24527 0bb3e6769.

69 Intergovernmental Panel on Climate Change (IPCC), *Climate Change and Land: An IPCC Special Report on Climate Change, Desertification, Land Degradation, Sustainable Land Management, Food Security, and Greenhouse Gas Fluxes in Terrestrial Ecosystems* (Cambridge University Press, 2019), accessed August 10, 2025, https://www.ipcc.ch/srccl/.

70 Megan W. Lang, James C. Ingebritsen, and Russell K. Griffin, *Status and Trends of Wetlands in the Conterminous United States 2009 to 2019* (Washington, DC: US Department of the Interior, Fish and Wildlife Service, 2024), 43pp.

71 "Ancestral land returned to Onondaga Nation in upstate New York," *AP News*, September 30, 2024, https://apnews.com/article/native-american-land-rights-onondaga-new-york-9f105760632d6bf7ce26a6e1c324f8a6.

72 The Santa Monica Mountains Fund, "Rewilding California Project Reaches Halfway Milestone!" *Santa Monica Mountains Fund Blog*, September 13, 2022, https://www.samofund.org/blog/rewilding-california-project-reaches-halfway-milestone.

73 National Council for the Social Studies, "National Curriculum Standards for Social Studies: Chapter 2—The Themes of Social Studies, Theme 2 Time Continuity and Change," *National Council for the Social Studies*, accessed August 10, 2025, https://www.socialstudies.org/national-curriculum-standards-social-studies-chapter-2-themes-social-studies.

74 National Council for the Social Studies, "National Curriculum Standards for Social Studies: Chapter 2—The Themes of Social Studies, Theme 2 Time Continuity and Change," *National Council for the Social Studies*, accessed August 10, 2025, https://www.socialstudies.org/national-curriculum-standards-social-studies-chapter-2-themes-social-studies.

75 National Council for the Social Studies, "National Curriculum Standards for Social Studies: Chapter 2—The Themes of Social Studies, Theme 3 People, Places and Environments," *National Council for the Social Studies*, accessed August 10, 2025, https://

www.socialstudies.org/national-curriculum-standards-social-studies-chapter-2-themes-social-studies.

76 Next-Generation Science Standards (NGSS), "Elementary Standards: Kindergarten Through Grade Five Disciplinary Core Ideas," *NGSS Lead States*, September 2017, accessed August 9, 2025, https://www.nextgenscience.org/sites/default/files/K-2DCI.pdf.

77 Next-Generation Science Standards (NGSS), "Elementary Standards: Third Through Fifth Grade Performance Expectations by Topic," *NGSS Lead States*, September 2017, accessed August 9, 2025, https://www.nextgenscience.org/sites/default/files/3-5Topic.pdf.

78 The Cloud Institute for Sustainability Education, "EfS Standards & Performance Indicators: Cultural Preservation & Transformation," *Cloud Institute for Sustainability Education*, accessed August 10, 2025, https://cloudinstitute.org/cloud-efs-standards-performanceindicators.

79 The Cloud Institute for Sustainability Education, "EfS Standards & Performance Indicators: Healthy Commons," *Cloud Institute for Sustainability Education*, accessed August 10, 2025, https://cloudinstitute.org/cloud-efs-standards-performanceindicators.

80 The Cloud Institute for Sustainability Education, "EfS Standards & Performance Indicators: Strong Sense of Place," *Cloud Institute for Sustainability Education*, accessed August 10, 2025, https://cloudinstitute.org/cloud-efs-standards-performanceindicators.

81 United Nations, "Goal 11: Make Cities and Human Settlements Inclusive, Safe, Resilient and Sustainable," *United Nations Sustainable Development Goals*, accessed August 10, 2025, https://sdgs.un.org/goals/goal11.

82 United Nations, "Goal 15: Protect, Restore and Promote Sustainable Use of Terrestrial Ecosystems, Sustainably Manage Forests, Combat Desertification, and Halt and Reverse Land Degradation and Halt Biodiversity Loss," *United Nations Sustainable Development Goals*, accessed August 10, 2025, https://sdgs.un.org/goals/goal15.

5 Water

Chapter Outline

The global supply of fresh water around the world is rapidly vanishing. This problem is only going to intensify in the years to come. I believe that educators have a responsibility to speak the truth to children about real world problems. Children are citizens of the world and they have a right to know what is going on and how they can take action. Their future is at stake.

—Marcie, Early Childhood Teacher

Introduction

Water covers 71 percent of our Earth and is essential for life. A typical healthy adult human can last two to three months without food,[1] but only about three days without water.[2] To say that water is an ever-present need for life as it is known, is not an exaggeration. Nor is the fact that humans have long organized their lives (knowingly or not) around access to clean water. However, shifting weather patterns brought on by climate change are altering landscapes and lifestyles around the globe. This has come with huge costs in human lives, property damage, and habitat loss. A United Nations Climate Change online resource states:

> Water and climate change are inextricably linked. Climate change affects the world's water in complex ways. From unpredictable rainfall patterns to shrinking ice sheets, rising sea levels, floods and droughts—most impacts of climate change come down to water. Climate change is exacerbating both water scarcity and water-related hazards (such as floods and droughts), as rising temperatures disrupt precipitation patterns and the entire water cycle.[3]

Surely such an important topic must receive a lot of attention in our system of education. Given that water is a natural element, we can expect the topic to be addressed in elementary school science curriculums. In addition, due to the intense relationship between humans and water, we can also expect the topic to be included in the social studies. In this chapter, we will begin by exploring how water is typically taught in these content areas. As with other chapters, this will be followed with an EcoJustice perspective on traditional approaches and ideas of what could and should be included. Next, we share information and resources to build teachers' background knowledge. Examples of instructional materials to help young people understand the challenges water issues present in the United States today, as well as ways that individuals, organizations and government are seeking to remedy the crises, are then provided. Lastly, we once again offer resources and guidance to support teachers if they choose to create their own materials for EcoJustice education in their classrooms.

The Conventional Approach

The Role of Science in Teaching About Water

> Pour yourself a glass of water and take a sip. Did you know that the water you've just swallowed is the same water that wooly mammoths, King Tutankhamun and the first humans drank? That's because Earth has been recycling water for over **4 billion years**!
>
> The world's water moves between lakes, rivers, oceans, the atmosphere and the land in an ongoing cycle called—you guessed it!—the **water cycle**. As it goes through this continuous system, it can be a liquid (water), a gas (vapor) or a solid (ice).[4]

The above text, from an online National Geographic resource, represents a typical approach to teaching elementary school students about water. The article continues by explaining phases of the water cycle: evaporation, condensation, precipitation, and collection. The information is presented in simplistic and factual terms, for example, "The fallen precipitation is then 'collected' in bodies of water—such as rivers, lakes and oceans—from where it will eventually evaporate back into the air, beginning the cycle all over again" (Figure 5.1).

The water cycle is typically taught to elementary school children through images like the one in Figure 5.1. While visuals can help children see the cycle, representations that are devoid of real-life and human images can lead students to feel disconnected from the

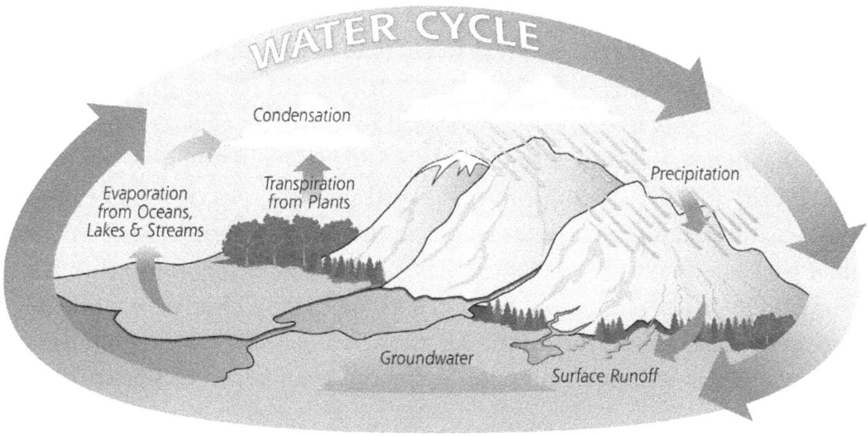

Figure 5.1. The water cycle. https://www.flickr.com/photos/90896682@N06/8265046380

process. This is especially important since humans have real-life impacts on the cycle and quality of water and are directly impacted by the health of the water cycle.

As part of understanding the water cycle, students will also learn that water can take the forms of liquid, gas, or a solid (ice). Beyond the water cycle, elementary school children will commonly learn about different water sources (surface water, groundwater, etc.) as well as topics related to water quality, conservation, and natural water disasters.

Students typically learn that there are natural bodies of water on the Earth's surface, such as lakes, rivers, and oceans, as well as water that is beneath the Earth's surface or frozen in glaciers. They will learn that approximately 71 percent of the Earth's surface is water, but that only about 1 percent can be used for drinking. These facts naturally lead to lessons on water conservation. The topic of water conservation is deemed important enough to be addressed on the US Environmental Protection Agency (EPA) website where teachers can find useful information and educational resources.

The EPA website highlights many ways children can help to conserve water usage, such as turning off the faucet when it's not needed while brushing one's teeth, taking showers instead of baths, or using a bucket of water and a sponge rather than a hose to wash a bike. Among the activities for use is a video game reminiscent of Pac-Man, where children can test their knowledge of how to conserve water. There are also worksheets for students, families, or teachers to use and lesson plan ideas. One lesson, *A Day in the Life of a Drop,* has the goals "To help students understand the connections between the source of the water they use; the ways their water use habits affect the environment and human health and ways to reduce their impacts by pledging to take steps to use water more efficiently."[5] An overview of the lesson highlights what students can potentially learn.

The initial focus of the lesson is on the importance of watersheds and students make connections to their own lives by identifying their local watershed. In the next stage of the lesson, students learn how water is transported from a local source and into their homes. The final stage of the lesson focuses on water efficiency so that students "come away from this activity with a greater understanding of why it is important to use water efficiently and what the effects on local water bodies can be when too much water is removed from the watershed at any given time."[6] The idea of a leaking faucet is introduced to demonstrate how much water can be wasted by this type of water inefficiency. Text included in the materials for the teacher states, "When we use water, we are taking it out of the watershed, and the amount of available freshwater goes down. We use water in many different ways and eventually return it to the environment in various conditions. How much we use and how we use it can have significant effects [on] other water uses, such as aquatic life uses, recreation, fishing, and the like."[7] Other than waste associated with behaviors in one's home, there is no mention of how water can be polluted and then returned to the water bodies, or how the water can even become contaminated before coming into homes.

Learning ways that individuals can protect water sources through the suggested methods is a great starting point for children. A Next-Generation Science Standard for kindergarten, K-ESS3-3: *Communicate solutions that will reduce the impact of humans on the land, water, air, and/or other living things in the local environment*, calls for students in the early grades to begin this process. However, as children mature, understanding larger scale threats to water sources, particularly in urban and lower-income areas, should also be understood if we hope to prepare a generation ready, able, and willing to address these needs. NGSS 3-ESS3-1 makes this clear as students are required to, *Make a claim about the merit of a design solution that reduces the impacts of a weather-related hazard.* In order to meet this standard in an authentic and meaningful way, students will need to explore real-world examples of how humans have failed to conserve water responsibly and what potential solutions exist. Without this, students could leave elementary school with the false impression that all that is needed to effectively conserve water is to turn the faucet off when they brush their teeth.

As students learn about Earth systems, weather, and climate, a commonly taught topic is natural water disasters. One government resource produced by the US Geological Survey and the US Department of the Interior,[8] offers teachers detailed lesson plans to address water disasters. A review of lessons on floods is instructive of the opportunities present with this resource. For example, the overview for lesson 2 is, "Students will explore the tools scientists use to track floods and the damage caused by floods. Students will also understand how floods affect low-lying areas and how humans have developed and live in these parts of our country."[9]

Through the suggested activities of lesson 2, students can explore threats to communities who live in coastal areas and even analyze damages caused by flooding. The focus for the tasks is explained as, "for students to experience how real scientists record information." A suggested culminating task is for students to analyze a picture of coastal flooding in New England brought on by a storm and based on their observations to "create a five-paragraph story. Write the story as the person living in one of the houses shown."[10]

Lesson 3 is designed for students to continue the study of flooding by gaining an understanding of the importance of floodplains. Once again students are exposed to lots of data and information, such as, "By 2050, a majority of U.S. coastal areas are likely to be threatened by 30 or more days of flooding each year."[11] The final lesson in the series, lesson 4, focuses on the role that barriers, both natural and human-made, can play to direct or delay floodwaters in order to lessen the severity or the timing of the flood's arrival. Once again important information is available to the students such as, flooding is the most frequent severe weather threat and the costliest natural disaster facing the United States; major hurricanes can create storm surges in coastal areas and heavy rain and flooding hundreds of miles inland; and, flash flooding is the #1 weather-related killer in the United States.[12]

One of the suggested activities for lesson 4 is for students to "watch the video Reducing Flood Risks by Restoring Coral Reefs to understand how barrier reefs can improve the negative effects of coastal floods." A follow-up activity is for the students to write a response to the question, "How would you use this knowledge if you were a scientist or engineer?" Lesson 4 and all of the learning experiences and content presented in the other lessons represent important information and many opportunities for students to gain an understanding of the challenges of floods and some methods to address the problem, as well as develop many academic and soft skills. However, the role humans are playing in creating conditions that worsen floods, contribute to climate change and shifting weather patterns, and the degradation of the coral reefs aren't addressed. Neither are socio-environmental issues such as who bears the costs when floods occur due to poor planning and management of systems? For example, in 2019 when impaired levees failed to hold back the swelling Arkansas, Mississippi, and Missouri rivers, inland flooding caused $20 billion in damages and left many farmers with destroyed crops.[13] Although farmers received financial support from emergency assistance and flood insurance, many were left to absorb huge losses.[14]

Students should learn about causes, consequences, and potential remedies for floods, as floods are the most common and among the deadliest disasters in the United States. This point is particularly important given warnings from scientists that global warming will continue to cause sea levels to rise and extreme weather patterns, such as heavy rains, which are expected to increase flood-prone areas by nearly half in this century.[15] Learning through real-life cases offers students the opportunity to explore the human dimensions of these disasters. One such case is Hurricane Katrina and the city of New Orleans.

In 2005, as Hurricane Katrina hit New Orleans, levees failed to hold back the rising waters, which caused massive flooding in the city, many deaths, destruction of neighborhoods, loss of homes, and forced relocation of thousands of people. Lower-income and Black people were particularly hard hit.[16] As the city was rebuilt, home prices soared, and many of the former residents could no longer afford to live in communities their families had inhabited for generations. The cost of floods is most often measured in destruction of property and the cost of rebuilding; however, the social and psychological impacts on people should also be understood. While the hurricane was a natural disaster, a federal investigation determined that the failure of the levees was caused by "negligent operation of the levees" by the army, US army corps of engineers,[17] and thus could have been avoided. For many of the residents of New Orleans, the event represents a history of negligent and unequal treatment of many of the nation's poor and people of color. Thus, if we truly want to prepare students in the upper elementary grades to meet standard 4-ESS3-2, *Generate and compare multiple solutions to reduce the impacts of natural Earth processes on humans*, they need to understand the varied factors that contribute to disasters, including the role of humans.

The Role of Social Studies in Teaching About Water

Where can and should students learn about the human dimensions of flooding, water pollution, loss of water sources, and so on? It might seem logical to think that social studies is where students will gain understandings of the relationship between humans and water; however, when it comes to the study of water, this relationship is usually reduced to the utilitarian value of water for settlement and advancement of civilizations.

In the elementary social studies curriculum, learning about the characteristics of different bodies of water is typical. Students learn facts such as, "Oceans are areas of salty water that fill enormous basins on the Earth's surface."[18] or the differences between a sea and a lake. These concepts are usually taught as part of geography and most often require students to memorize characteristics, which they then show mastery of through multiple-choice type assessments.

The significance of water is also taught in the context of how civilizations evolved. For example, the ancient Egyptians benefited from the flooding of the Nile River, which left behind sediments in the soil that supported the growth of crops. Students also learn that early civilizations began harnessing the power of water through irrigation. This advancement enabled surplus crops to be grown in Mesopotamia, which is considered one of the steps needed for civilization to develop.

In a typical elementary school curriculum, students learn about the role of water for trade. After all, Columbus was seeking a faster route to Asia when he set off from Spain in 1492. As students learn about the period leading up to European exploration and colonization, they once again learn that improved technology led to advancements in sailing and navigation that paved the way for more trade opportunities with foreign lands and ultimately the settlement of the Americas. Once Europeans began to settle in the present-day United States, students learn that the Jamestown settlement was chosen because of water. The *Historic Jamestowne* website explains the significance of water to the settlement as, "The site was surrounded by water on three sides (it was not fully an island yet) and was far inland; both meant it was easily defensible against possible Spanish attacks. The water was also deep enough that the English could tie their ships at the shoreline."[19] As settlement of the British colonies proceeds, students will learn that cities such as New York and Boston were established next to deep harbors that allowed ships access. The underlying narrative is limited to the usefulness of water bodies and how humans have mastered technology to use the water to achieve their goals.

The role that water has played in global conflicts is rarely, if ever, addressed. Yet humans have been fighting over access to this precious resource for centuries. In the United States, the battles span the history of European settlement up to the present day. One example is the Winnipesaukee Water War that occurred in the 1850s in New England. When powerful New England manufacturers needed energy to power their mills, they found a source in the New Hampshire lake region. Through a series of dams and canals, they were able to manipulate the flow of water, and by 1850 they controlled 45 miles of the Merrimack River, and they took control of 103 square miles of New Hampshire waters, including Winnipesaukee, Squam, Winnisquam, and Newfound lakes.[20]

The impact on the region was felt by farmers and local businesses: "As New Hampshire's waters drained away to Massachusetts, they carried away the wealth of the farmers and small business owners to the pocketbooks of powerful industrialists."[21] Local farmers fought back by trying to destroy dams and file lawsuits against the company. In the end, control of the waters became less of an issue when steam power came to replace water power in the Massachusetts factories. Most students will only learn of the New England textile industry as part of the growth of the US economy and a triumph of innovation and technology, rather than a struggle over water access that pitted independent farmers and merchants against large business interests. Competition over water continues to be an issue in the United States (e.g., CA farmers v. the state)[22] and globally, so why aren't students taught about this aspect over water?

Similarly, elementary and even secondary students rarely look at how lack of access to clean drinking water and adequate sanitation has shaped conflicts, caused disease and death, and led to responses by governments, international organizations, and aid groups. Therefore, it is also worth asking why students don't learn that access to clean water is considered to be a human right? As with other topics that have been discussed in previous chapters, the story of water as presented in elementary education traditionally can leave children thinking that in many ways humans have harnessed the power of water for their own gains and that threats concerning water come from nature. This narrative leaves out the role that humans have played in fighting over water, blocking others from sufficient water access, polluting water, and deepening water crises through land and building management practices, as well as actions causing climate change. We will next look at how this narrative can be reimagined to correct for these omissions and truly prepare young people for their future.

An EcoJustice Critique of Conventional Approach

Students need foundational knowledge to build upon. If we return to Bloom's taxonomy (discussed in detail in Chapter 1), we know that before students can get to the higher levels of applying and evaluating information, they first need to know it (knowledge/remember) and understand (comprehension) content. We know that these cognitive processes are necessary to move to the highest levels of creation (synthesis). Therefore, it is totally appropriate for students to learn about the water cycle, the forms that water takes, and so on, but an EcoJustice education calls on us to build on these concepts. Sadly, children today are experiencing the impacts of climate change and will be required to adapt and hopefully work to solve the problems this brings. Therefore, we can't ignore issues like the increased severity of storms and how this impacts the water cycle, particularly when it comes to natural disasters like flooding. Pillar I envisions *an education where students develop an understanding and value of the interconnectedness of all living beings and systems.* Among the components embedded in Pillar I are for students to: *acknowledge that our well-being is interconnected with the well-being of our planet; to accept responsibility for the part we play in the ecological web of life;* and *to care for the welfare of all beings.* What might teaching of the water cycle look like with these goals in mind?

The lesson referenced above, *Day in the Life of a Drop,* can easily be expanded on by teaching children that sometimes due to human actions, water can become contaminated and harmful to those who drink or bathe with it. The water crisis in Flint, Michigan, is a perfect and tragic example of how a water source was polluted with contaminants that corroded old lead pipes, which then released metal into the water that was piped into homes. This caused many health problems, including lead poisoning of children in the Flint community.[23] Even the drinking water in our nation's capital was found in 2024 to have thirty-seven contaminants, with thirteen at levels above the Environmental Working Group's health-based limits.[24] Learning about examples such as these can help children understand that this is a reality that needs action by people and governments.

Younger children can learn about the Flint water crisis through age-appropriate resources such as the book *Learning, Recycling and Becoming Little Heroes* written by Gale Glover to teach other children about the water crisis in her community of Flint, and the actions that even children took to help others. Glover explains, "Where I live, we have to drink bottled water and even brush our teeth with it. Then you're a hero . . . I've seen kids like as young as 3 years old out there volunteering, passing out water."[25] The model lessons shared in this chapter also highlight Flint, Michigan and how an eight-year-old girl helped hand out water to her community. By learning about the crisis, students can come to understand that human actions can impact the environment, animals, and other humans and see how interconnected we are. How else can we teach children to care for the welfare of others if we don't give them opportunities to understand the experiences of others? Children would also see great models of civic engagement among children and aspects of Pillar II are integrated: *An orientation toward innovative, action-oriented, and collaborative problem-solving; Accept our power as change agents;* and *Build skills of proactive citizenship.*

According to the World Health Organization, "1.4 million people die each year as a result of inadequate drinking-water, sanitation and hygiene. The vast majority of these deaths are in low- and middle-income countries."[26] These statistics should be enough to move people to learn about the crisis, what is being done and what can still be done to mitigate the death and disease caused by a lack of access to clean water and safe sanitation systems. However, in the increasingly isolationist "America First" attitude in the United States, this might seem to be the problem of "others." The reality is this is not only a situation in the developing world. According to a 2023 fact sheet by the United States Mission to the

UN, "more than two million Americans lack access to clean drinking water at home, and more than one million Americans don't have the plumbing required to flush a toilet."[27]

The notion that access to clean water is a human right is not well represented in the traditional elementary social studies curriculum, even though there are Americans today who don't have regular access to clean water. The plight of many Indigenous people living on reservations today is not taught, even when the situation violates treaties that were made between the US government and many Indigenous peoples, or given the fact that in the wealthiest nation in the world this is occurring. As social studies is the field tasked with helping children understand the rights and responsibilities of individuals, the role of government, and so on, teaching about human rights should be included.

Only two states in the United States recognize access to water as a human right. California has recognized this right under law since 2012, and Virginia took similar action in 2025, passing Joint Resolution 538 which

> affirms that access to clean, potable water in amounts sufficient for an acceptable standard of living is a fundamental human right. The resolution recognizes the essential role of water in public health, economic stability, and social well-being. It serves as a guiding principle for the Commonwealth, highlighting the state's responsibility to ensure safe and reliable water access for all residents, particularly marginalized and historically underserved communities.[28]

The opportunities to build on science and social studies lessons to address water scarcity and competition are clear. Students could examine what droughts are, why they are occurring more frequently, and how this is impacting life in different regions of the world. Students could conduct mini-research projects looking at a water crisis from different perspectives and consider different proposals. Learning about responses by individuals, organizations and governments at all levels can help the children see possibilities for taking action and better understand how our democratic system works. Modifications like these incorporate many components of Pillar I: *Think globally and act locally; Evaluate choices* and *decisions at multiple levels (self, community, state, country) through a systems lens.* Almost all of the components of Pillar II can be furthered through these learning experiences: *Value diverse knowledge and honor that knowledge is constructed from many and sometimes unexpected sources; Imagine new ideas and ways of being that challenge our socialized norms; Recognize the need and power of working in solidarity with others, across perceived difference, to achieve common goals;* and *Build skills of proactive citizenship.* Opportunities to study real-world issues from different perspectives allow for goals of Pillar III to be advanced: *Critically reads the world—uncovering and questioning the social, political, and economic forces that shape our lives; Ongoing self-education and information seeking that mines contradictions and tensions; Reflect and evaluate the ongoing process of our socialization and the mechanisms that shape our ways of being;* and *Change direction and/or one's mind when evidence suggests it is warranted.* Lastly, many elements of Pillar IV can also be fostered: *Connect ideas across disciplinary boundaries; Apply content knowledge in real world, interconnected contexts;* and *Understand the relevance and value of why they are learning what they are learning.*

When concepts like the water collection process and surface water are taught, students learn that some surfaces are more porous than others. The idea that when we pave over land with materials that aren't porous, drainage systems are needed can be explored as children can easily see puddles in the streets of their community or perhaps on the playground. Stormwater runoff and drainage systems can be introduced to older children through hands-on activities where they can create their own drainage systems. From here, children can learn that some urban areas don't have adequate drainage systems due to lack of resources or outdated systems. The city of Houston is an example of how increasingly more intense storms and heavy rains have wreaked havoc on urban areas. Houston is a flat, paved, low-lying terrain, which makes an effective drainage system paramount. Yet, in lower-income areas, the drainage systems have historically been neglected and were not sufficient to prevent massive flooding from Hurricane Beryl in 2024.[29] Children can view images from the floods and practice photo elicitation. They can also learn how community groups have been formed to respond to the needs of residents following flood disasters, and the role local and federal governments have played in relief and funding projects. Older students can engage in mapping activities where they explore the relationship between areas that tend to flood due to poor drainage systems and local economic factors such as average household income. In this way, *Pillar III: A commitment to investigating socio-environmental issues through the lens of power and* justice can be integrated as children begin to note patterns. Building on traditional science topics by including social studies content also represents *Pillar IV: Transdisciplinary approaches that focus on cross-curricular knowledge and connections rather than siloed thinking that leads to incomplete understandings.*

The opportunities to incorporate the EcoJustice Education Pillars by building on existing curriculum topics and traditional lessons are plentiful; however, we know that teacher confidence is paramount. The next section will help to build your background knowledge about some of the water-related issues of today.

Expanding Teacher Content Knowledge

We begin this section on expanding teacher knowledge regarding water use and water rights by first addressing why and how water is fundamental to life on Earth. Then, we wrestle with the contradictions of a reality where water is being polluted, commodified, dammed, diverted, used, and recycled every moment of every day in a discussion of access to freshwater. We introduce the role of water in climate change and how disruptions in climate are disrupting the predictability and patterns of the water cycle. We then discuss water pollution, broadly introducing The Clean Water Act and the Safe Drinking Water Act that are meant to safeguard US waterways and drinking water. In our section on pollution, we discuss the Flint, Michigan water crisis and the lasting impacts on city residents, as well as microplastics and how they are finding their way into human body tissues. Once again, we seek to honor the ways that Indigenous people have always stewarded and protected water and showcase the heroic activism of the Water Protectors at Standing Rock and briefly discuss how access to affordable, clean water and sanitation resources on Native American reservations continues to be an equity issue. This section concludes with an opportunity for you to hone your critical lens by connecting the dots across topics introduced here, illuminating the implications of household products and their impact on water resources and humans.

Why Water Is Foundational: Scientific Laws and Principles

Water is foundational to life on Earth. All life, with a few rare exceptions, is dependent upon water for its survival. Where and how water is available and useful to all living organisms is governed by a combination of physical laws, chemical principles, and biological processes. We often learned a few of these special rules about water in our time in science classrooms. For example, you might remember that water is a "*universal solvent*" but at the time did not really understand why or how that was important. Well, water can dissolve more substances than any other liquid, which makes it crucial to life as it helps facilitate chemical reactions in our body and in the environment, and it supports the transport of nutrients via the water content in our blood or the sap in a tree. You may also remember *osmosis and diffusion* and how osmosis is the movement of water across membranes (living and man-made). In the human body, the process of osmosis is the way that our kidneys keep our blood water levels stable or how our large intestine works to remove water from the foods we eat. This property of water is what allows for the human-engineered process called reverse osmosis, where salt is removed from ocean water in order to make fresh water. The *thermal properties of water*, its ability to absorb and release heat slowly, is what accounts for the Earth's capacity to regulate the climate and stabilize temperatures. It is this property of water that also prevents all organisms from freezing and overheating in their natural environments.

Finally, water's ability to move between phases—solid, liquid, gas—has allowed water to be cycled and recycled, allowing freshwater to be available for all living things. The water cycle is a common topic in many science classrooms across the K-12 curriculum and is something that many people remember learning about. However, as described in the introduction section, it is often taught devoid of humans and our human footprint. Water, like all matter on Earth, is never really created or destroyed. This means that water is renewable, but its availability as freshwater is limited to where it can be found, accessed, and utilized. This is one of the main reasons that freshwater is available in some places of the world and not others and why it is so essential in shaping ecosystems, climate, and all living things.

Factors Impacting Water Availability

Water is one of the most essential and contested resources on Earth, with access to clean freshwater varying dramatically around the world. This is due in part to natural landforms and geography, but it is also a product of human intervention. Infrastructure, economics, politics, and history have all played a role in limiting access to freshwater for many people across the globe. This section provides an overview of a few water issues that are pressing at this time. Beginning with the effects of climate change, we highlight the increasing strain the Earth has experienced as an intensification of droughts, floods, and water scarcity has been the signature struggle and root cause of many water-related issues. The scarcity and unpredictability in the water system created by climate change leads into a discussion of pollution from industrial, agricultural, and household sources that further degrade water quality and ecosystems. We end this section by highlighting Indigenous water rights, underscoring the need for justice, sovereignty, and sustainable stewardship rooted in traditional knowledge and legal recognition. By drawing upon examples from across the United States and beyond, we hope this section reveals the deep interconnections and tensions at play between power and socio-environmental justice when it comes to equitable water stewardship.

Climate Change, Flooding, and Sea Level Rise

Climate change is impacting the ways that water moves in the water cycle and having differential impacts on nations and cities all over the world. Specifically, as atmospheric temperatures are increasing, more water is evaporating from surface water, vegetation, and soil. This acceleration of the water cycle is increasing the odds of both severe drought and heavier precipitation that wreaks havoc on people and the environment.[30] When water evaporates over land areas, it creates more drought-like conditions. When conditions are right for rain events, there is more water raining down and with greater intensity. For example, in 2023, a heavy one-day rain from Mediterranean storm Daniel caused massive flooding across eastern Libya, breaching two dams that sent flooding water through the coastal city of Derna, destroying entire neighborhoods and sweeping bridges, cars, and people out to sea.[31] In 2023, California had record-setting rain and snowfall which increased vegetation. The increased vegetation was fuel for the devastating January 2025 wildfires that occurred once drought-like conditions returned to the region.[32]

The sheer volume of the Earth's oceans has allowed them to absorb the increased heat as a result of climate change; however, this hasn't come without a cost. Warmer ocean water has led to more intense and frequent hurricanes. The National Oceanic and Atmospheric Administration is predicting above normal hurricanes for the 2025 Atlantic hurricane season, citing warmer ocean temperatures leading to more higher category storms with stronger winds and greater rainfall.[33] 2025 marks the twentieth anniversary of Hurricane Katrina, when the Black-majority neighborhood of the Lower Ninth Ward was decimated by flood waters over 20 feet high due to a poorly maintained levee system. As of today, only a fraction of the original residents have returned, and Southern Louisiana is the most vulnerable part of the country to climate change due to its low-lying, low-income areas with neglected infrastructure that are prone to major flooding.[34] Hurricane Helene, which made landfall in Florida on September 26, 2024, brought massive flooding to southern states in the ensuing days, with parts of North Carolina experiencing over 30 inches of rain in a 24-hour period.[35] These storms are becoming more and more common and having social, economic, and environmental impacts on communities, but they are not the only way that climate change is disrupting the water cycle.

In addition to increased drought and precipitation, other aspects of the water cycle are impacted by climate change including glacial and snowpack melting which directly impacts sea level rise and displacement of diverse populations living at or below sea level. A recent study published in the journal *Science*, "estimates that glaciers globally will lose 39 (range, 15 to 55)% of their mass relative to 2020, corresponding to a global mean sea-level rise of 113 (range, 43 to 204) mm even if temperatures stabilized at present-day conditions."[36] The study goes on to state that with the current warming of 2.7 degrees Celsius, glaciers would disappear from the Western United States, the Russian Arctic, and Iceland and that glacial melt will continue for centuries even if climate warming stopped today.[37] Glacial melt is a serious cause for concern as it leads to sea level rise, and as freshwater stored in icecaps and snowpacks melts, it runs off to the seas where it becomes saltwater.

The people in the Pacific Island nations of Samoa, Tuvalu, Palau, the Cook Islands, and Fiji are not only experiencing and enduring the effects of sea level rise, they are also leading the fight to protect their countries from the impacts of the climate crisis. A 2024 NASA report showed irreversible sea level rise impacting the Pacific Island nations with a roughly 6-inch rise in sea level expected over the next 30 years.[38] Despite accounting for just 0.02 percent of global emissions, the Pacific islands are disproportionately impacted by rising sea levels with 90 percent of the population living within 5 kilometers of the coast and half the infrastructure within 500 meters of the sea.[39] However, the Pacific Island nations are fighting to protect their homes and the oceans. Young people in Tuvalu are planting mangrove trees to absorb rising tides and in Fiji, communities are cultivating heat-resistant corals to replace corals that have been bleached by ocean acidification as a result of increased CO_2 levels. These nations are also showing up to international conferences on climate change. At the February 2025 meeting of the Intergovernmental Panel on Climate Change (IPCC62) in Hangzhou, China, Pacific Island Nations continued to call for "1.5 to stay alive" referring to the 1.5 degree Celsius global temperature increase that is associated with the warming climate.[40] This rallying cry is a plea to the world from some of the nations most vulnerable to climate change.

Currently, 83.4 million people have been internally displaced as a result of conflict, violence, or natural disaster, and climate change is typically a contributing factor to all three of these causes.[41] In climate vulnerable Bangladesh, the number of internally displaced people due to natural disasters has risen for four consecutive years and reached 2.4 million in 2024, predominantly as a result of flooding during the monsoon season.[42] All of these climate-related issues speak to disruptions in the hydrologic (water) cycle, and as scarcity of freshwater increases, threats to water quality via pollution exacerbate the disparities in access to clean water.

Water Pollution

There are countless examples, nationally and globally, that highlight the many ways water has become polluted and contaminated by manufacturing, agriculture, wastewater and sewage, oil spills, and everyday household products (i.e., shampoos, household cleaners, lawn fertilizers, and weed killers). Exacerbating these direct polluting sources are the countless ways that water is indirectly polluted by old and failing infrastructure (i.e., pipes), runoff from densely populated areas, farms, and landfills, and erosion of sediment from deforestation. Exploring all of the pollutants and their impacts is beyond the scope of this section, but we wanted to review a brief history of water pollution that led to the creation of The Clean Water Act and The Safe Drinking Water Act and discuss the role each has played in reducing pollution in our ecosystems and drinking water.

Water pollution has existed as long as human civilization, but its recognition as a public health crisis emerged over the last few centuries in response to the industrial revolution and culminated in two landmark environmental laws—The Clean Water Act (CWA) in 1972 and The Safe Drinking Water Act (SDWA) in 1974. Early pollutants were primarily human and animal waste, other forms of organic waste, and early chemical waste. The eighteenth and nineteenth centuries saw the rise of industries like coal, petroleum, and steel which all dumped untreated waste into local bodies of water. Contaminants included bleach, acids, dyes, petroleum, and heavy metals. This time also saw the rise of cities where the increased concentration of people made managing sewage waste imperative. Outbreaks of typhoid occurred tied to exposure to raw sewage and contaminated seafood like oysters.[43] Many cities and towns are still dealing with pollutants dumped into rivers and lakes unchecked during this time, when little to no regulations existed to prevent contamination. Public response to pollution in waterways came to a roar when in 1969, fouled by industrial pollution, Ohio's Cuyahoga River caught on fire.

The image of a river on fire was a powerful symbol for the creation of the Clean Water Act in 1972. The Act was a direct response to widespread public outcry over polluted rivers and lakes and was passed to protect surface waterways and wetlands from pollution and destruction. There are multiple ways that the Clean Water Act works, including setting water quality standards for surface water, making sure it is clean enough for drinking and activities like swimming and fishing. Under the Act, any facility that is discharging pollutants into surface waters must obtain a permit, limiting the type and number of pollutants. This includes sewage treatment plants, something that the Act provided funding for to cities and towns, helping to ensure that water discharge was properly treated. Finally, the Clean Water Act was designed to protect wetlands and other small waterways that are ecologically significant for cleaning water, buffering against storms and flooding, and providing unique habitat for a diversity of species. To date, the law has prevented 700 billion pounds of pollutants from industry and wastewater from entering waterways.[44] However, in recent years, the Trump Administration, upheld by the Supreme Court, has reduced the wetland areas and streams under the law's protection and cut positions and funding to the Environmental Protection Agency (EPA), the regulatory agency that enforces the Clean Water Act. President Trump has proposed a 55 percent cut to the EPA budget for the 2026 Fiscal year[45] which would impact grant-funded programs "designed to boost access to clean air, water and land in communities living in substandard conditions or bearing a disproportionate burden of pollution."[46]

In 1974 the Safe Drinking Water Act was passed to protect drinking water and underground aquifers. It was designed as a consumer safeguard by setting maximum levels of contaminants like lead, arsenic, and bacteria in drinking water. It also required water utilities to test, monitor, and treat contaminants in the water. The Clean Water Act and the Safe Drinking Water Act work together to protect access to clean drinking water. Seventy-four percent of drinking water comes from surface water sources like rivers, lakes, and reservoirs, so the cleaner we keep these sources of water, the less treatment our drinking water needs. The EPA is also responsible for enforcement of the Safe Drinking Water Act, but with cutbacks and layoffs impacting the agency, their capacity to regulate and monitor violations of these laws has been compromised. In May 2025, the EPA announced its intentions to "eliminate or substantially delay urgently needed protections for up to 105 million people across the country whose drinking water is contaminated with PFAS at levels exceeding the 2024 standards."[47] PFAS, also known as forever chemicals because they don't break down easily in the environment, are synthetic chemicals that have been used in everything from nonstick frying pans to water-resistant fabrics. These chemicals accumulate in the living and nonliving environment and have been found in water, soil, rocks, and food, and may be linked to harmful health outcomes for humans and other organisms.[48] In response to this announcement, Food & Water Watch, a nonprofit organization whose mission is to protect people's health, communities, and democracy by advocating for sustainable food, clean water, and a livable climate, wrote:

> Today's decision to rollback the Biden EPA's rules was in response to a consolidated lawsuit from water utility associations and industrial associations, including the National Association of Manufacturers, the American Chemistry Council and Chemours. The chemical lobby has long-fought regulations on these toxic substances, while not disclosing a growing body of evidence linking their products to serious health problems. A Food & Water Watch report found the chemical industry spent more than $110 million from 2019–2022 alone on lobbying Congress on scores of bills, including many to address the crisis of PFAS contamination throughout the country. The Trump Administration has stacked the EPA with former executives and staff from the American Chemistry Council, including Nancy Beck and Lynn Ann Dekleva and lawyers like David Fotouhi, who have defended companies from PFAS pollution claims.[49]

The above decision is a clear example of corporate and industry influence over the regulatory agency designed to enforce and regulate them. The EPA was created in 1970 to protect public health, but it, like many other federal agencies, is now a place where former industry executives occupy high-ranking positions and in turn control the very regulations that limit their production and profits.

Similar to PFAS is another persistent and widespread pollutant that also accumulates up the food chain causing environmental and health risks. *Microplastics* and their smaller counterpart, *nanoplastics*, are small synthetic plastic particles that have been found in oceans, soils, the atmosphere, and the human body. A recent study revealed that microplastics and nanoplastics have been found in high concentrations in brain tissue, as well as in kidney and liver tissue of deceased humans.[50] The pathways for exposure to microplastics are multifold, including applications of certain makeups containing microplastics being absorbed directly by the skin, as well as ingestion of contaminated water or inhalation of airborne particles into the lungs. These pollutants are also found in the foods we eat and are reducing the photosynthetic capacity of contaminated plants, which could have an impact on food supply.[51] Microplastics have even been found near the summit of Mount Everest and in the Mariana Trench, the deepest part of the oceans.[52] Remember that plastic is a relatively recent invention (first synthesized in 1907[53]) and is designed to be used for brief periods of time but takes many hundreds of years to decompose. Therefore, the amplification and intensity of microplastics in our drinking water, our food, and our bodies will continue to be studied for their lasting health impacts. There are many types of microplastics and they can impact aquatic organisms by being directly ingested or moving up the food chain when a smaller organism is eaten by a larger one. Studies are being conducted on the impact of microplastics on aquatic systems and findings suggest that eating microplastics can clog up digestion and impact the liver function of fish and other organisms.[54] PFAS and microplastics highlight the ecological health risks posed by new and emergent contaminants in our water systems, but more traditional threats, such as pollution from aging and corroded pipes, continue to jeopardize drinking water quality and public health.

Pollution comes from many sources and impacts all of our water. Contaminated water can be most dangerous when it is coming from the pipes inside your home. The story of toxic drinking water in Flint, Michigan, is one example from the last decade that highlights once again that the burden of environmental justice issues falls on those most vulnerable, typically low-income communities. Although far from the only case of people being exposed to contaminated water, what happened in Flint, Michigan, shows the intersection of government negligence, poor water management systems, and aging infrastructure. Flint is a majority-black city with 40 percent of people living in poverty.[55] In 2014, a nearly bankrupt government, in an effort to save money, shifted the city water source from Lake Huron to the Flint River. The Flint River was an intermediate solution while a new pipeline was being built to another water source. Residents of Flint were assured the river was safe to drink by government officials with no corrosion control treatment in place for the water coming into homes. Most of the pipes that carried the water were aging iron and lead pipes and, without the corrosion control, the water reacted with the pipes, breaking down the lead and contaminating household drinking water. Bottled water became required for the residents of Flint, with millions of bottles sent and distributed for free up until 2018 when the then Michigan Governor Snyder declared the drinking water was safely restored.[56] Despite tests that showed that lead levels had been reduced and technically the water was "safe," the long-term physical, social, emotional, cognitive, and psychological impacts continue to haunt city residents.

NPR has a step-by-step look at how this socio-environmental crisis unfolded, and we encourage you to read it to see the multiple levels of deception and cover-up by state and local government officials that allowed this situation to exacerbate.[57] The most vulnerable to the contaminated water were children whose "elevated levels of lead in their blood doubled—and in some parts of the city, tripled. . . . There is no safe level of lead exposure. The neurotoxin harms nearly all of the body's functions, is linked to premature births and miscarriages, and has been shown to cause learning and behavior problems, among other ailments, in children."[58] Five years after the crisis, a study showed that one in four adults suffered from PTSD[59] and ten years later Flint residents still deal with ongoing physical, mental, and emotional challenges, with "rates of depression exceeding national averages for both children and adults. And almost half of the parents enrolled in the Flint Registry, which tracks the health of over 21,000 people affected by the water crisis, said that their children were living with behavioral problems as of 2022. These included attention issues, aggression, depression, hyperactivity, and trouble adapting."[60] The case of Flint, Michigan, received national attention, but there are many other vulnerable communities continuing to be exposed to contaminated water. Cities like Trenton, NJ,[61] and Chicago, IL,[62] are two cities currently experiencing unsafe drinking water conditions, and a California study revealed that "almost 400 water systems serving nearly a million Californians don't meet state requirements for safe and reliable drinking water supplies . . . more than two-thirds of these failing water systems serve communities of color, and more than half are in places struggling with poverty and pollution."[63] Vulnerable communities also include First Nations people, the original water protectors, who have been at the center of water rights and access battles, especially in the United States.

Indigenous Water Rights

As we discussed in Chapter 4, the legacy of settler colonialism has wrought much harm to Indigenous communities, whose dependence on access to clean water has been severely restricted due to displacement onto reservations. Indigenous communities also take seriously their responsibility as water protectors and seek to reduce harm to water resources wherever possible, especially when they are impacting their communities. In a beautiful opening to her piece entitled, *Indigenous Women and their connection to the Earth and Her Waters*, Kaya Hill, a Haudenosaunee from Six Nations of the Grand River territory, writes,

> Our Mother, the Earth, is home to all living beings. Water is the life blood of Mother Earth. Her waters not only cleanse and nourish her own body, but the bodies of each living being she carries. In this way, water represents the interconnection between all living beings. The Indigenous peoples of North America recognize this sacred relationship and interconnectedness, as water is an integral facet of our ways of life that have sustained our people for thousands of years. Traditional activities of many Indigenous nations depend on water for transportation, drinking, cleaning, and habitat for all of the living beings we depend on, such as the plants and animals that our ancestors relied on for sustenance.[64]

And the Native Women's Association of Canada writes,

> Water is considered sacred in many Indigenous communities and cultures around the world. For these communities, water is more than just a resource, it is a way of life and a crucial aspect of their cultural identity. Indigenous peoples have relied on water for their livelihood, spiritual practices, and traditional knowledge for generations. They have a deep understanding

> of their interconnectedness between water, land, and all living things. In many Indigenous cultures, water is seen as a living entity with its own spirit, and it is believed that humans have a responsibility to protect and care for it. For Indigenous peoples, water is not just a commodity, but a language, a community, and a source of knowledge and law.[65]

Both of these excerpts reflect a very different relationship to water than many of us raised in the United States are familiar with. While many of us participate in recreational activities that take place near and in water, so few of us hold any reverence or responsibility for our role in protecting these places. In contrast, Indigenous communities have been at the forefront of battles to remove dams from rivers, stop pipeline projects with the potential to contaminate drinking water, and demand affordable and accessible water for Native people living on reservations.

The Lakota phrase "Mní wičhóni," or "Water is life," became a powerful rallying call during the fight over the location of the Dakota Access Pipeline project. This project sought to move oil across the Missouri River in close proximity to the Standing Rock Sioux Tribal Land and in the path of Lake Oahe, the freshwater source for the reservation. Despite formal objections and legal challenges, in 2016, the Army Corps of Engineers approved the path of the pipeline buried under Lake Oahe.[66] Despite promises that the pipeline would not leak, hundreds of reported leaks had been documented at other locations along existing pipelines. In response, the Standing Rock Sioux Tribe, along with over one-hundred tribes from all over the world, protested the project on the grounds that the pipeline was violating Article II of the Fort Laramie Treaty, which guarantees the "undisturbed use and occupation" of reservation lands surrounding the proposed location of the pipeline and that any spill would damage their water supply and cultural lands.[67]

The protestors identified themselves as the Water Protectors and created encampments along the route of the pipeline to restrict building. A University of Arizona report investigating UN Human Rights Violations at the encampments found that "during the 7 months from September 2016 to February 2017, at least 76 different law enforcement agencies, 27 federal agencies, and private security firms hired by the oil company were present at some time. Law enforcement and private security donned heavy-duty riot gear and used military grade weapons against Water Protectors."[68] In an effort to stop the project, the Obama Administration refused to grant a federal easement for the pipe under Lake Oahe. However, within his first days of office in 2017, President Trump signed an executive order that resumed construction of the Dakota Access Pipeline and the project was completed and operational by summer 2017.[69] The activism of the Water Protectors took on many forms, including nonviolent actions (i.e., standing on the land to prevent construction, youth-led prayer runs to Washington, D.C.),[70] prayer ceremonies,[71] legal advocacy, media campaigns, and visual and spoken word art forms.[72] Solidarity and a shared sense of responsibility are some of the biggest lessons learned from Standing Rock, with thousands of people visiting the site in person and over a million people checking in on the Standing Rock Indian Reservation on Facebook.[73] The Dakota Access Pipeline protest gained spotlight attention and highlighted the Indigenous fight against big oil, but many Indigenous people living on reservations are involved in the everyday struggle to access clean water.

Native communities across the country lack access to clear water with one in ten Native Americans lacking access to clean water[74] and an estimated 48 percent of households on Native American reservations do not have access to reliable water sources, clean drinking water, or adequate sanitation.[75] In a US Senate Committee on Indian Affairs Oversight Hearing on Water as a Trust Resource, Heather Tanana, the initiative lead on universal access to Clean Water for Tribal Communities and a citizen of the Navajo Nation, shared in her testimony that,

> Native American households are more likely to lack adequate water services than any other group in the United States. Existing water infrastructure on reservations continues to deteriorate and inadequate water quality remains pervasive across Indian Country. According to the U.S. Water Alliance, while Black and Latinx households are almost twice as likely as white households to lack indoor plumbing, Native American households are about *19 times* as likely.[76]

Many Indigenous communities suffer from lack of access to water infrastructure, as well as exposure to contaminated drinking water. A 2021 report on the Universal Access to Clean Water for Tribes in the Colorado River Basin notes that the Hopi Tribe has suffered from arsenic-contaminated water since the 1960s when the initial drinking water system was first installed. This translates to an estimated 75 percent of people living on the Hopi land exposed to arsenic-contaminated water posing health risks like "diabetes, skin discoloration, cancer, blindness, and partial paralysis."[77] Once again this section provides only a tiny fraction of the ways that Indigenous communities in the United States continue to face extensive and profound water-related socio-environmental justice issues rooted in historical and ongoing inequities.

Implications of Current Water Issues on Our Ecological and Social Systems

Thinking about all the ways that water is used by humans and its significance to all ecological systems is important to honor. Access to clean water and water infrastructure is not a guarantee, even in the United States, as our discussion of Flint, Michigan and the Navajo Nation reveals. Water pollution is happening at every moment of our lives, either by industry, agriculture, or household use, and many of the pollutants that enter our waterways also enter into the tissues of plants and animals and accumulate up the food chain with the highest levels of toxic contamination in the human body! We don't often talk about the social and environmental justice impacts of water. Most of us turn on our faucets or flush our toilets without knowing where the water is coming from or where it goes. This level of ignorance can be changed by bringing in deeper explorations of water access into our schools with a focus on equity and connection between the science of the hydrologic and atmospheric systems that regulate our climate and the social forces that intersect with these systems. Below we highlight a few more statistics related to water use, water contamination, and access for humans and ecosystems, and the environmental justice implications for people in the United States.

- People who meet their recommended water intake through tap water ingest an additional 4,000 plastic particles annually, while those who drink only bottled water ingest an additional 90,000.[78]
- US oil refineries discharge nearly half a billion gallons of wastewater into waterways every day. That includes heavy metals like arsenic and mercury, oils and greases, and industrial salts. In 2021 alone, eighty-one refineries discharged 60,000 pounds of selenium, which causes mutations in fish. Those refineries also discharged nearly 16 million pounds of nitrogen, which creates algae blooms that suck oxygen from the water and kill fish.[79]
- Per- and polyfluoroalkyl substances (PFAS), also known as forever chemicals, have been found in public and private waters in all 50 states. 143 million people in communities throughout the United States have drinking water that has tested positive for PFAS.[80] These chemicals have been linked to thyroid disease, decreased fertility, endocrine disruption, cognitive problems, and immune system impacts (e.g., reduced response to vaccines).[81]
- Per EPA estimates, fifty-nine chemical fertilizer plants discharged nearly 90 million pounds of pollution into waterways in 2019. Pollutants include nitrogen, selenium, chromium, zinc, iron, nickel, cadmium, cyanide, and lead.[82]
- Inorganic chemical plants are some of the biggest industrial dischargers of toxic pollution in the United States. These plants make products like PVC and vinyl chloride, which recently made headlines after spilling in the train derailment at East Palestine, Ohio. The EPA estimates that 229 of these chemical plants dumped two billion pounds of pollution into our waterways in 2019 alone.[83]
- Today, almost four decades after the Clean Water Act's deadline for "fishable and swimmable" waters across the United States, 51 percent of assessed river and stream miles across the United States—more than 700,000 miles of waterways—remain impaired with pollution, as well as 55 percent of lake acres and 26 percent of estuary miles.[84]
- 10 percent of US households spend more than 4.5 percent of their annual income on water and sewer services, with the lowest-income decile paying an average of 6.8 percent of their income.[85]
- About two million people in the United States lack access to running water or indoor plumbing in their homes. Another thirty million people live where drinking water systems violate safety rules.[86]
- Older infrastructure is more likely to include lead pipes, which Congress banned in the 1980s due to the substantial health risks of lead exposure. Despite this Congressional ban, approximately fifteen to twenty-two million people nationally are still served by lead water lines.[87]
- There is a link between drinking water quality violations and social vulnerability in the United States, with violations disproportionately affecting the most vulnerable

communities. Approximately 70 percent of the population with drinking water violations ranked in the highest social vulnerability category, with many different social parameters, beyond income, linked to different drinking water quality violations.[88]

- There are five garbage patches of floating plastic in the oceans today. The largest one is the Great Pacific Garbage Patch and is roughly the size of Texas with more than 1.8 trillion pieces of plastic in the patch and weighing an estimated 100,000 tons.[89]
- One million marine animals are killed each year due to plastic debris in the ocean.[90]

Honing Your Critical Lens

How we use, access, distribute, and protect water highlights a connection between ecological limits, power, and inequity. Once again, we see that issues of water are complex and impacts on the water cycle have global implications that are not bounded by region or zip code. This means that lack of access to clean and affordable water is something that will impact everyone and therefore should be cared about by all. Sea level rise might be disproportionately impacting Pacific Island nations, but a large percentage of the world's population lives along coastlines and includes a wide range of socioeconomic categories. Hurricane Sandy destroyed many homes in affluent parts of New Jersey and Long Island, while Hurricane Katrina affected low-income communities in the Ninth Ward. These hurricanes cause similar damage; however, the important difference from an EcoJustice perspective is who had the means and access to rebuild and who is displaced and unable to return to their home. Water pollution similarly impacts everyone on the planet, but it is the most vulnerable communities, communities of color, Indigenous, rural, and low-income communities that are most often treated as disposable and suffer the compounded impacts of lack of access to clean and affordable water.

The perspective you take on issues of water access, water rights, water affordability, and water pollution matters—what you care about you will bring into your classroom. We always seek to empower you by illuminating connections that are intentionally left obscured. Our hope is that by expanding **your** understanding of how intricately connected water is to our lives and livelihoods on this planet, you can more confidently engage your students in critical discussions that connect the important laws and properties of water with the social and ecological relationships we hold with it. This section provided a brief introduction to water-related socio-environmental issues and our **Instructional Materials** in this chapter will provide lesson overviews and resources for teaching further about these topics in your elementary classrooms. We end this section with an opportunity for you to research and reflect about the role you and your everyday household products play in contributing to water pollution.

Research and Reflection Activity: We have so much control over how we use water in our homes and in our communities—how much we use and what we put down our drains, on our lawns, in our cars, and on our driveways, are our personal choices. But when we don't understand the implications of our choices, making ecological conscious decisions becomes difficult. Ttable 5.1 lists water toxins found in many common household products

Table 5.1. Toxic Chemicals in Household Products and Their Impacts

Chemical	Common Household Sources	Water and Environmental Impacts
Phthalates[a]	Air fresheners, vinyl flooring, detergents, personal care products	Disrupt endocrine systems in aquatic life; bioaccumulate in ecosystems
Triclosan[b]	Antibacterial soaps, toothpaste, deodorants	Harmful to algae and aquatic organisms; leads to antibiotic resistance
Ammonia[c]	Window cleaners, floor cleaners, polishing agents	Toxic to aquatic organisms even at low concentrations
Bleach (Sodium hypochlorite)[d]	Disinfectants, toilet bowl cleaners	Reacts with organic matter to form carcinogenic byproducts (THMs)
Phosphates[e]	Dishwasher and laundry detergents (less common today)	Causes algal blooms and dead zones in water bodies
Volatile Organic Compounds (VOCs)[f]	Aerosol sprays, air fresheners, paint thinners	Contaminate groundwater and contribute to smog
Per- and Polyfluoroalkyl Substances (PFAS)[g]	Stain-resistant sprays, nonstick cookware, water-repellent fabrics	Persistent in the environment; contaminate drinking water and affect human health
Bisphenol A (BPA)[h]	Plastic containers, canned food linings	Leaches into water; endocrine disruptor for both humans and wildlife
Synthetic Fragrances[i]	Personal care products, air fresheners, cleaners	Can contain phthalates and VOCs; toxic to aquatic organisms
Heavy Metals (Lead, Mercury, Cadmium)[j]	Old paint, batteries, thermometers, electronics	Bioaccumulate; highly toxic to marine and freshwater organisms

[a] Natural Resources Defense Council, "Fighting Phthalates," accessed August 10, 2025, https://www.nrdc.org/stories/fighting-phthalates.

[b] Environmental Working Group, "Down the Drain: Where Toxic Chemicals from Industrial Facilities End Up," accessed August 10, 2025, https://www.ewg.org/research/down-drain.

[c] Minnesota Department of Agriculture, "Ecological Effects of Ammonia," accessed August 10, 2025, https://www.mda.state.mn.us/ecological-effects-ammonia.

[d] The Momentum, "How Bleach Damages The Environment And Our Health," accessed August 10, 2025, https://www.themomentum.com/articles/how-bleach-damages-the-environment-and-our-health.

[e] US Environmental Protection Agency, "Indicators: Phosphorus," National Aquatic Resource Surveys, accessed August 10, 2025, https://www.epa.gov/national-aquatic-resource-surveys/indicators-phosphorus.

[f] US Environmental Protection Agency, "Volatile Organic Compounds' Impact on Indoor Air Quality," accessed August 10, 2025, https://www.epa.gov/indoor-air-quality-iaq/volatile-organic-compounds-impact-indoor-air-quality.

[g] Agency for Toxic Substances and Disease Registry, "Per- and Polyfluoroalkyl Substances (PFAS) and Your Health," accessed August 10, 2025, https://www.atsdr.cdc.gov/pfas/index.html.

[h] National Institute of Environmental Health Sciences, "Bisphenol A (BPA)," accessed August 10, 2025, https://www.niehs.nih.gov/health/topics/agents/sya-bpa.

[i] Environmental Working Group, "What is fragrance?" published July 2023, accessed August 10, 2025, https://www.ewg.org/news-insights/news/2023/07/what-fragrance.

[j] Environmental Working Group, "Harmful Heavy Metals: Why They're in Tap Water and How to Reduce Your Exposure," published May 2025, accessed August 10, 2025, https://www.ewg.org/news-insights/news/2025/05/harmful-heavy-metals-why-theyre-tap-water-and-how-reduce-your-exposure.

and their impact on aquatic life as well as terrestrial organisms like us. Read through the list and see where you might be able to make a different choice in what you consume. Also, ask yourself the important questions (see the questions listed here for some examples) that will help you further hone your critical lens. While many of these questions don't lend themselves to simple answers, thinking through them will reveal the connections between consumer choice, corporate power and profit-driven market decisions, and the regulatory role of government agencies like the EPA.

- Why are there so many toxic chemicals in our everyday products?
- Why are chemicals that are banned in other countries still legal to use in the United States?
- Why do some products use language like "natural" or "green" but still contain toxic chemicals?
- Why are products with toxic chemicals sometimes so cheap compared to more environmentally friendly products with less toxic chemicals? Who is then most vulnerable to exposure to toxic chemicals?
- Why are warning labels written in very small font so it is difficult for many to read?
- Who funds studies on chemicals in everyday household products?
- Do you have faith in the government regulatory agencies to protect us?

Standards and Goals for Teaching and Learning

With new knowledge about the relationship between the water cycle and climate change, water pollution and regulations, and activism for water justice, we hope you are starting to make connections to what you can teach in your elementary classrooms. This section broadly outlines the standards for social studies and science teaching at the elementary level that relate to these topics of study, as well as how the Cloud Institutes Education for Sustainability Content Standards and the UN Sustainable Development Goals can also be addressed and provide guidance to teachers.

Social Studies Standards from NCSS

Given that a basic premise of this book is that concepts of scarcity and economic competition drive actions and decisions that have consequences for people, the environment including all living beings, and the planet, the NCSS *Theme VII, Production, Distribution and Consumption* is again relevant. Under this theme students grapple with the idea of limited resources and how individuals, organizations, and nations should make decisions based on this concept. Students are encouraged to "consider the wider consequences of those decisions on groups, communities, the nation, and beyond,"[91] as we also call on students to do with the instructional ideas we present throughout this chapter.

Another relevant standard is *Theme VIII Science, Technology and Society.* Under this theme students explore how advances in science and technology have primarily impacted humans. Examples of technological breakthroughs that are relevant to the study of water in our lives are methods of irrigation and the building of dams and canals. NCSS suggests many lines of inquiry students should engage in when exploring the use and impact of technology. Some of these questions are particularly relevant for this chapter, such as: *How can we manage technology so that the greatest numbers of people benefit? How are disparate cultures, geographically separated but impacted by global events, offered hope by the science that may alleviate global problems? How can gaps in access to benefits of science and technology be bridged?*[92]

Additional NCSS standards that are critical for this chapter are *Theme 6 Power, Authority and Governance* and *Theme 10 Civic Ideals and Practices*. How decisions are made regarding water resources, the protection of, use of, and remediation when necessary, are extremely relevant. Students also need to learn about rights that they and others have and what role they can play in protecting those rights. Under Theme 6, students learn how decisions should be made in democratic societies and government's role in protecting fundamental rights and enacting laws. In Theme 10 they learn about the role that individuals and citizens can play to take action for responsible change and promote the principles of democracy.

While many of the NCSS C3 Indicators can apply to the study of humans' relationship to water, we will highlight only those we see as most relevant.

Textbox 5.1. Relevant NCSS C3 Inquiry Framework Indicators for Grades K-2[93]

D2.Eco.1.K-2. Explain how scarcity necessitates decision-making.
D2.Geo.1.K-2. Construct maps, graphs, and other representations of familiar places.
D2.Geo.2.K-2. Use maps, graphs, photographs, and other representations to describe places and the relationships and interactions that shape them.
D2.Geo.3.K-2. Use maps, globes, and other simple geographic models to identify cultural and environmental characteristics of places.
D2.Geo.4.K-2. Explain how weather, climate, and other environmental characteristics affect people's lives in a place or region.
D2.Geo.5.K-2. Describe how human activities affect the cultural and environmental characteristics of places or regions.
D2.Geo.12.K-2. Identify ways that a catastrophic disaster may affect people living in a place.
D2.Civ.1.K-2. Describe roles and responsibilities of people in authority.

D2.Civ.2.K-2. Explain how all people, not just official leaders, play important roles in a community.
D2.Civ.5.K-2. Explain what governments are and some of their functions.
D2.Civ.6.K-2. Describe how communities work to accomplish common tasks, establish responsibilities, and fulfill roles of authority.
D2.Civ.8.K-2. Describe democratic principles such as equality, fairness, and respect for legitimate authority and rules.
D2.Civ.9.K-2. Follow agreed-upon rules for discussions while responding attentively to others when addressing ideas and making decisions as a group.
D2.Civ.10.K-2. Compare their own point of view with others' perspectives.
D2.Civ.14.K-2. Describe how people have tried to improve their communities over time.
D2.His.4.K-2. Compare perspectives of people in the past to those of people in the present.

Textbox 5.2. Relevant NCSS C3 Inquiry Framework Indicators for Grades 3–5[94]

D2.Eco.1.3–5. Compare the benefits and costs of individual choices.
D2.Eco.2.3–5. Identify positive and negative incentives that influence the decisions people make.
D2.Geo.1.3–5. Construct maps and other graphic representations of both familiar and unfamiliar places.
D2.Geo.2.3–5. Use maps, satellite images, photographs, and other representations to explain relationships between the locations of places and regions and their environmental characteristics.
D2.Geo.3.3–5. Use maps of different scales to describe the locations of cultural and environmental characteristics.
D2.Geo.8.3–5. Explain how human settlements and movements relate to the locations and use of various natural resources.
D2.Geo.9.3–5. Analyze the effects of catastrophic environmental and technological events on human settlements and migration.
D2.Geo.12.3–5. Explain how natural and human-made catastrophic events in one place affect people living in other places.
D2.Civ.1.3–5. Distinguish the responsibilities and powers of government officials at various levels and branches of government and in different times and places.
D2.Civ.2.3–5. Explain how a democracy relies on people's responsible participation, and draw implications for how individuals should participate.

D2.Civ.8.3–5. Identify core civic virtues and democratic principles that guide government, society, and communities.
D2.Civ.10.3–5. Identify the beliefs, experiences, perspectives, and values that underlie their own and others' points of view about civic issues.
D2.Civ.12.3–5. Explain how rules and laws change society and how people change rules and laws.
D2.Civ.13.3–5. Explain how policies are developed to address public problems.
D2.Civ.14.3–5. Illustrate historical and contemporary means of changing society.
D2.His.4.3–5. Explain why individuals and groups during the same historical period differed in their perspectives.

Next-Generation Science Standards

In science classrooms, there is so much to explore when it comes to water, including where we find water, what forms water comes in, how water is needed for the survival of all living things, and how humans have learned that certain materials are good at cleaning water. Additionally, water lends itself to engineering design possibilities, as students can brainstorm solutions to water-related issues and design solutions to address these issues.

Textbox 5.3. Next-Generation Science Standards for Grades K-2

By grade 2 students understand:[95]

- All living things, including humans, have survival needs (water, air, and resources from the land) and their needs are related to the places they live. (K-ESS3-1, K-LS1-1)
- As a result of the survival needs of humans, we have had an impact on the land, water, air, and other living systems in our local environments, and our choices can minimize/maximize that impact. (K-ESS3-3)
- Accessing water for a variety of uses is a human process that changes the environment (K-ESS2-2)
- Humans have designed multiple solutions to manage the impact of water on land (e.g., irrigation, dams, reforestation, conservation). (2-ESS2-1)
- Drinking water comes from multiple sources, people access it in diverse ways, and water scarcity and lack of access to clean water can affect different communities. (2-ESS2-3)
- Certain materials can be used to filter or clear water that is polluted. (K-PS1-1)

Textbox 5.4. Next-Generation Science Standards for Grades 3–5

By grade 5 students understand:[96]

- Weather events like droughts, floods, and hurricanes can impact water access for communities, and more often than not, marginalized communities are disproportionately impacted by these events. (3-ESS3-1)
- Human activities have observable and measurable impacts on water access, erosion, and biodiversity. (4-ESS2-1)
- The Earth's spheres (hydrosphere, geosphere, biosphere, atmosphere) work together to cycle water, and disruptions of the Earth's spheres can affect ecosystems and human access to clear drinking water. (5-ESS2-1)
- Diverse communities have managed water differently over time, and this has led to the exploitation and protection of the Earth's resources and environment. (5-ESS3-1)
- Different materials have properties that can pollute and help clean water. (5-PS1-3, 5-PS1-4)

Cloud Institutes Education for Sustainability Content Standards

Two standards that have already been introduced are worth revisiting in a discussion on water. All living things need water to survive. This very basic truth aligns with the Cloud Standard related to the **laws and principles that govern the physical and biological world.** This standard reminds us that "all living things (including humans) are bound by the ecological principles and physical laws that are derived from nature"[97] including the water cycle that sustains the climate conditions for life to thrive. This standard also includes the application of the natural laws and principles by encouraging students to use their knowledge in the service of their lives, their communities, and the places in which they live, work, and study. This speaks to many aspects of this chapter on water—looking to Indigenous ways of being in relationship to water and the kinds of activism that were demonstrated at Standing Rock—but it also speaks to our collective responsibility to protect the most vulnerable communities when they are being exposed to contaminated water—similar to the solidarity shown to the residents of Flint, Michigan.

The second standard that we discussed in Chapter Four is the idea of a **Healthy Commons.** When thinking about water and water-related socio-environmental issues, this standard reminds us that water is a shared resource that we are all entitled to and responsible for. Embedded in this sentiment is the notion that all commons, especially water, must be protected for future generations and the best way to do this is through multiple social, legal, individual, and collective actions. The final standard that is significant to a discussion about water, especially when thinking about the water cycle and the ways humans are disrupting it through our heavy dependence on fossil fuels, is **System Dynamics and Change.** In describing the standard, the writers state, "A systems approach helps us understand the complexity of the world around us and encourages us to think in terms of relationships, connectedness and context." It is these relational and contextual connections that allow us to better understand the water cycle and the feedback loops that both regulate and disrupt this cycle.

United Nations Sustainable Development Goals

The UN SDGs include two goals related to water. The first is Goal 6, **Ensuring available and sustainable management of water and sanitation for all**.[98] This goal includes multiple target goals related to many topics discussed in this chapter, including equitable access to clean and affordable drinking water and to adequate sanitation for all. Additionally, the target goals include protecting freshwater ecosystems and drinking water sources through pollution reduction, as well as working with communities on developing local capacity to address water quality issues. Currently, the goals are not on track to be met by the 2030 deadline; however, progress is still being made toward them. The UN SDG website states that "between 2015 and 2022, the population using safely managed drinking water increased from 69% to 73%, the population using safely managed sanitation increased from 49% to 57% and the population using basic hygiene services increased from 67% to 75%." While this is progress, it still translates to roughly 2.2 billion people without access to safe drinking water and 3.5 billion people who lack access to adequate sanitation.[99]

Goal six primarily focuses on freshwater systems and their role in providing clean drinking water to the world's population. Goal 14 is meant to protect marine resources by **conserving and sustainably using the oceans, seas and marine resources for sustainable development**.[100] This goal is a response to multiple impacts on the ocean that are primarily the result of human action/interaction, including ocean acidification, eutrophication (increased nutrients from agricultural fertilizer runoff), and warming. Responding to the challenges of plastic pollution and overfishing is also included in this goal, as over one-third of global fish stocks have been overfished.[101] Progress on all of these goals has been challenging as global temperatures are still rising due to climate change, and ocean nutrient levels are still out of balance as a result of our industrialized food systems' heavy dependence on chemical inputs (see Chapter 6). However, many stories of hope exist, and in 2022, the UN published *Bringing Data to Life: SDG Human Impact Stories from Across the Globe*,[102] highlighting multiple local stories of success toward progress for all seventeen goals. This resource is definitely worth sharing with your class as it is inspiring, uplifting, and showcases the power of people and communities.

Applying EcoJustice Pillars to Chapter Instructional Materials

The provided instructional materials are models of the type of elementary instruction that can help students understand the socio-environmental issues related to water use and water rights. The instructional materials reflect our EcoJustice Education Pillars and are aligned to NCSS and Next-Generation Science Standards, as well as to Cloud Standards and the UN SDG goals. The flowchart in Figure 5.2 illustrates the knowledge, skills, and attitudes that we hope for a student to have upon completion of elementary school and the goals for the K-2 and 3–5 grade bands in order to reach the end goal. The instructional materials we model are designed with these goals in mind and are offered as examples of how they can be addressed in elementary education.

The instructional materials we offer in this chapter on Water Use and Water Rights are focused on teaching students to reflect upon the role that water plays in our lives and the livelihood of all life on our planet. Indigenous relationships to water differ from the Western, more distanced and commodified relationship to water that most of us are taught in our schools and homes. So, when thinking about how to bring lessons to children that integrate our EcoJustice Education Pillars and issues related to water, there were so many possibilities. For example, we could have focused on the overuse of pesticides and what that does to the water supply and ecosystems; or how droughts brought on by climate change are forcing migration on a global scale; or that plastics have leached into our water supply with a recent study supported by the NIH, finding a liter of bottled water has about 240,000 tiny pieces of plastic in it!![103] All of these are important topics that rely on knowledge from social studies and science and should be considered across the K-12 spectrum of education due to the current harms being caused

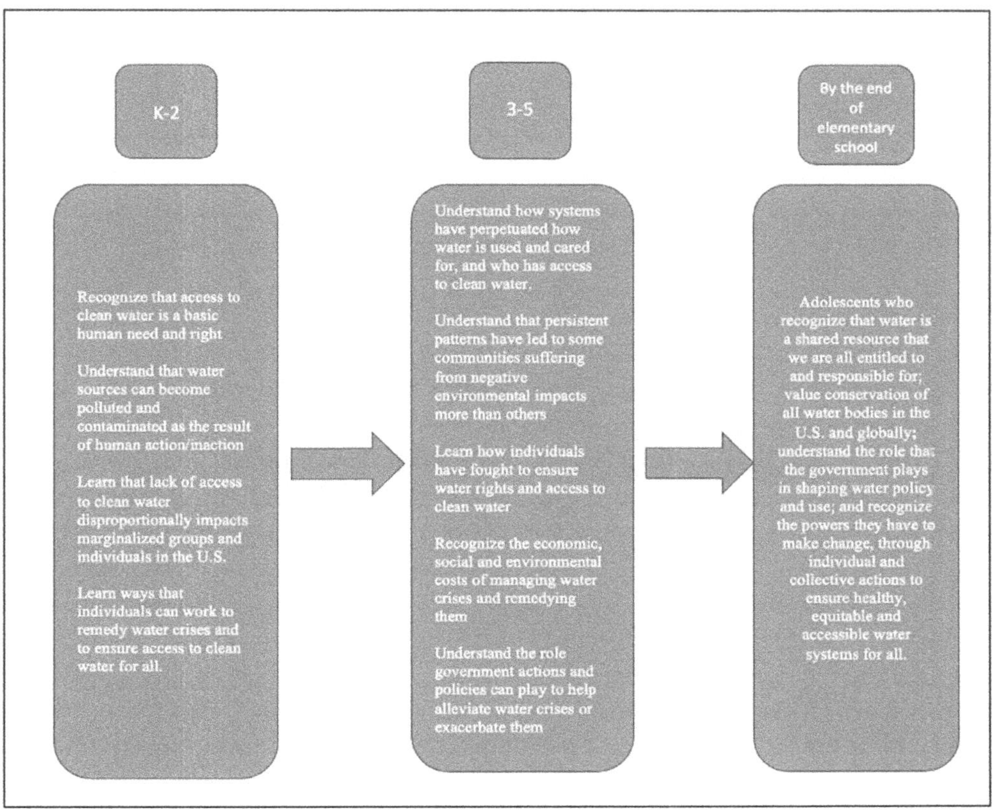

Figure 5.2. Flow chart K-5 to achieve an emerging EcoJustice consciousness related to water use. Author created.

and the potential for future ones. However, we chose to provide model lessons in this chapter that focus on the necessity of clean water for healthy living, ways that water can become polluted and how citizens and governments can and should play a role in ensuring that all have access to clean water.

At the most fundamental level, we all need water for life. It is astounding that given the state of modern medicine and technology, people are still developing illnesses and even dying from drinking contaminated water. Often the "access to clean water" discussion centers on countries that have been historically marginalized in the global economy, commonly grouped under the term "Global South." While it is true that the majority of the world's population most impacted by a lack of access to safely managed sanitation and water facilities live in countries often labeled the Global South, this doesn't mean that the United States isn't facing our own water crises.[104] We are concerned that when well-meaning teachers present the issue of access to clean water as a problem of countries that have been historically marginalized through colonialism and global economic inequality, hegemonic narratives about European superiority are inadvertently perpetuated. Therefore, we chose to focus on water crises in the United States, which also happen to be experienced by marginalized populations.

Given that EcoJustice Education seeks to protect all living beings in a sustainable way, we feel it is important to look at how historical inequalities are still playing out in the United States and the impacts on some of the most vulnerable populations, which include children growing up in poverty. The lessons presented can be adapted for all elementary grade levels. We start with a foundational lesson for the K-2 lessons by exploring how water becomes polluted and what actions can be taken to help reduce water pollution. This is built on through an exploration of a water crisis brought on by contaminated water piped into the homes of residents in Flint, Michigan. Children will learn about the crisis, but they will also learn about civic activism in the community. From here the lesson is designed so that students can reflect on how they can bring awareness to the need to keep water free from pollutants. By making posters, students are engaging in a form of civic engagement themselves, which is a central goal of social studies education. If time permits, all three lessons are suggested. If choices need to be made, any of the lessons could be implemented on their own; however, to integrate the EcoJustice Education Pillars, you might want to focus on the lessons related to Flint, Michigan.

We suggest that before you teach the concepts presented, refresh your own content knowledge by reviewing the topics in the **Introduction** and **Expanding Teacher Knowledge** sections and educate yourself more deeply on the ways that you and your students unknowingly contribute to water pollution (see the **Research and Reflection Activity** above for more guidance). This will prepare you to see the lessons through a more critical lens. Remember that exploring all of the topics we present through a critical lens will force you to wrestle with questions like: if water is a human right, why does everyone not have access to clean and affordable water, or why are toxic chemicals found in so many common household products and even children's toys? We hope that learning more about these topics empowers you to see the world a little differently and appreciate the role we all play in impacting water and the climate that regulates the Earth's water cycle.

Water Instructional Materials

I'm excited that students will be able to understand what water pollution is and that there is an activism piece in the lesson to have students learn and practice how to take action to protect water.

—Hannah, Early Childhood Teacher

I think it's extremely empowering for a classroom of elementary students to think deeply about something that (in most cases) is a part of their everyday lives. Most students in my classroom had their own water bottle that stayed on their desk every day. I always enjoyed lessons where students had to think about how often they "come across" water in their day-to-day life (brushing teeth, drinking water during meals, taking a bath). Students are learning about Indigenous voices and are being asked to reflect deeply on fairness and sustainability—all over a topic that they are extremely familiar with—WATER! Centering Native perspectives through the texts selected in these lessons help counter the dominant narratives oftentimes found in curriculum sets.

—Briana, Elementary Teacher

Textbox 5.5. K-2 EcoJustice Instructional Materials Water

Essential Question(s): What Role Can We Play in Protecting Clean Water?

Objectives
At the conclusion of the lessons, students will be able to:

- **Understand** that water can become polluted by both natural occurrences and human actions.
- **Brainstorm** actions they can take to help reduce water pollution.
- **Describe** actions that other individuals have taken to protect access to clean water in their community.
- **Create** posters to educate others on a water problem and actions that can be taken to help address the problem.

Standards:
Social Studies

- **D2.Geo.4.K-2.** Explain how weather, climate, and other environmental characteristics affect people's lives in a place or region.
- **D2.Geo.5.K-2.** Describe how human activities affect the cultural and environmental characteristics of places or regions.
- **D2.Geo.6.K-2.** Identify some cultural and environmental characteristics or specific places.
- **D2.Geo.12.K-2.** Identify ways that a catastrophic disaster may affect people living in a place.
- **D2.Civ.2.K-2**. Explain how all people, not just official leaders, play important roles in a community.

- **D2.Civ.6.K-2.** Describe how communities work to accomplish common tasks, establish responsibilities, and fulfill roles of authority.
- **D2.Civ.14.K-2**. Describe how people have tried to improve their communities over time.

Science

- **K-LS1-1:** Use observations to describe patterns of what plants and animals (including humans) need to survive.
- **K-ESS3-3:** Communicate solutions that will reduce the impact of humans on the land, water, air, and/or other living things in the local environment.
- **K-ESS2-2:** Construct an argument supported by evidence for how plants and animals (including humans) can change the environment to meet their needs.
- **2-ESS2-3:** Obtain information to identify where water is found on Earth and that it can be solid or liquid.

Materials:

Lesson 1

- The book, *A Cool Drink of Water* or the video of the read aloud at https://youtu.be/-WYlviGvZYA
- Photos of water collection around the world (can use the photos offered as examples or others) that represent different ways water is accessed.

Lesson 2

- Video—Water Pollution for Kids | Learn How to Keep Our Water Clean at https://www.youtube.com/watch?v=A3rLfrlUzY4&t=34s

Lesson 3

- *The Junior Scholastic* article, *Our Water Was Poison* for background information, images and the video, *Little Miss Flint,* used in the lesson at https://junior.scholastic.com/issues/2019-20/092319/our-water-was-poison.html?language=english#1020L

Important Vocabulary/Concepts:

- Clean Water
- Water Pollution
- Access
- Water Rights
- Protect
- Conservation
- Action
- Solution
- Lead
- Water Source

Note to Teacher: The images shared in the lessons can be used with proper citations or can simply be guides to finding similar pictures to incorporate into the lessons.

Instructional Materials Description and Overview:
The series of lessons begins with the students exploring how people around the world gain access to water. This is to help the children become aware of differences, but also of our shared dependence on water. From there the students begin to learn how water can become polluted. These ideas are expanded on in the next lesson along with considering actions we can all take to conserve water. The series concludes with the children learning about the contaminated water crisis that occurred in Flint, MI, and how one young girl took actions to help her community. The children are offered an opportunity to educate others on the necessity to protect our water systems by creating advocacy posters.

Lesson 1: Water and Life
ENGAGE: Lesson Introduction

- Show a picture or an actual glass of clean water to the children and ask who would like to drink it? (See a show of hands.)
- Show a picture or an actual glass of dirty water to the children and ask them who would like to drink it? (See a show of hands.)

EXPLORE: *Read Aloud A Cool Drink of Water*

- Tell the students they will listen to a book about water.
- Ask them to pay attention to all the different ways that people get water around the world.
- Read the book, *A Cool Drink of Water* (or show the video of the read aloud) https://youtu.be/-WYlviGvZYA
- After listening to the book:
    - Make a list with the children of some of the different ways that people get water.
    - Ask them, why do they think that people work hard to get water, for example, like riding on camels in the desert, or carrying jugs on their head? (you can show the pictures again).

EXPLAIN: Text Analysis and Discussion

- Explain that water is necessary to live.
- Explain to students that not everyone has water in their home or can get clean water easily.
- Ask the students why they think this happens?

ELABORATE: How Water Gets Polluted

- Explain that sometimes water can become polluted and therefore not safe to drink.
- Make two columns on a flipchart or whiteboard. On one side write "How Water becomes Polluted" and on the other side write, "Ways to help reduce water pollution."
    - For younger (K) students: Ask if they know what water pollution is? You can tell the students that *polluted water is simply dirty, unsafe water.*

- For older children (grades 1 and 2). Ask, if they know how water can get polluted? List the ideas mentioned.
- Tell the students that in the next lesson they will learn more about different ways that water can become polluted.

EXTEND: Photo Elicitation and Critical Dialogue

- Show the pictures below or similar ones and ask the children what they notice—prompt the students to notice details first.
- Ask students to think about where they can access water for drinking.

https://www.flickr.com/photos/52498245@N03/5202454566

https://www.flickr.com/photos/8788342@N08/798225432

https://www.flickr.com/photos/64607715@N05/8263306410

- Engage students in a critical dialogue about how people access water using the following prompts:
  - What do you notice in these pictures?
  - Which picture most connects to you and how you get drinking water?
  - Do you think all water can be drunk?
  - Why do you think it is important that everyone has access to clean drinking water?
  - What do you think happens when people don't have access to clean drinking water?
  - Do you think having access to clean drinking water is a human right?

EVALUATE: **Wrap-Up Activity/Assessment**

- For younger children: Ask the children to draw a picture of one way that people collect water that they would like to know more about.
- For older children: Ask them to write a question about one of the ways that people get water and to write one or two sentences about why they would like to know the answer to the question.

Lesson 2: Water and the Role We Play

ENGAGE: Lesson Introduction

- Choose from the questions the students had from the previous lesson and share a few with the class. (choose a few that relate to access to clean water).

EXPLORE: Video and Discussion on Water Pollution

- Tell the students they will continue to learn about how water can get polluted by watching a video.
- Show the video Water Pollution for Kids | Learn How to Keep Our Water Clean https://www.youtube.com/watch?v=A3rLfrIUzY4&t=34s
  - Stop the video at 4:28 minutes and discuss the different ways shown in the video that water can become polluted and add to the list from the previous lesson (if needed).
  - Tell them they will finish watching the video, and they should see what ideas are presented to help prevent water pollution.
  - Complete watching the video (the video can be stopped at 5:30 since the last minutes are a review of what was covered).

EXPLAIN: **Mini-lecture and Discussion**

- Review the list of the different ways that water can get polluted and discuss any points that students need clarified.
- Be sure to review that pollution can be caused naturally, but is usually caused by humans and that pollution is sometimes visible but sometimes invisible.

- Explain that even water that comes through our pipes can become polluted and therefore we have laws to protect our drinking water. Tell them in our country this works most of the time, but not always.

ELABORATE: **Actions We Can All Take to Protect Water**

- Ask the students to consider what actions they can take to help limit water pollution.
- Allow students to turn and talk to a partner to discuss ideas.
- Listen to the several ideas from students and list them on the board or flip chart.
- Tell the children to choose one idea from the list and explain they will make a poster to tell others why they should also take this action. Explain this will be a multi-day project that they will begin today; however, show the example of a poster (see the Appendix for a model) before they begin their work (younger children can simply draw a picture of an action they would like to take).
- You can provide the Template—*How to Raise Awareness with a Poster* from the Appendix to guide the students.

EXTEND: Sample Poster Analysis

- Show an image or poster that calls for water conservation that identifies a problem and a solution. Discuss the features with the children.
- Stress that the poster shows a problem (leaky faucet) and a way to help solve the problem (conservation).
- Ask what the children learned from the poster.
- Stress that the posters they create should also highlight a problem with lack of water or lack of access to clean water, and a way that people can help with the problem.
- Have students start working on their posters. Give time as needed to finish posters by the end of Lesson 3.

EVALUATE: **Wrap-Up Activity/Assessment**

- Children are informally assessed on their understanding of how water can become polluted and actions that can be taken to help prevent this based on their responses.

Lesson 3: Taking Action

ENGAGE: Lesson Introduction

Show the students the image below

- Ask the students what they think the picture is.
- Listen to a few ideas, then ask them how they think this might be connected to pollution in water?
- Listen to a few responses.

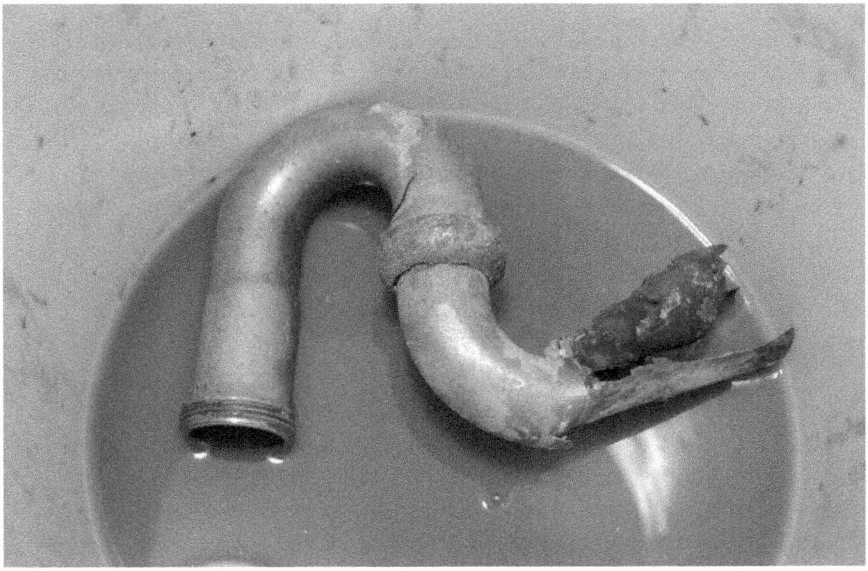

https://www.flickr.com/photos/21881956@N05/3828158533

EXPLORE: Video and Discussion

- Tell the students they will watch a video about a young girl who lived in a city in the United States where the pipes caused polluted water to come into the people's homes. You can explain that the image of the pipe shows how corroded the pipes were by lead.
- Show the video "Our Water Was Poison" at https://junior.scholastic.com/issues/2019-20/092319/our-water-was-poison.html?language=english#1020L
- After the video, ask the students the following questions:
  - How would they feel if their drinking water had poisonous lead or chemicals in it?
  - What actions did the girl in the video take to help her community?

EXPLAIN: Mini-Lecture

Provide the children with a brief overview of the Flint Michigan Water Crisis. *The Junior Scholastic* article can be used as a reference. The key points to raise are:

- State officials tried to save the city of Flint, Michigan, money by changing Flint's source of water from Lake Huron to the Flint River.
- The river water was polluted. It was full of contaminants that corroded the old lead pipes that released the metal into the water.
- Poisoned water went into people's homes and schools.
- Scientists say the water should have been treated with chemicals to prevent corrosion—but this never happened.

- Sometimes the water looked brown when it came from the faucet or smelled bad. Many people began to get rashes on their bodies, including children.
- The government said the water was fine, so the people kept drinking it and bathing with it.
- A local health center discovered that many children in Flint had high levels of lead in their blood from drinking the water. This can cause health problems and interfere with brain development.
- Finally, the people in Flint started to get help from the government, but it wasn't enough. That's why people like Mari took action.

ELABORATE: Action Posters

- Tell the children that everyone can take actions to help their community. Taking actions can help to protect clean water, which is why the children are making posters to educate others about actions they can take as well.
- Posters should include either: (A) a picture showing what they want others to know about the problem, or (B) a picture of what action the children want others to take. Older students should also include some text stating facts about the problem and why it is important for others to take action.
- Allow time for the children to work on their posters.
- Provide guidance to ensure that the message is clear on the posters.

EXTEND: Sharing Poster Messages

- Students will work on their posters. When they are completed, they can engage in constructive dialogue about the messages shared in the posters by their classmates.

EVALUATE: Wrap-Up Activity/Assessment

- Completing the posters might take several days.
- The children's posters will be assessed to see if they understood one (or more) ways that water can become polluted and listed one (or more) actions they and others could take to help reduce or prevent the type of water pollution they identified.

Textbox 5.6. 3–5 EcoJustice Instructional Materials Water

Essential Question(s):

- Is it fair if one group of people benefits by actions that harm another group of people?
- Does the government have a responsibility to protect people from harmful elements in the environment?
- Do people have a responsibility to protect the environment and safety of their community?

Objectives
At the conclusion of the lessons, students will be able to:

- **Explain** how human actions have caused environmental and health problems for some members of society.
- **Describe** actions that individuals can take to address an environmental crisis.
- **Describe** how people can come together to advocate for a policy.
- **Recognize** that some communities suffer from negative environmental impacts more than others.
- **Plan** a course of action to bring about a change they would like to see in their community, state, or nation.

Standards:
Social Studies

- **D2.Geo.2.3–5.** Use maps, satellite images, photographs, and other representations to explain relationships between the locations of places and regions and their environmental characteristics.
- **D2.Geo.5.3–5.** Explain how the cultural and environmental characteristics of places change over time.
- **D2.Geo.7.3–5.** Explain how cultural and environmental characteristics affect the distribution and movement of people, goods, and ideas.
- **D2.Geo.8.3–5.** Explain how human settlements and movements relate to the locations and use of various natural resources.
- **D2.Civ.2.3–5.** Explain how a democracy relies on people's responsible participation, and draw implications for how individuals should participate.
- **D2.Civ.6.3–5.** Describe ways in which people benefit from and are challenged by working together, including through government, workplaces, voluntary organizations, and families.
- **D2.Civ.9.3–5**. Use deliberative processes when making decisions or reaching judgments as a group.
- **D2.Civ.10.3–5.** Identify the beliefs, experiences, perspectives, and values that underlie their own and others' points of view about civic issues.
- **D2.Civ.12.3–5**. Explain how rules and laws change society and how people change rules and laws.

Science

- **3-ESS3-1:** Make a claim about the merit of a design solution that reduces the impacts of a weather-related hazard.
- **5-ESS3-1:** Obtain and combine information about ways individual communities use science ideas to protect the Earth's resources and environment.

Materials:
Lesson 1

- Map of Indian Lands of Federally Recognized Tribes of the United States at https://www.bia.gov/sites/default/files/dup/inline-files/idc1-028635.pdf

- *We Are the Water Protectors*, book or video of read aloud at https://www.bia.gov/sites/default/files/dup/inline-files/idc1-028635.pdf
- Video highlighting the Youth and Allies protest relay run https://americanindian.si.edu/nk360/plains-treaties/dapl

Lesson 2

- *The Water Lady: How Darlene Arviso Helps a Thirsty Navajo Nation*, book or video of a readaloud at https://www.youtube.com/watch?v=LzIPY7zh0fs
- Images of water jugs (included).
- Graphic of how we use water (included).

Lesson 3

- Map of the United States (can continue to use the map with the Native American Lands).
- Video: Navajo Nation has limited access to water (November, 2024) at https://www.youtube.com/watch?v=Mk3UyHSYLXU&t=9s

Important Vocabulary/Concepts:

- Petition
- Native American reservations
- Protest
- Legislature
- Congress
- Legislator
- A Bill

Note to Teacher:

This series of lessons relies on many graphics to help the students better understand the realities of water scarcity. You can use the graphics provided by finding them at the sites listed and then adding to a slideshow, or you can use similar, authentic images you find.

Instructional Materials Description and Overview:

This series of lessons focuses on the children learning about inequities with access to clean water here in the United States. Children will learn about the fight to stop the Dakota Access Pipeline and then about more recent efforts to bring clean water and sanitation to people of the Navajo Nation. The series concludes with the children learning about actions that can be taken to influence decisions in Congress.

Lesson 1: Lack of Access to Clean Water and the Water Protectors

ENGAGE: Lesson Introduction

- Project the map Indian Lands of Federally Recognized Tribes of the United States, available from the Bureau of Indian Affairs at: https://www.bia.gov/sites/default/files/dup/inline-files/idc1-028635.pdf
- Allow the students several minutes to note details on the map.

- Let several students share their observations.
- Then ask the class what they think the darker green spots on the map represent.
- If they don't know, explain that these spots represent Native American reservations. (Remind the students what they learned about land acknowledgments and Indian Removal in Chapter 4 on Land.)
- Explain that many (about 700,000) people live on reservations today.
- Tell the students that many Native Americans still practice the culture of their ancestors, but they have many challenges as well on the reservations.

EXPLORE: Book and Discussion

- Tell the students they will listen to a book, *We Are the Water Protectors* (or use the recorded read aloud at https://www.youtube.com/watch?v=0yLtBjVG0No) about a true fight that Native people had with the US Government and oil companies.
  - Stop the video at the points listed and ask the students the questions below:
    - At 0:45: What is the relationship between the Indigenous People in the story and water?
    - At 1:45: What do you think the "Black Snake" represents?
    - At 2:16: Why do you think the narrator says "We are still here?"
    - At 2:50: Who do the people stand for?
    - At 2:30: What does it mean to be a steward of the Earth?

EXPLAIN: Mini-lecture

- Show the students where the Dakota Access Pipeline is on the map.
- Explain that the pipeline was originally supposed to cross the Missouri River near Bismarck (the capital of North Dakota), *but it was moved over concerns that an oil spill at that location would harm the state capital's drinking water.*
- The Standing Rock Sioux opposed construction of the pipeline near their lands and water supply because they claimed that an oil spill would threaten their water supply and cultural resources as well.
- Tell the students that many Native people and supporters protested the building of the pipeline.

ELABORATE: Student Reflection and Small Group Discussions

- Read the Pledge at the end of the *We are the Water Protectors.*
- Ask the students, is there a cause you want to pledge to support?
- Tell students they will discuss this question in small groups and make a list of ideas that they share with the class.

EXTEND: Video and Critical Dialogue

- Explain that the class will watch a video of a group called Youth & Allies, who organized and ran a relay from Standing Rock Reservation to Washington, D.C., to protest the building of the pipeline.
- Show the students on the map how far this is.

- Tell the students that the young runners delivered a petition to the government telling them they didn't want the pipeline to be built. Define a petition as needed. Show the video highlighting the relay at https://americanindian.si.edu/nk360/plains-treaties/dapl
- After the video, ask the students:
  - Why did the youth run the relay to D.C.?
  - Do you think this was a good form of protest? (Protest can be defined as: expressing disagreement or disapproval of something publicly. It's a way to show that they don't like something and want it to change)
  - How else could the Native People protest?
- Allow students to share ideas for other forms of protest and record these on a flip chart.

EVALUATE: Wrap-Up Activity/Assessment

Exit ticket—What did you learn today about ways people can take action when they see a problem in their community?

Lesson 2: Water Consumption

ENGAGE: Lesson Introduction

- Show the students images of freshwater tanks and freshwater access on the Navajo Nation.
- Ask students to note details in the picture.
- Allow a few students to share some of the details they observed.
- Tell the students to talk to a partner and share their ideas about what they think is happening in the picture.
- Listen to a few of the students' ideas.

EXPLORE: Read Aloud and Discussion

- Tell the students they will listen to a book called *The Water Lady: How Darlene Arviso Helps a Thirsty Navajo Nation*
- Tell them they will learn about a boy named Cody and his family who live on a Navajo Reservation. Show them where the Navajo Reservation is on the map
- Read the book or show the video while reading aloud. The video can be stopped when the story ends at 9 minutes, or the teacher can choose to read the author's note ending at 10:20 https://www.youtube.com/watch?v=LzIPY7zh0fs
- Use the questions below to lead a discussion with the students:
  - Why didn't Cody's family have enough water?
  - What kind of things did his family need water for?
  - Why did Darlene bring water to the people?

- Do you think it is right that the people on the reservation have such little water?

EXPLAIN: Mini-Lecture

- Explain to the students that on many Native American reservations the people don't have access to clean water or enough water.
- There are many reasons for the situation. Some of the most common issues are:
    - Remote access—reservations are often far from cities and many services. Connecting remote homes to a centralized piped water system results in a higher cost per connection.
    - Quality of the land and infrastructure is often poor. When the US government negotiated treaties with Native Tribes, they promised to provide the necessities for life, such as clean water, but have often failed to do so.[10E]
    - The history of mining in the West has led to elevated levels of contaminants, such as arsenic and uranium, in groundwater sources near reservations.
    - Old and poor infrastructure to deliver the water, which can lead to chemicals leaching into the water, broken pipes, or not enough infrastructure to deliver water to all homes on reservations.

ELABORATE: Application activity

- Show the students a one-gallon jug of water and remind them that the people on Cody's reservation use 7 gallons of water a day on average versus the average American uses 100 gallons/day.
- Show the graphics of 7 gallons versus 100 gallons.
- Ask the students to brainstorm ways they think Americans typically use water.
- Show the students the image, "How do we use water?" and tell them this is how most American households are using water.
- Ask students how their lives and their families' lives would be different if they didn't have access to clean water every day and they had to use less. Students should discuss this in small groups or with a partner. Older students can write down their ideas.
- Have a discussion with the students about how their lives would be different if they had less water

7 Gallon Jugs. Author created.

100 Gallon Jugs. Author created.

https://19january2017snapshot.epa.gov/www3/watersense/our_water/understanding_your_bill.html

EXTEND: Photo Elicitation and Critical Dialogue

Ask students to think about what they are noticing in the images of water being used in excess and being conserved.

https://www.flickr.com/photos/26063220@N00/2746158589

https://www.flickr.com/photos/40322276@N04/10458706005

https://www.flickr.com/photos/74618946@N00/2632258770

- Engage students in a critical dialogue about how people waste and conserve water using the following prompts:
  - What do you notice in these pictures?
  - How do you connect to these pictures? Are any of these images familiar to you?
  - What do you think is happening in each of these pictures?
  - Why might these situations exist?
  - Why do you think it is important to conserve water?
  - What do you think happens when people don't conserve water?

EVALUATE: Wrap-Up Activity/Assessment

- Informally assess the students' understanding about average water use in America by listening to or reading their comments from the application activity.
- A formal assessment could be to require that students respond to the prompt: What have you learned about how the average person in the United States uses water each day?

Lesson 3: Water Consumption and Action

ENGAGE: Lesson Introduction

- Write or state the question: Should we all have a right to easy access to clean water?
- Allow the students to think about the question; older students can write a brief response.
- Allow a few students to share their ideas. Try to hear a variety of opinions. You might need to play devil's advocate by asking additional questions such as:
    - What if there isn't enough water for everyone?
    - What if some people live in an area that is close to water, but others don't, should they have to share?

EXPLORE: Video Analysis

- Explain that the people of the Navajo Nation have been fighting to get the government to help supply water to their people.
- Show the video *Navajo Nation has limited access to water* (November, 2024) https://www.youtube.com/watch?v=Mk3UyHSYLXU&t=9s
- Ask the students to discuss the following question:
    - Why do the Navajo people need help from the government?

EXPLAIN: Mini-lecture

- Explain that the people tried to get a law passed in Congress (the federal government) that would give the Navajo people the right to use water from the Colorado River.
- Explain that the name of the proposed law is *The Northeastern Arizona Indian Water Rights Settlement Agreement.*
- Show the students where the Colorado River is in relation to the Navajo Nation.
- Explain that people living in Colorado, Utah, Nevada, New Mexico, and Wyoming are worried that if the water from the river goes to the Navajo people, there might not be enough water for them. Show the students where those states are on the map.
- Explain that Congress has not yet voted on this possible law.

ELABORATE: Application activity

- Review with the students the different ways that people have tried to get access to clean water in their communities.
- List the points the students remember from the prior lessons.

- Tell them that sometimes people also write letters to lawmakers to tell them either a) how they hope they will vote on proposed laws or b) something that they want the legislator to take action on.
- Remind students of the list they made during Lesson 1 of the unit (keep the list available to show to the students). Ask if they would like to make any additions.
- Tell them they will now have an opportunity to choose one of the issues and work with others on a way to tell legislators what action they would like for them to take on the issue or to educate others about the issue so they might also take action. (help the students identify if their actions should be directed toward a local, state, or national legislature.)
- Organize the children into groups based on the topics they are interested in. If there are too many students interested in the same topic, create smaller groups so all will be able to contribute.
- Provide the students with the handout "Taking Action to Raise Awareness" found at the end of the lesson.

EXTEND: Photo Elicitation and Critical Dialogue

- Ask students to think about what kinds of water-related issues people might protest. Show them images of different water issues people have come together to protest about.

https://commons.wikimedia.org/w/index.php?curid=53433

https://www.flickr.com/photos/101009933@N05/9636580424

https://www.flickr.com/photos/45665234@N00/3879021351

- Engage students in a critical dialogue about the different water issues that people are protesting using the following prompts:
  - What do you notice in these pictures?
  - How do you connect to these pictures? Are any of these images familiar to you?
  - What kinds of water issues are mentioned in these images? Are any of these issues our community faces?
  - How are these water issues similar and how are they different?
  - Why do you think it is important for people to come together to protest these water issues?
  - What do you think can happen when people protest?

EVALUATE: **Wrap-Up Activity/Assessment**

Students will be assessed on the completion of the handout "Taking Action to Raise Awareness" and the supporting materials, for example, a letter, petition, poster that they create.

- Students should conduct additional research on the issue they choose so that they can make an effective argument.

Taking Action to Raise Awareness

In a representative government, we need to let the lawmakers know how we feel about social problems or changes we would like. This is important so that when they make new laws, they know what the people want and need. Below are some of the ways people communicate with their representatives. It also helps to make others aware of the issue and your goal so that they will also tell the representatives that they think the change is important.

Review the list below and consider which option your group thinks would be an effective way to tell representatives and others about the change your group wants.

- Write letters to the representatives.
- Make posters to get the attention of the representatives (and others who can also support your plan).
- Create a petition and get signatures to send to the representative(s).
- Create memes or videos to share on social media to inform others about the issues and get more support.
- Organize an event to get attention and support.
- Write and share a poem or song.
- Create a dance or piece of art.

Whichever action(s) you choose, it is very important to follow these steps: (1) Explain what the problem is you want fixed, (2) explain why you think this is an important problem to fix, (3) state what the change is you want, and (4) why this change would be good. Use the organizer below to make your plan. The chart below can be accessed in the Appendix or recreated and used for classroom instruction.

The Problem—What we think needs to be changed	The Goal—What is the change we would like
Actions—How we will advocate for our goal	Reasons—Why we think this is a good plan

Now that you are done planning, it is time to take action!

Community and Place-Based Learning Opportunities

This section invites teachers and parents to engage community members, outside school experts, and other local knowledge resources to extend the EcoJustice learning experiences that students are engaging with in classrooms. We know taking trips with students can be difficult, so sending these suggestions home to families might be a good idea. Additionally, we included inviting some speakers to visit your classroom to discuss in more detail their work as it relates to protecting local watersheds and waterways and providing access to clean water.

For this theme of water use and water rights, we suggest any of the following place-based learning experiences for you and your students:

For this theme of water use and water rights, we suggest any of the following place-based learning experiences for you and your students:

- Have students plan and/or participate in a local cleanup at/near a water body. This can be a beach, river, lake, creek, or other area near water. Have students collect and weigh the amount of trash removed and/or categorize litter into types (i.e., plastic, metal, glass, paper/cardboard, bulky items, textiles, personal items).
- Reach out to a local or state organization/nonprofit that is working on protecting watersheds in your region and take a tour of your watershed or have them visit your classroom. These might be state environmental protection or water conservation agencies or nonprofit organizations that are working to protect watersheds and waterways.
- Invite an Indigenous-based group that has worked on water protection in the community to speak to the class about their work as a water activist. Students will learn more about the ways Indigenous people are in relationship to water and how they have been stewards of water in the past and present.

- Have students conduct a photovoice project (see Appendix) on how they relate to water in their everyday life and their community.
- Have students track their water use over a period of time and measure individual and class data on water consumption. Brainstorm ways to conserve water at home, school, and more broadly.
- Create a rainwater collection barrel at the school to demonstrate how water runoff from roofs can be captured and used for watering gardens and other non-potable water needs.
- Create a rainwater garden with plants that are water-loving and help absorb water instead of allowing it to run off.
- Have students build a rain gauge to calculate rainfall totals. Use the data to discuss how rainwater moves on the different surfaces around the school community and what that means for water runoff.
- Students can engineer water filtration systems and demonstrate how water is cleaned. Introduce various "pollutants" and have students predict/observe how effective their filtration systems are at cleaning the polluted water. Allow for students to continuously improve their system based on controlled trials. Discuss different materials students used and what properties allow each to help with the filtration process.
- Make a closed terrarium system where students can observe the water cycle in action. Have students discuss what would happen in scenarios that mimic natural disruptions in the water cycle like heat, cold, contamination, and so on.

Teacher Turn

Now it is your turn. We understand how educators are always faced with the reality of a finite number of hours and days in the school year, coupled with the many demands on time, from assemblies, fire drills, and so on to state testing and mandated curriculum. This is why we encourage you to take small steps, to pick elements from our model lessons and make modifications as needed to fit your teaching needs, and/or use some of the resources we shared in this chapter to create your own lessons on some of these topics! Here we offer next steps for you to develop your own EcoJustice instructional materials that meet the needs of your school curriculum and your students' interests. As you have learned throughout this chapter, there are many EcoJustice issues that are linked to our current water use and water rights. Perhaps most important is for children to begin to understand that access to clean water is a human right, that water is an integral part of stabilizing our planet's climate and when humans disrupt the water cycle this can lead to social and environmental impacts. We invite teachers to dig deeper into any of the topics discussed in this chapter with your class by utilizing resources provided here, in our Appendices, and on our website, to create your own lessons.

A good place to start is to answer the following questions:

- Which standard fits with your school curriculum? (See the list in the Appendix of NCSS and NGSS standards we have identified as offering opportunities to incorporate our Pillars). Also look at the Cloud Standards and the SDGs for further connections to your curriculum and ideas.
- Which concepts are you and your students interested in learning more about? (e.g., water contamination at home and in the local community, water conservation efforts at school, use of plastic water bottles, etc.)
- Which resources (suggested or your own) would you like to use to expand your own understanding of these concepts?
- What pedagogical activities are most appropriate for your teaching context?

Remember that EcoJustice issues are often related to issues of access and equity as we saw with Indigenous communities' access to affordable and reliable water sources, clean drinking water, or adequate sanitation infrastructure. Additionally, in the United States, those who are most marginalized are also the most vulnerable to exploitation as we saw in Flint, Michigan, and other low-income communities across the country. We have put together many resources in our Appendices and on our website for you to build out an EcoJustice lesson including a lesson plan template, national social studies and science standards, chapter resources to expand your own thinking about EcoJustice issues, and common teaching strategies we have used in our own classrooms. You don't have to do this alone either. Include your students in the process of creating relevant and meaningful lessons for them. Tap into our EcoJustice Educators network to find other teachers who are also engaging in this work and set up co-planning dates. We are eager to support you on your journey toward becoming an EcoJustice conscious teacher!

Now it is your turn to take those next steps.

Notes

1 VeryWell Health, "How Long Can You Go Without Food?" *VeryWell Health*, April 5, 2025, https://www.verywellhealth.com/how-long-live-without-food-1132033.

2 MedicalNewsToday, "How Long Can You Live Without Water?" *MedicalNewsToday*, accessed August 10, 2025, https://www.medicalnewstoday.com/articles/325174.

3 United Nations, "Water—at the Center of the Climate Crisis," *United Nations Climate Action*, accessed August 10, 2025, https://www.un.org/en/climatechange/science/climate-issues/water.

4 National Geographic Kids, "The Water Cycle," *National Geographic Kids*, accessed August 10, 2025, https://kids.nationalgeographic.com/science/article/water-cycle.

5 U.S. Environmental Protection Agency, WaterSense, "A Day in the Life of a Drop," *Teachers' Guide*, May 2008, accessed August 10, 2025, https://www.epa.gov/sites/default/files/2017-02/documents/ws-ourwater-drop-guide.pdf.

6 U.S. Environmental Protection Agency, WaterSense, "A Day in the Life of a Drop," *Teachers' Guide*, May 2008, accessed August 10, 2025, https://www.epa.gov/sites/default/files/2017-02/documents/ws-ourwater-drop-guide.pdf.

7 U.S. Environmental Protection Agency, WaterSense, "A Day in the Life of a Drop," *Teachers' Guide*, May 2008, accessed August 10, 2025, https://www.epa.gov/sites/default/files/2017-02/documents/ws-ourwater-drop-guide.pdf.

8 U.S. Geological Survey, "Our Water Our Lives: Floods—Lesson 1," *Water Science School, US Geological Survey*, accessed August 10, 2025, https://www.usgs.gov/special-topics/water-science-school/our-water-our-lives-floods#Lesson%201.

9 U.S. Geological Survey, "Our Water Our Lives: Floods—Lesson 1," *Water Science School, US Geological Survey*, accessed August 10, 2025, https://www.usgs.gov/special-topics/water-science-school/our-water-our-lives-floods#Lesson%201.

10 U.S. Geological Survey, "Our Water Our Lives: Floods—Lesson 1," *Water Science School, US Geological Survey*, accessed August 10, 2025, https://www.usgs.gov/special-topics/water-science-school/our-water-our-lives-floods#Lesson%201.

11 U.S. Geological Survey, "Our Water Our Lives: Floods—Lesson 1," *Water Science School, US Geological Survey*, accessed August 10, 2025, https://www.usgs.gov/special-topics/water-science-school/our-water-our-lives-floods#Lesson%201.

12 U.S. Geological Survey, "Our Water Our Lives: Floods—Lesson 1," *Water Science School, US Geological Survey*, accessed August 10, 2025, https://www.usgs.gov/special-topics/water-science-school/our-water-our-lives-floods#Lesson%201.

13 Natural Resources Defense Council, "Flooding and Climate Change: Everything You Need to Know," *NRDC*, November 3, 2023, accessed August 10, 2025, https://www.nrdc.org/stories/flooding-and-climate-change-everything-you-need-know.

14 Zack Briggs, "Historic Flood Causes Financial Woes for Arkansas Farmers on the Road to Recovery," *KATV*, December 2, 2019, accessed August 10, 2025, https://katv.com/news/local/historic-flood-causes-financial-woes-for-arkansas-farmers-on-the-road-to-recovery.

15 Natural Resources Defense Council, "Flooding and Climate Change: Everything You Need to Know," *NRDC*, November 3, 2023, accessed August 10, 2025, https://www.nrdc.org/stories/flooding-and-climate-change-everything-you-need-know.

16 LSU Libraries, "Hurricane Katrina Impact on Communities," *Research Guides: Louisiana Hurricanes*, accessed August 10, 2025, https://guides.lib.lsu.edu/Hurricanes/KatrinaCommunities.

17 *The Guardian*, "Residents of New Orleans Comeback District Fear Port Development Could Kill the Renaissance," April 26, 2025, accessed August 10, 2025, https://www.theguardian.com/us-news/2025/apr/26/new-orleans-port-development-lower-ninth-ward.

18 National Geographic Kids, "Ocean Habitat," *National Geographic Kids*, accessed August 10, 2025, https://kids.nationalgeographic.com/nature/habitats/article/ocean.

19 U.S. National Park Service, "A Short History of Jamestown," *Historic Jamestowne, US National Park Service*, accessed August 10, 2025, https://www.nps.gov/jame/learn/historyculture/a-short-history-of-jamestown.htm.

20 New England Historical Society, "The Winnipesaukee Water War and the 1859 Fight for NH Property Rights," *New England Historical Society*, accessed August 10, 2025, https://

newenglandhistoricalsociety.com/winnipesaukee-water-wars-fighting-nh-property-rights/.

21 New England Historical Society, "The Winnipesaukee Water War and the 1859 Fight for NH Property Rights," *New England Historical Society*, accessed August 10, 2025, https://newenglandhistoricalsociety.com/winnipesaukee-water-wars-fighting-nh-property-rights/.

22 For more on the water battles between farmers and the state in CA look to: *The Los Angeles Times*, September 21, 2024, California cracks down on another Central Valley farm area for groundwater depletion, available at https://www.latimes.com/environment/story/2024-09-21/california-puts-another-farm-area-on-groundwater-probation.

23 Laura Anastasia, "Our Water Was Poison," *Junior Scholastic*, September 23, 2019, accessed August 10, 2025, ttps://junior.scholastic.com/issues/2019-20/092319/our-water-was-poison.html?language=english#1020L.

24 Rob Coleman, "What's in Washington D.C.'s Drinking Water?" *Environmental Working Group*, February 26, 2025, accessed August 10, 2025, https://www.ewg.org/news-insights/news/2025/02/whats-washington-dcs-drinking-water.

25 Natalie Zarowny, "Local Author Writes Children's Book About Flint Water Crisis," *ABC12 News*, December 9, 2021, accessed August 10, 2025, https://www.abc12.com/news/flint-water-emergency/local-author-writes-childrens-book-about-flint-water-crisis/article_38447c74-4f40-5002-a2b3-56878191a5ec.html.

26 World Health Organization, "Sanitation," *World Health Organization*, March 22, 2024, accessed August 10, 2025, https://www.who.int/news-room/fact-sheets/detail/sanitation.

27 United States Mission to the United Nations, "FACT SHEET: United States Announces $49 Billion in Commitments to Global Water Security and Sanitation," *United States Mission to the United Nations*, April 2023, accessed August 10, 2025, https://usun.usmission.gov/fact-sheet-united-states-announces-49-billion-in-commitments-to-global-water-security-and-sanitation/#:~:text=Today%2C%20more%20than%20two%20million,required%20to%20flush%20a%20toilet.

28 The Chisholm Legacy Project, "Virginia's Human Right to Water Resolution," *The Chisholm Legacy Project*, accessed August 10, 2025, https://thechisholmlegacyproject.org/policy/virginias-human-right-to-water-resolution/#:~:text=Virginia's%20House%20Joint%20Resolution%20538,is%20a%20fundamental%20human%20right.

29 Elena Bruess, "Poor Drainage Leaves Northeast Houston Residents with Full Ditches, Flooded Homes After Beryl," *Houston Landing*, July 9, 2024, accessed August 10, 2025, https://houstonlanding.org/poor-drainage-leaves-northeast-houston-residents-with-full-ditches-flooded-homes-after-beryl/.

30 Associated Press, "Climate Change Speeds up Water Cycle, Triggers More Extreme Weather," *AP News*, March 24, 2025, accessed August 10, 2025, https://apnews.com/article/climate-change-extremes-drought-flood-rain-hydrological-cycle-b1f3e71ec6bac03f7c72a16be2739b01.

31 PBS NewsHour, "How Climate Change is Affecting this Key Water Cycle, Triggering More Extreme Weather," *PBS NewsHour*, March 24, 2025, accessed August 10, 2025, https://www.pbs.org/newshour/nation/how-climate-change-is-affecting-this-key-water-cycle-triggering-more-extreme-weather.

32 SciTechDaily, "LA's Devastating Wildfire Crisis Didn't Start With a Spark—It Started With Rain," *SciTechDaily*, accessed August 10, 2025, https://scitechdaily.com/las-devastating-wildfire-crisis-didnt-start-with-a-spark-it-started-with-rain/.

33 National Oceanic and Atmospheric Administration, "NOAA Predicts Above Normal 2025 Atlantic Hurricane Season," *NOAA*, August 7, 2025, accessed August 10, 2025, https://www.noaa.gov/news-release/noaa-predicts-above-normal-2025-atlantic-hurricane-season.

34 Pia Herzan, "Who Dat in Lower Nine? The Role of Voluntariness in the Aftermath of Hurricane Katrina," *Voluntariness: History—Society—Theory*, August 2022, accessed August 10, 2025, https://www.voluntariness.org/who-dat-in-lower-nine/.

35 NOAA Climate.gov, "Hurricane Helene's Extreme Rainfall and Catastrophic Inland Flooding," *NOAA Climate.gov*, September 30, 2024, accessed August 10, 2025, https://www.climate.gov/news-features/event-tracker/hurricane-helenes-extreme-rainfall-and-catastrophic-inland-flooding.

36 Harry Zekollari et al., "Glacier Preservation Doubled by Limiting Warming to 1.5°C versus 2.7°C," *Science* 388, no. 6750 (May 29, 2025): 979–83, https://www.science.org/doi/10.1126/science.adu4675.

37 Damian Carrington, "Almost 40% of World's Glaciers Already Doomed Due to Climate Crisis—Study," *The Guardian*, May 29, 2025, accessed August 10, 2025, https://www.theguardian.com/environment/2025/may/29/almost-40-of-worlds-glaciers-already-doomed-due-to-climate-crisis-study.

38 Jet Propulsion Laboratory, "NASA Analysis Shows Irreversible Sea Level Rise for Pacific Islands," *Jet Propulsion Laboratory*, accessed August 10, 2025, https://www.jpl.nasa.gov/news/nasa-analysis-shows-irreversible-sea-level-rise-for-pacific-islands.

39 World Meteorological Organization, "Climate Change Transforms Pacific Islands," *World Meteorological Organization,* August 27, 2024, accessed August 10, 2025, https://wmo.int/media/news/climate-change-transforms-pacific-islands.

40 Secretariat of the Pacific Regional Environment Programme, "Pacific Amplifies Voice at Sixty Second Plenary Session of IPCC in China," *SPREP*, March 7, 2025, accessed August 10, 2025, https://www.sprep.org/news/pacific-amplifies-voice-at-sixty-second-plenary-session-of-ipcc-in-china.

41 Internal Displacement Monitoring Centre, "2025 Global Report on Internal Displacement (GRID)," *Internal Displacement Monitoring Centre*, accessed August 10, 2025, https://www.internal-displacement.org/global-report/grid2025/.

42 The Guardian, "Floods, Trauma, Displaced: Conflict, Climate Crisis and Safety in Bangladesh, Sudan, Colombia IDP Camps," May 23, 2025, accessed August 10, 2025, https://www.theguardian.com/global-development/2025/may/23/floods-trauma-displaced-conflict-climate-crisis-safety-bangladesh-sudan-colombia-idp-camps.

43 Food Safety News, "Oyster-Borne Typhoid Fever Killed 150 in Winter of 1924–25," *Editor's Note*, March 13, 2012, accessed August 10, 2025, https://www.foodsafetynews.com/2012/03/editors-note-in-the-winter/.

44 National Wildlife Federation, "Clean Water Act," *National Wildlife Federation*, accessed August 10, 2025, https://www.nwf.org/Our-Work/Waters/Clean-Water-Act.

45 Environmental Protection Network, "Trump FY26 EPA Skinny Budget Factsheet," *Environmental Protection Network*, May 2025, accessed August 10, 2025, https://www

.environmentalprotectionnetwork.org/wp-content/uploads/2025/05/Trump-FY26-EPA-Skinny-Budget-Factsheet.pdf.

46 Inside Climate News, "EPA Funding Cuts Target Disadvantaged Communities, Analysis Shows," January 5, 2025, accessed August 10, 2025, https://insideclimatenews.org/news/01052025/trump-epa-funding-cuts-target-disadvantaged-communities/.

47 Earthjustice, "EPA Announces Illegal Plan to Eliminate Restrictions for Toxic PFAS in Drinking Water," *Earthjustice*, 2025, accessed August 10, 2025, https://Earthjustice.org/press/2025/epa-announces-illegal-plan-to-eliminate-restrictions-for-toxic-pfas-in-drinking-water.

48 U.S. Environmental Protection Agency, "PFAS Explained," *US Environmental Protection Agency*, accessed August 10, 2025, https://www.epa.gov/pfas/pfas-explained.

49 Food & Water Watch, "Bowing to Industry Pressure, Trump's EPA Rolls Back PFAS Protections for Drinking Water," *Food & Water Watch*, May 14, 2025, accessed August 10, 2025, https://www.foodandwaterwatch.org/2025/05/14/bowing-to-industry-pressure-trumps-epa-rolls-back-pfas-protections-for-drinking-water/.

50 Alexander J. Nihart, Miguel A. Garcia, Elias El Hayek, Ngozi E. Ezike, Yasmin S. Hassan, Jessica A. Bartley, Zeenat Safdar, Prasanna V. Dwivedi, Marianna C. Viana, Brenda A. Wilson, Rohit R. Varma, Maria V. Sanchez, Evan L. Brittain, Rachael D. Seidler, and Frank J. Anania. "Bioaccumulation of Microplastics in Decedent Human Brains," *Nature Medicine* 31 (2025): 1114–19, https://www.nature.com/articles/s41591-024-03453-1.

51 Damian Carrington, "Microplastics Hinder Plant Photosynthesis, Study Finds—Threatening Millions with Starvation," *The Guardian*, March 10, 2025, accessed August 10, 2025, https://www.theguardian.com/environment/2025/mar/10/microplastics-hinder-plant-photosynthesis-study-finds-threatening-millions-with-starvation.

52 Damian Carrington, "Plastic Pollution Reaches World's Deepest Ocean Trench," *The Guardian*, December 20, 2018, accessed August 10, 2025, https://www.theguardian.com/environment/2018/dec/20/plastic-pollution-mariana-trench-deepest-point-ocean.

53 BeePlastic, "The Evolution of Bakelite: The World's First Fully Synthetic Plastic," *BeePlastic*, accessed August 10, 2025, https://www.beeplastic.com/blogs/plastic-insights/the-evolution-of-bakelite-the-worlds-first-fully-synthetic-plastic?srsltid=AfmBOoosno1MoPRlI-xZXvl10eBImZmzcQ8HsK-Rvyk_5--0jstiE-wM&.

54 American Fisheries Society Habitat Section, "Microplastics Pose a Serious Threat to Aquatic Ecosystem Health," *American Fisheries Society*, accessed August 10, 2025, https://units.fisheries.org/habitat/microplastics-pose-a-serious-threat-to-aquatic-ecosystem-health/.

55 NPR, "Lead-Laced Water in Flint: A Step-By-Step Look at the Makings of a Crisis," *NPR*, April 20, 2016, accessed August 10, 2025, https://www.npr.org/sections/thetwo-way/2016/04/20/465545378/lead-laced-water-in-flint-a-step-by-step-look-at-the-makings-of-a-crisis.

56 Great Lakes Now, "No More Free Bottled Water for Flint," *Great Lakes Now*, April 6, 2018, accessed August 10, 2025, https://www.greatlakesnow.org/2018/04/no-more-free-bottled-water-for-flint/.

57 NPR, "Lead-Laced Water in Flint: A Step-By-Step Look at the Makings of a Crisis," *NPR*, April 20, 2016, accessed August 10, 2025, https://www.npr.org/sections/thetwo-way/2016/04/20/465545378/lead-laced-water-in-flint-a-step-by-step-look-at-the-makings-of-a-crisis.

58 *The Guardian*, "Flint, Michigan, Water Crisis: Ten Years on, Residents Feel Left Behind," April 25, 2024, accessed August 10, 2025, https://www.theguardian.com/us-news/2024/apr/25/flint-michigan-water-crisis.

59 Boston University School of Public Health, "Five Years After Water Crisis, Nearly 1 in 4 Flint Residents Has PTSD," *Boston University School of Public Health*, accessed August 10, 2025, https://www.bu.edu/sph/news/articles/2022/five-years-after-water-crisis-nearly-1-in-4-flint-residents-has-ptsd/.

60 Harvard Public Health, "The Children of Flint, Ten Years Later," *Harvard Public Health*, accessed August 10, 2025, https://harvardpublichealth.org/environmental-health/the-children-of-the-flint-michigan-water-crisis-ten-years-later/.

61 Jeff Pillets, "Toxic Tap Water in Trenton: Lead, Copper, and Legionella Bacteria Found in Office Tower," *The Jersey Vindicator*, February 3, 2025, accessed August 10, 2025, https://jerseyvindicator.org/2025/02/03/toxic-tap-water-in-trenton-lead-copper-and-legionella-bacteria-found-in-office-tower/.

62 Benjamin Q. Huynh, Elizabeth T. Chin, and Mathew V. Kiang, "Estimated Childhood Lead Exposure From Drinking Water in Chicago," *JAMA Pediatrics* 178, no. 5 (2024): 473–9, https://doi.org/10.1001/jamapediatrics.2024.0133.

63 CalMatters, "Drinking Water of Almost a Million Californians Failed to Meet State Requirements," *CalMatters*, June 2024, accessed August 10, 2025, https://calmatters.org/environment/2024/06/california-drinking-water-failing-systems/.

64 The Indigenous Foundation, "Indigenous Women and Their Connection to the Earth and Her Waters," *The Indigenous Foundation*, accessed August 10, 2025, https://www.theIndigenousfoundation.org/articles/Indigenous-women-and-their-connections-to-Earth-and-water.

65 Native Women's Association of Canada, "Water is a Source of Life," *Native Women's Association of Canada*, accessed August 10, 2025, https://nwac.ca/policy/water-is-a-source-of-life.

66 Victoria Sutton, "Water is Life: We Should All Be Water Protectors," *Native News Online*, accessed August 10, 2025, https://nativenewsonline.net/opinion/water-is-life-we-should-all-be-water-protectors.

67 National Museum of the American Indian, "Standing Rock Sioux and Dakota Access Pipeline | Teacher Resource," accessed August 10, 2025, https://americanindian.si.edu/nk360/plains-treaties/dapl.

68 Seánna Howard et al., "Indigenous Resistance to the Dakota Access Pipeline: Criminalization of Dissent and Suppression of Protest," Report to the United Nations Special Rapporteur on the Rights of Indigenous Peoples, University of Arizona Rogers College of Law, Water Protector Legal Collective, submitted March 16, 2018, https://law.arizona.edu/sites/default/files/Indigenous%20Resistance%20to%20the%20Dakota%20Access%20Pipeline%20Criminalization%20of%20Dissent%20and%20Suppression%20of%20Protest.pdf.

69 Nick Tabor, "Standing Rock protests | Summary, Violence, & Outcome," *Encyclopaedia Britannica*, last modified 2025, accessed August 10, 2025, https://www.britannica.com/event/Standing-Rock-protests.

70 James Hill and Morgan Winsor, "Meet the Youths at the Heart of the Standing Rock Protests Against the Dakota Access Pipeline," *ABC News*, last modified February 23, 2017, accessed August 10, 2025.

71 Jenni Monet, "Military Force Criticized at Dakota Access Pipeline Protests," *PBS NewsHour*, published November 3, 2016, accessed August 10, 2025.
72 Creators, "How Art Immortalized #NoDAPL Protests at Standing Rock," *VICE*, accessed August 10, 2025.
73 Matt Pearce, "2 Years of Opposition, 1,172 Miles of Pipe, 1.3 million Facebook Check-ins. The Numbers to Know About the Standing Rock Protests," *Los Angeles Times*, published November 1, 2016, accessed August 10, 2025.
74 Sarah Sax, "Native Communities Cite Dismal Statistics on Lack of Access to Water at Senate Committee Hearing," *Medill on the Hill*, published September 28, 2023, accessed August 10, 2025.
75 Democratic Staff of the House Committee on Natural Resources, "How Congress has Blocked Access to Water for Native Families: Water Delayed Is Water Denied," released October 10, 2016, accessed August 10, 2025, https://democrats-naturalresources.house.gov/imo/media/doc/House%20Water%20Report_FINAL.pdf.
76 Heather Tanana, "Oversight Hearing on Water as a Trust Resource: Examining Access in Native Communities," *Testimony to the US Senate Committee on Indian Affairs*, September 27, 2023, accessed August 10, 2025, https://www.indian.senate.gov/wp-content/uploads/2023-09-27-HRG-Testimony-Tanana.pdf.
77 Heather Tanana et al., "Universal Access to Clean Water for Tribes in the Colorado River Basin: Executive Summary," *Water & Tribes Initiative*, released April 2021, accessed August 10, 2025, https://naturalresourcespolicy.org/docs/water-tribes/wti-executive-summary-4.2021.pdf.
78 Laura Parker, "You Eat Thousands of Bits of Plastic Every Year," *National Geographic*, published June 4, 2019, accessed August 10, 2025, https://www.nationalgeographic.com/environment/article/you-eat-thousands-of-bits-of-plastic-every-year#:~:text=A%20plastic%2Dfree%20diet?,%2C%20%E2%80%9Cbut%20we%20are.%E2%80%9D.
79 Environmental Integrity Project, "Oil's Unchecked Outfalls: Water Pollution from Refineries Endangers Public Health and the Environment," accessed August 10, 2025, https://environmentalintegrity.org/reports/oils-unchecked-outfalls/.
80 Environmental Working Group, "Mapping PFAS Chemical Contamination in the United States," accessed August 10, 2025, https://www.ewg.org/interactive-maps/pfas_contamination/.
81 Food & Water Watch, "PFAS: No Sticking, No Staining . . . And Not Going Anywhere," published June 15, 2022, accessed August 10, 2025, https://www.foodandwaterwatch.org/2022/06/15/pfas-no-sticking-no-staining-and-not-going-anywhere/.
82 Allison Kite, "EPA Sued Over Failure to Set, Update Pollution Limits for Oil Refineries, Plastics Plants and Others," *Kansas Reflector*, published April 15, 2023, accessed August 10, 2025, https://kansasreflector.com/2023/04/15/epa-sued-over-failure-to-set-update-pollution-limits/.
83 Food & Water Watch, "How the EPA Lets Dirty Industries Pollute Our Water," published May 8, 2023, accessed August 10, 2025, https://www.foodandwaterwatch.org/2023/05/08/elg-suit-industrial-water-pollution/.
84 Environmental Integrity Project, "The Clean Water Act at 50: Promises Half Kept at the Half Century Mark," published March 29, 2022, accessed August 10, 2025, https://environmentalintegrity.org/wp-content/uploads/2022/03/Revised-CWA-report-3.29.22.pdf.

85 Diego S. Cardoso and Casey J. Wichman, "Water Affordability in the United States," *Water Resources Research*, published 2022, accessed August 10, 2025, https://mleead.umich.edu/files/Event_LegislativeForum_2023/Water%20Affordability/Research%20Articles/Water%20Affordability%20in%20the%20United%20States.pdf.

86 Society for Risk Analysis, "Study Identifies U.S. Hotspots for Drinking Water Quality Violations and Lack of Access to Safe, Clean Water," published April 15, 2025, accessed August 10, 2025, https://www.sra.org/2025/04/15/study-identifies-u-s-hotspots-for-drinking-water-quality-violations-and-lack-of-access-to-safe-clean-water/.

87 National Partnership for Women & Families, "Clean Water and Reproductive Justice: Lack of Access Harms Women of Color," accessed August 10, 2025, https://nationalpartnership.org/report/clean-water-and-reproductive-health/.

88 Bridget R. Scanlon, Robert C. Reedy, Sarah Fakhreddine, Qingyang Yang, and Gregory Pierce, "Drinking Water Quality and Social Vulnerability Linkages at the System Level in the United States," *Environmental Research Letters* 18, no. 9 (2023): 094039, accessed August 10, 2025, https://iopscience.iop.org/article/10.1088/1748-9326/ace2d9.

89 The Ocean Cleanup, "The Great Pacific Garbage Patch," accessed August 10, 2025, https://theoceancleanup.com/great-pacific-garbage-patch/.

90 Sea Turtle Conservancy, "Marine Debris," accessed August 10, 2025, https://conserveturtles.org/threat/marine-debris/.

91 National Council for the Social Studies, "National Curriculum Standards for Social Studies: Chapter 2—The Themes of Social Studies," accessed August 10, 2025, https://www.socialstudies.org/national-curriculum-standards-social-studies-chapter-2-themes-social-studies#7.

92 National Council for the Social Studies, "National Curriculum Standards for Social Studies: Chapter 2—The Themes of Social Studies," accessed August 10, 2025, https://www.socialstudies.org/national-curriculum-standards-social-studies-chapter-2-themes-social-studies#8.

93 National Council for the Social Studies, *College, Career, and Civic Life (C3) Framework for Social Studies State Standards: Guidance for Enhancing the Rigor of K-12 Civics, Economics, Geography, and History*, accessed August 10, 2025, https://www.socialstudies.org/sites/default/files/c3/C3-Framework-for-Social-Studies.pdf.

94 National Council for the Social Studies, *College, Career, and Civic Life (C3) Framework for Social Studies State Standards: Guidance for Enhancing the Rigor of K-12 Civics, Economics, Geography, and History*, accessed August 10, 2025, https://www.socialstudies.org/sites/default/files/c3/C3-Framework-for-Social-Studies.pdf.

95 Next-Generation Science Standards (NGSS), "Elementary Standards: Kindergarten Through Grade Five Disciplinary Core Ideas," *NGSS Lead States*, September 2017, accessed August 9, 2025, https://www.nextgenscience.org/sites/default/files/K-2DCI.pdf.

96 Next-Generation Science Standards (NGSS), "Elementary Standards: Third Through Fifth Grade Performance Expectations by Topic," *NGSS Lead States*, September 2017, accessed August 9, 2025, https://www.nextgenscience.org/sites/default/files/3-5Topic.pdf.

97 Cloud Institute for Sustainability Education, "EfS Standards & Performance Indicators," accessed August 10, 2025, https://cloudinstitute.org/cloud-efs-standards-performance indicators.

98 United Nations, "Sustainable Development Goal 6: Ensure Availability and Sustainable Management of Water and Sanitation for All," accessed August 10, 2025, https://sdgs.un.org/goals/goal6.

99 United Nations, "Sustainable Development Goal 6: Ensure Availability and Sustainable Management of Water and Sanitation for All," *Progress and Info Section*, accessed August 10, 2025, https://sdgs.un.org/goals/goal6#progress_and_info.

100 United Nations, "Sustainable Development Goal 14: Conserve and Sustainably Use the Oceans, Seas and Marine Resources for Sustainable Development," accessed August 10, 2025, https://sdgs.un.org/goals/goal14.

101 United Nations, "Sustainable Development Goal 14: Conserve and Sustainably Use the Oceans, Seas and Marine Resources for Sustainable Development," accessed August 10, 2025, https://sdgs.un.org/goals/goal14.

102 United Nations, "Bringing Data to Life: SDG Human Impact Stories from Across the Globe," *The Sustainable Development Goals Report 2022 Flipbook*, accessed August 10, 2025, https://unstats.un.org/sdgs/report/2022/SDG2022_Flipbook_final.pdf.

103 National Institutes of Health, "Plastic Particles in Bottled Water," published January 23, 2024, accessed August 10, 2025, https://www.nih.gov/news-events/nih-research-matters/plastic-particles-bottled-water.

104 Macrotrends, "Clean Water Access by Country," accessed August 10, 2025, https://www.macrotrends.net/global-metrics/countries/ranking/clean-water-access-statistics.

105 U.S. Senate. Committee on Indian Affairs, "Water as a Trust Resource: Examining Access in Native Communities," *Oversight Hearing*, September 27, 2023, https://www.indian.senate.gov/wp-content/uploads/2023-09-27-HRG-Testimony-Tanana.pdf.

6

Food

Chapter Outline

These lessons are super exciting but what excites me the most is how they empower students to become problem solvers. These lessons don't just teach students what food systems are, they create the space for students to question what they are, reimagine what they could be, and find ways to participate in change. I also really got excited about students learning how everyday people are also driving and participating in what that change can look like—which is even more empowering for young students to see. This isn't just something they are learning about in a textbook, the videos help them see that it is happening in real time!

—Briana, Elementary Teacher

Introduction

We have probably all heard the adage, "You are what you eat," but if you look at foods that are produced and consumed in the United States, it appears that we either don't believe this or simply choose to ignore it. In the article, *The Relation of Diet and Health: You Are What You Eat*, published in 2022, the authors opened with the passage below:

> The intake of food is more than just a necessary process for ensuring the functionality of the human body. Nutritional components become a part of us, interacting with our gut microbiota, immune system and metabolism. For decades, it has been known that the occurrence and the course of a variety of typical Western diseases such as cancer, stroke and myocardial infarction are affected by diet. The common Western diet consists of highly processed foods and is rich of animal protein, trans-fatty acids and sugar. Recent research shows that a diet rich in red meat and processed meat leads to a high risk of cancer, especially colorectal cancer. Substantial evidence indicates that eating more vegetables and fruits and less meat is able to decrease overall cancer risk and improve health. Plant-based diets, in particular, are reported to be beneficial for health.[1]

The article is readily available on the National Library of Medicine website, which is part of the National Institutes of Health and is an organization described on a US government site as, "The National Library of Medicine (NLM) is a leader in research in biomedical informatics and data science and the world's largest biomedical library."[2] When the statements made by the authors are considered in light of data on food consumption patterns that show the average US resident consumes 224.6 lbs of meat every year,[3] approximately seventeen teaspoons of added sugars every day (two to three times the recommended daily allowance for men and women respectively),[4] that more than half of calories consumed at home by adults in the United States come from ultra-processed foods[5] and that approximately 41 percent of US adults and over 20 percent of twelve to nineteen year-olds are obese,[6] then the outlook is very grim. The situation is further complicated when factors such as socioeconomic status (SES), which is calculated based on one's income, level of education and occupation, are considered. For instance, individuals classified as lower SES are more likely to suffer from obesity and attendant diseases. This may be in part due to associated psychosocial stresses, such as the effects of living in impoverished neighborhoods and dealing with discrimination.[7] When all of this information is considered, the question becomes, are people denied adequate information on where our food comes from, how it is grown and processed, what the impacts are and/or lack access to healthy food, or do we simply not think in a meaningful way about what we eat?

Where do we learn about our relationship to food and the consequences for humans, animals, and the planet? When do we study factors in food production that impact what we eat, marketing strategies that influence our diets, or how access to healthy food choices varies from community to community and that personal choice is often limited by external factors? When do we help young people understand that there are systems in place that serve corporate or financial interests that can be at the expense of our health? Where in our education system do we prepare students to be critical consumers of food and to fight for a healthier and more just system of food production?

It is natural to assume that some information on how food impacts our health is taught in schools, particularly since public schools are charged with preparing individuals for productive adulthood. As we have done throughout this book, we will first explore how we are commonly taught about our relationship to food through what is and isn't taught, then we will examine the traditional approach through an EcoJustice lens. Later in the chapter, information will be offered to increase background knowledge of food production and consumption and the impacts on people, animals, and the environment. We will conclude with models of instructional methods and resources for teachers to draw on.

The Conventional Approach

While we will once again explore how children learn messages about food through both science and social studies lessons, we will begin with a quick review of standards for health education, since this is an obvious place to look for answers to the questions raised above. The Society of Health and Physical Educators (SHAPE) has developed National Health Education Standards that "serve as an important framework to address the holistic development of students and ensure consistency and quality in health education programs nationwide."[8] The standards are used by school districts to guide the development of local curriculum standards, thus a look at the standards for elementary school is useful to understand the content expected to be learned and the overall goals for health education. As you read through the standards for each grade band (Table 6.1), note which standards leave open room to explore some of the issues raised in the introduction regarding how our food is produced, what the impacts are and what role do we/can we play in this process.

The national standards are fairly broad and leave a lot of room for interpretation. For example, it's possible that when students are learning to *identify strengths and assets that support health and well-being,* they might learn to consider issues such as, were pesticides used to grow certain foods and what do we know about how this might affect one's health and the environment? Similarly, when students *examine how the environment affects personal and community health,* they might look at locally grown food options or the

Table 6.1. National Health Education Standards 2024

Pre K-Grade 2 Standards	Grades 3–5 Standards
1.2.1 Identify strengths and assets that support health and well-being. 1.2.2 Identify dimensions of wellness. 1.2.3 Identify ways to prevent or reduce risks for illnesses and injuries. 1.2.4 Describe health-promoting behaviors. 1.2.5 Explain the importance of health and well-being. 1.2.6 Identify how the environment affects personal and community health. 1.2.7 Explain when it is important to seek health care.	1.5.1 Explain how to build upon strengths and assets to support health and well-being. 1.5.2 Describe health-promoting behaviors for the dimensions of wellness. 1.5.3 Explain ways to prevent or reduce risks for illnesses and injuries. 1.5.4 Explain ways to engage in health-promoting behaviors, including how to manage health conditions. 1.5.5 Examine how health literacy supports health and well-being. 1.5.6 Examine how the environment affects personal and community health. 1.5.7 Explain when and why it is important to seek health care.

presence/absence of markets that sell whole foods, and not only processed foods. However, in each of these cases it would be up to the local school district or teacher to bring these topics to the curriculum.

We considered that states might provide teachers with more guidance, so we looked at the standards for our home state, specifically at the standards in the section labeled "Nutrition," and found that the standards are very brief, asking only that by the end of grade two students should know that "Nutritious food choices promote wellness and are the basis for healthy eating habits," and by the end of grade 5 they should understand "the principles of a balanced nutritional plan (e.g., moderation, variety of fruits, vegetables, limiting processed foods) assists in making nutrition related decisions that will contribute to wellness."[9] Although we are pleased that children are learning about healthy food choices, the standards don't consider how to explain to children that for some of them such choices will not be available and it is no fault of their own. Nor is it likely that the children would then explore why this is the case, either for them or children in other communities in the state.

What Is Learned About Food Through Science Education

Although the NGSS don't include a section labeled specifically as "food," food-related concepts are woven into **life science**, **Earth science**, and **engineering** standards across elementary grade levels. Starting in kindergarten, students begin to learn about the food chain. Students come to understand that for plants to grow, they need sunlight, food, and water, and similarly, humans and animals also need food to survive. As students progress through the primary grades, this will be expanded on, and they will learn that through the food chain, energy is transferred from one organism to another. Many terms and concepts will be introduced, such as food producer, primary consumer, apex predator, and decomposer. Images like the one below are used to help students visualize the process. Figure 6.1 presents a process where energy moves from one organism to the next, free from problems.

Beginning in third grade, there is an opportunity to expand on this process with standard **3-LS4-4** asking students to *Make a claim about the merit of a solution to a problem caused when the environment changes and the types of plants and animals that live there may change.* This can lead to an exploration of factors that can cause food chain disruptions, but human interaction is not specifically addressed.

By grade 5 students will learn about photosynthesis and how plants and crops grow with standard **5-LS1-1**—*Support an argument that plants get the materials they need for growth chiefly from air and water.* However, the use of pesticides or farming practices that deplete the soil and lead to a loss of biodiversity is never mentioned. Educators might seek out resources such as the *Pesticide Safety Curriculum* produced by the National Center for Farmworker Health, a private, not-for-profit corporation located in TX. This curriculum

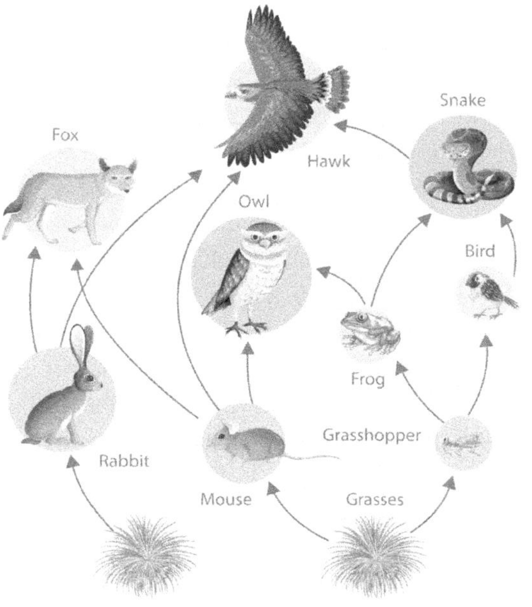

Figure 6.1. Example food chain. https://www.istockphoto.com/vector/education-poster-of-biology-for-food-chains-diagram-gm1318440579-405570281?searchscope=image%2Cfilm

provides resources for teachers, such as a slideshow for grades 1–3, which offers the information:[10]

- It is very important that fresh food be available for us. Food provides the ingredients that go together to make strong healthy bodies.
- Most fruits and vegetables come from large farms and orchards all over the country. Farming takes more work than a farmer can do alone.
- Many of the fruits and vegetables you buy in the grocery store were first hand-picked by the farmworkers.

A few slides later students learn, "Fruit and vegetables are sprayed with chemicals called pesticides. These chemicals kill bugs that live on fruits and vegetables. Pesticides are also poisonous to people and must be washed from the fruits and vegetables before we eat them. Sometimes farmworkers have to work in fields that have just been sprayed with pesticides."[11] On another slide the nature of migrant farm work is addressed and here the children would learn that families often have to move around to find work and that children must therefore change schools regularly. In this way some of the challenges farmworkers face are highlighted, but there is no elaboration about conditions that lead to these circumstances, or who is most affected and what are the consequences of this work. The following days in the curriculum focus on washing one's hands and how to protect oneself from pesticides.

We were pleased that the curriculum extended beyond what is typically taught to raise the issue of pesticides and introduce the human element of how food, fruits, and vegetables are produced. The curriculum also offers a model for teachers to build on the traditional science that is taught. However, there are missed opportunities for children to critique the existing system. Simple follow-up questions could extend the lesson to introduce children to more real-life problems associated with our food production system, such as: How do you think the children of migrant farmers feel about starting a new school all the time? Or, what do you think could be done so no one breathes or is exposed to pesticides?

Typical learning in elementary science lessons focuses the children's attention on the anatomy of plants and what is necessary for plants to survive. NGSS LS1.A *Structure and Function*, calls for students to identify the parts of the plant (roots, stems, leaves, flowers, fruits, seeds), and they learn that plants require air, sunlight, and water to survive. NCSS 2-LS2.2, *Develop a simple model that mimics the function of an animal in dispersing seeds of pollinating plants*, will help children understand the natural systems that are necessary for plant growth. However, the man-made factors that interfere with these systems, such as the endangerment of bees due to loss of habitats, pesticides, and climate change, are not addressed. Thus, in the early grades, children will understand the growth of plants as a natural process. Potentially without much consideration of the role humans play in impacting this process.

As children progress through the elementary school years, they will learn that plants are consumed by animals and humans. NGSS 5.LS2.1 calls for students *to develop a model to describe the movement of matter among plants, animals, decomposers, and the environment*. Students will learn that matter that is not food (air, water, decomposed materials in soil) is changed by plants into matter that is food. The role of plants in the food production process is further explored under NGSS LS2.A: Interdependent Relationships in Ecosystems. The Disciplinary Core Ideas for the standard are explained as:

> The food of almost any kind of animal can be traced back to plants. Organisms are related in food webs in which some animals eat plants for food and other animals eat the animals that eat plants. Some organisms, such as fungi and bacteria, break down dead organisms (both plants or plants parts and animals) and therefore operate as "decomposers." Decomposition eventually restores (recycles) some materials back to the soil. Organisms can survive only in environments in which their particular needs are met. A healthy ecosystem is one in which multiple species of different types are each able to meet their needs in a relatively stable web of life. Newly introduced species can damage the balance of an ecosystem.[12]

While students should come to understand the interconnectedness of natural systems in this process, it is interesting that, "Newly introduced species can damage the balance of an ecosystem" is mentioned without the context that this can be the result of human interactions. The use of pesticides in most large-scale agriculture in the United States has caused many disruptions to the ecosystem leading to the elimination of species and the introduction of new species. For instance, the National Center for Biotechnology Information website offers the information that "there is now overwhelming evidence that some of these chemicals do pose a potential risk to humans and other life forms and unwanted side effects to the environment. . . . In addition to killing insects or weeds, pesticides can be toxic to a host of other organisms including birds, fish, beneficial insects, and non-target plants."[13] The same article also explains that those who work in agriculture are particularly at risk due to exposure to chemicals in pesticides and that individuals from developing countries bear an unequal burden from this situation.

So, while we see that children will learn about the role of plants in the food chain, many detrimental side effects of current agricultural practices are not directly addressed and can therefore leave children with incomplete information needed to make healthy and ethical food choices, or call for changes in food systems to be made.

What Is Learned About Food in Social Studies Education

Once again, we turn to social studies to see how the topic of food is addressed and to the messages that are taught, directly or indirectly. Of all the topics we addressed in this book, food presented the biggest challenge when analyzing what we teach children in elementary school. The place where food is most prominent is on cultural days when children are encouraged to bring in an example of food that represents their ethnic or cultural background. This can lead to all kinds of food, both bought and prepared at home, to be served. Generally, the choices to be shared are based on what children like and will eat (not necessarily what is commonly eaten as part of a national tradition—think guinea pig in Ecuador). Discussion of where the food comes from, is it the food of the common people or the wealthy, what is the nutritional value of the food, and so on is rarely, if ever, had. In general, this practice offers a fun break from routine classroom practices, but it is hardly an opportunity to understand our relationship to food and the impact it has on humans, animals, and the land.

There are several other places where children are likely to see food in the elementary social studies curriculum. Children will likely learn that Indigenous People aided the early European settlers by teaching them how to grow crops, particularly corn. And of course, all children learn about the feast at the First Thanksgiving held after a successful harvest. This might lead to a class activity where students mimic the feast and share a meal together with slices of turkey, stuffing, and apple or pumpkin pie, all of which were foods not eaten at the original Thanksgiving. Surviving documents from the original meal describe a feast of "freshly killed deer, assorted wildfowl, a bounty of cod and bass, and flint, a native variety of corn harvested by the Native Americans, which was eaten as corn bread and porridge."[14] Therefore, we can see that the activity of replicating the First Thanksgiving meal has little reality in terms of the food and also obscures the true nature of the relationship between the Indigenous People and the settlers (as discussed in Chapter 4).

In another place in the curriculum, children will learn about the differences between rural, suburban, and urban communities. Pictures of each setting are most often used to help the children visualize characteristics and differences; therefore, they are likely to see pictures of farms for rural communities. Usually, fields of wheat or corn will be shown, which suggests that this type of monocultural (single crop) farming is natural. Or children will see pictures of cows grazing in fields or perhaps of an individual milking a cow, but images of cattle crammed into feedlots are not likely to be shown. In this way, children are shielded from less palatable aspects of food production.

Children in the upper grades will likely learn that the regions of the original thirteen colonies differed geographically, and this influenced the type of crops grown in each region. For instance, they usually learn that the Middle Colonies (New York, New Jersey, Pennsylvania, and Delaware) were known as the "Bread Basket" since the climate supported the large-scale farming of wheat. When they learn about Indigenous nations that populated North America prior to European settlement (which is usually how they learn about Indigenous Peoples), they learn about the relationship between culture and geography; thus, the Nations of the Plains hunted buffalo and the Inuit hunted and ate seal, whales, and other sea life.

Although food is present in elementary Social Studies education, it is not a focal point for investigation. Topics like how food production practices impact the environment or what the costs and benefits to humans, benefiting some at the expense of others, are not dealt with in the typical curriculum. In fact, children will likely come away from their elementary schooling with little understanding of food production and consumption and the environmental and social impacts.

An EcoJustice Critique of Conventional Approaches

How food is produced in the United States is having a detrimental impact on the environment, the health of most individuals, the welfare of many who are often the most vulnerable, and the economy. Many of these topics will be explored with more depth in the next section on Expanding Teacher Content Knowledge, but for now we must consider these realities when considering what an EcoJustice approach to teaching about food production and consumption in the United States could look like.

At the most basic level, students should learn where the food they eat is coming from. Most people don't know where the majority of the food they eat comes from beyond the grocery store, and so we experience a form of distancing by lacking this knowledge. Practices described above of showing bucolic scenes of farms add to this distancing in understanding food production. In the literal sense, so much of our food now travels hundreds, if not thousands, of miles from where it is grown to where it is sold and consumed. The distance food travels can be calculated in food miles, which is measured by the distance food travels from its production site to the consumer's plate, considering factors such as transportation mode, distance, and energy uses. Food miles are easy to grasp when we purchase produce that can't be grown in the climate we are located in. For many Americans, this means fresh produce like bananas and avocados often have high food miles.

However, even the more processed foods like peanut butter and pasta have associated food miles much higher than any fresh produce. This is because each ingredient is grown in a different part of the world and then sent to a location for manufacturing and then sent to the grocery store where it is purchased and eventually lands in our refrigerators or pantries.

On a practical level, students could engage in activities where they analyze products they commonly eat to calculate the food miles. Resources readily available such as Foodmiles.com. can be used to aid in this. The next step in the activity would be for students to learn about the emissions produced from various forms of transportation. Ultimately the students could devise grocery lists of food produced more locally or through more sustainable transportation in order to see the role that consumers play. In our section on *Community and Place-based Learning Opportunities*, we also introduce an activity to explore local food sources. When students experience learning such as this, we integrate multiple Pillars of EcoJustice Education. *Pillar I: An understanding and valuing of the interconnectedness of all living beings and systems* comes to life when children realize how the food we eat is transported and impacts the environment. Many of the components of this pillar are also addressed such as: *Accept responsibility for the part we play in the ecological web of life; Become conscious consumers and producers in all areas of existence; Understand that all actions have multiple consequences; Think globally and act locally;* and *Evaluate choices and decisions at multiple levels (self, community, state, country) through a systems lens.*

An EcoJustice approach would also address food insecurity and lack of access to healthy food choices for so many living in the United States today. The concept of a food desert, defined as regions where people have limited access to healthful and affordable food due to income, lack of local markets to supply fresh and whole foods, and transportation issues, could be introduced to students.. In the lessons we share for this theme, we showcase the book *Saturday at the Food Pantry* by Diane O'Neill to highlight how food insecurity exists in communities and some of the local efforts to offer supports. The story not only humanizes the issue but can help to destigmatize notions of poverty and food insecurity, as it is told through the experience of two school-aged children. Another resource, *The Good Garden: How One Family Went from Hunger to Having Enough* by Katie Smith Milway, highlights the movement to grow "good gardens," which can help communities located in food deserts. The lessons could be extended with mapping activities where students look at the distances to local supermarkets that sell fruits, vegetables, whole foods and foods with limited processing. This can be repeated with a contrasting community (from the one the children live in). If students are encouraged to look at communities where food deserts exist and to question how this occurs, *Pillar III: A commitment to investigating socio-environmental issues through the lens of power and justice*, and the component, *Critically reads the world—uncovering and questioning the social, political, and economic forces that shape our lives*, is integrated.

Students can also apply what they have learned about the relationship between what we eat and our health with analysis of the implications. Final activities could be student-created PSAs to raise awareness and even writing to local legislators to share what they learned, state their views on the subject, and ask for more information on what's being done. In this way, we are not only integrating Pillar I component; *Care for the welfare of all beings,* many elements of *Pillar II An orientation toward innovative, action-oriented, and collaborative problem-solving* are also addressed. The components of Pillar II; *Accept our power as change agents, Build skills of proactive citizenship,* and *Advocate for changes that focus on environmentally sustainable and just solutions and policies* are all addressed.

Distancing from our food sources also means we don't have to think about the practices used to grow food or house and slaughter the animals we eat. According to a 2021 USDA School Gardens Factsheet, "across the Nation schools are growing gardens to provide food for child nutrition programs, connect children to the source of their food, and create hands-on interdisciplinary classrooms."[15] The factsheet offers guidance on how to begin gardens, whether on plots of land or in boxes on window sills, with a focus on checking soil for lead levels, planting, watering, and harvesting. What is interestingly missing is guidance on how to talk about the use of pesticides in agriculture and the impacts on humans and the environment, or degradation of soil due to widespread farming practices. An EcoJustice perspective calls on teachers to introduce these topics while students are engaged in planting and harvesting food grown at school.

Students should be taught that chemicals that are used to eliminate insects and increase crop yields can be hazardous to those engaged in spraying them, but they can also leach into water systems and cause damage to local ecosystems. According to the Center for Biological Diversity, pesticides pose a "grave threat to organisms needed for healthy soil, biodiversity, and the fight against climate change."[16] Natural means of growing food without pesticides should be learned (and used in school gardens). Students could learn that by adding insect-deterring herbs such as chives or mint,[17] the need for pesticides can be reduced or eliminated. Worms can also be purchased and added to the soil to help. Worms break down organic matter, release nutrients into the soil through excreting, and allow air to circulate by traveling through the soil. Thus, students are learning that nature itself can help protect soil and aid in healthy growing practices. Besides, what elementary school child isn't fascinated by worms? Including this learning addresses several more components of the pillars: from Pillar I, *Protect and nurture the health and well-being of our Earth*, and from Pillar II: *Imagine new ideas and ways of being that challenge our socialized norms*. All of the approaches described thus far also integrate Pillar IV *Transdisciplinary approaches that focus on cross-curricular knowledge and connections rather than siloed thinking that leads to incomplete understandings,* as knowledge and skills from science and social studies are applied.

As discussed above, students learn in social studies what constitutes rural, suburban, and urban settings based mostly on their differences. What if instead they explored examples of how in all three settings people are finding ways to grow food for themselves and their local communities. The book, *City Green* by DyAnne DiSalvo-Ryan, is highlighted as a resource in one of our lessons we share at the end of this chapter. It is a story of how a community works together to grow an urban garden in an empty lot. Using books such as this can shift perspectives among children about who can produce food and where it can be grown. Another opportunity in social studies lessons is to explore the wisdom of food held among many Indigenous communities. Instead of teaching only that Squanto taught the colonists at Plymouth how to use fish to fertilize the soil, students could study how food has been used in Indigenous cultures for centuries in healing practices. What if students learned that "Native American traditional healing is identified by the National Institutes of Health/National Center for Complementary and Alternative Medicine (NCCAM) as a whole medical system that encompasses a range of holistic treatments used by Indigenous healers for a multitude of acute and chronic conditions or to promote health and wellbeing."[18] Or that high school student, Destany "Sky" Pete, of the Shoshone and Paiute Tribes of the Duck Valley Indian Reservation in Idaho and Nevada, discovered that Chokeberry pudding, a dessert traditional to her people, could fight cancer?[19] Students could come to understand that just as certain foods are harmful, others can be highly beneficial, as they also learn about Indigenous Peoples from an asset perspective. Including this information in the students' learning directly addresses Pillar II, component, *Value diverse knowledge and honor that knowledge is constructed from many and sometimes unexpected sources.*

The opportunities to incorporate knowledge of food systems and the implications of current practices are clearly present in both science and social studies. However, this is not likely to happen without support for teachers in how this can be done, a recognition among teachers that this should be done, and the confidence among teachers that they can incorporate this learning. The following sections will respond to these needs.

Expanding Teacher Content Knowledge

In this section on expanding teacher knowledge, we want to move beyond the conversation about nutrition and into a deeper and more critical discussion of food systems and how society as a whole has become dependent on industrialized agriculture. We reveal the damaging environmental and social impacts of modern food production on local ecology, natural resources, the climate, and humans. As part of this discussion, we connect to earlier chapters by addressing the consolidation of the food supply chain by a few multinational corporations and its impact on consumers, the challenge of land access, and the pollution of water by the agriculture industry. In response to the multifaceted and negative environmental and social effects of industrial agriculture, communities are developing local food systems to put control back into the hands of local, urban, and regenerative farms and the consumers they serve. We highlight some alternative food production models and acts of resistance by communities to see how reclaiming food systems is being mobilized across the country. As always, we end this section by providing a wealth of statistics that showcase the economic, ecological, and sociocultural implications of our modern industrialized food system and call on you to hone your critical lens by engaging in reflection and research about your own relationship to these topics.

Industrialized Agricultural and the Ecological Impact

Many people have a misguided image that our food still comes from a small farmer growing food and raising livestock to sell at local markets. However, most of the food we consume today is a product of an industrialized food system designed to maximize food production efficiently and at scale by using modern technology, scientific advancements, and concentrated methods for raising crops and livestock.[20] In fact, despite the fact that in 2021 about 89 percent of all farms were small family farms and operated on 45 percent of US agricultural land, they only produced 18 percent of the total value of food produced.[21] Family farms still exist at various sizes, but most of them are not selling directly to consumers, but rather are engaged in partnerships with multi- and transnational corporations that dictate growing practices, prices, and sell into the global market, rather than locally.

Many aspects of agriculture evolved around the same time and coalesced into our modern system of growing. The *Green Revolution*, an agricultural movement that started in the 1940s and continues today, is often the term used to mark the turn from local markets and traditional agricultural systems toward national and global food markets and more industrialized systems of growing. The legacy of the Green Revolution is pervasive throughout our modern systems of food production and has many detrimental consequences for the health and well-being of humans and non-humans alike. In this section, we will explore some of the consequences associated with widespread industrial agricultural practices.

Many features define the Green Revolution, but one large influence was the technological advancement in producing high-yield seed varieties through plant breeding. First developed in Mexico and the Philippines and then tested in India, this crop research was seeking to address the challenge of feeding a growing population and was a direct response to hunger and famine crises occurring globally. Danielle Nierenberg, co-founder and president of Food Tank, a nonprofit working toward positive transformation in how food is produced and consumed, reminds us that while the motivations for the Green Revolution were good, the focus to create high-yield varieties of starchy staple crops like wheat and rice provided nutrient-poor food. She states:

> We left behind a lot of Indigenous and traditional crops and traditional practices that were more nourishing. Millet and sorghum were, a long time ago, staple crops for many farmers and eaters in sub-Saharan Africa. But those were looked down upon. Because of Green Revolution practices, they were considered poor people's food. These are the foods now of the future because they're very nutritious. They're high in protein and vitamins and micronutrients, and they're resilient.[22]

She reminds us that much of the crops that were developed during this era are not climate-resilient and will be less productive as climate change impacts growing conditions globally.

The Green Revolution also heralded monoculture, or single crop farming, as an efficient and economical farming style; however, it led to many unintended environmental impacts.

When we see farms today, they look like fields and fields of the same crop—large areas of corn, wheat, and soybean dominate the Midwest landscape. *Monoculture* farming is in stark contrast to Indigenous and pre-industrial ways of growing food known as *polyculture*. Monoculture applies to both plants and animals raised on factory farms. Of the roughly 876 million acres of land that are in agricultural use in the United States, 25 percent is used to grow wheat, corn and soybean.[23] However, in the case of corn, only a small fraction of the corn is used for direct consumption. The majority of corn grown in the United States is used for animal feed and fuel. Roughly 44 percent of corn is fed to livestock and 44 percent is processed into ethanol, a biofuel that produces six pounds of carbon dioxide per gallon to produce.[24] Ten percent of corn is used as a food additive, including high fructose corn syrup, corn starch, corn oil, and many other products.[25] A quick search of ingredients that are derived from corn and used in food processing reveals there are over 1,800 corn derivatives used today.[26] One of the most significant impacts is that monoculture starkly contrasts with the ecological principles that we discussed in Chapter 2, particularly that biodiversity and the interconnectedness of systems and organisms determines the health and resiliency of an ecosystem. Monoculture reduces the diversity of plants and pollinator insects above ground, as well as destroys the soil food web that contributes to the nutrient density of food grown. Growing large amounts of single crops also requires intensive inputs, including fertilizers, pesticides, and herbicides to increase yields and reduce plant competition.[27]

Monoculture also applies to raising livestock. The United States has approximately 21,000 *concentrated animal feeding operations (CAFOs)* that produce an abundance of affordable meat (i.e., poultry, beef, pork). The EPA regulatory definition for a large CAFO is a facility holding more than 1,000 beef steers, 700 dairy cows, 2,500 pigs, or 125,000 chickens for 45 days with limited vegetation on site for animals to access.[28] As you can imagine, raising animals under these kinds of conditions also requires intensive technological and chemical inputs including large, energy-intensive facilities to house livestock, specialized feed to increase calories (corn!), and antibiotics to reduce infections from living in confinement.[29] As a result of this intensity of animal production, the 21,000 CAFOs each produce up to 1.6 million tons of waste annually. While the majority of the waste is animal manure, there are additional waste products that are found in excrement including hormones and other pharmaceutical products like antibiotics.[30] All of these waste products have been found in the meat we eat and water runoff that moves into local waterways during rain events.[31] CAFOs also produce large amounts of methane waste, a more powerful greenhouse gas than carbon dioxide, from animal digestive emissions (burps and farts) and methane off-gassing from liquid pools of manure. CAFO waste is but one example of where food production intersects with water pollution. Surprisingly, in agriculturally intensive states across the United States all of this pollution is legal, despite the cumulative environmental damage.[32]

Green Revolution plant varieties, grown in monoculture, have more intense requirements for growth and are dependent on inputs including *chemical fertilizers* (synthetic nutrients) to help support plant growth. Animal manure was historically the primary fertilizer input, but more intense amounts of chemical inputs were needed to grow the modified crops in large monoculture quantities. The use of chemical fertilizers increased dramatically with roughly 2 million tons of chemical fertilizers used per year in the mid-1940s to over 20 million tons used today.[33] Today, fertilizers like Miracle-Gro, marketed to the backyard gardener, are the same synthetic fertilizers used commercially. These fertilizers bypass the natural nutrient cycling in soil ecosystems which can, over time, degrade soil by disrupting the soil's natural nitrogen and carbon balance.[34] Fertilizer runoff is also a large environmental issue. During rain events, fertilizer runoff infiltrates groundwater and enters nearby lakes and rivers, causing increased nutrient loads in these aquatic systems. This increase in nutrients, particularly nitrogen and phosphorus is called *eutrophication* and allows for algae to grow rapidly. Excessive algae growth blocks sunlight from penetrating the depths of water bodies, reducing aquatic organisms capacity to photosynthesize, and the overall effect is a decrease in oxygen. A decrease in oxygen levels has negative impacts on organisms and can lead to *dead zones*, large areas where few organisms can survive. The Gulf of Mexico has a seasonal dead zone each summer as a result of agricultural runoff along the Mississippi River which can be as large as 8,000 square miles.[35] In 2024, the dead zone was 6,705 square miles, roughly the size of the state of New Jersey, resulting in 4 million acres of habitat loss for fish and other organisms.[36]

Growing plants using these Green Revolution practices also led to increased plant competition and pest pressure that was remediated with the use of chemical herbicides and pesticides. In 1962, Rachel Carson's *Silent Spring* revealed the ecological and human costs of the pesticide DDT by asking readers to reckon with the unintended consequences of this kind of chemical technological progress. Despite her warnings, herbicide and pesticide use dominate modern food production and comprise a massive global market. In 2024 global sales of herbicide were valued at $47.38 billion[37] and global sales of pesticides were valued at $108 billion.[38] It may surprise you to hear, but many crops have even been genetically modified to be resistant to chemical herbicides like glyphosate (more commonly known as Roundup).[39] Roundup is produced by Bayer, formerly Monsanto, and is by far the most common herbicide used in the industry. Between 2010 and 2014, an average of 266 million tons of glyphosate were utilized with an expected market value of $11.89 billion in 2025.[40] Growth in the glyphosate market continues despite the environmental and human costs. Bayer, one of the largest producers of glyphosate, has had over 170,000 roundup-related lawsuits filed against them due to the connection between exposure to glyphosate and certain forms of cancer.[41] A University of Washington research study found that exposure to glyphosate increases the chance of developing certain forms of cancer by 40 percent with the link between glyphosate and Non-Hodgkin Lymphoma stronger than previously reported studies suggested.[42] Bayer has paid millions of dollars in settlements to plaintiffs and is considering stopping production of Roundup in the United States if lawsuits continue.[43] Our dependence on an input-intensive food system (fertilizers, pesticides, herbicides) has allowed new markets to emerge in multiple sectors of the food supply chain—from seeds and chemical inputs to food processing, distribution, and grocery stores—all of these sectors are now controlled by a handful of multinational and transnational corporations.

Consolidation Along the Food Supply Chain

The common-sense assumption about our industrialized food system is that it is working how it should to get the most productivity from the land, labor, and material inputs in order to feed the demands of Earth's growing population. However, this model of growing food, which is the most common practice in the US and has been increasingly exported to many parts of the world, is unsustainable and ineffective. The global food system is the primary driver of biodiversity loss, with over half of the world's habitable land being used for agriculture, and still, nearly 600 million people are expected to face hunger by 2030.[44] This system of food production has been driven by the agribusiness monopoly and, as we have seen in previous chapters, when we have corporate power involved in food production, we have a profit-driven motive as opposed to a human rights motive. Many federal and state policies have upheld this model of food production and the industry has evolved to be even more extractive and monopolized than ever. Today, there are a handful of transnational corporations that control every aspect of the food supply chain. A 2025 report, *How Big Food Monopolies Threaten Food Security and Public Health*, explains:

> A small number of multinational corporations control the seeds that farmers are allowed to plant, the chemicals used to treat crops, the soil amendments that nourish the land, and the transportation networks that get food to our plates. From the farm to the grocery store shelf, the power is concentrated in the hands of just a few. This level of control doesn't just limit consumer choice—it makes our entire food system more fragile, more toxic, and ultimately, more dangerous.[45]

A joint investigation between *the Guardian* and Food and Water Watch revealed that despite the abundance of food on the shelves of grocery stores, the power of the consumer is largely an illusion.[46] As part of their investigation, they created a dynamic website that highlights corporate control over various food markets and the political power they wield via lobbying dollars that uphold government-subsidized industrial farming.[47]

Growing food at industrialized scale requires multiple agricultural inputs including fertilizers, pesticides, seeds, tools, and machinery. The corporate consolidation of these various sectors is a recent phenomenon, as Jennifer Clapp, author of *Titans of Industrial Agriculture: How a Few Giant Corporations Came to Dominate the Farm Sector and Why It Matters*, reminds us

> that just a few hundred years ago, agricultural inputs were not usually widespread market commodities. Farmers typically saved their own seeds to plant the next season; used available waste materials and crop rotations to ensure that plants received sufficient nutrients; intercropped plants to keep pests at bay; and used hand or horse-drawn implements that they could craft themselves to till the soil and harvest crops.[48]

Seeds used to be considered a form of commons, something to be freely distributed and shared. In fact, the US Department of Agriculture used to save and send seeds to farmers while also encouraging them to save and share seeds of their own.[49] Today, saving seed is rare as the seed industry has become increasingly privatized and most commercial farmers are forced to purchase new seeds each season. The seed market is dominated by a handful of corporations "that genetically engineer and mass produce seed alongside complementary inputs including fertilizers and pesticides."[50] Four agrichemical companies dominate the seed and chemical market, Bayer (Monsanto), BASF, Corteva, and Sinochem, controlling 60–70 percent of the global seed and agrochemical market.[51] According to Beyond Pesticides, a nonprofit committed to a future without the use of chemical pesticides, these four multinational corporations "are exerting increasing leverage over an agricultural system that concentrates power and wealth, while threatening health, the environment, and access to food."[52] High levels of corporate monopolization have occurred across all sectors of industrial agriculture including producers and growers, distributors, and grocers. In general, less competition among agribusinesses translates to higher prices and fewer choices for consumers while limiting overall access to healthy, nutrient-rich foods.

Food Access and Health Impacts

There is so much to think about when it comes to how our access to food has shaped our individual health and the health and well-being of communities at both national and global scales. Food access is not guaranteed, nor equitably distributed. Physical access, as well as economic and cultural barriers, exist across diverse contexts and contribute to food insecurity, hunger, and malnutrition. In this section, we will briefly discuss some of the causes of food insecurity globally and then zoom in to look at food access in the United States along with the social and economic impacts of food insecurity. We end with a discussion of who is most vulnerable to food insecurity across the country with an eye toward equity and justice.

The numbers are startling. Globally, one in eleven people faced hunger in 2023 and in Africa, one in five people. This amounts to approximately 733 million people worldwide experiencing hunger.[53] The reasons for hunger and malnutrition are threefold according to the World Food Programme: conflict, climate-related disturbances (i.e., flooding, drought, heatwaves), and economic inequality. Collectively, these causes have displaced people from their land, disrupted food markets, increased food prices, and caused damage to agricultural resources needed for cultivation.[54] Conflict, one of the primary causes of today's hunger crisis, is driving people away from their land and livelihoods, disrupting markets, increasing food prices, and destroying critical opportunities for development. Its devastating impact can be seen across hunger hotspots including Palestine, Sudan, Syria, Yemen, and Ukraine. Climate emergencies such as floods, droughts, and heatwaves also significantly contribute by destroying lives, livelihoods, and crops, while degrading soils and damaging infrastructure and agricultural assets. Economic inequalities exacerbate hunger. When food prices rise due to struggling economies and external factors—for example the war in Ukraine—the poorest people struggle even more to put nutritious food on the table. Additionally, around 30 percent of global food production is lost or wasted every year, with lack of access to food storage and processing technology and markets causing significant losses for many farmers.[55] Ironically, farmers are some of the most malnourished social groups, especially commodity crop farmers who grow primarily for global consumption. For every dollar spent by the consumer on food, the farmer's share is only 15.9 cents. The rest of the money goes to marketing, distribution, and retail.[56]

In the United States, 13.5 percent of people experienced some form of food insecurity in 2023.[57] Hunger in the United States is primarily tied to poverty (and other structural causes of poverty), lack of access to affordable housing (which leaves little income for food), and structural racism that has limited people of color and Indigenous Peoples' access to healthy and culturally relevant foods.[58] Children are one of the most vulnerable populations when it comes to food insecurity, as poor nutrition can disrupt physical, cognitive, and emotional development. As we discussed in Chapter 3, the role advertising plays in influencing perceptions and ideas is very powerful, and advertising is especially insidious when it comes to children. Today, children aged 2–11 years see more than 1,000 food and beverage-related advertisements per year, and the majority of the products seen are unhealthy.[59] Companies spend $14 billion each year on marketing to children, over 80 percent of which is for fast food and other ultra-processed foods like snacks, candy, and sodas.[60] By comparison, only one in ten food advertisements are for fruits or vegetables.[61] As a result of this confluence of factors, 17 percent of children aged six to seventeen suffer from obesity, with higher rates for non-Hispanic Black (23.5 percent), Hispanic (22.2 percent), and American Indian/Alaska Native (19.2 percent).[62] Obesity is heavily correlated to Type 2 diabetes. The Centers for Disease Control estimated that in 2023, 8.4 million adolescents (32.7 percent) aged eight to fourteen had prediabetes. The physical health effects of our highly processed diet have been documented extensively and include diabetes, high blood pressure, increased risk of heart attack, stroke, and other diseases.[63] For children, these forms of malnutrition and food insecurity are similar to stressors like houselessness or exposure to violence and are categorized as adverse childhood experiences (ACE) or potentially traumatic events and correlate to poor emotional and health outcomes later in life.[64]

Hunger is also a big barrier to learning, and many teachers have firsthand experience with students suffering from food insecurity. Students who experience food insecurity and associated traumas (i.e., poverty, inadequate healthcare, unsafe housing) may have impacted concentration, memory, moods, and social interactions.[65] Multiple studies show the importance of nutrition in the first years of life being significant for brain development and future cognitive functioning.[66] Children's healthy body and brain development and growth are at risk without access to the right balance of nutrients. These nutrient imbalances can reduce brain cell production, impact cell size and complexity, and even lead to less efficient communication between brain cells. The cumulative result is slower language development, impaired fine motor skills, and lower IQ, all making learning in schools more challenging.[67] Federally funded school meal programs have historically been some of the best defenses against food insecurity for school-aged children. Unfortunately, the 2025 budget bill passed by Congress has made changes to qualifications for food assistance, impacting the eligibility of many children for free and reduced lunch.[68]

Resistance and Alternative Food System Models

As you are probably piecing together by this overview, our industrialized agricultural model is designed not with the consumer's health or ecological principles in mind, but rather is driven by maximizing profits to large transnational agribusinesses. Because of this, many communities most impacted by food insecurity are seeking to reclaim control over the food they eat by growing their own food, creating food cooperatives, and creating other forms of community supported agriculture to increase access to nutrient-dense and affordable food. In urban communities across the country, culturally relevant urban farms are popping up and rural and urban networks are being revitalized to bring back local food systems and support local economies.[69] Regenerative farming is pushing for even more sustainable growing practices than organic farming and across the board, small farmers are reimagining the food supply chain to enhance local economies by creating local distribution networks and retail outlets.

All of these efforts speak to the idea of food sovereignty. *Food sovereignty* as defined by La Via Campesina, is "the right of peoples to healthy and culturally appropriate food produced through ecologically sound and sustainable methods, and their right to define their own food and agriculture systems."[70] Indigenous communities are at the heart of food sovereignty movements, as these communities hold deep food-related knowledge and wisdom that has been built up over thousands of years. The Indigenous Food Systems Network describes food sovereignty as "a specific policy approach to addressing the underlying issues impacting Indigenous Peoples and our ability to respond to our own needs for healthy, culturally adapted Indigenous foods." The network has identified four principles that guide the movement, including this first principle that speaks to the sacred and divine relationship to food. It states, "Food is a gift from the Creator; in this respect the right to food is sacred and cannot be constrained or recalled by colonial laws, policies and institutions. Indigenous food sovereignty is fundamentally achieved by upholding our sacred responsibility to nurture healthy, interdependent relationships with the land, plants and animals that provide us with our food."[71] Once again, we see a very different worldview when it comes to thinking about food, one that is rooted in deep ecological knowledge about how to grow and raise food for community consumption. Today, however, many Indigenous People living on reservations experience food insecurity. One in four Native Americans is likely to experience food insecurity compared to one in seven Americans overall,[72] and while Native Americans make up less than two percent of the population, they suffer from the highest rates of poverty leading to food insecurity, resulting in high incidence of diet-related diseases.[73]

Soul Fire Farm in Grafton, NY, co-founded by Leah Penniman, author of *Farming While Black*, began in 2010 with "the mission to end racism in the food system and reclaim our ancestral connection to land."[74] Soul Fire Farm's work is vast and offers on-farm opportunities for BIPOC growers and youth, as well as support for the development of community gardens in the Troy, Albany, and Schenectady areas of New York State that have been most impacted by food apartheid. Their reach continues to expand and their work is also rooted in food sovereignty. The farm has compiled a set of food sovereignty action steps that address policy, individual actions, and collective actions with a focus on dignity and economic viability for farmers, reparations for stolen land, and building community relations and support for historically underserved farmers.[75] The growing practices at Soul Fire Farm are rooted in "Afro-Indigenous agroforestry, silvopasture, wildcrafting, polyculture, and spiritual farming,"[76] all practices designed to regenerate the land they are stewarding.

Regenerative agriculture, rooted in Indigenous land stewardship practices, is gaining momentum in food production today and sharply contrasts with industrialized agriculture's extractive principles. Regenerative farmers study and respond to their unique contexts, specifically seeking to first understand the economic, community, and ecological factors that are shaping their growing space.[77] Reducing soil disturbance and supporting soil health are some of the key principles that distinguish regenerative agriculture along with a commitment to diversity—biodiversity, economic diversity, and social diversity.[78] As we have discussed previously, diversity is the key to the resiliency of any system, and integrating diverse plants and animals allows for stronger connections below and above ground, linking soil health to nutrient density in foods.

Reclaiming the food supply chain to support local economies is a big part of food sovereignty and puts power back into the hands of consumers. Local food growers, processors, and distributors are popping up all over and serving as food hubs and cooperatives designed to increase access to local foods. Examples include Rolling Harvest, a New Jersey—based food rescue working to connect local farms to areas experiencing food insecurity,[79] Zone 7, a New Jersey–based local food hub serving restaurants, retailers, schools, and box delivery service for customers in New Jersey, Pennsylvania, and New York,[80] and the Bucks County Foodshed Alliance, a nonprofit committed to connecting consumers and producers to improve access to local, sustainable, and healthy food.[81]

Farmers markets are also expanding across the country with over 8,000 markets operating throughout the United States and offering some of the most affordable places to purchase local and nutritious food. Many farmers markets take a form of food stamp or EBT, and the USDA has a local food directory that allows users to search by location for various forms of local food access, including farm markets, food hubs, and Community Supported Agriculture (CSAs).[82] When supply chains were stalled during the COVID-19 pandemic, local farms and farmers markets were able to respond and support communities.[83] The power of community supported agriculture as a safeguard to local food security cannot be overstated. We hope this brief overview of how local communities are attempting to remediate the broken and unsustainable food system that we are all dependent upon offers inspiration to you and ultimately your students.

Implications of Food Production, Quality, and Access on Our Social and Ecological Systems

Food is one of our most basic needs and yet many of us are dependent on a food system that does not care about the impact it has on human or ecological health. Most of us don't even know how our food is grown, where it is made, what is in the processed foods we are eating, or how the kinds of foods we ingest impact our overall health and well-being. Grocery stores continue to get bigger and carry products loaded with unhealthy and sometimes dangerous ingredients, and yet the parking lots and aisles are packed every day. Some communities don't even have access to a grocery store and everyone is experiencing food prices rise as the quality and quantity of product diminish. The intentionality of a food system that is designed to benefit the agribusiness and the multinational corporations that dominate the global food market seems unconscionable, but somehow is normalized by marketing, advertising, and monopolization of markets. Below we highlight some statistics that speak to the power and damage caused by our modern food system and illuminate the often hidden human and environmental costs.

- Sixty-two percent of land in the continental United States is used for agriculture, but only about 20 percent of that land is used to grow food that we eat.[84]
- Agriculture is a major user of ground and surface water in the United States, and irrigation accounted for 42 percent of the Nation's total freshwater withdrawals in 2015.[85]
- In the United States, Bayer and Corteva alone control 72 percent of the corn seed market and 66 percent of the soybean seed market manufacturer.[86]
- Of the more than seventy meat brands marketing to consumers and retailers under the guise of individual names and logos, just four corporations—Tyson, JBS, Cargill, and National Beef—are behind these brands.[87]
- In 2011, Driscoll's was estimated to supply around 90 percent of raspberry sales in conventional supermarkets. In 2017, the company controlled approximately a third of the US berry market, with 60 percent of the organic strawberry market. As the market leader in the over $6 billion US fresh berry market, Driscoll's has over 700 contract growers in the United States, Mexico, Chile, and Peru.[88]
- Four companies—Walmart, Costco, Kroger and Ahold Delhaize—control 65 percent of the food retail market.[89]
- Worldwide adult obesity has more than doubled since 1990, and adolescent obesity has quadrupled. Over 390 million children and adolescents aged 5–19 years were overweight in 2022, including 160 million who were living with obesity.[90]
- In 2023, one in three households headed by single moms and one in four households headed by single dads experienced food insecurity.[91]
- In 2023, households in the lowest-income quintile spent an average of $5,278 on food (representing 32.6 percent of after-tax income). Households in the middle-income quintile spent an average of $8,989 on food (representing 13.5 percent of after-tax income). Households in the highest income quintile spent an average of $16,996 on food (representing 8.1 percent of after-tax income).[92]
- The agricultural sector is among the top contributors of fossil fuels, responsible for 10–17 percent of global greenhouse gas emissions.[93]
- Air emissions from livestock operations make up 14.5 percent of global greenhouse gas emissions.[94]

- Methane emissions total 2.5 million metric tons from the 7 million dairy cows living on factory farms; 533,000 metric tons from the 12 million factory feedlot beef cattle; and 107,700 metric tons from the 72.2 million hogs living on factory farms.[95]
- 78 percent of global ocean and freshwater eutrophication is caused by agriculture.[96]
- Agricultural runoff is a leading cause of water pollution. Heavy rains, associated with climate change, increase runoff of fertilizers and pesticides into rivers, lakes, and oceans, cause hypoxia (oxygen depletion) and create "dead zones" like the one in the Gulf of Mexico.[97]
- 70 percent of global freshwater withdrawal is used for agriculture.[98]

Honing Your Critical Lens

Our modern food system is a globalized, industrialized, and unsustainable system for providing long-term, healthy, resilient food to communities. It also has direct and indirect impacts on our ecosystem health and is increasingly vulnerable to climate change. This brief discussion of food is an attempt to connect some of the dots within the vast machinery of the food system that are often intentionally left disconnected. Whether it is the erasure of traditional knowledge held by Indigenous communities about how to manage land for sustainable and healthy food production, or the fact that most corn grown in the United States is not for food but for fuel and animal livestock, our food system is a product of the interplay between corporate power, local, state, and federal policy, and the masses. Understanding these dynamics, like everything else we have been discussing in this book, will raise your awareness about the roles these actors have on food production, quality, and access, and open up opportunities for reimagination of food systems. There is hope and inspiration in witnessing individuals and communities take back power in what and how food is produced and accessed. With your new knowledge of our complex food system and the socio-environmental issues that have been created by this system, we hope you feel a more holistic understanding of this topic and feel excited to help your elementary students expand their own knowledge and make lasting connections of their own.

This section is a great starting point to dive deeper into food systems and food policy and learn more about what is in your food and where it comes from. The **Instructional Materials** provide ready-to-teach lessons that are both universal and customizable to your teaching context. Closing this section is an invitation to use our diverse media resources found on our website to explore a more specific topic related to food. We encourage you to expand your understanding of something meaningful and important to you that you might be able to bring into your classroom.

Free Write and Research Activity: There is so much to learn about our food system—who controls it, how food is grown and processed, the impacts of conventional and industrial agriculture, alternative food systems, food apartheid and access, nutrient-dense foods versus processed foods, the global food system, how our diet impacts our overall health, and so many other topics and ideas. Most of this is not part of our common knowledge or learning in schools, so dive deeper and begin by reflecting on some of these critical questions related to food. To expand your thinking further, the website contains a table with a list of media resources and the food-related topics they address.

- What did school teach me about how food is produced?
- What did school teach me about the relationship between food and health?
- What does my diet consist of and why do I choose to eat what I eat?
- Where do I shop for food? Why do I shop there?
- Why is there so much food in the grocery store but people are still going hungry?
- Do I waste food? Do I question the impacts of my food waste?
- Where does my produce come from? How was it grown?
- Where does my meat come from? How was it raised?
- Can I grow any of my own food?
- Does my community have spaces for community members to grow food?
- How much of my personal budget do I spend on food?

Standards and Goals for Teaching and Learning

With new knowledge about the social and environmental costs of modern food production and the diverse ways communities are coming together to address food access, we hope you are starting to make connections to what you can teach in your elementary classrooms. This section broadly outlines the standards for social studies and science teaching at the elementary level that relate to these topics of study, as well as how the Cloud Institutes Education for Sustainability Content Standards and the UN Sustainable Development Goals can also be addressed and provide guidance to teachers.

Social Studies Standards from NCSS

Once again it is not hard to determine that learning as we have described and is represented in the instructional materials that follow, easily reflects NCSS Themes and goals for learning. While many Themes can apply, the most prevalent are: **Theme 3 People, Places, and Environments** examines the relationships between individuals and their physical surroundings, including how geography influences human behavior and societal development, **Theme 7 Production, Distribution, and Consumption** examines economic systems and the processes involved in producing, distributing, and consuming goods and services, **Theme 8 Science, Technology, and Society** investigates the impact of scientific advancements and technological innovations on society and the environment, and **Theme 10 Civic Ideals and Practices** focuses on the principles of democracy, citizenship, and civic engagement, encouraging students to understand their roles and responsibilities in a democratic society.

Below is a list of NCSS C3 indicators to demonstrate how they align to topics discussed in this chapter and our model instructional materials.

Textbox 6.1. Relevant NCSS C3 Inquiry Framework Indicators for Grades K-2[99]

- **D2.Eco.1.K-2.** Explain how scarcity necessitates decision-making.
- **D2.Eco.2.K-2.** Identify the benefits and costs of making various personal decisions.
- **D2.Eco.4.K-2.** Describe the goods and services that people in the local community produce and those that are produced in other communites.
- **D2.Eco.5.K-2.** Identify prices of products in a local market.
- **D2.Geo.1.K-2.** Construct maps, graphs, and other representations of familiar places.
- **D2.Geo.2.K-2.** Use maps, graphs, photographs, and other representations to describe places and the relationships and interactions that shape them.
- **D2.Geo.5.K-2.** Describe how human activities affect the cultural and environmental characteristics of places or regions.
- **D2.Geo.8.K-2.** Compare how people in different types of communities use local and distant environments to meet their daily needs.
- **D2.Geo.9.K-2.** Describe the connections between the physical environment of a place and the economic activities found there.
- **D2.Geo.11.K-2.** Explain how the consumption of products connects people to distant places.
- **D2.Civ.2.K-2.** Explain how all people, not just official leaders, play important roles in a community.
- **D2.Civ.6.K-2.** Describe how communities work to accomplish common tasks, establish responsibilities, and fulfill roles of authority.
- **D2.Civ.14.K-2.** Describe how people have tried to improve their communities over time.

Textbox 6.2. Relevant NCSS C3 Inquiry Framework Indicators for Grades 3–5[100]

- **D2.Eco.1.3–5.** Compare the benefits and costs of individual choices.
- **D2.Eco.2.3–5.** Identify positive and negative incentives that influence the decisions people make.
- **D2.Eco.3.3–5.** Identify examples of the variety of resources (human capital, physical capital, and natural resources) that are used to produce goods and services.
- **D2.Eco.7.3–5.** Explain how profits influence sellers in markets.

- **D2.Eco.8.3–5.** Identify examples of external benefits and costs.
- **D2.Geo.1.3–5.** Construct maps and other graphic representations of both familiar and unfamiliar places.
- **D2.Geo.2.3–5.** Use maps, satellite images, photographs, and other representations to explain relationships between the locations of places and regions and their environmental characteristics.
- **D2.Geo.4.3–5.** Explain how culture influences the way people modify and adapt to their environments.
- **D2.Geo.5.3–5.** Explain how the cultural and environmental characteristics of places change over time.
- **D2.Geo.9.3–5.** Analyze the effects of catastrophic environmental and technological events on human settlements and migration.
- **D2.Geo.10.3–5.** Explain why environmental characteristics vary among different world regions.
- **D2.Geo.11.3–5.** Describe how the spatial patterns of economic activities in a place change over time because of interactions with nearby and distant places.
- **D2.Geo.12.3–5.** Explain how natural and human-made catastrophic events in one place affect people living in other places.
- **D2.Civ.2.3–5.** Explain how a democracy relies on people's responsible participation, and draw implications for how individuals should participate.
- **D2.Civ.9.3–5.** Use deliberative processes when making decisions or reaching judgments as a group.
- **D2.Civ.6.3–5.** Describe ways in which people benefit from and are challenged by working together, including through government, workplaces, voluntary organizations, and families.
- **D2.Civ.8.3–5.** Identify core civic virtues and democratic principles that guide government, society, and communities.

Next-Generation Science Standards

Explorations of food production and food sovereignty primarily connect to NGSS disciplinary core ideas in Life Science and Earth Sciences. These standards address the needs of all living things for survival, including the plants and animals that we eat. In the spirit of EcoJustice, these standards also honor that humans have had a differential impact on the land via food production and that there are systems of power that control food production and access. Elementary students can also engage in engineering design challenges to design simple solutions to food production challenges (i.e., how to manage water, control pests, manage food waste) or more broadly, designing a community or school garden space at or near your school.

Textbox 6.3. Next-Generation Science Standards for Grades K-2

By grade 2 students understand:[101]

- How food is grown, where food comes from, and who has access to healthy foods (K-LS1-1)
- Farming is a process of growing plants and raising animals, and innovations in farming typically mimic how plants and animals survive in nature (1-LS1-1)
- Plants need sunlight, water, and nutrients to grow (2-LS2-1)
- Bees, birds, bats, and other animals are part of the process of pollinating plants and dispersing seeds (2-LS2-2)
- Growing food and raising animals is a human process that changes the environment (K-ESS2-2)
- Food can be grown in diverse environments, and different foods grow in different parts of the world (K-ESS3-1)
- Humans can reduce the impact on the land, water, air, and other living things by growing food regeneratively and composting food waste (K-ESS3-3)

Textbox 6.4. Next-Generation Science Standards for Grades 3–5

By grade 5 students understand:[102]

- Plants and animals that we eat for food have unique life cycles that are often controlled by humans. (3-LS1-1)
- Plants and animals that we eat for food are influenced by the environment they are grown and raised in. (3-LS3-2)
- Environmental changes have disrupted food systems, and humans have attempted to solve these disruptions. (3-LS4-4)
- Plants have internal and external structures that support their survival, and the food we eat comes from all the parts of the plants. (4-LS1-1)
- Plants, animals, and decomposers are always exchanging matter, and plant and animal waste can be captured by humans and used for compost. (5-LS2-1)
- Regenerative farming practices are more resilient to weather-related hazards. (3-ESS3-1)
- Industrial agriculture production is heavily dependent on fossil fuels, and alternative farming methods, like regenerative agriculture, reduce pollution from fossil fuels. (4-ESS3-1)
- Individual communities use diverse farming practices to protect the Earth's resources and environment and ensure food sovereignty. (5-ESS3-1)

Cloud Institutes Education for Sustainability Content Standards

Thinking about how our food is produced is connected to an interesting and exciting Cloud Institute content standard, **Inventing the Future**. This standard asks, "What will it look like to unleash a quality of life for all within the means of nature?"[103] which is exactly what this chapter on food is wrestling with. We know that our current food system is unsustainable, and these standards invite students to envision and imagine a transformed, fair, and just future for themselves and their communities.

Many of the Cloud Institute content standards apply to food, but we will highlight a few more and how they are significant to an understanding of a sustainable, healthy, and culturally relevant food system. The first is **Principles That Govern the Physical and Biological World** as this reminds us that food production must also be within the limits of the Earth and honor the natural laws that sustain life on Earth. When it comes to our current system of food production, we have seen the ways that adding chemical inputs that are toxic to humans and other living organisms is misaligned with the laws of nature, the consequences of which we are seeing today in our nutrient-poor food and correlated human health. Two related and relevant standards applicable to conversations about food are **Cultures, Tradition and Change** and **The Many Ways of Knowing**. Together, these standards remind us of the inextricable link between the health of the planet and the health of the people, recognizing the ways knowledge informs our food production practices. Culturally relevant foods and cultivation practices are tied to the viability and resilience of diverse communities.

One final cloud standard worth discussing is **Sustainable Economics** as food production comes with a cost, a literal cost, as well as social and environmental costs that are often out of view of the consumer. As we discussed earlier, food is a multi-billion-dollar industry often benefiting multinational corporations and agribusinesses at the expense of small farmers and the consumer. Restructuring our food system so that it recognizes the role small farms that are producing food (not commodities) are playing in feeding local foodsheds and contributing to the health of local economies is important to teach people about, especially during times of economic stress like during recent inflation and COVID-19.

United Nations Sustainable Development Goals

UN SDG 2 is to **end hunger, achieve food security and improved nutrition and promote sustainable agriculture**. As you can see embedded in this goal are many aspects we have discussed in this chapter so far. Access to food is tied to both the production of food and the health of people and the planet. Anemia caused by malnutrition is most prevalent in women ages 15–49 and 148 million children under age 5 are experiencing stunted growth and development, and 45 million children under age 5 are experiencing low weight for height. Malnutrition also includes thirty-seven million children under age

5 who are overweight[104] from "exposure to high-fat, high-sugar, high-salt, energy-dense, and micronutrient-poor foods, which tend to be lower in cost but also lower in nutrient quality."[105] Much of the target goals with Goal two are geared toward addressing food security for vulnerable populations, including children under five as well as "adolescent girls, pregnant and lactating women and older persons."[106]

Goal two is also concerned with how food is produced and who is producing food. One of the target goals is to "ensure sustainable food production systems and implement resilient agricultural practices that increase productivity and production, that help maintain ecosystems, that strengthen capacity for adaptation to climate change, extreme weather, drought, flooding and other disasters and that progressively improve land and soil quality" and to "double the agricultural productivity and incomes of small-scale food producers, in particular women, Indigenous peoples, family farmers, pastoralists and fishers" by 2030.[107] Once again, we can see the tension of these goals and how they intersect with the policies of individual nations, like the United States who again, has recently defunded programs that support sustainable and climate-smart growing practices. Progress toward achieving SDG two goals has been slow. According to the 2023 report, "hunger affected 9.1 percent of the global population in 2023, up from 7.5 percent in 2019 (between 713 million and 757 million people globally and one in five in Africa). Nearly 2.33 billion people, or almost 3 in 10, faced moderate or severe food insecurity in 2023, which was 383 million more than in 2019."[108] Related targets for increasing small food producers and addressing food affordability have also had slow gains—all of which speak to the control that agribusiness has over the global food supply. Two hopeful stories are highlighted in the flipbook, *Bringing the Data to Life*, which highlights success stories from across the globe related to the UN Sustainable Development Goals.[109] The first shows the ways a group of villages in Bhutan have created a thriving chili pepper farming industry and, as a result, created stable income for villagers. The second story showcases two women in a province in Panama who began by creating school and community gardens to help feed children and are now part of the movement toward sustainable ecotourism in Panama.[110]

Applying EcoJustice Pillars to Chapter Instructional Materials

The provided lessons are models of the type of elementary instruction that can help students understand the socio-environmental issues related to food production and food sovereignty. The instructional materials reflect our EcoJustice Education Pillars and are aligned to NCSS and Next-Generation Science Standards, and draw inspiration from the Cloud Institute Standards and the UN SDGs. The flowchart in Figure 6.2 illustrates the knowledge, skills, and attitudes that we hope for a student to have upon completion of elementary school and the goals for the K-2 and 3–5 grade bands in order to reach the end goal. The instructional materials we model are designed with these goals in mind and are offered as examples of how they can be addressed in elementary education. Review the

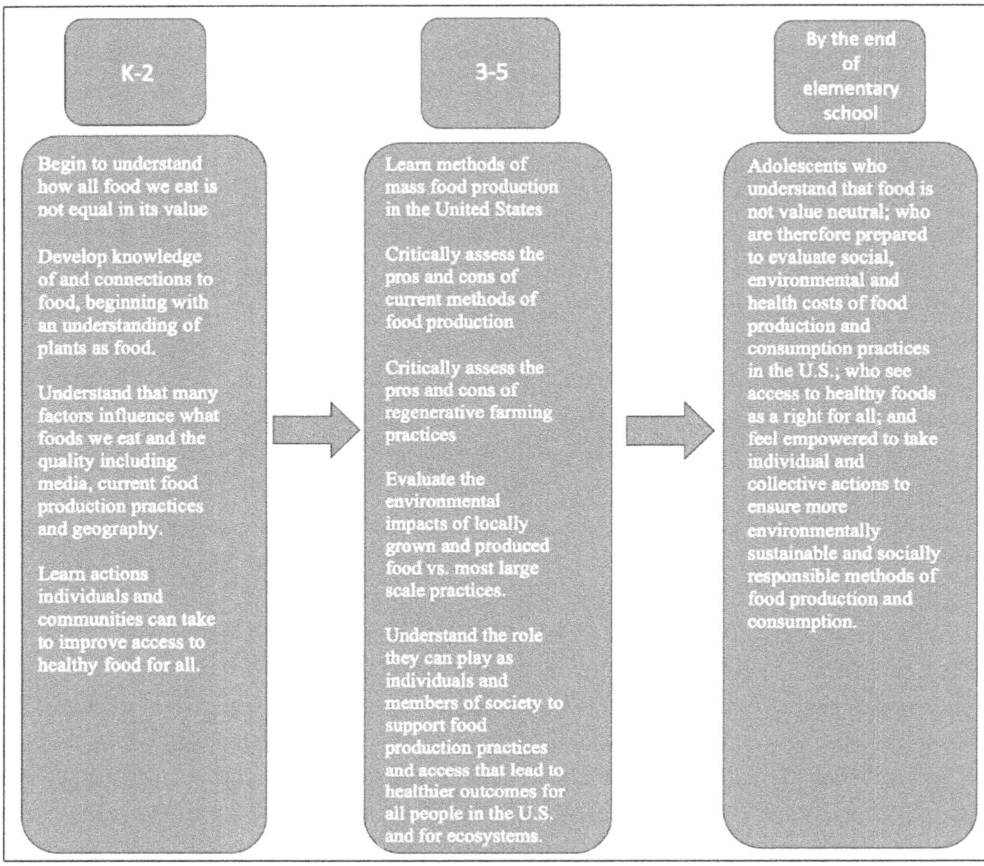

Figure 6.2. Flow chart K-5 to achieve an emerging EcoJustice consciousness related to food production and consumption. Author created.

progression and consider the types of learning experiences students will require to reach the stated goals for each grade band and for the end of elementary school.

In the instructional materials provided for our chapter on food production and sovereignty, we focus lessons on reconnecting young people with the knowledge of where our food comes from. In the K-2 lessons, students deepen their understanding of the relationship between food and the plant parts they eat, and in the grade 3–5 lessons students research the impacts of an industrialized food system. As a core pillar of EcoJustice education, helping young children see their interconnectedness with the natural and more human-managed plant and animal systems is something that can immediately spark interest and allow recognition that our well-being is connected to the food we eat. In both sets of lessons, there is also an exploration of food security and access, as this is one of the most pressing human rights violations millions of people endure worldwide.

We suggest that before you teach the concepts presented, refresh your own content knowledge on food production and access by reviewing topics presented in the **Introduction** and **Expanding Teacher Content Knowledge** sections. You can also do your own deep dive into a food topic of interest to you that you can transform into a lesson for your students using the list of films and shows provided on the website. Honing your understanding of the diversity of food systems will prepare you to see the lessons through a more critical lens, potentially challenging you and your students to question personal food choices. We live in a country where big box supermarkets are the norm and continue to expand. Food prices are rising, and we are too distanced from our food to truly understand why that is happening. However, there are ways to disrupt the dominance of the food industry—shop with a more critical lens (read ingredient lists and buy the cookies that don't use corn syrup as the main sweetener), grow your own food, and work with your neighbors to grow different foods for your community, shop at farmers markets, or join a CSA (community supported agriculture). Hopefully, by tying many of the ideas together from this book, you and your students can feel empowered to use your consumer dollar to make food choices that benefit your health and the health of the local economy and ecology. All lessons come with many resources that can be adapted to your classroom context, and remember that there is so much more to explore with your students through the lens of food that is relevant to science and social studies. For more ideas on class projects, field trip ideas, or class guests, check out the final section on **Community and Place-Based Learning Opportunities**.

> *Food Instructional Materials*
>
> *What struck me most was how invested the students became in brainstorming additional ways to use our school garden to support the wider community. After reading* City Garden, *I shared images of my town's own community garden, and the class was thrilled to see this real-world example in action. It solidified their understanding of how small initiatives can make a big impact.*
>
> *—Paige, Early Childhood Teacher*

Textbox 6.6. K-2 EcoJustice Instructional Materials Food

Essential Question(s):

- How can learning about the foods we eat and where they come from he p us make our community healthier and more food secure?

Objectives

At the conclusion of the lessons, students will be able to:

- **Identify** and name the six main parts of a plant (root, stem, leaf, flower, fruit, seed).
- **Categorize** foods we eat into each plant part (e.g., carrot as a root, celery as a stem, spinach as a leaf, broccoli as a flower, apple as a fruit, sunflower seed as a seed).
- **Describe** the function of each plant part and how it helps the plant grow
- **Explain** why people have different access to fresh and healthy foods.
- **Assess** multiple strategies that communities use to address food insecurity.

Standards:

Social Studies

- **D2.Eco.4.K-2.** Describe the goods and services that people in the local community produce and those that are produced in other communities.
- **D2.Eco.5.K-2.** Identify prices of products in a local market.
- **D2.Civ.2.K-2**. Explain how all people, not just official leaders, play important roles in a community.
- **D2.Civ.6.K-2.** Describe how communities work to accomplish common tasks, establish responsibilities, and fulfill roles of authority.
- **D2.Civ.14.K-2**. Describe how people have tried to improve their communities over time.

Science

- **K-LS1-1:** Use observations to describe patterns of what plants and animals (including humans) need to survive.
- **2-LS2-1**: Plan and conduct an investigation to determine if plants need sunlight and water to grow.
- **K-ESS2-2:** Construct an argument supported by evidence for how plants and animals (including humans) can change the environment to meet their needs.
- **K-ESS3-1**: Use a model to represent the relationship between the needs of different living things and the places they live.
- **K-ESS3-3:** Communicate solutions that will reduce the impact of humans on land, water, air, and other living things.

Materials:

Lesson 1

- Various fruits and vegetables that students are familiar with
- Poster paper or handout of plant parts with pre-printed word strips of the plant parts—root, stem, leaf, flower, fruit, seed
- Pots or trays, seed

Lesson 2

- Book or Read Aloud *Saturday at the Food Pantry* at https://www.youtube.com/watch?v=oYCuKS4Q7MI

Lesson 3

- Book or Read Aloud *City Green* at https://www.youtube.com/watch?v=6rm5gaurl4o

Important Vocabulary/Concepts:

- Plant parts—roots, stems, leaves, flowers, fruits, seeds
- Food insecurity/Food security
- Food pantry
- Community garden

- Whole foods
- Processed foods

Note to Teacher: This lesson assumes some prior knowledge of the parts of plants (roots, stem, leaves, flowers, fruits, seeds).

Instructional Materials Description and Overview:
In this set of instructional materials, students will begin by exploring some fruits and vegetables they are familiar with and connect these to the parts of the plant we eat. Students will review the parts of a plant, what plants need to survive, and begin to grow plants in the classroom. Next, students will learn about access to healthy and fresh fruits and vegetables and how access is not equal for all families in the United States. They will read the story, *Saturday at the Food Pantry*, and conduct class research about food insecurity statistics and resources in their community. The set of lessons ends with students brainstorming and implementing an action they can take as a class to address food insecurity in their community.

Lesson 1: Plant Parts and Food

ENGAGE: Lesson Introduction

- Have a table of different fruits and vegetables that students are familiar with.
- Have students observe the different fruits and vegetables and share some of their initial observations and questions.

EXPLORE: Categorizing Activity

- Put students into groups of 4–5.
- Provide each group with a food item that represents each of the different parts of a plant (for example, a potato or carrot for the root, celery for the stem, lettuce for leaves, broccoli for flowers, an apple for fruit, and a sunflower seed for seed). Each group should have six total food items. (Note: You can also use images of food.)
- Have students try to categorize the parts of the plants based on their observations and prior knowledge of plant parts. Ask them to record their ideas on a big chart paper using drawings and words (or use pre-printed word strips of the plant parts—root, stem, leaf, flower, fruit, seed).

EXPLAIN: Video and Class Discussion

- Have students share their poster of the plant and the parts of the plant that they eat.
- Ask students if they have a favorite part of the plant that they eat.
- Review plant parts and functions with students by watching the video Parts of Plants for Kids | Learn all about plant parts and their functions at https://www.youtube.com/watch?v=A-xScqCN0GA
- Using the video record on a chart paper, what plants need to grow and what part of the plant can help with this (e.g., leaves help capture sunlight, roots help collect water).

ELABORATE: **Application activity**

- Explain to students that they will plant their own seeds and try to grow food in the classroom (or a school garden).
- Have students plant seeds of fruits and vegetables that they would like to have access to in their classroom. (Note: Easy plants to grow, flower, and eat are herbs, lettuces, peas.)
- Review with students what they know about plants and what they need to grow.
- Set up a few pots or trays with soil and seeds.
- As a class, discuss what the plants will need each day to be sure they survive.
- Have students set up a schedule of who will take care of the plants each day and how they will be taken care of.
- Make observations of the plants each day.

EXTEND: Photo Elicitation and Critical Dialogue

Ask students to think about where they can buy fresh fruits and vegetables in their community. Show them images from local farm markets, supermarkets, bodegas, Walmart, Costco, and so on.

https://www.flickr.com/photos/23206546@N04/28024707592

https://www.istockphoto.com/photo/store-sign-over-boxes-of-produce-outside-of-a-bodega-in-washington-heights-nyc-gm2183683913-602558368?searchscope=image%2Cfilm

- Engage students in a critical dialogue about how people access fresh fruits and vegetables using the following prompts:
  - What do you notice in these pictures?
  - Do you think that all of the fruits and vegetables in these places taste the same?

- How do you connect to these pictures? Are any of these images familiar to you?
- Where do you think all of these fruits and vegetables came from? Do you think they were all grown the same?
- Why do you think it is important to eat fresh fruits and vegetables?
- What do you think happens when people don't have access to fresh fruits and vegetables?
- Do you think having access to fresh fruits and vegetables is a human right?

EVALUATE: Wrap-Up Activity/Assessment

- Choose one idea from class today to share with a table partner.
- Together write or draw your idea.

Lesson 2: Food Access and Insecurity

ENGAGE: Lesson Introduction

- Show students pictures of the interior of different refrigerators. Provide multiple examples that include fully stocked refrigerators, refrigerators with healthy foods, and a sparse refrigerator. Ask them to turn and talk a little about what they notice in the images.
- Engage students in a brief discussion about the differences they notice between the images of the refrigerators.
- Be sure to discuss further any observations that highlight:
  - The difference between whole, fresh foods and processed foods.
  - The little food available in the one fridge.
- Ask students to think a little bit about why these differences in refrigerator contents might exist.

EXPLORE: Read Aloud: *Saturday at the Food Pantry* by Diane O'Neill

- Remind students about the discussion from the first lesson about access to fresh fruits and vegetables.
- Read aloud or watch the video, Saturday at the Food Pantry: Kids Storytime by Diane O'Neill
- During and after the reading, engage in a class discussion using any of the following questions as prompts:
  - Why did Molly and her mom go to the food pantry? What does this tell us about their situation?
  - How does Molly feel when she sees her classmate Caitlin at the food pantry? Why do you think she felt this way?
  - How does Caitlin feel when Molly sees her? Why do you think she felt this way?
  - Molly's mom says, "Everybody needs help sometimes." What do you think she meant when she said that and how do we see this idea in the story?

  - Why do you think there are signs in the pantry saying how many of each item people can take? Do you think this is a good idea?
  - Why does Molly's mom hesitate to let her take cookies? What does this tell us about her feelings and worries?
  - Why is it important to have places like food pantries? How do they help people?

EXPLAIN: Food Insecurity Video

- Explain to the students that they will now watch a video about food insecurity, which is what Molly and Caitlin experienced in the story. Tell them to think about this term, and that after the video they will work as a class to define the term.
- Watch the video Child Food Insecurity Report on NBC Nightly News: Kids Edition at https://www.youtube.com/watch?v=RkRs73b0Enk
- Engage the students in a dialogue about the video using the following prompts:
  - Can you make any personal connections to the video?
  - Was there anything new that you learned in the video?
  - Did the video make you have any feelings? If so, what were they and how/where did you feel them?
  - Why do you think food insecurity exists in a country with so much wealth like ours, especially when we have more than enough food in our grocery stores to feed everyone who is hungry?
  - What questions do you have about food insecurity?
- Come up with a class definition for *food insecurity*

ELABORATE: Food Insecurity Class Research

- Have students share some of their questions about food insecurity and as a class do some research together exploring food insecurity and food access in your community. (Teachers can work with school librarians and media specialists to help young children learn how to conduct research by asking them to come up with key search terms, reading aloud some of the resources they find, helping students see why you, as the teacher, might like one resource over another, use Kiddle.co—a kids google-like search engine to find resources.)
  - If students struggle with coming up with questions, some questions might be:
    - What resources are available for families in our community to address food insecurity?
    - What role does our school play in supporting families facing food insecurity?
    - How many people are food insecure in our community?
    - How does food insecurity impact learning in school?
- Demonstrate for students how to do the research, ask for their help with doing the research, and read aloud answers to their questions.
- Record student questions and answers on poster paper.

EXTEND: Photo Elicitation and Critical Dialogue

- Explain to students that not everyone can always access healthy foods, and this often depends on what grocery stores and markets are available where they live, as well as the current cost of food and how much money a family can afford to spend on food. Share images that depict the cost of fresh food versus processed foods, lack of access to fresh food, fast food strips, and other relevant food-related images.
- Engage students in a critical dialogue about the lack of access to healthy foods:
    - What do you notice in these pictures?
    - Why do you think this situation exists?
    - Why is it important to eat healthy foods?
    - What happens when we don't have access to healthy foods?
    - What can we do about this situation?

EVALUATE: Wrap-Up Activity/Assessment

- Have students make a drawing of a lunch box of what they think a person their age needs to be healthy.

Lesson 3: What Can We Do to Address Food Insecurity?

ENGAGE: Lesson Introduction

- Review with students the idea of food insecurity.
    - Have them read aloud the class definition and any ideas they remember related to food insecurity.
    - Have students recall ideas from the reading, *Saturday at the Food Pantry*.

EXPLORE: Turn and Talk

- Ask students to turn and talk about the following questions:
    - Do you think food pantries are enough to help all the hungry people?
    - What are other ways communities can help people who might not have enough food?

EXPLAIN: Share Ideas

- Have students share their ideas about how the communities can help people who are food insecure.
- Write student responses on the board or poster.
- If creating a community garden comes up, use it as a jumping-off point to tell them they will read a book called *City Green* about a little girl who started a community garden in her community.
- Ask students to turn and talk about what they think a community garden is.
- Show them pictures of community gardens and ask them, "How might a community garden help address food insecurity?"

ELABORATE: Read Aloud: *City Green* by DyAnne DiSalvo-Ryan

- Read aloud or watch the video City Green by DyAnne DiSalvo-Ryan
- During the reading, ask a few prompting questions like:
  - What problems does Marcy notice in her neighborhood? How do these problems make her feel?
  - How do Marcy and her neighbors work together to solve the problem of the empty lot? What steps do they take?
  - Do you think she could have done this alone? Explain your thinking.
- After the reading is finished, engage in a class discussion using any of the following questions as prompts:
  - How does the community garden affect Marcy and the people who live in Marcy's neighborhood? What are some changes you notice?
  - Why do you think the author chose to write about a community garden?
  - What message do you think the book teaches?
  - Have you ever worked with others to make your neighborhood, school, or home a better place? What did you do, and how did it feel?

EXTEND: Photo Elicitation and Critical Dialogue

Show students images of community gardens like the ones below. Include images of people working together, food produced, and how they are often found in urban areas.

https://openverse.org/image/157e9d65-64f1-415a-8b0f-2a53b0a9690a?q=community+garden&p=8

https://openverse.org/image/99bd75ca-7a33-4cf3-bae4-9905484f085d?q=community+garden&p=15

https://www.flickr.com/photos/52271725@N07/8201727667

- Engage students in a critical dialogue about the power of community gardens:

- How do you connect to these images?
- What do you notice in these pictures?
- Why do you think this situation exists?
- How do community gardens connect to food insecurity?
- Why do you think it is important for communities to create gardens like this in neighborhoods?

EVALUATE: Design

- Have students design a school community garden and label what the plants would need to grow, what they would grow, and how they would take care of it.

Textbox 6.7. 3–5 EcoJustice Instructional Materials Food

Essential Question(s):

- What makes a strong and resilient food system?

Objectives
At the conclusion of the lessons, students will be able to:

- **Analyze** the environmental and social impacts of industrialized agriculture including both benefits (e.g., increased yields, efficiency) and harms (e.g., pollution, loss of biodiversity, labor issues).
- **Compare and contrast** industrialized agriculture with regenerative and urban agriculture.
- **Understand** what food insecurity is and how it is different from simply being hungry.
- **Identify** and **analyze** the causes (such as poverty, unequal distribution, barriers to access) and effects (on health, behavior, learning outcomes, and well-being) of food insecurity.
- **Explore** and evaluate possible solutions or interventions, including community programs, advocacy, and service projects.
- **Take action** to help reduce food insecurity in their own community.

Standards:
Social Studies

- **D2.Eco.1.3–5.** Compare the benefits and costs of individual choices.
- **D2.Eco.2.3–5.** Identify positive and negative incentives that influence the decisions people make.
- **D2.Eco.3.3–5.** Identify examples of the variety of resources (human capital, physical capital, and natural resources) that are used to produce goods and services.
- **D2.Eco.7.3–5.** Explain how profits influence sellers in markets.
- **D2.Eco.8.3–5.** Identify examples of external benefits and costs.
- **D2.Geo.1.3–5.** Construct maps and other graphic representations of both familiar and unfamiliar places.
- **D2.Geo.2.3–5.** Use maps, satellite images, photographs, and other representations to explain relationships between the locations of places and regions and their environmental characteristics.
- **D2.Geo.4.3–5.** Explain how culture influences the way people modify and adapt to their environments.
- **D2.Geo.5.3–5.** Explain how the cultural and environmental characteristics of places change over time.
- **D2.Geo.9.3–5.** Analyze the effects of catastrophic environmental and technological events on human settlements and migration.

- **D2.Geo.10.3–5.** Explain why environmental characteristics vary among different world regions.
- **D2.Geo.11.3–5.** Describe how the spatial patterns of economic activities in a place change over time because of interactions with nearby and distant places.
- **D2.Geo.12.3–5.** Explain how natural and human-made catastrophic events in one place affect people living in other places.
- **D2.Civ.9.3–5**. Use deliberative processes when making decisions or reaching judgments as a group.

NGSS Science Standards

- **3-LS1-1:** Develop models to describe that organisms have unique life cycles but all have birth, growth, reproduction, and death.
- **5-LS2-1:** Develop a model to describe the movement of matter among plants, animals, decomposers, and the environment.
- **3-ESS3-1:** Make a claim about the merit of a design solution that reduces the impacts of a weather-related hazard.
- **4-ESS3-1:** Obtain and combine information to describe that energy and fuels are derived from natural resources and their uses affect the environment.
- **5-ESS3-1:** Obtain and combine information about ways individual communities use science ideas to protect the Earth's resources and environment.

Materials:

Lesson 1

- Chromebook or Laptop for Research

Lesson 2

- Video: Regenerative Agriculture: Nourishing the Soil, Healing the Planet | Bioneer at https://www.youtube.com/watch?v=2j7DHDoaNvQ&t=73s
- Paper for Drawing Models/Visuals

Lesson 3

- Video What Is Food Insecurity? | At the Table at https://www.youtube.com/watch?v=UwVW4f_52n4
- Video: Just Food's Sheryll Durrant: Leading the Urban Agriculture Revolution against Food Apartheid in NYC at https://www.youtube.com/watch?v=UwVW4f_52n4
- Chromebook or Laptop for Research

Important Vocabulary/Concepts:

- Industrialized Agriculture
- Regenerative Agriculture
- Urban Agriculture
- Soil Health
- Biodiversity
- Ecosystem Services

- Mimicking Nature
- Cover Cropping
- Managed Grazing
- No-Till
- Perennial
- Annual
- Food Insecurity
- Food Apartheid
- Community Garden

Instructional Materials Overview: In this set of lessons on food production, students will begin by exploring industrialized farming processes and practices and learn how most food is grown conventionally, with heavy water and chemical inputs that are produced from fossil fuels. They will conduct their own research on aspects of the industrialized food system and investigate the socio-environmental impacts of industrialized agricultural practices. Students will then explore alternative agricultural systems including regenerative agriculture and urban agriculture as a way to reduce these social and environmental impacts and allow communities to regain control over the quality and cost of food. Food insecurity will be discussed and a class action will be taken to address food insecurity in their community.

Lesson 1: Industrialized Agriculture: Introduction and Research

ENGAGE: Lesson Introduction

- Have students draw a meal that they ate recently. Have them label the food and add any information about where the food came from.
  - Push the students to keep going back to the source.
    - Example: If a student shares that they ate a hamburger that came from Costco, have the student reflect on where Costco got the hamburger.
    - Try to get students to get to the original food source (Hamburger = cow).
- Ask students to share with a partner what food they ate and discuss the plants and animals that were part of their meal and where they think they came from.
- Have students share out to the whole class some of their foods and their thoughts about where this food comes from.
- Explain to students that they will explore more about how food moves from a farm to their plates.

EXPLORE: Research Activity

- Have students choose one item from their meal and record it in their notebook or on a handout.
- Have students research their item and try to learn more about where it comes from. Ask them to trace their food item back to its original plant or animal form.
- Have students share what they learned from their exploration.

EXPLAIN: **Photo Elicitation and Critical Dialogue**

- Explain to students that most food we eat today is produced by our industrialized agriculture system that is far removed from the farm ideal we often picture in our minds when we imagine farms and farmers.
- Show them images that are representative of practices associated with our industrialized food system including: Monoculture, CAFOs, Genetically Modified foods, Chemical inputs, Corporate Monopolies over production and seed.

https://www.flickr.com/photos/14922165@N00/4719020153

https://www.istockphoto.com/photo/feedlot-gm173688921-8244598?searchscope =image%2Cfilm

https://www.flickr.com/photos/137169575@N04/24443679794

- Ask students to talk in small groups about the images and what they notice. Have each group write down three ideas that they discussed and which pictures informed their discussion.

ELABORATE: **Preliminary research on Industrialized Agriculture**

- Break students into small groups and assign them a topic related to industrialized agriculture. Suggested topics include:
  - Industrial Agriculture and Concentrated Animal Feeding Operations (CAFOs)
  - Industrial Agriculture and Monoculture
  - Industrial Agriculture and Climate Change
  - Industrial Agriculture and Chemical Inputs
  - Industrial Agriculture and Soil Degradation
  - Industrial Agriculture and Water Use and Pollution
  - Industrial Agriculture and Genetically Modified Foods
  - Industrial Agriculture and Monopolies
- Have students use some of the following websites (as well as other internet resources) to learn more about the industrial agriculture practices and the social and environmental impacts of them:
  - What Is Industrial Agriculture and Why Is It Bad?—https://thehumaneleague.org/article/industrial-agriculture
  - What Is It and Why Is Industrial Agriculture Bad?—https://www.straydoginstitute.org/industrial-agriculture/
  - Food Mythbusters—https://realfoodmedia.org/programs/food-mythbusters/
  - What Is Organic Farming?—Earth.Org Kids—https://kids.earth.org/cl mate-change/organic-farming/

  - The Key to Feeding the World? It's Healthy Soil—YES! Magazine Solutions Journalism—https://www.yesmagazine.org/environment/2017/04/15/the-key-to-feeding-the-world-its-healthy-soil
  - 10 Things you Should Know About Industrial Farming—https://www.unep.org/news-and-stories/story/10-things-you-should-know-about-industrial-farming
  - Hidden Costs of Industrial Agriculture | Union of Concerned Scientists—https://www.ucs.org/resources/hidden-costs-industrial-agriculture
  - Zombie Soil: The Harmful Result of Industrial Farming—Earth911—https://earth911.com/business-policy/zombie-soil-the-harmful-result-of-industrial-farming/

- Give students options for how to present their research—slides, infographic, poster, script, video, collage
- Gallery walk with one presenter staying behind to share the project

EXTEND: Photo Elicitation and Critical Dialogue

Ask students to each choose one image from their research to co-create a photo elicitation activity for the class. Ask students to choose images that highlight the environment and/or social impact of industrialized agriculture. Examples might include people being exposed to chemical sprays, animal waste, and loss of soil and vegetation.

- Have each group lead a critical dialogue using the following prompts:

  - What do you notice in these pictures?
  - What do you know about what is going on in this picture?
  - Why do you think this situation exists?
  - How does this situation impact you/your community?
  - What do you think *you* can do about this situation?
  - What do you think we can do about this situation?

EVALUATE: Wrap-Up Activity/Assessment

- Ask students to share one thing they learned about industrialized agriculture from another group's research.

Lesson 2: Alternatives to Industrialized Agriculture

ENGAGE: Lesson Introduction

- Ask students to work in small groups to draw a visual model of industrialized agriculture on one half of a poster paper. Ask students to label some of the parts of their visual with ideas they learned from their classmates and their research (ideally have mixed groups of students from the prior research).

EXPLORE: Brainstorming Alternatives to Industrialized Agriculture

- Ask students to brainstorm and discuss with their group alternative models to industrialized agriculture. Have students write down ideas on a piece of paper.
- Have groups share ideas from their brainstorm with the whole class. Record student ideas on the board or chart paper.

EXPLAIN: Introduction to Regenerative Farming

- Explain to students that today they are going to learn about an alternative to industrialized agriculture called **regenerative farming**.
- Ask them to think about the word regenerative and ask them what images and ideas come to mind.
- Show a few pictures of different regenerative farms and ask students to observe the differences between these images and images they saw of industrial farms.

Jessica Reeder, CC BY-SA 2.0 https://creativecommons.org/licenses/by-sa/2.C, via Wikimedia Commons

https://www.flickr.com/photos/184594136@N08/49243424367

Anna Frodesiak, CC0, via Wikimedia Commons

- Have students turn and talk and together record at least three differences they notice.
- Allow students to share their ideas and record on the board.
- Create a class definition for **regenerative farming** based on student responses.

ELABORATE: Video on Regenerative Farming Principles

- Watch this video on Regenerative Farming Principles (See vocabulary terms for a list of words that might be new to students. When these words come up in the video, pause and explain or have students try to explain from context).
  - Video: Regenerative Agriculture: Nourishing the Soil, Healing the Planet | Bioneers: https://www.youtube.com/watch?v=2j7DHDoaNvQ&t=73s
- Have students take notes as they watch the video
- Have students share out some of their notes and write them on the board or chart paper
- Review the principles of regenerative farming using the Bioneers website Regenerative Agriculture Collection at https://bioneers.org/regenerative-agriculture/
- Be sure students feel confident with the principles/practices of regenerative farming

EXTEND: Visual Model Building for Regenerative Farming

- Have students create a visual model drawing of a farm or garden that utilizes regenerative farming practices.

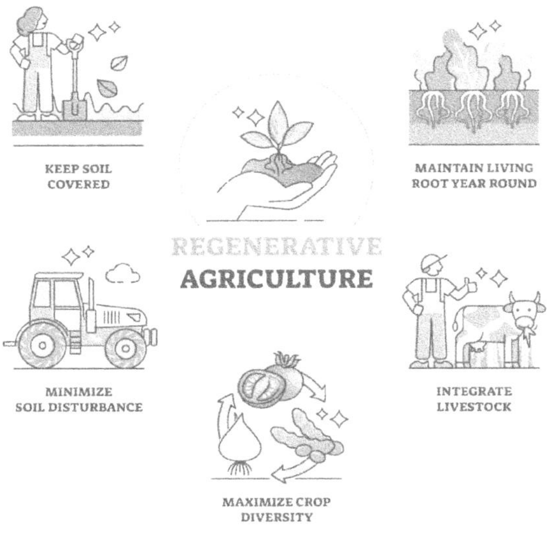

https://www.istockphoto.com/vector/regenerative-agriculture-method-for-soil-health-and-vitality-outline-diagram-gm1346337711-424136187?searchscope=image%2Cfilm

EVALUATE: Wrap-Up Activity/Assessment

- Have students write a three-sentence summary of their model that explains *why* regenerative farming is better for the environment and for people.

Lesson 3: Urban Farming and Feeding Communities
ENGAGE: Lesson Introduction: Video on Food Insecurity

- Watch the video What Is Food Insecurity? | At the Table at https://ny.pbslearningmedia.org/resource/what-is-food-insecurity-video/at-the-table/
- Have students turn and talk about what they saw and heard in the video
- Ask a few students to share their thoughts from the video and their turn and talk

EXPLORE: Group Brainstorm

- In small groups, have students discuss the following questions:
  - How does the video explain WHY there is food insecurity?
  - What solutions did you hear or see in the video that are trying to address food insecurity (e.g., food banks with culturally relevant food, changing policy that keeps food inaccessible in poor communities and communities of color)?
  - Do you think food pantries are enough to help all the hungry people? Why or why not?

EXPLAIN: Video on Urban Agriculture

- Tell students they will now watch a video of a community that is trying to address food insecurity through urban agriculture.
- Watch the video Just Food's Sheryll Durrant: Leading the Urban Agriculture Revolution against Food Apartheid in NYC at https://www.youtube.com/watch?v=UwVW4f_52n4
- Ask students to discuss in small groups
  - How does this video explain WHY there is food insecurity and how does it connect to the first video? (Marginalized communities—low-income and communities of color—experience food insecurity at higher rates than other communities)
  - How do you think urban agriculture can help address food insecurity?
  - How do you think urban agriculture is similar to or different from the other two models of food production researched so far—industrialized and regenerative agriculture?
  - What are other ways communities can help people who might be experiencing food insecurity? What are ways we can help people in our community who might be experiencing food insecurity?
- Have students share some of their thinking with the class from their small group discussions. Record student ideas about ways they can take action to address food insecurity.
- Discuss all the ideas as a class and choose one or two to do together (e.g., School/community garden, food donation, volunteer at a food bank, reduce food waste at school, raise awareness about food insecurity, write thank you notes to people who work at food pantries and other places that address food insecurity, write letters to community leaders or grocery stores to see how they can help with food insecurity).

ELABORATE: **Create a Plan for Your Action**

- Create a plan for your actions and implement your plan.
- Have small groups of students work on different parts of the plan (e.g., posters, labeling boxes, writing messages to community leaders, etc.).

EXTEND: Continue Work on Action

- Use additional class time as needed to allow students to continue working on the class action.

EVALUATE: **Wrap-Up Activity/Assessment**

- Class Discussion and drawing—Ask students to reflect on their action(s) and make a drawing that represents how they feel when they are helping address an issue in their community.

Community and Place-Based Learning Opportunities

This section invites teachers and parents to engage community members, outside school experts, and other local knowledge resources to extend the EcoJustice learning experiences that students are engaging with in classrooms. We know taking trips with students can be difficult, so sending these suggestions home to families might be a good idea. Additionally, we included inviting some speakers to visit your classroom to discuss in more detail their work as it relates to food production, food access, and food sovereignty.

For this theme of food production and sovereignty, we suggest any of the following community and place-based learning experiences for you and your students:

- Have students grow their own food, either in the classroom or on a larger scale in a school garden or greenhouse. Students can participate in the planning of the garden as well as in the preparation, cultivation, and harvesting of the garden. The garden can be used to teach many subject areas including math, integrative STEAM, and arts. Some important considerations for planting a school garden are:
  - Include students and parents as much as possible.
  - Check out neighboring school gardens and community gardens to learn more about what is being grown locally.
  - Plan who will be responsible for managing the garden in the summer, including weeding and watering.
  - Plant food crops that are best planted in May/June and can be harvested in September/October for your school year and growing zone.
  - Plant a three sisters garden or other Indigenous polyculture (e.g., beans, corn, sunflower, squash) that can be used to connect students to Traditional Ecological and Indigenous Knowledge.
  - Plant perennial foods like berries and fruits. If well mulched with woodchips or straw, they need less watering and overall maintenance and can provide food over many years.
- Visit a farm or invite a farmer or farmers to visit the classroom. There are so many types of farms, so be sure to include a diversity of growers to showcase the variety of ways people are reshaping local food systems. Consider inviting a multigenerational farmer as well as a historically underserved farmer (HUF), an urban grower, or other specialty crop farmers (e.g., fruit, flowers, vegetables, etc.), an oyster, bee, or worm farmer?
- Visit a farmers market and have students explore the types and prices of foods being sold. Many farmers markets require that the food travel under a certain distance, so the types of food available at different times of the year are important for students to note. Have students write interview questions for the farmers at the market and

allow them time to explore and shop. Do comparisons of food availability and prices to local grocery stores.

- Track food miles for your students' favorite snacks. Start with fresh produce—carrots, apples, mangoes, and then have them try to put together the food miles for a more complex snack with multiple ingredients. This type of exercise offers real-world math connections.
- Ask students to bring in their food waste for a week and collect it into a five-gallon bucket. Weigh the waste each day, integrating math concepts as well. Collect data about the types of food waste the class is collecting and engage in a discussion of how to reduce food waste and what food waste can be used for (Hint: compost!!!). Set up a composting system in your classroom—a bucket that is brought weekly to a drop location (many farmers markets have compost collection) or start a worm composting bin in your classroom.
- Create a map of your community foodshed. Locate where people buy food, what kinds of place each location is (big box supermarket—Costco, Walmart, family-owned grocery store, bodega, farmers market, restaurant, and so on). What transportation is needed to get to various food outlets.
- Visit and volunteer at a place that is meant to address food insecurity in your community. This might be a food pantry, food bank, community kitchen, or other type of meal center. Have students engage in the daily tasks as well as make observations about the kinds of foods that are available, who is visiting the pantry or kitchen, and how they feel while volunteering.
- Visit a community garden in an urban environment to learn more about how people living in cities are ensuring access to culturally relevant foods. Observe what and how people are growing food in small spaces with potentially contaminated soil through container gardening and other forms of raised beds. Learn more about how soil is being remediated in urban communities.
- Connect with people in the community who are saving seeds. Start a seed library! There are many interesting seed-saving farms and community projects that are ensuring access to diverse and culturally significant seeds. Invite a seed saver into your classroom to talk about the work they do, the places they have traveled to secure seeds, and the diversity of seeds they have saved and why they are significant. Ask them to help you start saving seeds in your own classroom. Have students save seeds from fruit they are eating, flowers they see, community gardens, and other sources. Check out the Seed Library Network[111] to learn more about how to get a seed-saving project started in your school!
- Have students keep a food journal for a week to see what they are eating on a daily basis. This allows for opportunities for individual and collective reflection on food access, cultural significance of food, and data analysis on foods being consumed.
- Invite a chef into your classroom who does education and outreach work. Have them speak to your students about their experiences with food, and if possible, do a cooking demonstration and recipe share in your classroom.

Teacher Turn

Now it is your turn. Here we offer next steps for you to develop your own EcoJustice instructional materials that meet the needs of your school curriculum and your students' interests. As you have learned throughout this chapter, there are many EcoJustice issues that are linked to our current food production and sovereignty. Perhaps most important is for children to begin to understand where their food comes from, that they have the power to make conscious choices about what they eat, that access to food in our country is not equitable, and that we have a right to demand more justice in our food system. We invite teachers to dig deeper into any of these issues with your class by utilizing resources provided in this chapter, on our website, and in our appendices to create your own lessons.

A good place to start is to answer the following questions:

- Which standard(s) fits with your school curriculum? (See the list in the Appendix of NCSS and NGSS standards we have identified as offering opportunities to incorporate our Pillars.) Also look at the Cloud Standards and the SDGs for further connections to your curriculum and ideas.
- Which concepts are you and your students interested in learning more about? (e.g., food insecurity, impact of food on human health, growing culturally relevant foods, etc.)
- Which resources (suggested or your own) would you like to use to expand your own understanding of these concepts?
- What pedagogical activities are most appropriate for your teaching context?

Remember that EcoJustice issues are often related to issues of access and equity since those with the most resources have the greatest access and those with the least material resources have the least access. Additionally, in the United States, those who are most marginalized are also the most vulnerable to exploitation. We have put together many resources in our Appendices and on our website for you to build out an EcoJustice lesson including a lesson plan template, national social studies and science standards, resources to expand your own thinking about EcoJustice issues, and common teaching strategies we have used in our own classrooms. You don't have to do this alone either. Include your students in the process of creating relevant and meaningful lessons for them. Tap into our EcoJustice Educators network to find other teachers who are also engaging in this work and set up co-planning dates. We are eager to support you on your journey toward becoming an EcoJustice conscious teacher!

Notes

1 Anja Lederer and R. Huber, "The Relation of Diet and Health: You Are What You Eat," *International Journal of Environmental Research and Public Health* 19, no. 14 (2022): 8501, accessed August 11, 2025, https://pmc.ncbi.nlm.nih.gov/articles/PMC9266141/.

2 National Library of Medicine, "National Library of Medicine | USAGov," accessed August 11, 2025, https://www.usa.gov/agencies/national-library-of-medicine.

3 Grace Hussain, "Meat Consumption in the U.S.: Is It Increasing or Decreasing?" *Sentient Media*, published 2023, accessed August 11, 2025, https://sentientmedia.org/meat-consumption-in-the-us/.

4 American Heart Association, "How Much Sugar Is Too Much?" accessed August 11, 2025, https://www.heart.org/en/healthy-living/healthy-eating/eat-smart/sugar/how-much-sugar-is-too-much.

5 Johns Hopkins Bloomberg School of Public Health, "Ultraprocessed Foods Account for More than Half of Calories Consumed at Home," published December 10, 2024, accessed August 11, 2025, https://publichealth.jhu.edu/2024/ultraprocessed-foods-account-for-more-than-half-of-calories-consumed-at-home.

6 Center for Sustainable Systems, University of Michigan, "U.S. Food System Factsheet," accessed August 11, 2025, https://css.umich.edu/publications/factsheets/food/us-food-system-factsheet.

7 Jesse L. Kwarteng, Amy J. Schulz, Gabriel B. Mentz, Barbara A. Israel, and Dawn W. Perkins, "Independent Effects of Neighborhood Poverty and Psychosocial Stress on Obesity Over Time," *Journal of Urban Health* 94, no. 6 (December 2017): 791–802.

8 Society of Health and Physical Educators (SHAPE America), "National Health Education Standards," published 2024, accessed August 11, 2025, https://www.shapeamerica.org/MemberPortal/standards/health/new-he-standards.aspx.

9 New Jersey Department of Education, "2020 New Jersey Student Learning Standards—Comprehensive Health and Physical Education," published June 2020, accessed August 11, 2025, https://www.nj.gov/education/standards/chp/Docs/2020_NJSLS-CHPE_Kto2.pdf.

10 Fred Hutchinson Cancer Research Center and University of Washington Child Health Center, *Pesticide Safety Elementary School Curriculum*, 5, accessed August 11, 2025, https://www.niehs.nih.gov/sites/default/files/health/assets/docs_p_z/pesticide_safety_elementary_school_curriculum_508.pdf.

11 Fred Hutchinson Cancer Research Center and University of Washington Child Health Center, *Pesticide Safety Elementary School Curriculum*, 6, accessed August 11, 2025, https://www.niehs.nih.gov/sites/default/files/health/assets/docs_p_z/pesticide_safety_elementary_school_curriculum_508.pdf.

12 "5-LS2-1 Ecosystems: Interactions, Energy, and Dynamics," *Next-Generation Science Standards*, accessed September 8, 2025, https://www.nextgenscience.org/pe/5-ls2-1-ecosystems-interactions-energy-and-dynamics.

13 Md Wasim Aktar, Dwaipayan Sengupta, and Ashim Chowdhury, "Impact of Pesticides Use in Agriculture: Their Benefits and Hazards," *Interdisciplinary Toxicology* 2, no. 1 (2009): 1–12, accessed August 11, 2025, https://pmc.ncbi.nlm.nih.gov/articles/PMC2984095/.

14 Sarah Jampel, "What Was Actually Served at the First Thanksgiving?" *Food52*, accessed August 11, 2025, https://food52.com/blog/20949-what-was-actually-served-at-the-first-thanksgiving.

15 USDA Food and Nutrition Service, "Using Gardens To Grow Healthy Habits in Cafeterias, Classrooms, and Communities," July 2021, accessed August 11, 2025, https://

www.nrcs.usda.gov/sites/default/files/2023-02/USDA-FNS%20School%20Gardens%20 factsheet.pdf.

16 Center for Biological Diversity, "Pesticides and Soil Health: The Center's Study on How Pesticides Harm Insects and Underground Ecosystems," accessed August 11, 2025, https://www.biologicaldiversity.org/campaigns/pesticides-and-soil-health/.

17 Craig Taylor, "6 Chemical-Free Gardening Techniques for a Healthy, Natural Garden," *Morning Chores*, accessed August 11, 2025, https://morningchores.com/chemical-free-gardening/.

18 Mary Koithan and Cynthia Farrell, "Indigenous Native American Healing Traditions," *The Journal for Nurse Practitioners* 6, no. 6 (June 2010): 477–8, accessed August 11, 2025, https://pmc.ncbi.nlm.nih.gov/articles/PMC2913884/.

19 Green Living Tribe, "High School Student Won Science Fair—Proved A Forgotten Native American Recipe Kills Cancer Cells in Just 24 Hours," https://greenlivingtribe.com/high-school-student-wins-sciences-fair-proves-a-forgotten-native-american-recipe-kills-cancer-cells-in-just-24-hours/.

20 Hazra Khatoon, "The Rise of Industrial Agriculture, Explained," *Sentient Media*, accessed August 11, 2025, https://sentientmedia.org/intensive-agriculture/.

21 Christine Whitt, Noah Miller, and Ryan Olver, "Eighty-nine Percent of All Farms are Small Family Farms and they Generated 18 Percent of Total Production Value in 2021," *US Department of Agriculture Economic Research Service*, published February 27, 2023, accessed August 11, 2025, https://www.ers.usda.gov/data-products/charts-of-note/chart-detail?chartId=105916.

22 PBS, "'No Silver Bullet Solution': Norman Borlaug and the Green Revolution," *American Experience*, accessed August 11, 2025, https://www.pbs.org/wgbh/americanexperience/features/no-silver-bullet-solution-norman-borlaug-and-green-revolution/.

23 U.S. Department of Agriculture, "Grains and Oilseeds Outlook for 2025," *Agricultural Outlook Forum 2025*, released February 27, 2025, accessed August 11, 2025, https://www.usda.gov/sites/default/files/documents/2025AOF-grains-oilseeds-outlook.pdf.

24 Kathryn Markham, "Corn: Food, Fuel, and Now . . . Fiber Too?" *Tellus: Stories of ARS Research*, accessed August 11, 2025, https://tellus.ars.usda.gov/stories/articles/corn-food-fuel-and-now-fiber-too.

25 U.S. Department of Agriculture Economic Research Service, "Corn and Other Feed Grains—Feed Grains Sector at a Glance," accessed August 11, 2025, https://www.ers.usda.gov/topics/crops/corn-and-other-feed-grains/feed-grains-sector-at-a-glance.

26 COB Foods, "The 1800+ (and counting!) Corn Derivatives You Never Would Have Guessed," accessed August 11, 2025, https://cobfoods.com/blogs/news/the-1800-and-counting-corn-derivatives-you-never-would-have-guessed.

27 Björn Ólafsson, "What Monoculture Farming Is, and Why It Matters," *Sentient Media*, accessed August 11, 2025, https://sentientmedia.org/monoculture/.

28 U.S. Environmental Protection Agency, "Animal Feeding Operations (AFOs)," accessed August 11, 2025, https://www.epa.gov/npdes/animal-feeding-operations-afos.

29 Heidi Wachter, "The CAFO Conundrum," *Experience Life*, published May 4, 2021, accessed August 11, 2025, https://experiencelife.lifetime.life/article/the-cafo-conundrum/.

30 Elise Pohl and Sang-Ryong Lee, "Local and Global Public Health and Emissions from Concentrated Animal Feeding Operations in the USA: A Scoping Review," *International*

Journal of Environmental Research and Public Health 21, no. 7 (2024): 916, accessed August 11, 2025, https://pmc.ncbi.nlm.nih.gov/articles/PMC11276819/pdf/ijerph-21–00916.pdf.

31 Farm Forward, "Farm Forward Finds Drugs in Certified Meat at Whole Foods," last updated April 4, 2022, accessed August 11, 2025, https://www.farmforward.com/news/farm-forward-finds-drugs-in-certified-meat-at-whole-foods/.

32 Kim Ferraro, "New CAFO Analysis Tells us What we Know and Fear," *Conservation Law Center*, published August 2024, accessed August 11, 2025, https://conservationlawcenter.org/new-cafo-analysis-tells-us-what-we-know-and-fear/.

33 Gary Hergert, Rex Nielsen, and Jim Margheim, "WWII Nitrogen Production Issues in Age of Modern Fertilizers," *Crop Watch*, University of Nebraska–Lincoln, published April 10, 2015, accessed August 11, 2025, https://cropwatch.unl.edu/fertilizer-history-p3/.

34 Mark Schonbeck and Organic Farming Research Foundation staff, "Understanding the Impact of Herbicides and Synthetic Fertilizers on Soil Health: What Research Tells Us," *Organic Farming Research Foundation*, accessed August 11, 2025, https://ofrf.org/news/understanding-the-impact-of-herbicides-and-synthetic-fertilizers-on-soil-health-what-research-tells-us/.

35 Greenly, "What Are Ocean Dead Zones?" accessed August 11, 2025, https://greenly.Earth/en-us/blog/ecology-news/what-are-ocean-dead-zones.

36 National Centers for Coastal Ocean Science, "Above Average Summer 2024 'Dead Zone' Measured in Gulf of Mexico," last updated July 29, 2024, accessed August 11, 2025, https://coastalscience.noaa.gov/news/above-average-summer-2024-dead-zone-measured-in-gulf-of-mexico/.

37 The Business Research Company, "Herbicides Market Report 2025—Herbicides Market Strategies and Outlook," accessed August 11, 2025, https://www.thebusinessresearchcompany.com/report/herbicides-global-market-report.

38 "Pesticides Market Size & Share | Growth Trends 2025–2037," *Research Nester*, published July 7, 2025, https://www.researchnester.com/reports/pesticides-market/7865.

39 Environmental Working Group, "Herbicides and GMO Crops," accessed August 11, 2025, https://www.ewg.org/herbicides-and-gmo-crops.

40 Consumer Shield, "Glyphosate Usage Trends, Risks, and Legal Battles (2025)," accessed August 11, 2025, https://www.consumershield.com/articles/glyphosate-usage-trends.

41 Simmons Hanly Conroy, "Weed Killer Roundup Lymphoma Lawsuit Settlements (2025)," accessed August 11, 2025, https://www.simmonsfirm.com/complex-litigation/monsanto-roundup/.

42 University of Washington News, "UW Study: Exposure to Chemical in Roundup Increases Risk for Cancer," published February 13, 2019, accessed August 11, 2025, https://www.washington.edu/news/2019/02/13/uw-study-exposure-to-chemical-in-roundup-increases-risk-for-cancer/; Luoping Zhang, Iemaan Rana, Rachel M. Shaffer, Emanuela Taioli, and Lianne Sheppard, "Exposure to Glyphosate-based Herbicides and Risk for Non-Hodgkin Lymphoma: A Meta-analysis and Supporting Evidence," *Mutation Research/Reviews in Mutation Research* 781 (2019): 186–206, accessed August 11, 2025, https://www.sciencedirect.com/science/article/abs/pii/S1383574218300887.

43 Carey Gillam, "New Study Adds to Evidence that Glyphosate Weed Killer Can Cause Cancer," *The New Lede*, June 10, 2025, https://www.thenewlede.org/2025/06/new-study-adds-to-evidence-that-glyphosate-weed-killer-can-cause-cancer/.

44 United Nations Department of Economic and Social Affairs, "Goal 2: End Hunger, Achieve Food Security and Improved Nutrition and Promote Sustainable Agriculture," *United Nations Sustainable Development Goals*, accessed August 11, 2025, https://sdgs.un.org/goals/goal2.

45 "How Big Food Monopolies Threaten Food Security and Public Health," *Green and Prosperous*, accessed August 11, 2025, https://www.greenandprosperous.com/blog/how-big-food-monopolies-threaten-food-security-and-public-health.

46 Gabrielle Canon, Alvin Chang, and Andrew Witherspoon, "Food Monopoly: Meals, Profits, Data Investigation," *The Guardian*, July 14, 2021, https://www.theguardian.com/environment/ng-interactive/2021/jul/14/food-monopoly-meals-profits-data-investigation.

47 Gabrielle Canon, Alvin Chang, and Andrew Witherspoon, "Food Monopoly: Meals, Profits, Data Investigation," *The Guardian*, July 14, 2021, https://www.theguardian.com/environment/ng-interactive/2021/jul/14/food-monopoly-meals-profits-data-investigation.

48 Jennifer Clapp, *Titans of Industrial Agriculture: How a Few Giant Corporations Came to Dominate the Farm Sector and Why It Matters* (Cambridge, MA: MIT Press, 2025).

49 Kristina Hubbard, "Seed Privatization and the Path Toward Equitable Exchange," *National Sustainable Agriculture Coalition*, March 2021, https://sustainableagriculture.net/wp-content/uploads/2021/03/Hubbard-Seeds-and-Breeds-Paper.pdf.

50 Billy Hackett, "Farmers Trapped in Unsustainable Cycle by Biotechnology, Seed Consolidation," *National Sustainable Agriculture Coalition*, July 9, 2021, https://sustainableagriculture.net/blog/farmers-trapped-in-unsustainable-cycle-by-biotechnology-seed-consolidation/.

51 Jennifer Clapp, "How a Few Giant Companies Came to Dominate Global Food," *Land and Climate Review*, accessed August 11, 2025, https://www.landclimate.org/how-a-few-giant-companies-came-to-dominate-global-food/.

52 "Pesticide, Seed, and Digital Agriculture Industry Concentrates Wealth and Power, Threatens Health," *Beyond Pesticides Daily News Blog*, January 13, 2023, https://beyondpesticides.org/dailynewsblog/2023/01/pesticide-seed-and-digital-agriculture-industry-concentrates-wealth-and-power-threatens-health/.

53 Food and Agriculture Organization of the United Nations, International Fund for Agricultural Development, United Nations Children's Fund, World Food Programme, and World Health Organization, *The State of Food Security and Nutrition in the World 2024: Financing to End Hunger, Food Insecurity and Malnutrition in All Its Forms* (Rome: FAO, 2024), https://doi.org/10.4060/cd1254en.

54 "Ending Hunger," World Food Programme, accessed August 11, 2025, https://www.wfp.org/ending-hunger.

55 Food and Agriculture Organization of the United Nations, "FAO Food Policy Series: Food Loss and Waste," *Featuring Robert VanOtterdijk and Camelia Bucatariu*, video, June 30, 2016, https://www.fao.org/platform-food-loss-waste/resources/multimedia/video/fao-food-policy-series-food-loss-and-waste/en.

56 "The Farmer's Share," *National Farmers Union*, accessed August 11, 2025, https://nfu.org/farmers-share/.
57 Matthew P. Rabbitt, Madeline Reed-Jones, Laura J. Hales, and Michael P. Burke, *Household Food Security in the United States in 2023* (Washington, DC: US Department of Agriculture, Economic Research Service, 2024), ERR-337, https://doi.org/10.32747/2024.8583175.ers.
58 "Understanding Poverty in America: Causes and Solutions," *Feeding America*, accessed August 11, 2025, https://www.feedingamerica.org/hunger-in-america/poverty.
59 Lisa M. Powell, Julien Leider, Rebecca Schermbeck, Aline Vandenbroeck, and Jennifer L. Harris, "Trends in Children's Exposure to Food and Beverage Advertising on Television: 2013–2022," *JAMA Network Open* 7, no. 8 (August 2024): e2426316, https://pmc.ncbi.nlm.nih.gov/articles/PMC11342137/.
60 "The Junk Food Industry is Targeting Our Children," *The Hill*, April 20, 2024, https://thehill.com/opinion/healthcare/4605533-the-junk-food-industry-is-targeting-our-children/.
61 Megan LoDolce, "Food Marketing to Children: A Wolf in Sheep's Clothing?" *Obesity Action Coalition*, Summer 2015, https://www.obesityaction.org/resources/food-marketing-to-children-a-wolf-in-sheeps-clothing/.
62 "Ages 6–17," *State of Childhood Obesity*, accessed August 11, 2025, https://stateofchildhoodobesity.org/demographic-data/ages-6-17/.
63 Charles H. Hennekens, Panagiota "Yiota" Kitsantas, Dawn Harris Sherling, Allison H. Ferris, Alicia Caceres, Katerina Benson, Alexandra Rubenstein, and Sarah K. Wood, "Alarming Surge: Global Crisis of Childhood Overweight and Obesity," *Florida Atlantic University Newsdesk*, August 7, 2023, https://www.fau.edu/newsdesk/articles/childhood-obesity-epidemic.
64 Asia Riviere and Jessica Kirchner, "Food is Medicine: Making Nutritious Food Accessible to All," *National Governors Association Center for Best Practices*, April 2025, https://www.nga.org/news/commentary/food-is-medicine-making-nutritious-food-accessible-to-all/.
65 "How Does Hunger Affect Learning?" *No Kid Hungry*, accessed August 11, 2025, https://www.nokidhungry.org/blog/how-does-hunger-affect-learning.
66 Benjamin Arnold, "Malnutrition Early in Life Sets Stage for Poor Growth and Death," *University of California, San Francisco News*, September 13, 2023, https://www.ucsf.edu/news/2023/09/426106/malnutrition-early-life-sets-stage-poor-growth-and-death.
67 "The Effects of Child Nutrition on Academic Performance: How School Meals Can Break the Cycle of Poverty," *World Food Program USA*, accessed August 11, 2025, https://www.wfpusa.org/news/effects-child-nutrition-academic-performance-how-school-meals-can-break-cycle-poverty/.
68 "Congress Passes Mega Bill that Harms School Meal Programs," *School Nutrition Association*, accessed August 15, 2025, https://schoolnutrition.org/sna-news/congress-passes-trumps-mega-bill-that-harms-school-meal-programs/.
69 "Sankofa Community Farm," *Bartram's Garden*, accessed August 15, 2025, https://www.bartramsgarden.org/farm/.
70 "La Via Campesina: International Peasants' Voice," *La Via Campesina*, accessed August 11, 2025, https://viacampesina.org/en/international-peasants-voice/.

71 "Indigenous Food Sovereignty," *Indigenous Food Systems Network*, accessed August 11, 2025, https://www.Indigenousfoodsystems.org/food-sovereignty.

72 "The Impact of the Coronavirus on Food Insecurity in 2020 & 2021," *Feeding America*, March 2021, https://www.feedingamerica.org/sites/default/files/2021-03/National%20Projections%20Brief_3.9.2021_0.pdf.

73 Jennifer Sowerwine, Megan Mucioki, Daniel Sarna-Wojcicki, and Lisa Hillman, "Reframing Food Security by and for Native American Communities: A Case Study Among Tribes in the Klamath River Basin of Oregon and California," *Food Security* 11, no. 3 (2019): 579–607, https://ourenvironment.berkeley.edu/sites/ourenvironment.berkeley.edu/files/user/profile2/main/publications/Sowerwine%20et%20al_Reframing%20Native%20American%20Food%20Insecurity.pdf.

74 "Leah Penniman," *Soul Fire Farm*, accessed August 11, 2025, https://www.soulfirefarm.org/leah-penniman/.

75 Soul Fire Farm, *Food Sovereignty Action Steps* (2018), https://docs.google.com/document/d/1dt0hicyhGdJSKlC3qyE1AbG9fdDrONjUh_M_bE0KMGs/edit?tab=t.0.

76 "Soul Fire Farm Programs," *Soul Fire Farm*, accessed August 11, 2025, https://www.soulfirefarm.org/programs/.

77 "Guide to Regenerative Agriculture," *Kiss the Ground*, accessed August 11, 2025, https://kisstheground.com/education/resources/regenerative-agriculture/.

78 "The Original Principles of Regenerative Agriculture," *Rodale Institute*, accessed August 11, 2025, https://rodaleinstitute.org/blog/original-principles-of-regenerative-agriculture/.

79 Rolling Harvest Food Rescue, "Connecting Local Farmers with Neighbors in Need," accessed August 15, 2025, https://rollingharvest.org/.

80 "Fresh From Zone 7," *Zone 7*, accessed August 11, 2025, https://www.freshfromzone7.com/.

81 Bucks County Foodshed Alliance, "Connecting Consumers, Producers and Other Stakeholders to Strengthen Our Farming Community and Improve the Availability of Local, Healthy, Sustainably Produced Food for Our Community," accessed August 15, 2025, https://bucksfoodshed.org/.

82 "USDA Local Food Portal," *US Department of Agriculture*, accessed August 11, 2025, https://www.usdalocalfoodportal.com/.

83 Edna Ledesma and Alfonso Morales, "The Pandemic Made Farmers Markets Essential Sources of Healthy Food for All Income Levels," *Blue Zones*, August 31, 2021, https://www.bluezones.com/2021/08/the-pandemic-made-farmers-markets-essential-sources-of-healthy-food-for-all-income-levels/.

84 Linda K. Breggin and Peter Lehner, *WBC 2024 Slides—Agriculture and the Environment* (Washington, DC: Environmental Law Institute, May 2024), https://www.eli.org/sites/default/files/files-pdf/WBC%202,024%20Slides%20-%20Agriculture%20and%20the%20Environment%20(Breggin%20&%20Lehner).pdf.

85 U.S. Department of Agriculture Economic Research Service, "Irrigation & Water Use," accessed August 11, 2025, https://www.ers.usda.gov/topics/farm-practices-management/irrigation-water-use.

86 Jennifer Clapp, "How a Few Giant Companies Came to Dominate Global Food," *Land and Climate Review*, February 2025, https://www.landclimate.org/how-a-few-giant-companies-came-to-dominate-global-food/.

87 Farm Action, "Behind the Brands: The Meatpacking Monopoly and the Illusion of Choice," accessed August 15, 2025, https://farmaction.us/behind-the-brands-the-meatpacking-monopoly-and-the-illusion-of-choice/.
88 Basel Musharbash, "Kings Over the Necessaries of Life: Monopolization and the Elimination of Competition in America's Agriculture System," *Farm Action*, September 2024, https://farmaction.us/wp-content/uploads/2024/09/Kings-Over-the-Necessaries-of-Life-Monopolization-and-the-Elimination-of-Competition-in-Americas-Agriculture-System_Farm-Action.pdf.
89 Toast, "Largest Grocery Chains," *Toast Blog: On the Line*, accessed August 11, 2025, https://pos.toasttab.com/blog/on-the-line/largest-grocery-chains.
90 World Health Organization, "Obesity and Overweight," accessed August 11, 2025, https://www.who.int/news-room/fact-sheets/detail/obesity-and-overweight#:~:text=Children%20in%20low%2D%20and%20middle,while%20undernutrition%20issues%20remain%20unsolved.
91 Feeding America, "Child Hunger in America," accessed August 11, 2025, https://www.feedingamerica.org/hunger-in-america/child-hunger-facts.
92 Megan Sweitzer and Victoria Davidenko, "Food Spending as a Share of Income Declines as Income Rises," *US Department of Agriculture Economic Research Service*, November 1, 2024, https://www.ers.usda.gov/data-products/chart-gallery/chart-detail?chartId=58372.
93 Food and Agriculture Organization of the United Nations, "Emissions Due to Agriculture: Global, Regional and Country Trends, 1961–2018," accessed August 11, 2025, https://openknowledge.fao.org/server/api/core/bitstreams/cc09fbbc-eb1d-436b-a88a-bed42a1f12f3/content; Global Alliance for the Future of Food, "Power Shift: Why We Need to Wean Industrial Food Systems Off Fossil Fuels," accessed August 11, 2025, https://story.futureoffood.org/power-shift/.
94 FoodPrint, "Food and the Environment," accessed August 11, 2025, https://foodprint.org/the-total-footprint-of-our-food-system/issues/food-and-the-environment/.
95 Food & Water Watch, *Factory Farms, Fracking, and the Methane Emergency* (Washington, DC: Food & Water Watch, July 2024), https://www.foodandwaterwatch.org/wp-content/uploads/2024/07/Methane_Fracking_FactoryFarms.pdf.
96 Hannah Ritchie, Pablo Rosado, and Max Roser, "Environmental Impacts of Food Production," *Our World in Data*, 2022, https://ourworldindata.org/environmental-impacts-of-food.
97 U.S. Environmental Protection Agency, "Climate Change Impacts on Agriculture and Food Supply," accessed August 11, 2025, https://www.epa.gov/climateimpacts/climate-change-impacts-agriculture-and-food-supply.
98 Hannah Ritchie and Max Roser, "Water Use and Stress," *Our World in Data*, 2018, https://ourworldindata.org/water-use-stress.
99 National Council for the Social Studies, *College, Career, and Civic Life (C3) Framework for Social Studies State Standards: Guidance for Enhancing the Rigor of K-12 Civics, Economics, Geography, and History*, accessed August 10, 2025, https://www.socialstudies.org/sites/default/files/c3/C3-Framework-for-Social-Studies.pdf.
100 National Council for the Social Studies, *College, Career, and Civic Life (C3) Framework for Social Studies State Standards: Guidance for Enhancing the Rigor of K-12 Civics,*

Economics, Geography, and History, accessed August 10, 2025, https://www.socialstudies.org/sites/default/files/c3/C3-Framework-for-Social-Studies.pdf.

101 Next-Generation Science Standards (NGSS), "Elementary Standards: Kindergarten Through Grade Five Disciplinary Core Ideas," *NGSS Lead States*, September 2017, accessed August 9, 2025, https://www.nextgenscience.org/sites/default/files/K-2DCI.pdf.

102 Next-Generation Science Standards (NGSS), "Elementary Standards: Third Through Fifth Grade Performance Expectations by Topic," *NGSS Lead States*, September 2017, Accessed August 9, 2025, https://www.nextgenscience.org/sites/default/files/3-5Topic.pdf.

103 Cloud Institute for Sustainability Education, "EfS Standards & Performance Indicators," accessed August 10, 2025, https://cloudinstitute.org/cloud-efs-standards-performance indicators.

104 United Nations, "Goal 2: End Hunger, Achieve Food Security and Improved Nutrition and Promote Sustainable Agriculture," accessed August 11, 2025, https://sdgs.un.org/goals/goal2#overview.

105 World Health Organization, "Obesity and Overweight," accessed August 11, 2025,https://www.who.int/news-room/fact-sheets/detail/obesity-and-overweight#:~:text=Children%20in%20low%2D%20and%20middle,while%20undernutrition%20issues%20remain%20unsolved

106 United Nations, "Goal 2: End Hunger, Achieve Food Security and Improved Nutrition and Promote Sustainable Agriculture—Targets and Indicators," accessed August 11, 2025, https://sdgs.un.org/goals/goal2#targets_and_indicators.

107 United Nations, "Goal 2: End Hunger, Achieve Food Security and Improved Nutrition and Promote Sustainable Agriculture—Targets and Indicators," accessed August 11, 2025, https://sdgs.un.org/goals/goal2#targets_and_indicators.

108 United Nations, "Goal 2: End Hunger, Achieve Food Security and Improved Nutrition and Promote Sustainable Agriculture—Progress and Info," accessed August 11, 2025, https://sdgs.un.org/goals/goal2#progress_and_info.

109 United Nations, *Bringing Data to Life: SDG Human Impact Stories from Across the Globe* (New York: United Nations, 2022), https://unstats.un.org/sdgs/report/2022/SDG2022_Flipbook_final.pdf.

110 National Geographic, "Looking for a Truly Remote, Off-the-Grid Adventure? Try Panama," accessed August 11, 2025, https://www.nationalgeographic.com/travel/article/panama-community-tourism-sostur.

111 Seed Library Network, "School Seed Libraries," accessed August 6, 2025, https://www.seedlibrarynetwork.org/school-seed-libraries.html.

Conclusion

Dear Educator,

Thank you for taking the time to read this book. We wanted to share with you a little more about our process of writing and why we think this work is so important at this moment in time. Our work on EcoJustice Education asks teachers to reimagine what classroom content and curriculum can look like. This is a big ask and a huge lift, and we don't expect it will happen overnight. Like other historical movements, change takes time, and we all play a part in either reproducing or transforming our existing sociocultural and environmental contexts. We also don't expect that educational policies and priorities will honor the complexity of EcoJustice Education, we understand the many reasons it cannot. From political to practical, EcoJustice Education will have to come from teachers themselves. From our care, desire, and belief that education and the children and youth we work with can be the changemakers and are entitled to the right to understand and shape the future contexts we all will be living in.

Since we began writing and have documented throughout this book, we have seen massive defunding and deregulation at the federal level, particularly the Environmental Protection Agency and any grants and projects related to Environmental Justice. We have seen money designated to support green energy and climate change initiatives be reallocated to commodity farmers, fossil fuel companies, and more mineral and resource extraction. Money that was meant to go to schools to support low-income families, food access, mental health services, and diversity and inclusion programming has been eliminated, and federal priorities for education include increasing privatization of public schooling, improving test scores, and greater surveillance and policing in schools. These policies will lead to further educational inequity and deep disparities across schools where the biggest losers will be the children and educators in the most marginalized, vulnerable, and historically segregated and disinvested communities.

These realities speak to a set of values that are incompatible with a future for our children where they celebrate and honor diversity, have access to healthy food, a healthy planet, and feel empowered to make the world a better place. Test preparation does not inspire children; it leaves them feeling more anxious and more disconnected from learning and from one another. And it is important to remember that this is deeply embedded in the current system of education. The more we feel disconnected, the more we see the world as a place full of division and cannot see the part we must play to live whole and healthy lives. It also goes without saying that the more we erase, devalue, and harm our social, built, and natural environments, the more they can be manipulated for economic gain, and what then is left to sustain life on our planet?

The message at the heart of this book, however, is hopeful. It is an active hope that honors that while we cannot know how things will unfold, we can anticipate and imagine the futures we can thrive in. What is most exciting is that you don't have to uproot everything about your classroom practice to be part of the EcoJustice Education movement. The standards, pedagogies, and practices are already there. The content exists in the real, lived experiences of you and your students and the communities in which you teach. The standards for science, social studies, ELA, and math are all present across the instructional methods we present and can be aligned to any EcoJustice lesson you create using resources from this text or your own inspiration and creativity. For us, it is worth the time and effort to reimagine K-5 classrooms as sites for social and EcoJustice because why wouldn't we want that? Why wouldn't we want to imagine the kinds of spaces that can challenge so much of the individual and competitive messaging we get in school and in life and replace that with messages that honor diversity, collectivity, solidarity, and community?

We have such deep faith in education and teachers as tools for change, and it is this hope that we seek to offer throughout the text and the lessons. We are not without agency as social actors, and we can look to historical and recent examples to see how individuals work together to exercise their democratic rights, organize, speak, and act against systems designed to oppress. As we come to the end of the writing process, we wanted to honor the challenge of writing this text during the latter half of 2024 and the first half of 2025. We feel it is important to have situated the text and the lessons at this moment as we are witnessing catastrophic climate change events locally and globally, people in power chipping away at the democratic ideals of the United States, and economic inequality continuing to shape the everyday lives of families across the country. This year has also been marked by mass protests, resistance efforts, economic boycotts of major corporations, and diverse coalitions organizing for resistance. All of these examples are signs of mass mobilization by individuals and communities and remind us of our collective power. We have also observed that individuals, now more than ever, seem to be offering grace to their neighbors, friends, relatives, and even strangers as trauma, healing, and self-care have become more acceptable and imperative. We invite you to seek out hopeful examples in your community that are related to sustainability and social movements. Do this with your students so together, inspiration and imagination can become the dominant force for change in your classroom.

We would be remiss if we didn't also honor that the dissonance we are experiencing at this moment can lead to confusing and difficult realities and emotions for all of us. While writing this book, we found ourselves having many difficult conversations. Conversations prompted by our research into the history and atrocities that are part of our collective past when it comes to issues of economics, land, water, and food. Many feelings arose for both of us, and they were hard to ignore and important to wrestle with. We would often stop one another and share something shocking we learned about or in dialogue piece together the past in light of current events and marvel at the voids our education system creates with its silence and erasure of diverse stories from the past and present. We invite you to engage in this process with your colleagues and your students.

Teachers do and will continue to play a role in shaping the future of our society and our country. We have power in our classrooms to teach true and complete history, to help our students learn the power of their own voices, experiences, and dreams for their lives, and to teach students how to ask critical questions and engage in critical dialogues that challenge existing assumptions. The lessons presented in this book were designed to do that and so much more. In this final section, we share the voices of the pre-service and in-service teachers we've worked with who have found meaning and purpose in EcoJustice Education. It is our hope that their experiences will inspire you, offer insights, and help you discover the value in this work.

This work has been guiding us for ten years together and many years before. We have collaborated on this text as science and social studies educators who have seen firsthand the excitement teachers feel when they are introduced to these kinds of lessons. We have also heard from teachers who have used the lessons in their K-5 classrooms and have told us about how impressed they are with the level of sophistication that young people are able to engage these topics with. These lessons have a real impact on the lives of children and the futures they are entitled to, and it is for you and for them that we have written this book. Throughout our years of working with teachers and introducing them to EcoJustice Education, we have seen two large areas for possibilities emerge. New possibilities and opportunities for teachers related to both classroom curriculum and pedagogies, and new possibilities for their students in terms of knowledge, critical thinking, and social-emotional learning. Below we share teacher experiences from a professional development (PD) where an overview of EcoJustice Education was provided along with hands-on engagement with multiple lessons included in this book.

New Possibilities for Teachers

New possibilities for teachers specifically highlight shifts teachers had upon recognition that they have more space for incorporating EcoJustice topics than previously thought possible. Upon participation in our EcoJustice PD, teachers were able to:

- Build their own teaching capacity on EcoJustice topics not typically taught in the curriculum.
- See socio-environmental topics and the associated instructional materials through a multidisciplinary lens.
- Strengthen their confidence to utilize student-centered pedagogies when engaging students in teaching about socio-environmental issues.

EcoJustice Topics

Instructional materials in this book exposed teachers to topics not typically found in their curriculum. Teachers identified the 3–5 Production and Consumption lesson on fast fashion and the 3–5 Land lesson on Land Acknowledgments particularly significant in expanding their own thinking. Two teachers reflected: "*Many students (and myself) aren't always sure where the things we buy come from—or think to look!*" and "*I am better educated on how to do a proper land acknowledgement, why we do them, and how to ensure they are honoring Indigenous people.*"

Cross-Curricular Connections

Across all the lessons introduced to teachers during the PD, connections were made to multiple disciplines including ELA (reading comprehension and writing), social studies (citizenship and immigration, economics, geography), science (plants, pollution, survival), and math (age-appropriate statistics, price comparisons, and spatial planning). These quotes from participants reflecting on multiple lessons sums up the transdisciplinary nature embedded in the instructional materials.

> *This lesson naturally integrates science, by reinforcing students' understanding of plant lifecycles and nutrition; social studies, through discussions on community, equity, and human rights; and language arts, as students practiced listening, speaking, and expressing their ideas during group conversations and reflections. Math was also woven in when we examined the price differences between healthy and unhealthy foods, allowing students to apply real-world math skills in a meaningful context. This interdisciplinary approach not only deepens their understanding of each subject but also helps them see how knowledge is connected and relevant to their everyday lives.*
>
> *—Elementary Teacher, K-2 Food Lesson*

> *These lessons support learning goals across content areas by offering an applicable understanding of how laws are made and how to influence change (civic literacy). They also create opportunities for students to develop empathy for others which will enhance their social-emotional understanding and the belief that they can make a change/ make a difference. There's also a deep understanding of environmental science and realizing how water scarcity affects not only ecosystems but human communities as well. These lessons create a strong interdisciplinary unit that ties together ELA, social studies, science, and civics.*
>
> *—Elementary Teacher, 3–5 Water Lesson*

> *Young children are fascinated with large numbers and not always exposed to them until they get to the upper elementary grades. Why not use the mapping activity to help them understand how far away China is during the piece about where pet toys are made? Estimating is such a fun group activity and an important math standard in the early elementary years. That can be compared to much smaller distances in the community they live in to help the students better comprehend that large of a distance. Money skills are also touched upon during the reading of Those Shoes. This social studies/science lesson connects seamlessly to ELA standards for the early elementary years. Those Shoes (a book highlighted in lessons on economics) lends itself beautifully to turn and talk or whole group discussions about economic disparity and character traits/choices. Asking the students to decide if they would have bought the shoes at the thrift*

store or not and then physically move to a specific corner in the room to verbally defend their decision is a wonderful way to practice their speaking/listening skills.

—Early Childhood Teacher, K-2 Production and Consumption Lesson

Student-Centered Pedagogies

Instructional materials are loaded with student-centered and dialogic approaches to building critical thinking skills. These included photoelicitation, interactive read alouds, individual and small group research and presentations, action-oriented activities, as well as community and place-based experiences. Teacher feedback overwhelmingly noted the ways lessons offered space for students to discuss their own thinking and relationship to ideas presented. Here are some of their comments about the lessons presented.

I am excited to get a conversation started with my young students about these topics and allow them to put together their own thoughts about access or lack of access. This could be the first time someone has ever asked them to think of these things or asked them what they think of these concepts.

—Early Childhood Teacher, K2 Economic Foundations Lesson

Lessons like this one excite me as a teacher because they go beyond surface-level learning and tap into my students' ability to think critically, care deeply, and take initiative. There's something incredibly rewarding about watching young children make real-world connections. Teaching lessons around food access, equity, and community involvement reminds me why I became a teacher in the first place: to empower students with knowledge that not only informs but also inspires.

—Elementary Teacher, K2 Food Lesson

These lessons are exciting because they don't just ask students to learn about water justice. Instead, they create the space for students to become water protectors themselves. That huge shift in learning (from passive learner to active learner) is what makes these series of lessons powerful, and exciting, for both the teacher and students.

—Elementary Teacher, 3–5 Water Lesson

These lessons offer value for both students and teachers by connecting real world issues with core elementary academic skills. Students are able to learn about food systems, justice, and what sustainability can look like—all while working collaboratively and with multiple opportunities for them to take ownership over their learning. As an educator, these lessons provide flexibility (since students are taking ownership over their learning) to differentiate and truly guide the conversation and learning in a way where co-learning is happening; instead of just stand and deliver.

—Elementary Teacher, 3–5 Food Lesson

Teachers quickly took ownership of the instructional materials and felt excited and empowered to modify materials for their individual contexts (i.e., working with multilingual learners, larger class sizes). We strongly encourage this as the lessons are not designed to be taught verbatim but rather teachers are invited to always use their deep knowledge about their students and their teaching context to make the lessons most relevant. Additionally, teachers recognized the ways they would be learning alongside their students about many of the socio-environmental issues presented throughout the book. One teacher stated, "*I am so excited at the idea of my students and I exploring these ideas together, I know that I don't know all there is to know about land acknowledgement but I appreciate that my students and I can discover that information together!*"

New Possibilities for Students

Teachers overwhelmingly expressed that the lessons taught students' knowledge of EcoJustice topics and are well designed to build skills and attitudes that support actions aligned with the goals and Pillars of EcoJustice Education.

Building Knowledge

Teachers recognized the potential to develop understandings among their students, regardless of the grade in school. This was evident in comments such as, "*this is accessible for K-2 students . . . this lesson allows them the space to formulate thoughts and engage with information that expands their understanding of the economics of our world,*" and "*It is great to look at water use and water rights and everyone needs water to survive. Students can see a clear connection to their lives.*" Forming understandings of land use and rights was also noted, "*I see that I can work with students to think about the land that we live on, who came before us, and who is native to this land and where are those people now?*" Another teacher shared, "*I think this is accessible for K-2 students, I think they are already noticing things about the world around them and this lesson allows them the space to formulate thoughts and engage with information that expands their understanding of the economics of our world.*" All of these teachers see that there is deep knowledge building that is happening in relation to elementary content.

Developing Skills

As discussed throughout the book, the EcoJustice Pillars speak to the skills required to address socio-environmental issues. The comments, "*I see the value in guiding students to think critically about land and ownership and why things are the way they* are," and "*I think students can get a better understanding of how a large corporation is impacting the Earth with their goods, but also bring it down to the individual level for students to see how they can make decisions that are good for the* environment," show the potential to support students in formulating reasoned and informed conclusions.

Initially, I had some reservations about introducing heavier topics such as food insecurity, worried it might be too abstract or overwhelming for this age group. However, I was pleasantly surprised by how quickly they connected the dots. When we discussed why we host a food drive each year or the purpose behind our school garden, they responded with thoughtful insights that showed a clear understanding of the issues. One student, in particular, suggested that communities could host a potluck night for families in need, not only to provide meals but also to bring people together. I found that idea to be especially clever and compassionate.

—Early Childhood Teacher, K-2 Food Lesson

Opportunities to Empower Students

EcoJustice Education seeks to develop an orientation toward action-oriented and collaborative problem-solving. After being introduced to the lessons, teachers recognized the power of the learning experiences to empower students as problem solvers and change agents. "*The lesson showed them that even at a young age, they can identify problems, feel empathy, and think creatively about solutions that impact their community*" and "*For K-2 students, that can be really exciting—to take home knowledge and teach their families. The students will truly feel like they are making a difference because it's something THEY can do themselves*" illustrate the potential teachers see for lessons to empower their students.

For my students, the great value I saw was that it gave them a voice and showed them that even at a young age, they can identify problems, feel empathy, and think creatively about solutions that impact their community. For me, it reaffirmed the importance of teaching meaningful, real-world content in age-appropriate ways. Watching my students connect academic knowledge to social responsibility reminded me that education isn't just about facts, it's about shaping compassionate, informed citizens.

—Early Childhood Teacher, K-2 Food Lesson

Finally, teachers highlight one of the most valuable aspects of engaging children and youth in EcoJustice Education—the social and emotional learning that is associated with these topics. Here are their insights about how these lessons offer space for learning that is rooted in building empathy, connection, and care.

Bringing these topics to younger students so they can truly understand what wants and needs are. Oftentimes in the younger grades, it is hard for students to differentiate. Also, the big emotions that come with not having your needs met or not having what you want.

—Early Childhood Teacher, K-2 Economic Foundations Lesson

The values I see in this lesson are that they establish community within the classroom by having students work and talk together about land and mindfulness learning as the lessons connect students to nature and land using their senses.

—Elementary Teacher, 3–5 Land Lesson

Similar to other lessons, these three lessons are a strong model of what interdisciplinary learning can look like. They hit key social studies standards by exploring economics, geography, and civics. There's also a science connection when thinking about environmental impacts. Last but

> *certainly not least, ELA is woven throughout each lesson. My favorite part of these lessons is definitely how they encourage social-emotional learning—not just learning about food justice and developing empathy, but collaboratively learning with their peers and setting goals while learning.*
>
> —*Elementary Teacher, 3–5 Food Lesson*

Thank you to the courageous and creative educators we have had the privilege of working with and the deep insights you have shared.

We have loved every minute of our work with teachers and introducing and supporting them in their efforts to bring EcoJustice Education into their classrooms. It is our sincerest hope this book is able to do the same for you.

Let's build a movement together.

In solidarity,
Greer and Marissa

Bibliography

"The 21st Century Skills Movement." *ASCD* 67, no. 1 (September 1, 2009). https://ascd.org/el/articles/the-21st-century-skills-movement.

64 Parishes. "Cancer Alley." *64 Parishes*. Accessed August 10, 2025. https://64parishes.org/entry/cancer-alley.

ACLU. "Racism by Design: The Building of Interstate 81." *ACLU*, August 10, 2025. Accessed August 10, 2025. https://www.aclu.org/news/racial-justice/racism-by-design-the-building-of-interstate-81.

Agency for Toxic Substances and Disease Registry. "Per- and Polyfluoroalkyl Substances (PFAS) and Your Health." Accessed August 10, 2025. https://www.atsdr.cdc.gov/pfas/index.html.

"Ages 6–17." *State of Childhood Obesity*. Accessed August 11, 2025. https://stateofchildhoodobesity.org/demographic-data/ages-6-17/.

Aktar, Md Wasim, Dwaipayan Sengupta, and Ashim Chowdhury. "Impact of Pesticides Use in Agriculture: Their Benefits and Hazards." *Interdisciplinary Toxicology* 2, no. 1 (2009): 1–12. Accessed August 11, 2025. https://pmc.ncbi.nlm.nih.gov/articles/PMC2984095/.

Amazon Frontlines. "Indigenous Women Put Their Bodies on the Line to Defend the Amazon." Accessed August 6, 2025. https://amazonfrontlines.org/chronicles/Indigenous-women-put-their-bodies-on-the-line-to-defend-the-amazon/.

American Association for the Advancement of Science. *Benchmarks for Science Literacy*. New York: Oxford University Press, 1993.

American Association for the Advancement of Science (AAAS). *Benchmarks for Science Literacy. Project 2061*. New York: Oxford University Press, 1993.

American Bar Association. "The Contemporary Relevance of Historic Black Land Loss." *ABA*, January 6, 2023. Accessed August 10, 2025. https://www.americanbar.org/groups/crsj/resources/human-rights/archive/contemporary-relevance-historic-black-land-loss/.

American Fisheries Society Habitat Section. "Microplastics Pose a Serious Threat to Aquatic Ecosystem Health." *American Fisheries Society*. Accessed August 10, 2025. https://units.fisheries.org/habitat/microplastics-pose-a-serious-threat-to-aquatic-ecosystem-health/.

American Heart Association. "How Much Sugar Is Too Much?" Accessed August 11, 2025. https://www.heart.org/en/healthy-living/healthy-eating/eat-smart/sugar/how-much-sugar-is-too-much.

Anastasia, Laura. "Our Water Was Poison." *Junior Scholastic,* September 23, 2019. Accessed August 10, 2025. https://junior.scholastic.com/issues/2019-20/092319/our-water-was-poison.html?language=english#1020L.

"Ancestral Land Returned to Onondaga Nation in Upstate New York." *AP News,* September 30, 2024. https://apnews.com/article/native-american-land-rights-onondaga-new-york-9f105760632d6bf7ce26a6e1c324f8a6.

Anderson, Lorin W. and David R. Krathwohl, eds. *A Taxonomy for Learning, Teaching, and Assessing: A Revision of Bloom's Taxonomy of Educational Objectives*. New York: Longman, 2001.

Anyon, Jean. "Social Class and School Knowledge." *Curriculum Inquiry* 11, no. 1 (1981): 3–42. https://doi.org/10.2307/1179509.

Arnold, Benjamin. "Malnutrition Early in Life Sets Stage for Poor Growth and Death." *University of California, San Francisco News*, September 13, 2023. https://www.ucsf.edu/news/2023/09/426106/malnutrition-early-life-sets-stage-poor-growth-and-death.

Associated Press. "Climate Change Speeds up Water Cycle, Triggers More Extreme Weather." *AP News*, March 24, 2025. Accessed August 10, 2025. https://apnews.com/article/climate-change-extremes-drought-flood-rain-hydrological-cycle-b1f3e71ec6bac03f7c72a16be2739b01.

Associated Press. "Miners Are Razing Forests to Meet Surging Demand for Metals and Minerals, Worsening Climate Emissions in Indonesia." *AP News*. Accessed August 9, 2025. https://apnews.com/article/mining-deforestation-indonesia-climate-emissions-3bf4395f4a16d6097727da0793e311e4.

Associated Press. "North American Grassland Birds in Peril, Spurring All-out Effort to . . ." *AP News*, August 25, 2023. Accessed August 10, 2025. https://apnews.com/article/grassland-birds-decline-endangered-species-climate-ce14337f33e77f190e245270bb3e6769.

Association for Experiential Education. "What Is Experiential Education?" Accessed August 6, 2025. https://www.aee.org/what-is-experiential-education.

Asthma and Allergy Foundation of America. *Asthma Disparities in America: A Roadmap to Reducing Burden on Racial and Ethnic Minorities*. 2020. http://aafa.org/asthmadisparities.

Bartram's Garden. "Sankofa Community Farm." Accessed August 15, 2025. https://www.bartramsgarden.org/farm/.

Basel Musharbash. "Kings Over the Necessaries of Life: Monopolization and the Elimination of Competition in America's Agriculture System." *Farm Action*, September 2024. https://farmaction.us/wp-content/uploads/2024/09/Kings-Over-the-Necessaries-of-Life-Monopolization-and-the-Elimination-of-Competition-in-Americas-Agriculture-System_Farm-Action.pdf.

Baskaran, Gracelin. "Why Responsible Mining Is a Human Rights Imperative." *Center for Strategic and International Studies*, December 1, 2023. https://www.csis.org/analysis/why-responsible-mining-human-rights-imperative.

Batchelor, Tom. "Mountains of Clothes Washed Up on Ghana Beach Show Cost of Fast Fashion." *The Independent*, August 3, 2022. https://www.independent.co.uk/climate-change/news/fast-fashion-ghana-clothes-waste-b2132399.html.

Baurick, Tristan. "Petrochemical Jobs Bypass Black Communities in Louisiana, Study Finds." *Environmental Health News*, August 2, 2023. Accessed August 10, 2025. https://www.ehn.org/petrochemical-jobs-bypass-black-communities-in-louisiana-study-finds.

Bealer, Alex W. and William Sauts Bock. *Only the Names Remain: The Cherokees and the Trail of Tears*. Boston: Little, Brown and Company, 1972.

BeePlastic. "The Evolution of Bakelite: The World's First Fully Synthetic Plastic." *BeePlastic*. Accessed August 10, 2025. https://www.beeplastic.com/blogs/plastic-insights/the-evolution-of-bakelite-the-worlds-first-fully-synthetic-plastic?srsltid=AfmBOoosno1MoPRlI-xZXvl10eBImZmzcQ8HsK-Rvyk_5--0jstiE-wM&.

Bellino, M. E. and G. Burroughs. "Learn Globally, Teach Locally: Developing an EcoJustice Stance among Preservice Teachers through a Critical Place-Based Pedagogical Model." In *Ecocritical Perspectives in Teacher Education*, edited by J. Lupinacci, A. Happel-Parkins, and R. Turner, Constructing Knowledge: Curriculum Studies in Action. Leiden: Brill, 2023.

Beverage Marketing Corporation. *U.S. Bottled Water Market – 2022: Key Trends and Forecasts.* New York: Beverage Marketing Corporation, 2022.

Bhattar, Kala. "A Wonderful World Withering Away: The Malignant Industry of Mining for Minerals." *UAB Institute for Human Rights Blog,* May 2, 2022. https://sites.uab.edu/humanrights/2022/05/02/a-wonderful-world-withering-away-the-malignant-industry-of-mining-for-minerals/.

"Big Steelmakers Failing to Make the Switch to Renewables, Survey Shows." *Reuters,* November 29, 2024. https://www.reuters.com/business/big-steelmakers-failing-make-switch-renewables-survey-shows-2024-11-29/.

Bigelow, Bill. "How My Schooling Taught Me Contempt for the Earth." *Rethinking Schools* 11, no. 1 (1996): 14–17.

Board of Governors of the Federal Reserve System. *Report on the Economic Well-Being of U.S. Households in 2019.* Washington, DC: Federal Reserve, May 2020. Accessed August 9, 2025. https://www.federalreserve.gov/publications/files/2019-report-economic-well-being-us-households-202005.pdf.

Booker, Cory. "A Conspiracy of Love." *Global Leadership Network.* Accessed August 10, 2025. https://www.globalleadership.org/article/conspiracy-love-cory-booker.

Boston University School of Public Health. "Five Years After Water Crisis, Nearly 1 in 4 Flint Residents Has PTSD." *Boston University School of Public Health.* Accessed August 10, 2025. https://www.bu.edu/sph/news/articles/2022/five-years-after-water-crisis-nearly-1-in-4-flint-residents-has-ptsd/.

Bowers, C. A. *Educating for Eco-Justice and Community.* Athens: University of Georgia Press, 2001.

Bowers, C. A. and Rebecca A. Martusewicz. "Ecojustice and Social Justice." In *Encyclopedia of the Social and Cultural Foundations of Education*, edited by Eugene F. Provenzo Jr. and Arlene Barry Provenzo. Thousand Oaks, CA: SAGE Publications, Inc., 2009.

Breggin, Linda K. and Peter Lehner. *WBC 2024 Slides – Agriculture and the Environment.* Washington, DC: Environmental Law Institute, May 2024. https://www.eli.org/sites/default/files/files-pdf/WBC%202024%20Slides%20-%20Agriculture%20and%20the%20Environment%20(Breggin%20&%20Lehner).pdf.

Briggs, Zack. "Historic Flood Causes Financial Woes for Arkansas Farmers on the Road to Recovery." *KATV,* December 2, 2019. Accessed August 10, 2025. https://katv.com/news/local/historic-flood-causes-financial-woes-for-arkansas-farmers-on-the-road-to-recovery.

Bringuier, Jean-Claude. *Conversations with Jean Piaget.* Chicago, IL: University of Chicago Press, 1980.

Bruess, Elena. "Poor Drainage Leaves Northeast Houston Residents with Full Ditches, Flooded Homes After Beryl." *Houston Landing,* July 9, 2024. Accessed August 10, 2025. https://houstonlanding.org/poor-drainage-leaves-northeast-houston-residents-with-full-ditches-flooded-homes-after-beryl/.

Bucks County Foodshed Alliance. "Connecting Consumers, Producers and Other Stakeholders to Strengthen Our Farming Community and Improve the Availability of

Local, Healthy, Sustainably Produced Food for Our Community." Accessed August 15, 2025. https://bucksfoodshed.org/.

Burroughs, Greer C. and Marissa E. Bellino. "Nurturing a Global EcoJustice Consciousness among Preservice Teachers through Critical Place-Based Learning." *Journal of Global Education and Research* 8, no. 1 (2024): 34–48.

Bush, George W. "Remarks by the President to Airline Employees." In *O'Hare International Airport*, Chicago, IL, September 27, 2001. The White House Archives.

"Bush Signs Stimulus Package into Law." *NBC News*, February 13, 2008. https://www.nbcnews.com/id/wbna23143814.

Caine, Renate Nummela and Geoffrey Caine. "Understanding a Brain-Based Approach to Learning and Teaching." *Educational Leadership* 48, no. 2 (October 1990): 66–70.

Calma, Justine. "The Trump Administration Faces a Fight over 'Biggest' Environmental Deregulatory Action in US History." *The Verge*, July 10, 2024. https://www.theverge.com/news/629128/trump-environmental-deregulation-epa.

CalMatters. "Drinking Water of Almost a Million Californians Failed to Meet State Requirements." *CalMatters*, June 2024. Accessed August 10, 2025. https://calmatters.org/environment/2024/06/california-drinking-water-failing-systems/.

Campa, Aydali, and Brett Chase. "Plans for I-55 Expansion in Chicago Raise Concerns Over Air Quality and Community Health." *Inside Climate News,* May 23, 2023. Accessed August 10, 2025. https://insideclimatenews.org/news/23052023/plans-for-i-55-expansion-in-chicago-raise-concerns-over-air-quality-and-community-health/.

Canon, Gabrielle, Alvin Chang, and Andrew Witherspoon. "Food Monopoly: Meals, Profits, Data Investigation." *The Guardian,* July 14, 2021. https://www.theguardian.com/environment/ng-interactive/2021/jul/14/food-monopoly-meals-profits-data-investigation.

Cardoso, Diego S. and Casey J. Wichman. "Water Affordability in the United States." *Water Resources Research*, Published 2022. Accessed August 10, 2025. https://mleead.umich.edu/files/Event_LegislativeForum_2023/Water%20Affordability/Research%20Articles/Water%20Affordability%20in%20the%20United%20States.pdf.

Carleton, David. "Old Deluder Satan Act of 1647 (1647)." *The First Amendment Encyclopedia. Middle Tennessee State University*, 2009. https://firstamendment.mtsu.edu/article/old-deluder-satan-act-of-1647/.

Carrington, Damian. "Almost 40% of World's Glaciers Already Doomed Due to Climate Crisis – Study." *The Guardian*, May 29, 2025. Accessed August 10, 2025. https://www.theguardian.com/environment/2025/may/29/almost-40-of-worlds-glaciers-already-doomed-due-to-climate-crisis-study.

Carrington, Damian. "Microplastics Hinder Plant Photosynthesis, Study Finds—Threatening Millions with Starvation." *The Guardian*, March 10, 2025. Accessed August 10, 2025. https://www.theguardian.com/environment/2025/mar/10/microplastics-hinder-plant-photosynthesis-study-finds-threatening-millions-with-starvation.

Carrington, Damian. "Plastic Pollution Reaches World's Deepest Ocean Trench." *The Guardian*, December 20, 2018. Accessed August 10, 2025. https://www.theguardian.com/environment/2018/dec/20/plastic-pollution-mariana-trench-deepest-point-ocean.

Casey, Michael. "DC Sues Federal Government Over Pollution in Anacostia River." *The Associated Press,* January 10, 2025. https://apnews.com/article/washington-dc-anacostia-pollution-environmental-cleanup-lawsuit-e00b90f883cfc83aeed341f43f69b7dc.

"CBRE Group, Inc. Reports Financial Results for Second-Quarter 2021." *CBRE Investor Relations*, July 29, 2021. https://ir.cbre.com/press-releases/detail/57/cbre-group-inc-reports-financial-results-for.

Center for Biological Diversity. "Pesticides and Soil Health: The Center's Study on How Pesticides Harm Insects and Underground Ecosystems." Accessed August 11, 2025. https://www.biologicaldiversity.org/campaigns/pesticides-and-soil-health/.

Center for International Environmental Law (CIEL). *Fossils, Fertilizers, and False Solutions: How Laundering Fossil Fuels in Agrochemicals Puts the Climate and the Planet at Risk.* Washington, DC: CIEL, October 6, 2022. Accessed August 10, 2025. https://www.ciel.org/reports/fossil-fertilizers/.

Center for Sustainable Systems, University of Michigan. "Environmental Justice Factsheet." CSS Pub. No. CSS17-16, 2024. Accessed August 10, 2025. https://css.umich.edu/publications/factsheets/sustainability-indicators/environmental-justice-factsheet.

Center for Sustainable Systems, University of Michigan. "U.S. Food System Factsheet." Accessed August 11, 2025. https://css.umich.edu/publications/factsheets/food/us-food-system-factsheet.

Centro de Estudios de la Realidad Puertorriqueña (CEREP). *The Caño Martín Peña Community Land Trust: A Tool for Equitable Development in Informal Settlements.* San Juan, PR: CEREP, 2015. https://martinpena.org/wp-content/uploads/2015/09/CMPLT_Report.pdf.

"Child Hunger in America." *Feeding America,* n.d. Accessed January 10, 2025. https://www.feedingamerica.org/hunger-in-america/child-hunger-facts.

Choi-Schagrin, Winston. "Many States Omit Climate Education. These Teachers Are Trying to Slip it in." *The New York Times,* Updated November 10, 2022. https://www.nytimes.com/2022/11/01/climate/middle-school-education-climate-change.html.

Clapp, Jennifer. "How a Few Giant Companies Came to Dominate Global Food." *Land and Climate Review*, February 2025. https://www.landclimate.org/how-a-few-giant-companies-came-to-dominate-global-food/.

Clapp, Jennifer. *Titans of Industrial Agriculture: How a Few Giant Corporations Came to Dominate the Farm Sector and Why It Matters.* Cambridge, MA: MIT Press, 2025.

Clay, Henry. "Speech on American Industry, 1824." *Bill of Rights Institute.* Accessed August 7, 2025. https://billofrightsinstitute.org/activities/henry-clay-speech-on-american-industry-1824.

"Climate Impact of Shipping." *Transport & Environment.* Accessed August 7, 2025. https://www.transportenvironment.org/topics/ships/climate-impact-shipping.

Cloud Institute for Sustainability Education. "EfS Standards & Performance Indicators." Accessed August 10, 2025. https://cloudinstitute.org/cloud-efs-standards-performanceindicators.

Coalition for Clean Air. "The Hidden Legacy of Highway Expansions." *Coalition for Clean Air,* September 28, 2023. Accessed August 10, 2025. https://www.ccair.org/the-hidden-legacy-of-highway-expansions/.

COB Foods. "The 1800+ (and counting!) Corn Derivatives You Never Would Have Guessed." Accessed August 11, 2025. https://cobfoods.com/blogs/news/the-1800-and-counting-corn-derivatives-you-never-would-have-guessed.

Cobb, Floyd and John Krownapple. *Belonging Through a Culture of Dignity: The Keys to Successful Equity Implementation.* San Francisco: Mimi & Todd Press, 2019.

Cobb, Jelani. “The Man Behind Critical Race Theory.” *The New Yorker*, September 13, 2021. https://www.newyorker.com/magazine/2021/09/20/the-man-behind-critical-race-theory.

Coleman, Rob. “What’s in Washington D.C.’s Drinking Water?” *Environmental Working Group*, February 26, 2025. Accessed August 10, 2025. https://www.ewg.org/news-insights/news/2025/02/whats-washington-dcs-drinking-water.

Columbia Center for Children’s Environmental Health. “Asthma.” *Columbia University Public Health*. Accessed August 10, 2025. https://www.publichealth.columbia.edu/research/centers/columbia-center-childrens-environmental-health/our-research/health-effects/asthma.

Columbus, Christopher. “Letter on the First Voyage.” March 1493. In *Columbus reports on his first voyage, 1493*. Translated and published by the Gilder Lehrman Institute of American History. Accessed August 9, 2025. https://www.gilderlehrman.org/history-resources/spotlight-primary-source/columbus-reports-his-first-voyage-1493.

“Common Core States 2025.” *World Population Review*. Accessed August 7, 2025. https://worldpopulationreview.com/state-rankings/common-core-states.

Consumer Shield. “Glyphosate Usage Trends, Risks, and Legal Battles (2025).” Accessed August 11, 2025. https://www.consumershield.com/articles/glyphosate-usage-trends.

Coolidge, Calvin. “The Press Under a Free Government.” Speech, American Society of Newspaper Editors, Washington, DC, January 17, 1925.

Costanza, Robert, Richard B. Howarth, Ida Kubiszewski, Shuang Liu, Chunbo Ma, Gaël Plumecocq, and David I. Stern. “Influential Publications in Ecological Economics Revisited.” *Ecological Economics* 123 (2016): 68–76. https://www.robertcostanza.com/wp-content/uploads/2017/02/2016_J_Costanza_InfluentialPublications.pdf.

Council for Economic Education. *Voluntary National Content Standards in Economics*, 2nd ed. New York: Council for Economic Education, 2010. https://www.councilforeconed.org/wp-content/uploads/2012/03/voluntary-national-content-standards-2010.pdf.

Creators. “How Art Immortalized #NoDAPL Protests at Standing Rock.” *VICE*. Accessed August 10, 2025. https://www.vice.com/en/article/how-art-immortalized-nodapl-protests-at-standing-rock-2/.

Cronon, William. *Changes in the Land: Indians, Colonists, and the Ecology of New England*. New York: Hill and Wang, 2011.

Declet-Barreto, Juan and Jacob Carter. “Superfund Site Cleanups Ignore Communities of Color.” *Union of Concerned Scientists Blog*, September 21, 2020. Accessed August 10, 2025. https://blog.ucs.org/juan-declet-barreto/superfund-site-cleanups-ignore-communities-of-color/.

Democratic staff of the House Committee on Natural Resources. “How Congress has Blocked Access to Water for Native Families: Water Delayed Is Water Denied.” Released October 10, 2016. Accessed August 10, 2025. https://democrats-naturalresources.house.gov/imo/media/doc/House%20Water%20Report_FINAL.pdf.

Deslauriers, Louis, Logan S. McCarty, Kelly Miller, Kristina Callaghan, and Greg Kestin. “Measuring Actual Learning versus Feeling of Learning in Response to Being Actively Engaged in the Classroom.” *Proceedings of the National Academy of Sciences* 116, no. 39 (2019): 19251–7.

“Digital 2025: Global Advertising Trends.” *DataReportal*. Accessed August 7, 2025. https://datareportal.com/reports/digital-2025-sub-section-global-advertising-trends.

Dobson, Jim. "The Top 20 Landowners In America, According To A New Report." *Forbes*, January 20, 2024. Accessed August 10, 2025. https://www.forbes.com/sites/jimdobson/2024/01/20/the-top-20-landowners-in-america-according-to-a-new-report/.

DoGoodPeople. "Responsible and Sustainable Consumption for Children: How Can You Teach Them?" *DoGoodPeople*. Accessed August 9, 2025. https://www.dogoodpeople.com/csr-trends/responsible-and-sustainable-consumption-for-children-how-can-you-teach-them/.

Earthjustice. "Cancer Alley Rises Up." *Earthjustice*. Accessed August 10, 2025. https://Earthjustice.org/feature/cancer-alley-rises-up.

Earthjustice. "EPA Announces Illegal Plan to Eliminate Restrictions for Toxic PFAS in Drinking Water." *Earthjustice*, 2025. Accessed August 10, 2025. https://Earthjustice.org/press/2025/epa-announces-illegal-plan-to-eliminate-restrictions-for-toxic-pfas-in-drinking-water.

Economic Policy Institute. "Housing Discrimination Underpins the Staggering Wealth Gap Between Blacks and Whites." *EPI*, December 12, 2017. Accessed August 10, 2025. https://www.epi.org/blog/housing-discrimination-underpins-the-staggering-wealth-gap-between-blacks-and-whites/.

Economic Policy Institute. "The Productivity–Pay Gap." 2021. https://www.epi.org/productivity-pay-gap/.

"The Effects of Child Nutrition on Academic Performance: How School Meals Can Break the Cycle of Poverty." *World Food Program USA*. Accessed August 11, 2025. https://www.wfpusa.org/news/effects-child-nutrition-academic-performance-how-school-meals-can-break-cycle-poverty/.

Einstein, Albert. *Quoted in Alice Caprice, The Ultimate Quotable Einstein*. Princeton, NJ: Princeton University Press, 2010.

Eisenstein, Charles. *Sacred Economics: Money, Gift, and Society in the Age of Transition*. Ebook. Berkeley, CA: Evolver Editions, 2011.

Ellen MacArthur Foundation. "Towards the Circular Economy Vol. 1: An Economic and Business Rationale for an Accelerated Transition." *Ellen MacArthur Foundation*, 2013.

ENLACE Caño Martín Peña. "Fideicomiso de la Tierra del Caño Martín Peña." *ENLACE*. Accessed August 10, 2025. https://martinpena.org/fideicomiso/.

Environmental Defense Fund. "New Report Finds Roughly 1 in 3 New Jersey Residents Lives Near a Mega-warehouse." *Environmental Defense Fund*, June 18, 2024. Accessed August 10, 2025. https://www.edf.org/media/new-report-finds-roughly-1-3-new-jersey-residents-lives-near-mega-warehouse.

Environmental Integrity Project. "The Clean Water Act at 50: Promises Half Kept at the Half Century Mark." Published March 29, 2022. Accessed August 10, 2025. https://environmentalintegrity.org/wp-content/uploads/2022/03/Revised-CWA-report-3.29.22.pdf.

Environmental Integrity Project. "Oil's Unchecked Outfalls: Water Pollution from Refineries Endangers Public Health and the Environment." Accessed August 10, 2025. https://environmentalintegrity.org/reports/oils-unchecked-outfalls/.

Environmental Protection Network. "Trump FY26 EPA Skinny Budget Factsheet." *Environmental Protection Network*, May 2025. Accessed August 10, 2025. https://www.environmentalprotectionnetwork.org/wp-content/uploads/2025/05/Trump-FY26-EPA-Skinny-Budget-Factsheet.pdf.

Environmental Working Group. "Down the Drain: Where Toxic Chemicals from Industrial Facilities End Up." Accessed August 10, 2025. https://www.ewg.org/research/down-drain.

Environmental Working Group. "Harmful Heavy Metals: Why They're in Tap Water and How to Reduce Your Exposure." Published May 2025. Accessed August 10, 2025. https://www.ewg.org/news-insights/news/2025/05/harmful-heavy-metals-why-theyre-tap-water-and-how-reduce-your-exposure.

Environmental Working Group. "Herbicides and GMO Crops." Accessed August 11, 2025. https://www.ewg.org/herbicides-and-gmo-crops.

Environmental Working Group. "Mapping PFAS Chemical Contamination in the United States." Accessed August 10, 2025. https://www.ewg.org/interactive-maps/pfas_contamination/.

Environmental Working Group. "Releases of Carcinogens and Other Toxic Chemicals from Industrial Facilities in Louisiana's Cancer Alley." *Environmental Working Group,* 2020. Accessed August 10, 2025. https://www.ewg.org/research/releases-carcinogens-cancer-alley.

Environmental Working Group. "What is Fragrance?" Published July 2023. Accessed August 10, 2025. https://www.ewg.org/news-insights/news/2023/07/what-fragrance.

Farm Action. "Behind the Brands: The Meatpacking Monopoly and the Illusion of Choice." Accessed August 15, 2025. https://farmaction.us/behind-the-brands-the-meatpacking-monopoly-and-the-illusion-of-choice/.

Farm Forward. "Farm Forward Finds Drugs in Certified Meat at Whole Foods." Last updated April 4, 2022. Accessed August 11, 2025. https://www.farmforward.com/news/farm-forward-finds-drugs-in-certified-meat-at-whole-foods/.

"The Farmer's Share." *National Farmers Union*. Accessed August 11, 2025. https://nfu.org/farmers-share/.

Federal Highway Administration. "Chapter 2: Effects of Roads on Wildlife Populations." In *Wildlife Crossing Structures Handbook: Design and Evaluation in North America.* Washington, DC: Federal Highway Administration, 2025. Accessed August 10, 2025. https://www.fhwa.dot.gov/clas/ctip/wildlife_crossing_structures/ch_2.aspx.

Federal Reserve. "Distribution of Household Wealth in the U.S. since 1962." *Survey of Consumer Finances*, 2021.

Feeding America. "Child Hunger in America." Accessed August 11, 2025. https://www.feedingamerica.org/hunger-in-america/child-hunger-facts.

Ferraro, Kim. "New CAFO Analysis Tells us What we Know and Fear." *Conservation Law Center*, Published August 2024. Accessed August 11, 2025. https://conservationlawcenter.org/new-cafo-analysis-tells-us-what-we-know-and-fear/.

Food & Water Watch. "Bowing to Industry Pressure, Trump's EPA Rolls Back PFAS Protections for Drinking Water." *Food & Water Watch*, May 14, 2025. Accessed August 10, 2025. https://www.foodandwaterwatch.org/2025/05/14/bowing-to-industry-pressure-trumps-epa-rolls-back-pfas-protections-for-drinking-water/.

Food & Water Watch. *Factory Farms, Fracking, and the Methane Emergency*. Washington, DC: Food & Water Watch, July 2024. https://www.foodandwaterwatch.org/wp-content/uploads/2024/07/Methane_Fracking_FactoryFarms.pdf.

Food & Water Watch. "How the EPA Lets Dirty Industries Pollute Our Water." Published May 8, 2023. Accessed August 10, 2025. https://www.foodandwaterwatch.org/2023/05/08/elg-suit-industrial-water-pollution/.

Food & Water Watch. "PFAS: No Sticking, No Staining . . . And Not Going Anywhere." Published June 15, 2022. Accessed August 10, 2025. https://www.foodandwaterwatch.org/2022/06/15/pfas-no-sticking-no-staining-and-not-going-anywhere/.

Food and Agriculture Organization of the United Nations. "Emissions due to Agriculture: Global, Regional and Country Trends, 1961–2018." Accessed August 11, 2025. https://openknowledge.fao.org/server/api/core/bitstreams/cc09fbbc-eb1d-436b-a88a-bed42a1f12f3/content.

Food and Agriculture Organization of the United Nations. "FAO Food Policy Series: Food Loss and Waste." *Featuring Robert VanOtterdijk and Camelia Bucatariu*. Video. June 30, 2016. https://www.fao.org/platform-food-loss-waste/resources/multimedia/video/fao-food-policy-series-food-loss-and-waste/en.

Food Safety News. "Oyster-Borne Typhoid Fever Killed 150 in Winter of 1924-25." *Editor's Note*, March 13, 2012. Accessed August 10, 2025. https://www.foodsafetynews.com/2012/03/editors-note-in-the-winter/.

FoodPrint. "Food and the Environment." Accessed August 11, 2025. https://foodprint.org/the-total-footprint-of-our-food-system/issues/food-and-the-environment/.

"Footprint Calculator – Measure your Impact." *Global Footprint Network*. Accessed August 7, 2025. https://www.footprintnetwork.org/resources/footprint-calculator/.

Fred Hutchinson Cancer Research Center and University of Washington Child Health Center. *Pesticide Safety Elementary School Curriculum*. Accessed August 11, 2025. https://www.niehs.nih.gov/sites/default/files/health/assets/docs_p_z/pesticide_safety_elementary_school_curriculum_508.pdf.

Freire, Paulo. *Pedagogy of the Oppressed*. Translated by Myra Bergman Ramos. New York: Herder and Herder, 1970.

"Fresh From Zone 7." *Zone 7*. Accessed August 11, 2025. https://www.freshfromzone7.com/.

Gillam, Carey. "New Study Adds to Evidence that Glyphosate Weed Killer Can Cause Cancer." *The New Lede*, June 10, 2025. https://www.thenewlede.org/2025/06/new-study-adds-to-evidence-that-glyphosate-weed-killer-can-cause-cancer/.

Giroux, Henry A. and Anthony N. Penna. "Social Education in the Classroom: The Dynamics of the Hidden Curriculum." *Theory & Research in Social Education* 7, no. 1 (1979): 21–42.

Global Alliance for the Future of Food. "Power Shift: Why We Need to Wean Industrial Food Systems Off Fossil Fuels." Accessed August 11, 2025. https://story.futureoffood.org/power-shift/.

"The Global Plastics Crisis." *Eco-Cycle*. Accessed August 7, 2025. https://ecocycle.org/our-programs/reducing-plastics/global-plastics-crisis/.

GOV.UK. "Rights of Way and Accessing Land: Use Your Right to Roam." *GOV.UK*. Accessed August 10, 2025. https://www.gov.uk/right-of-way-open-access-land/use-your-right-to-roam.

Grace Hussain, "Meat Consumption in the U.S.: Is It Increasing or Decreasing?" *Sentient Media*, Published 2023. Accessed August 11, 2025. https://sentientmedia.org/meat-consumption-in-the-us/.

Great Lakes Now. "No More Free Bottled Water for Flint." *Great Lakes Now*, April 6, 2018. Accessed August 10, 2025. https://www.greatlakesnow.org/2018/04/no-more-free-bottled-water-for-flint/.

"Great Spirit Prayer." *Native American Prayers*. Jesuit Resource, Xavier University. Accessed January 27, 2025. https://www.xavier.edu/jesuitresource/online-resources/prayer-index/native-american.

Green Living Tribe. "High School Student Won Science Fair – Proved A Forgotten Native American Recipe Kills Cancer Cells in Just 24 Hours." Accessed August 11, 2025. https://greenlivingtribe.com/high-school-student-wins-sciences-fair-proves-a-forgotten-native-american-recipe-kills-cancer-cells-in-just-24-hours/.

Greenly. "What Are Ocean Dead Zones?" Accessed August 11, 2025. https://greenly.Earth/en-us/blog/ecology-news/what-are-ocean-dead-zones.

Groover, Heidi. "Seattle-based Stanley Rides the Wave of Water Bottle, Tumbler Addiction." *The Seattle Times*, January 12, 2024. https://www.seattletimes.com/business/seattle-based-stanley-rides-the-wave-of-water-bottle-tumbler-addiction/.

Gruenewald, David A. "The Best of Both Worlds: A Critical Pedagogy of Place." *Educational Researcher* 32, no. 4 (May 2003): 3–12.

Gruenewald, David A. and Gregory A. Smith, eds. *Place-Based Education in the Global Age: Local Diversity*. New York: Lawrence Erlbaum Associates, 2008.

"Guide to Regenerative Agriculture." *Kiss the Ground*. Accessed August 11, 2025. https://kisstheground.com/education/resources/regenerative-agriculture/.

Hackett, Billy. "Farmers Trapped in Unsustainable Cycle by Biotechnology, Seed Consolidation." *National Sustainable Agriculture Coalition*, July 9, 2021. https://sustainableagriculture.net/blog/farmers-trapped-in-unsustainable-cycle-by-biotechnology-seed-consolidation/.

Hanh, Thich Nhat and Katherine Weare. *Happy Teachers Change the World: A Guide for Cultivating Mindfulness in Education*. Berkeley: Parallax Press, 2017.

Hansen, C. Bobbi. *Teaching with Superpowers: Ten Brain-Informed Practices*. Thousand Oaks, CA: Corwin Press, 2024.

Harvard Public Health. "The Children of Flint, Ten Years Later." *Harvard Public Health*. Accessed August 10, 2025. https://harvardpublichealth.org/environmental-health/the-children-of-the-flint-michigan-water-crisis-ten-years-later/.

Hedges, Chris. "Noam Chomsky Has 'Never Seen Anything Like This.'" Interview with Noam Chomsky. Common Dreams, April 19, 2010. https://www.commondreams.org/views/2010/04/19/noam-chomsky-has-never-seen-anything.

Henderson, J. A. "Out of Sight, Out of Mind: Global Connection, Environmental Discourse and the Emerging Field of Sustainability Education." *Cultural Studies of Science Education* 10, no. 3 (2015): 593–601.

Hennekens, Charles H., Panagiota "Yiota" Kitsantas, Dawn Harris Sherling, Allison H. Ferris, Alicia Caceres, Katerina Benson, Alexandra Rubenstein, and Sarah K. Wood. "Alarming Surge: Global Crisis of Childhood Overweight and Obesity." *Florida Atlantic University Newsdesk*, August 7, 2023. https://www.fau.edu/newsdesk/articles/childhood-obesity-epidemic.

Hergert, Gary, Rex Nielsen, and Jim Margheim. "WWII Nitrogen Production Issues in Age of Modern Fertilizers." *CropWatch*. University of Nebraska–Lincoln, Published April 10, 2015. Accessed August 11, 2025. https://cropwatch.unl.edu/fertilizer-history-p3/.

Herzan, Pia. "Who dat in Lower Nine? The Role of Voluntariness in the Aftermath of Hurricane Katrina." *Voluntariness: History – Society – Theory*, August 2022. Accessed August 10, 2025. https://www.voluntariness.org/who-dat-in-lower-nine/.

Hill, James and Morgan Winsor. "Meet the Youths at the Heart of the Standing Rock Protests Against the Dakota Access Pipeline." *ABC News*, Last modified February 23, 2017.

Accessed August 10, 2025. https://abcnews.go.com/US/meet-youth-heart-standing-rock-protests-dakota-access/story?id=45719115.

History.com Editors. "Manifest Destiny." *History*, Last modified December 1, 2017. https://www.history.com/topics/19th-century/manifest-destiny.

Hornaday, William T. "The Extermination of the American Bison." *DigiCat*, 2022.

"How Big Food Monopolies Threaten Food Security and Public Health." *Green and Prosperous*. Accessed August 11, 2025. https://www.greenandprosperous.com/blog/how-big-food-monopolies-threaten-food-security-and-public-health.

"How Does Hunger Affect Learning?" *No Kid Hungry*. Accessed August 11, 2025. https://www.nokidhungry.org/blog/how-does-hunger-affect-learning.

Howard, Seánna, Robert A. Williams Jr., Michelle Cook, Terry Janis, Andrea Carter, and the Water Protector Legal Collective. "Indigenous Resistance to the Dakota Access Pipeline: Criminalization of Dissent and Suppression of Protest. Report to the United Nations Special Rapporteur on the Rights of Indigenous Peoples." University of Arizona Rogers College of Law and Water Protector Legal Collective. Submitted March 16, 2018. https://law.arizona.edu/sites/default/files/Indigenous%20Resistance%20to%20the%20Dakota%20Access%20Pipeline%20Criminalization%20of%20Dissent%20and%20Suppression%20of%20Protest.pdf.

Hubbard, Kristina. "Seed Privatization and the Path Toward Equitable Exchange." *National Sustainable Agriculture Coalition*, March 2021. https://sustainableagriculture.net/wp-content/uploads/2021/03/Hubbard-Seeds-and-Breeds-Paper.pdf.

Human Rights Watch. "We're Dying Here: The Fight for Life in Louisiana's Fossil Fuel Sacrifice Zone." *Human Rights Watch*, January 25, 2024. Accessed August 10, 2025. https://www.hrw.org/report/2024/01/25/were-dying-here/fight-life-louisiana-fossil-fuel-sacrifice-zone.

Huynh, Benjamin Q., Elizabeth T. Chin, and Mathew V. Kiang. "Estimated Childhood Lead Exposure From Drinking Water in Chicago." *JAMA Pediatrics* 178, no. 5 (2024): 473–9. https://doi.org/10.1001/jamapediatrics.2024.0133.

"The Impact of the Coronavirus on Food Insecurity in 2020 & 2021." *Feeding America*, March 2021. https://www.feedingamerica.org/sites/default/files/2021-03/National%20Projections%20Brief_3.9.2021_0.pdf.

"Indigenous Food Sovereignty." *Indigenous Food Systems Network*. Accessed August 11, 2025. https://www.Indigenousfoodsystems.org/food-sovereignty.

Inequality Media. "About." Accessed August 7, 2025. https://www.inequalitymedia.org/about.

Inequality Media. "The 10 Biggest Myths About Our Economy." YouTube video, 8:28, Posted December 23, 2024. https://www.youtube.com/watch?v=HZ3j4hHMO5E.

Inside Climate News. "EPA Funding Cuts Target Disadvantaged Communities, Analysis Shows." January 5, 2025. Accessed August 10, 2025. https://insideclimatenews.org/news/01052025/trump-epa-funding-cuts-target-disadvantaged-communities/.

Institute for Policy Studies. "Billionaire Bonanza 2021: Wealth Windfalls, Tumbling Taxes, and Pandemic Profiteers." December 2021.

Institute for Policy Studies. "The Road to Economic Justice: Addressing the Racial Wealth Gap." 2020.

Institute for Policy Studies. "Wealth Transfer Report: How America's Wealthiest Families Use Inherited Wealth to Further Concentrate Power." 2021.

Intergovernmental Panel on Climate Change (IPCC). *Climate Change and Land: An IPCC Special Report on Climate Change, Desertification, Land Degradation, Sustainable Land Management, Food Security, and Greenhouse Gas Fluxes in Terrestrial Ecosystems.* Cambridge University Press, 2019. Accessed August 10, 2025. https://www.ipcc.ch/srccl/.

Intergovernmental Science-Policy Platform on Biodiversity and Ecosystem Services (IPBES). *Global Assessment Report on Biodiversity and Ecosystem Services.* Edited by E. S. Brondízio, J. Settele, S. Díaz, and H. T. Ngo. Bonn, Germany: IPBES Secretariat, 2019. Accessed August 9, 2025. https://ipbes.net/global-assessment.

Intergovernmental Science-Policy Platform on Biodiversity and Ecosystem Services (IPBES). *Summary for Policymakers of the Global Assessment Report on Biodiversity and Ecosystem Services of the Intergovernmental Science-Policy Platform on Biodiversity and Ecosystem Services.* Edited by S. Díaz, J. Settele, E. S. Brondízio, H. T. Ngo, M. Guèze, and others. Bonn, Germany: IPBES secretariat, 2019. Accessed August 9, 2025. https://doi.org/10.5281/zenodo.3553579.

Internal Displacement Monitoring Centre. "2025 Global Report on Internal Displacement (GRID)." *Internal Displacement Monitoring Centre.* Accessed August 10, 2025. https://www.internal-displacement.org/global-report/grid2025/.

IXL. "California Social Studies Standards - Grade 1." Accessed July 2024. https://www.ixl.com/standards/california/social-studies/grade-1.

Jampel, Sarah. "What Was Actually Served at the First Thanksgiving?" *Food52.* Accessed August 11, 2025. https://food52.com/blog/20949-what-was-actually-served-at-the-first-thanksgiving.

Jet Propulsion Laboratory. "NASA Analysis Shows Irreversible Sea Level Rise for Pacific Islands." *Jet Propulsion Laboratory.* Accessed August 10, 2025. https://www.jpl.nasa.gov/news/nasa-analysis-shows-irreversible-sea-level-rise-for-pacific-islands.

Johns Hopkins Bloomberg School of Public Health. "Ultraprocessed Foods Account for More than Half of Calories Consumed at Home." Published December 10, 2024. Accessed August 11, 2025. https://publichealth.jhu.edu/2024/ultraprocessed-foods-account-for-more-than-half-of-calories-consumed-at-home.

Josie Abugov. "Elementary School Next to Controversial Louisiana Chemical Plant to Shut Down Next Year." *NOLA.com*, November 7, 2024. https://www.nola.com/news/environment/louisiana-cancer-alley-pollution-environmental-justice-school/article_ea759872-9d33-11ef-95a3-3faf44318ad9.html

Judith Enck, Jan Dell, and Jennifer Congdon. "The Real Truth About the U.S. Plastics Recycling Rate: 2021 Facts and Figures." *Beyond Plastics and The Last Beach Cleanup*, May 4, 2022. Accessed August 7, 2025. https://static1.squarespace.com/static/5eda91260bbb7e7a4bf528d8/t/62b2238152acae761414d698/1655841666913/The-Real-Truth-about-the-US-Plastic-Recycling-Rate-2021-Facts-and-Figures-_5-4-22.pdf.

"The Junk Food Industry Is Targeting Our Children." *The Hill*, April 20, 2024. https://thehill.com/opinion/healthcare/4605533-the-junk-food-industry-is-targeting-our-children/.

Kabat-Zinn, Jon. *Wherever You Go, There You Are: Mindfulness Meditation in Everyday Life.* New York: Hyperion, 1994.

Kahn, Richard. "Producing Crisis: Green Consumerism as an Ecopedagogical Issue." *Green Theory & Praxis: The Journal of Ecopedagogy* 5, no. 1 (2010): i–iv.

Kazi, Ananna and Sarah Shidid. "Opinion: Let the Bronx Breathe—Address the Cross Bronx Expressway's Impact on Asthma." *City Limits*, October 6, 2023. Accessed August 10, 2025.

https://citylimits.org/opinion-let-the-bronx-breathe-address-the-cross-bronx-expressways-impact-on-asthma/.

Khatoon, Hazra. "The Rise of Industrial Agriculture, Explained." *Sentient Media*. Accessed August 11, 2025. https://sentientmedia.org/intensive-agriculture/.

Kilbourne, Jean. *Killing Us Softly 4: Advertising's Image of Women*. Directed by Sut Jhally. Northampton, MA: Media Education Foundation, 2010. DVD.

Kimmerer, Robin Wall. *Braiding Sweetgrass*. Ebook. Minneapolis, MN: Milkweed Editions, 2013.

Kimmerer, Robin Wall. *The Serviceberry: Abundance and Reciprocity in the Natural World*. Ebook. New York: Scribner, 2024.

Kite, Allison. "EPA Sued over Failure to Set, Update Pollution Limits for Oil Refineries, Plastics Plants and Others." *Kansas Reflector*, Published April 15, 2023. Accessed August 10, 2025. https://kansasreflector.com/2023/04/15/epa-sued-over-failure-to-set-update-pollution-limits/.

Klein, Naomi. *No Logo: Taking Aim at the Brand Bullies*. Toronto: Knopf Canada, 1999.

Koithan, Mary and Cynthia Farrell. "Indigenous Native American Healing Traditions." *The Journal for Nurse Practitioners* 6, no. 6 (June 2010): 477–8. Accessed August 11, 2025. https://pmc.ncbi.nlm.nih.gov/articles/PMC2913884/.

Kwarteng, Jesse L., Amy J. Schulz, Gabriel B. Mentz, Barbara A. Israel, and Dawn W. Perkins. "Independent Effects of Neighborhood Poverty and Psychosocial Stress on Obesity Over Time." *Journal of Urban Health* 94, no. 6 (December 2017): 791–802.

"La Via Campesina: International Peasants' Voice." *La Via Campesina*. Accessed August 11, 2025. https://viacampesina.org/en/international-peasants-voice/.

Lang, Megan W., James C. Ingebritsen, and Russell K. Griffin. 2024. *Status and Trends of Wetlands in the Conterminous United States 2009 to 2019*. U.S. Department of the Interior; Fish and Wildlife Service, Washington, DC, 43pp.

Lappé, Frances Moore. *EcoMind: Changing the Way We Think to Create the World We Want*. New York: Bold Type Books, 2011.

Layden, Samantha. "Land of the Free? Environmental Racism and Its Impact on Cancer Alley, Louisiana." *Keele University Extinction Project*. Accessed August 10, 2025. https://www.keele.ac.uk/extinction/controversy/canceralley/.

"Leah Penniman." *Soul Fire Farm*. Accessed August 11, 2025. https://www.soulfirefarm.org/leah-penniman/.

Lederer, Anja and R. Huber. "The Relation of Diet and Health: You Are What You Eat." *International Journal of Environmental Research and Public Health* 19, no. 14 (2022): 8501. Accessed August 11, 2025. https://pmc.ncbi.nlm.nih.gov/articles/PMC9266141/.

Ledesma, Edna and Alfonso Morales. "The Pandemic Made Farmers Markets Essential Sources of Healthy Food for All Income Levels." *Blue Zones*, August 31, 2021. https://www.bluezones.com/2021/08/the-pandemic-made-farmers-markets-essential-sources-of-healthy-food-for-all-income-levels/.

"Lenape and the Jersey Shore." *New Jersey Sea Grant Consortium*. Accessed August 7, 2025.

Leonard, Annie. *The Story of Stuff*. Directed by Louis Fox. Berkeley, CA: Free Range Studios, 2007. Video.

Livingston, Kelly. "New EPA Vehicle Standards Would cut US Emissions, Ramp up Pressure for more EVs." *ABC News*, March 20, 2024. https://abcnews.go.com/Politics/new-epa-vehicle-standards-cut-us-emissions-ramp/story?id=108278728.

LoDolce, Megan. "Food Marketing to Children: A Wolf in Sheep's Clothing?" *Obesity Action Coalition*, Summer 2015. https://www.obesityaction.org/resources/food-marketing-to-children-a-wolf-in-sheeps-clothing/.

Loewen, James W. "The Truth About the First Thanksgiving." *Monthly Review* 44, no. 6 (November 1992). Accessed August 10, 2025. https://monthlyreview.org/1992/11/01/the-truth-about-the-first-thanksgiving/.

Lowenstein, Ethan, Rebecca Martusewicz, and Lloyd Voelker. "Developing Teachers' Capacity for Ecojustice Education and Community-Based Learning." *Teacher Education Quarterly* 37, no. 4 (2010): 99–118.

Lowlander Center. "EPA Passes Air Quality Protection in 'Cancer Alley' and Beyond . . . but Federal Judge Overturns Decision." *Lowlander Center*, April 11, 2024. Accessed August 10, 2025. https://www.lowlandercenter.org/news-and-updates/2024/4/11/epa-passes-air-quality-protection-in-cancer-alley-and-beyond.

LSU Libraries. "Hurricane Katrina Impact on Communities." *Research Guides: Louisiana Hurricanes*. Accessed August 10, 2025. https://guides.lib.lsu.edu/Hurricanes/KatrinaCommunities.

Lupinacci, John and Althier M. Happel-Parkins. "Ecocritical Foundations: Toward Social Justice and Sustainability." In *The Social and Cultural Foundations of Education: A Reader*, edited by Josh D. Diem, 34–56. New York: Peter Lang, 2016.

Macrotrends. "Clean Water Access by Country." Accessed August 10, 2025. https://www.macrotrends.net/global-metrics/countries/ranking/clean-water-access-statistics.

Markham, Kathryn. "Corn: Food, Fuel, and Now . . . Fiber Too?" *Tellus: Stories of ARS Research*. Accessed August 11, 2025. https://tellus.ars.usda.gov/stories/articles/corn-food-fuel-and-now-fiber-too.

Marr, John S. and John T. Cathey. "New Hypothesis for Cause of Epidemic Among Native Americans, New England, 1616–1619." *Emerging Infectious Diseases* 16, no. 2 (2010): 281–6. Accessed August 10, 2025. https://pmc.ncbi.nlm.nih.gov/articles/PMC2957993/.

Martusewicz, Rebecca A. "EcoJustice for Teacher Education Policy and Practice: The Way of Love." *Issues in Teacher Education* 27, no. 2 (2018): 17–35.

McTighe, Jay and Grant Wiggins. *Understanding by Design Framework*. Alexandria, VA: Association for Supervision and Curriculum Development, 2012. https://files.ascd.org/staticfiles/ascd/pdf/siteASCD/publications/UbD_WhitePaper0312.pdf.

McTighe, Jay and Grant Wiggins. *Understanding by Design Guide to Advanced Concepts in Creating and Reviewing Units*. Alexandria, VA: ASCD, 2012.

MedicalNewsToday. "How Long can You Live Without Water?" *MedicalNewsToday*. Accessed August 10, 2025. https://www.medicalnewstoday.com/articles/325174.

Mele, Chris. "How did the 'Amazonification' of New Jersey happen?" *Delaware Currents*, May 2, 2023. Accessed August 10, 2025. https://delawarecurrents.org/2023/05/02/new-jersey-warehouses/.

Minnesota Department of Agriculture. "Ecological Effects of Ammonia." Accessed August 10, 2025. https://www.mda.state.mn.us/ecological-effects-ammonia.

Monet, Jenni. "Military Force Criticized at Dakota Access Pipeline Protests." *PBS NewsHour*, Published November 3, 2016. Accessed August 10, 2025. https://www.pbs.org/newshour/nation/military-force-criticized-dakota-access-pipeline-protests

Monticello Organization. "List of Suggested Activities for Lewis and Clark Studies." *Monticello*. Accessed August 10, 2025. https://www.monticello.org/research-education/for-educators/lewis-clark-study-resources/suggested-study-activities/.

Mozaffari, Sajjad, Behzad Heibati, Maritta S. Jaakkola, Taina K. Lajunen, Safa Kalteh, Hadi Alimoradi, Mahsa Nazari, Ali Karimi, and Jouni J. K. Jaakkola. "Effects of Occupational Exposures on Respiratory Health in Steel Factory Workers." *Frontiers in Public Health* 11 (2023): 1082874. https://pmc.ncbi.nlm.nih.gov/articles/PMC9971494/.

NAACP. "Reparations." *NAACP*, 2025. Accessed August 10, 2025. https://naacp.org/resources/reparations.

Namkung, Victoria. "How the Climate Crisis Fuels Devastating Wildfires: 'We have Tweaked Nature and Pissed it Off'." *The Guardian*, January 11, 2025. https://www.theguardian.com/us-news/2025/jan/11/wildfires-los-angeles-climate-crisis-john-vaillant.

Narin, Sun. "'Our Ancestors' Graves have been Drowned': Cambodian Dam Wipes Out Hill Tribe Way of Life." *Indigenous Peoples Major Group for Sustainable Development (IPMG)*, November 29, 2018. Accessed August 10, 2025. https://Indigenouspeoples-sdg.org/index.php/english/ttt/927-our-ancestors-graves-have-been-drowned-cambodian-dam-wipes-out-hill-tribe-way-of-life.

National Centers for Coastal Ocean Science. "Above Average Summer 2024 'Dead Zone' Measured in Gulf of Mexico." Last updated July 29, 2024. Accessed August 11, 2025. https://coastalscience.noaa.gov/news/above-average-summer-2024-dead-zone-measured-in-gulf-of-mexico/.

National Centers for Environmental Information. "Billion Dollar Weather and Climate Disasters." Last modified January 10, 2025. https://www.ncei.noaa.gov/access/billions/.

National Council for Geographic Education (NCGE). *Empowering Educators & Connecting Classrooms to the World*. NCGE, 2025. Accessed August 10, 2025. https://ncge.org/.

National Council for the Social Studies (NCSS). "Chapter 2—The Themes of Social Studies." In *National Curriculum Standards for Social Studies, Theme VII: Production, Distribution, and Consumption*. NCSS. Accessed August 9, 2025. https://www.socialstudies.org/national-curriculum-standards-social-studies-chapter-2-themes-social-studies.

National Council for the Social Studies. "College, Career, and Civic Life (C3) Framework for Social Studies State Standards." *NCSS Bulletin 113*, 2013. https://www.socialstudies.org/standards/c3.

National Council for the Social Studies. *The College, Career, and Civic Life (C3) Framework for Social Studies State Standards: Guidance for Enhancing the Rigor of K–12 Civics, Economics, Geography, and History*. Silver Spring, MD: NCSS, 2013. Accessed August 9, 2025. https://www.socialstudies.org/sites/default/files/c3/C3-Framework-for-Social-Studies.pdf.

National Council for the Social Studies. "Definition of Social Studies." Accessed July 2024. https://www.socialstudies.org/about/definition-social-studies

National Council for the Social Studies. "National Curriculum Standards for Social Studies: Chapter 2—The Themes of Social Studies." Accessed January 17, 2025. https://www.socialstudies.org/national-curriculum-standards-social-studies-chapter-2-themes-social-studies?check_logged_in=1#7.

National Council for the Social Studies. "National Curriculum Standards for Social Studies: Chapter 2—The Themes of Social Studies." Accessed August 10, 2025. https://www.socialstudies.org/national-curriculum-standards-social-studies-chapter-2-themes-social-studies#7.

National Council for the Social Studies. "National Curriculum Standards for Social Studies: Chapter 2—The Themes of Social Studies." Accessed August 10, 2025. https://www.socialstudies.org/national-curriculum-standards-social-studies-chapter-2-themes-social-studies#8.

National Council for the Social Studies. "National Curriculum Standards for Social Studies: Chapter 2—The Themes of Social Studies, Theme 3 People, Places and Environments." *National Council for the Social Studies*. Accessed August 10, 2025. https://www.socialstudies.org/national-curriculum-standards-social-studies-chapter-2-themes-social-studies.

National Geographic. "Looking for a Truly Remote, Off-the-Grid Adventure? Try Panama." Accessed August 11, 2025. https://www.nationalgeographic.com/travel/article/panama-community-tourism-sostur.

National Geographic Kids. "Ocean Habitat." *National Geographic Kids*. Accessed August 10, 2025. https://kids.nationalgeographic.com/nature/habitats/article/ocean.

National Geographic Kids. "The Water Cycle." *National Geographic Kids*. Accessed August 10, 2025. https://kids.nationalgeographic.com/science/article/water-cycle.

National Governors Association Center for Best Practices and Council of Chief State School Officers. *Common Core State Standards*. Washington, DC: National Governors Association Center for Best Practices, Council of Chief State School Officers, 2010. https://corestandards.org.

National Institute for Occupational Safety and Health (NIOSH). "Stress and Mental Health of Warehouse Workers." *NIOSH*, 2020. Accessed August 9, 2025. https://www.cdc.gov/niosh/.

National Institute of Environmental Health Sciences. "Bisphenol A (BPA)." Accessed August 10, 2025. https://www.niehs.nih.gov/health/topics/agents/sya-bpa.

National Institutes of Health. "Plastic Particles in Bottled Water." Published January 23, 2024. Accessed August 10, 2025. https://www.nih.gov/news-events/nih-research-matters/plastic-particles-bottled-water.

National Invasive Species Information Center. "Economic and Social Impacts." Accessed August 7, 2025. https://www.invasivespeciesinfo.gov/subject/economic-and-social-impacts.

National Library of Medicine. "National Library of Medicine | USAGov." Accessed August 11, 2025. https://www.usa.gov/agencies/national-library-of-medicine.

National Museum of the American Indian. "Standing Rock Sioux and Dakota Access Pipeline | Teacher Resource." Accessed August 10, 2025. https://americanindian.si.edu/nk360/plains-treaties/dapl.

National Oceanic and Atmospheric Administration. "NOAA Predicts Above Normal 2025 Atlantic Hurricane Season." *NOAA*, August 7, 2025. Accessed August 10, 2025. https://www.noaa.gov/news-release/noaa-predicts-above-normal-2025-atlantic-hurricane-season.

National Partnership for Women & Families. "Clean Water and Reproductive Justice: Lack of Access Harms Women of Color." Accessed August 10, 2025. https://nationalpartnership.org/report/clean-water-and-reproductive-health/.

National Research Council. *A Framework for K-12 Science Education: Practices, Crosscutting Concepts, and Core Ideas*. Washington, DC: The National Academies Press, 2012.

National Science Teaching Association. "Science Standards." Accessed July 2024. https://www.nsta.org/science-standards.

National University. "What is Social Emotional Learning (SEL): Why It Matters." Accessed August 6, 2025. https://www.nu.edu/blog/social-emotional-learning-sel-why-it-matters-for-educators/.

National Wildlife Federation. "Clean Water Act." *National Wildlife Federation*. Accessed August 10, 2025. https://www.nwf.org/Our-Work/Waters/Clean-Water-Act.

Native Women's Association of Canada. "Water is a Source of Life." *Native Women's Association of Canada*. Accessed August 10, 2025. https://nwac.ca/policy/water-is-a-source-of-life.

Natural Resources Defense Council. "Fighting Phthalates." Accessed August 10, 2025. https://www.nrdc.org/stories/fighting-phthalates.

Natural Resources Defense Council. "Flooding and Climate Change: Everything You Need to Know." *NRDC*, November 3, 2023. Accessed August 10, 2025. https://www.nrdc.org/stories/flooding-and-climate-change-everything-you-need-know.

New England Historical Society. "The Winnipesaukee Water War and the 1859 Fight for NH Property Rights." *New England Historical Society*. Accessed August 10, 2025. https://newenglandhistoricalsociety.com/winnipesaukee-water-wars-fighting-nh-property-rights/.

New Jersey Department of Education. "2020 New Jersey Student Learning Standards – Comprehensive Health and Physical Education." Published June 2020. Accessed August 11, 2025. https://www.nj.gov/education/standards/chp/Docs/2020_NJSLS-CHPE_Kto2.pdf.

New Jersey Department of Education. "Climate Change Education by Grade Band." Accessed July 2024. https://www.nj.gov/education/climate/learning/gradeband/.

Next-Generation Science Standards (NGSS). "Elementary Standards: Kindergarten Through Grade Five Disciplinary Core Ideas." *NGSS Lead States*, September 2017. Accessed August 9, 2025. https://www.nextgenscience.org/sites/default/files/K-2DCI.pdf..

Next-Generation Science Standards (NGSS). "Elementary Standards: Third Through Fifth Grade Performance Expectations by Topic." *NGSS Lead States*, September 2017. Accessed August 9, 2025. https://www.nextgenscience.org/sites/default/files/3-5Topic.pdf.

Next-Generation Science Standards. "5-LS2-1 Ecosystems: Interactions, Energy, and Dynamics." Accessed September 8, 2025. https://www.nextgenscience.org/pe/5-ls2-1-ecosystems-interactions-energy-and-dynamics.

Next-Generation Science Standards. Accessed July 2024. https://www.nextgenscience.org/.

NGSS Lead States. *Next-Generation Science Standards: For States, By States*. Washington, DC: The National Academies Press, 2013. https://www.nextgenscience.org.

Nihart, Alexander J., Miguel A. Garcia, Elias El Hayek, Ngozi E. Ezike, Yasmin S. Hassan, Jessica A. Bartley, Zeenat Safdar, Prasanna V. Dwivedi, Marianna C. Viana, Brenda A. Wilson, Rohit R. Varma, Maria V. Sanchez, Evan L. Brittain, Rachael D. Seidler, and Frank J. Anania. "Bioaccumulation of Microplastics in Decedent Human Brains." *Nature Medicine* 31 (2025): 1114–19. https://www.nature.com/articles/s41591-024-03453-1.

NOAA Climate.gov. "2024: An Active Year of U.S. Billion-Dollar Weather and Climate Disasters." Accessed August 7, 2025. https://www.climate.gov/news-features/blogs/beyond-data/2024-active-year-us-billion-dollar-weather-and-climate-disasters.

NOAA Climate.gov. "Hurricane Helene's Extreme Rainfall and Catastrophic Inland Flooding." *NOAA Climate.gov*, September 30, 2024. Accessed August 10, 2025. https://www.climate.gov/news-features/event-tracker/hurricane-helenes-extreme-rainfall-and-catastrophic-inland-flooding.

Noss, R. F. and R. L. Peters. *Endangered Ecosystems: A Status Report on America's Vanishing Habitat and Wildlife*. Washington, DC: Defenders of Wildlife, 1995.

NPR. “A Brief History Of How Racism Shaped Interstate Highways.” *NPR*, April 7, 2021. Accessed August 10, 2025. https://www.npr.org/2021/04/07/984784455/a-brief-history-of-how-racism-shaped-interstate-highways.

NPR. “Lead-Laced Water In Flint: A Step-By-Step Look At The Makings Of A Crisis.” *NPR*, April 20, 2016. Accessed August 10, 2025. https://www.npr.org/sections/thetwo-way/2016/04/20/465545378/lead-laced-water-in-flint-a-step-by-step-look-at-the-makings-of-a-crisis.

Ólafsson, Björn. “What Monoculture Farming Is, and Why It Matters.” *Sentient Media*. Accessed August 11, 2025. https://sentientmedia.org/monoculture/.

“The Original Principles of Regenerative Agriculture.” *Rodale Institute*. Accessed August 11, 2025. https://rodaleinstitute.org/blog/original-principles-of-regenerative-agriculture/.

Parker, Laura. “You Eat Thousands of Bits of Plastic Every Year.” *National Geographic*, Published June 4, 2019. Accessed August 10, 2025. https://www.nationalgeographic.com/environment/article/you-eat-thousands-of-bits-of-plastic-every-year#:~:text=A%20plastic%2Dfree%20diet?,%2C%20%E2%80%9Cbut%20we%20are.%E2%80%9D.

Patton, Mike. “A Historical Look At The Components of U.S. GDP: 1929 to 2011.” *Forbes*, December 30, 2014. https://www.forbes.com/sites/mikepatton/2014/12/30/a-historical-look-at-the-components-of-u-s-gdp-1929-to-2011/.

Paulo Freire. *Pedagogy of the Oppressed.* New York: Bloomsbury Publishing USA, 2018.

PBS. “‘No Silver Bullet Solution’: Norman Borlaug and the Green Revolution.” *American Experience*. Accessed August 11, 2025. https://www.pbs.org/wgbh/americanexperience/features/no-silver-bullet-solution-norman-borlaug-and-green-revolution/.

PBS. “The Truth Behind ‘40 Acres and a Mule.’” In *The African Americans: Many Rivers to Cross*. PBS. Accessed August 10, 2025. https://www.pbs.org/wnet/african-americans-many-rivers-to-cross/history/the-truth-behind-40-acres-and-a-mule/.

PBS NewsHour. “How Climate Change is Affecting this Key Water Cycle, Triggering More Extreme Weather.” *PBS NewsHour*, March 24, 2025. Accessed August 10, 2025. https://www.pbs.org/newshour/nation/how-climate-change-is-affecting-this-key-water-cycle-triggering-more-extreme-weather.

Pearce, Fred. “Why the Rush to Mine Lithium Could Dry Up the High Andes.” *Yale Environment 360*, September 21, 2022. https://e360.yale.edu/features/lithium-mining-water-andes-argentina.

Pearce, Matt. “2 Years of Opposition, 1,172 Miles of Pipe, 1.3 Million Facebook check-ins. The Numbers to Know About the Standing Rock Protests.” *Los Angeles Times*, Published November 1, 2016. Accessed August 10, 2025. https://www.latimes.com/nation/la-na-standing-rock-numbers-20161101-story.html.

People of Color Environmental Leadership Summit. *Principles of Environmental Justice.* Washington, DC: People of Color Environmental Leadership Summit, 1991.

“Pesticide, Seed, and Digital Agriculture Industry Concentrates Wealth and Power, Threatens Health.” *Beyond Pesticides Daily News Blog*, January 13, 2023. https://beyondpesticides.org/dailynewsblog/2023/01/pesticide-seed-and-digital-agriculture-industry-concentrates-wealth-and-power-threatens-health/.

Pillets, Jeff. “Toxic Tap Water in Trenton: Lead, Copper, and Legionella Bacteria Found in Office Tower.” *The Jersey Vindicator,* February 3, 2025. Accessed August 10, 2025. https://jerseyvindicator.org/2025/02/03/toxic-tap-water-in-trenton-lead-copper-and-legionella-bacteria-found-in-office-tower/.

"Plants as Medicine: Lenape Healing Traditions Continue Today." *Columbia University School of Nursing*, April 20, 2021. https://www.nursing.columbia.edu/news/plants-medicine-lenape-healing-traditions-continue-today.

"Plastics – Fueling Oil Demand, Climate Change and Pollution." *United Nations*. Accessed August 7, 2025. https://www.un.org/en/climatechange/science/climate-issues/plastics.

Pohl, Elise and Sang-Ryong Lee. "Local and Global Public Health and Emissions from Concentrated Animal Feeding Operations in the USA: A Scoping Review." *International Journal of Environmental Research and Public Health* 21, no. 7 (2024): 916. Accessed August 11, 2025. https://pmc.ncbi.nlm.nih.gov/articles/PMC11276819/pdf/ijerph-21-00916.pdf.

Powell, Lisa M., Julien Leider, Rebecca Schermbeck, Aline Vandenbroeck, and Jennifer L. Harris. "Trends in Children's Exposure to Food and Beverage Advertising on Television: 2013–2022." *JAMA Network Open* 7, no. 8 (August 2024): e2426316. https://pmc.ncbi.nlm.nih.gov/articles/PMC11342137/.

PYMNTS and LendingClub. *New Reality Check: The Paycheck-to-Paycheck Report: The Generational Divide Edition*. Boston: PYMNTS.com, 2023. https://www.pymnts.com/study/reality-check-paycheck-to-paycheck-consumer-planning-financial-emergency/.

Quattro, Christine. *Environmental Justice and Zoning Reform*. PAS Report 608. American Planning Association, 2023. Accessed August 10, 2025. https://www.planning.org/publications/report/9295614/.

Rabbitt, Matthew P., Madeline Reed-Jones, Laura J. Hales, and Michael P. Burke. *Household Food Security in the United States in 2023. ERR-337*. Washington, DC: U.S. Department of Agriculture, Economic Research Service, 2024. https://doi.org/10.32747/2024.8583175.ers.

Raworth, Kate. *Doughnut Economics: Seven Ways to Think Like a 21st-Century Economist*. London: Penguin Random House, 2017.

Research Nester. "Pesticides Market Size & Share | Growth Trends 2025–2037." Published July 7, 2025. https://www.researchnester.com/reports/pesticides-market/7865.

Retail Brew. "Here's Where Experts Say the Next Warehouse Hotspots Will Be." *Retail Brew*, November 1, 2022. Accessed August 10, 2025. https://www.retailbrew.com/stories/2022/11/01/here-s-where-experts-say-the-next-warehouse-hotspots-will-be.

Reuters. "Lawsuit Alleging Racism in Louisiana's Cancer Alley Revived on Appeal." *Reuters*, April 10, 2025. Accessed August 10, 2025. https://www.reuters.com/legal/government/lawsuit-alleging-racism-louisianas-cancer-alley-revived-appeal-2025-04-10/.

RioOnWatch. "Community Land Trusts in Latin America: Dialogues Between Brazil and Puerto Rico." *RioOnWatch*, October 26, 2021. Accessed August 10, 2025. https://rioonwatch.org/?p=68482.

Ritchie, Hannah, Pablo Rosado, and Max Roser. "Environmental Impacts of Food Production." *Our World in Data*, 2022. https://ourworldindata.org/environmental-impacts-of-food.

Ritchie, Hannah and Max Roser. "Water Use and Stress." *Our World in Data*, 2018. https://ourworldindata.org/water-use-stress.

Riviere, Asia and Jessica Kirchner. "Food is Medicine: Making Nutritious Food Accessible to All." *National Governors Association Center for Best Practices*, April 2025. https://www.nga.org/news/commentary/food-is-medicine-making-nutritious-food-accessible-to-all/.

Robyn Schelenz. "How the Indigenous Practice of 'Good Fire' Can Help Our Forests Thrive." *University of California*, April 6, 2022. https://www.universityofcalifornia.edu/news/how-Indigenous-practice-good-fire-can-help-our-forests-thrive.

Rodale, Robert and Maria Rodale. “The Original Principles of Regenerative Agriculture.” *Rodale Institute*. Accessed August 11, 2025. https://rodaleinstitute.org/blog/original-principles-of-regenerative-agriculture/.

Rolling Harvest Food Rescue. “Connecting Local Farmers with Neighbors in Need.” Accessed August 15, 2025. https://rollingharvest.org/.

Ross, Emma. “Fast Fashion Getting Faster: A Look at the Unethical Labor Practices Sustaining a Growing Industry.” *GW International Law and Policy Brief*, October 28, 2021. Accessed August 9, 2025. https://studentbriefs.law.gwu.edu/ilpb/2021/10/28/fast-fashion-getting-faster-a-look-at-the-unethical-labor-practices-sustaining-a-growing-industry/.

Rube, Teddy. “Rethinking Highway Construction as De Jure Segregation: A Case Study for Equal Protection Lawsuits.” *NYU Journal of Legislation & Public Policy Quorum*, October 9, 2023. Accessed August 10, 2025. https://nyujlpp.org/quorum/rube-rethinking-highway-construction-as-de-jure-segregation/.

Şahin, Şeyma and Abdurrahman Kiliç. “Effectiveness of the Project-based 6E Learning Model.” *European Journal of Open, Distance and E-Learning* 25, no. 1 (2023): 31–48.

Samson, Fred and Fritz Knopf. “Prairie Conservation in North America.” *BioScience* 44, no. 6 (1994): 418–21.

Sax, Sarah. “Native Communities Cite Dismal Statistics on Lack of Access to Water at Senate Committee Hearing.” *Medill on the Hill*, Published September 28, 2023. Accessed August 10, 2025. https://medillonthehill.medill.northwestern.edu/2023/09/native-communities-cite-dismal-statistics-on-lack-of-access-to-water-at-senate-committee-hearing/.

Scanlon, Bridget R., Robert C. Reedy, Sarah Fakhreddine, Qingyang Yang, and Gregory Pierce. “Drinking Water Quality and Social Vulnerability Linkages at the System Level in the United States.” *Environmental Research Letters* 18, no. 9 (2023): 094039. Accessed August 10, 2025. https://iopscience.iop.org/article/10.1088/1748-9326/ace2d9.

Schonbeck, Mark and Organic Farming Research Foundation staff. “Understanding the Impact of Herbicides and Synthetic Fertilizers on Soil Health: What Research Tells Us.” *Organic Farming Research Foundation*. Accessed August 11, 2025. https://ofrf.org/news/understanding-the-impact-of-herbicides-and-synthetic-fertilizers-on-soil-health-what-research-tells-us/.

Schonert-Reichl, Kimberly A., Eva Oberle, M. S. Lawlor, Diane Abbott, Kimberly Thomson, Tim F. Oberlander, and Adele Diamond. “Enhancing Cognitive and Social-Emotional Development through a Simple-to-Administer Mindfulness-Based School Program for Elementary School Children: A Randomized Controlled Trial.” *Developmental Psychology* 51, no. 1 (2015): 52–66.

School Nutrition Association. “Congress Passes Mega Bill that Harms School Meal Programs.” Accessed August 15, 2025. https://schoolnutrition.org/sna-news/congress-passes-trumps-mega-bill-that-harms-school-meal-programs/.

SciTechDaily. “LA’s Devastating Wildfire Crisis Didn’t Start With a Spark – It Started With Rain.” *SciTechDaily*. Accessed August 10, 2025. https://scitechdaily.com/las-devastating-wildfire-crisis-didnt-start-with-a-spark-it-started-with-rain/.

Scott, Robert E., Valerie Wilson, Jori Kandra, and Daniel Perez. “Botched Policy Responses to Globalization Have Decimated Manufacturing Employment with Often Overlooked Costs for Black, Brown, and Other Workers of Color: Investing in Infrastructure and Rebalancing Trade Can Create Good Jobs for All.” *Economic Policy Institute*, January 31, 2022. Accessed August 9, 2025. https://files.epi.org/uploads/239189.pdf.

Sea Turtle Conservancy. "Marine Debris." Accessed August 10, 2025. https://conserveturtles.org/threat/marine-debris/.

Secretariat of the Pacific Regional Environment Programme. "Pacific amplifies voice at Sixty Second Plenary Session of IPCC in China." *SPREP*, March 7, 2025. Accessed August 10, 2025. https://www.sprep.org/news/pacific-amplifies-voice-at-sixty-second-plenary-session-of-ipcc-in-china.

Seed Library Network. "School Seed Libraries." Accessed August 6, 2025. https://www.seedlibrarynetwork.org/school-seed-libraries.html.

Shalaby, Carla. *Troublemakers: Lessons in Freedom from Young Children at School*. New York: The New Press, 2017.

Sherman, General William T. "Special Field Orders, No. 15." January 16, 1865. In Special Field Orders No. 15. BlackPast. Accessed August 10, 2025. https://www.blackpast.org/african-american-history/special-field-orders-no-15/.

Sierra, M. E., S. N. Stephenson, et al. "The Value of Forests in Carbon Sequestration." *Nature* 507, no. 7492 (January 2014): 153–5. Accessed August 9, 2025. https://www.nature.com/articles/506153a.

Simmons Hanly Conroy. "Weed Killer Roundup Lymphoma Lawsuit Settlements (2025)." Accessed August 11, 2025. https://www.simmonsfirm.com/complex-litigation/monsanto-roundup/.

Society for Risk Analysis. "Study Identifies U.S. Hotspots for Drinking Water Quality Violations and Lack of Access to Safe, Clean Water." Published April 15, 2025. Accessed August 10, 2025. https://www.sra.org/2025/04/15/study-identifies-u-s-hotspots-for-drinking-water-quality-violations-and-lack-of-access-to-safe-clean-water/.

Society of Health and Physical Educators (SHAPE America). "National Health Education Standards." Published 2024. Accessed August 11, 2025. https://www.shapeamerica.org/MemberPortal/standards/health/new-he-standards.aspx.

Song, Lorraine. "How Social Media Fuels Impulse Purchasing." *SU Social*. Accessed August 7, 2025. https://susocial.com/how-social-media-fuels-impulse-purchasing/.

Soul Fire Farm. *Food Sovereignty Action Steps*. 2018. https://docs.google.com/document/d/1dt0hicyhGdJSKlC3qyE1AbG9fdDrONjUh_M_bE0KMGs/edit?tab=t.0.

"Soul Fire Farm Programs." *Soul Fire Farm*. Accessed August 11, 2025. https://www.soulfirefarm.org/programs/.

Sowerwine, Jennifer, Megan Mucioki, Daniel Sarna-Wojcicki, and Lisa Hillman. "Reframing Food Security by and for Native American Communities: A Case Study Among Tribes in the Klamath River Basin of Oregon and California." *Food Security* 11, no. 3 (2019): 579–607. https://ourenvironment.berkeley.edu/sites/ourenvironment.berkeley.edu/files/user/profile2/main/publications/Sowerwine%20et%20al_Reframing%20Native%20American%20Food%20Insecurity.pdf.

St. Julien, Gianna and Kimberley Terrell. Tulane Environmental Law Clinic. "A Horror Story – How the Law Simultaneously Addresses and Perpetuates Environmental Racism in Cancer Alley." *Global Network for Human Rights and the Environment*, September 9, 2024. Accessed August 10, 2025. https://gnhre.org/?p=18198.

Stanford Report. "Native Approaches to Fire Management Could Revitalize Communities, Stanford Researchers Find." August 27, 2019. https://news.stanford.edu/stories/2019/08/traditional-fire-management-help-revitalize-american-indian-cultures.

Stillerman, Karen Perry. "What a Second Trump Administration Means for Food and Farms." *Union of Concerned Scientists Blog*, June 28, 2024. https://blog.ucsusa.org/karen-perry-stillerman/what-a-second-trump-administration-means-for-food-and-farms/.

Stockholm Resilience Centre. "Planetary Boundaries." *Stockholm Resilience Centre*. Accessed August 9, 2025. https://www.stockholmresilience.org/research/planetary-boundaries.html.

Stop Warehouses And Trucking (S.W.A.T.). *Stop Warehouses and Trucking Official Website*. Hillsborough, NJ: Stop Warehouses And Trucking, 2025. Accessed August 10, 2025. https://www.swat-hb.org/.

Sutton, Victoria. "Water is Life: We Should All Be Water Protectors." *Native News Online*. Accessed August 10, 2025. https://nativenewsonline.net/opinion/water-is-life-we-should-all-be-water-protectors.

Sweitzer, Megan and Victoria Davidenko. "Food Spending as a Share of Income Declines as Income Rises." *U.S. Department of Agriculture Economic Research Service*, November 1, 2024. https://www.ers.usda.gov/data-products/chart-gallery/chart-detail?chartId=58372.

Tabor, Nick. "Standing Rock Protests | Summary, Violence, & Outcome." *Encyclopaedia Britannica*, Last modified 2025. Accessed August 10, 2025. https://www.britannica.com/event/Standing-Rock-protests.

Tanana, Heather, Jaime Garcia, Ana Olaya, Chelsea Colwyn, Hanna Larsen, Ryan Williams, Jonathan King, and the Water & Tribes Initiative Leadership Team. "Universal Access to Clean Water for Tribes in the Colorado River Basin: Executive Summary." *Water & Tribes Initiative*, Released April 2021. Accessed August 10, 2025. https://naturalresourcespolicy.org/docs/water-tribes/wti-executive-summary-4.2021.pdf.

Tanana, Heather. "Oversight Hearing on Water as a Trust Resource: Examining Access in Native Communities." *Testimony to the U.S. Senate Committee on Indian Affairs*, September 27, 2023. Accessed August 10, 2025. https://www.indian.senate.gov/wp-content/uploads/2023-09-27-HRG-Testimony-Tanana.pdf.

Taylor, Craig. "6 Chemical-Free Gardening Techniques for a Healthy, Natural Garden." *Morning Chores*. Accessed August 11, 2025. https://morningchores.com/chemical-free-gardening/.

TEACH SDGs. Accessed July 2024. http://www.teachsdgs.org/.

TeacherVision. "Chart Columbus's Voyages." *Columbus Day Full Lesson*. TeacherVision. Accessed August 10, 2025. https://www.teachervision.com/columbus-day/chart-columbuss-voyages.

TeacherVision. "Who Writes History? Rethinking Columbus Day." *Full Lesson*, TeacherVision. Accessed August 10, 2025. https://www.teachervision.com/social-studies-history/who-writes-history-rethinking-columbus-day.

TEKS Resource System. "Browse Standards." Accessed July 2024. https://www.teksresourcesystem.net/module/standards/Tools/Browse?StandardId=23759.

TerraCycle, Inc. *TerraCycle Official Website*. Trenton, NJ: TerraCycle, Inc., 2025. Accessed August 9, 2025. https://www.terracycle.com/en-US/.

The Business Research Company. "Herbicides Market Report 2025 – Herbicides Market Strategies and Outlook." Accessed August 11, 2025. https://www.thebusinessresearchcompany.com/report/herbicides-global-market-report.

The Chisholm Legacy Project. "Virginia's Human Right to Water Resolution." *The Chisholm Legacy Project*. Accessed August 10, 2025. https://thechisholmlegacyproject.org/policy/

virginias-human-right-to-water-resolution/#:~:text=Virginia's%20House%20Joint%20 Resolution%20538,is%20a%20fundamental%20human%20right.

The Cloud Institute for Sustainability Education. *The Benchmarks by The Cloud Institute*. Version 1.2. The Cloud Institute for Sustainability Education, 2017. Accessed August 9, 2025. https://cloud-institute.squarespace.com/s/EfS-Benchmarks_ver1x2.pdf

The Cloud Institute for Sustainability Education. "The EfS Benchmarks." Accessed July 2024. https://cloudinstitute.org/efs-benchmarks.

The Cloud Institute for Sustainability Education. "EfS Standards and Performance Indicators." Accessed January 27, 2025. https://cloudinstitute.org/cloud-efs-standards-performanceindicators.

The Cloud Institute for Sustainability Education. "EfS Standards & Performance Indicators: Cultural Preservation & Transformation." *Cloud Institute for Sustainability Education*. Accessed August 10, 2025. https://cloudinstitute.org/cloud-efs-standards-performanceindicators.

The Cloud Institute for Sustainability Education. "EfS Standards & Performance Indicators: Healthy Commons." *Cloud Institute for Sustainability Education*. Accessed August 10, 2025. https://cloudinstitute.org/cloud-efs-standards-performanceindicators.

The Cloud Institute for Sustainability Education. "EfS Standards & Performance Indicators: Strong Sense of Place." *Cloud Institute for Sustainability Education*. Accessed August 10, 2025. https://cloudinstitute.org/cloud-efs-standards-performanceindicators.

The Gilder Lehrman Institute of American History. "The Doctrine of Discovery, 1493." Accessed August 10, 2025. https://www.gilderlehrman.org/history-resources/spotlight-primary-source/doctrine-discovery-1493.

The Guardian. "Flint, Michigan, Water Crisis: Ten Years on, Residents Feel Left Behind." April 25, 2024. Accessed August 10, 2025. https://www.theguardian.com/us-news/2024/apr/25/flint-michigan-water-crisis.

The Guardian. "Floods, Trauma, Displaced: Conflict, Climate Crisis and Safety in Bangladesh, Sudan, Colombia IDP Camps." May 23, 2025. Accessed August 10, 2025. https://www.theguardian.com/global-development/2025/may/23/floods-trauma-displaced-conflict-climate-crisis-safety-bangladesh-sudan-colombia-idp-camps.

The Guardian. "Plan to Expand Texas Highway Stalled Over Environmental Racism Concerns." *The Guardian*, March 23, 2021. Accessed August 10, 2025. https://www.theguardian.com/us-news/2021/mar/23/plan-to-expand-texas-highway-stalled-over-environmental-racism-concerns.

The Guardian. "Residents of New Orleans Comeback District Fear Port Development Could Kill the Renaissance." April 26, 2025. Accessed August 10, 2025. https://www.theguardian.com/us-news/2025/apr/26/new-orleans-port-development-lower-ninth-ward.

The Indigenous Foundation. "Indigenous Women and Their Connection to the Earth and Her Waters." *The Indigenous Foundation*. Accessed August 10, 2025. https://www.theIndigenousfoundation.org/articles/Indigenous-women-and-their-connections-to-Earth-and-water.

The Momentum. "How Bleach Damages The Environment and Our Health." Accessed August 10, 2025. https://www.themomentum.com/articles/how-bleach-damages-the-environment-and-our-health.

The Ocean Cleanup. "The Great Pacific Garbage Patch." Accessed August 10, 2025. https://theoceancleanup.com/great-pacific-garbage-patch/.

The Ocean Cleanup. "The Ocean Cleanup Project: Annual Report 2020." *The Ocean Cleanup Foundation*, 2020. Accessed August 9, 2025. https://theoceancleanup.com.

The Santa Monica Mountains Fund. "Rewilding California Project Reaches Halfway Milestone!" *Santa Monica Mountains Fund Blog*, September 13, 2022. https://www.samofund.org/blog/rewilding-california-project-reaches-halfway-milestone.

The State of Rhode Island, Department of Environmental Management. "Tragedy of the Commons." Accessed January 27, 2025. https://dem.ri.gov/sites/g/files/xkgbur861/files/programs/bnatres/fishwild/outreach/critter-kits/balance-lesson01-tragedy-commons.pdf.

The Story of Stuff Project. "The Story of Stuff." Accessed August 7, 2025. https://www.storyofstuff.org/movies/story-of-stuff/.

The White House. "Ending Radical Indoctrination in K-12 Schooling." *Executive Order*, January 20, 2025. https://www.whitehouse.gov/presidential-actions/2025/01/ending-radical-indoctrination-in-k-12-schooling/.

Tishman Environment and Design Center, The New School. "New School Map Reveals Most Incinerators Pollute Low-Income and Communities of Color, Worsen Climate Change." *The New School*. Accessed August 7, 2025. https://www.newschool.edu/pressroom/pressreleases/2022/TishmanCenterIncineratorMap.htm.

Toast. "Largest Grocery Chains." *Toast Blog: On the Line*. Accessed August 11, 2025. https://pos.toasttab.com/blog/on-the-line/largest-grocery-chains.

Treehugger. "What Is Ecological Footprint? Definition and How to Calculate It." *Treehugger*. Accessed August 7, 2025. https://www.treehugger.com/what-is-ecological-footprint-4580244.

Truthout. "Tesla Paid Zero Federal Income Tax in 2024, Despite $2.3 Billion in Income." August 6, 2025. https://truthout.org/articles/tesla-paid-zero-federal-income-tax-in-2024-despite-2-3-billion-in-income/.

Turner, R. and R. Donnelly. "Case Studies in Critical Ecoliteracy: A Curriculum for Analyzing the Social Foundations of Environmental Problems." *Educational Studies* 49, no. 5 (2013): 387–408.

Turner, R. Kerry, W. J. Mitsch, and S. E. Jorgensen. "The Economic Value of Wetlands: A Global Perspective." *Wetlands Ecology and Management* 13, no. 1 (2005): 5–23.

U.S. Bureau of Economic Analysis (BEA). "Personal Consumption Expenditures by Type of Product." Accessed August 9, 2025. https://apps.bea.gov/iTable/?reqid=19&step=3&isuri=1&nipa_table_list=2017&categories=underlying.

U.S. Bureau of Labor Statistics. "Warehousing and Storage: NAICS 493." Last modified August 1, 2025. https://www.bls.gov/iag/tgs/iag493.htm.

U.S. Census Bureau. "Housing Vacancies and Homeownership, 2023 Q4." *U.S. Census Bureau*, January 30, 2024. Accessed August 10, 2025. https://www.census.gov/housing/hvs/.

U.S. Census Bureau. "Income and Poverty in the United States: 2023." September 10, 2024. https://www.census.gov/library/publications/2024/demo/p60-283.html.

U.S. Department of Agriculture. "Grains and Oilseeds Outlook for 2025." *Agricultural Outlook Forum 2025*, Released February 27, 2025. Accessed August 11, 2025. https://www.usda.gov/sites/default/files/documents/2025AOF-grains-oilseeds-outlook.pdf.

U.S. Department of Agriculture Economic Research Service. "Corn and Other Feed Grains – Feed Grains Sector at a Glance." Accessed August 11, 2025. https://www.ers.usda.gov/topics/crops/corn-and-other-feed-grains/feed-grains-sector-at-a-glance.

U.S. Department of Agriculture Economic Research Service. "Irrigation & Water Use." Accessed August 11, 2025. https://www.ers.usda.gov/topics/farm-practices-management/irrigation-water-use.

U.S. Environmental Protection Agency. "Animal Feeding Operations (AFOs)." Accessed August 11, 2025. https://www.epa.gov/npdes/animal-feeding-operations-afos.

U.S. Environmental Protection Agency. "Climate Change Impacts on Agriculture and Food Supply." Accessed August 11, 2025. https://www.epa.gov/climateimpacts/climate-change-impacts-agriculture-and-food-supply.

U.S. Environmental Protection Agency. "Frequent Questions Regarding EPA's Facts and Figures about Materials, Waste and Recycling." *EPA*. Accessed August 7, 2025. https://www.epa.gov/facts-and-figures-about-materials-waste-and-recycling/frequent-questions-regarding-epas-facts-and.

U.S. Environmental Protection Agency. "Guide to the Facts and Figures Report about Materials, Waste and Recycling." *EPA*. Accessed August 7, 2025. https://www.epa.gov/facts-and-figures-about-materials-waste-and-recycling/guide-facts-and-figures-report-about.

U.S. Environmental Protection Agency. "Indicators: Phosphorus." *National Aquatic Resource Surveys*. Accessed August 10, 2025. https://www.epa.gov/national-aquatic-resource-surveys/indicators-phosphorus.

U.S. Environmental Protection Agency (EPA). "National Overview: Facts and Figures on Materials, Wastes and Recycling." *EPA*. Accessed August 9, 2025. https://www.epa.gov/facts-and-figures-about-materials-waste-and-recycling/national-overview-facts-and-figures-materials.

U.S. Environmental Protection Agency. "New Toxics Release Inventory Data Reported." *EPA*. Accessed August 9, 2025. https://www.epa.gov/newsreleases/new-toxics-release-inventory-data-reported.

U.S. Environmental Protection Agency, Office of Land and Emergency Management. "Population Surrounding 1,857 Superfund Remedial Sites." *EPA*, September 2020. Accessed August 10, 2025. https://www.epa.gov/sites/default/files/2015-09/documents/webpopulationrsuperfundsites9.28.15.pdf.

U.S. Environmental Protection Agency. "PFAS Explained." *U.S. Environmental Protection Agency*. Accessed August 10, 2025. https://www.epa.gov/pfas/pfas-explained.

U.S. Environmental Protection Agency. "Research on Near Roadway and Other Near Source Air Pollution." *EPA*, 2025. Accessed August 10, 2025. https://www.epa.gov/air-research/research-near-roadway-and-other-near-source-air-pollution.

U.S. Environmental Protection Agency. "Rethinking Highways for Healthy Communities." *EPA*, 2024. Accessed August 10, 2025. https://www.epa.gov/smartgrowth/rethinking-highways-healthy-communities.

U.S. Environmental Protection Agency. "Study Finds Exposure to Air Pollution Higher for People of Color Regardless of Region or Income." *EPA*, September 20, 2021. Accessed August 10, 2025. https://www.epa.gov/sciencematters/study-finds-exposure-air-pollution-higher-people-color-regardless-region-or-income.

U.S. Environmental Protection Agency. "Volatile Organic Compounds' Impact on Indoor Air Quality." Accessed August 10, 2025. https://www.epa.gov/indoor-air-quality-iaq/volatile-organic-compounds-impact-indoor-air-quality.

U.S. Environmental Protection Agency, WaterSense. "A Day in the Life of a Drop." *Teachers' Guide*, May 2008. Accessed August 10, 2025. https://www.epa.gov/sites/default/files/2017-02/documents/ws-ourwater-drop-guide.pdf.

U.S. Geological Survey. "Our Water Our Lives: Floods—Lesson 1." *Water Science School. U.S. Geological Survey*. Accessed August 10, 2025. https://www.usgs.gov/special-topics/water-science-school/our-water-our-lives-floods#Lesson%201.

U.S. National Park Service. "A Short History of Jamestown." *Historic Jamestowne. U.S. National Park Service*. Accessed August 10, 2025. https://www.nps.gov/jame/learn/historyculture/a-short-history-of-jamestown.htm.

U.S. Senate. Committee on Indian Affairs. "Water as a Trust Resource: Examining Access in Native Communities." *Oversight Hearing*, September 27, 2023. https://www.indian.senate.gov/wp-content/uploads/2023-09-27-HRG-Testimony-Tanana.pdf.

"Understanding Poverty in America: Causes and Solutions." *Feeding America*. Accessed August 11, 2025. https://www.feedingamerica.org/hunger-in-america/poverty.

United Nations. *Bringing Data to Life: SDG Human Impact Stories from Across the Globe*. New York: United Nations, 2022. https://unstats.un.org/sdgs/report/2022/SDG2022_Flipbook_final.pdf.

United Nations. "Bringing Data to Life: SDG Human Impact Stories from Across the Globe." *The Sustainable Development Goals Report 2022 Flipbook*. Accessed August 10, 2025. https://unstats.un.org/sdgs/report/2022/SDG2022_Flipbook_final.pdf.

United Nations. "Goal 2: End Hunger, Achieve Food Security and Improved Nutrition and Promote Sustainable Agriculture." Accessed August 11, 2025. https://sdgs.un.org/goals/goal2#overview.

United Nations. "Goal 2: End Hunger, Achieve Food Security and Improved Nutrition and Promote Sustainable Agriculture – Progress and Info." Accessed August 11, 2025. https://sdgs.un.org/goals/goal2#progress_and_info.

United Nations. "Goal 2: End Hunger, Achieve Food Security and Improved Nutrition and Promote Sustainable Agriculture – Targets and Indicators." Accessed August 11, 2025. https://sdgs.un.org/goals/goal2#targets_and_indicators.

United Nations. "Goal 8: Promote Sustained, Inclusive and Sustainable Economic Growth, Full and Productive Employment and Decent Work for All." *United Nations Sustainable Development Goals*. Accessed August 9, 2025. https://www.un.org/sustainabledevelopment/economic-growth/.

United Nations. "Goal 11: Make Cities and Human Settlements Inclusive, Safe, Resilient and Sustainable." *United Nations Sustainable Development Goals*. Accessed August 10, 2025. https://sdgs.un.org/goals/goal11.

United Nations. "Goal 12: Ensure Sustainable Consumption and Production Patterns." *United Nations Sustainable Development Goals*. Accessed August 9, 2025. https://www.un.org/sustainabledevelopment/sustainable-consumption-production/.

United Nations. "Goal 15: Protect, Restore and Promote Sustainable Use of Terrestrial Ecosystems, Sustainably Manage Forests, Combat Desertification, and Halt and Reverse Land Degradation and Halt Biodiversity Loss." *United Nations Sustainable Development Goals*. Accessed August 10, 2025. https://sdgs.un.org/goals/goal15.

United Nations. "Sustainable Development Goal 6: Ensure Availability and Sustainable Management of Water and Sanitation for All." Accessed August 10, 2025. https://sdgs.un.org/goals/goal6.

United Nations. "Sustainable Development Goal 6: Ensure Availability and Sustainable Management of Water and Sanitation for All. Progress and Info." Accessed August 10, 2025. https://sdgs.un.org/goals/goal6#progress_and_info.

United Nations. "Sustainable Development Goals, Goal 12: Ensure Sustainable Consumption and Production Patterns." Accessed January 27, 2025. https://www.un.org/sustainabledevelopment/sustainable-consumption-production/.

United Nations. "Sustainable Development Goal 14: Conserve and Sustainably Use the Oceans, Seas and Marine Resources for Sustainable Development." Accessed August 10, 2025. https://sdgs.un.org/goals/goal14.

United Nations. "Water – At the Center of the Climate Crisis." *United Nations Climate Action*. Accessed August 10, 2025. https://www.un.org/en/climatechange/science/climate-issues/water.

United Nations Department of Economic and Social Affairs. "Goal 2: End Hunger, Achieve Food Security and Improved Nutrition and Promote Sustainable Agriculture." *United Nations Sustainable Development Goals*. Accessed August 11, 2025. https://sdgs.un.org/goals/goal2.

United Nations. Department of Economic and Social Affairs. "Transforming our world: the 2030 Agenda for Sustainable Development." Accessed July 2024. https://sdgs.un.org/2030agenda.

United Nations, Department of Economic and Social Affairs, Population Division. *World Urbanization Prospects: The 2018 Revision*. New York: United Nations, 2018. https://www.un.org/development/desa/en/news/population/2018-revision-of-world-urbanization-prospects.html.

United Nations General Assembly. "Transforming Our World: The 2030 Agenda for Sustainable Development." *Preamble*, October 21, 2015. https://sdgs.un.org/2030agenda.

United States Environmental Protection Agency. "Understanding Your Water Bill." Accessed September 8, 2025. https://19january2017snapshot.epa.gov/www3/watersense/our_water/understanding_your_bill.html.

United States Mission to the United Nations. "FACT SHEET: United States Announces $49 Billion in Commitments to Global Water Security and Sanitation." *United States Mission to the United Nations*, April 2023. Accessed August 10, 2025. https://usun.usmission.gov/fact-sheet-united-states-announces-49-billion-in-commitments-to-global-water-security-and-sanitation/#:~:text=Today%2C%20more%20than%20two%20million,required%20to%20flush%20a%20toilet.

University of Oxford. "$5 Trillion of Nature-Related Economic Risks Will Amplify Climate Change, Says Oxford Study." December 14, 2023. https://www.ox.ac.uk/news/2023-12-14-5-trillion-nature-related-economic-risks-will-amplify-climate-change-says-oxford.

University of Washington News. "UW Study: Exposure to Chemical in Roundup Increases Risk for Cancer." Published February 13, 2019. Accessed August 11, 2025. https://www.washington.edu/news/2019/02/13/uw-study-exposure-to-chemical-in-roundup-increases-risk-for-cancer/.

USDA Food and Nutrition Service. "Using Gardens To Grow Healthy Habits in Cafeterias, Classrooms, and Communities." July 2021. Accessed August 11, 2025. https://www.nrcs.usda.gov/sites/default/files/2023-02/USDA-FNS%20School%20Gardens%20factsheet.pdf.

"USDA Local Food Portal." *U.S. Department of Agriculture*. Accessed August 11, 2025. https://www.usdalocalfoodportal.com/.

VeryWell Health. "How Long Can You Go Without Food?" *VeryWell Health*, April 5, 2025. https://www.verywellhealth.com/how-long-live-without-food-1132033.

Wachter, Heidi. "The CAFO Conundrum." *Experience Life*, Published May 4, 2021. Accessed August 11, 2025. https://experiencelife.lifetime.life/article/the-cafo-conundrum/.

Washington Post. "We Mythologize Highways, But They've Damaged Communities of Color." *Made By History*, January 19, 2023. Accessed August 10, 2025. https://www.washingtonpost.com/made-by-history/2023/01/19/interstate-highways-black-neighborhoods/.

"What Is the Composition of Stainless Steel? Full Guide & Key Components." *Jindal Stainless*, September 30, 2024. https://www.jindalstainless.com/blog/a-complete-guide-to-stainless-steel-compositions/.

Whitt, Christine, Noah Miller, and Ryan Olver. "Eighty-nine Percent of All Farms are Small Family Farms and They Generated 18 Percent of Total Production Value in 2021." *U.S. Department of Agriculture Economic Research Service*, February 27, 2023. Accessed August 11, 2025. https://www.ers.usda.gov/data-products/charts-of-note/chart-detail?chartId=105916.

Wiggins, Grant and Jay McTighe. "From Common Core Standards to Curriculum: Five Big Ideas." 2012. https://exemplars.com/sites/default/files/inline-files/McTighe%20Wiggins%20From%20Common%20Core%20Standards%281%29.pdf

World Economic Forum. "The Future of Jobs Report 2023: Introduction – The Global Labour Market Landscape in 2023." *World Economic Forum*, 2023. Accessed August 9, 2025. https://www.weforum.org/publications/the-future-of-jobs-report-2023/in-full/1-introduction-the-global-labour-market-landscape-in-2023/.

World Health Organization. "Obesity and Overweight." Accessed August 11, 2025. https://www.who.int/news-room/fact-sheets/detail/obesity-and-overweight#:~:text=Children%20in%20low%2D%20and%20middle,while%20undernutrition%20issues%20remain%20unsolved.

World Health Organization. "Sanitation." *World Health Organization*, March 22, 2024. Accessed August 10, 2025. https://www.who.int/news-room/fact-sheets/detail/sanitation.

World Meteorological Organization. "Climate Change Transforms Pacific Islands." *World Meteorological Organization*, August 27, 2024. Accessed August 10, 2025. https://wmo.int/media/news/climate-change-transforms-pacific-islands.

World Wildlife Fund. "Living Planet Report 2024." *World Wildlife Fund*, October 10, 2024. Accessed August 9, 2025. https://www.worldwildlife.org/publications/2024-living-planet-report.

WWNO. "In Louisiana's 'Cancer Alley,' Most Oil and Gas Jobs Go to White Workers, New Research Says." *WWNO*, October 6, 2023. Accessed August 10, 2025. https://www.wwno.org/coastal-desk/2023-10-06/in-louisianas-cancer-alley-most-oil-and-gas-jobs-go-to-white-workers-new-research-says.

Zárate, Lorena. "By the People, For the People: Social and Environmental Revitalisation of the Caño Martín Peña, Puerto Rico." *Urbanet*, June 7, 2022. Accessed August 10, 2025. https://www.urbanet.info/cano-martin-pena/.

Zarowny, Natalie. "Local Author Writes Children's Book About Flint Water Crisis." *ABC12 News*, December 9, 2021. Accessed August 10, 2025. https://www.abc12.com/news/flint-water-emergency/local-author-writes-childrens-book-about-flint-water-crisis/article_38447c74-4f40-5002-a2b3-56878191a5ec.html.

Zekollari, Harry, Lilian Schuster, Fabien Maussion, et al. "Glacier Preservation Doubled by Limiting Warming to 1.5°C versus 2.7°C." *Science* 388, no. 6750 (May 29, 2025): 979–83. https://www.science.org/doi/10.1126/science.adu4675.

Zhang, Luoping, Iemaan Rana, Rachel M. Shaffer, Emanuela Taioli, and Lianne Sheppard. "Exposure to Glyphosate-based Herbicides and Risk for Non-Hodgkin Lymphoma: A Meta-analysis and Supporting Evidence." *Mutation Research/Reviews in Mutation Research* 781 (2019): 186–206. Accessed August 11, 2025. https://www.sciencedirect.com/science/article/abs/pii/S1383574218300887.

Ziner, Feenie. *Squanto*. Hamden, CT: Linnet Books, 1988 [1965].

Appendix A
Lesson Plan Template

Lesson Essential Question(s):
What are the overarching themes you want to address?

Relevant Standards:
Draw on inspiration from the NGSS, the NCSS Themes and C3 Inquiry Indicators, The Cloud Standards and the UN SDGs.

Learning Objectives:
What do you want students to know or be able to do as a result of the learning experience?

Materials:
What resources would be useful to teach this topic?
Review the resources presented in the Appendix, on our website, or in the Instructional Materials for ideas.

Lesson Plan
What learning experiences are well-suited to help the students reach the learning objectives and your goals for the lesson?
Use a strategy presented in the model instructional learning materials, one from the Appendices, our companion website, or one of your own!
Consider:

- *How will you begin the lesson to capture the students' attention and activate their prior knowledge?*
- *What new content or skill will you need to teach them or provide them with?*
- *What activity will enable the students to meaningfully apply what they have learned, build skills, and extend their understanding?*
- *How will you conclude the lesson so that the students can reflect on what they learned and make connections?*

Assessment Plan
How will you determine if the learning objectives have been met?
Consider both informal and formal methods to assess the students' learning.

Appendix B
Relevant National Council for the Social Studies Standards (NCSS)

Economic Indicators for Student Learning from NCSS C3 Inquiry

Framework for Grades K-2

Textbox B.1.

D2.Eco.1.K-2. Explain how scarcity necessitates decision-making.
D2.Eco.2.K-2. Identify the benefits and costs of making various personal decisions.
D2.Eco.4.K-2. Describe the goods and services that people in the local communities produce and those that are produced in other communities.
D2.Eco.5.K-2. Identify prices of products in a local market.
D2.Eco.6.K-2. Explain how people earn income.
D2.Eco.7.K-2. Describe examples of costs of production.
D2.Eco.10.K-2. Explain why people save.
D2.Eco.12.K-2. Describe examples of the goods and services that governments provide.
D2.Eco.13.K-2. Describe examples of capital goods and human capital.

Economic Indicators for Student Learning from NCSS C3 Inquiry

Framework for Grades 3–5

Textbox B.2.

D2.Eco.1.3-5. Compare the benefits and costs of individual choices.
D2.Eco.2.3-5. Identify positive and negative incentives that influence the decisions people make.

D2.Eco.3.3-5. Identify examples of the variety of resources (human capital, physical capital, and natural resources) that are used to produce goods and services.
D2.Eco.7.3-5. Explain how profits influence sellers in markets.
D2.Eco.8.3-5. Identify examples of external benefits and costs.

Geography Indicators for Student Learning from NCSS C3 Inquiry

Framework for Grades K-2

Textbox B.3.

D2.Geo.1.K-2. Construct maps, graphs, and other representations of familiar places.
D2.Geo.2.K-2. Use maps, graphs, photographs, and other representations to describe places and the relationships and interactions that shape them.
D2.Geo.3.K-2. Use maps, globes, and other simple geographic models to identify cultural and environmental characteristics of places.
D2.Geo.4.K-2. Explain how weather, climate, and other environmental characteristics affect people's lives in a place or region.
D2.Geo.5.K-2. Describe how human activities affect the cultural and environmental characteristics of places or regions.
D2.Geo.6.K-2. Identify some cultural and environmental characteristics or specific places.
D2.Geo.7.K-2. Explain why and how people, goods, and ideas move from place to place.
D2.Geo.8.K-2. Compare how people in different types of communities use local and distant environments to meet their daily needs.
D2.Geo.9.K-2. Describe the connections between the physical environment of a place and the economic activities found there.
D2.Geo.10.K-2. Describe changes in the physical and cultural characteristics of various world regions.
D2.Geo.11.K-2. Explain how the consumption of products connects people to distant places.
D2.Geo.12.K-2. Identify ways that a catastrophic disaster may affect people living in a place.

Geography Indicators for Student Learning from NCSS C3 Inquiry

Framework for Grades 3–5

Textbox B.4.

D2.Geo.1.3-5. Construct maps and other graphic representations of both familiar and unfamiliar places.
D2.Geo.2.3-5. Use maps, satellite images, photographs, and other representations to explain relationships between the locations of places and regions and their environmental characteristics.
D2.Geo.3.3-5. Use maps of different scales to describe the locations of cultural and environmental characteristics.
D2.Geo.4.3-5. Explain how culture influences the way people modify and adapt to their environments.
D2.Geo.5.3-5. Explain how the cultural and environmental characteristics of places change over time.
D2.Geo.6.3-5. Describe how environmental and cultural characteristics influence population distribution in specific places or regions.
D2.Geo.7.3-5. Explain how cultural and environmental characteristics affect the distribution and movement of people, goods, and ideas.
D2.Geo.8.3-5. Explain how human settlements and movements relate to the locations and use of various natural resources.
D2.Geo.9.3-5. Analyze the effects of catastrophic environmental and technological events on human settlements and migration.
D2.Geo.10.3-5. Explain why environmental characteristics vary among different world regions.
D2.Geo.11.3-5. Describe how the spatial patterns of economic activities in a place change over time because of interactions with nearby and distant places.
D2.Geo.12.3-5. Explain how natural and human-made catastrophic events in one place affect people living in other places.

Civics Indicators for Student Learning from NCSS C3 Inquiry

Framework for Grades K-2

D2.Civ.1.K-2. Describe roles and responsibilities of people in authority.
D2.Civ.2.K-2. Explain how all people, not just official leaders, play important roles in a community.
D2.Civ.5.K-2. Explain what governments are and some of their functions.
D2.Civ.6.K-2. Describe how communities work to accomplish common tasks, establish responsibilities, and fulfill roles of authority.
D2.Civ.8.K-2. Describe democratic principles such as equality, fairness, and respect for legitimate authority and rules.
D2.Civ.9.K-2. Follow agreed-upon rules for discussions while responding attentively to others when addressing ideas and making decisions as a group.
D2.Civ.10.K-2. Compare their own point of view with others' perspectives.
D2.Civ.14.K-2. Describe how people have tried to improve their communities over time.

Civics Indicators for Student Learning from NCSS C3 Inquiry

Framework for Grades 3–5

Textbox B.5.

D2.Civ.1.3-5. Distinguish the responsibilities and powers of government officials at various levels and branches of government and in different times and places.
D2.Civ.2.3-5. Explain how a democracy relies on people's responsible participation, and draw implications for how individuals should participate.
D2.Civ.6.3-5. Describe ways in which people benefit from and are challenged by working together, including through government, workplaces, voluntary organizations, and families.
D2.Civ.8.3-5. Identify core civic virtues and democratic principles that guide government, society, and communities.
D2.Civ.9.3-5. Use deliberative processes when making decisions or reaching judgments as a group.
D2.Civ.10.3-5. Identify the beliefs, experiences, perspectives, and values that underlie their own and others' points of view about civic issues.

D2.Civ.12.3-5. Explain how rules and laws change society and how people change rules and laws.
D2.Civ.13.3-5. Explain how policies are developed to address public problems.
D2.Civ.14.3-5. Illustrate historical and contemporary means of changing society.

History Indicators for Student Learning from NCSS C3 Inquiry

Framework for Grades K-2

D2.His.1.K-2. Create a chronological sequence of multiple events.
D2.His.2.K-2. Compare life in the past to life today.
D2.His.3.K-2. Generate questions about individuals and groups who have shaped a significant historical change.
D2.His.4.K-2. Compare perspectives of people in the past to those of people in the present.

History Indicators for Student Learning from NCSS C3 Inquiry

Framework for Grades 3–5

Textbox B.6.

D2.His.1.3-5. Create and use a chronological sequence of related events to compare developments that happened at the same time.
D2.His.2.3-5. Compare life in specific historical time periods to life today.
D2.His.3.3-5. Generate questions about individuals and groups who have shaped significant historical changes and continuities.
D2.His.4.3-5. Explain why individuals and groups during the same historical period differed in their perspectives.
D2.His.5.3-5. Explain connections among historical contexts and people's perspectives at the time.

Appendix C

Relevant Next-Generation Science Standards (NGSS)

Textbox C.1.

Engineering Design K-2

Students who demonstrate understanding can:

K-2-ETS1-1.	Ask questions, make observations, and gather information about a situation people want to change to define a simple problem that can be solved through the development of a new or improved object or tool.
K-2-ETS1-2.	Develop a simple sketch, drawing, or physical model to illustrate how the shape of an object helps it function as needed to solve a given problem.
K-2-ETS1-3.	Analyze data from tests of two objects designed to solve the same problem to compare the strengths and weaknesses of how each performs.

Textbox C.2.

Engineering Design 3–5

Students who demonstrate understanding can:

3-5-ETS1-1.	Define a simple design problem reflecting a need or a want that includes specified criteria for success and constraints on materials, time, or cost.
3-5-ETS1-2.	Generate and compare multiple possible solutions to a problem based on how well each is likely to meet the criteria and constraints of the problem.
3-5-ETS1-3.	Plan and carry out fair tests in which variables are controlled and failure points are considered to identify aspects of a model or prototype that can be improved.

Table C.1. Next Generation Science Standards Highlighting Progressions in Earth and Space Science

Earth and Space Science Progression		
Standard	**K-2 Performance Expectation**	**3–5 Performance Expectation**
ESS2.A Earth materials and systems	Wind and water change the shape of the land. (Dams) 2-ESS2-1 Earth's Systems | Next-Generation Science Standards	Four major Earth systems interact. Rainfall helps to shape the land and affects the types of living things found in a region. Water, ice, wind, organisms, and gravity break rocks, soils, and sediments into smaller pieces and move them around. 4-ESS2-1 Earth's Systems | Next-Generation Science Standards 5-ESS2-1 Earth's Systems | Next-Generation Science Standards
ESS2.C The roles of water in Earth's surface Processes	Water is found in many types of places and in different forms on Earth. 2-ESS2-3 Earth's Systems | Next-Generation Science Standards	Most of Earth's water is in the ocean and much of the Earth's fresh water is in glaciers or underground. 5-ESS2-2 Earth's Systems | Next-Generation Science Standards
ESS2.D Weather and climate	Weather is the combination of sunlight, wind, snow or rain, and temperature in a particular region and time. People record weather patterns over time K-ESS2-1 Earth's Systems | Next-Generation Science Standards	Climate describes patterns of typical weather conditions over different scales and variations. Historical weather patterns can be analyzed. 3-ESS2-1 Earth's Systems | Next-Generation Science Standards 3-ESS2-2 Earth's Systems | Next-Generation Science Standards
ESS2.E Biogeology	Plants and animals (including humans) can change their local environment. K-ESS2-2 Earth's Systems | Next-Generation Science Standards	Living things (including humans) can affect the physical characteristics of their environment. 4-ESS2-1 Earth's Systems | Next-Generation Science Standards
ESS3.A Natural resources	Living things need water, air, and resources from the land, and they live in places that have the things they need. Humans use natural resources for everything they do. K-ESS3-1 Earth and Human Activity | Next-Generation Science Standards	Energy and fuels humans use are derived from natural sources and their use affects the environment. Some resources are renewable over time, others are not. 4-ESS3-1 Earth and Human Activity | Next-Generation Science Standards
ESS3.B Natural hazards	In a region, some kinds of severe weather are more likely than others. Forecasts allow communities to prepare for severe weather.K-ESS3-2 Earth and Human Activity | Next-Generation Science Standards	A variety of hazards result from natural processes; humans cannot eliminate hazards but can reduce their impacts. 3-ESS3-1 Earth and Human Activity | Next-Generation Science Standards 4-ESS3-2 Earth and Human Activity | Next-Generation Science Standards
ESS3.C Human impacts on Earth systems	Things people do can affect the environment, but they can make choices to reduce their impacts. K-ESS2-2 Earth's Systems | Next-Generation Science Standards K-ESS3-3 Earth and Human Activity | Next-Generation Science Standards	Societal activities have had major effects on the land, ocean, atmosphere, and even outer space. Societal activities can also help protect Earth's resources and environments. 5-ESS3-1 Earth and Human Activity | Next-Generation Science Standards

Table C.2. Next Generation Science Standards Highlighting Progressions in Life Science

Life Science Progression		
Standard	**K-2 Performance Expectation**	**3–5 Performance Expectation**
LS1.A Structure and function	All organisms have external parts that they use to perform daily functions. 1-LS1-1 From Molecules to Organisms: Structures and Processes | Next-Generation Science Standards	Organisms have both internal and external macroscopic structures that allow for growth, survival, behavior, and reproduction. 4-LS1-1 From Molecules to Organisms: Structures and Processes | Next-Generation Science Standards
LS1.B Growth and development of organisms	Parents and offspring often engage in behaviors that help the offspring survive. 1-LS1-2 From Molecules to Organisms: Structures and Processes | Next-Generation Science Standards	Reproduction is essential to every kind of organism. Organisms have unique and diverse life cycles. 3-LS1-1 From molecules to Organisms: Structures and Processes | Next-Generation Science Standards
LS1.C Organization for matter and energy flow in organisms	Animals obtain food they need from plants or other animals. Plants need water and light. K-LS1-1 From Molecules to Organisms: Structures and Processes | Next-Generation Science Standards	Food provides animals with the materials and energy they need for body repair, growth, warmth, and motion. Plants acquire material for growth chiefly from air, water, and process matter and obtain energy from sunlight, which is used to maintain conditions necessary for survival. 5-PS3-1 Energy | Next-Generation Science Standards 5-LS1-1 From Molecules to Organisms: Structures and Processes | Next-Generation Science Standards

LS2.A Interdependent relationships in ecosystems	Plants depend on water and light to grow, and also depend on animals for pollination or to move their seeds around. 2-LS2-1 Ecosystems: Interactions, Energy, and Dynamics | Next-Generation Science Standards 2-LS2-2 Ecosystems: Interactions, Energy, and Dynamics | Next-Generation Science Standards	The food of almost any animal can be traced back to plants. Organisms are related in food webs in which some animals eat plants for food and other animals eat the animals that eat plants, while decomposers restore some materials back to the soil. 5-LS2-1 Ecosystems: Interactions, Energy, and Dynamics | Next-Generation Science Standards
LS2.B Cycles of matter and energy transfer in ecosystems	[Content found in LS1.C and ESS3.A]	Matter cycles between the air and soil and among organisms as they live and die. 5-LS2-1 Ecosystems: Interactions, Energy, and Dynamics | Next-Generation Science Standards
LS2.C Ecosystem dynamics, functioning, and resilience	NA	When the environment changes some organisms survive and reproduce, some move to new locations, some move into the transformed environment, and some die. 3-LS4-4 Biological Evolution: Unity and Diversity | Next-Generation Science Standards
LS4.D Biodiversity and humans	A range of different organisms lives in different places. 2-LS4-1 Biological Evolution: Unity and Diversity | Next-Generation Science Standards	Populations of organisms live in a variety of habitats. Change in those habitats affects the organisms living there. 3-LS4-4 Biological Evolution: Unity and Diversity | Next-Generation Science Standards

Table C.3. Next Generation Science Standards Highlighting Progressions in Physical Science

Physical Science Progression		
Standard	**K-2 Performance Expectation**	**3–5 Performance Expectation**
PS1.A Structure of matter (includes PS1.C Nuclear processes)	Matter exists as different substances that have observable different properties. Different properties are suited to different purposes. Objects can be built up from smaller parts. 2-PS1-1 Matter and Its Interactions | Next-Generation Science Standards 2-PS1-2 Matter and Its Interactions | Next-Generation Science Standards 2-PS1-3 Matter and Its Interactions | Next-Generation Science Standards	Matter exists as particles that are too small to see, and so matter is always conserved even if it seems to disappear. Measurements of a variety of observable properties can be used to identify particular materials. 5-PS1-1 Matter and Its Interactions | Next-Generation Science Standards 5-PS1-3 Matter and Its Interactions | Next-Generation Science Standards
PS3.D Energy in chemical processes and everyday life	Sunlight warms Earth's surface.	Energy can be "produced," "used," or "released" by converting stored energy. Plants capture energy from sunlight, which can later be used as fuel or food. 4-PS3-4 Energy | Next-Generation Science Standards 5-PS3-1 Energy | Next-Generation Science Standards

Appendix D
Planning to Take Action

Table D.1.

The Problem—What we think needs to be changed	The Goal—What is the change we would like
Actions—How we will advocate for our goal	Reasons—Why we think this is a good plan

Now that you are done planning, it is time to take action!

Appendix E
Our School Community Project

Table E.1.

Something we want to change in our school community to make it a positive place for everyone is . . .	Our plan to work with others to make this change is . . .
Before Picture (how we see the problem now)	After Picture (what we would like to see change)

Appendix F
Template and Model of Awareness Poster

Bold Title/Slogan

Textbox F.1.

The Issue and Why It Matters
(Add some facts and include a picture)

Textbox F.2.

Call to Action (CTA)
(List some of the actions you want others to take. Can add visuals)

Textbox F.3.

End with a Catchy Slogan
(This is your final message to get people's attention)

Sample Awareness Poster

Textbox F.4.

Save Water, Save Our Future!

Water is a limited resource—Only about 1 percent of Earth's water is fresh and safe for people to use.
We need it to live—People, animals, and plants all need clean water every day.
It protects nature—Saving water helps rivers, lakes, and oceans stay healthy for fish and wildlife.
It helps everyone—When we conserve water, there's more to share with communities around the world who don't always have enough.
What you can do to help

- ***Turn off the tap while brushing your teeth***
- ***Take short showers instead of long baths.***
- ***Don't waste clean drinking water—only pour what you'll drink.***

Protect our Water, Protect our Lives!

Appendix G
Gallery Walk Strategy

Rationale:
The Gallery Walk strategy enables students to explore multiple texts or images to make connections to content, apply prior knowledge, and learn from peers.

Teachers often use this strategy as a way to have students share their work with peers, examine multiple images or documents, or respond to a collection of excerpts. The activity is great to introduce a new topic, assessing students' understanding of recent learning, or simply for them to react to text.

Preparation:
Select the "text" that you plan to use. This can be graphics, excerpts from readings or speeches, student work, and so on.

Place the text selections around the room so that there is room between the items so that several students may gather around each item in order to discuss and analyze it. The items can be hung on walls or placed on tables.

Procedure:

- Organize the class into small groups of two to three students.
- Explain that each group should remain together to travel around the room to discuss and analyze the item, or respond to a prompt the teacher has given. The prompt could be a matching activity where students match a concept to each picture, or open-ended reactions of what students think the message it, and so on.
- After students have had enough time to see all of the items, have them return to their seats and follow up with a discussion or writing task.

Variation:
This activity can also be done with individuals viewing items independently followed by a class discussion or another follow-up activity.

Appendix H
Cost/Benefit Analysis Tool

Part of rational decision-making is weighing pros and cons, or in economic terms, costs and benefits. This worksheet helps students develop this skill. The activity can be used first with something the child wants after they have learned what wants and needs are.

Table H.1.

What Is Something I Want or Something I Would Like to Have Happen?	Is This a Want or a Need?	What Is an Action I Can Take That Would Help Me to Achieve My Goal?

Table H.2.

What Are the Costs of This Action (cons)?	What Are the Benefits of This Action (pros)?

Textbox H.1.

Based on my chart, what do I think is the best decision to make?

Appendix I
Town Hall Meeting Simulation

Rational:
This town hall meeting activity is designed to expose students to a town hall meeting process and to analyze the active role citizens can play in influencing policy at the local level. Conducting a simulated town hall meeting helps students understand this process to exercise skills of participatory democratic citizenship. Any issue of public concern can be selected for a town hall meeting role-play; however, *it is important that there be multiple perspectives on the issue.* A role/character worksheet is attached that can be used to help the students prepare.

Procedure:
Step 1: Introduction (Suggested)

- Review different methods citizens can utilize to inform elected officials about their views on issues.
- Ask students to consider which methods they think are most likely to influence officials and why.
- Explain that the class will experience the method of attending a town hall meeting through a role-play activity.

Step 2: Preparation
Introduce the relevant background information to the students. This can be in the form of reading an article, a children's book, or based on content the students have been learning.

- Assign roles to the students (the roles should represent various stakeholders and views. The Role/Character worksheet can be used to help students prepare).
- Assign students to each of the roles identified for the activity.
  - Small groups of students can be assigned the same role.
  - A few students must be assigned to act as the public officials who will officiate the meeting. Their job will be to lead the meeting and listen carefully to the citizens' statements. They will need to consider these views when they make a policy recommendation.
  - If additional roles are needed, some students can be assigned to play members of the press. Their job would be to report on the meeting.
- Distribute the background reading materials and allow all groups time to prepare.
- The students should work together to identify the perspective of their role and prepare statements to express this view. Inform the students speakers will all be allowed the

same amount of time to speak during the activity, generally 3 minutes is sufficient. Some of these students can also prepare visuals to represent their views. Citizens often carry signs or wear buttons that state their views.

- Students who have been assigned one of the roles should prepare statements to express their assigned perspective.—Public officials should brainstorm policy proposals (they will need to present a proposal after the meeting has been concluded).
- The students acting as public officials should familiarize themselves with the background information. They can also consider questions they might want to ask during the meeting to learn more about the views of those who will speak. They should also prepare to lead the meeting.
- Members of the Press (if assigned) should prepare a summary of the issue as part of the news story.

Step 3: The Town Hall Meeting

- A public official should call the meeting to order and state the purpose of the meeting. Then the officials should allow time for the citizens to speak (approximately 3 minutes).
- The citizens take turns delivering their prepared statements and answering any questions the officials may have. The public officials can ask questions after hearing from the citizens.
- After all the citizens have delivered their statements, the public officials should review the issues and the views expressed and then state their policy recommendation. (The elected officials can be given 5–10 minutes to conduct this stage. During this time, the members of the press can give their reports or students can be asked to reflect on their experience to prepare for the class discussion.)
- Members of the press should take notes during the meeting. When the meeting is over, the press should prepare a written or oral summary of the event.

Step 4: Class Discussion

When the activity has concluded, lead the students in a discussion about the activity. The following questions can be used to help students reflect on the experience.

- Did you personally agree with the perspective of the role you were assigned?
- Was it difficult to present your position or decide on what action to take?
- Which statements were most persuasive?
- Do you agree with the policy recommendations made?
- What has this taught you about the role citizens can play in the public policymaking process?
- How important do you think it is for citizens to attend public meetings?
- Can you relate the activity to current or past public issues?

Appendix J
Photovoice

Timeline

Textbox J.1.

Talk about topic and photovoice project (example: Water and climate change)
Students take pictures of photovoice topic
Students add captions to photos
Students share pictures in small group or whole class and engage in critical dialogue
Students write a narrative about the topic using a selection of pictures

Photovoice is a method that can (be):

- Used as a tool to build knowledge together.
- Used as a tool to connect and discuss what we see, what we know, and how we experience something.
- Provide opportunities for you to share knowledge that contributes to your local communities.
- Provide opportunities to generate research questions that can be investigated.

My goal(s) for this project is (are) . . .

Textbox J.2.

Questions we will ask of all images we look at together:

- What do you see here?
- Why did you take this picture?
- What is really happening here?
- How does this relate to our lives?
- Why does this condition exist?

- What can we do about it?
- Where is the social studies in this picture? How can we connect our learning about our community and relationships to this picture?
- Where is the science in this picture? How can we connect our learning about water and climate to this picture?
- How could this image educate others?
- What do some of our pictures have in common?
- Are there any images or issues that are really different that stand out?
- What further questions can we ask about this picture?

Textbox J.3.

Daily Reflections:

Use any of the following prompts to write a short reflection each day.

- Something new I learned today was . . .
- The most interesting part of our conversation was . . .
- Something that surprised me today was . . .
- Something I wanted to learn more about is . . .
- Something I am now wondering about is . . .
- Feel free to make up your own!!!

Daily Reflection

Textbox J.4.

Daily Reflection

Textbox J.5.

Daily Reflection

Textbox J.6.

Final Reflection (for today think about the entire project and write a little something about your thoughts and feelings about the photovoice learning experience.)

Textbox J.7.

Photovoice Narrative: Use the following sentence starters to support the writing of your narrative (Feel free to use your own style but you can use these if you get stuck). You can use your narrative as a script to make a recording to go along with your image.

- This is a picture of . . .
- I took this picture because . . .
- What I see happening in this picture is . . .
- This relates to my life because . . .
- This is happening because . . .
- We can address this issue by . . .
- This picture connects to things we have been learning about in school like . . .
- We can learn____________from this picture.
- In our groups we all had similar pictures about . . .
- Some of our pictures were really different, like . . .
- This picture makes me wonder about . . .
- If I were to do further research about this situation I would want to know . . .

Textbox J.8.

Appendix K

Photoelicitation Handout

For each image, record ideas in the table.

Table K.1.

Photo Number	Feeling	Thought	Connection	Question
1				
2				
3				
4				
5				
6				
7				
8				
9				
10				

Index

Note: Page number in *italics* refer to figures and tables

About the Authors

Greer Burroughs is an associate professor at The College of New Jersey in the Department of Elementary and Early Childhood Education. She teaches courses in multicultural approaches to elementary social studies and environmental sustainability education.

Marissa Bellino is an associate professor in the Department of Secondary Education at the College of New Jersey. She teaches courses in environmental sustainability education, social foundations of education, methods in science teaching, and critical pedagogy.

Greer and Marissa have engaged pre-service and in-service teachers in critical place-based learning experiences locally and abroad to build their skills and orientation toward EcoJustice Education. They have published and presented extensively on this work.